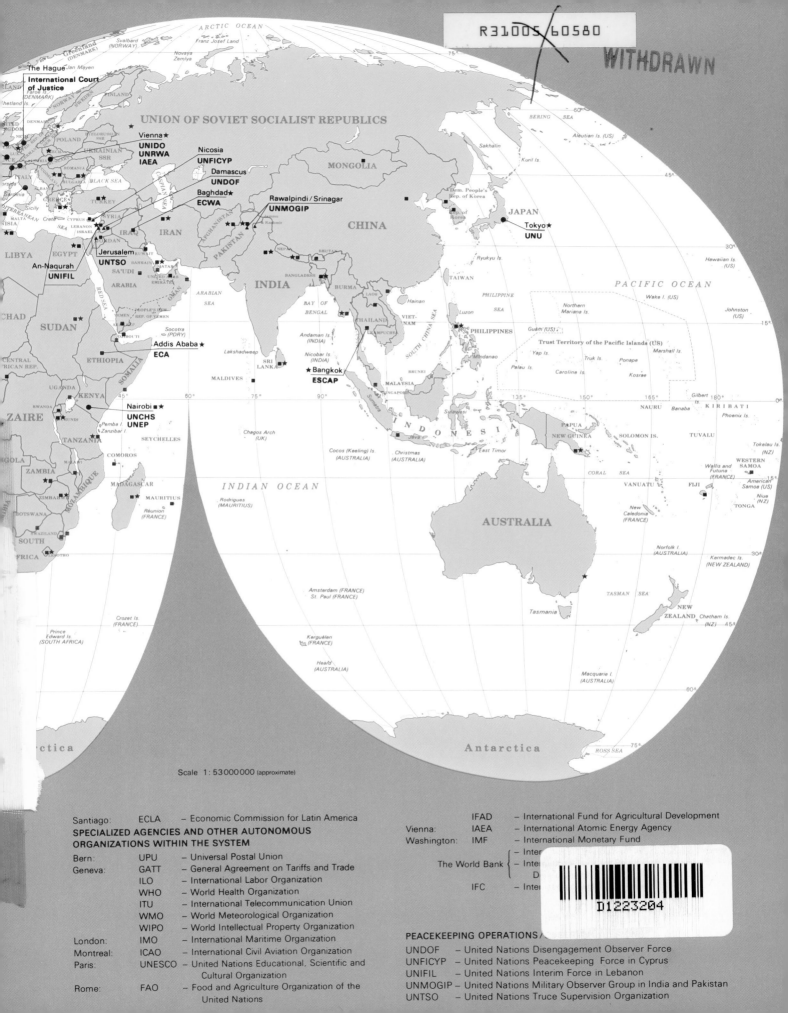

Scale 1:53000000 (approximate)

Santiago: ECLA — Economic Commission for Latin America

SPECIALIZED AGENCIES AND OTHER AUTONOMOUS ORGANIZATIONS WITHIN THE SYSTEM

Bern:	UPU	— Universal Postal Union
Geneva:	GATT	— General Agreement on Tariffs and Trade
	ILO	— International Labor Organization
	WHO	— World Health Organization
	ITU	— International Telecommunication Union
	WMO	— World Meteorological Organization
	WIPO	— World Intellectual Property Organization
London:	IMO	— International Maritime Organization
Montreal:	ICAO	— International Civil Aviation Organization
Paris:	UNESCO	— United Nations Educational, Scientific and Cultural Organization
Rome:	FAO	— Food and Agriculture Organization of the United Nations

	IFAD	— International Fund for Agricultural Development
Vienna:	IAEA	— International Atomic Energy Agency
Washington:	IMF	— International Monetary Fund
The World Bank	{ Inter...	— Inter... D...
	IFC	— Inter...

PEACEKEEPING OPERATIONS A...

UNDOF	— United Nations Disengagement Observer Force
UNFICYP	— United Nations Peacekeeping Force in Cyprus
UNIFIL	— United Nations Interim Force in Lebanon
UNMOGIP	— United Nations Military Observer Group in India and Pakistan
UNTSO	— United Nations Truce Supervision Organization

Volume 1

A practical guide to the geographic, historical, political, social, & economic status of all nations, their international relationships, and the United Nations system.

WORLDMARK
ENCYCLOPEDIA
OF THE NATIONS

UNITED NATIONS

WORLDMARK PRESS, LTD.
PUBLISHER

JOHN WILEY & SONS, INC.
EXCLUSIVE WORLD DISTRIBUTOR
New York Chichester
Brisbane Toronto Singapore

Goode projection of the world Copyright by the University of Chicago.

Typography by U.S. Lithograph Inc., New York, N.Y.

Preparation of lithographic negatives for maps by
John Dreyer & Co., Inc., New York, N.Y.

Production by the Maple-Vail Book Manufacturing
Group, Binghamton, N.Y.

Printed in the United States of America

LIBRARY OF CONGRESS CATALOGING IN PUBLICATION DATA

Main entry under title:
Worldmark encyclopedia of the nations.
Includes bibliographies and index.
Contents: v.1. The United Nations—v.2. Africa—
v.3. Americas—[etc.]
1. Geography—Dictionaries. 2. History—Dictionaries.
3. Economics—Dictionaries. 4. United Nations.
5. Political Science—Dictionaries.
G63.W67   1984   910′.3′21   83-26013
ISBN 0-471–88622-X (Wiley)

Staff

Editor and Publisher	MOSHE Y. SACHS
Executive Editor	GEOFFREY M. HORN
Senior Editor	LOUIS BARRON
Chief Copy Editor and Consulting Editor	MARY JANE ALEXANDER
Associate Editors	DONNA AMOS
	ROY CREGO UNA HILDEBRANDT
Contributing Editors	WALTER R. FOX
	DEBORAH GALE ROBERT HALASZ
	KATHRYN PAULSEN PATRICIA A. RODRIGUEZ
	IRINA RYBACEK SARA STEINMETZ

Cartography and Art Staff

Senior Cartographic Editor	MIKLOS PINTHER
Cartographer and Art Director	STEVEN R. AUSTIN
Associate Cartographer	SUDSAI POOLSUK
Artists	PAT EBNER MARGARET Z. LEE
	JOHN K. McDONALD ALASTAIR R. NOBLE
	GARY S. TONG VERA TOSTANOSKI

United Nations Volume Staff

Editor UN Section	ROBERT N. KENNEY
Associate UN Editor	SARAH ANN MARTIN
Indexer	ROSLYN FRIEDMAN

General Staff

Copy Editors and Proofreaders	LOUIS DOYLE
	MARCIA D. HORN MAXINNE LEIGHTON
	MARTIN MITCHELL PAULINE PIEKARZ
	ISABEL STEIN BIFF TAIBI
	PHILIP THOMPSON JOHN WILLIAMS
Typists	LAURA BELL ROSEMARIE T. KRIST
	ERIC NOOTER PATRICIA E. O'CONNOR
	BARBARA W. STANKOWSKI JEAN WOLFF

Acknowledgments

A basic part of the editorial preparation of the *Worldmark Encyclopedia of the Nations* consists of keeping continuously abreast of the work of governments. The editors wish to express their gratitude to the many government officials the world over who so kindly gave their cooperation. Grateful acknowledgment is made for the invaluable material, used throughout the encyclopedia, drawn from the mass of documents issued by the United Nations and its specialized agencies. Gratitude is expressed for the assistance given by numerous officials of the United Nations, the specialized agencies, and the intergovernmental and nongovernmental organizations.

To Louis Barron, the publisher expresses profound indebtedness for his unique contribution in setting the scholarly standard of this encyclopedia in its First Edition and for his dedication to maintaining that standard in subsequent editions.

Special acknowledgment must be given to Miklos Pinther, Chief, Cartographic Unit of the United Nations, for his painstaking devotion to this encyclopedia's particular mapping needs, and to Fredric M. Kaplan, Editor of *Encyclopedia of China Today*, for past and current help.

Gratitude for assistance in updating articles on the activities of their agencies for the *United Nations* volume is expressed to James Quackenbush, Director, Washington Office, ILO; Peter Ozorio, Information Officer, WHO; Tony Loftas, Chief, Information Materials Production Branch, FAO; René Lefort, Office of Public Information, UNESCO; Frank Vogo, Director of Public Affairs, World Bank; Azizali Mohammed, Director, External Relations Department, IMF; A. G. El-Zanati, Chief, Central Library, ITU; Roger Kohn, Information Officer, IMO; L. Rubins, Counselor, UPU; Hans-Friedrich Meyer, Acting Director of Public Information, IAEA; Marc Peeters, External Relations Officer, WMO; A. Pillepich, Deputy Registrar, International Court of Justice; and John Croome, Director, External Relations and Information Division, GATT.

Special thanks is also extended to the many members of individual offices and departments of the United Nations for assistance in revising and rewriting material, including Edith Ward, Center for Transnational Corporations; John von Arnold, UNDP; Anthony Hewett, UNICEF; Thijs Bienefelt, UNFPA; John Miles, UNRWA; Zia Rizvi, UNHCR; Thomas Tanaka, Division of Non-Self-Governing Territories, Purchasing and Transportation Department; and Jean-Claude Faby, UNEP.

The editors wish to express their gratitude for the exceptional help extended by the governments of the following nations: Afghanistan, Albania, Antigua and Barbuda, Australia, Austria, Bahamas, Bahrain, Bangladesh, Barbados, Belgium, Bhutan, Bolivia, Botswana, Brazil, Bulgaria, Cameroon, Chad, Chile, China, Cuba, Cyprus, Czechoslovakia, Denmark, Ecuador, Egypt, Fiji, France, Finland, Gabon, German Democratic Republic, Ghana, Greece, Guatemala, Guinea-Bissau, Haiti, Honduras, Iceland, Iran, Ireland, Israel, Jamaica, Japan, Jordan, Kampuchea (Democratic Kampuchea), Kenya, Korea (ROK), Kuwait, Laos, Liberia, Libya, Liechtenstein, Luxembourg, Madagascar, Malaysia, Maldives, Malta, Mauritius, Mexico, Monaco, Morocco, Netherlands, Niger, Nigeria, Norway, Oman, Pakistan, Papua New Guinea, Paraguay, Philippines, Qatar, Rwanda, St. Lucia, San Marino, Sa'udi Arabia, Senegal, Singapore, Spain, Sri Lanka, Sudan, Suriname, Sweden, Switzerland, Tanzania, Thailand, Turkey, Tuvalu, Uganda, United Arab Emirates, United Kingdom, Uruguay, Viet-Nam, Yemen Arab Republic, Zambia, Zimbabwe.

The following individuals and agencies deserve special acknowledgment for their generous assistance: Monica Peralta Ramos, Academic and University Affairs, Embassy of the Argentine Republic; Merle Fabian, Librarian, Canadian Embassy, and Sheila Purse, Librarian, Canadian Consulate General; Paul Robert Mangouta, Economic Counselor, Permanent Mission of the People's Republic of the Congo to the UN; Ronald A. Shillingford, Director, Investment Promotion North America, Dominica Industrial Development Corp.; Piedad de Suro, Counselor for Cultural and Press Affairs, Embassy of Ecuador; Margaret Foster, Documentation Section, Press and Information Division, French Embassy; Inge Godenschweger, German Information Center (FRG); Greek National Tourist Organization; Ágnes Sebes, Deputy Head, Department of Encyclopedias, Akadémiai Kiadó, Hungary; Narendra Kumar, Consul for Press and Public Relations, Consulate General of India; Sambas Wirakusumah, Educational and Cultural Attache, Embassy of the Republic of Indonesia; Cornelio Zani, Director, Consumer Goods Division, Italian Trade Commission; Choijiljavyn Bold, Second Secretary, Permanent Mission of the Mongolian People's Republic to the UN; Alfredo Valencia, Counselor for Commercial Affairs, and Domingo Da-Fineo, Counselor, Embassy of Peru; Andrzej Dobrzynski, First Secretary, Embassy of the Polish People's Republic; Ann Mulrane, Portuguese Embassy; Ilie Puscas, Third Secretary, Cultural Affairs, Embassy of the Socialist Republic of Romania; Joel G. Toney, Counselor and Deputy Permanent Representative to the UN, Mission of St. Vincent and the Grenadines; Delarey van Tonder, Third Secretary, Information, Embassy of South Africa, and T. L. van Zyl, Assistant Editor, *Standard Encyclopedia of Southern Africa*; Javier Malagón, Cultural Attaché, Embassy of Spain; Murhaf Jouejati, Consultant, US Arab Chamber of Commerce (Syria); Coordination Council for North American Affairs (Taiwan); Henri Bersoux, Coordinator, Togo Information Service, and Stanley Cleveland, Togo Investment Board; Trinidad and Tobago Industrial Development Corp.; Arlette Ben-Dali, Permanent Mission of Tunisia to the UN; A. N. Kulakov, Soviet Encyclopedia Publishing House (USSR); Albert Short, Director and Department of Defense Adviser, Office of Micronesian Negotiations (US Pacific Dependencies); British Information Services, New York (UK); Youri Ivanov, Director, UN Statistical Office; Monsignor Eugenio Sbarbaro, Apostolic Delegation, Vatican; Gonzalo Palacios, Counselor for Cultural Affairs, Embassy of Venezuela; Nena Crnec, Yugoslav Chamber of Economy; Jill Penfold, Zimbabwe Mission to the UN.

The editors gratefully acknowledge the cooperation of the following financial institutions: African Development Bank, Asian Development Bank, Reserve Bank of Australia, Central Bank of the Bahamas, Bahrain Monetary Authority, Bangladesh Bank, Central Bank of Barbados, National Bank of Belgium, Bank of Bhutan, Bank of Botswana, National Bank of Bulgaria, Banque de la République du Burundi, Bank of Canada, Banque Centrale des États de l'Afrique de l'Ouest (BCEAO), Banco Central de Chile, Bank of China, Banco de la República (Colombia), Státní Banka Československá (Czechoslovakia), Danmarks Nationalbank (Denmark), Banco Central de la República Dominicana, Central Bank of Egypt, Banco de Guinea Ecuatorial (Equatorial Guinea), Banco Central de Reserva de El Salvador, National Bank of Ethiopia, Bank of Finland, Deutsche Bundesbank (FRG), Banco de Guatemala, Bank of Greece, Bank of Guyana, Hongkong and Shanghai Banking Corp., National Bank of Hungary, Central Bank of Iceland, State Bank of India, Inter-American Development Bank, Central Bank of Ireland, Bank of Israel, Banca d'Italia, Central Bank of Jordan, Central Bank of Kenya, Bank of Korea (ROK), Central Bank of Kuwait, Central Bank of Lesotho, Lesotho Monetary Authority, Banque sdu Liban (Lebanon), National Bank of Liberia, National Bank of Liechtenstein, Banque Internationale à Luxembourg, Reserve Bank of Malawi, Bank Negara Malaysia, Central Bank of Malta, Banque Centrale de Mauritanie, Banco de Mexico, De Nederlandsche Bank n.v., Nepal Rastra Bank, Revenue Bank of New Zealand, Banque de Développement de la

République du Niger, Central Bank of Nigeria, State Bank of Pakistan, Bank of Papua New Guinea, Banco de Portugal, Sa'udi Arabian Monetary Agency, Central Bank of Seychelles, Bank of Sierra Leone, Monetary Authority of Singapore, Central Bank of Solomon Islands, Central Bank of Somalia, Banco de España (Spain), Central Bank of Ceylon (Sri Lanka), Central Bank of Swaziland, Sveriges Riksbank (Sweden), Bank of Taiwan, Bank of Tanzania, Bank of Thailand, Bank of Tonga, Central Bank of the Republic of Turkey, Bank of England (UK), Banco Central de Venezuela, Bank of Western Samoa, Narodna Banka Jugoslavije (Yugoslavia), and Reserve Bank of Zimbabwe.

The editors also wish to acknowledge that, in preparing the present edition, they have drawn freely upon the publications of the following agencies and organizations, among others: American Jewish Committee, American Society of Civil Engineers, Americas Watch, American Telephone & Telegraph Co., Caribbean Tourism Association, Council for Mutual Economic Assistance, Statistical Office of the European Communities (EUROSTAT), Helsinki Watch, International Iron and Steel Institute, International Institute for Strategic Studies, International Road Federation, International Union for Conservation of Nature and Natural Resources, Lloyd's Bank, Motor Vehicle Manufacturers Association of the United States, NATO, Nordic Statistical Secretariat, OAS, OECD, OPEC, PAHO, Population Council, Population Reference Bureau, Price Waterhouse, UNFPA, UNDP, UNEP, UNESCO, UNHCR, UNRWA, UN Statistical Office, US Agency for International Development, US Arms Control and Disarmament Agency, US Board of Geographic Names, US Department of Commerce, US Department of Defense, US Department of Energy, US Department of State, US Maritime Administration, US Public Health Service, WHO, World Bank, World Environment Center, World Insurance Congress, and World Tourism Organization.

Continental endsheets were adapted from maps provided by the Government of the United States. Endsheets for the *United Nations* volume were adapted from the *Descriptive Map of the United Nations*.

The publisher wishes to acknowledge his gratitude to the late Simha Amir for having made feasible the establishment of this encyclopedia. Appreciation is expressed to Joseph R. Vergara of Harper & Row for his advice and encouragement and for helping the encyclopedia to achieve recognition as a basic reference work.

Grateful acknowledgment for editorial liaison assistance is extended to Robert B. Polhemus of John Wiley & Sons, Inc., and to Nat Bodian for his untiring promotion of this work.

The author of the first edition (1960) of the *United Nations System*, and the second edition (1963) *United Nations*, was John H. E. Fried, Professor of Political Science, City University of New York (Lehman College).

Contents

Foreword

to the First Edition

This encyclopedia is different from all others produced in recent years. It is not simply a collection of miscellaneous facts for ready reference. It resembles more the pioneer work of those encyclopedists who ushered in the era of enlightenment in 18th-century France, in that it mirrors the life of men and nations at a great turning point in history, when the national state system of absolute sovereignties has to find new adjustments under the sovereignty of science. The old safeguards for security—mountains and oceans—no longer hold against the impact of an atomic age. The United Nations is the mirror of this new world in which international life becomes more and more interdependent. The political framework is therefore filled in by a comprehensive survey of the major interests of people everywhere. Such an encyclopedia should prove a valuable guide to the understanding not only of the United Nations but of our time.

JAMES T. SHOTWELL
6 August 1874–17 July 1965
Chairman, Editorial Advisory Board
First Edition

From the

Introduction

to the First Edition

The swift course of domestic and world events, part of a hastened process of change, requires an enormous increase of basic understanding by peoples of the multiple factors influencing the tempo and direction of national developments. The pattern of intercultural penetration and cross-fertilizing exchanges of scientific and technological knowledge rests upon a concept of fundamental unity of diverse approaches to the central objective of all human endeavors: the creation of a better world, with general equality of opportunity to all individuals, everywhere.

Within a planet shrunk into community bounds by the progress of communications there are no substantial sectors of mankind still completely isolated from the main currents of 20th-century thought and action. A growing sense of identification among men is fostered by the adoption of certain basic standards of human rights and the slow growth of supranational law rooted in the fundamental principles that are common to all juridical systems.

No period in history has witnessed such accelerated search for adequate answers to the riddles that have so long beset humanity. Metaphysical explanations of the universe and of the individual's place within it vie with each other in the vast and only superficially explored realm of emotions; rationalized conceptions of economic and social philosophies contend in the marketplace of personal loyalties with a violence that frequently threatens to rend asunder the fabric of overall unity; and the march forward of freedoms and improvements in the status of people througout our earth is largely clouded by the supercharged treatment of political affairs in the media of mass communication.

At a time when people everywhere are truly eager for accurate, comprehensive, and timely information about themselves and their neighbors in the closely related various geographic areas, the vastness and multiplicity of the field to be covered promotes reporting that serves little the needs of the average person: it is either too detailed in breadth and depth, so that only specialists can profit from its availability, or sketchy and fragmentary, to the point where it contributes more to confusion than enlightenment of the users.

A specific reason has made necessary a new approach to analytical and basic data on each country, as a separate political unit, and as a member of the vast family of nations all constitute together: the universality of their interest in the maintenance of international peace and security through the joint exercise of agreed-upon powers to restrain violence; to police disturbed areas where peaceful relations are endangered; to promote the application of legal procedures to the adjudication of their differences; and to strike at the very sources of controversy, which are rooted in the deep chasms among their economic and social standards and their consequent basic inequalities of status.

So-called realists may continue to voice their belief that conflict among nations is an outgrowth of their dynamic development, and that only practical arrangements which create "balances" of power can establish an equilibrium within the diverse segments of the world; and theorists of the biological inevitability of war still proclaim the materialistic concept that only a concentration of authority in the hands of some overwhelmingly strong state can eliminate actual armed conflict and bring to subjected peoples the "benefits" of a freedomless "pax romana." But mankind has made great strides since the days of empires, the conquest of colonial dependencies, the plagues and misery that fixed the general expectation of human life under thirty years, and the spiritual darkness of illiteracy and isolation from the mainstreams of culture of variegated philosophical, religious, and scientific concepts.

Under principles of ethics the peoples and the nations emerged as possessors of rights and bearers of responsibilities, and morality took its place in the councils of power. The advancement toward a universal rule of law has been too slow for the idealists and yet most encouraging to those who believe that peaceful evolutionary progress achieves more durable results than violent revolutionary change. The steady process of codification of generally recognized juridical principles and the formulation of new ones through general consensus constitute one of the most hopeful signs of this restless era of change. International compacts such as the Covenant of the League of Nations and the Charter of the United Nations incorporate moral concepts side by side with legal standards. They recognize that there are both ethical and juridical duties and rights that must be observed by states in their reciprocal relations and in respect of their inhabitants, subjects, and citizens.

So far-reaching are the changes already wrought within the world community, particularly for its less developed segments, that the normal processes of history have lost considerable significance in the face of new realities recently created.

Feeling that none of the encyclopedias and specialized sources of information do sufficient justice to these accomplishments in political freedom, economic development, social progress, and the practice of international cooperation, Worldmark Press, Inc., decided to publish a basically new encyclopedia devoted to the nations.

After identifying the outward symbols of each state: the *capital*, a *map*, the *flag*, the *national anthem*, the *monetary unit*, the system of *weights and measures, holidays,* and *time,* each article proceeds to cover, as thoroughly as available data permit, 50 individual phases of the country's life, so as to furnish an overall picture of its present as rooted in the past evolution of its institutions, customs, and traditions. A precise definition of *location, size, and extent* of the individual territory is given, so that the reader can visualize, as a living reality, that which the map depicts graphically. *Topography, climate,* and *flora and fauna* supplement the other natural physical features of the respective nation.

More than by any other factor, countries are what they are because of man's exertions to create his own environment, so *population, ethnic groups,* and *language* are the next items covered. Together with the section devoted to *religion,* they give a basic understanding of the demographic phenomena that determine the basic institutions, political, economic, and social, of each sovereign unit.

Transportation and *communications* follow in the description of the positive factors working for the consolidation of each country's internal unity and of the reconstruction of the wider oneness of mankind.

Next there is a *historical survey,* in most cases kept brief because of the availability of comprehensive ones in other sources of general information.

As the result of individual national experience various types of *governmental authority* have been either adopted from the similar experience of other peoples or created to meet different requirements. In the operation of governments, there are diverse types of machinery which correspond to particular political philosophies and which the citizens control through *political parties.*

Local governmental structures supplement the system of deliberative and executive authorities in charge of public interests.

Knowledge of the organizational pattern of the *judiciary* acquires considerable importance for all kinds of individual and corporate activities within a particular nation, so information is furnished thereon.

The internal stability of a country and its international security are made clear by adequate data on the organization and potential of the *armed forces.*

Because the pattern of *migrations* has undergone great changes, information on their effect upon demographic developments in each state is of deep significance for any evaluation of manpower prospects and consumer potentials.

No nation is an isolated unit itself. The extent to which each government engages in *international cooperation* is a useful indicator of its concern with the peaceful handling of potential sources of tensions and conflicts.

One of the phases of internal development with an international impact relates to the wide range of the economy. This encyclopedia deals comprehensively with *income, labor, agriculture, animal husbandry, fishing, forestry, mining, energy and power, industry, domestic trade, foreign trade, balance of payments, banking, insurance, securities, public finance, taxation, customs and duties, foreign investment,* and *economic policy.*

It also gives information on *health, social welfare,* and *housing,* important in the economically less developed nations as a mainspring of economic activity and financial investment for what is called the infrastructure, vital as a prerequisite of other actions to promote production, employment, higher standards of living and, in general, a broader enjoyment of basic human rights and fundamental freedoms.

The domestic activities mentioned in the two previous paragraphs aim to help in the struggle against illiteracy which, even in more advanced countries, reduces the number of citizens actively engaged in political life and is instrumental in the growth and maintenance of discriminatory practices and arbitrary stereotypes within each nation and between many nations. It is of the utmost importance to know the *educational* facilities available for supplying trained political leaders, administrators, economists, social workers, medical personnel, and technicians. And to data on teaching establishments is added information on *libraries and museums* and on the *organizations* set up by the people of each country to promote their collective interests and welfare.

The *press* and other media of information and enlightenment constitute an important index of the cultural standing of the people; the degree of their freedom is the best evidence of the intellectual maturity of government and governed, and a significant indicator of the degree to which essential human rights in the field of opinion are truly respected.

Perhaps the most effective way to advance reciprocal understanding is by contacts among peoples of different countries and with each other's natural environment. The conditions which must be met for the purposes of *tourism* are fully explained.

Dependencies for which each individual state assumes international responsibilities are described in detail. Finally a brief roll of *famous persons* is a biographical listing of national figures. An up-to-date *bibliography* closes each nation's description.

But in our day and era nations are not islands unto themselves, busy solely with internal problems of varying magnitude. The field of exclusively domestic concern is shrinking under the tremendous impact of easy communications among nations.

While the United Nations and regional organizations of states, directly or through their subsidiary or associated organs, may and do deal with practically every field of human interest, other organizations restrict their jurisdiction to the more specific areas of economic or social matters. They handle issues at the universal and at the close neighborhood levels and, large or small, they each play a part in the process of international cooperation to improve and give constructive meaning to the relations among peoples. Even military pacts have gradually broadened the scope of their concern as a result of the finding that merely negative aims do not afford by themselves the stability and coherence for which they were brought into being. The Secretary-General of the United Nations, Mr. Dag Hammarskjöld, has repeatedly stated his views that any collective action conducted outside the United Nations, but consonant with the spirit of its charter, can be considered as cooperation toward the fundamental objectives of the world organization.

Because we live under the impact of global issues that affect every individual, for good or for ill, and because also of the advance of democratic processes domestically and internationally, more and more people are now actively concerned with the course of world affairs. The best channels to voice their hopes are the governments democratically elected and responsible to the wishes of the citizenry. When the people disagree with their authorities, whose judgment must necessarily take into account factors not always of public knowledge, the people then can use their nongovernmental bodies to express their prevailing views.

The *Worldmark Encyclopedia of the Nations* is a pioneer effort. It is our earnest hope that this first edition may prove a truly useful tool to everyone.

BENJAMIN A. COHEN
18 March 1896–12 March 1960
Editor-in-Chief, First Edition

Preface

The purpose of this encyclopedia is to offer the reader a portrait of the world—the individual nations and their main meeting ground, the United Nations system. Each country and organization is here viewed as it might be reflected in a world mirror and not as seen from the perspective of any one nation.

The world view was achieved by constantly seeking to adhere to a supranational attitude. Belief in the basic mutuality of interests of the people of all lands and in the work of international organizations guided the editors in their approach to the material and its presentation.

The standard treatment of fifty features has been applied uniformly to all countries, regardless of their size, strength, position, or prominence on the world scene. This schema not only serves as a means for comparative study but also affords the reader balanced knowledge of the new and lesser-known nations.

The editors have endeavored to transmit to the reader the realities of today's existence. To this end, specific details are related to other aspects of a particular country and to the world as a whole. Care has been taken to present these interrelationships not only in dealing with social, political, and historical aspects, but also in treating economic, statistical, and organizational material. In this Silver Anniversary Edition, new attention has been given to *environment, science and technology*, and such important indicators of *social development* as population planning and the role of women.

It was this supranational attitude that attracted the late Dr. Benjamin A. Cohen, former undersecretary of the United Nations, to assume the editorship-in-chief of the First Edition. Ben Cohen's personal appeal and stature impelled hundreds of people, many with specialized talents and in positions usually not accessible to publishers, to contribute to this work. The *Worldmark Encyclopedia of the Nations* would not have had its wealth of resources but for him.

Thus, we had the unique opportunity of sending each article to an official authority for factual checking and general appraisal. The authority, either a representative of the country or the international organization in question, went over the material and made suggestions that were evaluated for inclusion in the article. The practice of consulting such authorities was continued in the preparation of subsequent editions. Indeed, many of them assisted in bringing up to date the articles dealing with their countries or organizations.

The new material on individual nations and the updating of the information on the United Nations system required the physical enlargement of the encyclopedia. This expansion reflects the growth of United Nations membership since 1945. The United Nations had 51 charter members. By the time of our First Edition (1960), there were 82 member nations; by the Second Edition (1963), 110; by the Third Edition (1966), 122; by the Fourth Edition (1971), 127; by the Fifth Edition (1976), 144; and by the present Silver Anniversary Edition (1984), 158.

The First Edition, in one volume, contained 119 country articles; the present edition, in five volumes, contains 172, including new articles on 12 newly independent or emerging nations and on the increasingly important polar regions. Coverage of the United Nations has been extensively revised and expanded, reflecting the fact that the United Nations system, with all its departments, agencies, commissions, committees, and working groups, has now become active in virtually every walk of life, from human rights to agriculture, from education to atomic energy.

Carved in stone, opposite the home of the United Nations, is an inscription taken from Isaiah: " . . . and they shall beat their swords into plowshares, and their spears into pruning hooks: nation shall not lift up sword against nation, neither shall they learn war any more." The Prophets' sense of moral justice, which was the foundation of their vision of peace as expressed in this inscription, has not yet been accepted as a basis for political behavior. Indeed, developments in recent years have cast a dark shadow over the United Nations. The passage of resolutions and the toleration of practices inconsistent with the spirit of the Charter have not only instilled doubt about the effectiveness of the organization as a political instrument but have also undermined the spirit of fairness and cooperation that once characterized the work of the specialized agencies. In the 1930s, the world witnessed the loss of moral force and then the political decline of the League of Nations. No friend of peace could wish its successor a similar fate. It is the fervent hope of the editors of this encyclopedia that political influences will not further undermine the substantive achievements of the United Nations.

The problems of peace preoccupy the minds of people everywhere. The ever-intensifying complexities of our times, while serving to increase the responsibility of a larger number of persons, often also augment the individual's feeling of helplessness. Yet, knowledge of other lands and ability to see their people as fellow human beings can enable the individual to overcome this feeling of helplessness and to act for himself and others. In this spirit this work was conceived and is offered, with the hope that it may not only find many specific uses, but may bring into focus a broader world view for the reader, and thus contribute to international understanding.

MOSHE Y. SACHS
Editor and Publisher

Notes
to the Sixth Edition

GENERAL NOTE: In compiling data for incorporation into the Sixth Edition of the *Worldmark Encyclopedia of the Nations*, substantial efforts were made to enlist the assistance of the government and central bank or monetary agency of every nation in the world, as well as of all pertinent UN agencies, who cooperated by supplying data and by revising and updating materials relevant to their sphere of interest. Material received from official sources was reviewed and critically assessed by the editors as part of the process of incorporation. Materials and publications of the UN family and of intergovernmental and nongovernmental organizations throughout the world provided a major fund of geographic, demographic, economic, and social data; in compiling historical and political data, primary materials generated by governments were supplemented by data gathered from numerous other sources.

For the Sixth Edition, fresh and corroborating data were sought for every entry, with special efforts taken to augment the scope of prior coverage in mapping; flags and crests; currency; population; religions; history; armed forces; international cooperation; energy and power; economic development (including economic development assistance); social development (including population planning and the role of women); tourism, travel, and recreation (including sports); famous persons; and bibliography. While the familiar format of 50 sections was retained, the sections on banking and securities as well as the sections on communications and press were combined, in order to make room for new sections on environment (5) and science and technology (29). In addition, the section on migration was moved in order to integrate it more fully with coverage of population and ethnic groups.

We have tried in our transliterations to strike a balance between the sometimes conflicting claims of familiarity to the reader, fidelity to the original pronunciation, compliance with a country's own transliteration preference (as expressed in its official English-language publications), and overall consistency of treatment. In general, we have adopted the most familiar usage as the preferred choice, reserving the more literal transliteration to parentheses at first mention; e.g., Kuwait (Al-Kuwayt), Gamal Abdel Nasser (Jamal 'Abd an-Nasir). In the case of China, whose government has gone to great lengths to familiarize the English-speaking world with its new transliteration system, we have in most cases adopted the official pinyin spellings, relegating to parenthetical mention the names in their Wade-Giles form; e.g., Beijing (Peking), Mao Zedong (Mao Tse-tung).

The reader's attention is directed to the Glossary of Special Terms (pp. 259–60) of this volume) for explanations of key terms and concepts essential to a fuller understanding of the text.

COUNTRY NAMES: Country names are reported (as appropriate) in three forms: the short-form name, as commonly used in the text; the English version of the official name; and the official name in the national language(s). When necessary, textual usages of some short-form names have been rectified, usually through the substitution of an acronym for the official name, in order to strike a better balance between official usages and universal terminology. Thus the following changes in short-form names have been adopted throughout (except in historical context to preserve accuracy): East Germany: GDR (German Democratic Republic); West Germany: FRG (Federal Republic of Germany); North

Korea: DPRK (Democratic People's Republic of Korea); South Korea: ROK (Republic of Korea); North Yemen: YAR (Yemen Arab Republic); South Yemen: PDRY (People's Democratic Republic of Yemen). In addition, the following usages have been adopted to reflect official name changes since the Fifth Edition—from the Gilbert Islands to Kiribati, from New Hebrides to Vanuatu, from Rhodesia to Zimbabwe, from South West Africa to Namibia, and from the Territory of the Afars and the Issas (formerly French Somaliland) to Djibouti. In all current membership lists and contemporary contexts, the country name China should be taken to mean the People's Republic of China, or mainland China; the country controlled by the government of the Republic of China is given as Taiwan.

MAPS: All maps have been fully updated, and where necessary, new maps have been drafted and outdated maps redrawn. In the few instances where disputes exist over the designation of a place-name in an international zone, editorial discretion has been applied (e.g., the designation "Persian Gulf" has been retained). Spellings on the individual country maps reflect national usages and recognized transliteration practice. In the case of some internationally prominent place-names, both conventional English spellings and national-language versions are supplied; e.g., Moscow (Moskva), Rome (Roma), Jerusalem (Yerushalayim, Al-Quds). To clarify national boundaries and landforms, light shading has been applied to waters, and darker shading to lands not within that nation's jurisdiction. A line of alternating dashes and dots signifies an internationally recognized boundary; a line consisting only of dashes signifies a disputed or undemarcated boundary. Cross-hatching has been used to designate certain disputed areas.

FLAGS AND NATIONAL EMBLEMS: All depictions of flags, flag designations, and national emblems have been reviewed and, where necessary, corrected or changed to reflect their official usage as of 1984; in each case, official sources were sought for corroboration. In general, the term "national flag" denotes the civil flag of the nation. New and revised flags and emblems were in most cases provided by Dr. Whitney Smith, Executive Director, Flag Research Center, Winchester, Mass.

CURRENCY: Where not otherwise specified, currency conversion factors cited in the Sixth Edition are market rates as of 31 October 1983. The list of nominal New York closing quotations compiled by the Chase Manhattan Bank was the principal source used. Other trading rates were generously provided by Deak-Perera.

WEIGHTS AND MEASURES: The general world trend toward adoption of the metric system is acknowledged through the use of metric units and their nonmetric (customary or imperial) equivalents throughout the text. The two exceptions to this practice involve territorial sea limits, which are reported in nautical miles, and various production data, for which (unless otherwise stated) units of measure reflect the system in use by the country in question. All tons are metric tons (again, unless otherwise indicated), reflecting the practice of the UN in its statistical reporting. For a complete listing of conversion factors and an explanation of symbols used in the text, see p. 266 of this volume.

HOLIDAYS: Except where noted, all holidays listed are official public holidays, on which government offices are closed that would normally be open. Transliterations of names of Muslim holidays have been standardized. For a fuller discussion on these points, and for a description of religious holidays and their origins and meanings, see the Glossary of Religious Holidays in this volume (pp. 261–63).

LOCATION, SIZE AND EXTENT: The length of international boundary segments, the total lengths of national boundaries, and the territorial extent of each country appear in roman type when data were derived from official governmental sources of the country concerned; *italic type* indicates data derived from the UN and other sources. Rounding was used in the process of converting most figures. The reader may find differences in the length of boundaries of neighboring countries printed in roman type (thus signifying official governmental sources); such apparent discrepancies often reflect divergent measurement methodologies applied by individual countries.

ENVIRONMENT: The lists of common names for endangered species were compiled from basic data provided to Worldmark Press by the International Union for Conservation of Nature and Natural Resources, Environmental Monitoring Unit, Cambridge, and reflect the known status of endangered animal species as of 1983.

POPULATION: National population estimates, population growth rates, rural-urban ratios, life-expectancy estimates, and 1985–90 projections of population, crude birthrate, crude death rate, and net natural increase, where not provided by the countries, were derived from *Demographic Indicators of Countries: Estimates and Projections as Assessed in 1980*, published by the UN Department of International Economic and Social Affairs in 1982.

RELIGIONS: Estimates of religious adherents as of mid-1980, where not supplied by the countries, were based on David B. Barrett (ed.), *World Christian Encyclopedia* (Oxford University Press, 1982).

ARMED FORCES: In most cases, data on weaponry and personnel were derived from *The Military Balance* (1982–83 and 1983–84 editions), published by the International Institute for Strategic Studies in London. Figures for arms imports and exports are in current US dollars and were computed from *World Military Expenditures and Arms Transfers, 1971–80* (US Arms Control and Disarmament Agency, 1983).

BALANCE OF PAYMENTS: Balance of payments tables were computed from the monthly *International Financial Statistics* and other IMF publications.

ECONOMIC DEVELOPMENT: *US Overseas Loans and Grants and Assistance from International Organizations: Obligations and Loan Authorizations, July 1, 1945–September 30, 1982* (US Agency for International Development, 1983) and various OECD publications were the principal sources of the data on official development assistance.

MEDIA: Circulation data in most cases follow the *1982 Editor & Publisher International Year Book*.

FAMOUS PERSONS: Entries are based on information available through March 1984. Where a person noted in one country is known to have been born in another, the country (or, in some cases, city) of birth follows the personal name, in parentheses.

BIBLIOGRAPHY: Bibliographical listings are provided as a guide to further reading on the country in question and are not intended (for reasons of limitation of space) as a comprehensive listing of references used in research for the country article. Effort was made to provide a broad sampling of works on major subjects and topics as covered by the article; the bibliographies provide, wherever possible, introductory and general works for use by students and general readers, as well as classical studies, recent contributions, and other works regarded as seminal by area specialists.

Contributors

Shown below are contributors of country articles to the present and previous editions, in most cases followed by their affiliation or status at the time the contribution was made. Following each contributor's name is a list of the country article(s) written and/or updated; note that many articles have been written and/or revised by several contributors since the First Edition. Country names are given in the form in which they appear in the present edition; e.g., Rhodesia is listed as Zimbabwe. An asterisk (*) following the country name indicates an entirely new article written for the present edition.

ABOUCHAER, TOUFIC. Second Secretary, Embassy of Syria, Washington, D.C.: SYRIA (in part).

ALBA, VICTOR. Author, *Transition in Spain: From Franco to Democracy*: SPAIN.

ALISKY, MARVIN. Director of Center for Latin American Studies and Professor of Political Science, Arizona State University: URUGUAY.

ANTHONY, JOHN. Assistant Professor of Middle East Studies, School of Advanced International Studies, Johns Hopkins University: BAHRAIN (in part), QATAR (in part), UNITED ARAB EMIRATES (in part).

ARNADE, CHARLES W. Chairman, The American Idea, and Professor of History, University of South Florida: BOLIVIA.

ASHFORD, DOUGLAS E. Department of Political Science, Cornell University: MOROCCO, TUNISIA.

AUMANN, MOSHE. Counselor, Embassy of Israel, Washington, D.C.: ISRAEL (in part).

BARBER, WILLIAM J. Associate Professor of Economics, Wesleyan University: MALAWI (in part), ZAMBIA (in part).

BARRON, MURIEL T.: CANADA.

BASS, ELIZABETH M. Economist-Editor, Research Project on National Income in East Central Europe, New York: ALBANIA, BULGARIA, CZECHOSLOVAKIA (in part), POLAND (in part), ROMANIA.

BENNETT, NORMAN. Professor of History, Boston University: MAURITIUS.

BERG, ELLIOT J. Professor of Economics, University of Michigan: MAURITANIA.

BERG, NANCY GUINLOCK: BENIN, GUINEA, MALI, MAURITANIA, MOROCCO, SENEGAL, TOGO.

BERNSTEIN, MARVIN. Professor of History, State University of New York at Buffalo: ECUADOR.

BIRNS, LAURENCE R. Director, Council on Hemispheric Affairs: BOLIVIA, CHILE, CUBA, PARAGUAY.

BOSTON UNIVERSITY, AFRICAN STUDIES CENTER. John Harris, Professor of Economics and Director of African Studies Center; James C. Armstrong, Head, African Studies Library, Editors; Norman Bennett, Professor of History, Boston University: LIBYA, RWANDA, TUNISIA; Valerie Plave Bennett, Energy Resources Co.: GHANA; Heinz A. Bertsch: BURUNDI; Edouard Bustin, Professor of Political Science, Boston University: ZAIRE; Sid A. Chabawe: ALGERIA; Tobias Chizengeni: BOTSWANA, LESOTHO, SWAZILAND; William D. Coale: LIBERIA; Leon Cort: IVORY COAST; Bernardo P. Ferraz, Fellow, Massachusetts Institute of Technology: ANGOLA (in part),

GUINEA-BISSAU (in part), MOZAMBIQUE (in part); Kathleen Langley, Associate Professor of Economics, Boston University: EGYPT, NIGERIA; Jay I. Mann: MADAGASCAR; Sandra Mann: NIGER, UPPER VOLTA; Marcos G. Namashulua, Instructor, Political Science, Brandeis University: ANGOLA (in part), GUINEA-BISSAU (in part), MOZAMBIQUE (in part); Jeanne Penvenne: CAPE VERDE, SÃO TOMÉ AND PRÍNCIPE, UGANDA; Stella Silverstein: GAMBIA; Henry Steady: SIERRA LEONE; Dominique Western: CHAD.

BRADBURY, R.W. Professor of Economics, College of Business Administration, University of Florida: MEXICO.

BUTWELL, RICHARD. Dean for Arts and Science, State University of New York at Fredonia: AUSTRALIA, BURMA, ISRAEL, KAMPUCHEA, LAOS, NEW ZEALAND, SINGAPORE, THAILAND, TURKEY, VIET-NAM.

CARTER, GWENDOLEN M. Director, Program of African Studies, Northwestern University: SOUTH AFRICA.

CASTAGNO, ALPHONSO A. Director, African Research and Studies Program, Boston University: SOMALIA.

CASTAGNO, MARGARET. Author, *Historical Dictionary of Somalia*: SOMALIA.

CHANG, A.S. Hong Kong Correspondent, Institute of Foreign Studies, Tokyo; formerly Professor of Economics, National Chi-nan University, Shanghai: CHINA.

COLEMAN, JAMES S. Director, African Studies Program, and Professor of Political Science, University of California, Los Angeles: NIGERIA, TOGO.

COLLINS, ROBERT O. Professor of History, University of California, Santa Barbara: SUDAN.

CORDERAS, DESCÁRREGA, JOSÉ. Royal Geographical Society, Valverde (Spain): ANDORRA, SPAIN.

COWAN, L. GRAY. Dean, School of International Affairs, State University of New York, Albany: CENTRAL AFRICAN REPUBLIC, CHAD, CONGO, GABON.

CUMINGS, BRUCE G. Professor of Political Science, Swarthmore College: DEMOCRATIC PEOPLE'S REPUBLIC OF KOREA, REPUBLIC OF KOREA.

CZIRJAK, LASZLO. Associate, Columbia University: GERMAN DEMOCRATIC REPUBLIC, HUNGARY, ROMANIA.

DE GALE, SIR LEO. G.C.M.G., C.B.E., Governor-General, Government of Grenada: GRENADA.

DUNKLE, JOHN R. Associate Professor of Geography and Physical Science, University of Florida: CUBA.

EVANS, LAURENCE. Professor of History, Harpur College: JORDAN, SYRIA.

EYCK, F. GUNTHER. Professorial Lecturer in History and International Relations, American University:

AUSTRIA, BELGIUM, FRANCE, FEDERAL REPUBLIC OF GERMANY, LUXEMBOURG, NETHERLANDS, SWITZERLAND.

FALL, BERNARD B. Professor of Government, Howard University: KAMPUCHEA, LAOS, VIET-NAM.

FINLAND, GOVERNMENT OF. STATISTICAL OFFICE, Helsinki: FINLAND.

FLETCHER, N.E.W. Personal Assistant to the Governor-General, Government of Grenada: GRENADA.

FLETCHER, WILLARD ALLEN. Professor and Chairman, Department of History, College of Arts & Sciences, University of Delaware: BELGIUM, CYPRUS, GREECE, LUXEMBOURG, MALTA, NETHERLANDS, NETHERLANDS AMERICAN DEPENDENCIES, SWITZERLAND.

FONER, PHILIP S. Professor of History, Lincoln University: CUBA.

GANJI, MOHAMMAD H. Professor Emeritus, Tehran University; Chancellor, Amir Showkatul-Mulk University, Birjand, Iran: IRAN.

GOUTTIERRE, THOMAS E. Dean, International Studies and Programs; Director, Center for Afghanistan, University of Nebraska at Omaha: AFGHANISTAN.

GREENHOUSE, RALPH. US Information Agency: MALAYSIA.

HEINTZEN, HARRY. African Department, Voice of America: MALI, NIGER.

HISPANIC AMERICAN REPORT. Ronald Hilton, Editor; Donald W. Bray, Ronald H. Chilcote, James Cockcroft, Timothy F. Harding, Sir Harold Mitchell, Assistant Editors; Ann Hartfiel, Andrew I. Rematore, Editorial Assistants; Eugene R. Braun, Marjorie Woodford Bray, Lee Ann Campbell, Jorge Caprista, Manuel Carlos, Frances Chilcote, Nancy Clark, Richard L. Cummings, Carlos Darquen, Anthony Dauphinot, Nicholas H. Davis, Joan E. Dowdell, Jerome Durlak, Pan Eimon, Peter L. Eisenberg, Richard Eisman, Claire E. Flaherty, Charles Gauld, Hugh Hamilton, Timothy Harding, Paul Helms, Raymond D. Higgins, Saul Landau, Wendy Lang, Joyce Lobree, Thomas Marks, Marilyn Morrison, Frank Odd, Molly Older, D. Wingeate Pike, Gabriel Pinheiro, Luis Ponce de León, Kenneth Posey, James Purks, Lawrence L. Smith, Maud Maria Straub, Linda Striem, David F. Thompson, Pamela Throop, Alice Wexler, Ann Wyckoff, Allen Young, Michael J. Zimmerman, Contributors: ARGENTINA, BOLIVIA, BRAZIL, CHILE, COLOMBIA, COSTA RICA, CUBA, DOMINICAN REPUBLIC, ECUADOR, EL SALVADOR, GUATEMALA, HAITI, HONDURAS, MEXICO, NICARAGUA, PANAMA, PARAGUAY, PERU, URUGUAY, VENEZUELA.

HOFFMAN, GEORGE W. Professor of Geography, University of Texas at Austin: AUSTRIA, FRANCE, ITALY, LIECHTENSTEIN, SWITZERLAND, YUGOSLAVIA.

HUNSBERGER, WARREN S. Professor of Economics, American University (with the assistance of Alan D. Smith, Information Officer, Consulate-General of Japan, New York): JAPAN.

INDOCHINA RESOURCE CENTER. Washington, D.C., D. Gareth Porter, Director: KAMPUCHEA (in part), LAOS (in part), VIET-NAM (in part).

INGHAM, KENNETH. Director of Studies, Royal Military Academy, Sandhurst: UGANDA (in part).

INGRAMS, HAROLD. Adviser on Overseas Information, Colonial Office, London: TANZANIA.

INTERNATIONAL INSTITUTE FOR AERIAL SURVEY AND EARTH SCIENCES. F. J. Ormeling, Head of Cartography Department; C. A. de Bruijn, P. Hofstee, A. B. M. Hijl, Department of Urban Surveys: NETHERLANDS.

ITZKOWITZ, NORMAN. Associate Professor of Oriental Studies, Princeton University: SA'UDI ARABIA (in part), YEMEN ARAB REPUBLIC.

KANTOR, HARRY. Professor of Political Science, Marquette University: COSTA RICA.

KAPLAN, FREDRIC M.: AUSTRALIA, CHINA, CYPRUS, JAPAN, DEMOCRATIC PEOPLE'S REPUBLIC OF KOREA, LAOS, MALAYSIA, MONGOLIA, NEPAL, SINGAPORE, TAIWAN, UNITED STATES OF AMERICA, VIET-NAM.

KARCH, JOHN J. Professorial Lecturer, Institute for Sino-Soviet Studies, George Washington University: ALBANIA, BULGARIA, CZECHOSLOVAKIA, GERMAN DEMOCRATIC REPUBLIC, HUNGARY, POLAND, ROMANIA, YUGOSLAVIA.

KINGSBURY, ROBERT C. Assistant Professor of Geography, Indiana University: INDIA, THAILAND, TRINIDAD AND TOBAGO.

KISH, GEORGE. Professor of Geography, University of Michigan: FRANCE, FEDERAL REPUBLIC OF GERMANY, ITALY, PORTUGAL, SPAIN, SWITZERLAND.

KOLEHMAINEN, JOHN I. Chairman, Department of Political Science, Heidelberg College: FINLAND.

KOLINSKI, CHARLES J. Professor of History, Florida Atlantic University: PARAGUAY.

KOSTANICK, HUEY LOUIS. Professor of Geography, University of Southern California: CYPRUS, GREECE.

KRANZ, WALTER. Press and Information Officer, Principality of Liechtenstein: LIECHTENSTEIN.

LEE, ROBERT H.G. Assistant Professor of History, State University of New York at Stony Brook: TAIWAN.

LEMARCHAND, RENE. Director, African Studies Center, University of Florida: BURUNDI, RWANDA, ZAIRE.

LENGYEL, EMIL. Professor of History, Fairleigh Dickinson University (in collaboration with Catherine Logan Camhy): EGYPT.

LEWIS, H.A.G. O.B.E., Fellow, Royal Geographical Society (United Kingdom): SEYCHELLES, UNITED KINGDOM, UNITED KINGDOM AFRICAN DEPENDENCIES, UNITED KINGDOM AMERICAN DEPENDENCIES, UNITED KINGDOM ASIAN AND PACIFIC DEPENDENCIES.

LEWIS, WILLIAM H. Department of Anthropology and Sociology, American University: ETHIOPIA, LIBYA.

LICHTENSTADTER, ILSE. Center for Middle Eastern Studies, Harvard University: IRAQ.

LINDO, WILLIAM. Government Information Services, Government of Belize: BELIZE (in part).

LUX, WILLIAM R. Assistant Professor of History, University of Alabama: BARBADOS, CHILE, COLOMBIA, FRENCH AMERICAN DEPENDENCIES, GUYANA, JAMAICA, MEXICO, NETHERLANDS AMERICAN DEPENDENCIES, PERU, TRINIDAD AND TOBAGO, UNITED KINGDOM AMERICAN DEPENDENCIES, VENEZUELA.

McGUIRE, CARL. Professor of Economics, University of Colorado: EGYPT.

McINTIRE, ROBERT C. Associate Professor and Chairman, Department of Political Science, Millikin University: ANTIGUA AND BARBUDA,* ST. CHRISTOPHER AND NEVIS,* TURKS AND CAICOS ISLANDS.*

McLELLAN, ROBERT S. US Information Agency: ITALY, PORTUGAL, SPAIN.

MARKS, HENRY S. Professor of History, Northeast Alabama State Junior College: COSTA RICA, DOMINICAN REPUBLIC, EL SALVADOR, GUATEMALA, HAITI, HONDURAS, NICARAGUA, PANAMA.

MATHEWS, THOMAS G. Secretary-General, Association of Caribbean Universities and Research Institutes, Puerto Rico. DOMINICA,* ST. LUCIA,* ST. VINCENT AND THE GRENADINES.*

MENDELL, MARCIA EIGEN.: JAMAICA, PERU (in part), TRINIDAD AND TOBAGO.

MILLER, NATHAN. Associate Professor of History, University of Wisconsin, Milwaukee: UNITED STATES.

MILNE, R. S. Professor of Political Science, University of British Columbia: NEW ZEALAND.

MORTIMER, MOLLY. Former Commonwealth Correspondent, *The Spectator*, London. BRUNEI,* KIRIBATI,* TUVALU,* VANUATU.*

MOSELEY, EDWARD. Assistant Professor of History, University of Alabama: ARGENTINA.

NEW YORK UNIVERSITY, DEPARTMENT OF POLITICS. I. William Zartman, Editor; John Entelis, Oladipo Coles, Jeffrey Knorr, Marie-Daniele Harmel, Contritors: ALGERIA, EGYPT, ETHIOPIA, GUINEA, IVORY COAST, LIBERIA, MALI, MAURITANIA, MOROCCO, NIGER, SENEGAL, SIERRA LEONE, TUNISIA, UPPER VOLTA.

NICHOLSON, NORMAN L. Professor of Geography, University of Western Ontario: CANADA.

O'DELL, ANDREW C. Professor of Geography, University of Aberdeen: NORWAY, SWEDEN.

OH, JOHN K. C. Professor of Political Science, Marquette University: DEMOCRATIC PEOPLE'S REPUBLIC OF KOREA, REPUBLIC OF KOREA.

OLIVER, ROBERT T. Head, Department of Speech, Pennsylvania State University: REPUBLIC OF KOREA.

PANORAMA DDR. Berlin: GERMAN DEMOCRATIC REPUBLIC.

PATAI, RAPHAEL. Editor, The Herzl Press: JORDAN.

PAYNE, WALTER A. Professor of History, University of the Pacific: EL SALVADOR, GUATEMALA, HONDURAS, PANAMA.

PETROV, VICTOR P. Professor of Geography, California State College: MONGOLIA, TAIWAN.

POLAND, EMBASSY OF. Washington, D.C.: POLAND.

POLK, WILLIAM R. Director, Adlai E. Stevenson Institute, University of Chicago: LEBANON (in part).

PRAGOPRESS. Prague: CZECHOSLOVAKIA.

PRICE, GEORGE. Premier, Government of Belize: BELIZE (in part).

RASHIDUZZAMAN, M. Professor of Political Science, Glassboro State College: BANGLADESH.

REINES, BERNARD: CANADA, SINGAPORE, UNITED KINGDOM, ZAIRE, ZIMBABWE.

ROBINSON, KENNETH E. Director, Institute of Commonwealth Studies, and Professor of Commonwealth Affairs, University of London: BENIN, GUINEA, IVORY COAST, MADAGASCAR, SENEGAL.

ROBINSON, RICHARD D. Lecturer on Middle Eastern Studies, Center for Middle Eastern Studies, Harvard University: TURKEY.

ROSBERG, CARL G., JR. Associate Professor of Political Science, University of California: KENYA.

ROTBERG, ROBERT I. Professor of Political Science and History, MIT: DJIBOUTI,* NAMIBIA.*

RUPEN, ROBERT A. Associate Professor of Political Science, University of North Carolina: MONGOLIA.

SANDS, WILLIAM. Editor, *The Middle East Journal*: LEBANON, LIBYA, SAʿUDI ARABIA.

SHABAD, THEODORE. Correspondent, *The New York Times*: ALBANIA, BULGARIA, CHINA, DEMOCRATIC PEOPLE'S REPUBLIC OF KOREA (in part), MONGOLIA, ROMANIA, UNION OF SOVIET SOCIALIST REPUBLICS, VIET-NAM (in part).

SHEPHERD, GEORGE. Professor of Political Science, University of Denver: SUDAN.

SMITH, ALAN HEPBURN. Associate Professor of Finance, Marquette University; formerly Permanent Secretary, Ministry of Finance, Ghana: GHANA.

SORICH, RICHARD. East Asian Institute, Columbia University: CHINA.

SOVIET ENCYCLOPEDIA PUBLISHING HOUSE: UNION OF SOVIET SOCIALIST REPUBLICS (in part).

STEVENS, RICHARD P. Director, African Language and Area Center, Lincoln University: GABON, SWAZILAND.

SYRACUSE UNIVERSITY, FOREIGN AND COMPARATIVE STUDIES PROGRAM. Peter Dalleo: KENYA; Thomas C. N. Evans: ZAMBIA; Robert G. Gregory, Professor of History: ZIMBABWE; Elisabeth Hunt: TANZANIA; Roderick J. Macdonald, Professor of History: MALAWI (in part); Thomas F. Taylor: ETHIOPIA.

SYRACUSE UNIVERSITY, PROGRAM OF EAST AFRICAN STUDIES. Fred G. Burke, Director; John R. Nellis, Administrative Assistant; and Gary Gappert, Nikos Georgulas, Richard Kornbluth: ETHIOPIA, KENYA, MALAWI, TANZANIA, ZAMBIA, ZIMBABWE.

VANDENBOSCH, AMRY. Director Emeritus, Patterson School of Diplomacy and International Commerce, University of Kentucky: INDONESIA, MALAYSIA, SRI LANKA.

VIVIANI, NANCY. Department of Economics, Australian National University: AUSTRALIA, FIJI, MALDIVES, NAURU, PAPUA NEW GUINEA, TONGA.

WAGNER, EDWARD W. Associate Professor of Korean Studies, Harvard University: DEMOCRATIC PEOPLE'S REPUBLIC OF KOREA, REPUBLIC OF KOREA.

WENNER, MANFRED W. Associate Professor of Political Science, University of Northern Illinois: PEOPLE'S DEMOCRATIC REPUBLIC OF YEMEN, YEMEN ARAB REPUBLIC.

WERNSTEDT, FREDERICK L. Associate Professor of Geography, Pennsylvania State University: PHILIPPINES.

WIEDNER, DONALD L. Chairman, Department of History, Temple University: EQUATORIAL GUINEA.

WILBER, DONALD N. Author, *Iran Past and Present*: AFGHANISTAN (in part), IRAN, PAKISTAN.

WILMINGTON, MARTIN W. Professor of Economics, Pace College: SUDAN.

WINDER, R. BAYLY. Chairman, Department of Near Eastern Languages and Literatures, New York University: SAʿUDI ARABIA (in part).

WOLFE, GREGORY D. Portland State University: HONDURAS.

WRIGHT, WINTHROP R. Professor of History, University of Maryland: SURINAME.

YUGOSLAV FEDERAL COMMITTEE FOR INFORMATION: YUGOSLAVIA.

THE UNITED NATIONS
SYSTEM

THE UNITED NATIONS SYSTEM

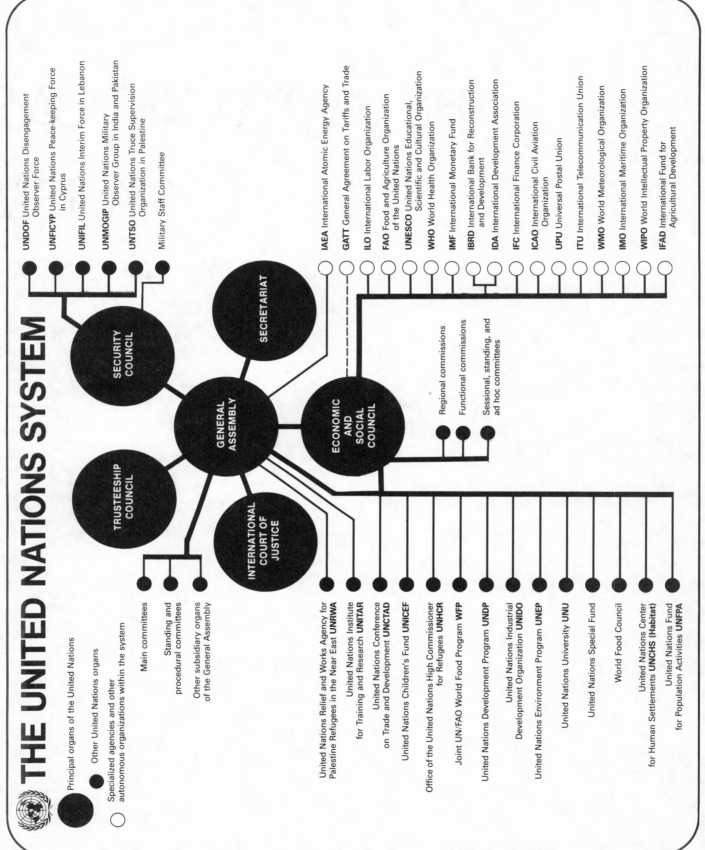

Principal organs of the United Nations

Other United Nations organs

Specialized agencies and other autonomous organizations within the system

SECURITY COUNCIL

SECRETARIAT

TRUSTEESHIP COUNCIL

GENERAL ASSEMBLY

ECONOMIC AND SOCIAL COUNCIL

INTERNATIONAL COURT OF JUSTICE

Main committees

Standing and procedural committees

Other subsidiary organs of the General Assembly

Regional commissions

Functional commissions

Sessional, standing, and ad hoc committees

UNDOF United Nations Disengagement Observer Force

UNFICYP United Nations Peace-keeping Force in Cyprus

UNIFIL United Nations Interim Force in Lebanon

UNMOGIP United Nations Military Observer Group in India and Pakistan

UNTSO United Nations Truce Supervision Organization in Palestine

Military Staff Committee

IAEA International Atomic Energy Agency

GATT General Agreement on Tariffs and Trade

ILO International Labor Organization

FAO Food and Agriculture Organization of the United Nations

UNESCO United Nations Educational, Scientific and Cultural Organization

WHO World Health Organization

IMF International Monetary Fund

IBRD International Bank for Reconstruction and Development

IDA International Development Association

IFC International Finance Corporation

ICAO International Civil Aviation Organization

UPU Universal Postal Union

ITU International Telecommunication Union

WMO World Meteorological Organization

IMO International Maritime Organization

WIPO World Intellectual Property Organization

IFAD International Fund for Agricultural Development

United Nations Relief and Works Agency for Palestine Refugees in the Near East **UNRWA**

United Nations Institute for Training and Research **UNITAR**

United Nations Conference on Trade and Development **UNCTAD**

United Nations Children's Fund **UNICEF**

Office of the United Nations High Commissioner for Refugees **UNHCR**

Joint UN/FAO World Food Program **WFP**

United Nations Development Program **UNDP**

United Nations Industrial Development Organization **UNIDO**

United Nations Environment Program **UNEP**

United Nations University **UNU**

United Nations Special Fund

World Food Council

United Nations Center for Human Settlements **UNCHS (Habitat)**

United Nations Fund for Population Activities **UNFPA**

Reproduced by permission of the United Nations.

STRUCTURE OF THE UNITED NATIONS SYSTEM

The UN system is often referred to as a "family" of organizations. The Charter of the UN, signed in San Francisco on 26 June 1945, defined only six main organs of the new world body, each with specific tasks and functions. However, because it was impossible to foresee all the demands that might be made on the organization, provision was made for extending its capacities as the need arose. Thus three of the main organs are specifically empowered to establish "such subsidiary organs" as may be considered necessary for the performance of their functions. In addition, Article 57 of the Charter provides that the various independent agencies, established by intergovernmental agreement, having international responsibilities in economic, social, cultural, educational, health, and related fields, "shall be brought into relationship" with the UN. Since the signing of the Charter, the UN has founded numerous subsidiary organs and has entered into relationship with 17 independent organizations. Reproduced opposite is a chart of the UN showing the various organs and bodies within the system as of October 1983.

For assistance in interpreting the chart, a brief survey of the UN's main organs, the different categories of subsidiary organs, and the related agencies is given below. A detailed description of the functioning of each of the main organs and an account of the work of selected subsidiary organs are contained in later chapters of the UN section of this volume. The structure and work of the UN-related agencies are described in individual chapters.

MAIN ORGANS OF THE UN

1. *The General Assembly,* composed of representatives of all member states, is the UN's central deliberative body, empowered to discuss and make recommendations on any subject falling within the scope of the Charter itself. It also decides the budget for the whole organization and determines—alone or with the Security Council—part of the composition of the other main organs, including the Security Council.

2. *The Security Council,* a 15-member body, has primary responsibility for maintaining international peace and security. In times of crisis it is empowered to act on behalf of all member states and to decide on a course of collective action that is mandatory for the entire membership. The charter names five states as permanent members of the Council: China, France, the UK, the USSR, and the US (those that were chiefly responsible for the defeat of the Axis powers in 1945). The remaining Council members are elected by the General Assembly for two-year terms.

3. *The Economic and Social Council (ECOSOC)* is assigned the task of organizing the UN's work on economic and social matters and the promotion of human rights. It consists of 54 members elected for three-year terms by the General Assembly.

4. *The Trusteeship Council* operates the UN trusteeship system. It is composed of member nations administering trust territories, the permanent members of the Security Council, and a sufficient number of other members, elected by the Assembly for three-year terms, to ensure an equal division of administering and non-administering powers.

5. *The International Court of Justice (ICJ)* is the principal judicial organ of the UN. It consists of 15 judges elected by the General Assembly and the Security Council voting independently.

6. *The Secretariat* is the administrative arm of the organization. Its staff is headed by a secretary-general appointed by the General Assembly upon the recommendation of the Security Council.

SUBSIDIARY ORGANS OF THE UN

The UN Charter specifically confers the right to create subsidiary organs upon the General Assembly, the Security Council, and ECOSOC. The subsidiary bodies fluctuate in number from year to year, according to the changing requirements of the main organ concerned. Both the General Assembly and ECOSOC, for instance, continually create new bodies to assist them in their ever-expanding activities and dissolve others which have completed their work. In many cases, the newly established bodies are intended to take over the functions of several existing ones. Some of the subsidiary organs in turn set up their own subsidiary units—working groups, subcommittees, and the like.

Subsidiary Organs of the General Assembly

The Assembly's subsidiary organs range in complexity and status from temporary committees to highly organized, semiautonomous institutions that maintain their own secretariats or administrative departments. The names of the 14 semiautonomous bodies or institutions in existence in 1983 (all but two of which were set up under the joint aegis of the Assembly and ECOSOC) appear in the lower left-hand column of the chart opposite. The remaining subsidiary organs are too numerous to list; the chart merely indicates their principal types: main committees, standing and procedural committees, and "other subsidiary organs." The committees comprise representatives of all member states and are formally reconstituted at each regular Assembly session to discuss the various items on the agenda for that year. (For further information on the work and constitution of these committees, see the chapter on the General Assembly.)

The standing committees are the Advisory Committee on Administrative and Budgetary Questions and the Committee on Contributions (see the chapter on the UN Budget). Both of these committees are maintained continuously, and their memberships are reelected on a staggered basis. Procedural committees include the 29-member General Committee, which is responsible for scrutinizing the Assembly's agenda prior to its adoption by the plenary (see the chapter on the General Assembly), and the 9-member Credentials Committee, which examines the credentials of delegations sent to the Assembly (see the chapter on Membership, under the heading "Representation of Nations in the UN"). Like the main committees, both of these procedural committees are constituted anew at every session. The category "other subsidiary bodies" encompasses the large number of substantive committees set up ad hoc by General Assembly resolutions to study subjects of interest to the Assembly—for example, the peaceful uses of outer space, apartheid in South Africa, and independence for colonial territories. These committees, whose members are elected by the Assembly or appointed by the Assembly's president, usually meet several times a year. At each regular session of the Assembly, they report on their deliberations. They continue to exist for as long as is considered necessary. Even when their mandate seems completed, they are not necessarily formally disbanded, but may be adjourned indefinitely and reactivated when the need arises. It is through these committees that the Assembly accomplishes most of its work outside the spheres of responsibility that are specifically entrusted to ECOSOC, the Trusteeship Council, or the various semiautonomous bodies referred to above.

Subsidiary Organs of the Security Council

Six of the Security Council's subsidiary organs are shown on the chart. The last one in the top right-hand column is a permanent body. The Military Staff Committee, as provided for in the Charter, is to advise the Security Council on the military aspects of maintaining international peace. However, the Military Staff Committee secretariat, though it holds regular formal meetings, has never been consulted on any of the UN's peacekeeping operations (see the chapters on the Security Council and on Maintaining Peace and Security). The five other subsidiary bodies shown on the chart in the top right-hand column were set up, as their names suggest, to conduct the Council's peacekeeping operations in the areas specified. (For further information on the work of these bodies, see the chapter on Maintaining Peace and Security under the heading "Some Case Histories of UN Action.")

In addition to the subsidiary organs shown on the chart, the Council maintains three permanently constituted committees of the whole: one to examine the provisional rules of the Council's procedure, the second to consider the admission of new members of the UN, and the third to consider meetings of the Council away from Headquarters. The committee on the admission of members did not meet from 1949 to 1971, but since then has met regularly. The committee to examine the Council's provisional rules of procedure has not met since 1953. The Committee on Council meetings away from Headquarters was constituted in 1972 before the Council held meetings in Addis Ababa, and convened again to prepare for the Council session in Panama the following year.

The Council has twice specified that it was acting under Chapter VII of the Charter, which deals with "action with respect to threats to the peace, breaches of the peace, and acts of aggression."

In 1966, it imposed mandatory economic sanctions against the illegal regime in Southern Rhodesia; and in 1977 it imposed a mandatory arms embargo against South Africa. In both cases, the Council set up committees to monitor compliance with its resolutions by member states.

Subsidiary Organs of ECOSOC

As indicated on the chart, ECOSOC's subsidiary organs are of four types: (1) the semiautonomous bodies shown in the left-hand column; (2) regional commissions; (3) functional commissions; and (4) sessional, standing, and ad hoc committees. Further information on these organs is included in the chapter on the Economic and Social Council.

UN RELATED AGENCIES

The 15 specialized agencies that have been brought into relationship with the UN—and which are named in the lower right-hand column of the chart—are separate autonomous organizations with their own policy-making and executive organs, secretariats, and financial arrangements. The precise nature of their relationship with the UN is defined by the terms of special agreements that were established with ECOSOC and subsequently approved by the General Assembly, as provided for in Article 63 of the Charter. Since Article 63 also empowers ECOSOC to coordinate the activities of the specialized agencies through consultation and recommendations, they are required to report annually to the Council.

Mention should be made here of the special status of the General Agreement on Tariffs and Trade (GATT). For the sake of convenience, GATT is listed on the chart just above the specialized agencies. It is a treaty establishing a code of conduct on international trade and providing machinery for reducing and stabilizing tariffs. The treaty was concluded pending the creation of a specialized agency to be known as the International Trade Organization, whose draft charter was completed in 1948 but was never ratified by the important trading powers (for further details, see the chapter in this volume on GATT). Nonetheless, GATT is regarded as part of the UN system and maintains a close working relationship with the world body.

The International Atomic Energy Agency (IAEA), which appears above GATT on the chart, is distinguished from the other agencies in that it was specifically established under the aegis of the UN and is therefore considered a category by itself. The IAEA reports annually to the General Assembly and only "as appropriate" to ECOSOC. Because of the nature of its work, IAEA also reports to the Security Council, again only "as appropriate."

COMPARISON WITH THE LEAGUE OF NATIONS

The League of Nations grew out of the catastrophe of World War I (1914–18). Though the idea of the establishment of a body in which the nations of the world could settle their disagreements had been put forth periodically since antiquity, the League, created at the 1919 Paris Peace Conference, was the first organization of sovereign states designed to be universal and devoted to the settlement of disputes and the prevention of war. The League's failure to prevent the outbreak of World War II in 1939 did not destroy the belief in the need for a universal organization. On the contrary, it bred a determination to learn from the mistakes of the past and to build a new world body more adequately equipped to maintain international peace in the future.

The differences between the League of Nations and the UN begin with the circumstances of their creation. First, whereas the Covenant of the League was formulated after hostilities were ended, the main features of the UN were devised while war was still in progress. The more comprehensive powers assigned to the UN for the preservation of peace may well owe something to the urgent conditions in which it was conceived. Second, the Covenant was drawn up in an atmosphere of divided attention at the Paris Peace Conference and was incorporated as part of the peace treaty with Germany. Although countries were permitted to ratify the Covenant and the treaty separately, the link between them was not good psychology and contributed, for example, to the unwillingness of the US Senate to ratify the Covenant. In contrast, the UN Charter was drafted as an independent legal instrument at a conference especially convened for the purpose. Third, the Covenant was hammered out behind closed doors, first by the five major powers of the era—France, Italy, Japan, the UK, and the US—and eventually in conjunction with nine other allied nations. The final text of the UN Charter, on the other hand, was the product of combined efforts of 50 states represented at the 1945 San Francisco Conference and therefore took into account the views of the smaller nations, especially their concern to give the new organization far-reaching responsibilities in promoting economic and social cooperation and decolonization.

VOTING

Under the Covenant, decisions of the League could be made only by unanimous vote. This rule applied both to the League's Council, which had special responsibilities for maintaining peace (the equivalent of the UN's Security Council), and to the all-member Assembly (the equivalent of the UN's General Assembly). In effect, each member state of the League had the power of the "veto," and, except for procedural matters and a few specified topics, a single "nay" killed any resolution. Learning from this mistake, the founders of the UN decided that all its organs and subsidiary bodies should make decisions by some type of majority vote (though, on occasion, committees dealing with a particularly controversial issue have been known to proceed by consensus). The rule of unanimity applies only to five major powers —France, China, the UK, the US, and the USSR—and then only when they are acting in their capacity as permanent members of the Security Council. The Security Council also proceeds by majority vote, but on substantive (though not on procedural) matters it must include the concurring votes of all the permanent members.

CONSTITUTIONAL POWERS TO PREVENT WAR AND END AGGRESSION

The Charter was designed to remedy certain constitutional defects and omissions in the Covenant which the founders of the UN believed had been partly responsible for the League's inability to halt the drift toward a second world war in the 1930s. These defects and omissions included the absence of any provision imposing a total ban on war; the provision of a too rigid procedure for negotiating disputes between states; and the failure to vest the Council with sufficient powers to prevent the outbreak of hostilities or to terminate hostilities that had already begun.

The Covenant forbade military aggression but did not reject the limited right of a state to start a war, provided it had first submitted the dispute to arbitration, judicial decision, or the Council of the League. If one party accepted the findings of the negotiating body and the second did not, the first might then resort to war legally after a "cooling-off" period.

The Charter recognizes no circumstances under which a nation may legally start a war. Article 51 does guarantee the right to individual and collective self-defense, which is a right to respond to an illegal armed attack but not to initiate one. If the Security Council decides that a "threat to the peace" exists, it has the power to order collective enforcement measures. These are mandatory for all member states and may include economic sanctions or military measures, but the power has rarely been invoked. (See the chapter on Maintaining Peace and Security.)

MEMBERSHIP

The League never became the universal organization that had been envisaged. Moreover, it failed to secure or retain the membership of certain major powers whose participation and cooperation were essential to make it an effective instrument for preserving the peace. Despite President Wilson's advocacy, the US did not join, and the USSR joined only in 1934, when the League had already shown itself unable to contain the aggressive policies of Germany, Italy, and Japan. The three aggressor states themselves withdrew their membership during the 1930s to pursue their expansionist aims. The UN, on the other hand, is approaching the goal of universality, with only a few smaller countries still unrepresented. By the end of 1983 its membership had reached 158.

PROMOTION OF HUMAN WELFARE

The UN Charter not only lays down specific injunctions for international economic and social cooperation, based on respect for the principle of equal rights and self-determination of peoples, but it has established a special organ—the Economic and Social Council—to conduct the organization's activities in this sphere. Throughout its existence the UN, together with its specialized agencies, has gradually assumed primary responsibility for assisting the economic and social development of nonindustrialized member nations, most of them former colonial territories that joined the world body long after it was founded. The UN's many projects have become the cornerstone of the development policies adopted by almost all these countries. Since the Covenant of the League contained no provisions for a coordinated program of economic and social cooperation, there can be no comparison between the respective achievements of the two organizations in this respect. Nevertheless, the League performed valuable work in several fields—notably, in eliminating the illegal sale of women and children, or the "white slave" trade; providing assistance for refugees; reducing traffic in opium and other dangerous narcotics; and getting nations to lessen trade restrictions.

ADMINISTRATION OF COLONIAL TERRITORIES

Instead of sharing the colonial possessions of their defeated enemies as the traditional spoils of victory, the founding members of the League, with admirable foresight and restraint, regarded these territories as international mandates, and certain member states were designated to administer them on behalf of the world organization. This mandate system in a modified form was continued in the trusteeship system evolved by the founders of the UN. However, unlike the Covenant, the Charter expressly stipulates that the administering countries have an obligation to promote the progressive development of the territories placed in their charge toward self-government or independence.

BALANCE SHEET OF THE LEAGUE OF NATIONS

The League failed in its supreme test. It failed to contain the aggressive action of the Axis powers—Japan, Germany, and Italy —and thus halt the drift toward a new world war. From 1931, Japan, a permanent member of the League's Council, waged a war of aggression against China, in defiance of both the Council and the Assembly. Although the League did impose economic sanctions against Italy, another permanent member of the Council, when it wantonly invaded Ethiopia in 1935, support was half-hearted and the action unsuccessful. The League was unable to do anything against the illegal reoccupation of the Rhineland in 1936 by Germany, still another permanent member of the Council, nor could it offer more than verbal protests against German and Italian intervention in the Spanish Civil War, the forcible incorporation of Austria into Germany in March 1938 and of Czechoslovakia into Germany a year later. The cumulative effect of these failures strengthened Hitler's belief in the impotence not only of the League itself but also of its principal remaining members. During the summer of 1939, when the world moved ever closer toward the abyss, and even when Hitler's armies marched into Poland on 1 September 1939, not a single member called for a meeting of the League's Council or Assembly.

The League's balance sheet in political matters was not wholly negative, however. It was able, for example, to settle the dispute between Finland and Sweden over the Åland Islands, strategically located in the Gulf of Bothnia; the frontier controversy between Albania, Greece, and Yugoslavia; the potentially explosive border situation between Greece and Bulgaria; and the dangerous conflicts between Poland and Germany over Upper Silesia and between Germany, Poland, and Lithuania over Memel. Through the League's Permanent Court of Justice, a border controversy between Czechoslovakia and Poland was straightened out, as were the disputes between Britain and Turkey over the Mosul area and between France and Britain over the nationality of Maltese residents in the French protectorates of Morocco and Tunisia. The League also stopped the incipient war between Peru and Colombia over territorial claims in the upper Amazon basin.

In addition to these successsful peacekeeping activities, the League financially assisted the reconstruction of certain states, notably Austria, and was responsible for administering the Free City of Danzig and the Saar Territory. (The latter was transferred to Germany following a plebiscite in 1935.) It also carried out important humanitarian work. Some of its nonpolitical activities continued throughout World War II, and its secretariat did valuable preparatory work for the emerging UN. The League of Nations was not officially dissolved until April 1946, five months after the new world body came into being.

THE UN'S GREATER SCOPE

The field of activity and the responsibilities of the UN are considerably more extensive than those of the League. Of the 15 specialized agencies in the UN system, only three—the ILO, the ITU, and the UPU—antedate the UN. The League, furthermore, never sponsored any such enterprises as those undertaken by, for example, the UN Development Program, the UN Environment Program, or the World Food Program. Membership in the League did not oblige a nation to join the Permanent Court of Justice, whereas all members of the UN are automatically parties to the Statute of the International Court of Justice, which is an integral part of the Charter.

Like the League, the UN has recorded several important successes in halting local armed conflicts and the spread of disputes —for example, in the Congo, Kashmir, and, over long periods, in Cyprus. However, it has proved unable to take effective action in any situation where the interests of either the US or the USSR are closely involved or where the two giant powers seem committed to opposite sides of disputes involving smaller nations. Thus it was unable to check the Soviet invasion of Hungary in 1956 and of Czechoslovakia in 1968; it was unable to take any action to halt the fighting that raged in Indochina during most of its life; and it has not succeeded in settling the prolonged crisis that has periodically erupted in Arab-Israeli wars in the Middle East, long a major arena in the US–USSR power struggle.

The UN's ineffectuality in such situations has caused a loss of confidence in its relevance in international political relations. Nor is it a source of consolation that there is no discernible drift toward a world war, for in most cases where the US and the USSR have found themselves almost at the point of actual confrontation, as in the 1962 Cuban crisis, they have tended to resolve their differences bilaterally, not under the aegis of the UN.

On the other hand, if the two great powers do not always find it convenient to allow the UN to play too decisive a role in political matters, they find it equally impractical to bypass the world organization altogether. Unlike the League, the UN is the center of a network of organizations whose activities reach into many aspects of the national life of every member state. As such, it has come to be regarded as an indispensable part of the machinery for conducting multiple-level international relations. Benefiting by the fear of a global or nuclear war, the UN is likely to continue to display much greater strength and vitality than the League ever could.

THE MAKING OF THE UNITED NATIONS

The creation of the UN at the San Francisco Conference in June 1945 was the culmination of four years of concentrated preparation. During these years, the idea of a world organization to replace the League of Nations was first debated and then fleshed out. Many of the important principles of the UN adopted at San Francisco derived from earlier conferences.

DEVELOPMENTS LEADING TO THE SAN FRANCISCO CONFERENCE

1. *The Inter-Allied Declaration (London Declaration) of 12 June 1941.* In a dark hour of World War II representatives of the UK, Australia, Canada, New Zealand, and the Union of South Africa, of the governments-in-exile of Belgium, Czechoslovakia, Greece, Luxembourg, the Netherlands, Norway, Poland, and Yugoslavia, and of General Charles de Gaulle of France assembled at St. James's Palace in London. It was there that they each pledged not to sign a separate peace and declared: "The only true basis of enduring peace is the willing cooperation of free peoples in a world in which, relieved of the menace of aggression, all may enjoy economic and social security. . . . " Ten days later, Hitler launched his attack against the Soviet Union.

2. *The Atlantic Charter of 14 August 1941.* British Prime Minister Winston S. Churchill and US President Franklin D. Roosevelt met aboard the cruiser USS *Atlanta* off the coast of Newfoundland and signed a declaration giving the first indication that the two powers would strive for the creation of a new world organization once peace was restored. In it they announced "certain common principles . . . of their respective countries . . . for a better future for the world: the need for a secure peace; the abandonment by all nations of the use of force; the disarmament of aggressors; and the establishment of a wider and permanent system of general security."

3. *The United Nations Declaration of 1 January 1942.* With the Japanese attack on Pearl Harbor on 7 December 1941 and the entry of the US into the war, the conflict assumed even wider dimensions. Japan's initial successes were staggering, and it was clear that the coalition against the Axis Powers (Germany, Italy, Japan, and their allies) would need to be strengthened.

On New Year's Day 1942 in Washington, D.C., representatives of 26 states signed a declaration whose preamble called for subscription "to a common program of purposes and principles embodied in the . . . Atlantic Charter" and explicitly referred to the need for promoting respect for human rights on an international basis. In that declaration the phrase "united nations" made its first official appearance. It had been coined by President Roosevelt to express the unity of the signatory nations in their determination to withstand the onslaught of the Axis Powers. The declaration subsequently was signed by the governments of 21 additional states.

4. *The Moscow Declaration of 30 October 1943.* This declaration laid the foundation for the establishment of a new world body to replace the League of Nations. Meeting at a time when victory seemed in sight, the US, British, and Soviet foreign ministers and an ambassador from China drew up the Declaration of Four Nations on General Security, which recognized "the necessity of establishing at the earliest practicable date a general international organization based on the principle of sovereign equality of all peace-loving States, and open to membership by all such States, large and small, for the maintenance of international peace and security."

5. *Dumbarton Oaks Conference, Washington, 21 August–7 October 1944.* The Dumbarton Oaks conference was the first big-power meeting convoked specifically to discuss the establishment of a new world organization. At the beginning of the conference, the delegations offered widely differing proposals. On some of these divergent views they eventually reached agreement. For example, the British and Soviet delegations accepted an American position that favored a strong role for the General Assembly as the organ in which all member states would be represented and which, therefore, would be the most "democratic" of the UN organs. There was agreement that a small Security Council should be "primarily responsible for the maintenance of international peace and security" and that the big powers should have the right of veto in that body. However, a deadlock developed over a Soviet proposal that a big power might exercise this right in disputes in which it was itself involved. This the US and the British refused to accept.

6. *Yalta Conference, February 1945.* The resultant deadlock was resolved at a meeting in Yalta attended by Prime Minister Churchill, President Roosevelt, and Marshal Stalin. The "Yalta formula," actually a compromise proposed by the US and rejected by the USSR at Dumbarton Oaks, provided that if any of the Big Five powers was involved in a dispute, it would not have the right to veto Security Council recommendations for peaceful settlement of the issue, but would be able to veto a Council decision to invoke sanctions against it. After some initial objections from Churchill, the three leaders at Yalta also managed to agree on the basic principles of a trusteeship system for the administration of certain dependent territories under the aegis of the projected world body.

On 11 February 1945, the three leaders announced that a conference would be convened in San Francisco on 25 April 1945 for the "earliest possible establishment of a general international organization" along the lines proposed at Dumbarton Oaks.

THE SAN FRANCISCO CONFERENCE, 25 APRIL–26 JUNE 1945

Despite the sudden death of President Roosevelt in early April, the United Nations Conference on International Organization convened as scheduled. President Roosevelt had been working on his speech to the conference before he died. That never-delivered address contained the often-quoted words: "The work, my friends, is peace; more than an end of this war—an end to the beginning of all wars; . . . as we go forward toward the greatest contribution that any generation of human beings can make in this world—the contribution of lasting peace—I ask you to keep up your faith. . . . "

China, the USSR, the UK, and the US acted as the sponsoring powers, and 46 other states participated, comprising all those that had signed the Declaration of United Nations of 1 January 1942 or had declared war on the Axis Powers by March 1945. The huge conference was attended by 282 delegates and 1,444 other officially accredited persons from those 50 countries, and by representatives of scores of private organizations interested in world affairs (50 from the US alone). The daily output of documents averaged half a million sheets.

Major Modifications to the Dumbarton Oaks Draft for the UN Charter

After much debate, the smaller and medium-sized nations succeeded in restricting the Big Five's use of the veto in the Security Council. Herbert V. Evatt, then deputy prime minister of Australia, who was in the forefront of that fight, declared:

> In the end our persistence had some good effect. The Great Powers came to realize that the smaller powers would not accept a Charter unless certain minimum demands for restriction of the veto were accepted, viz., that there should be no veto upon the placing of items on the [Security Council] agenda and no veto on discussion [in the Security Council]. . . . If this vital concession had not been won, it is likely that discussion of matters in the open forum of the Security Council would have been rendered impossible: If so, the United Nations might well have broken up.

Another major change resulted from the desire of the smaller nations to give the world organization more responsibilities in social and economic matters and in colonial problems. Accordingly, the Economic and Social Council and the Trusteeship Council were given wider authority than was provided for in the Dumbarton Oaks draft, and they were made principal organs of the UN.

Creation of a New World Court

The conference also unanimously adopted a constitution—called the Statute—for an International Court of Justice to be incorporated as a main organ of the UN and to succeed the Permanent Court of Justice established by the League of Nations. The Statute, which had originally been drafted by jurists from 44 nations meeting in Washington in April 1945, became part of the Charter of the UN.

Unanimous Acceptance of the Charter

The UN Charter touches on so many delicate and complex matters that its unanimous acceptance has often been ascribed to the particularly auspicious circumstances prevailing in the spring of 1945. In spite of some dissonance, the San Francisco Conference was imbued with a spirit of high mission. The Charter was worked out within two months. It was signed by 50 nations in its five official languages in an impressive ceremony on 26 June 1945. The official languages were Chinese, English, French, Russian, and Spanish. The sixth official UN language, Arabic, was not adopted until 1973.

ESTABLISHMENT OF THE UN, 24 OCTOBER 1945

The new world body officially came into being on 24 October 1945, when the Charter had been duly ratified by all permanent members of the Security Council and a majority of the other original signatory powers. This date is universally celebrated as United Nations Day.

SUBSEQUENT CHARTER AMENDMENT

Like other political constitutions, the UN Charter contains provisions for its own amendment. Amendments to the Charter come into force when they have been adopted by a vote of two-thirds of the members of the General Assembly and ratified by two-thirds of the UN member states, including all the permanent members of the Security Council.

The amendments that have been adopted are essentially adjustments to take account of the huge increase in UN membership, which has more than tripled since 1945. As originally constituted, the 11-member Security Council and the 18-member Economic and Social Council were considered adequate to reflect the different interests of the various geographical groupings of states within the organization. However, the admission to the UN during the late 1950s and early 1960s of large numbers of newly decolonized African, Asian, and Caribbean countries created additional groupings. To accommodate their interests without jeopardizing those of the older groups, the General Assembly, at its 18th session in 1963, adopted amendments to Articles 23, 27, and 61 of the Charter. The first amendment enlarged the membership of the Security Council to 15; the second required that decisions of the Security Council be made by an affirmative vote of 9 members (formerly 7); the third enlarged the membership of the Economic and Social Council to 27. All three amendments officially came into force on 31 August 1965.

The Economic and Social Council was enlarged to 54 by an amendment to Article 61 of the Charter which was adopted by the General Assembly at its 26th session in 1971 and became operative on 24 September 1973.

Charter Review. A general conference of UN members "for the purpose of reviewing the Charter may be held at a date and place to be fixed by a two-thirds vote of the members of the General Assembly and a vote of any seven members [amended to nine, as of 1965] of the Security Council." In addition, the Charter provided that if such a conference were not held by the tenth regular assembly session (in 1955), the proposal to call such a conference should be placed on the agenda. Accordingly, the 1955 Assembly considered the matter and decided that a general review conference should be held at an "appropriate" but unspecified date in the future. A committee consisting of the full UN membership was established to consider the time and place at which the conference should be held. The Security Council concurred in the Assembly's decision by a vote of 9 to 1, with 1 abstention. The committee met every two years until September 1967 without recommending a conference. It then became inactive, recommending that any member state might request it to meet.

At its 1974 session the General Assembly established a 42-member Ad Hoc Committee on the Charter to consider specific proposals from governments for "enhancing the ability of the United Nations to achieve its purposes." The committee reported to the 1975 Assembly session that there was a fundamental divergence of opinion on the necessity for carrying out a review of the Charter, and made no recommendations for action. The Assembly decided, however, to continue the committee as a Special Committee on the Charter of the UN and on the Strengthening of the Role of the Organization, and increased its membership to 47. In pursuit of its mandate, the Committee has met every year since 1975 and has reported to each session of the Assembly.

PURPOSES AND PRINCIPLES

The UN has three chief aims. The first is to maintain international peace; or, in the words of the preamble to the Charter, "to save succeeding generations from the scourge of war, which twice in our lifetime has brought untold sorrow to mankind." The second aim is to establish effective machinery to ensure international security, thereby reducing the fear of war. To reduce the fear of war is to reduce the danger of war, for only when nations cease to feel threatened will they cease preparing for war. And only when they cease preparing for war will they be able to devote their energies to building the essential infrastructure for peace, by eliminating the underlying causes of conflict —poverty, ignorance, bigotry, and oppression.

To better the lot of humanity through improvement in economic and social conditions, raised standards of health and education, and promotion of respect for fundamental human rights and freedoms is therefore the third aim of the UN, assisted by its related agencies. Freedom from war and the fear of war is necessary for making the world a better place to live in. And conversely, making the world a better place to live in is necessary for preserving the peace. It is a reciprocal relation. The UN's peacekeeping functions and what former Secretary-General U Thant termed its "peacebuilding activities" are thus complementary and interdependent aspects of the total work of the organization.

PURPOSES
The aims of the UN are embodied in a set of purposes and principles contained in Articles 1 and 2 of the Charter, which are summarized below.

1. To maintain international peace and security, and to that end: to take effective collective measures for the prevention and removal of threats to the peace, and for suppression of acts of aggression or other breaches of the peace, and to bring about by peaceful means, and in conformity with the principles of justice and international law, adjustment or settlement of international disputes or situations which might lead to a breach of the peace.

2. To develop friendly relations among nations based on respect for the principles of equal rights and self-determination of peoples, and to take other appropriate measures to strengthen universal peace.

3. To achieve international cooperation in solving international economic, social, cultural, or humanitarian problems, and in promoting and encouraging respect for human rights and for fundamental freedoms for all without distinction as to race, sex, language, or religion.

4. To be a center for harmonizing the actions of nations in attaining these common ends.

PRINCIPLES
In pursuit of these purposes, the Charter stipulates that the UN and its members are to act in accordance with the following principles:

1. That the organization is based on the sovereign equality of all its members.

2. That all members are to fulfill in good faith their Charter obligations.

3. That they are to settle their international disputes by peaceful means and without endangering peace, security, and justice.

4. That they are to refrain in their international relations from the threat or use of force against other states.

5. That they are to give the UN every assistance in any action it takes in accordance with the Charter, and shall not assist states against which the UN is taking preventive or enforcement action.

6. That the UN shall also ensure that states which are not members act in accordance with these principles insofar as is necessary to maintain international peace and security.

7. That nothing in the Charter is to authorize the UN to intervene in matters that are essentially within the domestic jurisdiction of any state, though this principle is not to prejudice the application of enforcement measures made necessary in the event of a threat to or breach of the peace.

MEMBERSHIP

As of 23 September 1983, the UN had 158 member states.

ROSTER OF THE UN

(*Original Members Who Signed the Charter at San Francisco)

Afghanistan	19 November 1946
Albania	14 December 1955
Algeria	8 October 1962
Angola	1 December 1976
Antigua and Barbuda	11 November 1981
*Argentina	24 October 1945
*Australia	1 November 1945
Austria	14 December 1955
Bahamas	18 September 1973
Bahrain	21 September 1971
Bangladesh	17 September 1974
Barbados	9 December 1966
*Belgium	27 December 1945
Belize	25 September 1981
Benin	20 September 1960
Bhutan	21 September 1971
*Bolivia	14 November 1945
Botswana	17 October 1966
*Brazil	24 October 1945
Bulgaria	14 December 1955
Burma	19 April 1948
Burundi	18 September 1962
*Byelorussia	24 October 1945
Cameroon	20 September 1960
*Canada	9 November 1945
Cape Verde	16 September 1975
Central African Republic	20 September 1960
Chad	20 September 1960
*Chile	24 October 1945
*China	24 October 1945
*Colombia	5 November 1945
Comoros	12 November 1975
Congo	20 September 1960
*Costa Rica	2 November 1945
*Cuba	24 October 1945
Cyprus	20 September 1960
*Czechoslovakia	24 October 1945
*Denmark	24 October 1945
Djibouti	20 September 1977
Dominica	18 December 1978
*Dominican Republic	24 October 1945
*Ecuador	21 December 1945
*Egypt	24 October 1945
*El Salvador	24 October 1945
Equatorial Guinea	12 November 1968
*Ethiopia	13 November 1945
Fiji	13 October 1970
Finland	14 December 1955
*France	24 October 1945
Gabon	20 September 1960
Gambia	21 September 1965
German Democratic Republic	18 September 1973
Germany, Federal Republic of	18 September 1973
Ghana	8 March 1957
*Greece	25 October 1945
Grenada	17 September 1974
*Guatemala	21 November 1945
Guinea	12 December 1958
Guinea-Bissau	17 September 1974
Guyana	20 September 1966
*Haiti	24 October 1945
*Honduras	17 December 1945
Hungary	14 December 1955
Iceland	19 November 1946
*India	30 October 1945
Indonesia	28 September 1950
*Iran	24 October 1945
*Iraq	21 December 1945
Ireland	14 December 1955
Israel	11 May 1949
Italy	14 December 1955
Ivory Coast	20 September 1960
Jamaica	18 September 1962
Japan	18 December 1956
Jordan	14 December 1955
Kampuchea	14 December 1955
Kenya	16 December 1963
Kuwait	14 May 1963
Laos	14 December 1955
*Lebanon	24 October 1945
Lesotho	17 October 1966
*Liberia	2 November 1945
Libya	14 December 1955
*Luxembourg	24 October 1945
Madagascar	20 September 1960
Malawi	1 December 1964
Malaysia	17 September 1957
Maldives	21 September 1965
Mali	28 September 1960
Malta	1 December 1964
Mauritania	27 October 1961
Mauritius	24 April 1968
*Mexico	7 November 1945
Mongolia	27 October 1961
Morocco	12 November 1956
Mozambique	16 September 1975
Nepal	14 December 1955
*Netherlands	10 December 1945
*New Zealand	24 October 1945
*Nicaragua	24 October 1945
Niger	20 September 1960
Nigeria	7 October 1960
*Norway	27 November 1945
Oman	7 October 1971
Pakistan	30 September 1947
*Panama	13 November 1945
Papua New Guinea	10 October 1975
*Paraguay	24 October 1945
*Peru	31 October 1945
*Philippines	24 October 1945
*Poland	24 October 1945
Portugal	14 December 1955
Qatar	21 September 1971
Romania	14 December 1955
Rwanda	18 September 1962
St. Christopher and Nevis	23 September 1983
St. Lucia	18 September 1979
St. Vincent and the Grenadines	16 September 1980
São Tomé and Príncipe	16 September 1975
*Sa'udi Arabia	24 October 1945

Senegal	28 September 1960
Seychelles	21 September 1976
Sierra Leone	27 September 1961
Singapore	21 September 1965
Solomon Islands	19 September 1978
Somalia	20 September 1960
*South Africa	7 November 1945
Spain	14 December 1955
Sri Lanka	14 December 1955
Sudan	12 November 1956
Suriname	4 December 1975
Swaziland	24 September 1968
Sweden	19 November 1946
*Syria	24 October 1945
Tanzania	14 December 1961
Thailand	16 December 1946
Togo	20 September 1960
Trinidad and Tobago	18 September 1962
Tunisia	12 November 1956
*Turkey	24 October 1945
Uganda	25 October 1962
*Ukraine	24 October 1945
*USSR	24 October 1945
United Arab Emirates	9 December 1971
*UK	24 October 1945
*US	24 October 1945
Upper Volta	20 September 1960
*Uruguay	18 December 1945
Vanuatu	15 September 1981
*Venezuela	15 November 1945
Viet-Nam	20 September 1977
Western Samoa	15 December 1976
Yemen, People's Democratic Republic of	14 December 1967
Yemen Arab Republic	30 September 1947
Yugoslavia	24 October 1945
Zaire	20 September 1960
Zambia	1 December 1964
Zimbabwe	25 August 1980

The roster does not take account of the several federations or unions of states that were created or dissolved during membership. Thus Syria, an original member, ceased independent membership on joining with Egypt to form the United Arab Republic in 1958. On resuming its separate status in 1961, Syria also resumed separate membership, which is still officially dated from the country's original day of entry. Tanganyika and Zanzibar joined the UN as separate states in 1961 and 1963, respectively, but in 1964 merged to form the United Republic of Tanzania with a single membership officially dated from Tanganyika's day of entry. Similarly, Malaya, which joined in 1957, merged with the British territories of Singapore, Sarawak, and Sabah to form the Federation of Malaysia with a single membership officially dated from Malaya's day of entry. When Singapore left the federation in 1965, it took up separate membership.

ADMISSION OF MEMBERS

In the words of Article 4 of the Charter, membership in the UN is open to all "peace-loving states which accept the obligations contained in the present Charter and, in the judgment of the Organization, are able and willing to carry out these obligations." The original members are the states that participated in the San Francisco Conference, or that had previously signed the United Nations Declaration of 1 January 1942, and subsequently signed and ratified the Charter.

The procedure of admission is as follows. A state wishing to join submits an application to the secretary-general in which it formally states its acceptance of the Charter obligations. The application is forwarded to the Security Council. If the Council, by a vote of at least nine members (formerly seven), including all the permanent members, recommends the application, membership becomes effective on the day it is approved by a two-thirds majority of the General Assembly. In other words, if any of the Council's permanent members vetoes it, or it fails to obtain a sufficient majority in the Council, the application does not reach the Assembly at all.

Up to 1955 there were bitter controversies and years of stalemate in the Security Council over the applications of some countries. Usually one or more of the Big Five was on bad terms with the applying state, or it would choose to withhold consent as a bargaining point against the other big powers. Finally, on 14 December 1955, by a compromise, 16 countries were admitted together. Since then, new applications have only exceptionally inspired controversy. Most of the applicants have been newly independent states which have signalized their freedom by applying for membership immediately. In almost all cases they have been admitted without delay and by unanimous vote.

The outstanding exceptions are the applications of the Republic of Korea (ROK), which applied in January 1949; the Democratic People's Republic of Korea (DPRK), which applied in February 1949; South Viet-Nam, which applied in December 1951; and North Viet-Nam, which applied in December 1951. The two Viet-Nams and the ROK sought action on their applications in 1975. The Security Council, by a narrow vote, decided not to take up the ROK's application, and the US subsequently vetoed membership for the Viet-Nams, citing as a reason the Council's earlier refusal to consider the membership application of the ROK. In response to a General Assembly recommendation, however, the Security Council in 1977 recommended the admission of the newly established Socialist Republic of Viet-Nam, and that country became a member in September 1977.

WITHDRAWAL FROM MEMBERSHIP

While the Covenant of the League of Nations contained provisions for the legal withdrawal of members, the UN Charter deliberately omits all reference to the subject. The majority feeling at the San Francisco Conference was that provisions for withdrawal would be contrary to the principle of universality and might provide a loophole for members seeking to evade their obligations under the Charter.

Thus when the first—and so far the only—case of withdrawal arose, the procedure had to be improvised ad hoc. On 1 January 1965, Indonesia, which then was pursuing a policy of active confrontation against the newly formed Federation of Malaysia, announced that it would withdraw from the UN and its related agencies if Malaysia were to take its elected seat on the Security Council. Three weeks later, Indonesia's foreign minister officially confirmed withdrawal in a letter to the secretary-general who, after consultations with the Indonesian mission to the UN, merely noted the decision and expressed hope that Indonesia would in due time "resume full cooperation" with the world body. Following a coup later in 1965, Indonesia sent a telegram to the secretary-general just before the opening of the 1966 Assembly session announcing its decision to "resume full cooperation with the UN." Arrangements were made to ensure that Indonesia's reentry would take place with minimum formality. Hence it was decided that Indonesia need not make a formal reapplication via the Security Council, but that the matter could be handled directly by the Assembly. Citing the telegram as evidence that Indonesia regarded its absence from the UN as a "cessation of cooperation" rather than an actual withdrawal, the Assembly's president recommended that the administrative procedure for reinstating Indonesia could be taken. No objections were raised, and Indonesia was immediately invited to resume its seat in the Assembly. In short, the problems raised by the first case of withdrawal from the UN were solved by treating it as if it had not been a matter of withdrawal at all. (Although South Africa withdrew from three of the UN's related agencies—UNESCO, FAO, ILO—because of the anti-apartheid sentiments of their members, it did not withdraw from the UN itself, despite numerous Assembly resolutions condemning apartheid and recommending stringent sanctions.)

SUSPENSION AND EXPULSION

The Charter provides that a member against which the Security Council has taken preventive or enforcement action may be suspended from the exercise of the rights and privileges of membership by the Assembly upon the recommendation of the Security Council. However, only the Security Council, not the Assembly, has the power to restore these rights. Any member that "has persistently violated the Principles" of the Charter may be expelled from the UN by the same procedure. By September 1983 no cases of suspension of rights or expulsion had been recommended or considered by the Council. Many states had called for the expulsion of South Africa because of its apartheid policies, but no formal proposal to this effect had been made.

At its twenty-ninth session, in 1974, the General Assembly called upon the Security Council to review the relationship between the UN and South Africa in the light of the constant violation by South Africa of the principles of the Charter and Universal Declaration of Human Rights. The Council considered a draft resolution submitted by Cameroon, Iraq, Kenya, and Mauritania that would have recommended to the Assembly the immediate expulsion of South Africa under Article 6 of the Charter. Owing to the negative votes of three permanent members (France, UK, US), the draft resolution was not adopted. After the Council had reported back to the Assembly on its failure to adopt a resolution, the president of the Assembly, Abdelaziz Bouteflika of Algeria, ruled that the delegation of South Africa should be refused participation in the work of the Assembly's twenty-ninth session. His ruling was upheld by 91 votes to 22, with 19 abstentions.

Although remaining a member of the UN, South Africa was not represented at subsequent sessions of the General Assembly.

REPRESENTATION OF NATIONS IN THE UN

The members of the UN are nations, not governments. Whereas the UN may concern itself with the character of a government at the time a nation applies for admission and may occasionally defer admission on these grounds (Franco Spain, for example, applied for membership in 1945–46 but was not admitted until 1955), once a nation becomes a member any governmental changes thereafter do not affect continuance of membership—provided, of course, the nation continues to fulfill its Charter obligations. Nor, under the Charter, is the admission of a new nation dependent upon whether other nations individually recognize and have diplomatic relations with the government concerned. Though the relations of individual members with a nation applying for membership will affect the voting in the Security Council and the General Assembly, strictly speaking the only consideration enjoined by the Charter is the judgment by the members that the applying nation as represented by its government is "willing and able" to carry out its UN obligations. As a result, there are several nations in the UN that do not recognize or have diplomatic relations with each other.

Nations have to be represented at UN proceedings by delegations that are specifically authorized by their governments to speak on their behalf. Thus when a new ambassador appears, or when a new session of a UN organ convenes, it is necessary to examine the credentials of persons claiming to represent member states. The Credentials Committee must be satisfied that the person was duly appointed by his government and that that government is the official government of the respective member nation. The matter can become controversial at the UN if, for example, two rival governments both claim to be the only legitimate government of a member state and each demands that its own representative be seated. An outstanding case in point was China; the unresolved issue of its representation in the UN had been one of the most important and controversial items on the Assembly's agenda.

At its twenty-sixth session, in 1971, however, the Assembly decided "to restore all its rights to the People's Republic of China and to recognize the representatives of its government as the only legitimate representatives of China to the United Nations, and to expel forthwith the representatives of Chiang Kai-shek from the place which they unlawfully occupy at the United Nations and in all the organizations related to it."

UNITED NATIONS HEADQUARTERS AND FACILITIES

THE HEADQUARTERS BUILDINGS

When the UN came into being on 24 October 1945, it had no home. On 11 December 1945, the US Congress unanimously invited the UN to make its headquarters in the US. In February 1946 the General Assembly, meeting for its first session in London, voted for the general vicinity of Fairfield and Westchester counties, near New York City, but sites near Philadelphia, Boston, and San Francisco were also considered during 1946. Then came the dramatic offer by John D. Rockefeller Jr. to donate $8.5 million toward the purchase of properties along the East River in midtown Manhattan. The City of New York rounded out the zone and granted rights along the river frontage. By November 1947 the Assembly approved the architectural plans, and nine months later the UN concluded a $65 million interest-free loan agreement with the US government. The director of planning for UN headquarters was Wallace K. Harrison of the US. The international board of design consultants included G. A. Soilleux, Australia; Gaston Brunfaut, Belgium; Oscar Niemeyer, Brazil; Ernest Cormier, Canada; Ssu-ch'eng Liang, China; Charles le Corbusier, Switzerland; Sven Markelius, Sweden; Nikolai D. Bassow, USSR; Howard Robertson, UK; and Julio Vilamajo, Uruguay.

The first structure to be completed, in the spring of 1951, was the 39-story marble and glass Secretariat building. In 1952, the Conference building (with the three council halls designed by Scandinavians) and the General Assembly building were ready.

Thus it was five or six years before the UN was permanently housed. In the interim, the Secretariat was established provisionally at Hunter College in the Bronx, New York, and in August 1946 the United Nations moved to the Sperry Gyroscope plant at Lake Success, Long Island. Several General Assembly sessions took place in the New York City Building at Flushing Meadow, and in 1948 and 1951 the Assembly met in Paris at the Palais de Chaillot.

A library building at the headquarters site, erected and equipped through a $6.6 million donation by the Ford Foundation, was dedicated in 1961 to the memory of former Secretary-General Dag Hammarskjöld.

Various equipment and works of art for the Conference and Assembly buildings have been donated by member governments. A unique feature of the Assembly building is the Meditation Room. The dimly lit "room of stillness" contains at its center a block of iron ore illuminated by a thin shaft of light from the ceiling. This block symbolizes, in the words of Dag Hammarskjöld, "an altar to the God of all." Since iron ore is basic material for plowshares as well as swords, the block is also intended to aid the meditator in making the proper choice.

For a small fee, visitors may join one of the Secretariat's tours of the headquarters buildings, conducted by a staff of 50 guides in at least 25 languages. The number of visitors to headquarters averages one million per year and there have been more than 26 million since the tours were begun.

Capacity

Because of the increase in the number of member states, the conference rooms and the Plenary Hall have been expanded several times on a temporary basis. A major and more permanent expansion of staff and meeting facilities at Headquarters was undertaken in the early 1980s.

More than 16,000 men and women from some 150 countries comprise the UN staff—about one-third of them at Headquarters and the other two-thirds at UN offices and centers around the globe.

INTERNAL SERVICES

Library. The Dag Hammarskjöld Library contains 400,000 volumes and 15,000 periodicals. The library is for official use by the permanent missions and the Secretariat. Outside researchers may also be accommodated.

Documents Services. Most of the UN documents are produced in mimeographed form for the use of members and the Secretariat. Headquarters houses one of the world's largest mimeographing and printing plants.

Some documents are issued as UN publications for sale to the public. Sales in 1982 grossed almost $6.5 million, yielding more than $980,000 in net profit.

Conference Services. Headquarters, together with the UN's offices in Geneva and Vienna, provide the interpreters, translators, précis writers, editors, and conference personnel required for the many UN meetings throughout the world, as well as for other meetings held under UN auspices.

Telecommunications System. The UN has its own telecommunications system. Headquarters is linked by radio with the offices in Geneva and Vienna, which in turn provide liaison with UN organs and offices in different parts of the world.

UN Postal Administration

UN stamps are issued under separate agreements with the postal authorities of the US, Switzerland, and Austria and are valid for postage only on mail deposited at UN headquarters in New York and at the UN offices in Geneva and Vienna. UN stamps may be obtained by mail, across the counter, or automatically through the Customer Deposit Service in New York, Geneva, or Vienna. Only revenue from the sale of stamps for philatelic purposes is retained by the UN; in 1982 such sales netted the UN $6.5 million. In addition to producing revenue, UN stamp designs publicize the work of the organization and its related agencies.

PUBLIC INFORMATION SERVICES

At its first session, in 1946, the General Assembly decided to create a special Department of Public Information in the Secretariat. Recognizing that the UN's aims cannot be achieved unless the world is fully informed of its objectives and activities, the General Assembly directed that DPI should work to promote the fullest possible informed understanding of UN affairs. Accordingly, the UN provides a steady stream of official information on its activities, covering virtually all media—press, publications, radio, television, films, photographs, and exhibits.

Press, Publications, and Photographic Services

DPI provides information to news correspondents and facilitates their access to meetings, documents, and other news sources. In any given year several thousand press releases are issued at headquarters, including accounts of meetings, texts of speeches, announcements of special programs, and background or reference papers. DPI holds daily briefings and helps to arrange press conferences for members of delegations and senior members of the Secretariat and the specialized agencies.

Booklets, pamphlets, and leaflets covering the work of the UN are published in many languages. The *UN Chronicle,* published in English, French, Spanish, and Arabic, reports on UN activities during the preceding month. DPI also issues a *Yearbook of the United Nations*.

To illustrate UN activities in the field, photo missions are periodically undertaken throughout the world. The photographs obtained, together with extensive coverage of events at UN headquarters and other principal conference centers, are widely used by newspapers, periodicals, book publishers, and government information agencies. Posters and photo display sets are published to engage public interest.

Radio, TV, and Film Services

A major responsibility of DPI is to assist the accredited correspondents of national and commercial broadcasting organizations in their coverage of the UN's work. In radio, correspondents may use studios and recording equipment at headquarters, and New York is linked with distant capitals by shortwave or radiotelephone. Film and television correspondents may receive visual coverage of principal meetings of the Security Council and the General Assembly, as well as of press conferences and briefings. Satellite transmissions carry this material around the world.

DPI broadcasts meetings of principal UN organs by shortwave, and produces its own radio programs in some 24 languages, reaching listeners in more than 100 countries. UN films and television programs are not only for television, but also for groups in schools, universities, and voluntary organizations.

Division for Economic and Social Information (DESI)

Other elements of DPI are organized on the basis of the medium, but DESI on that of a subject—economic and social affairs. It coordinates information services of the UN, issues publications, and conducts "encounters" for journalists.

UN Information Centers

In 1983, 63 UN Information Centers in as many cities around the world were disseminating information about UN aims and activities to some 150 countries and territories. The centers maintain up-to-date reference libraries of UN publications and documentation and answer public inquiries. DPI material is locally translated by the centers, which work closely with local media, information agencies, educational authorities, and nongovernmental organizations. The centers also inform headquarters on local UN activities which, in turn, are publicized by DPI.

PRIVILEGES AND IMMUNITIES

The Charter provides that in all territory of its member states the UN shall hold whatever legal capacity, privileges, and immunities are necessary for the fulfillment of its purposes, and that representatives of member states and officials of the UN shall have a status allowing them independent exercise of their functions. On 13 February 1946, the General Assembly adopted the Convention on the Privileges and Immunities of the United Nations. As of December 1982, 119 countries, including the US, had acceded to this convention. UN staff on official business can travel on a *laissez-passer* issued by the UN.

Countries that have acceded to the convention exempt the salaries of UN officials from taxation, except Canada, Laos, Turkey, and the US, where special reservations apply. These salaries, however, are subject to a "staff assessment" which is internal UN taxation. The UN itself is exempt from all direct taxes, customs duties, and export and import restrictions on articles for official use.

Practically all member states have established permanent missions to the UN in New York. Their personnel enjoy privileges and immunities similar to those of diplomatic missions.

HEADQUARTERS AGREEMENT BETWEEN THE UN AND THE US

A special headquarters agreement, signed by Secretary-General Trygve Lie and US Secretary of State George C. Marshall at Lake Success on 26 June 1947, has been in force since 21 November 1947. It defines the 18 acres of land in New York City located between 42nd and 48th Streets and First Avenue and the Franklin D. Roosevelt Drive as the Headquarters District of the United Nations. Subsequently, by supplemental agreements between the UN and the US, additional office space located in buildings in the vicinity has been included in the Headquarters District. The Headquarters District is "under the control and authority of the United Nations as provided in this agreement." It is the seat of the UN, and the agreement stipulates that the district "shall be inviolable." Federal, state, and local personnel on official duty (for example, a policeman intent on making an arrest) may enter it only with the consent of the secretary-general. The UN may make regulations for the area; and US federal, state, and local law, insofar as it is inconsistent with UN regulations, does not apply here. Otherwise, the US courts would have jurisdiction over actions and transactions taking place in the Headquarters District. The UN may expel persons from it for violations of regulations. In such cases, and generally for the preservation of law and order, US authorities have to provide a sufficient number of police if requested by the secretary-general. "No form of racial or religious discrimination shall be permitted within the Headquarters District." Other detailed provisions in the agreement between the UN and the US deal with the important matter of the accessibility of the seat of the UN to non-US citizens.

EMBLEM AND FLAG OF THE UN

The General Assembly adopted an official seal and emblem for the organization.

Emblem. The UN emblem depicts in silver against a light blue background a map of the earth, projected from the North Pole, and encircled by two symmetrical olive branches. It is a slight modification of a design selected by the US Office of Strategic Services for buttons used at the San Francisco Conference in 1945. The particular shade of blue is now officially called United Nations blue.

Flag. The first UN flag was used in Greece in 1947 in a region where there was fighting. The flag had the UN emblem in white against a background of United Nations blue.

Display of UN Flag. The flag may be displayed not only by the UN and specialized agencies and by governments but also by "organizations and individuals to demonstrate support of the United Nations and to further its principles and purposes." It is considered "especially appropriate" to display the UN flag on national and official holidays, on UN Day, 24 October, and at official events in honor of the UN or related to the UN.

UN Flag Code and Regulations. The Code prohibits the use of the emblem except for UN publications and conferences and other officially approved uses.

THE UNITED NATIONS BUDGET

THE UN BUDGET

Under the Charter it is the task of the General Assembly to "consider and approve the budget of the Organizaton" and to apportion the expenses of the UN among the member nations. From an administrative standpoint, the expenditures of the UN may be said to fall into two categories: expenditures that are included in what is termed the "regular budget," to which all members are obliged to contribute; and expenditures for certain high-cost items or programs, for which are established separate, or "extrabudgetary," accounts or funds, financed by special arrangements that do not necessarily involve obligatory payments by UN members.

Included in the regular budget are operating costs at UN Headquarters and all overseas UN offices; the expenses of the International Court of Justice; expenditures for certain technical programs, and for special missions, such as the UN Truce Supervision Organization in Palestine (UNTSO); and debt services charges, which are also listed as "special expenses."

Extrabudgetary accounts cover the work of the many subsidiary bodies of the UN that are financed either wholly or in part by voluntary contributions from government and other sources. These include the UN Children's Fund (UNICEF) and the UN Development Program (UNDP). The administrative expenses of the Office of the High Commissioner for Refugees are included in the regular UN budget, but its programs are financed through a special account. The salaries of the professional staff of the UN Relief and Works Agency for Palestine Refugees (UNRWA) are provided for in the regular budget, but the other costs of its operation are defrayed from a special account. Special accounts have also been used to finance the costly UN peacekeeping operations along the borders of Israel, in the Congo, and in Cyprus. All told, these extrabudgetary accounts greatly exceed the regular UN budget in most years. The much publicized financial crisis of the UN, which came to a head in 1964 and was still unresolved at the end of 1982, arose chiefly over the financing of peacekeeping operations in the Middle East and in the Congo. (See the section below on Proposals to Ease the UN's Financial Difficulties.)

SUBSIDIARY ORGANS ASSISTING THE ASSEMBLY IN FINANCIAL MATTERS

The General Assembly has established two permanent subsidiary organs concerned with administrative and budgetary affairs.

The Advisory Committee on Administrative and Budgetary Questions is responsible for expert examination of the UN budget and the administrative budgets of the specialized agencies. The committee's 16 members, elected by the Assembly for staggered 3-year terms, serve as individuals, not as government representatives.

The Committee on Contributions advises the Assembly on the apportionment of the expense of the UN among the member nations. Its 18 members are elected for 3-years terms and also serve as individuals.

PROCEDURE FOR DETERMINING THE REGULAR BUDGET

Every other summer, the secretary-general presents detailed budget and appropriations estimates for the following biennium. Until 1974 there were annual budgets. These estimates are reviewed and sometimes revised by the Advisory Committee and are later debated in the Assembly. At the end of its debate, the Assembly approves the budget in the form of a three-part resolution which lists: (1) the total appropriations and the estimates for the major items of expenditures; (2) the estimates of anticipated income from sources other than assessments on member nations; and (3) the distribution scale for the financing of the appropriations for the period in question.

APPROPRIATIONS (GROSS) FOR THE REGULAR BUDGET OF THE UN, 1946–1983

YEAR	APPROPRIATION	YEAR	APPROPRIATION
1946	$ 19,390,000	1963	92,876,550
1947	28,616,568	1964	101,327,600
1948	39,285,736	1965	108,472,800
1949	43,204,080	1966	121,080,530
1950	44,520,773	1967	133,084,000
1951	48,925,500	1968	141,787,750
1952	50,547,660	1969	156,967,300
1953	49,869,450	1970	168,956,950
1954	48,528,980	1971	194,627,800
1955	50,228,000	1972	208,650,200
1956	50,683,350	1973	233,820,374
1957	53,174,700	1974–75	606,033,000
1958	61,121,900	1976–77	745,813,800
1959	61,657,100	1978–79	996,372,900
1960	65,734,900	1980–81	1,339,151,200
1961	71,649,300	1982–83	1,472,961,700
1962	85,818,220		

Aside from the regular budget, the Assembly also allots a certain amount of money for unforeseen and extraordinary expenses and determines the level of the UN's working capital fund, to which member nations advance sums in proportion to their assessed contributions to the regular budget. The fund—$100 million—is used to finance appropriations pending receipt of contributions and may also be drawn upon by the secretary-general for other purposes determined by the Assembly.

Since the expenses of the organization can never be precisely predicted, the secretary-general reviews actual expenditures for the current year at each regular session of the Assembly and proposes adjustments in the original appropriations. Usually, a supplemental budget is voted, but occasionally the Assembly votes reductions.

BUDGET ESTIMATES FOR 1982–83
A. Items of Expenditure

The amount of $1,472,961,700 was appropriated as the revised gross expenditures for 1982–83, as follows:

1. *Overall policy-making, direction, and coordination:* $38,849,500
2. *Political and Security Council affairs; peacekeeping activities:* $84,326,800
3. *Political affairs, trusteeship, and decolonization:* $21,106,700
4. *Economic, social, and humanitarian activities:* $469,918,600
5. *International justice and law:* $22,018,500
6. *Public information:* $64,635,000
7. *Common support services:* $511,002,000

8. *Special expenses:* $17,220,300
9. *Staff assessment:* $207,802,500
10. *Capital expenditures:* $36,081,800

B. Income Estimates

It was estimated that gross expenditures would be offset to the amount of $257,059,900, derived as follows:

1. *Income from staff assessment:* $211,123,800
2. *General income:* $32,194,500
3. *Revenue-producing activities:* $13,741,600

UN Staff Assessment. Under UN regulations, a percentage of the earnings of the entire UN staff is deducted in lieu of taxes and credited to "income." In order to avoid double taxation of staff members of US nationality, these are reimbursed by the UN for the taxes (federal, state, and city) levied on their UN earnings. The withholdings from the salaries of UN personnel of all other nationalities are credited to the member states' accounts against their assessed contributions.

C. Net Expenditures

After taking into account staff assessments and other items of income, the net estimated amount remaining to be raised through assessed contributions from member states for the biennium 1982–83 totaled $1,215,901,800.

ASSESSED CONTRIBUTIONS OF MEMBER STATES TO THE REGULAR BUDGET

The scale of contributions of member states is established by the General Assembly on the recommendation of its Committee on Contributions. The basic original criterion for the apportionment of UN expenses was the ability to pay, with comparative estimates of national income taken as the fairest guide. Other factors, such as the comparative income per capita, the ability of contributors to obtain foreign exchange, and, until 1974, dislocation of national economies arising out of World War II, were also taken into account. In this way, the US share was at first 39.89%, gradually declining to 31.52% for 1971–73. Since the early 1950s, the next highest share has been that of the USSR. Until then, it was that of the UK.

In 1972, the Assembly established a ceiling on the rate of assessment of the highest contributor, set at 25%. At the same time, it lowered the minimum rate of assessment to 0.02% (later lowered to 0.01%) and requested the Committee on Contributions to give attention to the special economic and financial problems of developing countries.

In an effort to introduce what it termed greater fairness and equity in the scale of assessments, the Assembly in 1981 requested the Committee on Contributions to prepare a set of guidelines for the collection of more uniform and comparable data and statistics from member states, and to study alternative methods to assess "the real capacity of member states to pay." This question will again be considered by the Assembly in 1984.

Under the scale of assessments adopted for the period 1983–85, the seven largest contributors, listed in order, are the US, the USSR, Japan, the FRG, France, the UK, and Canada. The complete scale is as follows:

Member State	Percent
Afghanistan	0.01
Albania	0.01
Algeria	0.13
Angola	0.01
Antigua and Barbuda	0.01
Argentina	0.71
Australia	1.57
Austria	0.75
Bahamas	0.01
Bahrain	0.01
Bangladesh	0.03
Barbados	0.01
Belgium	1.28
Belize	0.01
Benin	0.01
Bhutan	0.01
Bolivia	0.01
Botswana	0.01
Brazil	1.39
Bulgaria	0.18
Burma	0.01
Burundi	0.01
Byelorussia	0.36
Cameroon	0.01
Canada	3.08
Cape Verde	0.01
Central African Republic	0.01
Chad	0.01
Chile	0.07
China	0.88
Colombia	0.11
Comoros	0.01
Congo	0.01
Costa Rica	0.02
Cuba	0.09
Cyprus	0.01
Czechoslovakia	0.76
Denmark	0.75
Djibouti	0.01
Dominica	0.01
Dominican Republic	0.03
Ecuador	0.02
Egypt	0.07
El Salvador	0.01
Equatorial Guinea	0.01
Ethiopia	0.01
Fiji	0.01
Finland	0.48
France	6.51
Gabon	0.02
Gambia	0.01
German Democratic Republic	1.39
Germany, Federal Republic of	8.54
Ghana	0.02
Greece	0.40
Grenada	0.01
Guatemala	0.02
Guinea	0.01
Guinea-Bissau	0.01
Guyana	0.01
Haiti	0.01
Honduras	0.01
Hungary	0.23
Iceland	0.03
India	0.36
Indonesia	0.13
Iran	0.58
Iraq	0.12
Ireland	0.18
Israel	0.23
Italy	3.74
Ivory Coast	0.03
Jamaica	0.02
Japan	10.32
Jordan	0.01
Kampuchea	0.01
Kenya	0.01

Kuwait	0.25	US	25.00
Laos	0.01	Upper Volta	0.01
Lebanon	0.02	Uruguay	0.04
Lesotho	0.01	Vanuatu	0.01
Liberia	0.01	Venezuela	0.55
Libya	0.26	Viet-Nam	0.02
Luxembourg	0.06	Western Samoa	0.01
Madagascar	0.01	Yemen, People's Democratic Republic of	0.01
Malawi	0.01	Yemen Arab Republic	0.01
Malaysia	0.09	Yugoslavia	0.46
Maldives	0.01	Zaire	0.01
Mali	0.01	Zambia	0.01
Malta	0.01	Zimbabwe	0.02
Mauritania	0.01		
Mauritius	0.01	TOTAL	100.00
Mexico	0.88		
Mongolia	0.01		
Morocco	0.05		
Mozambique	0.01		
Nepal	0.01		
Netherlands	1.78		
New Zealand	0.26		
Nicaragua	0.01		
Niger	0.01		
Nigeria	0.19		
Norway	0.51		
Oman	0.01		
Pakistan	0.06		
Panama	0.02		
Papua New Guinea	0.01		
Paraguay	0.01		
Peru	0.07		
Philippines	0.09		
Poland	0.72		
Portugal	0.18		
Qatar	0.03		
Romania	0.19		
Rwanda	0.01		
St. Lucia	0.01		
St. Vincent and the Grenadines	0.01		
São Tomé and Príncipe	0.01		
Sa'udi Arabia	0.86		
Senegal	0.01		
Seychelles	0.01		
Sierra Leone	0.01		
Singapore	0.09		
Solomon Islands	0.01		
Somalia	0.01		
South Africa	0.41		
Spain	1.93		
Sri Lanka	0.01		
Sudan	0.01		
Suriname	0.01		
Swaziland	0.01		
Sweden	1.32		
Syria	0.03		
Tanzania	0.01		
Thailand	0.08		
Togo	0.01		
Trinidad and Tobago	0.03		
Tunisia	0.03		
Turkey	0.32		
Uganda	0.01		
Ukraine	1.32		
USSR	10.54		
United Arab Emirates	0.16		
UK	4.67		

Contributions by Nonmember States

States that are not members of the UN but participate in certain of its activities (principally the International Court of Justice, the regional economic commissions, the UN Conference on Trade and Development, the UN Industrial Development Organization, and the control of narcotic drugs) contribute toward expenses of such activities according to the following scale.

	Percent
Korea, People's Democratic Republic of	0.05
Korea, Republic of	0.18
Liechtenstein	0.01
Monaco	0.01
Nauru	0.01
San Marino	0.01
Switzerland	1.10
Tonga	0.01
Vatican	0.01

PROPOSALS TO EASE THE UN'S FINANCIAL DIFFICULTIES

By and large, the regular budget has never created major disputes among the member states, and most governments have usually paid their dues relatively punctually. However, since 1963 the USSR has refused as a matter of principle to contribute to certain items in the regular budget, such as the UN Commission for the Unification and Rehabilitation of Korea until its dissolution by a consensus vote of the 1973 Assembly, or to those parts of the regular budget devoted to the redemption of UN bonds (a method of raising funds for certain UN peacekeeping operations). France has taken a similar stand in connection with the redemption of the bonds. Furthermore, a number of countries have refused to contribute to the special accounts for peacekeeping operations in the Congo and the Middle East. It was chiefly these controversial expenditures which precipitated the UN's financial emergency in the mid-1960s.

In July 1962, the International Court of Justice, at the request of the General Assembly, issued an advisory opinion in which it declared that the expenses of the first UN Emergency Force in the Middle East and the UN Force in the Congo constituted expenses of the organization within the meaning of Article 17, paragraph 2, of the Charter, and should thus be borne by member states as apportioned by the Assembly. The Assembly accepted the Court's opinion in December 1962, but debate over peacekeeping operations and the financial difficulties continued. The emergency still existed in 1982. A number of other factors, moreover, have contributed to the precariousness of the financial position of the organization, notably the lateness of many member states in paying their assessed contributions, the currency fluctuations of the 1970s (marked by two devaluations of the US dollar, on which the UN budget is based), and inflation.

Several Assembly working groups and committees studied the financial position of the UN between 1965 and 1982 without leading to a resolution of the problem. The 1972 Assembly set up a special account for voluntary contributions to help to clear up the UN deficit.

By 1983, 28 countries had contributed over $42 million to the account.

Meanwhile, the deficit continued to grow, reaching over $100 million in 1977 and an expected $300 million by 1983. Since 1975 a special Negotiating Committee on the Financial Emergency has kept the matter under review. One partial solution being considered involves the issuance of special postage stamps devoted to conservation and the protection of nature, with a portion of the revenue from sales earmarked for those causes.

THE GENERAL ASSEMBLY

First of the UN organs established by the Charter, the General Assembly is the pivot of the entire organization. All member states are represented in it. Each country, large or small, has one vote, and each country decides the way in which it chooses its own representatives.

FUNCTIONS AND POWERS

The central position of the Assembly within the organization is firmly established in a series of Charter provisions encompassing an extraordinarily wide range of functions and powers. First are the provisions setting forth the Assembly's powers as the major deliberative body of the UN. With two exceptions (described below), the Assembly has the right to discuss and make recommendations on any subject that falls within the scope of the Charter itself, including the functions and powers of the other organs. Hence, it is in the Assembly that all of the UN's important projects (except for the Security Council's peacekeeping operations) originate: on political questions, disarmament, economic and social welfare, human rights, decolonization of dependent territories, and development of international law.

The second group of Charter provisions defining the pivotal position of the Assembly concerns the financing of the UN. The Assembly is empowered to "consider and approve" the budget of the organization (which includes that of the International Court of Justice at The Hague), and it also has the right to determine how the expenses shall be apportioned among the member nations.

Lastly, the Assembly's pivotal position is secured by provisions that give it specific powers in relation to the other organs. Thus both the Economic and Social Council and the Trusteeship Council are constituted under the direct authority of the Assembly to carry out designated tasks in their respective spheres. The administrative arm of the UN, the Secretariat, is also at the disposition of the Assembly. The Assembly's powers, however, are much more limited where the Security Council and International Court of Justice are concerned. Designed in some respects to be more powerful than the Assembly, the Security Council is in no way answerable to the Assembly for its activities—although it is required to make an annual report and, when necessary, special reports. Also, whereas the Assembly is empowered to make recommendations to the Council concerning the maintenance of international peace, it cannot give the Council instructions. In the case of the International Court of Justice, any attempt to render its activities answerable to the Assembly would have prejudiced the independent status that is normally accorded to judiciary bodies throughout the world. Nevertheless, inasmuch as the Assembly not only has budgetary power but also elects the nonpermanent members of the Security Council and, concurrently with the Security Council, all the judges of the International Court, it can be said to exercise an appreciable degree of indirect control over both these bodies.

Thus the one main UN organ on which all member states have the constitutional right to be represented is able to make its will felt throughout the organization, and indeed the entire UN system. Because its powers closely resemble those of a national parliament, the General Assembly has often been described as a "world parliament." Parliamentary powers are not to be confused, though, with governmental powers. Except insofar as the Economic and Social Council, the Trusteeship Council, and the Secretariat are

bound to carry out its requests, the Assembly has no power to legislate and cannot enforce its decisions upon individual member nations. The only sanctions that the Assembly can wield against an uncooperative member are the suspension of the rights and privileges of membership and expulsion from the organization, but even these sanctions can be invoked only on the recommendation of the Security Council. In effect, then, all Assembly decisions are merely recommendations whose sole force is one of moral obligation. At the end of this chapter an attempt is made to assess their effectiveness on this score.

Charter Restrictions on the Assembly's Power to Discuss and Recommend

The Charter imposes two major restrictions on the Assembly's powers to discuss and make recommendations. The first is embodied in the principle set out in Article 2, paragraph 7 of the Charter, which states that "Nothing contained in the present Charter shall authorize the United Nations to intervene in matters which are essentially within the domestic jurisdiction of any state or shall require the Members to submit such matters to settlement. . . . " This principle is not so restrictive as it might seem, for whether a given issue is or is not of a domestic character is decided by the Assembly itself. The Assembly can and often does override by majority vote the attempt of a member nation to bar a particular topic from debate by invoking Article 2, paragraph 7 of the Charter. The most notable case in point is the Assembly's annual discussion of South Africa's apartheid policy despite South Africa's contention that the matter is within its domestic jurisdiction and without international implications.

The second restriction is to be found in Article 12 of the Charter, which states that while the Security Council is exercising its functions respecting any international dispute or crisis, "the General Assembly shall not make any recommendations with regard to that dispute . . . unless the Security Council so requests." This stipulation, then, clearly establishes the absolute primacy of the Security Council over the General Assembly in times of crisis. Here, the main object of the founders of the UN was to ensure against the possibility of the smaller nations forming a majority bloc to interfere with any decisions that might be taken by the Big Five acting in concert as permanent members of the Security Council, where each possesses the right of veto. (For a discussion of the veto right, see the chapter on the Security Council.)

Extension of the Assembly's Power to Discuss and Recommend through the "Uniting for Peace Resolution"

Designed to secure maximum unity of action in moments of acute danger, Article 12 in fact proved to be the chief obstacle to action of any kind during successive crises in the years just after World War II. The effectiveness of the entire system presupposed a spirit of unanimity among the great powers in their determination to end a particular dispute that appeared to threaten international peace and security. But on each occasion when the great powers might have been expected to display unanimity, the USSR and the other four permanent members of the Security Council took opposite sides in the dispute. As a result, precisely because each of them possessed the veto, all Council action was deadlocked. Meanwhile, the Assembly, prevented from taking action of its own accord because of Article 12, was forced to stand helplessly by.

It was the seriousness of the prolonged Korean crisis that finally impelled the Assembly to take steps to break through its constitutional straitjacket. Following a deadlock in the Council, when the USSR vetoed a US-sponsored resolution in connection with the entry of the People's Republic of China into the Korean conflict on the side of North Korea, the Assembly convened an emergency special session to discuss the situation and adopted a resolution that enabled it to circumvent the restrictions imposed by Article 12. This act, which came to be known as the "Uniting for Peace Resolution," provides that if the Security Council, because of lack of unanimity among its permanent members, fails to exercise its primary responsibility in the maintenance of peace, in a case where there appears to be a threat to the peace, breach of the peace, or act of aggression, the Assembly shall consider the matter immediately with a view to making recommendations to members for collective measures, including if necessary the use of armed force. Although the Uniting for Peace Resolution thus considerably extends the Assembly's powers with respect to maintenance of international peace and security, it in no way represents an attempt to usurp the Security Council's prerogatives when that body is functioning smoothly. Nor does it attempt to arrogate to the Assembly the enforcement powers that the Charter accorded to the Security Council alone. Even under the Uniting for Peace Resolution, the Assembly can only recommend that members undertake collective peacekeeping measures; it cannot oblige them to do so. Nor can the Assembly impose peacekeeping action against the will of the parties to a dispute. It must obtain their explicit consent to the presence of UN personnel—observer commissions, mediators, troops—in their territories.

Since the Korean War, the General Assembly has authorized one large-scale peacekeeping operation, the first UN Emergency Force (UNEF) in the Middle East (1956–67). All subsequent operations have been authorized by the Security Council. (See the discussion of peacekeeping operations in the chapter on Maintaining Peace and Security.)

ORGANIZATION

Sessions

The General Assembly meets once a year in regular sessions that begin on the third Tuesday in September. Usually these sessions last about three months, ending before Christmas, but there is no fixed time limit, and several times the Assembly has adjourned to continue the session after the holidays. Special sessions on a particular topic may be held at the request of the Security Council, or of a majority of UN members, or of one member if the majority of members concur. To implement the terms of the Uniting for Peace Resolution, an emergency special session may be called within 24 hours at the request of the Security Council on the vote of any nine members, or by a majority of UN members, or by one member if the majority concur.

Sessional Committees

Most of the Assembly's substantive work during its regular session is conducted through seven "Main Committees" which are reconstituted at every session. Each main committee is composed of representatives of all member nations.

Six of the main committees are officially designated by numbers. The *First Committee* deals with political and security issues, including disarmament. The *Second Committee* deals with economic and financial matters, including technical assistance and the work of the specialized agencies. The *Third Committee* reviews social problems and human rights issues, including the work of the appropriate specialized agencies. The *Fourth Committee* handles problems of granting independence to colonial and trust territories. The *Fifth Committee* deals with the administrative and budgetary matters of the organization. The *Sixth Committee* debates legal questions, including the general development and codification of international law. The seventh is the *Special Political Committee*, which was originally created in 1948 as an ad hoc committee of the whole to discuss the Palestine question. Never disbanded, it was subsequently retained as an additional main committee to assist the First Committee in dealing with political issues.

The Assembly maintains two other sessional committees, both of which deal with Assembly procedure. However, neither of these is a committee of the whole. The *General Committee,* composed of the Assembly president, the 21 vice-presidents, and the chairmen of the main committees, examines the provisional agenda of each session and makes recommendations to the Assembly on the inclusion or exclusion of items and on their assignment to the appropriate main committee. The *Credentials Committee* is a nine-member body appointed by the Assembly at the beginning of the session to examine the credentials of representatives and work out any problems that might arise in this connection.

Plenary Meetings

Since all the main committees are committees of the whole, the distinction between the Assembly meeting in committee and meeting in plenum is largely one of protocol. Always conducted by the president or a vice-president of the Assembly, plenary meetings are much more formal affairs. Normally, no one below the rank of head of delegation may actively participate in the proceedings, and no one is allowed to speak from his chair but must go to the speaker's rostrum. (None of the conference rooms in which the committees meet is provided with a speaker's rostrum.) The Assembly Hall itself is reserved for plenary meetings and rarely used by the committees.

It is in plenary that all formal or ceremonial functions occur: the opening and closing of the Assembly session, election of officers and members of other organs, the final decisions on all agenda items, and addresses by heads of state or government or by other high national officials who visit the UN while the Assembly is in session. Plenary meetings also constitute the forum for the statements of general policy that the head of each member delegation is entitled to make as part of what is known as the "general debate," which takes place during the first three weeks or so of the regular session.

Voting Procedure

Each member of the General Assembly and its committees has one vote. Article 18 of the Charter decrees that Assembly decisions on "important" questions shall be made by a two-thirds majority of the members present and voting. Among the important questions specified are recommendations with regard to maintenance of peace and security; election of the nonpermanent members of the Security Council and of the members of the Economic and Social Council and the Trusteeship Council; the admission of new UN members, suspension of rights and privileges of membership, and expulsion of members; questions relating to the operation of the trusteeship system; and budgetary questions. Decisions on other questions, including the determination of additional categories of important questions requiring a two-thirds majority vote, are made by a simple majority of the members present and voting. The phrase "members present and voting" means members casting either affirmative or negative votes; members that abstain are considered as not voting. Thus, although the number of abstentions is usually listed for information purposes, it does not count in the final tally as to whether a resolution has received the requisite majority—provided that the rules of quorum have been observed. A quorum is constituted when a majority of the members are present: no decision may be taken without one. The president of the Assembly, however, may declare a meeting open and permit the debate to proceed when at least one-third of the members are present. The chairman of a main committee may open a meeting when one-quarter of the members are present.

Voting may be by a show of hands, by roll call, or in certain instances, such as elections, by secret ballot. The normal method was intended to be by a show of hands, but any member can request a roll call. There has been an increasing tendency to do so, especially on the more contentious issues. Before a roll-call vote is taken, a lot is drawn to determine the country that is to vote first. Starting with that country, voting proceeds according to the alphabetical order of the official names of states in English. Mechanical voting equipment was installed in the Assembly Hall and first used at the 1965 session. Similar equipment is used in two conference rooms.

Seating Arrangements
The Charter allows each member state a maximum of five representatives in the General Assembly. Most members, in addition to their five representatives, send five alternative representatives and a number of advisers to each session. Six seats are assigned to every delegation in the Assembly Hall. Both in the hall and in committee rooms, delegations are seated in alphabetical order according to the official names of the countries in English. The seating is rearranged before each session by drawing lots to select the country with which the alphabetical seating will start.

Election of Officers
At each regular session, the General Assembly constitutes itself anew. During the opening meetings, the main officers are elected, to serve until the end of the session. If a special or emergency session is called, it is normally presided over by officers elected the previous September.

The first officer to be elected is the president of the Assembly. Delegates vote by secret ballot, and a simple majority suffices. In choosing the president, regard has to be paid to the equitable geographical rotation of the office among the following groups of states: African states, Asian states, East European states, Latin American states, and West European and other states. By tacit agreement, no representative of a permanent member of the Security Council is ever elected president of the Assembly or chairman of a committee.

PRESIDENTS OF THE GENERAL ASSEMBLY

First session, 1946–47, Paul-Henri Spaak, Belgium
Second session, 1947, Oswaldo Aranha, Brazil
Third session, 1948–49, Herbert V. Evatt, Australia
Fourth session, 1949, Carlos P. Romulo, Philippines
Fifth session, 1950–51, Nasrollah Entezam, Iran
Sixth session, 1951–52, Luis Padilla Nervo, Mexico
Seventh session, 1952–53, Lester B. Pearson, Canada
Eighth session, 1953, Mrs. Vijaya Lakshmi Pandit, India
Ninth session, 1954, Eelco N. van Kleffens, Netherlands
Tenth session, 1955, José Maza, Chile
Eleventh session, 1956–57, Prince Wan Waithayakon, Thailand
Twelfth session, 1957, Sir Leslie Munro, New Zealand
Thirteenth session, 1958–59, Charles Malik, Lebanon
Fourteenth session, 1959, Victor Andrés Belaúnde, Peru
Fifteenth session, 1960–61, Frederick H. Boland, Ireland
Sixteenth session, 1961–62, Mongi Slim, Tunisia
Seventeenth session, 1962, Muhammad Zafrulla Khan, Pakistan
Eighteenth session, 1963, Carlos Sosa Rodríguez, Venezuela
Nineteenth session, 1964–65, Alex Quaison-Sackey, Ghana
Twentieth session, 1965, Amintore Fanfani, Italy
Twenty-first session, 1966, Abdul Rahman Pazhwak, Afghanistan
Twenty-second session, 1967–68, Corneliu Manescu, Romania
Twenty-third session, 1968, Emilio Arenales, Guatemala
Twenty-fourth session, 1969, Miss Angie E. Brooks, Liberia
Twenty-fifth session, 1970, Edvard Hambro, Norway
Twenty-sixth session, 1971, Adam Malik, Indonesia
Twenty-seventh session, 1972, Stanislaw Trepczynski, Poland
Twenty-eighth session, 1973–74, Leopoldo Benites, Ecuador
Twenty-ninth session, 1974–75, Abdelaziz Bouteflika, Algeria
Thirtieth session, 1975, Gaston Thorn, Luxembourg
Thirty-first session, 1976, Hamilton S. Amerasinghe, Sri Lanka
Thirty-second session, 1977, Lazar Mojsov, Yugoslavia
Thirty-third session, 1978, Indalecio Liévano, Colombia

Thirty-fourth session, 1979, Salim A. Salim, Tanzania
Thirty-fifth session, 1980, Rüdiger von Wechmar, Federal Republic of Germany
Thirty-sixth session, 1981, Ismat T. Kittani, Iraq
Thirty-seventh session, 1982, Imre Hollai, Hungary
Thirty-eighth session, 1983, Jorge E. Illueca, Panama

First special session, 1947, Oswaldo Aranha, Brazil
Second special session, 1948, José Arce, Argentina
Third special session, 1961, Frederick H. Boland, Ireland
Fourth special session, 1963, Sir Muhammad Zafrulla Khan, Pakistan
Fifth special session, 1967, Abdul Rahman Pazhwak, Afghanistan
Sixth special session, 1974, Leopoldo Benites, Ecuador
Seventh special session, 1975, Abdelaziz Bouteflika, Algeria
Eighth special session, 1978, Lazar Mojsov, Yugoslavia
Ninth special session, 1978, Lazar Mojsov, Yugoslavia
Tenth special session, 1978, Lazar Mojsov, Yugoslavia
Eleventh special session, 1980, Salim A. Salim, Tanzania
Twelfth special session, 1982, Ismat T. Kittani, Iraq

First emergency special session, 1956, Rudecindo Ortega, Chile
Second emergency special session, 1956, Rudecindo Ortega, Chile
Third emergency special session, 1958, Sir Leslie Munro, New Zealand
Fourth emergency special session, 1960, Victor Andrés Belaúnde, Peru
Fifth emergency special session, 1967, Abdul Rahman Pazhwak, Afghanistan
Sixth emergency special session, 1980, Salim A. Salim, Tanzania
Seventh emergency special session, 1980, Salim A Salim, Tanzania
Eighth emergency special session, 1981, Rüdiger von Wechmar, Federal Republic of Germany
Ninth emergency special session, 1982, Ismat T. Kittani, Iraq

Following the election of the president, the main committees of the Assembly are officially constituted and retire to elect their own officers. Here again the matter of equitable geographical representation arises, and it is precisely regulated by a resolution adopted by the Assembly in 1963. Of the seven committee chairmen, three must be chosen from Africa and Asia and one each from Eastern Europe, Latin America, and Western Europe. The seventh chairmanship rotates in alternate years between representatives from Latin America and from Western Europe.

The final officers to be elected are the Assembly's 21 vice-presidents. Of these, 16 are elected in accordance with a geographical pattern. The remaining five represent the permanent members of the Security Council: China, France, the USSR, the UK, and the US.

AGENDA OF THE ASSEMBLY
Under the Assembly's rules of procedure, the provisional agenda for a regular session must be issued no later than 60 days before the opening. However, up to 30 days before the opening, the secretary-general, any of the other principal organs of the UN, or any member of the UN may request the inclusion of supplementary items. Additional items may also be included at a later stage, even after the session has formally started, if a majority of the Assembly agree.

Normally, the agenda includes well over 100 items. The great majority of substantive (that is to say, nonprocedural) items arise out of decisions made by previous sessions of the Assembly, and their inclusion in the agenda is automatic. Thus the Assembly frequently requests the secretary-general, a special committee, or another UN organ to submit a special report on a given topic. The report, at the time it is due, becomes an automatic agenda item. There also are several items that the Assembly is obliged to consider at each session under the Charter—for example, the annual report of the secretary-general on the work of the UN and the reports of the three councils. Moreover, certain items placed on the agenda by particular members of the UN come up at session after session because the sponsors are not satisfied with the Assembly's previous action on these matters.

Adoption of the Agenda

The adoption of the agenda is not a mere formality. The Assembly has to approve the entire agenda and may amend or delete any item by majority vote. A decision by the Assembly to reject a particular member's request to have an item placed on the agenda could have considerable political significance. It is the function of the 29-member General Committee (which could be described as the steering committee) to make recommendations to the Assembly on the inclusion of requested items in the agenda. Most of the pros and cons of including a controversial item in the agenda are thrashed out in this committee rather than in the plenary, and the committee's proceedings sometimes afford a preview of the positions countries will take on certain questions when they come up for substantive debate. Another important function of the General Committee is to recommend the assignment of agenda items to the various main committees for debate. It may also recommend that an important item be debated in the plenary without being referred to a committee.

EFFECTIVENESS OF THE ASSEMBLY

Depending on the nature of the question and on the views of the majority, Assembly debates may lead to one or a combination of the following: recommendations, phrased in varying degrees of urgency, to individual countries or to all countries; initiation of studies and reports; creation of new UN organs, committees of inquiry, and permanent special bodies assigned specific tasks; adoption of international covenants, treaties, and agreements.

Significance of the Enlarged Membership and Changing Voting Patterns

Since 1960, when the impact of the number of newly independent African and Asian nations first began to make itself felt in the UN, the Assembly's voting patterns have undergone a marked alteration. Until then, the majority of controversial resolutions had tended essentially to reflect a simple East-West division of opinion. In the resulting lineup of votes, the Western view, marshaled under the leadership of the US, easily attained comfortable majorities on most issues, since it was supported not only by the countries of Western Europe but by the Latin American states as well. The formation of what has come to be known as the "Afro-Asian group," coupled with the general detente in East-West relations, introduced a new element into the voting equation.

Interested in wielding influence within the world body and preoccupied with the problems of development and decolonization rather than with cold-war issues as such, African and Asian countries sought to unite themselves into an independent or "nonaligned" voting bloc. On occasion, the unity of the group is split by divided interests. This occurs most frequently in major political issues of special importance to the big powers, when some small countries may find it expedient to associate themselves with the big power on which they are dependent for financial aid. At other times, notably on items connected with economic development, African and Asian nations may join the developing countries of the Latin American group in order to create a formidable voting bloc that can force through requests to which the highly

developed nations, from East and West alike, may be reluctant to accede.

Then again, the emergence of what is in effect a floating third voting force in the Assembly has resulted in the creation of special alliances as occasion demands. For example, the Soviet bloc and the nonaligned groups often combine to defeat or harry the West on colonial issues. It has also opened up possibilities for striking voting bargains on individual draft resolutions. Accordingly, one group may support an initiative taken by a second group on a given item in exchange for support by the latter for an initiative taken by the first group on a different item.

The indiscriminate wielding of voting strength by small members that are without power as sovereign nations is subject to the law of diminishing returns. Indeed, many small nations have shown indications of growing restraint, realizing that there is little point in pushing through resolutions requiring, for example, increased expenditure on economic development, if the big powers, which have to foot most of the bill, are not prepared to implement them. Similarly, they have recognized that there is nothing to be gained from trying to compel the big powers to go beyond their own pace in agreeing upon measures for disarmament or for resolving their differences on peacekeeping issues.

One important outcome of the growing recognition by the small nations of the practical limitations of their voting strength, coupled with the complementary realization by the Western powers that they no longer can be certain of majority support, even on items of particular importance to them, has been a general recourse wherever possible to compromise resolutions that command unanimous or nearly unanimous support. However, notwithstanding this partial solution to the problems created by the emergence of a floating third voting force in the Assembly, the big powers, especially those from the West, have become increasingly dissatisfied with this situation, and some of their leaders have come to question the principle of "one country, one vote."

The fact that a resolution receives an overwhelming majority vote does not guarantee its effectiveness. Nor does the fact that a resolution was adopted by a slender margin necessarily mean that it will serve no purpose. In general it may be said that a resolution will be effective insofar as its adoption is not regarded by any country as inimical to its national interests. As long as a country feels that its interests are directly prejudiced by the terms of a resolution, that resolution is usually a dead letter. Hence, for example, the total ineffectiveness of more than three decades of resolutions calling upon the big powers to agree on measures for general and complete disarmament; or upon South Africa to abandon its racially discriminatory system of apartheid.

The most effective resolutions, then, are those that concern matters on which all members are prepared to accept a degree of compromise (though this acceptance may not necessarily be reflected in the actual voting) and establish goals that all members are eager to achieve or to which they have no objection. For like the UN itself, resolutions can be only as effective as the membership wants them to be.

THE SECURITY COUNCIL

Under the Charter, the Security Council is assigned the primary responsibility for maintaining international peace and security. To facilitate its work as guardian of the peace and to ensure quick and effective action when required, the Council is vested with certain powers and attributes not accorded the other organs of the UN. Thus the Council is the only UN body with powers commensurate with those of a world government, since it is empowered by the Charter to enforce its decisions and prescribe them as a course of action legally binding upon all UN members. However, its governmental prerogatives can be invoked only in times of gravest crisis and under explicit conditions laid down in the Charter. Otherwise, the Council, like the General Assembly, can merely recommend and advise.

Another distinctive feature of the Council is the membership and voting privileges accorded to the five countries that were chiefly responsible for the defeat of the Axis nations in World War II and, at the time of the San Francisco Conference, were regarded as militarily the most powerful countries in the world. By the terms of these privileges, China, France, the USSR, the UK, and the US were each accorded permanent membership on the Council and the right to veto singlehandedly any substantive decision adopted by the majority of the other members. The underlying consideration here was the desire to preserve the unanimity of the Big Five; that is, to ensure that no peacekeeping action would be taken against the will of a country considered sufficiently powerful to oppose the Council's decision with military force and so open up the possibility of a third major international war. Today the US and the USSR are universally acknowledged to be in a class by themselves as military powers. But the powers of the other permanent members in the Council, including the right to veto, are and will probably remain unchanged. As all five countries were actually specified by name in the relevant Charter provisions, an amendment or revision of the Charter would be required to name different nations as permanent Council members. In turn, a Charter amendment requires ratification by all five permanent members of the Security Council before it can come into force. In 1971, a major change was brought about without altering the names of permanent members. The Assembly voted that the right to represent China belonged to a delegation which the People's Republic of China would name and expelled the delegation from the Republic of China (Taiwan).

COMPOSITION

To expedite decision and action, the membership of the Security Council was deliberately restricted to a small number. Originally an 11-member body, it was subsequently enlarged to 15 members by a Charter amendment that came into effect on 31 August 1965.

With five seats permanently assigned, the remaining ten are ifilled by other UN members elected by secret ballot in the General Assembly for two-year terms. Five seats on the Security Council become vacant each year. Nonpermanent members of the Security Council are ineligible for immediate reelection upon retirement. In electing the nonpermanent members of the Security Council, the Assembly is required to pay due regard to the past and potential contribution of nations to the maintenance of international peace and security, as well as to equitable geographic distribution. In view of the power of the Council, nations attach great importance to the choice of the nonpermanent members.

The problem of ensuring equitable geographical distribution of members elected to the Security Council has not been easy to resolve. Prior to the Council's enlargement, there had been a long-standing difference of views on a "gentlemen's agreement" reached in the early days of the UN that was intended to guarantee that the six nonpermanent seats would be so distributed that one of the seats would always be held by a Soviet bloc country. But until 1960 only Poland and the Ukrainian SSR were elected, and each served for only one two-year term. In the 1959 election, Poland and Turkey competed for the nonpermanent Council seat for the two-year term 1960–61. After 52 ballots, the Assembly gave the seat to Poland on the basis of the following compromise: though elected for two years, Poland would resign its seat at the end of the first year and Turkey would be the sole candidate to fill the unexpired term. Under a similar arrangement, Romania held a seat for 1962, resigning it for 1963 to the Philippines. To avoid the recurrence of such situations after the enlargement of the Council, the Assembly at its 18th session, in 1963, adopted a resolution that established a fixed pattern for the geographical distribution of the 10 nonpermanent seats: 5 from African and Asian nations, 1 from East European nations, 2 from Latin American nations, and 2 from West European and other nations.

Composition of the Security Council for 1983: Permanent members: China, France, USSR, UK, and US. Nonpermanent members: Guyana, Jordan, Malta, Netherlands, Nicaragua, Pakistan, Poland, Togo, Zaire, and Zimbabwe.

GENERAL FUNCTIONS AND POWERS

The functions and powers assigned to the Security Council under the Charter relate to four categories of responsibilities: (1) maintenance of international peace and security; (2) formulation of plans for establishing a system for the regulation of armaments; (3) UN trusteeship responsibilities in trust territories designated as strategic areas; (4) organizational functions—namely, considering applications for UN membership, recommending suspension of and restoring a country's rights and privileges of membership, recommending the expulsion of a member state, electing (in conjunction with the Assembly) the judges of the International Court of Justice, and recommending to the Assembly candidates for the office of secretary-general.

Of these four categories, only the first is discussed in this chapter. The Council's responsibility for formulating a system for the regulation of armaments is elaborated in the chapter on disarmament; its responsibilities in respect to strategic trust territories are described in the chapter on the Trusteeship Council; and its various organizational functions are considered in the chapters on Membership, the International Court of Justice, and the Secretariat.

MAINTAINING INTERNATIONAL PEACE AND SECURITY

By the very act of joining the world body, all members "confer on the Security Council primary responsibility for the maintenance of international peace and security, and agree that in carrying out its duties under this responsibility the Security Council *acts on their behalf*" (italics added). They also consent "to accept and carry out" the decisions of the Council on any peacekeeping action that may be required. Under Article 39 of the Charter, the

Council's powers to take such enforceable decisions come into effect only when there has risen a definite "threat to the peace," an actual "breach of the peace," or a particular "act of aggression." Only if the Council decides that one of these circumstances prevails may it invoke its power to take a course of enforcement action that constitutes a legally binding commitment on all UN members. With regard to disputes between states that, in the opinion of the Council, have not yet led to a definite threat to the peace or do not constitute an actual breach of the peace or an act of aggression, it may merely recommend measures for a peaceful settlement.

The extreme caution with which the founders of the UN assigned governmental prerogatives to the Council is reflected in the fact that its powers with regard to its peacekeeping functions are set out in two quite separate chapters of the Charter. Chapter VI establishes its advisory functions in assisting the peaceful settlement of disputes. Chapter VII defines the kind of action it may take in the event of threats to the peace, breaches of the peace, and acts of aggression.

Peaceful Settlement of Disputes

Under the Charter, the parties to any dispute "the continuance of which is likely to endanger the maintenance of international peace and security" are enjoined to seek a settlement of their own accord by peaceful means. These include "negotiation, enquiry, mediation, conciliation, arbitration, judicial settlement, resort to regional agencies or arrangements. . . ." When can the Security Council itself intervene? On this point, the Charter is as unrestrictive as possible. By no means does every "situation" of conflicting interests lead to an actual dispute. Yet the Security Council need not wait until a situation has given rise to friction before taking action. It may take the initiative of investigating any dispute, or any situation that might lead to international friction or give rise to a dispute, in order to determine whether the continuance of the dispute or situation is likely to endanger the maintenance of international peace and security. Moreover, any nation, whether a member of the UN or not, has the right to bring voluntarily any dispute or threatening situation before the Council (or before the General Assembly). Should the parties to a dispute fail to settle their differences by peaceful means of their own choice, they are bound under the terms of the Charter to refer the problem to the Council.

Once the Council has decided to intervene in a dispute, it can take several courses of action. It may recommend one of the methods of settlement listed in the Charter; or it may itself determine and recommend other "procedures or methods of adjustment" that it deems appropriate; or, if it considers that the continuance of the dispute is likely to endanger international peace and security, it can decide to recommend substantive terms of settlement.

What is an "appropriate" procedure or method of settlement? And what kind of specific, substantive recommendations can the Security Council make? Purposely, the Charter has left this to the Council's discretion.

An example of a major conflict during which the Security Council recommended both procedures and substantive terms for peaceful settlement was the struggle that eventually led to the independence of the Dutch East Indies. In that instance, the Security Council was unable to prevent bloodshed, but it forestalled the spread of the conflict, and it helped in the emergence of the new state of Indonesia.

On 1 August 1947, the Security Council called upon the Netherlands and Indonesia to cease hostilities and settle their dispute by arbitration or other peaceful means. It then offered, on 25 August 1947, to assist in the settlement through a Good Offices committee, with whose help a truce was signed. Later, negotiations for a final settlement ran into a snag, and eventually hostilities were resumed. On 28 January 1949, the Security Council called upon the Netherlands to discontinue all military opera-

tions for a final settlement ran into a snag, and eventually hostilities were resumed. On 28 January 1949, the Security Council called upon the Netherlands to discontinue all military operations and release political prisoners immediately and unconditionally. It also called upon Indonesia to cease guerrilla warfare. In addition, it recommended various measures, including the establishment of an interim federal government of Indonesia and the holding of elections within a certain period of time.

By way of contrast is the UK-Albania case of 1947, where a mere recommendation of method of settlement proved sufficient in a dispute that otherwise might have had serious repercussions. The conflict revolved around the shelling by Albanian coastal batteries of two British warships and the mining of the Corfu Channel by Albania, which caused damage to two British destroyers and loss of life. On 3 April 1947, the Council recommended that the case be immediately referred to the International Court of Justice. Both parties complied.

Threats to the Peace, Breach of the Peace, and Acts of Aggression

If in its opinion there is a threat to the peace, the Council has the duty to maintain peace and security by preventing the outbreak of actual hostilities. If there has been a breach of the peace or an act of aggression, its duty is to restore international peace and security.

The Security Council is empowered by the Charter to call upon the parties to comply with any provisional measures it deems necessary or desirable. Such immediate instructions to the quarreling states are intended, without prejudice to the rights of the parties, to prevent an aggravation of the conflict. For example, the Council may demand the immediate cessation of hostilities and withdrawal of the forces from the invaded territory. If either or both parties do not comply with these demands, the Security Council "shall duly take account" of the failure to comply. In this event, the farthest-reaching prerogative of the Security Council can come into play—namely, the right to institute sanctions against the recalcitrant state or states.

Here again, the discretion of the Security Council is very wide. When the Council finds that a threat to the peace, breach of the peace, or act of aggression exists, it is authorized, though not compelled, by the Charter to invoke sanctions. Even if its first provisional demands are not heeded, it may continue to press for peaceful settlement or take various other actions, such as the dispatch of a commission of inquiry, short of sanctions. On the other hand, the Council is free to invoke whatever enforcement measures it may consider necessary under the circumstances. It need not begin with the mildest, but may, as in the Korean conflict, immediately start with the severest type of sanction—namely, the use of military force—if it considers that less drastic measures would be inadequate.

Types of Sanctions. The Charter does not provide an exhaustive list of sanctions that the Security Council may invoke, but it mentions two types: sanctions not involving the use of armed forces and military sanctions.

Sanctions not involving the use of armed forces may be of two kinds. One is the severance of diplomatic relations with one or more of the belligerent states. The other is economic sanctions, including partial or complete interruption of economic relations and communications—rail, sea, and air traffic, postal and telegraphic services, radio, and others. The purpose is to isolate the country or countries against which they are directed physically, economically, and morally. For example, a would-be aggressor that is denied certain strategic materials may be compelled to cease hostilities. If successful, such measures have great advantages over military sanctions. They impose fewer burdens on the participating countries and fewer hardships on the population of the areas of conflict. They also avoid the danger that once military action on behalf of the UN has been taken, war may spread.

Military sanctions, the Charter stipulates, may include (1) demonstrations by air, sea, or land forces, (2) blockade, or (3) "other operations by air, sea, and land forces," the latter including actual military action against the offending country or countries.

Once the Security Council has decided on specific sanctions, all members of the United Nations are under legal obligation to carry them out. The Security Council may, however, at its discretion, decide that only certain member states shall take an active part. On the other hand, the Security Council may demand that even nonmember states participate in economic sanctions to make them effective. The Charter also stipulates that before any member state not represented on the Security Council is called upon to provide armed forces, that country must, upon its request, be invited to participate in the Council's deliberations with a right to vote on the employment of its own contingents.

There have been only two cases in which the Council has invoked its powers to impose sanctions in a decision taken explicitly under Chapter VII of the Charter. In December 1966 the Council imposed mandatory economic sanctions against the illegal Smith regime in Rhodesia, and in November 1977, it imposed a mandatory arms embargo against South Africa. (The Council had instituted a voluntary arms embargo against South Africa in 1963 on the grounds that arms supplied to that country were being used to enforce its policy of apartheid.) Apart from these two cases, the Council deliberately has refrained from designating a serious dispute as a threat to peace, a breach of the peace, or an act of aggression, precisely to avoid acting explicitly within the terms of Chapter VII.

The Council's reluctance to invoke its ultimate prerogatives is attributable to two main factors. The first is a genuine feeling that in most cases punitive measures are inappropriate and may be harmful to the chances for an eventual peaceful settlement. The arrangement and wording of the provisions on the UN security system make it clear that peace is to be preserved whenever possible without recourse to force. The second major factor is that, in successive serious international disputes, one or two of the permanent members have taken different positions from the other three or four so that in most cases the Council's sympathies were divided between the opposing parties. Not only does division between the permanent members preclude punitive measures against one side, but it also seriously inhibits definitive action of any kind. For example, the initial action of sending a UN command into Korea was made possible only by the absence of the USSR from the Council at the time (in protest against the Council's decision on Chinese representation). Had the Soviet Union been there, it would be assumed to have vetoed the necessary resolutions. An example of the reverse situation is the issue of South Africa's apartheid policies. Since 1960 the African nations have appealed regularly to the Council to institute mandatory economic sanctions against South Africa in the hope of forcing it to terminate the apartheid system. The USSR has frequently expressed itself in favor of such a move, but the Western permanent members—in particular South Africa's major trading partners, the UK and the US—have been reluctant to impose economic sanctions.

SECURITY COUNCIL PEACEKEEPING PRACTICE

Peacekeeping operations are not mentioned in the Charter, yet they, as opposed to enforcement measures, are the means the Council has most frequently used to maintain the peace. It has dispatched observer commissions and troops in several crises. The UN Operation in the Congo (UNOC) numbered 20,000 at the maximum; other operations have used troops in more limited numbers. (Details of the Security Council's major peacekeeping operations and those undertaken by the Assembly are contained in the chapter on Maintaining Peace and Security.)

With the exception of Korea, the formula has always been that the disputants themselves must expressly invite the Council to take peacekeeping measures. The formula permits the Council to act in the maintenance of peace and security even though it may not have resolved its own differences on recommending terms of a settlement. Generally, the peacekeeping operations undertaken by the Council have represented a kind of holding action. Furthermore, they fall under no explicit provision either of Chapter VI or of Chapter VII of the Charter. The prospect of amending the Charter to accommodate current practice appears remote. Nevertheless, UN forces in 1983 were still on duty in Kashmir, the Middle East, and Cyprus. With the financial participation of the USSR and the participation of the troops of a Warsaw Pact country, Poland, in the second UN Emergency Force (UNEF) in the autumn of 1973, a consensus of the membership on the legality and desirability of peacekeeping operations seemed to be near, though China had abstained in the vote in the Council that set up the second UNEF. This contrasts sharply with the rooted disagreement about the legality of Assembly operations carried out under the Uniting for Peace Resolution, which is mentioned in the chapter on Maintaining Peace and Security.

ARMED FORCES FOR THE UNITED NATIONS

Although the Charter contains provisions to equip the Council with armed forces in case of need (the Covenant of the League of Nations contained no such provisions), these requirements have not been implemented. Under the Charter, all UN members "undertake to make available to the Security Council, on its call and in accordance with a special agreement or agreements, armed forces, assistance, and facilities, including rights of passage, necessary for the purpose of maintaining international peace and security." These agreements were to determine the number and types of military forces to be provided by the nations, their degree of readiness, their location, and so on. And they were to come into effect only after ratification by the countries concerned according to their respective constitutional requirements. (With this in mind, the US Congress in December 1945 passed the "UN Participation Act" authorizing the President of the US to negotiate a special agreement with the Security Council on the detailed provision of US forces, which agreement would then require approval by legislative enactment or joint resolution of the US Congress.) The troops and weapons would remain part of each country's national military establishments. They would not become international forces, but they would be pledged to the UN and, at the request of the Security Council, would be placed at its disposal.

However, the plan to place armed forces at the disposition of the Security Council required wide international agreement on a number of steps before it could be put into operation. The Charter provides for the establishment of a Military Staff Committee composed of the chiefs of staff (or their representatives) of the five permanent members to advise and assist the Council on all questions relating to its military requirements. The first task the Council assigned the Military Staff Committee was to recommend the military arrangements to be negotiated with member states. The Committee was never able to reach agreed positions that could serve as the basis for negotiation and at an early date took on the characteristics of a vestigial organ.

Although the arrangements for the provision of armed forces foreseen in the Charter have not been realized, the UN has nevertheless been able to establish peacekeeping forces on the basis of voluntary contributions of troops by member states, often organizing these within 48 hours. Only once, in the case of the UK in Cyprus, has a permanent member of the Council contributed a contingent to a peacekeeping force. It is specified in the resolution establishing the two UN forces on border strips separating Israel from Egypt and from Syria that contingents shall not be drawn from permanent members. However, France, the USSR, and the US contribute military observers, as opposed to contingents, to the UN Truce Supervision Organization (UNTSO), which was set up at the time of the signing of armistice agreements between Israel and neighboring states in 1949.

ORGANIZATION OF THE SECURITY COUNCIL

The Security Council is organized to function continuously. It is not permanently in session, but it meets as often as necessary. Hence, a representative from each member state must always be available so that in an emergency the Council can convene at once. Chairmanship rotates among the Council's member states according to their English alphabetical order, a new president (as the chairman is called) presiding every month. It is up to the president to decide whether to preside during the discussion of a question that directly concerns his own country.

Council members normally are represented by the heads of their permanent missions to the UN, who have the status of ambassador. Any state that is not currently a Council member but is a party to a dispute under consideration by the Council must be invited to send representatives to participate in the proceedings, though without the right to vote. (In these circumstances the disputing states concerned usually send a high government official, very often the foreign minister.) When the Council is discussing a matter other than an actual dispute, the decision to invite the participation of any UN member states whose interests are directly affected is left to its discretion. The Council has usually acceded to requests for such invitations. It has also granted representatives of national liberation organizations the opportunity to speak at a number of meetings. The Council has held sessions away from its New York headquarters on two occasions, in Addis Ababa in 1972 and in Panama in 1973.

VOTING IN THE SECURITY COUNCIL

Each member of the Council has one vote. On questions of procedure, a motion is carried if it obtains an affirmative vote of any nine members. On substantive matters, a resolution requires the affirmative votes of nine members, including the concurring votes of the permanent members. However, any member, whether permanent or nonpermanent, must abstain from voting in any decision concerning the peaceful settlement of a dispute to which it is a party. (When the Council consisted of only 11 members, the number of affirmative votes required was 7.)

The Veto

In the Council, as in other organs of the UN, efforts to achieve consensus decisions have increased. But the veto power and its exercise by permanent members remains a central characteristic of the mechanism of the Council. Though the word "veto" does not occur in the Charter, it is the common-usage term for the power of any of the five permanent members to defeat a resolution by voting "nay."

By no means do all negative votes cast in the Council by its permanent members constitute an exercise of their veto power. This occurs only when the resolution would otherwise have obtained the requisite number of affirmative votes. Moreover, by long-standing practice, the Charter provision stipulating that all substantive resolutions must obtain the concurring votes of the permanent members has been interpreted to mean that, provided a permanent member does not actually vote "nay," a resolution may still be carried.

Significance of the Veto

The veto power, then, is the constitutional instrument for giving expression to the requirement—discussed at the opening of this chapter—that, before the Council invokes its authority in peacekeeping action, the big powers should first resolve their differences on how a particular crisis should be handled. But though the principle of ensuring unanimity among the big powers was the major consideration underlying the institution of the veto, it was not the only one. A complementary consideration was the need of the major powers to ensure that their decisions would not be overridden by a majority vote of the smaller nations. In effect, conferring the right of veto upon a few powerful countries was tacit acknowledgement of the natural conflict that exists between their interests and those of the less powerful nations. It was a recognition of the fact that, despite differing social systems and power rivalry, the large countries often share more interests with each other than they do with smaller nations having social systems and tenets similar to their own. And it was for exactly this reason that the smaller countries represented at the San Francisco Conference made strenuous but unsuccessful efforts to prevent the institution of the veto power in the Charter.

THE ECONOMIC AND SOCIAL COUNCIL

Many of the United Nations' most outstanding accomplishments to date are in the economic and social fields. Under Article 55 of the Charter, the organization is committed to promote:

"a) higher standards of living, full employment, and conditions of economic and social progress and development;

b) solutions of international economic, social, health, and related problems; and international cultural and educational cooperation;

c) universal respect for, and observance of, human rights and fundamental freedoms for all without distinction as to race, sex, language, or religion."

The responsibility for UN activities aimed at the achievement of these goals is vested in the General Assembly and, under its authority, the Economic and Social Council (ECOSOC).

FIELDS OF ACTIVITY

The activities of ECOSOC, carried out through its subsidiary bodies in cooperation with the specialized agencies, have touched all aspects of human well-being and affected the lives of people everywhere. A list of the major spheres of activity supervised by the Council is given below; the chapters on Economic and Social Development, Technical Cooperation Programs, Social and Humanitarian Assistance, and Human Rights contain further information on matters directly under its purview.

Economic Development. Although this field encompasses both developed and developing nations, emphasis is focused on the problems of the latter group. Specific items dealt with include evaluating long-term projections for the world economy; fostering international trade, particularly in commodities, between industrialized and nonindustrialized countries; improving the international flow of private and public capital; promoting industrialization and the development of natural resources; resolving related political and legal issues, such as permanent sovereignty over natural resources and land reform; developing programs of technical assistance and cooperation for developing nations; and applying the latest innovations of science and technology to improve the industrialization of developing countries.

Social Progress. Among the social problems handled under the aegis of ECOSOC are housing, population, international traffic in narcotic drugs, the welfare of children in the developing countries, and the status of the world's refugees.

Human Rights. ECOSOC and its subsidiary organs have elaborated a series of important principles for the promotion of fundamental freedoms. Measures include the Universal Declaration of Human Rights and a number of declarations and recommendations on specific rights—for example, the rights of women, freedom of information and the press, and racial equality.

Related Special Problems. An example of a special problem of interest to ECOSOC is the improvement of statistical techniques, since efficient statistics are essential to economic and social development. Work in this field includes techniques to improve world statistics in specific economic branches, such as industry and finance, the standard of national statistical services, and methods of comparing statistics from different countries.

Problems Dealt with by the UN-Related Agencies. The 15 specialized agencies, the General Agreement on Tariffs and Trade (GATT), and the International Atomic Energy Agency (IAEA) undertake a wide range of activities in the economic and social fields. It is a function of ECOSOC to coordinate these activities. Accounts of each of the 17 related agencies will be found in the separate chapters devoted to them.

FUNCTIONS AND POWERS

Under the Charter, ECOSOC is authorized to make or initiate studies, reports, and recommendations on economic, social, cultural, educational, health, and related matters; to make recommendations to promote respect for, and observance of, human rights; to prepare draft conventions for submission to the General Assembly on matters within its competence; to call international conferences on matters within its competence and in accordance with rules prescribed by the UN; to enter into agreements, subject to the approval of the General Assembly, with specialized agencies; to coordinate the activities of the specialized agencies; to obtain regular reports from the specialized agencies; to perform, with the approval of the Assembly, services at the request of member nations or the specialized agencies; to consult with nongovernmental agencies whose work is related to matters dealt with by the Council; to set up subsidiary organs to assist its work; and to perform any other functions that may be assigned to it by the Assembly.

COMPOSITION

Originally, ECOSOC consisted of 18 members, but the amendments to the Charter that came into force on 31 August 1965 raised the number to 27. Another amendment that came into force on 24 September 1973 increased the membership to 54.

When ECOSOC was constituted in January 1946, the General Assembly elected ECOSOC's first 18 members for staggered terms: 6 members each for one, two, and three years, respectively. Subsequently, all terms were for three years, so that each year one third of the membership is elected by the Assembly.

The Assembly resolutions adopting the amendments to the Charter which increased the membership of ECOSOC also laid down an equitable pattern for the geographical distribution of the additional seats. The 54 members are elected so as to include 14 African states, 11 Asian states, 10 Latin American states, 13 Western European and other states, and 6 socialist states of Eastern Europe. Elections are by a two-thirds majority vote on a secret ballot in the Assembly, and immediate reelection of members is permissible. Although the permanent members of the Security Council have no privileged position on ECOSOC and the Charter does not guarantee them membership in ECOSOC, it has been the custom to reelect them continuously. In general, the Assembly has less difficulty in agreeing on its ECOSOC selections than in filling Security Council vacancies. Moreover if, in the opinion of ECOSOC, a matter on its agenda is of particular concern to a UN member not represented on the Council, it may invite that state to participate in its discussions, but without a vote.

In 1983 the composition of ECOSOC was as follows: Algeria, Argentina, Austria, Bangladesh, Benin, Botswana, Brazil, Bulgaria, Burundi, Byelorussia, Cameroon, Canada, China, Colombia, Congo, Denmark, Djibouti, Ecuador, Fiji, France, FRG, GDR, Greece, India, Japan, Kenya, Lebanon, Liberia, Luxembourg, Malaysia, Mali, Mexico, Netherlands, New Zealand, Nicaragua, Norway, Pakistan, Peru, Poland, Portugal, Qatar, Romania, Saint Lucia, Sa'udi Arabia, Sierra Leone, Sudan, Suriname, Swaziland, Thailand, Tunisia, USSR, UK, US, and Venezuela.

PROCEDURE

ECOSOC normally holds two sessions each year, one at UN headquarters in the spring and one in Geneva in the summer. A president and four vice-presidents are elected by the Council for each year. The Council also holds an organizational session in January to plan its program of work for the year.

Other ECOSOC sessions may be called at the request of a majority of its members, of the General Assembly, of the Security Council, of the president of the ECOSOC, with the approval of the four vice-presidents, of the Trusteeship Council, of any member of the UN, or of a specialized agency, if the president of the Council and the four vice-presidents agree.

Each of the 54 members in the Council has one vote. The big powers possess no veto or other special voting privilege. A proposal or motion before the Council may be adopted without a vote unless a member requests one. When a vote is taken, decisions are carried by a simple majority of the members present.

SUBSIDIARY ORGANS

As indicated in the chapter on the structure of the UN System, ECOSOC accomplishes its substantive work through numerous subsidiary organs in the form of commissions, standing committees, ad hoc committees, and special bodies. In Article 68, the Charter specifically states that the Council "shall set up commissions in economic and social fields and for the promotion of human rights. . . . " Several types of commissions and other organs have been set up within this provision, including the regional economic commissions, to deal with economic problems in the different geographical areas of the world; and the functional commissions, to handle matters connected with social progress and human rights.

Regional Commissions

There are 5 regional commissions: the Economic Commission for Europe (ECE); the Economic and Social Commission for Asia and the Pacific (ESCAP); the Economic Commission for Latin America (ECLA); the Economic Commission for Africa (ECA); and the Economic Commission for Western Asia (ECWA). Each has its own staff members, who are considered part of the regular staff of the UN. Regional commission expenditures come out of the regular UN budget. The organization and work of the regional commissions are considered in detail in the chapter on Economic and Social Development.

Functional Commissions

The Council has six functional commissions and two subcommissions:

Statistical Commission. Composed of 24 members elected by ECOSOC for staggered 4-year terms. Composition in 1983: Argentina, Australia, Austria, Brazil, Czechoslovakia, Ecuador, Finland, France, Ghana, Hungary, India, Iraq, Ireland, Japan, Kenya, Libya, Malaysia, Mexico, Nigeria, Spain, Togo, Ukraine, USSR, UK.

Population Commission. Composed of 27 members elected by ECOSOC for staggered 4-year terms. Composition in 1983: Bolivia, China, Ecuador, Finland, France, Greece, Honduras, Hungary, Indonesia, Japan, Mexico, Morocco, Netherlands, Nigeria, Norway, Peru, Rwanda, Sierra Leone, Sri Lanka, Sudan, Thailand, Ukraine, USSR, UK, US, Zaire, Zambia.

Commission for Social Development. Composed of 32 members elected by ECOSOC for staggered 4-year terms. Composition in 1983: Argentina, Austria, Byelorussia, Central African Republic, Chile, Costa Rica, Cyprus, Ecuador, El Salvador, Finland, France, Ghana, India, Indonesia, Italy, Kenya, Liberia, Madagascar, Mongolia, Morocco, Netherlands, Panama, Philippines, Poland, Sudan, Sweden, Thailand, Togo, Turkey, Ukraine, USSR, US.

Commission on Human Rights. Composed of 43 members elected by ECOSOC for staggered 3-year terms. Composition in 1983: Argentina, Australia, Bangladesh, Brazil, Bulgaria, Canada, China, Colombia, Costa Rica, Cuba, Cyprus, Finland, Fiji, France, FRG, Gambia, Ghana, India, Ireland, Italy, Japan, Jordan, Libya, Mexico, Mozambique, Netherlands, Nicaragua, Pakistan, Philippines, Poland, Rwanda, Senegal, Tanzania, Togo, Uganda, Ukraine, Uruguay, USSR, UK, US, Yugoslavia, Zaire, Zimbabwe.

Commission on the Status of Women. Composed of 32 members elected by ECOSOC for staggered 4-year terms. Composition in 1983: Australia, Canada, China, Cuba, Czechoslovakia, Egypt, France, GDR, Guatemala, Honduras, India, Indonesia, Italy, Japan, Kenya, Lesotho, Liberia, Mexico, Nigeria, Norway, Pakistan, Philippines, Sierra Leone, Spain, Sudan, Trinidad and Tobago, Ukraine, USSR, UK, US, Venezuela, Zaire.

Commission on Narcotic Drugs. Composed of 30 members elected by ECOSOC for staggered 4-year terms. Composition in 1983: Argentina, Austria, Bahamas, Belgium, Bulgaria, Colombia, France, FRG, Hungary, India, Italy, Japan, Korea (ROK), Madagascar, Malawi, Malaysia, Mexico, Nigeria, Norway, Pakistan, Panama, Senegal, Spain, Thailand, Turkey, USSR, UK, US, Yugoslavia, Zaire.

Subcommission on Prevention of Discrimination and Protection of Minorities. Composed of 26 persons elected for 3-year terms by the Commission on Human Rights from nominations of experts made by UN members.

Subcommission on Illicit Drug Traffic and Related Matters in the Near and Middle East. Composed of 5 persons nominated by their governments in consultation with the secretary-general and subsequently confirmed by the Council.

All commissions meet biennially with the exception of the Commission on Human Rights, which meets annually. The Subcommission on Prevention of Discrimination meets annually and the Subcommission on Illicit Drug Traffic biennially.

Other Subsidiary Organs

Article 68 of the Charter provides that in addition to the commissions specifically mentioned in the Charter, ECOSOC should establish "such other commissions as may be required for its functions." With two exceptions, however, the other subsidiary organs created have not been given the name "commission." Instead, ECOSOC has established committees and special bodies of varying kinds.

In 1983, these other subsidiary organs included: Committee for Program and Coordination; Committee for Development Planning; Commission on Human Settlements; Committee on Nongovernmental Organizations; Committee on Crime Prevention and Control; Committee on Science and Technology for Development; Committee on Review and Appraisal; Committee on Natural Resources; Commission on Transnational Corporations; Committee on Negotiations with Intergovernmental Agencies. Special bodies assisting the work of ECOSOC are those listed on the left-hand column on the chart on the structure of the UN, which report to both ECOSOC and the General Assembly: UN Conference on Trade and Development (UNCTAD); UN Children's Fund (UNICEF); Office of the UN High Commissioner for Refugees (UNHCR); Joint UN/FAO World Food Program (WFP); UN Development Program (UNDP); UN Industrial Development Organization (UNIDO); UN Environment Program (UNEP); UN University (UNU); UN Special Fund; World Food Council; UN Center for Human Settlements (UNCHS-Habitat); and UN Fund for Population Activities (UNFPA).

RELATIONS WITH NONGOVERNMENTAL ORGANIZATIONS (NGO's)

The Charter empowers ECOSOC to make arrangements to consult with international organizations of private citizens, known as nongovernmental organizations (NGO's) and distinguished from intergovernmental organizations (IGO's). Consultations with NGO's bring informed opinion other than that of governments and their officials before ECOSOC and provide it with a source of special experience and technical knowledge. NGO's granted consultative status are divided into two categories. Those in Category I are organizations with a general interest in the work of ECOSOC, and their activities are particularly germane to the Council and the UN as a whole. Those in Category II are organizations with an interest in some particular aspect of the work of ECOSOC. In June 1982, 31 NGO's were listed in Category I and 239 in Category II. Another 523 were listed on the NGO roster for consultation as occasion arises. All such officially recognized organizations may send observers to the public meetings of ECOSOC and its commissions and may submit memoranda for circulation. Representatives of Category I organizations are entitled to participate in ECOSOC debates and to propose items for the agenda. Representatives of Category II organizations may, with the permission of the chair, make oral statements at ECOSOC meetings.

Consultative status in Category II has been granted to nearly all important international businessmen's associations, cooperative societies, farmers' organizations, trade unions, and veterans' organizations; to leading professional groups, such as associations of architects, engineers, lawyers, newspaper publishers and editors, social welfare workers, tax experts, and many others;

and to various women's and youth associations. Many associations formed along denominational lines—Greek Orthodox, Jewish, Muslim, Protestant, and Roman Catholic—also have consultative status. Most organizations that enjoy such official UN standing are international, in that they have members in more than one country. An organization whose membership is restricted to one particular country may obtain consultative status only with the consent of its government.

ORGANIZATION OF INTERNATIONAL CONFERENCES

In accordance with a Charter provision, ECOSOC from time to time calls for the convening of international conferences on special world problems falling within its sphere of competence. Thus in recent years the UN has held conferences on such subjects as the environment, population, food, housing, and the status of women. These conferences have led to the establishment of the UN Environment Program, the World Food Council, the Center for Human Settlements (Habitat), and other programs and to the adoption of world plans of action for the environment, clean water, population, the aging, the disabled, and other subjects of international concern.

THE TRUSTEESHIP COUNCIL

Unlike the other main organs of the UN, the Trusteeship Council was established for the purpose of executing a closely defined system of operations. This is the trusteeship system, which was devised to adapt the League of Nations mandate system to meet the requirements of a new era.

THE MANDATE SYSTEM OF THE LEAGUE OF NATIONS

In its political aspect, the history of the world could be read as the history of the creation and disintegration of successive empires, a chain of vicious cause and effect that brought much bloodshed and wretchedness. After World War I, however, a concerted effort was made for the first time, in a limited way, to break the chain. Recognizing that colonies are a source of friction and jealousy among wealthy nations, the victorious Allies decided not to appropriate for themselves the colonies of their defeated enemies. Instead, those territories belonging to Imperial Germany and the Ottoman Empire that were considered unable to function as independent states were placed under international administration supervised by the League of Nations.

The founders of the League created three types of mandates for the administration of these territories by nations acting as "Mandatories of the League of Nations." Class A mandates covered territories that were considered to be ready to receive independence within a relatively short period of time; these territories were all in the Middle East—Iraq, Palestine, and Transjordan, administered by the UK; and Lebanon and Syria, administered by France. Class B mandates covered territories for which the granting of independence was a distant prospect; these territories were all in Africa—the Cameroons and Togoland, each of which was divided between British and French administration; Tanganyika, under British administration; and Ruanda-Urundi, under Belgian administration. To the territories classified under Class C mandates virtually no prospect of self-government, let alone independence, was held out; these included South West Africa, administered by the Union of South Africa; New Guinea, administered by Australia; Western Samoa, administered by New Zealand; Nauru, administered by Australia under mandate of the British Empire; and certain Pacific islands, administered by Japan.

The terms of the mandate system implied an acknowledgment of the right of the peoples of the colonial territories belonging to states defeated in war to be granted independence if they were thought to have reached a sufficiently advanced stage of development. But no provision was made in the League Covenant specifying that the countries designated to administer the mandated territories should take steps to prepare these peoples for eventual self-determination.

THE UN TRUSTEESHIP SYSTEM

Although the Covenant of the League forbade wars of aggression —that is, wars of conquest—the League's founding members did not see the need to underwrite this provision in a positive assertion of the principle of equal rights and self-determination of peoples. The UN Charter embodies an implicit recognition of the belief that denial of equal rights and peoples' right to self-determination is a potential cause of war. Thus Article 1 of the Charter sets forth as a basic purpose of the UN "to develop friendly relations among nations based on respect for the principle of equal

rights and self-determination of peoples, and to *take other appropriate measures to strengthen universal peace.*" (Italics added.) Article 76, which sets out the main objectives of the international trusteeship system that was to replace the mandate system of the League, leaves no doubt of the value attached to its role as a means of assisting the UN, in the words of the preamble to the Charter, "to save succeeding generations from the scourge of war." The article reads as follows:

The basic objectives of the trusteeship system, in accordance with the purposes of the United Nations laid down in Article 1 of the present Charter, shall be:

(a) to further international peace and security;

(b) to promote the political, economic, social, and educational advancement of the inhabitants of the trust territories, and their progressive development towards self-government or independence as may be appropriate to the particular circumstances of each territory and its peoples and the freely expressed wishes of the peoples concerned, and as may be provided by the terms of each trusteeship agreement;

(c) to encourage respect for human rights and for fundamental freedoms for all without distinction as to race, sex, language, or religion, and to encourage recognition of the interdependence of the peoples of the world; and

(d) to ensure equal treatment in social, economic, and commercial matters for all members of the United Nations and their nationals, and also equal treatment for the latter in the administration of justice. . . .

As well as emphasizing the importance of the trusteeship system as an instrument for peace, Article 76 defines the framework for the elaboration of obligations that the countries designated to administer the territories placed under UN trusteeship must undertake toward the peoples concerned. In essence, these obligations amounted to a pledge on the part of the administering authorities to work toward the liquidation of the trusteeship system itself by preparing the peoples in trust territories for independence, or at least self-government.

The Trust Territories and Their Administering Authorities

The Charter does not specify the actual territories to be placed under UN trusteeship. Article 77 merely states that the system shall apply to three categories: (1) territories still under mandate; (2) territories "detached from enemy states as a result of the Second World War"; and (3) territories voluntarily placed under the system by states responsible for their administration.

On the question of designating the administrators of trust territories, the Charter is equally nonspecific. It states simply that the individual trusteeship agreements shall designate the authority in each case, which may be "one or more states or the Organization itself." The provision that the UN itself may serve as an administering authority is a compromise solution that was inserted when it was decided at the Charter conference to abandon an ambitious plan, originally proposed by China and initially supported by the US, to make the UN directly responsible for the administration of all trust territories.

It was decided that the powers that had administered mandates on behalf of the League of Nations were to conclude agreements with the new world organization and administer the same territories that were still dependent. There was one exception. The Pacific islands, which after World War I had been given to Japan as Class C mandates, were, by a special arrangement embodied in the Charter, classified as a strategic area to be administered by the US under a modified trusteeship.

As a result of agreements worked out by the Assembly, 11 trust territories were placed under UN trusteeship, and 7 countries were designated as administering authorities. These figures exclude the former German colony of South West Africa, which after World War I had been mandated to the Union of South Africa, because South Africa refused to place the territory under UN trusteeship. The distribution of the territories and their respective administering authorities was as follows.

In East Africa: Ruanda-Urundi administered by Belgium; Somaliland by Italy; Tanganyika by the UK.

In West Africa: Cameroons administered by the UK; Cameroons by France; Togoland by the UK; Togoland by France.

In the Pacific: Nauru, administered by Australia and on behalf of New Zealand and the UK; New Guinea by Australia; Western Samoa by New Zealand; the Pacific islands of the Marianas, Marshalls, and Carolines by the US.

In 1983, only the Pacific islands remained within the trusteeship system. The other 10 territories had either achieved separate independence or, on being granted self-determination, had chosen to unite themselves with other independent states (see the chapter on Independence of Colonial Peoples).

THE TRUSTEESHIP COUNCIL

The fact that the Trusteeship Council was made a main organ of the United Nations is evidence of the importance attached to the role of the trusteeship system. The Council's functions, however, are decidedly more limited than those of the other main organs for it acts, as the case may be, under the direct responsibility of the General Assembly in respect to trusteeships not involving areas designated as strategic, and of the Security Council in respect of trusteeships relating to areas designated as strategic. The Charter provisions make it clear that the Trusteeship Council only "assists" the General Assembly and the Security Council in implementing the trusteeship system. It has a purely executive capacity in supervising the day-to-day operations of the system.

Composition

The Charter provides that the Council is to be composed of three groups of members: the countries administering trust territories; permanent members of the Security Council that do not administer trust territories; and a number of other UN members elected for three-year terms by the General Assembly to ensure an equal division between administering and nonadministering countries in the Council. Until 1960, the Council consisted of 14 members: 7 administering members; 2 permanent nonadministering members; and 5 other nonadministering countries elected for three-year terms by the Assembly. As the various trust territories gained independence, the size and composition of the Council changed. The Assembly decided that after 1968 the Council would be composed only of administering powers and the nonadministering permanent members of the Security Council. On 16 September 1975, when Papua New Guinea, which includes the former trust territory of New Guinea, achieved independence, Australia ceased to be a member of the Council. This left a membership of five: one administering power, the US, and four nonadministering permanent members of the Security Council.

Procedure

Each member of the Trusteeship Council has one vote. Decisions are made by a simple majority vote. The permanent members of the Security Council have no veto or other special voting privileges. Before 1968, the Council held two regular sessions a year and afterwards, one. Special sessions may be called on the decision of the majority of the members or at the request of the Security Council or the General Assembly. The president and vice-president are elected at the beginning of each regular session and serve for one year.

Powers

In carrying out its supervisory and administrative functions, the Council was specifically authorized to consider reports submitted by the administering authority; to accept petitions and examine them in consultation with the administering authority; to provide for periodic visits to the trust territories at times agreeable to the respective administering authorities; and to formulate a questionnaire on the political, economic, social, and educational progress in each trust territory, which the administering authorities were required to answer.

OPERATION OF THE TRUSTEESHIP SYSTEM

Trusteeship and Strategic Area Agreements

Since trusteeship territories are merely entrusted to the administering authorities, the precise terms of the agreement had to be carefully prescribed for each territory and approved by a two-thirds vote of the General Assembly or by the Security Council, as the case might be.

Article 82 of the Charter provides that there may be designated in any trusteeship agreement a strategic area or areas, which may include part or all of the trust territory concerned. In such cases, all trusteeship functions of the UN are to be exercised by the Security Council.

In fact, there exists only one strategic area agreement—that concluded between the UN and the US government on the Pacific islands mandated to Japan after World War I. Most of the general provisions of the other trusteeship agreements are included in it, but the right of accessibility to the area is curtailed, and supervision by the UN is made dependent on US security requirements. The US is also authorized to close certain areas for security reasons, as in connection with nuclear fission experiments.

The Role of the Administering Authorities

Administering countries have full legislative, administrative, and judicial powers over the territories entrusted to them. If they so desire, they may administer the trust territory in conjunction with one of their own colonies. Thus, the trust territory of Ruanda-Urundi was united administratively with the Belgian Congo, and Australia established an administrative union between the trust territory of New Guinea and its own dependency, Papua. However, UN trusteeship territories are not under the sovereignty of the administering authorities, which govern them only on behalf of the UN.

The Work of the Trusteeship Council

In essence, the work of the Council consists in the exercise of the powers specifically granted to it by the Charter for the purpose of supervising the operation of the trusteeship system and ensuring that the administering authority is carrying out its obligations as laid down by the trusteeship agreement.

The work of the Trusteeship Council diminished progressively as, one by one, ten of the eleven trust territories either achieved independence or, on being granted self-determination, chose to unite themselves with another independent state. In 1983 there remained only one trust territory, the Pacific Islands, which is designated a strategic area.

THE INTERNATIONAL COURT OF JUSTICE

The International Court of Justice, sometimes referred to as the World Court, was established at the San Francisco Conference in 1945. It is a successor to and resembles the Permanent Court of International Justice created at the time of the League of Nations, but its competence is wider, because membership in the League did not automatically require a nation to join the Permanent Court. The International Court, however, is a principal organ of the UN, so that all UN members automatically become parties to its Statute, which, modeled on that of the Permanent Court, was adopted as an integral part of the Charter. By joining the UN, each country binds itself, in the words of the Charter, "to comply with the decision of the International Court of Justice in any case to which it is a party." If any party to a case violates this obligation, the other party "may have recourse to the Security Council, which may, if it deems necessary, make recommendations or decide upon measures to be taken to give effect to the judgment."

The Charter further provides that nonmembers of the UN may also become parties to the Statute of the Court "on conditions to be determined in each case by the General Assembly upon the recommendation of the Security Council." Three such countries —Liechtenstein, San Marino, and Switzerland—have become parties to the Statute in this way.

The rules under which the Court is constituted and by which it functions are laid down in the Statute and detailed in rules adopted by the Court itself. The seat of the Court is the Peace Palace at The Hague in the Netherlands, but it can meet elsewhere if it so desires. The judges are bound "to hold themselves permanently at the disposal of the Court."

The Court is funded from the regular budget of the UN, to whose members its services are otherwise free of charge.

JUDGES OF THE COURT

The Court consists of 15 independent judges, known as "members" of the Court. They are elected "from among persons of high moral character" without consideration of nationality, except that no two judges of the same nationality may serve concurrently. They must be persons possessing the qualifications required in their respective countries for appointment to the highest judicial offices or be jurists of recognized competence in international law. No judge of the International Court of Justice may exercise any political or administrative function or engage in any professional occupation. "When engaged on the business of the Court," judges enjoy diplomatic privileges and immunities. A newly elected judge must "make a solemn declaration in open court that he will exercise his powers impartially and conscientiously." A judge cannot be dismissed except by a unanimous decision of the other judges that "he has ceased to fulfill the required conditions." No such dismissal has ever occurred.

As in any court, a judge may disqualify himself from sitting on a particular case. The Statute enumerates certain conditions under which this is obligatory—for example, if a judge was previously involved in the case as a member of a commission of inquiry.

Significance of Nationality of Judges

The Statute declares specifically that a judge has the right to sit on a case in which his own country is a party. Furthermore, any country that is a party to a case before the Court may add "a person to sit as judge" on that case if there is not already a judge of its nationality on the Court. If there are "several parties in the same interest," they may add only one judge to the bench. Such ad hoc judges are chosen by the respective states themselves and may, or may not, be nationals of the states choosing them.

Nomination and Election of Judges

Two international conferences at The Hague, in 1899 and 1907, contemplated the establishment of a permanent international court. The conferees were unable to agree on a system for electing judges. They did agree, however, on a convention establishing a Permanent Court of Arbitration. That convention provides that each country party to it name four jurists as arbitrators who will be available to consider a concrete matter for international arbitration. When the Permanent Court of International Justice was established after World War I, a solution was found for the difficult problem of electing judges. The legal experts named as potential arbitrators under the Hague convention were given the right to nominate candidates, and the League of Nations elected the judges from among these nominees. This system has in essence been preserved by the UN. To ensure that candidates are not mere government nominees, they are proposed by the groups of jurists already established in the Permanent Court of Arbitration or by similar groups specially constituted in countries not members of that Court; no national group may nominate more than four persons, and only two of those may bear the nationality of the group.

The list of candidates so nominated then goes to the UN. To be elected to a judgeship on the Court, a candidate must obtain an absolute majority in the Security Council and the General Assembly, both bodies voting independently and simultaneously. If more than one candidate of the same nationality obtains the required votes, the eldest is elected. On these occasions, Liechtenstein, San Marino, and Switzerland, the three nonmembers of the UN that are parties to the Statute of the Court, vote in the Assembly. In electing judges to the Court, delegates are requested to bear in mind that "the main forms of civilization" and "the principal legal systems of the world" should be represented at all times on the international tribunal.

Terms of Judgeships

Judges are elected for nine years. To stagger the expiration of terms, the terms of five of the judges named in the first election (1946) expired at the end of three years, and the terms of five others at the end of six years, as determined by lot. Hence, five judges are now elected every three years. Reelection is permissible and frequently occurs. Every three years, the Court elects its president and vice-president from among the judges. Unless reelected, judges chosen to fill a casual vacancy serve only for the remainder of their predecessor's term.

The composition of the Court as of 1 September 1983 is shown on the following list. Terms expire on 5 February of the year given in parentheses.

Taslim Olawale Elias, Nigeria (1985), President
José Sette-Camara, Brazil (1988), Vice-president
Manfred Lachs, Poland (1985)
Platon D. Morozov, USSR (1988)
Nagendra Singh, India (1991)
José M. Ruda, Argentina (1991)
Hermann Mosler, FRG (1985)

Shigeru Oda, Japan (1985)
Roberto Ago, Italy (1988)
'Abdallah El-Khani, Syria (1985)
Stephen M. Schwebel, US (1991)
Sir Robert Jennings, UK (1991)
Guy Ladreit de Lacharrière, France (1991)
Kéba Mbaye, Senegal (1991)
Mohammed Bedjaoui, Algeria (1988)

Normally, all judges sit to hear a case, but nine judges (not counting an ad hoc judge) constitute a quorum. The Statute of the Court makes provision for the formation of chambers either for summary procedure, for particular categories of cases, or for an individual case. Since 1945 only one case has been referred to a chamber, namely that concerning the delimitation of the maritime boundary in the Gulf of Maine area, to deal with which the Court in 1981 formed a chamber consisting of four judges and an ad hoc judge. A judgment delivered by a chamber is considered as rendered by the Court.

PROCEDURE OF THE COURT
All questions are decided by a majority vote of the judges present. If the votes are equal, the president has the casting, or deciding, vote. The judgments have to be read in open court and are required to state the reasons on which they are based and the names of the judges constituting the majority. Any judge is entitled to append to the judgment a personal opinion explaining his concurrence or dissent. All hearings are public unless the Court decides, whether at the request of the parties or otherwise, that the public not be admitted.

Judgments are final and without appeal. An application for revision will be considered by the Court only if it is based on the discovery of some decisive fact that at the time of the judgment was unknown to both the Court and the party seeking revision. Should a dispute arise concerning the meaning or scope of a judgment, the Court shall construe it on the request of any party.

In order to simplify and expedite recourse to it, the Court amended its Rules of Court in 1972. A completely overhauled set of Rules, incorporating those amendments, was adopted in 1978.

COMPETENCE AND JURISDICTION OF THE COURT
Only states can be parties in cases before the Court. Hence, proceedings may not be instituted by or against an individual, corporation, or other entity that is not a state under international law. However, if certain rules are satisfied, a state may take up a case involving one of its nationals. Thus the *Nottebohm Case—Liechtenstein* vs. *Guatemala*—judgment of 6 April 1955, involved a claim by the former state in respect of injuries sustained by a German-born, naturalized citizen of Liechtenstein as a result of certain measures Guatemala had taken during World War II.

All countries that are parties to the Statute have automatic access to the Court and can refer to it any case they wish. In addition, the Security Council may recommend that a legal dispute be referred to the Court.

Under the Charter, nations are not automatically obliged to submit their legal disputes for judgment. At the San Francisco Conference it had been argued by some that the Court should be given compulsory jurisdiction and that UN members should bind themselves to accept the Court's right to consider legal disputes between them. This would have meant that if one member filed a case against another member, the Court would automatically, and without reference to the second member concerned, have the right to try the case. The proposal was rejected because some delegates feared that such a provision might make the Statute unacceptable to their countries. Moreover, it was generally felt that since the disputants in an international court are sovereign states, they should not be summoned against their will to submit to the Court's jurisdiction. Thus the Court cannot proceed to adjudicate a case unless all parties to the dispute have in some way consented that it should do so. Such consent comes about in one of three main ways:

1. Through specific agreement between the parties to submit a dispute to the Court. This is the simplest method and the one employed in several recent cases. Since the creation of the Court, eight cases have been brought before it in this way.

2. Through specific clauses contained in treaties and conventions. Many treaties and conventions expressly stipulate that disputes that may arise under them, such as a claim by one country that a treaty has been violated by another country, will be submitted to the Court for decision. More than 430 treaties and conventions, including peace treaties concluded after World War II, contain clauses to this effect, which attests to the readiness of countries to agree in advance to accept judicial settlement.

3. Through voluntary recognition in advance of the compulsory jurisdiction of the Court in specified types of disputes. Article 36 of the Statute states that all parties to the Statute

may at any time declare that they recognize as compulsory *ipso facto* and without special agreement, in relation to any other state accepting the same obligation, the jurisdiction of the Court in all legal disputes concerning: (a) the interpretation of a treaty; (b) any question of international law; (c) the existence of any fact which, if established, would constitute a breach of international obligation; (d) the nature or extent of the reparation to be made for the breach of an international obligation.

Such declarations may be made for only a limited period if desired, and with or without any conditions; or they may state that they will become operative only when a particular country or number of countries accept the same obligation. The most far-reaching reservation that has been attached to a declaration is the condition that the Court must not adjudicate any dispute that the country itself determines to be an essentially domestic matter. In effect, this leaves the country free to deny the Court's jurisdiction in most cases in which it might become involved; and in general, the practical significance of many of the declarations is severely limited by the right to make conditions. As of September 1983, declarations recognizing the compulsory jurisdiction of the Court were in force in 47 states.

The jurisdiction of the Court therefore comprises all legal disputes which the parties to the Statute refer to it and all matters specifically provided for in the UN Charter or in treaties and conventions in force. In the event of a dispute as to whether the Court has jurisdiction, the Statute provides that the matter shall be decided by the Court. Article 38 of the Statute requires that in deciding the disputes submitted to it, the Court shall apply: (a) international conventions establishing rules recognized by the contesting states; (b) international custom as evidence of a general practice accepted as law; (c) the general principles of law recognized by civilized nations; (d) judicial decisions and teachings of the most highly qualified publicists of the various nations as a subsidiary means for determining the rules of law. In certain cases, however, if the parties concerned agree, the Court may decide a case *ex æquo et bono*—that is, by a judgment in equity taken simply on the basis of what the Court considers is right and good.

Advisory Opinions
The Charter provides that the General Assembly and the Security Council may request the Court to give an advisory opinion on any legal question and that other UN organs and specialized agencies, when authorized by the General Assembly, may also request advisory opinions on legal questions arising within the scope of their activities. In such cases, the Court does not render a judgment but provides guidance for the international body concerned. Thus advisory opinions by their nature are not enforceable, and, though the bodies may receive them with respect,

they may not necessarily find it politic to act on them. In some cases, however, the requesting body will be committed to abide by the Court's decision.

Extrajudicial Functions of the Court
Many international conventions, treaties, and other instruments confer upon the International Court of Justice or its president the function of appointing umpires or arbitrators in certain eventualities. Furthermore, even when no treaty provision to this effect exists, the Court or individual judges may be requested to carry out functions of this nature.

Review of the Role of the Court
In 1970, citing the relative lack of activity of the Court, nine member states sponsored a General Assembly agenda item on a review of the role of the Court. In an explanatory memorandum, they noted that the situation at that time was "not commensurate with either the distinction of the judges or the needs of the international community." Proposals for remedying the situation included a revision of the Court's Statute and rules of procedure, the appointment of younger judges and/or shorter terms of office, and wider acceptance of the Court's compulsory jurisdiction.

The subject was debated at four subsequent sessions of the General Assembly, culminating in the adoption in 1974 of a resolution designed to strengthen the role of the Court. The recommendations included: the possible insertion of clauses in treaties which would provide for submission to the Court of disputes arising from differences in their interpretation or application; acceptance of the compulsory jurisdiction of the Court with as few reservations as possible; and greater recourse to the Court by UN organs and specialized agencies for advisory opinions.

SURVEY OF COURT PRACTICE
Since the Court's inauguration in 1946, states have submitted 47 legal disputes to it and international organizations have requested 17 advisory opinions.

Legal Disputes. Of the 47 cases submitted to the Court by states, 15 were withdrawn by the parties or removed from the list for some other reason. In 9 others, the Court found that, under its Statute, it lacked jurisdiction. The remaining cases on which the Court has rendered judgment encompassed a wide range of topics, including: sovereignty over disputed territory or territorial possessions; the international law of the sea; commercial interests or property rights either of states or of private corporations and persons (examples of these types of disputes are given in the case histories below).

Many of the cases, including some that fall into the three categories just described, involve differences in interpretations of specific bilateral or multilateral treaties and other legal instruments. Thus, in the case of the rights of US citizens in Morocco—*France* vs. *US*—the Court found, on 27 August 1952, that the prohibiting of certain imports into Morocco had violated US treaty rights. But it rejected the US claim that its citizens in principle were not subject to the application of Moroccan laws unless they had received the US's prior assent.

Advisory Opinions. The 17 advisory opinions requested by the General Assembly, Security Council, or authorized specialized agencies likewise have dealt with a variety of matters. The Court, on 16 October 1975, rendered an opinion in response to the request of the Assembly made at its 1974 session. This concerned Western Sahara, which was passing from Spanish administration. Morocco, Mauritania, and Algeria, all bordering states, took conflicting positions on ties of sovereignty which might have existed before the territory came under Spanish administration. The court concluded that no ties of territorial sovereignty between Western Sahara and the Kingdom of Morocco or the Mauritanian entity had existed. In the decolonization of the territory, therefore, the principle of self-determination through the free expression of the will of its people should apply in accordance with the relevant Assembly resolution. Another opinion

concerned the question of whether the costs of the peacekeeping operations in the Middle East and the Congo could, within the scope of Article 17 of the Charter, be regarded as expenses of the organization to be financed by contributions of member states, as assessed by the General Assembly. In its opinion, issued on 20 July 1962, the Court concluded that the expenses of both operations could be regarded as expenses of the UN within the meaning of Article 17 of the Charter.

SOME CASE HISTORIES OF DISPUTES SUBMITTED TO THE COURT
For convenience, the following sample case histories have been drawn from the three categories of legal disputes indicated above.

Disputes over Territorial Claims and Territorial Possessions
In the *Case Concerning Sovereignty over Certain Frontier Land* —Belgium vs. *Netherlands*—the Court traced developments that had begun before the 1839 separation of the Netherlands from Belgium, and in its judgment, on 20 June 1959, decided that sovereignty over the disputed plots belonged to Belgium.

In a dispute regarding sovereignty over certain islets and rocks lying between the British Channel island of Jersey and the French coast—the *Minquier and Ecrehos Islands Case*—the UK and France invoked historical facts going back to the 11th century. The UK started its argument by claiming title from the conquest of England in 1066 by William, Duke of Normandy. France started its argument by pointing out that the dukes of Normandy were vassals of the king of France and that the kings of England after 1066, in their capacity as dukes of Normandy, held the duchy in fee from the French kings. The Court decided, on 17 November 1953, that "the sovereignty over the islets and rocks of the Ecrehos and Minquier groups, insofar as these islets and rocks are capable of appropriation, belongs to the United Kingdom."

The first case involving two Asian countries, *Cambodia* vs. *Thailand,* was filed with the Court, in October 1959, as the *Case Concerning the Temple of Preah Vihear.* It concerned, as stated by Cambodia, "a sacred place of pilgrimage and worship for the Cambodian population." On 15 June 1962, the Court found, 9 to 3, that the temple was in Cambodian territory and that therefore Thailand must withdraw any military or police forces or other guards it had stationed there; it further held, by 7 to 5, that Thailand must restore to Cambodia any works of art that might, since Thailand's occupation of the temple area in 1954, have been removed.

Disputes Relating to the Law of the Sea
The Corfu Channel Case (UK vs. Albania), the first case decided by the Court, was brought before it at the suggestion of the Security Council. The facts were as follows. On 22 October 1946, two UK destroyers passing through the Corfu Channel off the Albanian coast struck mines whose explosion caused the death of 46 seamen and damage to the ships. The British thereupon mineswept the Channel. Albania claimed that it had not laid the mines. The Court found Albania "responsible under international law for the explosions . . . and for the damage and loss of human life that resulted therefrom" and determined the compensation due to the UK at £843,947, equivalent to approximately $2.4 million. The Court also found that the British minesweeping activities in Albanian territorial waters had violated international law. The unanimous rejection by the Court of the British claim that the action was justified under the principle of "self-protection" constituted the first judicial finding that the use of force for self-help is in certain circumstances contrary to international law.

In 1981, Canada and the US submitted to a chamber of the Court a question as to the course of the maritime boundary dividing the continental shelf and fisheries zones of the two countries in the Gulf of Maine area. A dispute relating to the delimitation of the continental shelf between Libya and Malta was referred to the Court in 1982 by means of a special agreement specifically concluded for this purpose. Final judgments in these two cases have not yet been rendered.

Disputes Involving Commercial Interests and Property Rights

The Anglo-Iranian Oil Co. Case. On 1 May 1951, Iran passed a law terminating the concessions of the Anglo-Iranian Oil Co. and expropriating the company's refinery at Abadan, the largest in the world. On 26 May, the UK instituted proceedings against Iran before the International Court. On 5 July, the Court ordered important "interim measures" enjoining the two governments to refrain from any action that might aggravate the dispute or hinder the operation of the company. The company was to continue under the same management as before nationalization, subject to such modification as agreed to by a special supervisory board, which the Court requested the two governments to set up. A year later, however, on 22 July 1952, the Court in its final judgment ruled that it lacked jurisdiction and lifted the "interim measures." The Court found that the 1933 agreement, which gave the Iranian concession to the Anglo-Iranian Oil Co. and which the UK claimed had been violated by the act of nationalization, was merely a concessionary contract between Iran and a foreign corporation. The Court ruled that the interpretation of such a contract was not one of the matters regarding which Iran had accepted the compulsory jurisdiction of the Court. The controversy was settled by negotiations in 1953, after the Mossadegh regime in Iran had been replaced by another government.

The Barcelona Traction Case—Belgium vs. *Spain*—arose out of a 1948 adjudication by a provincial Spanish law court of bankruptcy of a company incorporated in Canada with subsidiaries operating in Barcelona. Belgium was seeking reparation for damages alleged to have been sustained by Belgian shareholders in the company as a result of the Spanish court's adjudication, which Belgium claimed was contrary to international law. The Court, on 5 February 1970, found that the Belgian government lacked standing to exercise diplomatic protection of Belgian shareholders in a Canadian company with respect to measures taken against that company in Spain.

THE SECRETARIAT

CHARTER REQUIREMENTS

The Charter lays down very few requirements governing the establishment of the sixth main organ of the UN. Such requirements as are specified may be conveniently listed under the following headings.

Composition. The Charter states simply: "The Secretariat shall comprise a Secretary-General and such staff as the Organization may require."

Appointment of Staff. With regard to the secretary-general, the Charter merely stipulates that he "shall be appointed by the General Assembly upon the recommendation of the Security Council." In other words, the Security Council first must agree on a candidate, who then must be endorsed by a majority vote in the General Assembly. The other members of the Secretariat are to be appointed by the secretary-general "under regulations established by the General Assembly." The Charter stipulates that the "paramount consideration" in the employment of staff "shall be the necessity of securing the highest standards of efficiency, competence, and integrity." However, to this consideration is added an important rider—namely, that "due regard shall be paid to the importance of recruiting the staff on as wide a geographical basis as possible."

Functions of the Secretariat. The duties of the general staff are not specified beyond an instruction that an appropriate number shall be permanently assigned to ECOSOC and the Trusteeship Council, and "as required, to the other organs of the United Nations." With respect to the functions of the secretary-general, the Charter states only that he shall be "the chief administrative officer of the Organization," and that he shall "act in that capacity" at all meetings of the Assembly and the three councils, and that he shall also perform "such other functions as are entrusted to him by these organs." Apart from these general requirements, the Charter accords the secretary-general one specific duty and one specific power: he must make an annual report to the Assembly on the work of the organization, and he has the right to bring to the attention of the Security Council any matter that "in his opinion may threaten the maintenance of international peace and security."

The single restriction on the Secretariat is that "in the performance of their duties the Secretary-General and the staff shall not seek nor receive instructions from any government or from any authority external to the Organization," and that "they shall refrain from any action which might reflect on their position as international officials responsible only to the Organization." As a corollary to this injunction, the Charter puts member nations under the obligation to "respect the exclusively international character of the responsibilities of the Secretary-General and the staff and not to seek to influence them in the discharge of their responsibilities."

APPOINTMENT OF THE SECRETARY-GENERAL

Since the Charter is silent on the qualifications for secretary-general and on his term of office, these decisions had to be made by the first Assembly, in January 1946. It was agreed that, in making its recommendations to the Assembly, the Security Council should conduct its discussions in private and vote in secret, for the dignity of the office required avoidance of open debate on the char-

acter of the candidate. The Assembly also decided that the term of office would be five years (the League of Nations' secretary-general was elected for ten years), and that the secretary-general would be eligible for reappointment.

The permanent members of the Security Council have tacitly agreed that the secretary-general should not be a national of one of their own countries.

STRUCTURE AND COMPOSITION OF THE SECRETARIAT

The Secretariat services the other organs of the UN and administers the programs and policies laid down by them. As the scope and range of UN activities have widened, the staff of the Secretariat has increased in number and its organizational pattern has increased in complexity. The major elements of the Secretariat, variously designated as offices, departments, programs, conferences and the like, are headed by officials of the rank, but not necessarily the title, of undersecretary-general or assistant secretary-general. In 1983 there were 51 officials at those two levels in New York and at other UN offices, including deputies to the heads of some of the larger elements.

The Secretariat includes the executive office of the secretary-general and offices or departments for General Assembly, Security Council, trusteeship and decolonization, and economic and social affairs. There is an office of legal affairs, a department of public information, and a department that provides documents, interpretation, and other services for UN meetings and conferences. A department of administration and management deals with financial and personnel matters, communications, field operations services, and the management of UN buildings. The 17 related agencies, including the 15 specialized agencies, being related to the UN by special agreements, are autonomous and have their own secretariats.

Directly below the ranks of undersecretary and assistant secretary-general are what the office of personnel refers to as "D-level" staff: directors of main subdepartments and chiefs of specific bureaus within the major organizational units. Below them is the stratum of "P-level" staff: personnel with professional qualifications as administrators, specialists, technical experts, statisticians, translators, editors, interpreters, and so on. And below them is the army of general services, or "G-level," personnel, which includes administrative assistants, clerical workers, secretaries, typists, and the like. Manual workers, such as building maintenance staff, are separately classified.

P-level personnel and above are recruited in the various member countries of the UN and, when serving outside their own country, are entitled to home-leave travel, repatriation grants, and related benefits. General service personnel include a variety of nationalities, but they are recruited locally and are not selected according to any principle of geographical representation. The majority of G-level staff at headquarters are Americans.

Organizational Distribution of Staff, 1983

As of 30 June 1983, the UN Secretariat consisted of 16,219 staff members holding permanent appointments or temporary appointments of one year or more. Of this total, 11,118 represented posts financed from the regular budget, while 5,101 were in the Secretariat posts financed from extra-budgetary sources.

In addition, there were 10,296 staff members serving nine related UN organs. Of these, three were financed from the regular budget, as follows: UN Relief and Works Agency for Palestine Refugees in the Middle East, 91 posts; International Civil Service Commission, 45; and International Court of Justice, 37. Two were financed in part from the regular budget and in part from extra-budgetary sources, as follows: Office of the UN High Commissioner for Refugees, 1,417 posts; and International Trade Centre, 268. The remaining four related UN organs were financed entirely from extra-budgetary sources, as follows: UN Development Program, 5,513 posts; UN Children's Fund, 2,775; UN Institute for Training and Research, 51; and UN University, 99.

By category, the 11,118 regular staff of the Secretariat consisted of 3,673 in the professional or higher categories, 7,307 in the general service of related categories, and 138 technical cooperation project personnel. Of the 5,101 extra-budgetary Secretariat posts (mainly field service), 533 were professional or higher posts, 1,895 were project personnel, and 2,673 were general service or related posts. Those serving with related UN organs consisted of 1,885 in professional or higher categories, 731 project personnel, and 7,680 in general service or related categories.

Problems of Staff Appointment According to Equitable Geographical Distribution

All UN senior staff members are appointed by the secretary-general under regulations established by the Assembly. Some of the appointments, such as the high commissioner for refugees, are subject to confirmation by the General Assembly. Staff recruitment, in general, is handled by the Office of Personnel, salary scales and other conditions of employment being determined by the General Assembly.

UN member governments attach great importance to having a fair proportion of their nationals employed in the Secretariat. However, equitable representation has proved almost impossible.

The 1962 Assembly recommended that in applying the principle of equitable geographical distribution the secretary-general should take into account the fact of membership, members' financial contributions to the UN, the respective populations of the member countries, the relative importance of posts at different levels, and the need for a more balanced regional composition of the staff at D-level. It further recommended that in confirming permanent contracts (UN staff are initially hired on the basis of two-year contracts), particular account should be taken of the need to reduce underrepresentation.

The 1975 Assembly reaffirmed previously defined aims for UN recruitment policy and mentioned the following specifically: development of an international civil service based on the highest standards of efficiency, competence, and integrity; equitable geographic distribution, with no post, department, or unit to be regarded as the exclusive preserve of any member state or region; the recruitment of a greater number of qualified women for professional and senior level posts; and the correction of imbalances in the age structure of the Secretariat.

The General Assembly called in 1978 for an increase in the number of women in posts subject to geographical distribution to 25% of total staff over a four-year period. The secretary-general reported in 1983 that the number of female staff in the professional and higher categories had increased to 22.3% of the total, compared to 16.3% in 1973.

In June 1983, 143 of 157 member states were represented in the Secretariat. Of the 14 unrepresented states, 5 were in Asia and the Pacific, 4 in Africa, 3 in the Middle East, and 1 each in Eastern Europe and in North America and the Caribbean. There were also 25 under-represented states, which means that the number of their nationals in posts subject to geographical distribution was less than the lower limit of their desirable ranges of representation. Of the under-represented states, there were 5 each in Africa and Western Europe, 4 each in Eastern Europe and the Middle East, 3 in Asia and the Pacific, and 2 each in Latin America and in North America and the Caribbean.

In 1972, the Assembly created an International Civil Service Commission and in 1974 approved its statute. The commission commenced operations in 1975. It is responsible for making recommendations to the Assembly for the regulation and coordination of service within the UN, the specialized agencies, and other international organizations which are part of the UN system and accept the commission's statute. The commission is composed of 15 independent experts, appointed in their individual capacities for four-year staggered terms.

THE EVOLVING ROLE OF THE SECRETARIAT

The UN's administrative arm has developed largely in accordance with the demands made upon it. In the process, it has evolved a distinctive character of its own, in keeping with its status as a constitutionally defined organ of the world body.

The secretary-general has played the most significant part in shaping the character of the Secretariat. As chief administrative officer, the secretary-general has wide discretionary powers and latitude to administer as he thinks fit. As Mrs. Eleanor Roosevelt, a former chairman of the UN Commission on Human Rights, noted in 1953, the secretary-general "partly because of the relative permanence of his position (unlike the president of the General Assembly who changes every year) and partly because of his widely ramified authority over the whole UN organization, tends to become its chief personality, its embodiment and its spokesman to the world."

The first five secretaries-general have striven to develop and maintain the positive functions of the Secretariat. Although each has had his own views on the role of the office, all have shared the belief that the Secretariat is the backbone of the UN system. The most eloquent statement of that belief was probably made by Dag Hammarskjöld in an address at the University of California in 1955: ". . . the United Nations is what member nations made it, [but] within the limits set by government action and government cooperation, much depends on what the Secretariat makes it." He went on to say that in addition to the Secretariat's function of providing services and facilities for governments in their capacity as members of the UN, the Secretariat also "has creative capacity. It can introduce new ideas. It can, in proper forms, take initiatives. It can put before member governments findings which will influence their actions." Stressing the fact that members of the Secretariat serve as international officials rather than as government representatives, Hammarskjöld concluded that "the Secretariat in its independence represents an organ, not only necessary for the life and proper functioning of the body, but of importance also for its growth. . . . "

THE POLITICAL ROLE OF THE SECRETARY-GENERAL

From the outset, the secretary-general has played a crucial part in helping to settle crises that have troubled nations since the end of World War II. In practice, the role has gone far beyond what might be anticipated from a reading of the terse Charter provisions for the office. Yet the role has been developed precisely through a skillful exploitation of the potentialities inherent in these provisions.

The deliberative organs of the UN are political bodies intended to function as forums where the interests of governments can be represented and reconciled. The secretary-general and the Secretariat embody the other aspect of the UN, which is also intended to be a place where people may speak not for the interests of governments or blocs but as impartial third parties. The secretary-general is consistently working in a political medium but doing so as a catalytic agent who, in person or through special missions, observers, and mediators, uses his influence to promote compromise and conciliation.

Under the Charter, the secretary-general has the right to bring to the attention of the Security Council any matter which, in his opinion, might threaten international peace and security. This goes beyond any power granted the head of an international organization before the founding of the UN. The Charter requires that he submit to the Assembly an annual report on the work of the organization. In this report he can state his own views and convey his voice to the world's governments. The secretary-general's role has also been considerably enhanced by exploiting the Charter provision that he shall perform "such other functions" as are entrusted to him by the main organizational units of the United Nations.

The role of the secretary-general has varied with the man and the time and circumstances in which he has had to work. This chapter contains an outline account of the initiatives taken by the five secretaries-general, and of the reactions these provoked among the big powers in successive crises.

BIOGRAPHIES OF THE SECRETARIES-GENERAL

The first secretary-general, Trygve Lie of Norway, was appointed for a five-year term on 1 February 1946. On 1 November 1950, he was reappointed for three years. He resigned on 10 November 1952 and was succeeded by Dag Hammarskjöld of Sweden on 10 April 1953. On 26 September 1957, Hammarskjöld was appointed for a further five-year term beginning 10 April 1958. After Hammarskjöld's death in a plane crash in Africa on 17 September 1961, U Thant of Burma was appointed secretary-general on 3 November 1961, to complete the unexpired term. In November 1962, U Thant was appointed secretary-general for a five-year term beginning with his assumption of office on 3 November 1961. On 2 December 1966, his mandate was unanimously renewed for another five years. However, at the end of his second term U Thant declined to be considered for a third. The General Assembly appointed Kurt Waldheim of Austria to succeed him on 22 December 1971, for a five-year term beginning 1 January 1972. In December 1976, Mr. Waldheim was reappointed for a second five-year term which ended on 31 December 1981. He was succeeded by Javier Pérez de Cuéllar of Peru, who was appointed by the General Assembly on 15 December 1981 for a five-year term beginning on 1 January 1982.

Trygve Lie
Born in Oslo, Norway, 1896; died Geilo, Norway, 30 December 1968. Law degree from Oslo University. Active in his country's trade union movement from the age of 15, when he joined the Norwegian Trade Union Youth Organization. At 23, became assistant to the secretary of the Norwegian Labor Party. Legal adviser to the Norwegian Trade Union Federation (1922–35). Elected to the Norwegian parliament (1935). Minister of justice (1935–39). Minister of trade, industry, shipping, and fishing (1939–40). After the German occupation of Norway in 1940 and until the liberation of Norway in 1945, he was, successively, acting foreign minister and foreign minister of the Norwegian government in exile in London. A prominent anti-Nazi, he rendered many services in the Allied cause during World War II. For example, he was instrumental in preventing the Norwegian merchant marine, one of the world's largest, from falling into German hands. Reelected to parliament in 1945. He headed the Norwegian delegation to the San Francisco Conference.

Dag Hjalmar Agne Carl Hammarskjöld
Born in Jönkönpirg, Sweden, 1905; died near Ndola, Northern Rhodesia, 17 September 1961. Studied at Uppsala and Stockholm universities; Ph.D., Stockholm, 1934. Secretary of Commission on Unemployment (1930–34). Assistant professor of political economy, Stockholm University (1933). Secretary of the Sveriges Riksbank (Bank of Sweden, 1935–36); chairman of the board (1941–45). Undersecretary of state in the Swedish ministry of finance (1936–45). Envoy extraordinary and financial adviser to the ministry of foreign affairs (1946–49). Undersecretary of state (1949). Deputy foreign minister (1951–53). Delegate to the Organization for European Economic Cooperation (OEEC; 1948–53). Vice-chairman of the Executive Committee of the OEEC (1948–49). Swedish delegate to the Commission of Ministers of the Council of Europe (1951–52). Hammarskjöld was a member of the Swedish Academy, which grants the Nobel prizes, and vice-president of the Swedish Tourist and Mountaineers' Association.

U Thant
Born in Pantanaw, near Rangoon, Burma, 1909; died New York, 25 November 1974. Educated at University College, Rangoon. Started career as teacher of English and modern history at Pantanaw High School; later headmaster. Active in development and modernization of Burma's educational system. Author and freelance journalist. Books include a work on the League of Nations (1932), *Democracy in Schools* (1952), and *History of Post-War Burma* (1961). After Burma's independence, became Burma's press director (1947), director of broadcasting (1948), secretary in the ministry of information (1949–53). Chief adviser to his government at many international conferences. Member of Burma's delegation to the 1952 General Assembly. In 1957, moved to New York as head of Burma's permanent delegation to the UN. Vice-president of the 1959 Assembly session.

Kurt Waldheim
Born in Sankt Andrä-Wördern, Austria, 21 December 1918. Studied at the Consular Academy of Vienna and took an LL.D. at the University of Vienna. Member of the delegation of Austria in negotiations for Austrian State Treaty, London, Paris, and Moscow (1945–47). First secretary of Austria's legation to France (1948–51). Counselor and head of personnel division, ministry

of foreign affairs, Vienna (1951–55). Permanent observer of Austria to the UN (1955–56). Minister, embassy to Canada, Ottawa (1956–58), and ambassador (1958–60). Director-general, political affairs, ministry of foreign affairs, Vienna (1960–64). Ambassador and permanent representative of Austria to the UN (1964–68 and 1970–71). Chairman of UN Outer Space Committee (1965–68 and 1970–71). Austrian minister of foreign affairs (1968–70). Unsuccessful candidate for the presidency of Austria in 1971. Author of *The Austrian Example,* on Austria's foreign policy.

Javier Pérez de Cuéllar
Born in Lima, Peru, 19 January 1920. Graduated from the law faculty of Catholic University, Lima (1943). Joined Peruvian ministry of foreign affairs (1940) and the diplomatic service (1944). Served as secretary at Peruvian embassies in France, UK, Bolivia, and Brazil. Returned to Lima (1961) as director of legal and personnel departments, ministry of foreign affairs. Served as ambassador to Venezuela, USSR, Poland, and Switzerland. Member of Peruvian delegation to the 1st General Assembly (1946) and of delegations to the 25th through 30th sessions (1970–75). Permanent representative of Peru to the UN (1971–75). Served as UN secretary-general's special representative in Cyprus (1975–77); UN undersecretary-general for special political affairs (1979–81); and secretary-general's personal representative in Afghanistan (1981). After resigning from the UN, he returned to the ministry of foreign affairs and voluntarily separated from the service of his government on 7 October 1981. He is a former professor of diplomatic law at the Academia de Guerra Aérea del Peru. Author of *Manual de derecho diplomático* (Manual of International Law; 1964).

DEVELOPMENTS UNDER TRYGVE LIE
First Term, 1946–51
Trygve Lie was recommended for appointment as the first secretary-general by the Security Council on 30 January 1946, in a compromise between Western delegations and the USSR. He was appointed by the Assembly on 1 February 1946 by a vote of 46 to 3.

Trygve Lie had not yet been in office three months when he assumed the initiative of advising the Security Council on the Secretariat's interpretation of the Charter. The Council was considering its first case, the Iranian complaint against the USSR. The Secretary-General delivered a legal opinion that differed sharply from that of the Security Council. The Council did not accept his interpretation, but it upheld his right to present his views. After setting this precedent, Lie submitted legal opinions on other matters.

During Lie's first term as secretary-general, East-West tension charged the UN atmosphere. As the world situation became increasingly threatening, the political role of the secretary-general expanded. Lie took definite stands on three issues, each of which earned him the dislike of some of the permanent members of the Security Council. The issues were Chinese representation, a plan for the general settlement of the cold war, and UN military action in the Korean War.

Chinese Representation. By the end of 1949, a number of states, including the USSR and the UK—permanent members of the Security Council—had recognized the mainland government, the People's Republic of China. In January 1950 the USSR representatives, having failed to obtain the seating of the representatives of the People's Republic, began boycotting UN meetings at which China was represented by delegates of the Republic of China, based on Taiwan. In private meetings with delegations, Lie tried to solve the impasse. He adduced various reasons, including a ruling of the International Court of Justice, for the thesis that nonrecognition of a government by other governments should not determine its representation in the UN.

Trygve Lie's Twenty-Year Peace Plan. Lie developed an extraordinary initiative during the first half of 1950. In a letter to the Security Council dated 6 June 1950, approximately two weeks before the outbreak of the Korean War, he said, "I felt it my duty to suggest a fresh start to be made towards eventual peaceful solution of outstanding problems." In his *Twenty-Year Program for Achieving Peace through the United Nations,* Lie proposed new international machinery to control atomic energy and to check the competitive production of armaments, and the establishment of a UN force to prevent or stop localized outbreaks.

Armed with these proposals and other memoranda, including the one on Chinese representation, Lie journeyed first to Washington, then to London, to Paris, and finally to Moscow. He held conversations not only with foreign ministers and high-ranking diplomats, but with US President Harry S Truman; British Prime Minister Clement Attlee; French President Vincent Auriol; and Soviet Premier Joseph Stalin. Lie's reception was most cordial in Moscow, warm in Paris and friendly in London, but cool in Washington.

The international picture changed abruptly, however, with the outbreak of the Korean War. The attitude of a number of governments toward Lie changed dramatically as well.

The Korean War. An outstanding example of the Secretary-General's taking a stand on an issue was Lie's intervention in the emergency meeting of the Security Council on 24 June 1950. He unequivocally labeled the North Korean forces aggressors because they had crossed the 38th parallel; declared that the conflict constituted a threat to international peace; and urged that the Security Council had the "clear duty" to act. After the Council (in the absence of the Soviet delegate) had set in motion military sanctions against the DPRK, Lie endorsed that course for the UN and rallied support from member governments for the UN military action in Korea. This brought him into sharp conflict with the USSR, which accused him of "slavish obedience to Western imperialism" and to the "aggression" which, in the Soviet view, the US had committed in Korea.

As the Korean conflict grew more ominous with the intervention of the People's Republic of China, Lie played an active role in getting cease-fire negotiations under way in the field. At the same time, he fully identified himself with the military intervention in Korea on behalf of the UN.

Extension of Lie's Term as Secretary-General
Lie's first term as secretary-general was to expire on 31 January 1951. In the Security Council, the USSR vetoed a resolution recommending him for a second term. Subsequently, the USSR announced it would accept anyone other than Lie who was acceptable to the other members of the Council. The US announced it would veto anyone but Lie. The Council was unable to recommend a candidate for the office of secretary-general to the Assembly, a situation unforeseen in the Charter. A resolution in the Assembly to extend Lie's term by three years, beginning 1 February 1951, was carried 46 to 5, with 8 abstentions. The negative votes were cast by the Soviet bloc.

The USSR maintained normal relations with Lie until the expiration of his original term, 31 January 1951. Thereafter, it stood by its previous announcement that the extension of the term was illegal and that it would "not consider him as Secretary-General." By the fall of 1951, however, its nonrecognition policy toward Lie subsided.

Lie's Resignation
Other complications were facing Lie, and on 10 November 1952 he tendered his resignation to the General Assembly.

Subsequently, Lie again became active in the public affairs of his native Norway. But he allowed some time to elapse in deference to a resolution adopted by the General Assembly in 1946 which states that "because a Secretary-General is a confidant of many governments," no member government "should offer him . . . immediately upon retirement, any governmental position in which his confidential information might be a source of embarrassment to other Members, and on his part a [retired] Secretary-General should refrain from accepting any such position."

DEVELOPMENTS UNDER DAG HAMMARSKJÖLD

First Term, 1953–58

A stalemate had seemed unavoidable in the Security Council's attempt to agree on a successor to Trygve Lie who could be recommended to the Assembly for appointment as secretary-general. Then France proposed Dag Hammarskjöld of Sweden. On 31 March 1953, he was recommended by a vote of 10 to 0, with China abstaining, possibly because Sweden had recognized the People's Republic of China. The Assembly accepted Lie's resignation and appointed Hammarskjöld on 7 April 1953. The results of the secret ballot were 57 to 1, with 1 abstention.

Hammarskjöld's activities in the political field were more numerous and far-reaching than Lie's had been. Both the General Assembly and the Security Council repeatedly relied on his initiative and advice, and entrusted important tasks to him.

The 1954 General Assembly set a precedent when it asked the Secretary-General to seek the release of 11 US fliers who were held prisoners by mainland China. The Assembly resolution left the course of action entirely to his judgment. After various preparations, Hammarskjöld flew to Peking for personal negotiations with that government, and the 11 were released. This success greatly increased the readiness of the Assembly to rely on the Secretary-General as a troubleshooter.

The Suez Crisis. Grave responsibilities were entrusted to the Secretary-General by the Assembly in connection with the establishment and operation of the UN Emergency Force (UNEF). On 4 November 1956, at the height of the crisis resulting from British, French, and Israeli intervention in Egypt, the Secretary-General was requested to submit a plan within 48 hours for the establishment of a force "to secure and supervise the cessation of hostilities." The Assembly approved his plan and, at his suggestion, appointed Major-General E. L. M. Burns, Chief of Staff of the UN Truce Supervisory Organization (UNTSO), as the chief of UNEF. The Assembly authorized the Secretary-General to take appropriate measures to carry out his plan, and an advisory committee of seven UN members was appointed to assist him. Hammarskjöld flew to Egypt to arrange for the Egyptian government's consent for UNEF to be stationed and to operate in Egyptian territory. He was given the task of arranging with Egypt, France, Israel, and the UK the implementation of the cease-fire and an end to the dispatch of troops and arms into the area, and was authorized to issue regulations and instructions for the effective functioning of UNEF.

Second Term, 1958–61

On 26 September 1957, after endorsement by the Security Council, the General Assembly reelected Hammarskjöld for a new five-year term, until 10 April 1963.

Hammarskjöld's Views on Developing the Role of Secretary-General. Even before the Middle East crisis of 1956, Hammarskjöld had pointed to the need for the secretary-general to assume a new role in world affairs. On his reelection, Hammarskjöld told the Assembly that he considered it to be the duty of the secretary-general, guided by the Charter and the decisions of the main UN organs, to use his office and the machinery of the organization to the full extent permitted at each stage by practical circumstances. But he then declared: "I believe it is in keeping with the philosophy of the Charter that the Secretary-General be expected to act also *without such guidance*, should this appear to him necessary in order to help in *filling a vacuum* that may appear in the systems which the Charter and traditional diplomacy provide for the safeguarding of peace and security." (Italics added.) In other words, inaction or stalemate either at the UN or outside of it may be the justification for the secretary-general to act on his own.

Thus in 1958, Hammarskjöld took an active hand in the Jordan-Lebanon crisis. After a resolution for stronger UN action failed to carry in the Security Council, he announced that he would nevertheless strengthen UN action in Lebanon and "accept the consequences" if members of the Security Council were to disapprove; but none did. In the fall of 1959, the USSR made it known that it did not favor a visit by the Secretary-General to Laos and, in particular, the assignment of a special temporary "UN ambassador" there. Yet Hammarskjöld did go to Laos to orient himself on the situation in that corner of Southeast Asia and assigned a high UN official as the head of a special mission to Laos. In March 1959, Hammarskjöld sent a special representative to help Thailand and Cambodia settle a border dispute. He did this at their invitation, without specific authorization by the Security Council or the General Assembly. The dispute was settled.

In his report to the 1959 Assembly, he said, "The main significance of the evolution of the Office of the Secretary-General . . . lies in the fact that it has provided means for smooth and fast action . . . of special value in situations in which prior public debate on a proposed course of action might increase the difficulties . . . or in which . . . members may prove hesitant. . . . "

The Congo Crisis. By far the greatest responsibilities Hammarskjöld had to shoulder were in connection with the UN Operation in the Congo (designated by its French initials, ONUC). This is described more fully in the chapter on Maintaining Peace and Security.

On 12 and 13 July 1960, respectively, President Joseph Kasavubu and Premier Patrice Lumumba of the newly independent country each cabled the Secretary-General asking for UN military assistance in view of the arrival of Belgian troops and the impending secession of Katanga. At Hammarskjöld's request, the Security Council met on the night of 13 July. He gave his full support to the Congo's appeal and recommended that the Council authorize him to "take the necessary steps" to set up a UN military assistance force for the Congo, in consultation with the Congo government and on the basis of the experience gained in connection with the UN Emergency Force in the Middle East. The Security Council so decided.

Since the Congo operation thus initiated was of much greater dimensions than the UNEF operation, the responsibilities imposed upon the Secretary-General were correspondingly heavier. For though the Security Council and the General Assembly guided Hammarskjöld, he himself had to make extraordinarily difficult decisions almost daily, often on highly explosive matters that arose as a result of serious rifts within the Congo government and many other factors.

Various member governments, including certain African countries, the USSR, and certain Western countries, criticized Hammarskjöld for some actions the UN took or failed to take in the Congo. At times, he had to face the possibility that some country that had contributed military contingents to the UN force would withdraw them.

When it became known in February 1961 that Lumumba, who had been deposed by Kasavubu early in September 1960 and later detained by the Léopoldville authorities, had been handed over by them to the Katanga authorities and subsequently murdered, Hammarskjöld declared that the UN was blameless for the "revolting crime." But several delegates claimed that he should have taken stronger measures to protect Lumumba.

The "Troika" Proposal. The USSR had asked for Hammarskjöld's dismissal long before the assassination of Lumumba. Premier Khrushchev, as head of the Soviet delegation to the 1960 General Assembly, accused Hammarskjöld of lacking impartiality and of violating instructions of the Security Council in his conduct of the UN Operation in the Congo. He also proposed a basic change in the very institution of the secretary-general: since the secretary-general had become "the interpreter and executor of decisions of the General Assembly and the Security Council," this one-man office should be replaced by a "collective executive organ consisting of three persons each of whom would represent a certain group of states"—namely, the West, the socialist states, and the neutralist countries; the institution of a "troika" would guarantee that the UN executive organ would not act to the detriment of any of these groups of states.

Hammarskjöld rejected the accusations against his impartiality; declared he would not resign unless the member states for which the organization was of decisive importance or the uncommitted nations wished him to do so; and received an ovation from the overwhelming majority of the delegations. He also stated that to replace the one-man secretary-general by a three-man body would greatly alter the character and limit the scope of the UN.

Outside the Soviet bloc there had been little support for a troika proposal, but some "subtroika" proposals were advanced. Hammarskjöld in turn suggested that his five top aides, including a US and a Soviet citizen, advise the secretary-general on political problems. Discussions of the question were interrupted by his death.

Death of Dag Hammarskjöld

In view of dangerous developments in the Congo, Hammarskjöld flew there in September 1961. On the night of the 17th, the plane carrying him from Léopoldville to a meeting with the Katanga secessionist leader at Ndola, Northern Rhodesia, crashed in a wooded area about 16 km (10 mi) west of Ndola airport. Hammarskjöld and all 15 UN civilian and military personnel traveling with him, including the crew, were killed. The exact cause of the tragedy has not been determined. An investigation commission appointed by the General Assembly reported several possibilities: inadequate technical and security preparations for the flight; an attack on the plane from the air or the ground; sabotage; or human failure by the pilot.

DEVELOPMENTS UNDER U THANT
First Term, 1961–66

For a few weeks after Hammarskjöld's death, UN activities were guided under an informal arrangement by some of the top UN officials. The problem was not only finding a successor but also resolving the controversial question of the number and responsibilities of his top collaborators. Eventually, the Security Council accepted U Thant's proposal that, if elected, he would decide about the top posts in the Secretariat. On 3 November 1961, following the Security Council's unanimous recommendation, the General Assembly unanimously appointed U Thant as acting secretary-general until 10 April 1963 (when Hammarskjöld's term would have expired). On 30 November 1962, the General Assembly, again on the recommendation of the Security Council, unanimously appointed U Thant secretary-general for a term ending 3 November 1966.

U Thant's approach to his office was different from that of Hammarskjöld, whose dynamic conception of the secretary-general's political role had aroused such opposition in the Soviet bloc. Thant did not take the same initiatives as his predecessor, but he consistently sought to use the prestige of his office to help settle disputes. Moreover, both the Assembly and the Security Council assigned him to mediate in extremely delicate situations. In his annual reports, he put forth proposals on basic issues—for example, disarmament and economic and social cooperation—and many of his suggestions were adopted.

An early example of a successful initiative taken by U Thant was in connection with the long-standing dispute between Indonesia and the Netherlands over the status of West Irian. The territory, formerly known as West New Guinea, had belonged to the Dutch East Indies, and Indonesia now claimed it as its own. In December 1961, fighting broke out between Dutch and Indonesian troops. Appealing to both governments to seek a peaceful solution, the Secretary-General helped them arrive at a

settlement. That settlement, moreover, brought new responsibilities to the office of the secretary-general: for the first time in UN history a non-self-governing territory was, for a limited period, administered directly by the world organization.

The Cyprus Operation. Intercommunal clashes broke out in Cyprus on Christmas Eve 1963, and were followed by the withdrawal of the Turkish Cypriots into their enclaves, leaving the central government wholly under Greek Cypriot control. A "peacemaking force" established under British command was unable to put an end to the fighting, and a conference on Cyprus held in London in January 1964 ended in disagreement. In the face of the danger of broader hostilities in the area, the Security Council on 4 March 1964 decided unanimously to authorize U Thant to establish a UN Peace-keeping Force in Cyprus (UNFICYP), with a limited three-month mandate of preventing the recurrence of fighting and contributing to the maintenance of law and order and return to normal conditions. The force was to be financed on the basis of voluntary contributions. The Council also asked the Secretary-General to appoint a mediator to seek an agreed peaceful settlement of the Cyprus problem.

The report of U Thant's mediator, Galo Plaza Lasso, was transmitted to the Security Council in March 1965, but rejected by Turkey. Plaza resigned in December 1965 and the function of mediator lapsed.

Another crisis occurred in November 1967, but threatened military intervention by Turkey was averted, largely as a result of US opposition. Negotiations conducted by Cyrus Vance for the US and José Rolz-Bennett on behalf of the Secretary-General led to a settlement. Intercommunal talks were begun in June 1968, through the good offices of the Secretary-General, as part of the settlement. The talks bogged down, but U Thant proposed a formula for their reactivation under the auspices of his special representative, B. F. Osorio-Tafall. Talks resumed in 1972, after Thant had left office.

The India-Pakistan War of 1965 and Conflict of 1971. Hostilities between India and Pakistan broke out in Kashmir in early August 1965 and soon spread along the entire length of the international border from the Lahore area to the sea. At the behest of the Security Council, whose calls of 4 and 6 September for a cease-fire had gone unheeded, U Thant visited the subcontinent from 9 to 15 September. In his report to the Council the Secretary-General proposed certain procedures, including a possible meeting between President Ayub of Pakistan and Prime Minister Shastri of India, to resolve the problem and restore the peace.

The Council, on 20 September, demanded a cease-fire and authorized the Secretary-General to provide the necessary assistance to ensure supervision of the cease-fire and withdrawal of all armed personnel. For this purpose, U Thant strengthened the existing UN military observer group in Kashmir and established the UN India-Pakistan Observation Mission (UNIPOM) to supervise the cease-fire and withdrawals of troops along the border outside Kashmir.

At a meeting organized by Premier Kosygin of the Soviet Union in January 1966 in Tashkent (USSR), the leaders of India and Pakistan agreed on the withdrawal of all troops; this was successfully implemented under the supervision of the two UN military observer missions in the area. UNIPOM was disbanded in March 1966, having completed its work.

Following the outbreak of civil strife in East Pakistan in March 1971 and the deterioration of the situation in the subcontinent that summer, U Thant offered his good offices to India and Pakistan and kept the Security Council informed under the broad terms of Article 99 of the Charter. When overt warfare broke out in December, the Security Council appealed to all parties to spare the lives of innocent civilians. Pursuant to a decision by the Security Council, U Thant appointed a special representative to lend his good offices for the solution of humanitarian problems after the cease-fire of 18 December 1971. This was followed by the independence of Bangladesh. (See the section on UNHCR in the chapter on Social and Humanitarian Assistance for an account of UN operations in the area.)

U Thant's Stand on the Viet-Nam War. Throughout his tenure, U Thant was deeply concerned with the question of Viet-Nam. By tacit consent, the question was never formally debated in the Assembly and only cursorily touched upon in the Security Council. Until the opening of the Paris peace talks in 1968, the Secretary-General was unremitting in his efforts to persuade the parties in the conflict to initiate negotiations on their own. In 1966 he put forward a three-stage proposal to create the conditions necessary for discussion, but this was ignored by the US.

After the Paris talks began, U Thant deliberately refrained from making any public statements on Viet-Nam "in order to avoid creating unnecessary difficulties" for the parties. He broke this silence only once, when on 5 May 1970 he expressed his deep concern "regarding the recent involvement of Cambodia in the war."

Second Term, 1966–71

Many observers believe that U Thant's disappointment at the US's negative response toward his plan for Viet-Nam peace talks was largely responsible for his initial decision, announced early in September 1966, that he would not "be available" for reappointment when his term of office expired on 3 November of that year. Dismayed by this development, and having no other candidate in mind, all factions among the UN membership made a concerted effort to persuade U Thant to change his mind. The Security Council even went so far as to issue, on 29 September 1966, a consensus asking him to reconsider his decision. By 3 November 1966, he still had not reached a decision but offered to remain in office until the end of the regular Assembly session in December, to ensure continuity of administration during that period. U Thant later consented to accept another term, and on 2 December 1966 the Security Council's unanimous recommendation for his reappointment was unanimously endorsed by the Assembly.

U Thant's second term of office was dominated by the protracted Middle East crisis that arose in the aftermath of the Six-Day War in 1967. His quick action in removing UNEF troops from the Suez area at the request of the UAR just before that war began occasioned much criticism and some misunderstanding (see the section on the Middle East in the chapter on Maintaining Peace and Security).

Of the two other major political conflicts during the period 1967–70, the savage civil war in Nigeria and the Soviet invasion of Czechoslovakia on 20 August 1968, only the latter was debated at the UN. The political aspects of the Nigerian situation were never raised in either the Assembly or the Security Council out of deference to the African countries themselves, whose main object was to keep external intervention to a minimum. However, as the troops of the federal government of Nigeria began to penetrate more deeply into the eastern region (which had announced its secession from the Federation and proclaimed itself an independent state under the name of Biafra), the various humanitarian organs of the UN became increasingly concerned about the plight of the people there. Accordingly, in August 1968 the Secretary-General took the initiative of sending a personal representative to Nigeria to help facilitate the distribution of food and medicine.

At the request of its six Western members, the Security Council decided to debate the situation in Czechoslovakia, despite the protests of the USSR. On 23 August 1968, 10 members voted for a resolution condemning the Soviet action, which the USSR vetoed. Another resolution requesting the Secretary-General to send a representative to Prague to seek the release of imprisoned Czechoslovak leaders was not put to a vote. In view—as one UN text puts it—of the "agreement reached on the substance of the problem during the Soviet-Czechoslovak talks held in Moscow from August 23 to 26," no further action was taken by the Council. However, it is worth noting that U Thant was among the first world figures publicly to denounce the invasion. At a press briefing on 21 August at UN Headquarters, he expressed unequivocal dismay, characterizing the invasion as "yet another serious blow to the concepts of international order and morality which form the basis of the Charter of the United Nations . . . and a grave setback to the East-West détente which seemed to be re-emerging in recent months."

DEVELOPMENTS UNDER KURT WALDHEIM

In the autumn of 1971, many names, including that of Kurt Waldheim of Austria, were mentioned as possible successors to U Thant, who declined to stand for a third term. The Security Council met in three closed sessions. The People's Republic of China, which had voted against Kurt Waldheim, abstained on the third ballot and he was recommended to the General Assembly on 21 December for appointment. The following day, the Assembly appointed him secretary-general by acclamation for a five-year term, from 1 January 1972 to 31 December 1976.

The Situation in the UN. When Kurt Waldheim was named secretary-general of the UN at the end of 1971, it was a vastly different organization from the one that U Thant had taken over on the death of Dag Hammarskjöld a decade before. At the end of 1960, counting the 14 new members admitted that year, there were 101 member states. At the end of 1971, there were 132. Most of the new members were small states, former colonies, which had attained independence immediately before their admission to the UN. At the same time, the representatives of the most populous country in the world, the People's Republic of China, with close to 800 million inhabitants, were occupying China's seat at the UN, having displaced delegates of the Republic of China (Taiwan) as the legitimate representatives of the Chinese people by the decision of the 1971 Assembly.

During Waldheim's tenure, the new composition of the UN evidenced itself in different and more complex alignments. In earlier years, the principal divisions had been between the Western bloc and the socialist countries of Eastern Europe. Now the third-world countries—generally small or of medium size and sometimes very small, with populations under 1 million—could easily dominate the voting in the Assembly. Years before, the US had sought to bypass the Soviet veto in the Security Council by acting through the Assembly, notably in the case of the Korean conflict. In the 1970s, and dramatically during the regular and special sessions of 1974 and 1975, the third world exercised its strength. In some cases, principles theretofore accepted as fundamental in the UN were ignored. On most issues, the socialist countries and the third-world countries voted together. The Western group was frequently at odds with the majority, and the questions of the effectiveness of the Assembly resolutions and the consistency with the Charter of some of its recently adopted procedures figured in public and private discussion and the press in Western countries.

The complexion of the Security Council was also changed with the substitution of the representatives of Peking for those of Taiwan. The Council was strengthened in that it more faithfully reflected world political realities and now heard the voice of the nation with the world's largest population. China declared it wished to be considered a developing country. It aspired to leadership of the third world and was at pains to distinguish itself from the "superpowers," the US and the USSR. Its interests conflicted especially with those of the USSR, and strong exchanges between the two powers became a feature of Security Council and Assembly debates.

The Middle East situation was no closer to solution than it had been for decades, and the petroleum crisis, which transferred immense economic power into Arab hands in the first half of the 1970s, eventuated in increased tension in the Middle East.

It is against a background of turmoil, new power alignments, and widespread uncertainty about the ability of the UN to preserve peace, that Kurt Waldheim's work as secretary-general must be considered.

First Term, 1972–76

Two overriding concerns shaped Waldheim's secretary-generalship: concern for the preservation of the peace and concern for the evolution of world economic arrangements that would effect a more equitable distribution of the world's wealth.

Two other specific questions were also of special concern to Waldheim in his first five years: the financial position of the UN and terrorism. The financial position of the UN had been rendered precarious by the practice of some member states, including the USSR, France, and the US, of withholding or threatening to withhold their share of funds obligated to the UN for activities they question. When Waldheim took office, the crisis had become an emergency and he dealt with it vigorously throughout his tenure. In September 1972 he placed the question of terrorism on the Assembly agenda against the wishes of many member states. It was the first time a secretary-general had ever placed a substantive item on the agenda of the Assembly.

Although Kurt Waldheim came to the position of secretary-general with a reputation as a classical diplomat of the old school, he was more of an activist than his predecessor. He traveled extensively in pursuit of his objectives, exerting every effort to gain a principal role for the UN.

Financial Status of the UN. Waldheim acted decisively and immediately, both to reduce costs at the UN Secretariat and to bring in contributions from member nations. By leaving 300 staff positions vacant and by reducing paperwork 15%, he was able to save $6 million in office expenses in his first nine months as secretary-general. As to income, Waldheim persuaded a number of countries to pay their annual contributions in advance, so that 1972 bills could be paid. Making a visit to Paris, he induced France, for the first time, to include its share of the interest on the UN bond issue along with its advance payment.

Waldheim's austerity measures in the Secretariat saved another $3.9 million in 1972, but the devaluation of the US dollar had serious effects on the UN because about 40% of UN expenditures in the 1972–73 budget had to be made in other currencies purchased with devalued dollars. Waldheim continued to leave vacant positions in the Secretariat unfilled in 1972, but had to recommence recruiting after that to avoid impairing operations.

The US contribution to the UN was historically the highest single assessment, and by the early 1970s stood at 31.5% of the budget. In October 1973, the US Congress reduced the US share to 25% of the UN budget—116 other nations also had their contributions reduced by the UN. The difference was made up by increasing the assessments of Japan, China, and 10 other members, and by admitting to membership the two Germanys. Waldheim helped to bring these changes about, fostering the notion that any country paying more than 25% of the UN's expenses could wield excessive influence.

Peacekeeping and Peacemaking. In 1972, on his own authority, Waldheim undertook a number of missions on behalf of peace. Visiting Cyprus, he temporarily calmed the Turkish community's concern over reported arms shipments to the Greek-dominated government. He visited the island again in 1973 in pursuit of reconciliation. After the hostilities in 1974, he was able to bring Greek and Turkish leaders together for negotiations, and he presided over the Geneva talks regarding Cyprus.

Waldheim's efforts to conciliate in the Viet-Nam War were rebuffed by both sides in 1972. He then tried, without success, to end the war through action by the Security Council. He visited

the two Yemens to try to mediate a border dispute in 1972, and in the same year tried to mediate between India and Pakistan.

In the long-continued Arab-Israeli disputes, Waldheim made many efforts to lead toward a satisfactory settlement and was praised for the speed with which he organized the UN Emergency Force, between the armies of Egypt and Israel, at the request of the Security Council in October 1973.

Striving for a New International Economic Order. The sixth special session of the Assembly, in the spring of 1974, and the seventh special session, in September 1975, resulted in a number of decisions and proposals for bridging the gap between the rich and the poor nations and building a "new international economic order." The seventh special session was, in Waldheim's words, "a major event, even a turning point, in the history of the United Nations and showed a new and highly promising capacity of the organization to achieve practical results through consensus and through negotiation. . . . I believe that the need to make the United Nations work and to use it to build a more peaceful and prosperous world is widely recognized. . . . Economic imbalance does not lend itself to the building of an orderly and peaceful world. Some redress of this imbalance should now be viewed as an objective in itself, as part of *realpolitik*, and not just as an idealistic approach. . . . I believe that development assistance should be given to those in need with a view to fostering economic growth and to creating better living conditions for the people of the recipient countries in a spirit of international cooperation. . . . "

Exercising the Moral Authority of the UN. Incidents of terrorism increased in the early 1970s. In September 1972, during the XXth Olympiad in Munich, 11 Israeli athletes were killed by Palestinians of the Black September group. Waldheim expressed himself strongly about the event and put the question of terrorism on the agenda of the 1972 Assembly. A number of Arab and African countries took exception to his initiative. They argued that attention should be focused on the causes of terrorism. Though the Assembly had condemned aerial hijacking a little earlier, the resolution it adopted on terrorism did not condemn the practice but called for a study of its causes. After OPEC officials were attacked by terrorists in 1975, the sentiment for more ample UN action against terrorism grew among third-world countries.

The moral authority of the UN has frequently been exercised by the secretary-general through humanitarian enterprises. In Bangladesh in 1972 Waldheim organized the largest relief project ever undertaken by the UN, in order to prevent starvation and get the war-ravaged new country on its feet. In early 1974 Waldheim visited five nations in western Africa that had been devastated by prolonged drought and were receiving substantial UN aid. His implementation and personal direction of humanitarian operations were seen after earthquakes in Nicaragua and Guatemala, and in the wake of natural and man-made disasters in many other parts of the world.

Second Term, 1977–81

In December 1976, Waldheim was reappointed for a second five-year term, from 1 January 1977 to 31 December 1981.

Based on the "hard experience" of the first five years, Waldheim entered his second term of office with few illusions about the organization. To some extent, he wrote, it was still in search of its identity and its true role: "It tends to react rather than foresee, to deal with the effects of a crisis rather than anticipate and forestall that crisis." The history of the UN since its founding, he wrote, "has essentially been the story of the search for a working balance between national sovereignty and national interests on the one hand and international order and the long-term interests of the world community on the other." He said he was not discouraged, however, and he urged governments—particularly the major powers—to turn away from the age-old struggle for spheres of influence and to honor and respect their obligations and responsibilities under the Charter.

In the aftermath of the Israeli invasion of southern Lebanon, the Security Council decided in March 1978 to dispatch a UN peacekeeping force to the area to confirm the withdrawal of Israeli forces, ensure that the area was not used for hostile acts, and help restore the authority of the Lebanese government. Waldheim reported that by mid-June, the UN Interim Force in Lebanon (UNIFIL) had established satisfactory arrangements with the Palestine Liberation Organization (PLO) and that Israeli forces had withdrawn from UNIFIL's area of operations; other objectives had not been realized, however, and UNIFIL remained on the scene.

In 1978 Waldheim called for an effort to improve and streamline the workings of the UN, beginning with the General Assembly, the agenda of which should be reviewed, he said, and items of lesser interest removed. He noted that the Assembly had grown in three decades from a body of 50 members with an agenda of 20 items to a gathering of some 150 members and an agenda of more than 130 items.

Waldheim traveled extensively in East Asia in early 1979 and again in 1980 to get a first-hand view of developments in that area, particularly Indo-China, where, in the aftermath of the Viet-Nam War, there was an exodus of refugees, by land and sea, from that country. With the tide of these and other refugees from Laos and Kampuchea rising daily, Waldheim convened a meeting in Geneva in June 1979 to help alleviate the problem.

In May, pursuing a "good offices" mission in Cyprus, Waldheim convened a high-level meeting which called for a resumption of intercommunal talks. The talks were subsequently resumed but broke down shortly thereafter. Waldheim again exerted his best efforts beginning in late 1979, as did the UN itself, in search of solutions to unexpected crises touched off by the Soviet invasion of Afghanistan and the taking of American diplomatic personnel as hostages in Iran. From the outset, his efforts were directed at freeing the hostages and settling relations between Iran and the US and, for this purpose, he went to Tehran himself, as did a UN commission of inquiry. Waldheim noted that the war between Iran and Iraq, which began in September 1980, had resisted all efforts, both within and outside the UN, to find a peaceful solution. He offered his own good offices for this purpose and appointed Olof Palme, former Swedish prime minister, as his special representative. As regards the Afghanistan crisis, he appointed Javier Pérez de Cuéllar of Peru as his personal representative.

DEVELOPMENTS UNDER JAVIER PÉREZ DE CUÉLLAR

In his first report to the General Assembly, in September 1982, on the work of the organization, Pérez de Cuéllar commented on the inability of the UN to play an effective and decisive role in its capacity to keep the peace and serve as a forum for negotiations. Time after time, he said, "we have seen the Organization set aside or rebuffed, for this reason or for that, in situations in which it should and could have played an important and constructive role." He saw this trend as dangerous for the world community and for the future, and criticized the tendency of governments to resort to confrontation, violence, and even war in pursuit of what were perceived as vital interests, claims, or aspirations. In the Falkland Islands crisis, for example, despite intensive negotiations which he had conducted with the full support of the Security Council, it had proved impossible to avoid a major conflict. When a UN peacekeeping operation, such as the one in Lebanon, was bypassed, as was the case when Israeli troops invaded Lebanon in June 1982, the credibility of both the UN and of peacekeeping operations as such was severely shaken, he said.

In order to reverse this most dangerous course, the most urgent goal was to reconstruct the Charter concept of collective action for peace and security, Pérez de Cuéllar stressed. One means would be more systematic, less last-minute use of the Security Council, with the Council keeping an active watch on dangerous situations to avoid crises or defuse them at an early stage. The secretary-general should play a more forthright role in bringing potentially dangerous situations to the attention of the Council, and it was his intention, he said, to develop a wider and more systematic capacity for fact-finding in potential conflict areas. He recommended that member states, especially members of the Security Council, urgently study means to strengthen peacekeeping operations, and examine the reasons for the reluctance of parties to some conflicts to resort to the Council or to use UN machinery. He appealed to all governments to make a serious effort to reinforce "the protective and preemptive ring of collective security" and to look beyond short-term national interests.

Despite the subsequent interest in the proposals contained in his first report, Pérez de Cuéllar wrote—one year later—that actual developments had been "far from encouraging." Reporting again to the General Assembly in September 1983, he said that the year had been a frustrating one in the search for peace, stability, and justice for those who believed the UN was the best available instrument to achieve those ends. Perhaps more than any other factor, he said, it was the weakening of the commitment of all nations, especially the permanent members of the Security Council, to cooperate within the framework of the UN in dealing with threats to peace and security, that had led to the "partial paralysis" of the organization.

Aside from conflict control, the main objective of the Security Council, and the basic idea of the Charter, he said, should be to develop an effective common approach to potential threats to peace and security, and to assist and, if necessary, to put pressure on the conflicting parties to resolve their differences peacefully. It was necessary to persevere in the effort to move from words to action. For his own part, the Secretary-General said that he had kept the Council informed of the responsibilities entrusted to him and had, within the Secretariat, initiated steps in order to be alerted in advance to potential problems. He added that he looked forward to working with the Council to develop a wider and more systematic capacity for fact-finding in potential conflict areas.

As Secretary-General, he noted that he was the repository of many injunctions to use his best efforts and to report on a wide variety of problems that no one had been able to solve. In this context, he warned against the substitution of resolutions for action. Decisions of various organs should be the beginning, not the end, of government concern and action. Contributing to the implementation of UN decisions, he added, should be an integral part of the foreign policy of member states to a far greater extent than at present.

Again, Pérez de Cuéllar blamed "short-term national interests," old resentments and fears, and ideological differences as being responsible for obscuring the vision of the Charter, and he noted that in most conflict situations "the will to compose differences seems weak or absent." The times demanded a return to the far-sighted statesmanship of the immediate postwar years, not a retreat from it, he said. The value of multilateral diplomacy was being questioned and international institutions were not functioning as intended. "The machinery is running and the wheels are turning," he declared, "but it is not moving forward as it should," and this applied not only to the United Nations but also, in different degrees, to regional organizations and to many international agencies.

The Secretary-General appealed to member states to find the means to push the machinery into forward motion again. "If we do not do this," he stressed, "we run the risk of being caught, immobile and in the open, in a new international storm too great for us to weather." A source of real encouragement, he said, was the proposal of the chairman of the recent conference of nonaligned countries, Indira Gandhi, that the UN should be strengthened by a meeting of heads of state "to give a fresh collective look at some of the major problems of the world."

MAINTAINING PEACE AND SECURITY

The first purpose of the UN, as stated in Article 1 of its Charter, is the maintenance of international peace and security. To this end, the organization is required "to take effective collective measures for the prevention and removal of threats to the peace, and for the suppression of acts of aggression or other breaches of the peace, and to bring about by peaceful means . . . adjustment or settlement of international disputes or situations which might lead to a breach of the peace."

BASIC CHARTER PROVISIONS

The basic provisions of the Charter defining the functions of the Security Council and the General Assembly are summarized here but fuller accounts will be found in the chapters on those bodies, which complement the present chapter.

1. *Relative Powers of the Security Council and the General Assembly.* The Council has "primary responsibility" in questions of peace and security. It has been invested with special powers enabling it to decide, on behalf of the entire UN membership, to take collective action when peace is threatened (Articles 39–42). The Council is further empowered to negotiate agreements with individual members of the UN for the provision of armed forces necessary to maintain international security, and to determine how many members shall participate in any collective action undertaken (Articles 43–48).

The General Assembly, on the other hand, is empowered merely to consider and make recommendations, either to the Security Council or to particular states, on matters pertaining to peace and security. Moreover, it may discuss but may not make actual recommendations on any special dispute between nations that is currently under consideration by the Council (Articles 11, 12). However, though the Assembly is not expressly empowered to take action, neither is it expressly prohibited from doing so. In the only Charter provision touching on the subject, paragraph 2 of Article 11—which is the focus of conflicting interpretation in the long-standing constitutional controversy on the financing of certain Assembly-sponsored peacekeeping operations—the actual wording is as follows: "Any such question [of peace and security] on which action is necessary shall be referred to the Security Council by the General Assembly either before or after discussion."

2. *Bringing a Dispute or Serious Situation Before the UN.* Although the Charter firmly establishes the primacy of the Security Council over the Assembly in matters of peace and security, it does not stipulate that disputes or serious situations must be discussed in the Council before they are discussed by the Assembly. A dispute may be brought before the UN in a variety of ways specified in the Charter without order of preference. One or more of the disputing parties may bring the matter before the Security Council voluntarily, or the Security Council itself may choose to exercise its constitutional right to investigate a dispute at its own discretion; or any UN member, whether or not it is involved in the dispute, may propose the matter for discussion by the Assembly; or a non-UN member that is a party to the dispute may—under certain conditions—bring it to the attention of the Assembly; or the Security Council may ask the Assembly to discuss the matter.

Despite these liberal provisions, the Charter does not stipulate that all political disputes should be brought before the UN. Article 33, for example, enjoins UN members "first of all" to seek a solution to their differences on their own initiative (though if they fail to take this initiative, the Security Council is empowered to call upon them to do so). Only after their efforts to achieve a peaceful settlement have proved fruitless are the disputing parties obliged by the Charter to refer the matter to the Security Council. Again, the UN was never intended by its founders to be regarded as the sole international agency for dealing with political disputes. Thus Article 52 states: "Nothing in the present Charter precludes the existence of regional arrangements or agencies for dealing with such matters relating to the maintenance of international peace and security as are appropriate for regional action. . . . " Members participating in such regional arrangements or agencies "shall make every effort to achieve pacific settlement of local disputes through such regional arrangements or by such regional agencies before referring them to the Security Council." Accordingly, several border disputes between African states are currently under consideration by the Organization of African Unity (OAU) instead of the UN. Likewise, the Organization of American States (OAS) has been given the task of settling a number of disputes that have arisen between nations in its region.

However, it cannot be claimed that Charter obligations are necessarily the chief reason that a number of disputes have failed to make their appearance before the UN. The postwar era has seen many cases of important disputes that were not before any international agency during the crucial moment and were subsequently allowed to linger on, quiescent though unresolved, without any serious attempt at even bilateral negotiation. The question of the future status of Berlin is the most outstanding case of this type—the situation in Viet-Nam being an example of a dispute that did not remain quiescent. The reasons for the failure of the UN to discuss these two major issues are largely self-evident. In the absence of any will on the part of the US or the USSR to negotiate on them through UN machinery, consideration could only jeopardize the survival of the organization itself. With respect to the numerous unresolved disputes between smaller nations, the reasons for UN inaction vary with the individual circumstances.

POLITICAL BACKGROUND TO THE UN'S PEACEKEEPING ACTION

The UN's efforts to preserve peace and security are the most contentious aspect of its entire work. This is due to the inherently political nature of its role and to the fact that both the Security Council and the General Assembly are essentially political bodies, not courts of law which apportion blame and impartially hand down judgments drawn from a set of established legal codes. Their task in disputes brought before them is to find a compromise solution which is at once satisfactory to all parties, based on the political realities of the world situation, and consistent with the principles of the Charter. In this way, each local dispute brought before the UN automatically becomes a dispute involving the entire membership, as nations express differing views on the appropriate action to be taken by consensus of the membership.

The involvement of the general membership in all disputes is precisely what the founders of the UN intended—as a means of ensuring collective international responsibility for political solutions that are both just and realistic. But in order to provide a counterweight to the unavoidable taking of sides, they established the principle of unanimity among the great powers by bestowing the right of veto on the permanent members of the Security Council. The workability of this principle in practice presupposed a basic measure of cooperation among the great powers. As events turned out, however, unanimity among the great powers proved to be a chimera. Within a year of the signing of the Charter, the world was in the throes of the cold war, and the US and USSR were engaged in a fierce power struggle. The effects of this unexpected political development on the UN's work in maintaining peace and security were immediate and devastating. Each dispute between the smaller nations that came before the UN was subsumed under the developing power struggle between the giants. As a result, the Security Council was deadlocked again and again by the Soviet veto. Furthermore, the Charter requirements for agreement on the provision of armed forces for the UN could not be met.

Where the USSR looked to the Security Council and the veto as its power instrument in the UN, the US looked to the support of the majority vote in the Assembly. To circumvent the Soviet veto in the Council, and being at that time confident of majority support for most of its substantive policy objectives, the US spearheaded a drive to turn the Assembly into a body for action in periods of international crisis. This drive culminated in the adoption in 1950 of the Uniting for Peace Resolution, which empowered the Assembly to undertake collective measures for maintaining or restoring peace when the Security Council found itself unable to act in times of emergency (for the terms of the resolution, see the chapter on the General Assembly). It was the US, represented by Secretary of State Dean Acheson, that originated the proposal for the resolution. Although some of the small nations expressed reservations about certain clauses, most of them were eager to participate more fully in the UN's peace and security responsibilities. Only India and Argentina abstained in the vote, and only the Soviet bloc voted against, branding the move as illegal and contrary to the Charter.

The Uniting for Peace Resolution has been invoked in three major crises: the Korean War, the Suez crisis, and the Congo crisis (for details, see below under Case Histories). In all three instances the Security Council found itself deadlocked, and Assembly action was deemed essential by the majority of members. Nevertheless, despite its proven usefulness as an instrument of restoring peace in these instances, the resolution seems unlikely to be invoked in future disputes. Certain countries questioned the legality of the resolution and of the Assembly's action taken thereunder, and they felt justified on these grounds in refusing to contribute to the costs of the Suez and Congo peacekeeping operations. This opened the way for a major constitutional controversy, which came to a head in 1964–65, and brought the UN to a virtual standstill and threatened to split the entire organization. The controversy has remained quiescent since then because the main countries concerned, in order to preserve the UN, tacitly agreed not to make an issue of their differences. Nevertheless, the controversy is still unresolved, and its continued existence has subtly influenced the nature of subsequent UN peacekeeping operations.

TYPES OF ACTION TAKEN BY THE UN
The UN has two main responsibilities with respect to the political disputes that are brought before it: helping the parties concerned to arrive at a pacific settlement of the issue that caused the dispute; and maintaining the peace if animosities threaten to erupt into violence or restoring the peace if hostilities have already broken out.

Depending on the nature of the issue—and on the extent of agreement between the great powers on the course of action to be taken—the UN may either discuss the matter and make rec-

ommendations or it may actually intervene. On occasion, the mere public airing of disputes has been followed by a rapid settlement. Two early cases in point were the requests lodged with the Security Council during 1946 by Iran for the withdrawal of Soviet troops and by Lebanon and Jordan for the withdrawal of British and French troops from their territories. In both instances, despite some great-power altercation in the Council, the offending troops were withdrawn within the year. On other occasions, when the UN has confined its efforts to discussion and recommendation, the dispute has either been resolved outside the UN or it has simply been allowed to lapse unresolved. An example of the former was the 1953 Anglo-Egyptian agreement on the evacuation of British troops from the Sudan and the termination of British administration of the area, which followed an Egyptian complaint to the Security Council in 1947. An example of a dispute being allowed to lapse occurred when the UN failed to take action on the charge, brought by Ireland and Malaya to the Assembly in 1959, that the People's Republic of China had violated the human rights and fundamental freedoms of the people of Tibet.

In keeping with the dual nature of its responsibilities, action by the UN may take two forms: peacemaking or peacekeeping. Although the two kinds of intervention may be undertaken simultaneously in reaction to a single dispute, they are usually applied as separate aspects of the work in hand and kept quite distinct from each other. In its efforts to assist the parties to reach a substantive settlement of the issue under dispute, the UN may dispatch to the scene investigation or conciliation bodies (special committees or commissions consisting of selected UN members); the secretary-general may send his representatives or take on the mission himself. There is no set formula. Peacekeeping action, on the other hand, generally falls into one of two categories, depending on the seriousness of the situation. In cases where the dispute is still relatively under control, the UN may undertake observer operations involving the stationing of UN personnel in the area on a quasi-permanent basis to supervise cease-fire and truce lines and to conduct immediate investigations of any complaints of violations. If full-scale hostilities have broken out, military operations may be necessary to bring the fighting to a halt and to maintain the peace until a final settlement has been reached.

The UN has been much more successful at peacekeeping than at peacemaking. In the introduction to his 1966 report, the secretary-general called attention to the danger of forgetting that peacekeeping is only a means to an end. Paradoxically, the continued presence of UN peacekeeping forces, while providing "time and quiet" for the solution of a dispute, may lessen the sense of immediacy of the parties who must reach a durable agreement.

The system for the maintenance of international peace and security established by the Charter has by no means been put fully into practice. In an era when imposed solutions are no longer acceptable, that system has increasingly been supplemented by a process of decision-making based on consensus.

Since the inception of the UN, peacemaking missions have been undertaken in over 40 different cases of dispute. In those cases where the dispute has finally been resolved, the settlement usually has been due to the labors of the UN's teams. An example of failure was the attempt to negotiate compliance by South Africa with the International Court's 1950 opinion on its obligations in South West Africa (see the chapter on Independence of Colonial Peoples). An example of success was the establishment of Indonesia as an independent state in 1949 (for the UN's work in that case, see the chapter on the Security Council).

In contrast to its extensive peacemaking activities, the UN, as of 1983, had mounted peacekeeping operations in only 14 cases: (1) the Balkan boundary disputes—observer group in Greece from 1952 to 1954; (2) the Arab-Jewish conflict over the establishment of Israel—observer group patrolling borders since 1948;

(3) the India-Pakistan dispute over Kashmir—observer group patrolling borders since 1949; (4) the Suez crisis—UN emergency force on borders from 1956 to 1967; (5) simultaneous allegations by Jordan and Lebanon of UAR intervention in their internal affairs—observer group in Lebanon during 1958 and a special representative in Jordan since 1958; (6) the Congo crisis—UN forces in Congo from 1960 to 1964; (7) Indonesia-Netherlands dispute over future status of West New Guinea—a temporary administrative authority in the territory in 1962–63; (8) the overthrow of the royalist regime in Yemen—observer mission, 1963–64; (9) outbreak of hostilities between Greek and Turkish communities in Cyprus—UN force on island since 1964; (10) outbreak of civil strife in the Dominican Republic (plus US dispatch of troops and USSR charge of US interference)—representative of the secretary-general sent May 1965 to help negotiate cease-fire, remaining until October 1966 to report to the Security Council on the general situation; (11) establishment of a new emergency force between Israeli and Egyptian positions after the renewal and cessation of full-scale hostilities in October 1973; (12) establishment of a disengagement observer force between Israeli and Syrian positions following the October 1973 war—the force in place since June 1974; (13) establishment of an interim force in Lebanon following the Israeli invasion of southern Lebanon in 1978; and (14) deployment of observers in the Beirut area following the June 1982 Israeli invasion of southern Lebanon.

In addition, the UN undertook an enforcement operation in Korea, 1950–53.

SOME CASE HISTORIES OF UN ACTION

The following descriptions are of actions taken—both peacemaking and peacekeeping—in cases where, except for the Congo, the situation remains unstable or where at least part of the original peacemaking or peacekeeping machinery has had to continue in operation. The special case of Korea is also included. The cases are arranged in order of the dates when disputes in the areas indicated were first brought before the UN.

The Middle East

Establishment of Israel. In April 1947 the General Assembly at a special session established a Special Committee on Palestine to make recommendations for the future status of the British mandate. The resulting partition plan, which divided Palestine into an Arab and a Jewish state, with an international regime for the city of Jerusalem, was adopted by the Assembly in November of the same year. A UN Palestine Commission was established to carry out the recommendations, and the Security Council was requested to implement the plan. The date for termination of the British mandate and withdrawal of British troops was 1 August 1948. However, violent fighting broke out between the Arab nations and the Jewish community in Palestine. The Security Council thereupon established a Truce Commission consisting of Belgium, France, and the US, while the Assembly authorized a UN Mediator for Palestine to replace the Palestine Commission. On 14 May 1948, the Jewish state of Israel was proclaimed. Almost immediately, the Arab nations instituted full-scale armed action. Following a four-week truce at the request of the Security Council, hostilities were renewed on 8 July. This time the Security Council, invoking Chapter VII of the Charter, ordered the governments concerned to desist from further military action and proclaimed a cease-fire. (Until the case of Rhodesia in December 1966, that was the only occasion on which the Council had expressly invoked Chapter VII in deciding upon a course of action, though it did not at the time make use of the Chapter VII provisions for instituting sanctions or military action.)

Through the UN mediator, the Council then established a UN Truce Supervision Organization (UNTSO) of military observers from different countries, with a headquarters in Jerusalem, and assigned it the task of patrolling the frontiers. Fighting continued, however, and the mediator was assassinated in September 1948.

During its regular session in the fall of 1948, the General Assembly established a three-member Conciliation Commission (France, Turkey, and the US) to negotiate a settlement and the UN Relief for Palestine Refugees (later replaced by UNRWA; see chapter on Social and Humanitarian Assistance). Following negotiations with the acting UN mediator in the first half of 1949, Israel, Egypt, Jordan, Lebanon, and Syria signed armistice agreements. The agreements provided for mixed armistice commissions to check on their implementation. UNTSO was continued in operation to observe the cease-fire and was still in existence in 1983, investigating complaints of armistice violations and reporting to the Security Council. Likewise, the Conciliation Commission continues to function, still trying to fulfill its mandate from the Assembly to assist the parties concerned to negotiate a final settlement of all issues.

The Suez Crisis. In July 1956, Egypt nationalized the Suez Canal. In September, after Egypt's rejection of the London Conference plan for international control of the canal, France and the UK informed the Security Council that Egypt's attitude was endangering the peace. Israel invaded Egypt's Gaza Strip the following month, and a Council resolution calling for a cease-fire and the withdrawal of Israeli troops was vetoed by France and the UK. France and the UK began armed intervention in the area, and thereafter the situation was handled exclusively by the Assembly under the Uniting for Peace Resolution. It established the UN Emergency Force (UNEF) to secure and supervise cessation of hostilities. Since Israel would not permit UNEF contingents on territory under its control, the force was stationed on the Egyptian side of the demarcation line. Withdrawal of British and French forces was completed by December 1956 and of Israeli forces by March 1957. The canal was cleared by April of the same year, and Egypt declared it open to international traffic (Israeli ships were barred, however).

The Six-Day War, 1967. By the mid-1960s, the tension between Israel and the Arab countries had begun to manifest itself in frequent and sometimes major hostilities across the various armistice borders. On 18 May 1967, the UAR, which two days previously had begun deploying troops to the armistice demarcation line in the Sinai peninsula, officially requested Secretary-General U Thant to withdraw all UNEF units from the area. After consultations with the UNEF Advisory Committee, U Thant ordered the withdrawal of the force that evening.

U Thant's prompt compliance with the UAR's request aroused severe criticism in Israel and other quarters. His view was that both legal and practical considerations required him to act without delay. In subsequent reports he pointed out that UNEF was not an enforcement operation ordered by the Security Council but a peacekeeping operation dependent on the consent of the host country. His unilateral decision to disband the force was, however, probably the most controversial of his career as secretary-general. Some of his critics challenged the legal validity of his stand, while many others believed that he could have used his office to try to persuade the UAR at least to agree to a postponement of its request for UNEF's withdrawal, which they felt only helped pave the way for the crisis that followed.

The UAR occupied the fortress Sharm el-Sheikh, which commands the Strait of Tiran at the mouth of the Gulf of Aqaba, and on 22 May 1967 declared the Gulf closed to Israeli ships and to other ships bound for Israel with strategic goods. Israel found its sole direct access to the Red Sea blockaded and considered the blockade, together with the military agreement the UAR had recently signed with Jordan, a justified *casus belli*. Regarding the assurances of help it had received from Western countries in the course of concentrated diplomatic activity intended to avert the impending war as insufficient, it simultaneously attacked the UAR, Jordan, and Syria on 5 June. Within three days it had deeply penetrated the territory of each country.

The Security Council, in emergency session, demanded a cease-fire on 6 June 1967. Israel announced that it would accept a cease-fire provided the other parties accepted. Jordan announced acceptance on 7 June, the UAR on 8 June, and Syria on 9 June, and a cease-fire accordingly took effect on 10 June. Violations of the cease-fire, especially along the Israel-Syria border, continued until 13 June, when the secretary-general was able to report the "virtual cessation" of all military activity. By this time, Israel had voluntarily withdrawn its forces from much of the territory it had occupied but had retained control of several areas regarded as essential to its security—namely, the whole of the UAR's Sinai peninsula up to the Suez Canal, including Sharm el-Sheikh and the Gaza Strip; the Jordanian part of the city of Jerusalem and the West Bank area of the Jordan River; and the Golan Heights in Syrian territory overlooking the Sea of Galilee. On 14 June, the Security Council adopted a resolution calling upon Israel to ensure the "safety, welfare and security" of the inhabitants of the occupied areas and upon the "governments concerned" scrupulously to respect the humanitarian principles governing the treatment of prisoners of war contained in the 1949 Geneva Conventions.

An emergency special session of the General Assembly, held from 19 June to 21 July 1967, failed to produce a resolution which might serve as the frame of reference for a settlement. The division of opinion between the supporters of the Arabs, including the Soviet bloc and several African and Asian countries, and the supporters of the Israeli position, including the US and several Western countries, was too deep to be bridged. But the Assembly did adopt, by a vote of 99 in favor with 20 abstentions, a resolution declaring invalid Israel's proclamation on 28 June that Jerusalem would thenceforward be a unified city under Israeli administration.

For many months, the Security Council was equally unsuccessful in the attempt to devise an acceptable formula for establishing permanent peace in the area. Finally, on 22 November 1967, after weeks of quiet diplomacy and closed discussions, it adopted Resolution 242, which has remained the basis of UN efforts to achieve a definitive settlement. The resolution, based on a British draft, establishes certain principles for a peaceful settlement without going into contentious specifics or prescribing priorities. The principles include withdrawal of Israeli forces from occupied areas (the text deliberately avoided requesting withdrawal from "all" occupied areas, in view of Israel's declaration that it would not give up certain strategic places, including Jordanian Jerusalem); an end to states of belligerency; respect for the rights of all states in the area to peaceful existence; and an affirmation of the need to guarantee free navigation through international waterways, settle the long-standing Palestine refugee problem, and guarantee the territorial integrity and political independence of the countries involved. All parties—except, initially, Syria—accepted the formula.

The October War, 1973. Full-scale hostilities broke out again in the Suez Canal and Israel-Syria sectors on 6 October 1973. The Security Council met four times without considering any draft resolutions and on 12 October decided to reconvene at a later date after consultations. It did so on 21 October at the request of the US and the USSR and the next day adopted a resolution calling for the immediate cessation of all military activities. It also decided that negotiations between the concerned parties for a just and durable peace should begin at once. China did not participate in this or other votes on the question. Israel, Syria, and Egypt agreed to comply, each stating conditions.

The UN Emergency Force (UNEF), bearing the same name as the 1956–67 UN operation in the area, was established by the Council on 25 October 1973. Its personnel were to be drawn from member states, with the exception of the permanent members of the Security Council, and its eventual strength was to be 7,000. As the Force was assembled, it took up stations in zones of disengagement between Israel and Egypt.

The Peace Conference on the Middle East was convened on 21 December 1973 in Geneva under the auspices of the UN and the cochairmanship of the US and the USSR. The work of the Conference came to fruition at kilometer 101 on the Cairo-Suez road on 18 January 1974, when the chief of staff of the Egyptian Armed Forces and the chief of staff of the Israel Defense Forces signed an Agreement on Disengagement of Forces with the UNEF commander as witness. The agreement was brought into effect on 25 January 1974.

It was not until 31 May 1974, in Geneva, that Syria and Israel signed an Agreement on Disengagement. It called for the creation of a UN Disengagement Observer Force (UNDOF) and specified that it did not represent a peace agreement but a step toward peace. On the same day, after the signing, the Security Council adopted a resolution jointly sponsored by the US and the USSR which set up UNDOF. China and Iraq did not participate in the vote. The strength of UNDOF was to be 1,250, its components to be drawn from members of the UN that were not permanent members of the Security Council. Since that time, its mandate has been extended every six months by the Council.

The establishment of UNEF and UNDOF following the October war and the convening of the Peace Conference on the Middle East were of the greatest significance for UN peacekeeping endeavors in that they marked the first occasion on which the USSR participated.

Lebanon, 1978–82. On 15 March 1978, following a Palestinian commando raid in Israel, Israeli forces invaded southern Lebanon. On 19 March the Security Council called on Israel to cease its military action against Lebanese territory and decided to establish a UN Interim Force in Lebanon (UNIFIL) to confirm the withdrawal of Israeli forces and assist the Lebanese government in ensuring the return of its effective authority in the area.

The mandate of the 6,000-man UNIFIL has been extended by the Council through 1983. Perhaps its greatest crisis occurred on the morning of 6 June 1982, when Israeli forces, comprising two mechanized divisions with air and naval support, moved into Lebanese territory, bypassing positions occupied by UNIFIL. The Israeli invasion was followed by a few days of intensive exchanges of fire with PLO and Syrian forces and by Israeli air attacks on targets in the Beirut area. In subsequent days and weeks, the Security Council met numerous times to demand a cease-fire, withdrawal of Israeli forces, and respect for the rights of the civilian population.

UNIFIL's mandate was enlarged to extend protection and humanitarian assistance to the population of the area; an international survey mission was established to assess the situation on the spot; a UN observer group was deployed in and around Beirut to ensure that a cease-fire was fully observed by all concerned; and, at Lebanon's request, a 4,000-man multinational force, composed of contingents from France, Italy, and the US (and later the UK), was deployed in the Beirut area.

On the morning of 18 September 1982, UN observers reported fighting in the area of the Sabra and Shatila refugee camps in the southern suburbs of Beirut, which was at that time under Israeli military control. Two teams of UN observers reached the camps that morning and found many clusters of bodies of men, women, and children in civilian clothing who appeared to have been massacred in groups of 10 or 20. The observers received information from the Lebanese army that the units seen in the refugee camp area were in fact Kataeb (Phalange) units mixed with Lebanese de facto forces coming from southern Lebanon.

Upon receiving the first reports of the killings, the secretary-general issued a statement expressing shock and horror and called urgently for an end to the violence. Meeting in emergency special session on 24 September, the General Assembly condemned the massacre of Palestinian and other civilians at the camps and called for an investigation of the extent of the killings.

In his 1982 report on the situation in the Middle East, the secretary-general commented that after so many years of debate, the issues dividing the opposing sides were now well known. In order to reconcile the basic aspirations and vital interests of all the parties, he believed a settlement must meet the following conditions: withdrawal of Israeli forces from occupied territories; respect for and acknowledgment of the sovereignty, territorial integrity, and political independence of every state in the area and their right to live in peace within secure and recognized boundaries; and a just settlement of the Palestinian problem based on recognition of the legitimate rights of the Palestinian people, including self-determination. In this connection, he noted, the question of Jerusalem remained of primary importance.

Korea

At the end of World War II, the Allied powers agreed that Soviet troops would accept the Japanese surrender north of the 38th parallel in Korea and that US forces would accept it south of that line. The two occupying powers established a joint commission to set up a provisional government for the country. The commission could not come to an agreement, and the US brought the matter to the General Assembly in September 1947. In November the Assembly created a Temporary Commission on Korea to facilitate nationwide elections. However, since the commission was denied access to northern Korea, it was able only to supervise elections in the southern half of the country. These elections took place in May 1948, and in August the US transferred governmental and military functions to the duly elected ROK government. A separate government meanwhile was established in the north. In December 1948 the Assembly, over the objection of the USSR, established a seven-member UN Commission on Korea (UNCOK) to replace the Temporary Commission and to seek reunification.

On 25 June 1950, both UNCOK and the US informed the Security Council that the DPRK had attacked the ROK that morning. The Council met the same day and (the USSR being absent at the time in protest against a Council decision on Chinese representation) declared the attack to be a breach of the peace. The Council called for a cease-fire, withdrawal of North Korean forces to the 38th parallel, and the assistance of member states to the ROK. As the fighting continued, the Council on 27 June recommended that UN members furnish assistance to the ROK to repel the attack and restore peace and security. On the same day, the US announced that it had ordered its own air and sea forces to give cover and support to the South Korean troops. On July 7, the Council voted to recommend that states make forces available to a UN Unified Command under the US. (It should be noted that though the Council had used the language of Chapter VII of the Charter—"breach of the peace," etc.—it did not specifically invoke the chapter itself or use its constitutional power thereunder to order all states to comply with its decision.) In all, 16 nations supplied troops—Australia, Belgium, Canada, Colombia, Ethiopia, France, Greece, Luxembourg, Netherlands, New Zealand, Philippines, Thailand, Turkey, South Africa, the UK, and the US; the ROK also placed its troops under the UN Command.

On 1 August 1950, the USSR returned to the Security Council (having by then been absent for six months) and declared that all the actions and decisions that had previously been taken by the Council were illegal. On 6 November the USSR vetoed a resolution proposed by the US. As a result of the ensuing deadlock, the Assembly virtually took over the handling of the entire situation (the Security Council even agreeing unanimously, on 31 January 1951, to remove the item from its agenda). The legalistic device by which the Assembly voted itself competent to continue with collective measures that under the Charter are the exclusive preserve of the Security Council was the Uniting for Peace Resolution.

Even before the Council became deadlocked, the Assembly had considered an agenda item entitled "The Problem of the Independence of Korea." Under this item, it established the Commission for the Unification and Rehabilitation of Korea (UNCURK) to replace UNCOK. Then, on 6 November 1950, events were given a new twist of intensity when the People's Republic of China entered the war on the side of the DPRK. The Assembly promptly added the agenda item entitled "Intervention of the Central People's Government of the People's Republic of China in Korea." Under this item, the Assembly in December established the UN Korean Reconstruction Agency (UNKRA), and a three-member Cease-fire Group that included the president of the Assembly to determine a basis for ending hostilities. Following China's refusal to cooperate, the Assembly in February 1951 adopted a resolution that that government had engaged in aggression. It also established a Good Offices Committee and an Additional Measures Committee to supplement the Cease-fire Group. Truce negotiations began in July 1951, but fighting continued until 1953, when an armistice agreement was signed on 27 July. A year later, the Assembly called for the political conference that had been provided for in the armistice agreement. The conference was held between April and June 1954, but it failed to resolve problems and negotiate reunification of the country. UNKRA ceased operations in 1960, and UNCURK was dissolved by a consensus vote of the 1973 Assembly.

On 18 November 1975, the Assembly adopted two resolutions —one with Western support, the other with that of the socialist states—which were to some extent conflicting, but which both favored dissolution of the UN Command at an early date. The first resolution called for negotiations among the DPRK, the ROK, China, and the US. The second called for negotiations between the DPRK and the US. The DPRK declared it would not participate in negotiations with the ROK. In April 1983, in its annual report to the Security Council on the UN Command, the US stated that the following countries were represented on the Command: Australia, Canada, Philippines, Republic of Korea, Thailand, UK, and US.

The India-Pakistan Subcontinent

The state of Kashmir (officially, Jammu and Kashmir) was originally one of the princely states of British India. Under the partition plan and the Indian Independence Act of 1947, it became free to accede to either India or Pakistan. The maharajah requested accession to India, and India accepted the accession. The dispute between India and Pakistan began in January 1948 when India complained that tribesmen were invading Kashmir with the active assistance of Pakistan. Pakistan countered by declaring that Kashmir's accession to India was illegal. The Security Council, after asking the parties to mediate, called for withdrawal of Pakistani nationals, reduction of Indian forces, and arrangement of a plebiscite on Kashmir's accession to India. A UN Commission for India and Pakistan (UNCIP) was sent to mediate in July 1948. By 1949 UNCIP had effected a cease-fire and was able to state that principles on a plebiscite had been accepted by both governments. In July 1949 agreement was reached on a cease-fire line, and UNCIP appointed a group of military observers to watch for violations. However, it was unable to reach agreement on terms for the demilitarization of Kashmir prior to plebiscite.

In March 1951, after several attempts at further negotiation had failed, the Security Council decided to continue the observer group—now called the UN Military Observer Group for India and Pakistan (UNMOGIP)—to supervise the cease-fire within Kashmir itself. Despite continued mediation, the differences between the parties remained. The Council repeatedly considered the matter without achieving appreciable progress.

In August 1965, however, there was a sudden outbreak of serious hostilities. UNMOGIP reported clashes between the regular armed forces of both India and Pakistan, and fighting continued into September, although the Security Council had twice called for a cease-fire. Following a report that fighting had spread to the international border between India and West Pakistan, the Council on September 20 requested that both sides issue orders for a cease-fire within two days and withdraw their forces to originally held positions. The cease-fire was accepted by both states, but continuous complaints of violations were made by each side. Accordingly, the Council requested the secretary-general to increase the size of the military observer group in Kashmir and to establish a separate group on the India–West Pakistan border.

On 5 November 1965, the Council urged that a meeting between the parties be held as soon as possible and that a plan for withdrawal containing a time limit for execution be developed. The secretary-general appointed a representative to meet with authorities of both countries on the question. On 17 February 1966, the secretary-general informed the Council that a plan and rules for withdrawals had been worked out. He also stated that on 10 January the prime minister of India and the president of Pakistan had agreed at Tashkent, where they had met at the initiative of the USSR, that their respective forces would be withdrawn to their original positions by 25 February. Thus, though the crisis remains quiescent, the conflict itself is unresolved, and UNMOGIP is still in operation.

In 1971, another conflict between the two countries broke out, this time in connection with the civil strife in East Pakistan, which later became the independent state of Bangladesh. As nearly 10 million refugees streamed into neighboring India, tension increased in the subcontinent. The secretary-general conveyed his serious concern to the president of Pakistan and the prime minister of India and, with the consent of the host governments, set up two large-scale humanitarian programs. One of these, with the UN high commissioner for refugees as the focal point, was for the relief of the refugees in India. The other was for the assistance to the distressed population in East Pakistan. The secretary-general's actions were subsequently unanimously approved by the General Assembly.

On 20 July 1971, the secretary-general drew the attention of the president of the Security Council to the steady deterioration of the situation in the region, which he described as a potential threat to peace and security. He noted that humanitarian, economic, and political problems were involved, and he indicated that the UN should play a more forthright role to avert further deterioration. In October of that year, he offered his good offices to the governments of India and Pakistan, but India declined. Clashes broke out between the two countries and on 3 December, the secretary-general notified the Security Council under Article 99 of the Charter that the situation constituted a threat to international peace and security.

After a cease-fire had put an end to the fighting on 17 December 1971, the Council adopted a resolution demanding the strict observance of the cease-fire until withdrawal of all armed forces to their previous positions should take place. The Council also called for international assistance in the relief of suffering, and it authorized the secretary-general to appoint a special representative to lend his good offices for the solution of humanitarian problems. During 1972, the refugees, with UN assistance, returned to their homeland. The UN relief operation helped pave the way for the rehabilitation of the shattered economy of Bangladesh, which became a member of the UN in 1974. This developed into the largest humanitarian operation in the history of the UN. (See the section on UNHCR in the chapter on Social and Humanitarian Assistance.)

The Congo

One week after the Democratic Republic of the Congo, a former Belgian colony, had become independent on 30 June 1960, troops of the Force Publique mutinied against the Belgian officers, demanding higher pay and promotions. As violence and general disorder spread rapidly throughout the country, Belgium rushed troops to the area to protect its extensive mining interests. On 11 July, Katanga, the richest province of the country by virtue of its Belgian-controlled copper mines, proclaimed its secession from the new state. The following day, President Kasavubu and Prime Minister Patrice Lumumba appealed for UN military assistance "to protect the national territory against acts of aggression committed by Belgian metropolitan troops."

In a series of meetings the Security Council called for the withdrawal of Belgian troops and authorized the secretary-general to provide such military and technical assistance as might be necessary. It called upon Belgium to withdraw from Katanga in August and announced that it would be necessary for UN forces to enter Katanga, whose secessionist president, Moise Tshombe, refused to dismiss Belgian troops. A struggle for power developed between President Kasavubu and Prime Minister Lumumba and the latter clashed with Secretary-General Hammarskjöld over the role of UN forces, demanding that they subdue Katanga. In Council discussions, the West supported Kasavubu and the Secretary-General, while the USSR supported Lumumba and severely criticized the Secretary-General.

In September 1960, Kasavubu and Lumumba each "dismissed" the other from office, and in New York the Security Council was deadlocked. As a result, it once again invoked the Uniting for Peace Resolution and called an emergency session of the Assembly. Meeting in response to that call, the Assembly authorized the Secretary-General to continue assisting in the restoration of law and order in the Congo. Toward the end of the month, a new caretaker government was installed in the Congo by Colonel Mobutu, with the approval of President Kasavubu, and the country sought admission to the UN. Both Kasavubu and Lumumba sent delegations to New York, but in the end the Assembly accepted the credentials of the Kasavubu representatives.

Subsequent Assembly missions attempted to reconcile the various factions within the country, and in June 1961 an accord was reached to end Katanga's secession. But strife in the Congo continued with bewildering twists and turns for four years. Finally, in February 1964, Secretary-General U Thant announced that the objective of the UN operation—the removal of foreign troops, particularly the foreign mercenaries in Katanga—had been largely completed. In June 1964, the UN Operation in the Congo (UNOC), which at its peak strength had totaled some 20,000 officers and men, was disbanded.

Cyprus

Cyprus was granted independence from British rule in 1960 through agreements signed by the UK, Greece, and Turkey. Under these agreements, Cyprus was given a constitution containing certain unamendable provisions guaranteeing specified political rights to the Turkish minority community. The three signatory powers were constituted guarantors of Cyprus' independence, each with the right to station troops permanently on the island.

The granting of independence had been preceded by a prolonged conflict between the Greek and Turkish communities on the future status of Cyprus. The Greek Cypriots, 80% of the total population, originally had wanted some form of union with Greece, thereby provoking a hostile reaction among the Turkish Cypriots, who countered by demanding partition. Each side was supported in its aims by the country of its ethnic origin. Independence did nothing to alleviate dissension on the island. Both sides were dissatisfied with the constitution that had been granted them, but their aims were diametrically opposed. The Turks wanted partition or a type of federal government, whereas the Greeks wanted a constitution free of outside controls and of provisions perpetuating the division between the two communities.

After three years of continuous tension, culminating in a major incident on 21 December 1963, the Cyprus government (under Greek Cypriot President Makarios) complained to the Security Council on 27 December 1963 that Turkey was interfering in its internal affairs and committing acts of aggression. Against a background of mounting violence on the island, the Council considered the matter but did not immediately take any peacekeeping action. With the consent of Cyprus, British troops had been trying to restore order during the crisis. However, in mid-February 1964, the UK informed the Security Council that its efforts to keep the peace would have to be augmented. Accordingly, on 4 March 1964, the Council unanimously authorized the establishment of the UN Force in Cyprus (UNFICYP) for a three-month period and at the same time requested the secretary-general to designate a UN mediator to promote a substantive settlement. UNFICYP became operational on 27 March 1964, with a mandate to prevent the recurrence of fighting, help maintain law and order, and promote a return to normal conditions.

A coup d'etat on 15 July 1974 by Greek Cypriot and Greek elements opposed to President Makarios forced the latter to flee the country. This was followed by military intervention by Turkey, whose troops subsequently established Turkish Cypriot control over the northern part of Cyprus. Four days after a cease-fire came into effect on 16 August 1974, the UN high commissioner for refugees was asked to coordinate humanitarian assistance in Cyprus, where more than 200,000 persons had been dislocated as a result of the hostilities.

Concurrent with the functioning of UNFICYP, the UN has been active in promoting a peaceful solution and an agreed settlement of the Cyprus problem. This task, first entrusted to a mediator, has since 1968 been carried out through the good offices of the secretary-general. Within that framework, a series of intercommunal talks between representatives of the Greek and Turkish Cypriot communities, as well as high-level meetings, have been held since 1974 in a effort to reach a just and lasting solution. The most recent talks were resumed in August 1980, following extensive consultations by the secretary-general and his representatives with the parties, and beginning in September were held weekly in Nicosia.

In the meantime, UNFICYP has continued its task of supervising the cease-fire and maintaining surveillance over the buffer zone between the cease-fire lines. As of 1 August 1983, the Force (including civilian police) numbered 2,355 men, with contingents from Australia, Austria, Canada, Denmark, Finland, Ireland, Sweden, and the UK.

DISARMAMENT

The UN Charter is emphatic in denouncing the "scourge of war," and it lists the maintenance of international peace and security as the first of the UN's basic purposes. To the Security Council the Charter assigns the task of formulating plans for the "regulation of armaments" to be submitted to UN members with a view to establishing an appropriate system of controls. The General Assembly is explicitly authorized by the Charter to consider "principles governing disarmament and the regulation of armaments." Since—aside from a brief attempt in the early years—the Security Council has not initiated disarmament plans, UN concern with disarmament has been expressed almost exclusively by the General Assembly. However, the Assembly has no power to conduct actual negotiations, but only to make recommendations.

At the start of the discussions on disarmament, the basic disagreements were concerned with which aspects of disarmament should have priority. On the issue of whether nuclear or conventional disarmament should come first, the Western powers chose conventional disarmament, whereas the Eastern European powers gave priority to nuclear disarmament. Each side accused the other of seeking to retain the arms in which it had superiority, at the same time aiming at disarming the other side of weapons in which the latter had more strength. Eventually it was agreed that conventional and nuclear disarmament must be carried out in a balanced manner, although there has been no agreement as to what such a balance constitutes.

Eastern European powers wanted priority for concrete disarmament measures without specific provisions to ensure, by international means, against possible violations, while the West insisted upon effective verification of any agreements reached. The view has been accepted that disarmament and verification must go hand in hand. The USSR contended that the Western powers wanted arms verification and control as a means of collecting military intelligence, and the West countered that on-site inspection was necessary to ensure that there were no evasions of disarmament agreements.

Discussion has centered also on the question whether political settlements should precede disarmament. The West sought priority for political settlement, while the USSR and its allies insisted on agreement on disarmament measures first. Participants in disarmament talks have also been concerned with the problem of whether increased security should come before disarmament or after. The majority of states now take the view that the two questions should be dealt with simultaneously.

The USSR has generally maintained that disarmament plans should be contained in a single treaty, whereas the West's view is that general and complete disarmament should be started with less comprehensive measures. The difference in view has been largely settled in this way: while negotiations proceed for an agreement on general and complete disarmament, other disarmament measures might be undertaken in the hope that this would create confidence.

Another subject of discussion has been the question whether technical studies on the specific details of disarmament measures and their verification should have priority over agreements in principle. Western powers have given priority to technical studies, the USSR to agreements in principle. Their discussions have given the world a clearer understanding of the problems involved.

However, in spite of some significant agreements in the field of limitation of armaments, particularly since 1962, little progress has been made towards the reduction of armaments.

CHRONOLOGY OF DEVELOPMENTS, 1946–62

Separate Consideration of Atomic and Conventional Armaments, 1946–50

In its first resolution, adopted unanimously on 24 January 1946, the General Assembly established a UN Atomic Energy Commission to work out a plan to put the production of atomic energy under international control and inspection and to eliminate atomic weapons and other weapons of mass destruction. However, no agreement could be reached by the commission in the atmosphere of distrust among the big powers.

On the initiative of the US, at that time the only power possessing atomic weapons, the commission concentrated its study on the so-called Baruch Plan for an International Atomic Development Authority. The proposed authority was to have a worldwide monopoly "on all phases of the development and use of atomic energy, starting with the raw material." The USSR rejected the plan, arguing that it could not submit to an agency that might refuse the USSR the necessary permission to carry out work it regarded as essential to advance its peaceful atomic energy program. The Soviet counterproposal called for immediate prohibition of the production, stockpiling, and use of atomic weapons and for the destruction of all existing stocks. It was impossible to obtain West-East agreement on three essential questions: (1) whether establishment of effective verification procedures or the outlawing of nuclear weapons should come first; (2) whether verification functions should be exercised by an international system of on-site inspections as proposed by the Baruch Plan, or by individual governments, as proposed by the USSR; (3) whether decisions in the atomic field should require a simple majority vote or Big Five unanimity. By the spring of 1948, the Atomic Energy Commission was hopelessly deadlocked.

In the meantime, on 13 February 1947, the Security Council had created a Commission for Conventional Armaments, composed of the 11 nations then seated on the Council. This commission's debates ended when, on 27 April 1950, a USSR proposal to exclude from its membership the representative of the Republic of China was rejected, and the USSR representative left the commission.

UN Disarmament Commission, 1952

After the two separate commissions were dissolved, a new start was made in January 1952 when a single UN Disarmament Commission was formed under the Security Council. The new body was to prepare proposals for the regulation, limitation, and balanced reduction of all armed forces and all armaments, nuclear and conventional alike, and it was to propose an effective system of international control of atomic energy to ensure that atomic energy would be used only for peaceful purposes. The debates in the full 11-member Disarmament Commission ended inconclusively in October 1952. In November, the first hydrogen bomb, whose force dwarfed that of the Hiroshima-type atomic bomb, was tested by the US at Eniwetok (now Enewetak). In August of the following year, a hydrogen bomb was exploded by the USSR.

Negotiations, 1953–57

The 1953 General Assembly adopted a resolution suggesting that the Disarmament Commission should establish "a subcommittee consisting of representatives of the Powers principally involved which should seek in private an acceptable solution." The subcommittee, composed of representatives of Canada, France, the USSR, the UK, and the US, held a number of meetings in the following two years. By the autumn of 1955, its efforts aimed at drawing up a comprehensive disarmament plan had ended in deadlock. Thereafter, it limited itself to considering partial disarmament plans. These efforts, too, had resulted in stalemate by the autumn of 1957.

The 1957 Assembly enlarged the Disarmament Commission from 11 to 25 nations, against the strenuous opposition of the USSR, which had proposed that the commission should embrace the entire UN membership. On the grounds that the 25-member body was heavily weighted in favor of the West, the USSR declined to participate in its work. The 1958 Assembly enlarged the Commission to comprise all members of the UN.

Geneva Conference on Nuclear Testing, 1958

In 1958 some significant developments began to take place outside the UN. Nuclear-weapons tests were discontinued by the USSR in the spring of 1958 and by the UK and US as of 31 October 1958. As a result of direct correspondence between the heads of government of the USSR and the US, a conference of experts met in Geneva in July–August 1958 to study methods of detecting violations of a possible ban on nuclear tests.

These experts, from four Western and four Eastern European countries, unanimously reported that violation of an agreement concerning nuclear-weapons tests within certain specific limits could be detected. Although the role of the UN was limited to that of host, the secretary-general was represented by a personal representative and the conference reported to the UN on its work. After 1958 the conference was organized on a more or less continuous basis, remaining in existence until March 1962.

Ten-Nation Committee with East-West Parity, 1959

In the summer of 1959 the foreign ministers of France, the USSR, the UK, and the US agreed that disarmament negotiations would "most effectively advance" if held outside the UN framework in a 10-nation disarmament committee, based on equal East-West representation. The committee was composed of five Western countries—Canada, France, Italy, the UK, and the US—and five Soviet-bloc countries—Bulgaria, Czechoslovakia, Poland, Romania, and the USSR. This became the first group to discuss "general and complete" disarmament.

The committee was quickly deadlocked on the issue of whether to begin with plans for general and complete disarmament, as the USSR proposed, or to start with partial measures, as the US and its allies suggested.

Assembly Emphasis on General and Complete Disarmament, 1959

A feeling of great urgency, but also a spirit of unprecedented initiative and unity, characterized the disarmament debates in the 1959 General Assembly. Two major new plans were submitted to the Assembly: a UK plan, avowedly "pragmatic," and a Soviet plan, avowedly "radical." Many delegates emphasized that the two plans were not too dissimilar. Both would abolish the ability of all states to wage war and reduce all military forces and armaments to the requirements of internal security.

In the three-week debate that followed in the Assembly's Political and Security Committee, many proposals and suggestions were discussed, virtually without acrimony or mutual recrimination. Finally, on 20 November 1959, the Assembly adopted unanimously and without a formal vote the first resolution ever to be sponsored by all member nations. In it the Assembly declared that it was "striving to put an end completely and forever to the arma-

ments race," and stated "that the question of general and complete disarmament is the most important one facing the world today." The resolution transmitted to the Disarmament Commission and to the 10-nation disarmament committee "for thorough consideration" the UK and USSR disarmament plans and all other proposals and suggestions made during the Assembly debate.

Collapse of Negotiations, 1960–61

The shooting down of a US airplane on photo reconnaissance over the Soviet Union (the "U-2 incident"), and the subsequent breakup of the summit meeting between the leaders of France, the USSR, the UK, and the US in early May 1960, greatly worsened the international climate. Revised versions of the Soviet and Western plans were thereafter submitted to the East-West 10-nation committee in Geneva. But at the end of June, the five Eastern delegates walked out of the committee, and no talks on disarmament were held for almost a year.

US-USSR Agreement on Eight Principles of Negotiation, 1961

In the spring of 1961, the US and the USSR began top-level discussions to reopen formal disarmament talks. On 20 September 1961, they submitted to the General Assembly at the opening of its 16th regular session a Joint Statement of Agreed Principles for Disarmament Negotiations. Eight principles were set forth, dealing with (1) the stated goal of negotiations—a program ensuring that disarmament was to be "general and complete" and was to be accompanied by reliable procedures for the maintenance of peace; (2) the reduction of nonnuclear weapons and facilities to such levels as might be agreed to be necessary for the maintenance of internal order and provision of agreed manpower for a UN peace force; (3) the main elements of the disarmament program; (4) implementation of the disarmament program in an agreed sequence of stages within specified time limits; (5) the balance of armaments to be maintained throughout the disarmament process; (6) the need for international control under an International Disarmament Organization to be created within the framework of the UN; (7) the need during and after disarmament to strengthen institutions for maintaining world peace; and (8) the need for speedy and continuous talks to reach these goals.

These principles were endorsed unanimously by the 1961 Assembly and have served as the basic terms of reference for all subsequent discussions on general and complete disarmament. But differences remained on how the principles should be applied.

Addition of Nonaligned Nations to the East-West Disarmament Body. Upon endorsing the joint US-USSR agreement on disarmament principles, the Assembly urged the two powers to replace the moribund 10-nation disarmament committee by a larger committee so as to include "nonaligned" nations which might be able to bridge the differences between the two factions. By the end of the session, the US and the USSR had agreed that a new 18-member body should be set up. The Eighteen-Nation Disarmament Committee (ENDC) consisted of the members of the 10-nation committee and Brazil, Burma, Ethiopia, India, Mexico, Nigeria, Sweden, and the United Arab Republic (Egypt and Syria). France did not participate, stating it hoped the disarmament question could later be discussed among powers that could effectively contribute to a solution.

In 1969, the membership was enlarged to 26 and the name was changed to the Conference of the Committee on Disarmament (CCD). At the General Assembly's first special session devoted to disarmament in 1978, the Conference was rearranged and became the Committee on Disarmament. It now has 40 members.

STATUS OF NEGOTIATIONS ON MAJOR DISARMAMENT ISSUES SINCE 1962

Developments Concerning General and Complete Disarmament

Owing primarily to improved international relations, the atmosphere of disarmament negotiations from 1962 until the beginning of 1964 was markedly more cooperative than in previous years. Both the US and the USSR submitted plans for phased general and complete disarmament, and both agreed to discuss a number of "collateral measures," designed to lessen international tension, that could be implemented prior to an overall disarmament treaty. US proposals included a verified freeze on the number of nuclear-delivery vehicles and a verified cessation of the production of fissionable material for nuclear weapons. Soviet proposals included a nonaggression pact between NATO and the Warsaw Pact countries and a reduction in military budgets. In April 1964, the US and USSR made a simultaneous announcement of respective cutbacks in their production of fissionable material. From May to September 1964, the ENDC was deadlocked over the question of which of the numerous "collateral measures" proposed should be given priority of debate. The committee adjourned in September 1964 and did not reconvene until January 1965, in response to a request of the Disarmament Commission, which had met a month earlier. Since then, it has concentrated on the banning of underground nuclear testing, chemical and biological weapons, and weapons of mass destruction on the seabed, and preventing the proliferation of nuclear weapons.

The elaboration of a comprehensive program dealing with all aspects of the problem of the cessation of the arms race and general and complete disarmament under effective international control was proposed by the Assembly in 1969. While today that remains the ultimate goal of all efforts exerted in the field of disarmament, it is no longer regarded as an objective to be achieved through a single and comprehensive instrument. UN comprehensive disarmament efforts have been combined with efforts to achieve agreement on specific issues.

Basic Differences Between the US and USSR Disarmament Plans. Both plans submitted by the US and the USSR in 1962 were similar in that they were intended to be an embodiment of the principles agreed to in 1961. Both envisaged disarmament as a three-stage process, and both provided for establishment of peacekeeping machinery and an International Disarmament Organization to implement controls. The crucial difference between the two plans lay in the proposed sequence of disarmament moves. As has frequently been the case, US anxiety that violations might go undetected was matched by Soviet fear of what it terms "legalized espionage." The two drafts, as amended from time to time during the following years, were discussed extensively. While the debate did not lead to agreement on general and complete disarmament, it generated some action on partial measures.

SALT I and SALT II. The 1968 General Assembly urged the US and the USSR to initiate bilateral talks on strategic arms limitation. The two powers held the first series of Strategic Arms Limitation Talks (SALT I) between November 1969 and May 1972 and began a second series (SALT II) in November 1972. Technically speaking, SALT was not directly related to the UN, but the talks were closely followed there and comments were made on their progress. SALT I was brought to a conclusion on 26 May 1972 in Moscow when US President Nixon and Soviet Premier Brezhnev signed a treaty on antiballistic missile (ABM) systems and an interim agreement on strategic offensive arms.

Salt II began the following autumn, but little progress was made until President Ford and Premier Brezhnev met at Vladivostok in November 1974. At that meeting, they agreed that further SALT negotiations would be based on the understanding that both sides would have a certain agreed number of strategic delivery vehicles and of missiles equipped with multiple independently targetable warheads (MIRV's). SALT II was finally signed on 18 June 1979. The treaty sets an initial aggregate number of strategic delivery vehicles at 2,400 for each side, to take effect six months after its ratification and entry into force. Within these totals, each side could determine the composition of the types of weapons up to certain limits. The number of warheads for each type of weapon

was also limited. Verification was based on "national technical means" such as satellites and monitoring of test signals. While the treaty has not yet been ratified, the US and USSR continue to abide by its provisions.

Chemical and Biological Warfare. A group of 14 experts appointed by the secretary-general reported in 1969 that were chemical and bacteriological (biological) weapons ever to be used on a large scale in war, no one could predict how enduring the effects would be and how they would affect the structure of society and the environment. In December 1969, the General Assembly, after considering the experts' report, adopted a resolution stating that chemical and biological methods of warfare had always been viewed with horror and condemned by the international community, and calling for adherence to the 1925 Protocol for the Prohibition of the Use in War of Asphyxiating, Poisonous or Other Gases, and of Bacteriological Methods of Warfare.

Socialist and most nonaligned states favored a convention banning the development of all chemical and bacteriological weapons jointly. Western powers believed it more practical to ban biological weapons first because of the complexities of a ban on chemical weapons. The USSR and other Socialist countries agreed in March 1971 to treat the two questions separately. In August of that year, the US and the USSR submitted identical texts of a draft convention on bacteriological questions to the CCD, which approved the draft. The Assembly in December commended the Convention on the Prohibition of the Development, Production and Stockpiling of Bacteriological (Biological) and Toxin Weapons and on Their Destruction. The treaty, the first in modern times to provide for the elimination of existing weapons, entered into force in 1975; by October 1983, 87 states were parties to it.

In 1972 the USSR and the other Socialist members of the CCD tabled a draft convention on the prohibition of chemical weapons based largely on the convention on the prohibition of biological weapons. The US held that adequate verification of a comprehensive ban on chemical weapons presented problems of great complexity and that consequently a convention on the subject was premature. Towards the end of the 1973 session of the CCD, Japan suggested a treaty that would be comprehensive in aim, but of a scope that would be expanded gradually. In July 1974, the USSR and the US announced that they had agreed to consider a joint initiative in the CCD aimed at the conclusion, as a first step, of an international convention dealing with the most lethal methods of chemical warfare.

Negotiations between the US and the USSR were initiated in 1976, and both countries submitted joint reports in 1979 and 1980 on progress achieved. The General Assembly in 1980 expressed regret that the talks had not yet resulted in the elaboration of a joint initiative. In 1980 also, the Committee on Disarmament established an ad hoc Working Group on Chemical Weapons.

Environmental Warfare. The US and the USSR issued a joint statement on environmental warfare in July 1974. In 1976, the General Assembly adopted the Convention on the Prohibition of Military or Any Other Hostile Use of Environmental Modification Techniques. Under the convention, states undertake not to engage in "military or any other hostile use of environmental modification techniques having widespread, long-lasting or severe effect as a means of destruction, damage or injury to any other state party." The term "environmental modification techniques" is defined as "any technique for changing—through the deliberate manipulation of natural processes—the dynamics, composition or structure of the Earth, including its biota, lithosphere, hydrosphere and atmosphere, or of outer space." The convention came into force in 1978; by the end of 1982, 37 states had become parties to it.

The Seabed. When discussions on banning weapons of mass destruction from the seabed began in 1968, the US and the USSR had widely diverging positions on the question. By 1969 they had resolved their differences and accepted amendments to a draft they jointly presented to the General Assembly. This failed to be adopted because the smaller powers believed their vital interests were being ignored.

In 1970, the CCD submitted to the Assembly the text of a draft treaty to prohibit the emplacement of weapons of mass destruction on the seabed, and in December the Assembly adopted a resolution commending the Treaty on the Prohibition of the Emplacement of Nuclear Weapons and Other Weapons of Mass Destruction on the Seabed and the Ocean Floor and in the Subsoil Thereof. The US and the USSR supported the resolution. The treaty entered into force in 1972; by October 1983, 73 states had become parties to it. (See also the chapter on the Law of the Sea.)

Outer Space. In 1966, the General Assembly commended the Treaty on Principles Governing the Activities of States in the Exploration and Use of Outer Space, Including the Moon and Other Celestial Bodies. The treaty entered into force in 1967; by October 1983, 103 states had become parties to it. In 1979, the Assembly adopted the Agreement Governing the Activities of States on the Moon and Other Celestial Bodies. (See also the chapter on the Peaceful Uses of Outer Space.)

Negotiations between the US and the USSR on the control of anti-satellite systems began in 1978 but were suspended in 1979 without any substantial results having been achieved. In 1981, and again in 1983, the USSR submitted to the Assembly draft treaties on the prohibition of the stationing of weapons of any kind in outer space.

Conventional Weapons. While giving primary emphasis to the prohibition of the use of nuclear weapons, the General Assembly has also been concerned with conventional weapons, particularly napalm and other incendiary weapons. Following a conference held in Geneva in 1979–80, the Assembly welcomed the adoption by the conference of the Convention on Prohibitions or Restrictions on the Use of Certain Conventional Weapons Which May Be Deemed to Be Excessively Injurious or to Have Indiscriminate Effects, and of three protocols—on nondetectable fragments, on the use of mines, booby traps, and other devices, and on the use of incendiary weapons. The convention was opened for signature on 10 April 1981.

Disarmament Decades. In 1969, on the proposal of Secretary-General U Thant, the General Assembly designated the 1970s as a Disarmament Decade. Despite some progress both within and outside the UN, the Assembly at the midpoint of the decade expressed deep concern at "the meager achievements of the Disarmament Decade in terms of truly effective disarmament and arms limitation agreements." It established an ad hoc committee open to participation by all member states which would undertake a fundamental review of the role of the UN in the field of disarmament.

The first special session of the General Assembly devoted to disarmament, held in 1978, adopted by consensus a Final Document outlining measures which should be taken in the near future, as well as steps to prepare the way for later negotiations. The special session also recognized the importance of increasing public awareness of the dangers of the arms race, of mobilizing public opinion in support of disarmament, and of creating an atmosphere conducive to progress in disarmament negotiations.

To these ends, the UN in recent years has increased the flow of information on disarmament subjects to governments, nongovernmental organizations, and the media and, through them, to the general public. In 1978, the Assembly decided that the week beginning 24 October (UN Day) should be observed each year as Disarmament Week, and in 1980 it proclaimed the Second Disarmament Decade. At the opening meeting of the second special session of the General Assembly devoted to disarmament in 1982, a World Disarmament Campaign was launched. Its purposes are to inform, to educate, and to generate public understanding of and support for UN objectives in the field of arms limitation and disarmament.

Negotiations for a Comprehensive Nuclear Test-Ban Treaty

The problem of nuclear testing has been discussed annually in the Assembly since 1954, after the US began experiments in its Pacific proving grounds in March 1954. In 1958 the nuclear powers (then the UK, US, and USSR) made the first responsive move toward alleviating the anxiety of the world over the harmful radiation effects of continued testing, by establishing a three-power Geneva conference to negotiate a test-ban treaty. Although the conference accomplished nothing appreciable, private negotiations among the three powers led in 1963 to a partial test-ban treaty—the Treaty Banning Nuclear Weapons Tests in the Atmosphere, in Outer Space and Under Water. The treaty was signed in August by the representatives of the UK, US, and USSR meeting in Moscow. By October 1983, 124 countries were parties to the treaty. Neither France nor China had ratified it. At the time the treaty was drafted, France was already a nuclear power and China was well on the way to becoming one, and both countries have conducted atmospheric tests since the treaty came into force. At the 1974 Assembly, however, France announced its decision to stop nuclear testing in the atmosphere beginning in 1975.

During its 1963 session, the Assembly, and in particular the nonaligned nations, made strenuous efforts to persuade the US and USSR to extend the partial test-ban treaty to include a ban on underground tests. Pending such an agreement, the nonaligned powers urged that the nuclear countries accept an informal "interim arrangement" for banning underground tests. This the nuclear powers steadfastly refused to do. Nor did they accept any of the numerous compromise proposals put forward by the eight nonaligned members of the ENDC to reconcile the technical differences between the US and Soviet positions on an underground test ban. At a summit meeting in Moscow in July 1974, the USSR and the US announced an agreement setting a limit of 150 kilotons on underground nuclear tests. This limit went into effect in 1976. That same year, the US and the USSR signed the Peaceful Nuclear Explosions Treaty, which places the same limit of 150 kilotons on any underground explosion for peaceful purposes and limits any group explosion to an aggregate yield of 1,500 kilotons.

Beginning in 1977, the UK, US, and USSR engaged in negotiations on extending the test ban to prohibit underground tests. In 1979 the UK, reporting for the three parties, said that a large measure of agreement had been reached. In 1980, however, the trilateral talks came to a halt and have not been resumed. In the Committee on Disarmament, a working group was established in 1982 to discuss outstanding issues with a view to making further progress toward a comprehensive nuclear test ban.

Basic Differences Between the US and USSR on an Underground Test Ban. The obstacle that long prevented the conclusion of even a partial test-ban treaty was the difficulty of establishing adequate methods of control and verification. The US has always insisted in every sphere of its disarmament plans on the need for strict international control, backed by appropriate verification procedures. The USSR, on the other hand, tends to believe that these stringent US demands, if implemented, would constitute an infringement on national sovereignty, tantamount to an attempt at legalized espionage. The partial test-ban treaty largely owes its existence to the fact that technical progress by 1963 had made it possible for each nuclear power to ascertain exclusively from observations conducted in its own territory whether another nuclear power was conducting tests in any of three environments—the atmosphere, outer space, or under water. The failure to develop similar methods for distinguishing underground tests—below a certain threshold of magnitude—from natural seismic activity caused the deadlock on an underground test ban.

Lately, however, there has been wide agreement that seismic identification techniques are so effective that most underground tests could be identified. Still, the US and a number of other Western nations have maintained that some on-site inspections would be essential to identify the nature of low-magnitude events that might have military importance. In 1976 the USSR agreed to on-site inspection of the country concerned "if convincing grounds" were presented in the request for such inspections.

Prevention of Nuclear Proliferation

In the early years of the atomic era, it had been assumed that only a very few highly industrialized nations would be able to afford to manufacture nuclear weapons. Owing to the unexpected simplification of nuclear production processes, however, by the mid-1960s some 20 nations, including relatively small countries, were recognized as possessing nuclear capability. In the absence of a nonproliferation treaty and a comprehensive test ban, international conflicts sorely tempt some of these countries to consider developing nuclear weapons.

Although the General Assembly had already discussed the problem of nuclear proliferation at earlier sessions, during 1965 and 1966 it devoted the greater part of its disarmament debates to this matter. The discussions were lent a special note of urgency by the sudden emergence of China as a proven nuclear power. The concern felt at China's nuclear bomb explosions of October 1964 and May 1965 deepened into real alarm when its first nuclear missile was tested in October 1966.

Following prolonged and difficult negotiations, the USSR and the US tabled identical draft treaties in the Disarmament Committee in August 1967. A final draft of the treaty was commended in a resolution overwhelmingly adopted by the Assembly in June 1968. The Treaty on the Non-Proliferation of Nuclear Weapons entered into force in March 1970. By July 1983, 121 countries were parties to it. France and China have continued to refuse to join it.

The treaty prohibits the spread of nuclear weapons under international safeguards, contains provisions for promoting peaceful uses of nuclear energy, makes nuclear material available for peaceful purposes to nonnuclear-weapon states, and provides for negotiations for an early end to the arms race.

In May 1974, India, which was not a party to the treaty, announced that it had carried out "a peaceful nuclear explosion experiment" on 18 May. India's Atomic Energy Commission stated that India "had no intention of producing nuclear weapons."

In accordance with the provisions of the treaty, a conference of the parties to it was held in Geneva in 1975 to review its operation. One of the problems the conference discussed was the widespread demand for nuclear reactors owing to the need for new sources of fuel. The fact that a capability for producing peaceful nuclear explosions is indistinguishable from a capability for the production of nuclear weapons constitutes a thorny issue in efforts to halt the proliferation of those weapons.

While the treaty does not mandate inspection by the IAEA, the IAEA has concluded safeguards agreements with the US, the UK, and France on their nuclear facilities other than those related to national security. In 1983, the IAEA started discussions with the USSR on the conclusion of a similar agreement. (See also the section on safeguards in the chapter on the IAEA.)

Establishment of Nuclear-Free Zones. The idea of nuclear-free zones has been discussed in the General Assembly and elsewhere on many occasions since 1956. In 1959, the Antarctic Treaty became the first treaty to put into practice the concept of the nuclear-weapon-free zone; it prohibits in the Antarctic region any military maneuvers, weapon tests, building of installations, or the disposal of radioactive wastes produced by military activities. In the 1960s, the General Assembly adopted declarations on the denu-clearization of Latin America (1963) and of Africa (1965), and the regional organizations in both areas worked on the texts of draft treaties.

In February 1967, the Treaty for the Prohibition of Nuclear Weapons in Latin America (Treaty of Tlatelolco) was signed. The treaty prohibits the stationing, manufacture, acquisition, or use of nuclear weapons in Latin America. It entered into force in April 1968; by October 1983, 31 states were parties to it.

Two protocols have been added to the treaty. Protocol I provides that the extraterritorial powers (France, the Netherlands, the UK, and the US) controlling certain territories situated within the Latin American geographical zone would undertake to apply the statute of denuclearization in those territories. Protocol II provides that the nuclear-weapons powers would undertake fully to respect the status of denuclearization of Latin America and also would not use or threaten to use nuclear weapons against the parties to the treaty. All major powers except France have ratified Protocol I. Protocol II has been ratified by all five nuclear-weapon states.

The idea of making Africa a nuclear-weapon-free zone dates back to 1960. A 1964 summit conference of the heads of state and government of the OAU approved a Declaration on the Denuclearization of Africa. In 1965, the General Assembly, strongly supporting the idea, called upon all states not to transfer nuclear weapons, scientific data, or technical assistance in any form that might be used to aid in the manufacture or use of nuclear weapons in Africa.

South Africa has not renounced the acquisition of nuclear weapons and refuses to accept IAEA safeguards on all of its nuclear facilities. In view of the possibility that South Africa might have already acquired a nuclear weapon, the 1982 General Assembly called upon all nations to terminate any nuclear collaboration with South Africa and demanded that South Africa submit all its nuclear installations and facilities to IAEA inspection.

The Assembly has also called for efforts toward the establishment of nuclear-weapon-free zones in the Middle East and South Asia, and in 1971 it adopted the Declaration of the Indian Ocean as a Zone of Peace. In 1974 the Assembly decided that a study of the question of nuclear-weapon-free zones in all its aspects should be undertaken by an ad hoc group of government experts under the auspices of the CCD. After considering the CCD report in 1975, the Assembly adopted a declaration containing a definition of the concept of nuclear-weapon-free zones and of the principal obligation of nuclear-weapon states toward nuclear-weapon-free zones. In 1982 the Assembly decided that a further study should be undertaken to review and supplement the 1975 study.

Proposals for a World Disarmament Conference

The idea for a world disarmament conference was formulated at the first conference of heads of state or government of nonaligned countries, held in Belgrade in 1961. The idea was discussed at several subsequent conferences of nonaligned countries and in the General Assembly, which in 1965 endorsed the idea of convening a world disarmament conference.

In 1971, the USSR revived the idea, and the Assembly stated that consideration should be given to the convening of a world disarmament conference open to all states. Since then the item has appeared on the agenda of the Assembly each year. The Assembly set up a special committee on the question in 1972, and the following year it established an Ad Hoc Committee on the World Disarmament Conference. The ad hoc committee has submitted reports annually to the Assembly, in which it has repeatedly stated that, notwithstanding differences of view that have been hindering progress toward the convening of a world disarmament conference, there exists a widespread feeling that such a conference would be a useful forum for disarmament efforts.

PEACEFUL USES OF OUTER SPACE

In October 1957, the USSR launched the first sputnik into orbit around the earth. The following year, the General Assembly for the first time debated the question of outer space. Two items were proposed for inclusion on the agenda: "The Banning of the Use of Cosmic Space for Military Purposes, the Elimination of Foreign Bases on the Territories of Other Countries, and International Cooperation on the Study of Cosmic Space," proposed by the USSR; and a "Program for International Cooperation in the Field of Outer Space," proposed by the US. The very titles of these items indicate the differences that initially existed between the two powers in regard to an international accord on the uses of outer space. The USSR proposed that the first order of business should be a ban on armaments in space but wished to link this with the dismantling of US overseas military bases. The US preferred to avoid the disarmament issue altogether in this connection and wished merely to emphasize that it was the common aim of mankind to ensure the use of outer space for peaceful purposes. This disagreement provoked a series of disputes over the composition and terms of reference of the special UN body that should be established to deal with outer-space problems. The USSR wanted a body with East-West parity, while the US preferred a body more broadly geographic in representation.

Owing to these differences, the 1958 Assembly merely set up an 18-member ad hoc committee to deal with questions of outer space. It included only 3 member states from the Soviet bloc, which, on account of the composition of the committee, declared they would not take part in its work. The committee was eventually reduced to 13 participants.

After intensive negotiations, the 1959 Assembly set up the permanent 24-nation Committee on the Peaceful Uses of Outer Space. Its membership was increased to 28 in 1961, 37 in 1974, 47 in 1977, and 53 in 1980. In 1983 the members were: Albania, Argentina, Australia, Austria, Belgium, Benin, Brazil, Bulgaria, Cameroon, Canada, Chad, Chile, China, Colombia, Czechoslovakia, Ecuador, Egypt, France, FRG, GDR, Greece, Hungary, India, Indonesia, Iran, Iraq, Italy, Japan, Kenya, Lebanon, Mexico, Mongolia, Morocco, Netherlands, Niger, Nigeria, Pakistan, Philippines, Poland, Romania, Sierra Leone, Spain, Sudan, Sweden, Syria, USSR, UK, US, Upper Volta, Uruguay, Venezuela, Viet-Nam, and Yugoslavia.

In 1962 the committee constituted itself into two subcommittees of the whole—one to deal with scientific and technical cooperation, the other with the task of evolving outer-space law. The committee has also established working groups of the whole to deal with navigational satellites (1966), direct broadcast satellites (1968), remote sensing of the earth by satellites (1969), and the use of nuclear power sources in outer space (1979).

DEVELOPMENTS IN SCIENTIFIC AND TECHNICAL COOPERATION

Scientific and technical cooperation within the framework of the UN grew out of Assembly action on the basis of recommendations of the committee, and has increased over the years. It covers various fields of activity, including:

Exchange of Information. The UN Secretariat produces annual reports on national and cooperative international projects. Since 1961, a growing number of countries and international organizations have provided the committee with information on space activities and programs.

Public Registry of Launchings of Space Vehicles. An essential requirement for international cooperation in outer-space development is that launchings of space vehicles, together with scientific data on the results of such launchings, be made public. In 1961 the Assembly decided unanimously that the UN "should provide a focal point" for such information and requested the secretary-general to open a public registry for this purpose. The information is transmitted to the outer-space committee for review and is then placed in the registry.

The USSR and the US regularly supply appropriate data, as do Australia, Canada, the FRG, France, Italy, Japan, and the UK.

Cooperation with Specialized Agencies and Other International Organizations. By the terms of its 1961 resolution on outer space, the Assembly requested the WMO to submit reports to the outer-space committee on the international cooperation required in weather research. The following year, it endorsed steps taken under WMO auspices which resulted in the establishment of the World Weather Watch, incorporating meteorological satellites into its operational system. The same resolution also requested the ITU to submit reports on cooperation required to develop effective space communications. In the ensuing years, this cooperative effort embraced other specialized agencies and international organizations having special interests in matters related to outer space, including: ICAO, ILO, IMO, the European Space Agency, INTELSAT, INMARSAT, INTERSPUTNIK, ICSU, and IAF.

Education and Training. The Assembly has emphasized the need to train personnel from countries not yet advanced in space activities. The Secretariat distributes a periodically revised directory of information taken from UN documents and carries out an educational program on space applications. The program creates an awareness of the potential of space applications for development, especially in developing countries, through technical panels, seminars, and workshops, and the administration of fellowships offered by member states for education and training.

UN CONFERENCES ON OUTER SPACE

Originally recommended by the General Assembly in 1959, the first UN Conference on the Exploration and Peaceful Uses of Outer Space was held in August 1968 in Vienna. It examined the practical benefits to be derived from space research and the opportunities for international cooperation available to nations without space capability, with special reference to the needs of the developing countries. Seventy-eight member states and a large number of international organizations attended. The participants submitted some 200 papers dealing primarily with space applications. They reviewed 10 years of space research in practical applications—communications, meteorology, navigation, education—as well as economic and legal questions pertaining to international cooperation, and practical benefits.

In August 1982, the Second UN Conference on the Exploration and Peaceful Uses of Outer Space (called UNISPACE 82) was held in Vienna with 94 state participants and 45 observers representing intergovernmental and nongovernmental organizations. The conference dealt with the entire gamut of space sciences, technologies, and applications from scientific, technical, political, economic, social, and organizational points of view. It also considered the legal implications of issues on the agenda and discussed growing international concern relating to military activities in outer space.

The report of the conference, adopted by consensus, dealt with matters relating to the prevention of an arms race in space, the needs and possibilities for technology transfer, coordination in the use of the geostationary orbit, remote sensing of earth resources from space, the use of direct-broadcasting satellites, space transportation and space platform technologies, protection of the near-earth environment, the role of the UN, and other matters. The recommendations of the conference were seen as an agenda for nations and organizations to follow in carrying out space activities in the coming decades.

DEVELOPMENT OF INTERNATIONAL LAW ON OUTER SPACE

The early work of the legal subcommittee was marked by disputes that delayed progress on the development of outer-space law. The majority of members stressed the dangers of spectacular scientific advances without corresponding legal obligations and safeguards.

In originally proposing the formulation of an international legal code on outer space, the Assembly had recommended that such a code be based, insofar as possible, on the existing body of international law (including the UN Charter) and the principle of freedom of space exploration for all states. But the USSR and the US differed on certain fundamental issues from the time the question was first debated in the Assembly in 1959. The most important difference was on the relation between the prevention of armaments in space and disarmament on earth.

The breakthrough in this quasi-procedural deadlock came as part of the general East-West détente that followed the partial nuclear test-ban treaty signed in August 1963. During its 1963 autumn session, the Assembly was able to adopt by acclamation two important measures relating to restricting the use of outer space to peaceful purposes. The first was a resolution calling upon all states to refrain from placing in orbit objects carrying nuclear weapons or other weapons of mass destruction. The second was a resolution embodying a Declaration of Legal Principles Governing the Activities of States in the Exploration and Use of Outer Space. Though not an agreement with binding force, as the USSR had wished, it was regarded as the forerunner to a full legal treaty to be drawn up in the future.

Treaty on Principles Governing the Activities of States in the Exploration and Use of Outer Space, Including the Moon and Other Celestial Bodies. This treaty, which the General Assembly unanimously acclaimed in 1966 and which came into force on 10 October 1967, was based on drafts submitted individually by both the US and the USSR. The 17 articles of the treaty state that the exploration and use of outer space shall be carried out for the benefit of all countries and shall be the province of all mankind; that outer space and celestial bodies are not subject to national appropriation by claim of sovereignty or any other means; and that exploration shall be carried on in accordance with interna-

tional law. Parties to the treaty undertake not to place in orbit any objects carrying nuclear weapons, install such weapons on celestial bodies, or otherwise station them in outer space. The moon and other celestial bodies shall be used by all parties exclusively for peaceful purposes, and military bases or maneuvers on celestial bodies shall be forbidden. States shall regard astronauts as envoys of mankind in outer space and shall render them all possible assistance in case of accident, distress, or emergency landing. Parties launching objects into outer space are internationally liable for damage caused by such objects or their component parts. The principle of cooperation and mutual assistance shall be followed in space exploration. Harmful contamination of the moon and other celestial bodies shall be avoided. All stations, installations, equipment, and space vehicles on the moon and other celestial bodies shall be open for inspection to representatives of other states on a reciprocal basis.

Agreement on the Rescue of Astronauts, the Return of Astronauts, and the Return of Objects Launched into Outer Space. Under this agreement, which came into force on 3 December 1968, contracting parties agree to procedures for assistance to spacecraft personnel in the event of accident or emergency landing, and for the return of space objects.

Convention on International Liability for Damage Caused by Space Objects. This convention, which entered into force on 1 September 1972, provides a procedure for the presentation and settlement of claims.

Convention on Registration of Objects Launched into Outer Space. Under this agreement, which came into force on 15 September 1976, a central register of objects launched into space was established and is maintained by the secretary-general, with mandatory registration, as well as notification to the secretary-general of voluntary markings of such objects. Assistance is provided to states requesting help in the identification of hazardous objects or those causing damage.

Agreement Governing the Activities of States on the Moon and Other Celestial Bodies. Adopted by the Assembly on 5 December 1979, this agreement describes the moon and its natural resources as the common heritage of mankind, and it reserves the moon for exclusively peaceful purposes. It bars the emplacement of nuclear or other weapons of mass destruction on the moon, and also prohibits the placing in orbit, or in any other trajectory to or around the moon, of objects carrying such weapons, and the establishment of military bases, the testing of any type of weapons, and the conduct of military activities on the moon.

Currently, the work of the committee is directed to the legal implications of the remote sensing of the earth from space, consideration of the possibility of supplementing the norms of international law relevant to the use of nuclear-power sources in outer space, and matters relating to the definition and delimitation of outer space and outer-space activities.

LAW OF THE SEA

The earth is essentially a liquid planet, with more than 70% of its surface covered by water. Although geographically divided and labeled continents, islands, seas, and oceans, when viewed from outer space the earth appears as one large body of water interspersed with lesser land masses. The ebb and flow of the world's oceans thus provide a common link for the more than 110 nations whose shorelines are washed by their waters. But despite these universal characteristics, this last earthly frontier has become an arena for disputes: fishing rights and varying claims of national jurisdiction, the right of exploitation of the sea's mineral resources, responsibility for the protection of the environment, the right of innocent passage of ships, and free access to the sea for landlocked countries.

As early as 1945, the US, in the first modification of the doctrine of "freedom of the seas," proclaimed US jurisdiction over the natural resources of its continental shelf "beneath the high seas" (that is, beyond US territorial limits). Other nations quickly followed suit with similar claims. In a move to clarify these and other changes in international law, the UN in 1958 convened the first Conference on the Law of the Sea, which resulted in the adoption of four conventions prepared earlier by the International Law Commission. The conventions dealt with the territorial sea and contiguous zones, the high seas, fishing and conservation of living resources, and the continental shelf (see the chapter on International Law). Subsequent developments, however, revealed serious defects in the conventions, and a second conference was convened in 1960. However, it failed to resolve disagreements over the breadth of the territorial sea.

A sense of urgency was again given to the problems connected with the law of the sea when in 1967 Malta warned the General Assembly that there was a danger that technically equipped countries might wish to appropriate the ocean floor for their national use, not only to develop its immense resources but also for defense and other purposes. Malta's delegate, Arvid Pardo, remarked that the "dark oceans" were "the womb" of life: from the protecting oceans life had emerged. Man was now returning to the ocean depths, and his penetration "could mark the beginning of the end for man, and indeed for life as we know it . . . it could also be a unique opportunity to lay solid foundations for a peaceful and increasingly prosperous future for all peoples."

Reacting to the Malta proposal, the Assembly set up the Committee on the Peaceful Uses of the Seabed and the Ocean Floor beyond the Limits of National Jurisdiction, called the Seabed Committee, to study various aspects of the problem and to indicate practical means to promote international cooperation. The principal results of the committee's work were embodied in a Declaration of Principles proclaiming that the seabed and ocean floor and its resources beyond national jurisdiction "are the common heritage of mankind," and that no nation should exercise sovereignty or rights over any part of the area. The declaration, adopted by the Assembly in 1970, also called for the establishment of an international regime to govern the exploration and exploitation of the sea's resources for the benefit of mankind.

At the same session, the Assembly commended the Treaty on the Prohibition of the Emplacement of Nuclear Weapons and Other Weapons of Mass Destruction on the Seabed and Ocean Floor and in the Subsoil Thereof, which had been drafted by the Conference of the Committee on Disarmament following discussion of the question in the Seabed Committee. The treaty entered into force in 1972.

THIRD LAW OF THE SEA CONFERENCE

The work of the Seabed Committee laid the groundwork for a conference of plenipotentiaries that was given a mandate to draft a single convention dealing with all matters related to the law of the sea. The first session of the Third UN Conference on the Law of the Sea met at headquarters in New York in December 1973 and dealt with procedural matters. The second session met in Caracas in 1974, and the third in Geneva in 1975.

The conference, at both the Caracas and the Geneva sessions, decided not to engage in formal debates or the formal statement of national positions, but to devote most of its available time to informal consultations. The procedure was designed to allow the greatest flexibility possible to participating states and to prevent premature commitment to fixed positions that would be difficult to change in the process of drawing up a comprehensive agreement. The Caracas session issued a working document setting forth the different alternatives for each item before the conference. At the Geneva session, a single informal negotiating text was drawn up and circulated to governments. Over the next eight years, in negotiations in three main committees of the conference and in special negotiating and working groups, the text was to undergo several major revisions.

UN CONVENTION ON THE LAW OF THE SEA

The final text of the new convention was approved by the conference at UN headquarters on 30 April 1982, by a vote of 130 in favor, with 4 against (Israel, Turkey, US, and Venezuela) and 17 abstentions. Following the signing of the Final Act of the conference in Jamaica on 10 December 1982, the convention was opened for signature for a period of two years; it will enter into force one year after it has been ratified by 60 states.

The convention covers almost all human uses of the seas —navigation and overflight, resource exploration and exploitation, conservation and pollution, fishing, and shipping. Its 321 articles and 9 annexes constitute a guide for behavior by nations in the world's oceans, defining maritime zones, laying down rules for drawing boundaries, assigning legal duties and responsibilities, and providing machinery for settlement of disputes.

Territorial Sea. Coastal states would exercise sovereignty over their territorial sea of up to 19.3 km (12 mi) in breadth, but foreign vessels would be allowed "innocent passage" through those waters for purposes of peaceful navigation.

Straits Used for International Navigation. Ships and aircraft of all countries would be allowed "transit passage" through straits used for international navigation, as long as they proceeded without delay and without threatening the bordering states; states alongside the straits would be able to regulate navigation and other aspects of passage.

Archipelagic States. Archipelagic states, consisting of a group or groups of closely related islands and interconnecting waters, would have sovereignty over a sea area enclosed by straight lines drawn between the outermost points of the islands; all other states would enjoy the right of passage through sea lanes designated by the archipelagic states.

Exclusive Economic Zone. Coastal states would have sovereign rights in a 322-km (200-mi) exclusive economic zone with respect to natural resources and certain economic activities, and would also have certain types of jurisdiction over marine science research and environmental protection; all other states would have freedom of navigation and overflight in the zone, as well as freedom to lay submarine cables and pipelines. Landlocked and other geographically disadvantaged states would have the opportunity to participate in exploiting part of the zone's fisheries when the coastal state could not harvest them all. Highly migratory species of fish and marine mammals would be accorded special protection.

Continental Shelf. Coastal states would have sovereign rights over the continental shelf (the national area of the seabed) for the purpose of exploring and exploiting it; the shelf would extend at least 322 km (200 mi) from shore, and 563 km (350 mi) or more under specified circumstances. Coastal states would share with the international community part of the revenue they would derive from exploiting oil and other resources from any part of their shelf beyond 322 km (200 mi). A Commission on the Limits of the Continental Shelf would make recommendations to states on the shelf's outer boundaries.

High Seas. All states would enjoy the traditional freedoms of navigation, overflight, scientific research, and fishing on the high seas; they would be obliged to adopt, or cooperate with other states in adopting measures to conserve living resources.

Islands. The territorial sea, exclusive economic zone, and continental shelf of islands would be determined in accordance with rules applicable to land territory, but rocks that could not sustain human habitation or economic life would have no economic zone or continental shelf.

Enclosed or Semienclosed Seas. States bordering enclosed or semienclosed seas would be expected to cooperate on management of living resources and on environmental and research policies and activities.

Landlocked States. These states would have the right of access to and from the sea and would enjoy freedom of transit through the territory of transit states.

International Seabed Area. A "parallel system" would be established for exploring and exploiting the international seabed area. All activities in this area would be under the control of the International Seabed Authority to be established under the convention. The Authority would conduct its own mining operations through its operating arm, called the "Enterprise," and would also contract with private and state ventures to give them mining rights in the area, so that they could operate in parallel with the Authority. The first generation of seabed prospectors, called "pioneer investors," would have guarantees of production once mining was authorized.

Marine Pollution. States would be bound to prevent and control marine pollution from any source and would be liable for damage caused by violation of their international obligations to combat marine pollution.

Marine Scientific Research. All marine scientific research in the exclusive economic zone and on the continental shelf would be subject to the consent of the coastal state, but coastal states would in most cases be obliged to grant consent to foreign states when the research was to be conducted for peaceful purposes.

Development and Transfer of Marine Technology. States would be bound to promote the development and transfer of marine technology "on fair and reasonable terms and conditions," with proper regard for all legitimate interests, including the rights and duties of holders, suppliers, and recipients of technology.

States would be obliged to settle by peaceful means their disputes over the interpretation or application of the convention. They would have to submit most types of disputes to a compulsory procedure entailing decisions binding on all parties. Disputes could be submitted to an International Tribunal for the Law of the Sea, to be established under the convention; to the International Court of Justice; or to arbitration. Conciliation would also be available, and, in certain circumstances, submission to conciliation might be compulsory.

With the signing of the convention, a preparatory commission was established to pave the way for the two major institutions to be set up under the convention—the International Seabed Authority, with headquarters in Jamaica, and the International Tribunal for the Law of the Sea, to be located in Hamburg, FRG.

The commission is to draft rules, regulations, and procedures for deep-seabed mining and other matters of concern to the future International Seabed Authority, and is also to implement a special regime that will allow "pioneer investors" in seabed mining development to acquire internationally recognized rights.

Establishment of the preparatory commission and of the pioneer investment scheme was provided for in two resolutions adopted by the conference on 30 April 1982 as part of a package with the convention.

ECONOMIC AND SOCIAL DEVELOPMENT

Article 55 of the Charter, on international economic and social cooperation, calls on the UN to promote higher standards of living, full employment, and conditions of economic and social progress and development. The fostering of economic and social development, however, was only one of several objectives specified in the Charter, and no special emphasis was accorded to it. The League of Nations and the early ILO were concerned primarily with defensive or protective action—the protection of countries against diseases that might cross international frontiers; prevention of international traffic in women and children and in illicit drugs; protection of workers against unfair and inhumane conditions of labor. Such early action in the economic and social fields was taken in a climate of thought that hardly recognized the concept of economic development.

Toward the middle of this century, however, the idea of development as a major objective of international cooperation took root in the international scene, and the major goal of the UN and the specialized agencies in the economic and social fields came to be promoting the development of the less developed countries.

THE RICH AND THE POOR NATIONS

The UN's preoccupation with development is rooted in the sharp division of its membership between rich and poor nations, a division that the secretary-general has frequently characterized as a leading long-term threat to world peace and security.

In 1945, when the UN was established, this sharp dichotomy could not be drawn between its members. The wealth of Europe had been wasted by the ravages of war. Only the US could claim to be rich, and even the US, with the depression of the 1930s still a fresh memory, could not be confident of lasting prosperity. What made the challenge of development central to the thinking of every aspiring country was the rapidity with which the countries of Western Europe recovered their prosperity and went on to attain higher levels of economic and social well-being than they had ever experienced before. Meanwhile, economic expansion continued apace in the more prosperous countries that had not been directly hurt by the war—the US, Canada, Australia, and New Zealand. And within a few years, in Asia, the miracle of Japan's recovery and growth was matching Europe's postwar record.

Nothing comparable occurred among the colonial peoples and former colonial peoples. Tropical Asia, Africa, and Latin America had been cultivated in preceding generations largely as appendages to industrial Europe and North America—on the one hand supplying essential primary commodities not commonly found in the temperate regions and on the other hand serving as profitable markets for consumer goods produced in the temperate regions. The peoples of these economically underdeveloped areas made rapid political progress in the postwar era. Significant economic progress was also recorded in a number of these countries, so that by the late 1950s it was considered not only tactful but proper to refer to them as "developing" rather than "underdeveloped" nations. As a group, however, the developing countries were far outdistanced in economic growth by the temperate zone industrialized countries, which were finding the postwar era the most propitious in history for their development. Before the UN had completed its first 15 years, it was abundantly evident that a very disturbing gap had opened up between the industrialized and the developing nations and that, despite very substantial foreign aid efforts, the gap was growing broader year by year.

SCOPE OF THE UN'S WORK

The international community was not slow to recognize the political and economic dangers inherent in such an imbalance of national wealth. As early as 1946, when "recovery" rather than "development" dominated UN thinking on economic matters, the General Assembly requested ECOSOC to study ways and means of furnishing advice to nations desiring help in developing their resources. As a result the UN, in cooperation with the specialized agencies of the UN system, began its first programs of technical assistance.

This chapter describes the principles and goals of the UN development effort, considered mainly within the framework of the UN development decades first launched in the early 1960s, and summarizes the work of the regional economic commissions. Programs of technical cooperation undertaken by the UN and its related organizations are described in the chapter on Technical Cooperation Programs, and programs for social development in the chapter on Social and Humanitarian Assistance. The work of the specialized agencies for economic and social development is described in the separate chapters on those agencies.

FIRST UN DEVELOPMENT DECADE

The first UN Development Decade was launched by the General Assembly in December 1961. It called on member states to intensify their efforts to mobilize support for measures required to accelerate progress toward self-sustaining economic growth and social advancement in the developing countries. With each country setting its own target, the objective would be a 5% minimum rate of growth of aggregate national income at the end of the decade.

Member states were asked to pursue policies designed to enable the developing countries to sell more of their products at stable and remunerative prices in expanding markets in order to finance more of their economic development, and to follow policies designed to ensure developing countries an equitable share of earnings from extraction and marketing of their natural resources by foreign capital. Member states were also called on to pursue policies that would lead to an increase in the flow of developmental resources to developing countries on mutually acceptable terms, and that would stimulate the flow of private capital to developing countries on mutually satisfactory terms. The Assembly recommended that the flow of international capital and assistance to developing countries should be about 1% of the combined national incomes of the economically advanced countries.

In his appraisal of the decade at midpoint (1965), the secretary-general noted the harsh fact that many of the poorest economies had continued to grow most slowly, while the growth rate in the economically advanced market economies had accelerated. The gap between the per capita incomes of the developing countries and those of the developed countries had also widened. Two-thirds of the world's population living in the less developed regions of the world still had less than one sixth of the world's income. In 1962 annual per capita income in those regions averaged $136, while that of the population of the economically advanced market economies in North America and Western Europe averaged $2,845 and $1,033, respectively.

The secretary-general reported in 1969 that the slower progress in development had been accompanied by the emergence or aggravation of major imbalances which imperiled future growth. Without greater progress in food production and the more effective control of communicable diseases, the necessary conditions for steady economic and social development could hardly be said to have been laid. However, the secretary-general pointed out that the experience of a few countries had undoubtedly demonstrated that "given a favorable constellation of circumstances and policies, an adequate and sustained pace of development can be achieved." He also said that acceptance of development as a fundamental objective had gradually wrought a desirable change in attitudes and modes of action on the part of developing countries. Public decisions were no longer made solely in response to immediate expediency, and policies and programs previously decided in relative isolation were gradually being integrated and harnessed to a common purpose. At the international level, the secretary-general noted that the institutional machinery for the review and advancement of international policies had been considerably strengthened by the creation of such bodies as the UN Conference on Trade and Development (UNCTAD), the Advisory Committee on Science and Technology, and the Committee for Development Planning.

The first UN Development Decade ended in December 1970 with one of its major goals, the attainment of a 5% growth rate, unattained in the developing countries. During the period 1960–67, those countries achieved an annual rate of increase in their total domestic product of about 4.6%; but in view of the population increase, the increase in their per capita gross product was only about 2%. The Assembly concluded that one of the reasons for the slow progress was the absence of a framework of international development strategy.

SECOND UN DEVELOPMENT DECADE

At its 25th session, in 1970, the General Assembly adopted a resolution outlining an international development strategy for the second UN Development Decade—the 1970s. The main objective of the plan was to promote sustained economic growth, particularly in the developing countries, to ensure a higher standard of living, and to facilitate the process of narrowing the gap between the developed and developing countries. The Assembly declared that the developing countries bore primary responsibility for their development but that their efforts would be insufficient without increased financial assistance and more favorable economic and commercial policies on the part of the developed countries.

Under the goals and objectives of the second decade, the Assembly stated that the average annual rate of growth in the gross product of the developing countries as a whole should be at least 6%, with the possibility of attaining a higher rate in the second half of the decade. Such a rate of growth would imply an average annual expansion of 4% in agricultural output and 8% in manufacturing output.

The Assembly also stated that it was essential to bring about a more equitable distribution of income and wealth for promoting social justice and efficiency of production; to raise substantially the level of employment; to achieve a greater degree of income security; to expand and improve facilities for education, health, nutrition, housing, and social welfare; and to safeguard the environment. Thus qualitative and structural changes in society must go hand in hand with rapid economic growth, and existing disparities—regional, sectoral, and social—should be substantially reduced. The Assembly believed that developing countries must bear the main responsibility for financing their development. To this end, they were asked to pursue sound fiscal and monetary policies and remove institutional obstacles through the adoption of appropriate legislative and administrative reforms. At the same time, each economically advanced country was called upon to endeavor to provide annually to developing countries financial resource transfers of a minimum net amount of 1% of its gross national product. A major part of financial resource transfers to the developing countries should be provided in the form of official development assistance.

Progress achieved during the first half of the decade was reviewed by the General Assembly in 1975. The Assembly noted that the gap between the developed and the developing countries had increased alarmingly during the first half of the decade, but it found the generally gloomy picture lightened by one element —the developing countries had emerged "as a more powerful factor, as a necessary consequence of the new and growing perception of the reality of interdependence." The Assembly also found that some of the aggregate targets set in the strategy for the decade had been met or exceeded, "owing mainly to the developing countries' own efforts and, to a certain extent, to external factors such as the commodity boom" (a short-lived rise in commodity prices between 1972 and 1974). Those aggregates, however, did not reflect the variation in achievement among developing countries, for many countries did much worse than the average. A major area of shortfall was in agriculture, where less than half the target rate of 4% annual growth was realized by the developing countries as a whole.

The Assembly further noted that the net flow of financial resources from developed countries in the form of official development assistance had decreased in real terms and as a percentage of gross national product. It stated that the poor performance of most of the developed market countries in this regard was due to "a lack of political will" to reach the target of 0.7% by the middle of the decade. In addition, the burden of debt-service payments of developing countries had continued to increase in relation to their export earnings.

The Assembly urged governments to continue to seek new areas of agreement and to widen existing ones by addressing themselves to the following issues: the extension of preferential treatment in favor of developing countries in trade and other areas; the transfer of resources to developing countries on a predictable, continuous, and assured basis; the increased financing of development in developing countries in accordance with their national plans and priorities through new approaches such as access on favorable terms to the capital markets of developed countries; and the full and effective participation of developing countries in the international economic system, and their contribution to its functioning.

NEW INTERNATIONAL ECONOMIC ORDER

In September 1973, in Algiers, the Arab petroleum-exporting countries discussed the possible uses of oil as a political weapon. When a new Arab-Israeli conflict broke out on 6 October, the Arab countries reduced the flow of oil to Europe and Japan and suspended exports to the US, the Netherlands, and Portugal. The embargo against the US was lifted in March 1974, that against the Netherlands in July 1974, and that against Portugal after a new regime instituted a policy leading to independence for African territories under Portuguese administration. But the measures taken by the petroleum-exporting countries marked a turning point for the world economy. Members of the Organization of Petroleum-Exporting Countries (OPEC) undertook a long-term study of the collective fixing of oil prices and increased them periodically thereafter.

On 31 January 1974, President Boumedienne of Algeria requested a special session of the General Assembly to consider the question of all raw materials and relations between developed industrial and developing states. Within two weeks, 70 nations endorsed his proposal.

Sixth Special Session of the General Assembly. The special session was held in April-May 1974 and adopted a declaration and program of action on the establishment of a new international economic order. The declaration and program of action called for a fundamental change in the international economic order, in the absence of which the gap between developing and developed countries would only continue to widen. Such a change would require the industrial countries to make adjustments in their policies and economies for the benefit of the poorer countries, which in turn were determined to control their own resources.

The program of action called for efforts to link the prices of exports of developing countries to the prices of their imports from developed countries. It suggested the formation of producers' associations, orderly commodity trading, increased export income for producing developing countries, and improvement in their terms of trade. It also looked to the evolution of an equitable relationship between prices of raw materials, primary commodities, and semimanufactured goods exported by developing countries, and the raw materials, primary commodities, food, manufactured and semimanufactured goods, and capital equipment imported by them.

In the declaration, UN member states proclaimed their determination to work urgently for "the establishment of a new international economic order based on equity, sovereign equality, interdependence, common interest, and cooperation among all states, irrespective of their economic and social systems, which shall correct inequalities and redress existing injustices, make it possible to eliminate the widening gap between the developed and the developing countries and ensure steadily accelerating economic and social development in peace and justice for present and future generations."

Though the program and declaration were adopted without a vote and enthusiastically supported by almost all developing and socialist countries, most Western European and other industrialized states with market economies entered reservations, often very far-reaching. They warned against constraints to the flow of trade which might result from the establishment of producers' associations and argued that nationalization should be carried out in accordance with the existing rules of international law.

Charter of Economic Rights and Duties of States. At its regular session in 1974, the Assembly adopted a Charter of Economic Rights and Duties of States. The charter affirms that every state has the right freely to exercise full permanent sovereignty over its wealth and natural resources, to regulate foreign investment within its national jurisdiction, and to nationalize, expropriate, or transfer the ownership of foreign property. The charter provides that appropriate compensation should be paid in cases of nationalization and that any controversies should be settled under the domestic laws of the nationalizing states unless all states concerned agree to other peaceful means. It also sets forth the right of states to associate in organizations of primary producers in order to develop their national economies.

Seventh Special Session of the General Assembly. The Assembly held a seventh special session devoted to development and international cooperation in September 1975. The polemical atmosphere in which the program and declaration on the new international economic order and the charter on the economic rights and duties of states had been adopted was replaced by a pragmatic one. Negotiations were carried on chiefly in private meetings between "contact groups" representing the developing countries and the Western European and other states with market economies. The market economy states at the time of the session were the buyers of approximately three-quarters of the exports of the developing countries; consequently, agreement among the two groups was essential to significant progress. At the close of the session, the secretary-general declared that it had been "about *change* rather than the smoother management of the status quo." The socialist, market economy, and developing groups of countries all expressed satisfaction with the results.

These results were embodied in a 12-page resolution that proposed a large number of initiatives and was unanimously adopted by the Assembly. It reaffirmed the target, originally defined in the strategy for the second Development Decade, of 0.7% of the gross national product of developed countries to be devoted to official assistance to the developing countries. It called for the accumulation of buffer stocks of commodities in order to offset market fluctuations, combat inflationary tendencies, and assure grain and food security. The resolution also called for a restructuring of the economic and social sectors of the UN system so as to make it more capable of dealing with problems of international economic cooperation and development in a comprehensive and effective manner.

In 1979 the Assembly called for the launching, at the third special session on development in 1980, of a round of global and sustained negotiations on international economic cooperation for development. The negotiations, however, failed to achieve the hoped-for progress at the special session held in September 1980, but at the Assembly's regular session that year, an international development strategy for the third UN Development Decade was adopted by consensus.

THIRD UN DEVELOPMENT DECADE
In the new International Development Strategy adopted by the General Assembly for the third UN Development Decade, beginning on 1 January 1981, organs, organizations, and bodies of the UN system were requested to assist appropriately in the implementation of the strategy and in the search for new avenues of international cooperation for development. In the strategy, governments pledged themselves, individually and collectively, to fulfill their commitment to establish a new international economic order based on justice and equity, and to subscribe to the goals and objectives of the strategy and translate them into reality by adopting a coherent set of interrelated, concrete, and effective policy measures in all sectors of development.

The strategy sets forth goals and objectives for an accelerated development of the developing countries in the period 1981–90, including: (1) a 7% average annual rate of growth of gross domestic product; (2) a 7.5% annual rate of expansion of exports and an 8% annual rate of expansion of imports of goods and services; (3) an increase in gross domestic savings to reach about 24% of gross domestic product by 1990; (4) a rapid and substantial increase in official development assistance by all developed countries, to reach or surpass the agreed international target of 0.7% of gross national product of developed countries; (5) a 4% average annual rate of expansion of agricultural production; and (6) a 9% annual rate of expansion of manufacturing output. Other goals and objectives of the strategy include the attainment, by the year 2000, of full employment, of universal primary school enrollment, and of life expectancy of 60 years as a minimum, with infant mortality rates no higher than 50 per 1,000 live births.

The strategy also sets out a series of policy measures—in international trade, industrialization, food and agriculture, financial resources for development, international monetary and financial issues, science and technology for development, energy, transport, environment, human settlements, disaster relief, and social development, as well as in technical cooperation, including cooperation among developing countries themselves, and special measures for the least-developed countries and for geographically disadvantaged countries, such as island and landlocked developing countries.

It calls for a review and reappraisal of the development strategy to be carried out by the General Assembly in 1984.

DEVELOPMENT PLANNING
Almost all the organizations in the UN family contribute in one way or another to development planning—by helping to evolve and introduce new planning methods, by assisting governments in establishing realistic growth targets, and by trying to ensure

that overall plans take account of the needs of the different sectors of society.

Within the UN, problems relating to development planning are the concern of ECOSOC's Committee for Development Planning and the UN Center for Development Planning, Projections, and Policies. The activities of the Center include the preparation of studies on economic and social progress, technical assistance relating to development planning and policies, dissemination of information on the subject, and the organization of seminars and workshops.

The 24-member Committee for Development Planning, established in 1966, is a consultative body which meets annually to consider problems encountered in implementing development plans and to provide analyses and information relating to implementation of the international development strategy for the third UN Development Decade.

In addition, the UN Secretariat provides an account of the state of the world economy through its annual publication of the *World Economic Survey,* which has appeared every year since 1948. Statistical data, considered indispensable for economic and social development planning, also appears in a number of UN publications, including: the *Statistical Yearbook, Demographic Yearbook, Yearbook of National Account Statistics, Yearbook of International Trade Statistics, World Energy Supplies, Commodity Trade Statistics, Population and Vital Statistics Report,* and *Monthly Bulletin of Statistics.*

SCIENCE AND TECHNOLOGY FOR DEVELOPMENT

A major event of the first UN Development Decade was the UN Conference on the Application of Science and Technology for the Benefit of the Less Developed Countries, held in Geneva in 1963. The conference focused world attention on the practical possibilities of accelerating development through the application of advances in science and technology and on the need for reorienting research towards the requirements of the developing countries.

A second conference, the UN Conference on Science and Technology for Development, held in Vienna in 1979, adopted a program of action designed to put science and technology to work for the economic development of all countries, particularly the developing countries. It recommended the creation by the General Assembly of a high-level intergovernmental committee on science and technology for development, open to all states, and the establishment of a voluntary fund, to be administered by UNDP.

The program of action consists of 65 recommendations divided into three target areas: strengthening the science and technology capacities of developing countries; restructuring existing patterns of international scientific and technological relations; and strengthening the role of the UN system in science and technology and the provision of increased financial resources.

Endorsing the recommendations of the Vienna conference, the General Assembly decided to establish an Intergovernmental Committee on Science and Technology for Development, to be open to all states, and to create within the Secretariat a Center for Science and Technology. In 1981, the Assembly established long-term arrangements for the UN Financing System for Science and Technology for Development, which became operative on 1 January 1982 and which has as its purpose the financing of a broad range of activities intended to strengthen the endogenous scientific and technological capacities of developing countries.

TRANSNATIONAL CORPORATIONS

Since the end of World War II, the role of multinational or transnational corporations in international commerce has been growing, but information on their activities has been fragmentary and often closely held. Some of these corporations command resources greater than those of most governments represented at the UN. Their relationship with developing countries has frequently been troubled, but they can provide capital, managerial expertise, and technology that are all urgently required for development and often would be hard to come by in any other way.

In 1972, ECOSOC requested the secretary-general to appoint a group of eminent persons to study the impact of transnational corporations on development and international relations. The secretary-general appointed a group of 20 economists, government officials, and corporation executives from all parts of the world. The group met in 1973 and heard testimony from 50 witnesses in public hearings—a procedure new to the UN—and in 1974 issued a report recommending the creation of a permanent commission on transnational corporations under ECOSOC and an information and research center in the UN Secretariat.

In December 1974, ECOSOC established an intergovernmental Commission on Transnational Corporations to furnish a forum within the UN system regarding such corporations; promote an exchange of views about them among governments, intergovernmental organizations, business, labor, and consumers; assist ECOSOC to develop the basis for a code of conduct on the activities of transnational corporations; and develop a comprehensive information system on their activities.

The commission meets annually. At its second session, held in Lima in March 1976, it gave priority to the elaboration of a code of conduct and recommended that ECOSOC establish an Intergovernmental Working Group on a Code of Conduct, composed of at least four members of the commission from each regional group, to undertake this task. The working group held 17 sessions from 1977 to 1982 and produced a draft code in which several paragraphs had not been agreed upon. The commission held a special session in March and May of 1983 to finalize the code, but agreement could not be reached.

In 1982, ECOSOC established an Intergovernmental Group of Experts on International Standards of Accounting and Reporting. The group reviews issues which give rise to divergent accounting and reporting practices of transnational corporations, and identifies areas where efforts at harmonization appear necessary.

The four other priorities for the commission's program of work are: establishment of an information system to advance understanding of the nature of transnational corporations and their effects on home and host countries, developing and developed nations; research into the effects of their operations; technical assistance; and work leading to a more precise definition of the term "transnational corporations."

The UN Center on Transnational Corporations (UNCTC) was established by ECOSOC as part of the UN Secretariat in 1974. The functions of the center are to develop a comprehensive information system on the activities of transnational corporations, using data from governmental, corporate, and other sources; to analyze and disseminate the information to all governments; to provide technical assistance and strengthen the capacity of host countries (especially developing countries) in their dealings with transnational corporations; and to carry out political, legal, economic, and social research, particularly research to help in devising a code of conduct.

NATURAL RESOURCES AND ENERGY

The importance of natural resources for economic development was emphasized in 1970 when ECOSOC established the Committee on Natural Resources. The committee develops guidelines for advisory services to governments, reviews arrangements to coordinate UN activities in natural resources development, and evaluates trends and issues concerning natural resources exploration and development, as well as prospects for selected energy and mineral resources.

In 1973 the General Assembly established the UN Revolving Fund for Natural Resources Exploration, which began operation in 1975. The fund, financed from voluntary contributions, is intended to provide additional risk capital for mineral exploration in developing countries. In 1981 the fund was authorized to extend its exploration activities to geothermal energy.

During the 1970s, with the rise and volatility of costs for petroleum which affected the economies of all countries, particularly those of the poorer countries, and the growing awareness that known supplies of petroleum would, in the long run, be unable to meet global requirements, more attention was focused on new and renewable sources of energy. This led to the General Assembly's decision to convene, in Nairobi in August 1981, the UN Conference on New and Renewable Sources of Energy. The conference examined different alternative forms of energy, including solar energy, biomass energy, wind power, hydropower, fuelwood and charcoal, peat, and the use of draft animals for energy purposes. It adopted the Nairobi Program of Action for the Development and Utilization of New and Renewable Sources of Energy as a blueprint for national and international action.

Endorsing the Nairobi program later that year, the Assembly decided to establish an Interim Committee on New and Renewable Sources of Energy to launch implementation of the program and to recommend ways and means of mobilizing financial and other resources for the development of new and renewable sources of energy.

During the 1970s the Committee on Natural Resources played an important role in focusing world attention on the status of the global stock of water resources to meet human, commercial, and agricultural needs. As a result of an initiative of the committee, the UN Water Conference was convened in 1977 in Mar del Plata, Argentina. The conference adopted an action plan to guide international efforts to effectively manage, develop, and use water resources. In 1980 the General Assembly launched the International Drinking Water Supply and Sanitation Decade (1981–90).

REGIONAL ECONOMIC COMMISSIONS

The five regional economic commissions—serving Europe, Asia and the Pacific, Latin America, Africa, and Western Asia—were established by ECOSOC in recognition of the fact that many economic problems are best approached at the regional level. The commissions work to raise the level of economic activity in their respective regions, as well as to maintain and strengthen economic relations among countries within and outside regions. All actions taken by the commissions are intended to fit within the framework of overall UN economic and social policies. The commissions are also empowered, with the agreement of the governments concerned, to make recommendations directly to member governments and to the specialized agencies.

The commissions are subsidiary organs of ECOSOC to which they report annually. The secretariats of the commissions—each headed by an Executive Secretary with the rank of Undersecretary General—are integral parts of the UN staff and their budgets form part of the regular UN budget.

An important part of the work of all the regional commissions is the preparation of regional studies and surveys, particularly annual economic and social surveys which are published at the headquarters of each commission. Supplementing these are bulletins and periodicals covering a wide range of subjects—agriculture, population, transport and communications, energy, industry, housing and building—which are widely used as sources of information by governments, business and industry, educational institutions, other UN organs, and the press.

Economic Commission for Europe (ECE)

The Economic Commission for Europe (ECE), with headquarters in Geneva, was established in 1947 to help mobilize concerted action for the economic reconstruction of postwar Europe and to increase European economic activity among countries both within and outside the region. To these goals was added that of providing governments with economic, technological, and statistical information. Begun as an experiment at a time when severe postwar shortages of some commodities and surpluses of others made economic cooperation in Europe a necessity, ECE soon became a permanent UN instrument and one of the few institutions providing a forum for the consideration of economic problems of Europe as a whole.

ECE priority objectives include the development of trade, scientific and technical cooperation, improvement of the environment, and long-term planning and projections as a basis for formulation of economic policy. Through meetings of policy makers and experts, through publications of economic analyses and statistics, and through study tours and exchanges of technical information, the commission provides a link between governments having different economic and social systems and belonging to different subregional organizations.

Plenary meetings of the commission are held annually; its subsidiary organs meet throughout the year. These include committees on agriculture, coal, electric power, gas, inland transport, steel, timber, development of trade, housing, the chemical industry, and water. There are also senior advisers to ECE on problems of the environment and on science and technology. A conference of European statisticians operates as a permanent body under the joint auspices of ECE and the Statistical Commission of the United Nations.

ECE works closely with a number of specialized agencies, particularly ILO and FAO; with other intergovernmental organizations; and with nongovernmental organizations, which ECE has consulted frequently for their expertise in particular subjects.

Membership and Budget. The ECE region covers Europe and North America. On 1 July 1983, the following countries were members of ECE: Albania, Austria, Belgium, Bulgaria, Byelorussia, Canada, Cyprus, Czechoslovakia, Denmark, Finland, France, FRG, GDR, Greece, Hungary, Iceland, Ireland, Italy, Luxembourg, Malta, Netherlands, Norway, Poland, Portugal, Romania, Spain, Sweden, Switzerland, Turkey, Ukraine, USSR, UK, US, and Yugoslavia.

Appropriations for ECE from the regular UN budget for 1982/83 totaled $23.7 million.

Economic and Social Commission for Asia and the Pacific (ESCAP)

The Economic and Social Commission for Asia and the Pacific (ESCAP), with headquarters in Bangkok, serves a region that contains more than half the world's population. ESCAP was established in 1947 as the Economic Commission for Asia and the Far East to promote reconstruction and economic development of the region. Its name was changed in 1974 to reflect equal concern with economic growth and social progress and to clarify its geographic scope.

ESCAP's activities help identify common problems and facilitate cooperation for economic and social development at the national and international levels. It provides technical assistance and advisory services to governments on request, aids member countries in attracting necessary assistance from outside sources, and acts as a clearinghouse of information.

The commission's nine committees deal with agricultural development; development planning; industry, housing, and technology; natural resources; population; social development; statistics; trade; and shipping, transport, and communications. In addition, ESCAP has established a "special project" on energy, an environmental coordinating unit, a study group on government information systems, and, since July 1980, an Asian and Pacific Development Center which serves to integrate four regional institutions.

Other subsidiary bodies include a task force on integrated rural development; a UN development advisory team for the South Pacific; a joint Center on Transnational Corporations/ESCAP unit on transnational corporations; a Statistical Institute for Asia and the Pacific; a committee for coordinating prospecting for mineral resources in Asian offshore areas; a typhoon committee; and a committee for coordination of investigations of the Lower Mekong Basin. The work program of the latter includes delta development projects, tributary projects (some 13 dams have been completed and 9 are under construction), agriculture and fishery programs, environmental studies, and social development and public health.

Membership and Budget. On 1 July 1983, the following countries were members of ESCAP: Afghanistan, Australia, Bangladesh, Bhutan, Burma, China, Fiji, France, India, Indonesia, Iran, Japan, Kampuchea, Laos, Malaysia, Maldives, Mongolia, Nauru, Nepal, Netherlands, New Zealand, Pakistan, Papua New Guinea, Philippines, Republic of Korea, Singapore, Solomon Islands, Sri Lanka, Thailand, Tonga, USSR, UK, US, Viet-Nam, and Western Samoa. Associate members were: Brunei, Cook Islands, Guam, Hong Kong, Kiribati, Niue, Trust Territory of the Pacific Islands, Tuvalu, and Vanuatu.

Appropriations for ESCAP from the regular UN budget for 1982/83 totaled $29.1 million.

Economic Commission for Latin America (ECLA)
The Economic Commission for Latin America (ECLA), with headquarters in Santiago, was established in 1948 to help Latin American governments promote the economic development of their countries and improve living standards. To this end, ECLA undertakes studies and research of the various sectors of the Latin American economy, analyzes economic and social conditions and trends of the region, reviews the progress of development plans and programs, and works to strengthen economic relations among the countries of the region and between those countries and the rest of the world.

ECLA's initial stress on economic growth and trade was later complemented with emphasis on employment, income distribution, and other social aspects of development. In recent years, ECLA has expanded its activities to include research in such areas as the environment, the development and transfer of technology, and the role and control of transnational corporations. ECLA coordinates its work with other UN organs, as well as with the specialized agencies and other international organizations operating in the region.

The secretariat of ECLA is organized into the following divisions: economic development; social development; natural resources and environment; transport and communications; international trade and development; statistics and quantitative analysis; operations; and economic projections. In addition, two joint divisions deal with two important sectors of the region's economy—the ECLA/UNIDO industrial development division and the ECLA/FAO agricultural division.

Two other major bodies form part of the ECLA system: the Latin American Institute for Economic and Social Planning (ILPES), which provides governments with training and advisory services; and the Latin American Demographic Center (CELADE), which offers training and technical advice on population matters as they relate to development.

ECLA meets biennially; a committee of the whole carries on intersessional work.

Membership and Budget. On 1 July 1983, the following countries were members of ECLA: Antigua and Barbuda, Argentina, Bahamas, Barbados, Belize, Bolivia, Brazil, Canada, Chile, Colombia, Costa Rica, Cuba, Dominica, Dominican Republic, Ecuador, El Salvador, France, Grenada, Guatemala, Guyana, Haiti, Honduras, Jamaica, Mexico, Netherlands, Nicaragua, Panama, Paraguay, Peru, Saint Lucia, Saint Vincent and the Grenadines, Spain, Suriname, Trinidad and Tobago, UK, US, Uruguay, and Venezuela. Associate members were: Montserrat, Netherlands Antilles, and Saint Christopher and Nevis.

Appropriations for ECLA from the regular UN budget for 1982/83 totaled $44.8 million.

Economic Commission for Africa (ECA)
The Economic Commission for Africa (ECA), with headquarters in Addis Ababa, was established in 1958. It was the first intergovernmental organization in Africa whose geographical scope covered the whole of a continent in which economic and social conditions differed widely and where many countries and dependent territories were among the poorest in the world. ECA's chief objective is the modernization of Africa, with emphasis on both rural development and industrialization. Its work has been marked by a sense of urgency and a determination to match the rapid pace of African political progress with economic and social progress. In carrying out its functions, ECA works closely with the OAU and various organizations of the UN system.

The commission's sessions are held biennially at the ministerial level and are known as the Conference of Ministers. An executive committee meets between sessions to ensure more frequent contacts between ECA and member states and to assist the executive secretary in carrying out the commission's program of work.

The approach of ECA is primarily at the level of its four subregions: North Africa, East Africa, Central Africa, and West Africa. ECA members have made it clear that the subregional approach is to be regarded as a necessary first step and that pan-African economic integration remains the goal.

Work priorities outlined by the executive secretary for the 1980s and 1990s include the development of agriculture, increased food production, and increased production of raw materials for industry; the removal of market constraints on production and distribution; the promotion of economic cooperation among African countries and between African and other developing countries in ways that would avoid new forms of domination or vulnerability; the physical integration of the continent in line with the goals of the UN Transport and Communications Decade for Africa (1978–88); and greater control and sovereignty over natural resources and the environment.

Assisting in the task of economic cooperation and integration are a number of regional centers—Multinational Programming and Operational Centers (MULPOCS)—which since 1977 have assisted in implementing ECA programs directly in the field.

Membership and Budget. On 1 July 1983, the following countries were members of ECA: Algeria, Angola, Benin, Botswana, Burundi, Cameroon, Cape Verde, Central African Republic, Chad, Comoros, Congo, Djibouti, Egypt, Equatorial Guinea, Ethiopia, Gabon, Gambia, Ghana, Guinea, Guinea-Bissau, Ivory Coast, Kenya, Lesotho, Liberia, Libya, Madagascar, Malawi, Mali, Mauritania, Mauritius, Morocco, Mozambique, Niger, Nigeria, Rwanda, São Tomé and Príncipe, Senegal, Seychelles, Sierra Leone, Somalia, Sudan, Swaziland, Tanzania, Togo, Tunisia, Uganda, Upper Volta, Zaire, Zambia, and Zimbabwe. (South Africa is a member, but in 1963 it was suspended by ECOSOC from participation in the work of ECA "until conditions for constructive cooperation have been restored by a change in its racial policy.")

Appropriations for ECA from the regular UN budget for 1982/83 totaled $37.3 million.

Economic Commission for Western Asia (ECWA)
A regional economic commission for the Middle East was first proposed in 1947–48. A commission which would include the Arab nations and Israel proved to be out of the question, however, and in 1963 the small UN Economic and Social Office in Beirut (UNESOB) was set up. For 11 years, UNESOB assisted governments in economic and social development and provided them with consultants in fields such as community development, demography, industrial development planning, and statistics.

In 1972 Lebanon revived the issue of a regional commission for the area and, in August 1973, ECOSOC established the Economic Commission for Western Asia (ECWA) to supersede UNESOB. Israel is not a member.

ECWA began operations on 1 January 1974, with provisional headquarters in Beirut. As defined by the resolution establishing ECWA, its task is to initiate and participate in measures for facilitating concerted action for the economic reconstruction and development of Western Asia, for raising the region's level of economic activity, and for maintaining and strengthening the economic relations of countries of the region both among themselves and with other countries of the world.

In pursuit of these goals, ECWA undertakes or sponsors studies on economic, social, and development-related topics; collects, evaluates, and disseminates economic, technical, and statistical information; and provides consultancy services at the request of countries of the region. For this latter purpose, ECWA has at its disposal a group of regional advisers who offer their technical expertise in a number of different fields, including statistics and national accounts; development planning; human resources development; population; transport and communications; industry; and natural resources.

ECWA maintains close liaison with other UN organs and specialized agencies, and with intergovernmental organization in the region such as the League of Arab States and the Arab Fund for Economic and Social Development. Its secretariat consists of eight substantive divisions and units dealing with technical cooperation, statistics, program planning and coordination, and program evaluation.

In 1976, ECWA decided to move its operations to 'Amman, Jordan, for one year because of the conflict in Lebanon. Later the same year, it decided to accept the offer of the government of Iraq for Baghdad to be the site of its permanent headquarters.

Membership and Budget. On 1 July 1983, the following countries were members of ECWA: Bahrain, Egypt, Iraq, Jordan, Kuwait, Lebanon, Oman, Qatar, Sa'udi Arabia, Syria, United Arab Emirates, Yemen (Peoples Democratic Republic), and Yemen Arab Republic. The PLO was also a member.

Appropriations for ECWA from the regular UN budget for 1982/83 totaled $19.5 million.

TECHNICAL COOPERATION PROGRAMS

The International Development Strategy for the third UN Development Decade calls for a renewed emphasis on technical cooperation and a significant increase in the resources provided for this purpose. It recognizes that technical cooperation makes an essential contribution to the efforts of developing countries to achieve self-reliance through its broad role of facilitating and supporting investment, research, and training, among other things.

UN programs of technical cooperation may be grouped in three categories: (1) the UN regular program of technical cooperation, which includes activities financed under the portion of the UN regular budget set aside for technical cooperation activities; (2) activities funded by the UN Development Program; and (3) extrabudgetary activities, which include projects financed by contributions provided directly to the executing agencies by multilateral funding organizations within or outside the UN system, other than UNDP, and by unilateral or bilateral contributions from governments and nongovernmental organizations.

In order to consolidate under one authority the responsibilities and resources within the UN Secretariat in support of technical cooperation activities, the General Assembly, in March 1978, set up the Department of Technical Cooperation for Development (DTCD). As an executing agency for UNDP and a principal operational arm of the Secretariat, DTCD executes projects financed from the regular program of technical cooperation and from extrabudgetary sources, providing technical expertise, training materials, and direct advisory assistance to governments in the formulation, implementation, and evaluation of country and intercountry programs and specific projects.

UN technical cooperation programs and projects help governments establish a more effective framework for growth by aiding in preparing comprehensive plans to ensure balanced economic and social development and the best use of available financial, physical, and human resources; in investigating and making maximum use of natural resources such as water, minerals, and energy supplies; in modernizing and expanding transport facilities; and in improving statistical, budgetary, and administrative services.

UN DEVELOPMENT PROGRAM (UNDP)

Since before 1950, the UN system has been engaged in a growing effort that by the early 1980s was absorbing more than 85% of all its resources. That effort has two main thrusts. The first, and most important, is supporting the vigorous drive of the world's developing countries to provide their own people with the essentials of a decent life—including adequate nutrition, housing, employment, earnings, education, health care, consumer goods, and public services. The second, and closely related, aim is to help these countries increase their output of commodities, raw materials, and manufactured items which the whole world increasingly needs—as well as to ensure them a fair return.

The UN Development Program (UNDP) is the UN's major arm—and the world's largest channel—for international technical cooperation in these fields. Working with nearly every government on earth—and with 35 international agencies—UNDP helps support some 5,000 development projects in Asia, Africa, Latin America, the Arab States, and parts of Europe. Though they involve a broad spectrum of activities, all these projects focus on one basic target—the fuller and better use of available natural resources and human talents and energies.

Evolution of UNDP

Although the UNDP came into formal existence only in January 1966, it really began 20 years earlier, for it grew out of two long-established UN institutions.

In 1948 the General Assembly had decided to appropriate funds under its regular budget to enable the secretary-general to supply teams of experts, offer fellowships, and organize seminars to assist national development projects at the request of governments. About the same time, many of the specialized agencies had also begun to undertake similar projects. However, no sooner had the Regular Programs of Technical Assistance, as they were called, begun to operate than it became apparent that the money that could be spared from the regular budget would not suffice to meet demand. In 1949 the Assembly set up a separate account for voluntary contributions toward technical assistance and decided to make this a central account to finance the activities not only of the UN itself but also of the specialized agencies. Machinery was established for distributing financial resources and coordinating projects, and the whole enterprise was called the Expanded Program of Technical Assistance (EPTA), to distinguish it from the UN's technical assistance financed under the regular budget. The venture proved remarkably successful. Ten years after it had begun operations, EPTA was financing technical assistance in some 140 countries and territories. Between 1950 and 1960, the number of governments contributing funds had grown from 54 to 85 and the total annual contributions had risen from $10 million to $33.8 million.

In 1958 the Assembly felt that it would be desirable to broaden the scope of UN technical assistance to include vital large-scale preinvestment surveys and feasibility studies on major national development projects which would lay the groundwork for subsequent investment of capital. These surveys and studies necessarily involved a much greater financial outlay than the kind of technical assistance then being undertaken, and the Assembly decided to set up a new institution which would be run along lines similar to those of EPTA. Thus the Special Fund was established to act as a multilateral channel for voluntary contributions toward preinvestment projects and as a coordinating center for the work of the various UN agencies. The Special Fund began operations in 1959; within three years, 86 governments had pledged a total of $110,836,585.

In January 1964, the secretary-general formally proposed to ECOSOC that EPTA and the Special Fund be merged into a single enterprise. The advantages to be derived from the merger were a pooling of resources, simplification of procedures, improvement in overall planning, elimination of duplication, reduction in overhead administrative costs, and a general strengthening of UN development aid. By August 1964, ECOSOC had adopted recommendations for the merger, but due to the political situation at the 1964 Assembly, no action could be taken until the following year. On 22 November 1965, the Assembly unanimously voted to consolidate the two operations, effective 1 January 1966, as the UN Development Program (UNDP).

Structure and Organization

Administrator and Governing Council. The UNDP is headed by an administrator, who is responsible to a 48-nation Governing Council for all aspects of program operations. The council—representing every geographic region and both donor and recipient countries—reports to the General Assembly through ECOSOC. In addition to setting overall policy guidelines, the governing council examines and approves the volume of assistance allocated to each country over successive five-year cycles, and must similarly approve all country programs. Its decision-making almost always takes place by "consensus" rather than by recorded voting.

Regional Bureaus. Regional bureaus, located at headquarters, cover Africa, Asia, Latin America, and the Arab States. (There is also an office for Europe.) The bureaus serve as the administrator's principal links with the field. Together with specialized divisions for program policy, technical advice, and finance and administration, they also furnish the UNDP's resident representatives with day-to-day operational support. UNDP's own administrative costs represent 12.5% of total annual UNDP expenditures. The UN agencies' administrative costs for the UNDP program constitute an additional 9.9% (including outlays for recruiting thousands of experts).

Resident Representatives. Resident representatives, heading field offices in 114 nations, function as field-level leaders of the UN development system. They are responsible for seeing that UNDP-assisted country programs and their projects are carried out as effectively and efficiently as possible. They act as chief liaison officers between government planning authorities and the executing agencies; help blueprint all activities from formulation to follow-up; and are responsible for ensuring that personnel, equipment, and facilities are utilized to best advantage. In a growing number of countries, they also help governments coordinate aid from all sources and plan overall development activities.

UNDP's field offices also perform a growing variety of non-project-related development activities which are nonetheless of considerable importance to UNDP's goals and to the needs of its national partners. These services, financed through administrative support and agency overhead costs, include development planning advice, both at national and sectoral levels, by UNDP resident representatives and field office staffs; technical advice and general problem-solving, frequently at the request of the sectoral ministry concerned, by senior agricultural and industrial development advisers and other agency personnel within field offices; follow-up investment advice and services; use of the field office as a focal point for government needs in the event of emergencies caused by natural or man-made disasters; assistance in the formulation, management, and evaluation of country programs themselves; and increasing participation in the coordination of other external assistance and in the achievement of well-balanced, effective national development programs.

Functions and Guiding Principles

If the known needs of the developing countries for technical assistance were the only measure required to justify the existence of UNDP and to govern the scale of the resources made available to it, an unbroken pattern of substantial growth would have been automatically established. But "more of the same" is not the response that the problems and opportunities of the developing countries call for. The nature of UNDP and the activities it finances are constantly changing. In part, this is a reflection of the evolving requirements and interests of the countries. It is also a function of concern at the global level over development problems and issues.

In the early 1970s, UNDP had to demonstrate its ability to replace a basic structure, which had served it well in its formative stages, with a "second generation" mechanism designed to determine the nature of UNDP's market with greater discrimination and to deliver the required product with more efficiency. The cumulative impact of a number of intensive inquiries into development and development assistance—by the Pearson Commission, by the UN Committee for Development Planning, by Sir Robert Jackson's study of the capacity of the UN development system,

and by some of the major donor countries individually—helped to fashion the new look of UNDP. They coincided in many of their findings: on the need for the more deliberate matching of country requests for assistance to available resources, for the introduction of forward and coordinated planning and programming, for more careful and appropriate project design, and for greater quality, timeliness, and efficiency of implementation.

The consideration of these matters by the UNDP governing council in 1970 produced a consensus on the future of UNDP that was endorsed by the General Assembly in the same year, translated into organizational and procedural changes in 1971, and brought substantially into effect during the next few years. The pivotal change was the introduction of "country programming"—the programming of UNDP assistance at the country level for periods up to five years ahead, involving the identification of the role and phasing of UNDP inputs in specified areas within each country's development objectives.

By the end of 1982, nearly 150 country programs were in place and functioning. These exercises, together with a similar approach to regional, interregional, and global activities, are designed to achieve the most rational and efficient utilization of resources.

A necessary counterpart to the introduction of UNDP country programming was administrative reform. The most important change has involved a substantial shift of power and responsibility for effective technical cooperation at all stages away from headquarters and into the field, where the governments look to the UNDP resident representatives for leadership of the UN development system at the country level. New guidelines for the selection of resident representatives imply that, first and foremost, they should be effective managers of the country programs, for it is they who cooperate directly with the governments, approving many projects on the administrator's behalf. In addition, they must intervene to help ensure more efficient implementation and more effective use of the results of project assistance, and they must be ready to play, when requested, a vital part in the coordination of assistance from other programs with that provided by the UNDP. In fact, under the restructuring of the UN development system mandated by the General Assembly, most UNDP resident representatives have been designated as resident coordinators for *all* development activities.

In 1975 UNDP further revised its programming principles to include "new dimensions" in technical cooperation designed primarily to foster greater self-sufficiency among developing countries by relying more heavily on their own skills and expertise in the development process. Accordingly, UNDP redefined its role in technical cooperation to stress results achieved, rather than inputs required from the industrialized nations.

The purpose of technical cooperation, in this view, is to promote increasing autonomy in regard to the managerial, technical, administrative, and research capabilities required to formulate and implement development plans in the light of options available.

In general terms, UNDP has a mandate—laid down by its establishing legislation—to make its assistance available to all countries where it can be effective in meeting priority needs, provided those countries are members of the UN or one of its affiliated agencies. This broad frame of reference is essential for protecting two of UNDP's most valuable assets—its universality and its large measure of freedom from political problems and pressures.

Planning and Programming

In the planning and programming of UNDP assistance, the largest role is played by the developing countries themselves. The process involves three basic steps.

First, an estimate is made of the financial resources expected to be available to UNDP over a five-year period. This estimate is then divided up into Indicative Planning Figures (IPFs) for each country assisted. The IPFs are approved, and adjusted from time to time, by the UNDP's governing council.

Next, with its IPF as a guide, each government draws up a "country program," outlining its priorities for UNDP assistance and allocating its share of UNDP resources among those priorities. Country programming formulation—in which the UNDP's resident representative and locally based officials of other UN agencies usually participate—takes a number of factors into account. Among these are a country's overall development plans, the domestic resources it can call on for carrying out those plans, and the assistance expected from external sources other than UNDP. Each country program is then submitted to the governing council for approval.

The third step involves preparation of individual project requests —again usually in consultation with advisers from the UN system. These requests delineate each project's main objectives, its duration, its cost, and the respective responsibilities of the government and the UN system.

Allocation of Funds

IPFs for 1972–76, the first programming cycle, were largely determined by applying the same percentage of total UNDP resources actually committed to each country from 1967 through 1971 to the total of projected UNDP resources for the years 1972 through 1976.

Completely new criteria were established by the governing council for the 1977–81 "second cycle." Of the country programming resources expected to be available during those years, 92.5% was allocated largely on the basis of a formula involving each country's population and its per capita gross national product—with this second factor being given somewhat greater weight in calculating each country's allocation.

Under the new criteria, about 13% of total resources was devoted to regional programs aimed at fostering development cooperation among neighboring countries or at making expertise economically available to several governments from a single regional base. There was also a separate IPF for global and interregional projects such as "breakthrough" research in high-nutrition grains usable worldwide.

On an overall basis during the third cycle (1982–86), countries with per capita GNPs of $500 a year or less will receive 80% of total UNDP funding, as compared with 52% in the 1977–81 period and 40% in the 1971–76 period.

INDICATIVE PLANNING FIGURES (IPFS) FOR
1982–86
(in thousands of US dollars)

COUNTRY OR TERRITORY	IPF 1982–86
Afghanistan	71,500
Albania	10,250
Algeria	20,000
Angola	41,500
Antigua and Barbuda	1,765
Argentina	20,000
Bahamas	2,400
Bahrain	2,500
Bangladesh	201,000
Barbados	2,500
Belize	1,650
Benin	33,500
Bermuda	550
Bhutan	36,500
Bolivia	19,500
Botswana	8,500
Brazil	30,000
British Virgin Islands	300
Brunei	200
Bulgaria	6,000
Burma	102,000
Burundi	48,500
Cameroon	27,500
Cape Verde	11,250
Cayman Islands	560
Central African Republic	29,500
Chad	52,000
Chile	20,000
China	134,900
Colombia	22,000
Comoros	12,000
Congo	11,000
Cook Islands	1,400
Costa Rica	5,000
Cuba	20,500
Cyprus	5,000
Czechoslovakia	2,500
Djibouti	5,250
Dominica	2,300
Dominican Republic	12,000
Ecuador	15,000
Egypt	56,000
El Salvador	15,250
Equatorial Guinea	11,750
Ethiopia	112,000
Fiji	5,000
Gabon	6,000
Gambia	14,250
Ghana	40,000
Greece	6,000
Grenada	2,100
Guatemala	13,000
Guinea	44,500
Guinea-Bissau	21,750
Guyana	8,500
Haiti	38,000
Honduras	16,000
Hong Kong	500
Hungary	3,500
India	252,000
Indonesia	106,000
Iran	20,000
Iraq	15,000
Ivory Coast	16,500
Jamaica	7,500
Jordan	15,000
Kampuchea	25,500
Kenya	52,000
Kiribati	1,300
Korea, Democratic People's Republic of	24,750
Korea, Republic of	18,000
Laos	52,500
Lebanon	10,000
Lesotho	22,250
Liberia	13,500
Libya	5,000
Madagascar	49,000
Malawi	53,000
Malaysia	15,000
Maldives	7,000
Mali	65,000
Malta	2,500
Mauritania	24,500
Mauritius	7,000
Mexico	20,000
Mongolia	10,000
Montserrat	700
Morocco	27,000
Mozambique	74,000
Namibia	7,750
Nauru	60
Nepal	98,000
Netherlands Antilles	1,500
Nicaragua	9,500
Niger	45,000
Nigeria	55,000
Niue	1,000

Oman	4,000
Pacific Islands, Trust Terr. of	1,000
Pakistan	118,000
Panama	7,500
Papua New Guinea	13,500
Paraguay	9,750
Peru	25,000
Philippines	46,000
Poland	6,000
Portugal	4,000
Romania	7,500
Rwanda	45,000
St. Christopher and Nevis	1,300
St. Lucia	2,100
St. Vincent and the Grenadines	3,250
São Tomé and Príncipe	2,000
Sa'udi Arabia	10,000
Senegal	33,000
Seychelles	1,600
Sierra Leone	32,500
Singapore	7,500
Solomon Islands	4,000
Somalia	48,000
Sri Lanka	76,000
Sudan	58,500
Suriname	3,500
Swaziland	5,750
Syria	15,000
Tanzania	72,000
Thailand	43,000
Togo	21,750
Tokelau	950
Tonga	2,500
Trinidad and Tobago	5,000
Tunisia	15,000
Turkey	20,000
Turks and Caicos Islands	850
Tuvalu	1,140
Uganda	59,500
United Arab Emirates	1,000
Upper Volta	55,000
Uruguay	10,000
Vanuatu	2,000
Venezuela	10,000
Viet-Nam	118,000
Western Samoa	5,250
Yemen, People's Democratic Rep. of	22,250
Yemen Arab Republic	30,000
Yugoslavia	7,500
Zaire	79,000
Zambia	21,250
Zimbabwe	24,250

Implementation in the Field

UNDP is primarily a financing, overall programming, and monitoring organization. The bulk of the field work it supports is actually carried out by 35 international agencies of the UN development system. These are: the UN itself—DTCD; 13 specialized agencies —FAO, IAEA, ICAO, IFAD, ILO, IMO, ITU, UNESCO, UPU, World Bank, WHO, WIPO, and WMO (plus WTO); the 5 regional economic commissions—ECA, ECE, ECLA, ECWA, and ESCAP, and 4 regional development banks and funds—ADB, AFESD, AsDB, and IDB; and 11 UN-related agencies— HABITAT, UNCTAD, UNCTC, UNDRO, UNEP, UNFDAC, UNFPA, UNHCR, UNICEF, UNIDO, and WFP.

These agencies perform three major functions. They serve as "data banks" of development knowledge and techniques in their respective specialties. They help governments plan the individual sectors in their country programs for UNDP assistance. Finally, as a rule, they recruit the international experts, purchase the equipment, and procure the specialized contract services needed for project execution.

The decision as to which agency will implement any given project is made by UNDP in consultation with the government of the developing country concerned. Though a single agency is always in charge of a particular project, two or more often collaborate in providing the services required.

UNDP itself directly implements a modest number of projects, especially in fields that demand a mix of different competences and a multidisciplinary approach. On an expenditure basis, about 5% of total activities are being executed in this way.

The progress of field work is carefully monitored through periodic reviews, involving UNDP field office staffs, government officials, and experts of the UN implementing agencies. A modern computer-based management information system provides a continuous flow of operational data from the field. When required, special missions are sent to the field to evaluate project work.

Systematic efforts are made to stimulate follow-up investments on surveys, feasibility studies, and other appropriate projects. These activities—which often begin at very early stages of project implementation—involve cooperation with all likely and acceptable sources of finance: internal and external, public and private. By 1983, the cumulative total of follow-up investment exceeded $50 billion.

In a larger sense, however, most projects have a "built-in" follow-up component, because they are deliberately planned to create permanent institutions or facilities whose total operation will be taken over by national personnel. Thus many projects —particularly in training, applied research, and development planning—not only continue but significantly expand their work after UNDP support ends.

In 1982 UNDP was supporting over 4,600 technical and investment support projects in some 150 developing countries and territories. These projects involved a total cost, on completion, of nearly $7 billion, of which over half was being borne through contributions in cash or kind by recipient countries. The $660 million in 1982 field expenditures by UNDP financed the project work of 9,080 experts and technical consultants, provided 8,760 fellowships to developing country nationals for study abroad, and furnished $222 million worth of equipment and services.

Activities supported fell into five basic categories:

1. Locating and assessing development resources—through surveys of land for farming, pasturage, and forestry; of water for irrigation, hydropower, fisheries, and human consumption; of minerals and fuels; and of manufacturing, commercial, export/import, and tourism opportunities.

2. Activating resources—through feasibility studies to identify and define capital needs and to provide the financial and technical data required for productive investment.

3. Improving resource utilization—through education and professional, vocational, and technical training.

4. Expanding and conserving resources—through basic and applied research, the appropriate selection and adaptation of technologies, the fostering of innovative approaches, and the strengthening of domestic technological capabilities.

5. Allocating resources wisely—through comprehensive economic and social planning, regional as well as national, with special emphasis on meeting the needs of the least developed countries and of the poorest segments of society.

Financing

UNDP is financed in two ways. First, the developing countries themselves pay, on the average, more than half the costs of their UNDP-assisted projects. These funds are used for the salaries of local personnel, construction and maintenance of project buildings and facilities, and the purchase of locally available supplies and services. Second, almost every member of the UN and its associated agencies makes a yearly voluntary contribution to the UNDP's central resources. From 1975 to 1982, contributions totaled $5,083 million.

In the period 1977–80, approximately 90% of the voluntary contributions to UNDP came from a group of 15 nonrecipient Western countries. Five countries accounted for more than 55% of the voluntary contributions: the US (18.4%), Sweden (10.5%), the Netherlands (10.4%), the FRG (8.3%), and Denmark (8.3%). During the 1970s, recipient developing countries raised their contributions quite substantially.

A breakdown of all UNDP-supported projects by type of project, economic or social sector, executing agency, and geographic region in which the assistance is concentrated shows the following:

Projects Approved as of September 1982

ESTIMATED COST
(US dollar equivalent)

	NUMBER OF PROJECTS	TOTAL	UNDP	GOVERNMENT COUNTERPART CONTRIBUTION
BY TYPE OF PROJECT				
Country	4,088	6,247,373,403	2,568,921,615	3,678,451,788
Regional	457	576,345,500	369,337,385	207,008,115
Interregional	75	48,220,600	44,873,727	3,346,873
Global	22	92,416,766	91,854,485	562,281
TOTALS	4,642	6,964,356,269	3,074,987,212	3,889,369,057
BY SECTOR				
Agriculture, forestry, and fisheries	900	1,430,504,751	799,376,151	631,128,600
Industry	780	1,177,081,014	357,011,358	820,069,656
Transport and communications	513	1,116,318,869	388,127,939	728,190,930
Natural resources	472	722,435,427	380,563,800	341,871,627
General development issues, policy, and planning	602	609,046,830	367,036,225	242,010,605
Education	275	467,100,376	207,880,012	259,220,364
Employment	253	363,421,582	175,313,711	188,107,871
Science and technology	202	350,014,195	132,417,842	217,596,353
Health	249	305,107,004	137,563,450	167,543,554
Population	6	94,388,734	4,252,833	90,135,901
International trade and development finance	143	89,775,844	65,949,475	23,826,369
Human settlements	84	80,648,966	49,540,418	31,108,548
Social conditions and equity	80	74,684,089	19,125,845	55,558,244
Culture	54	49,620,277	26,029,874	23,590,403
Humanitarian aid and relief	25	33,744,376	8,063,479	25,680,897
Political affairs	4	463,935	462,800	1,135
BY AGENCY				
FAO	888	1,389,345,775	749,648,688	639,697,087
UNIDO	741	1,067,422,749	305,223,517	762,199,232
UN	596	795,312,999	397,117,155	398,195,844
UNESCO	361	570,930,997	251,361,238	319,569,759
ILO	349	570,875,488	241,819,795	329,055,693
ICAO	175	435,622,277	181,913,471	253,708,806
UNDP	342	332,502,824	218,978,994	113,523,830
ITU	141	270,487,860	101,697,806	168,709,054
WHO	202	256,123,936	97,512,766	158,611,170
IBRD	153	254,967,224	150,487,107	104,480,117
IMO	51	211,444,070	34,204,327	177,239,743
IAEA	27	155,604,838	26,521,921	129,082,917
WMO	77	133,318,957	57,273,048	76,045,909
UNCHS	80	117,232,744	58,861,663	58,371,081
UNCTAD	140	89,127,365	69,158,245	19,969,120
AsDB	28	48,467,327	18,873,527	29,593,800
ESCAP	23	35,137,566	18,436,094	16,701,472
ECA	27	32,136,589	30,825,589	1,311,000
UNV	55	20,352,850	17,751,663	2,601,187
ECWA	5	16,938,070	3,798,070	13,140,000
UPU	36	14,623,789	11,974,217	2,649,572
ECE	4	10,706,631	2,482,011	8,244,620
ECLA	7	7,247,821	6,276,979	970,842
AFESD	1	6,900,320	6,900,320	—
WIPO	11	3,477,640	3,277,301	200,339
WTO	8	2,382,663	1,594,026	788,637
UNCTC	11	1,438,617	1,393,980	44,637
BY REGION				
Africa	1,522	2,362,393,653	1,088,738,900	1,273,654,753
Asia and the Pacific	1,490	1,949,530,229	1,106,988,735	842,541,494
Europe	514	1,265,138,876	294,190,709	970,948,167
Arab states	724	689,814,617	360,492,366	329,322,251
Latin America	295	556,841,528	87,848,290	468,993,238
Interregional	75	48,220,600	44,873,727	3,346,873
Global	22	92,416,766	91,854,485	562,281

Associated Programs

The UNDP administrator is also responsible for several associated programs, including the following:

UN Capital Development Fund (UNCDF), established in 1966, provides limited amounts of "seed financing" for such social infrastructure as low-cost housing, water supply in drought areas, rural schools, and hospitals—and for such "grass-roots" productive facilities as agricultural workshops, cottage-industry centers, and cooperatives and credit unions. The least developed countries, and others in similar need, receive their assistance on grant terms. As of May 1983, 36 countries had contributed a total of $16.8 million to UNCDF resources.

Revolving Fund for Natural Resources Exploration, created by the General Assembly in 1974, helps underwrite searches for economically useful mineral deposits which developing countries could not otherwise carry out because of the high risk factor involved. Repayment is required only when new minerals are actually produced. Activities were under way in 1982 in more than 20 countries, when the fund's capitalization stood at $5.4 million.

UN Volunteers (UNV), activated in 1970, provides a channel for qualified private citizens, particularly young people, to become directly involved in development. Since the beginning of the UNV program, nearly 1,200 volunteers have served in less-developed countries. At the end of 1982, 500 UN volunteers were assigned in these countries. Most of these volunteers work on UNDP-assisted projects—as agriculturalists, foresters, veterinarians, engineers, mechanics, economists, architects, teachers and teacher-trainers, nurses, and sociologists. It is estimated that the kind of expertise provided by UN volunteers might double during the 1980s to 2,000 a year.

Other UNDP affiliates include UNFPA, described later in this chapter, and UNSO, described in the chapter on Social and Humanitarian Assistance.

UN CONFERENCE ON TRADE AND DEVELOPMENT (UNCTAD)

The need for a permanent UN body to deal with trade in relation to development was one of the major recommendations made by the first UN Conference on Trade and Development (UNCTAD), which met in Geneva in the spring of 1964. Later that year, the General Assembly, noting that international trade was an important instrument for economic development and that there was a widespread desire among developing countries for a comprehensive trade organization, decided to establish UNCTAD as one of its permanent organs.

The main purposes of UNCTAD are to promote international trade with a view to accelerating economic development; to formulate principles and policies on international trade; to initiate action for the adoption of multilateral trade agreements; and to act as a center for harmonizing trade and development policies of governments and regional economic groups.

Since the initial session of the Conference in Geneva in 1964, five sessions have been held, usually at four-year intervals—at New Delhi (1968), Santiago (1972), Nairobi (1976), Manila (1979), and Belgrade (1983).

To carry out the functions of the conference between sessions, the Assembly established a 55-member Trade and Development Board (expanded in 1976 to include all UNCTAD members) to implement conference decisions and to make or initiate studies and reports on trade and related development problems. The board, which reports annually to the General Assembly through ECOSOC, serves also as the preparatory body for sessions of the conference.

The trade and development board has seven committees: on commodities; manufactures; invisibles and financing related to trade; shipping; preferences; transfer of technology; and economic cooperation among developing countries. Other subsidiary bodies include special committees and intergovernmental groups.

The UNCTAD secretariat, located at Geneva, services the conference, the board, and its subsidiary bodies. It is headed by a secretary-general who is appointed by the UN secretary-general and confirmed by the General Assembly.

Export promotion and marketing are the responsibility of the International Trade Center, which is operated jointly by UNCTAD and GATT. The center focuses attention on export-market opportunities and helps developing countries to train personnel in marketing and export-promotion techniques and to set up the institutions and training programs necessary to build up modern export-promotion services.

A major achievement of the Nairobi session of UNCTAD in 1976 was the adoption of an Integrated Program for Commodities, aimed at setting remunerative and just prices for the primary commodities of developing countries that would take account of world inflation, monetary changes, and the cost of manufactured imports. As part of the program, the Nairobi session agreed that steps would be taken for the negotiation of a common fund for the financing of buffer stocks which would be held or sold as conditions required, thus helping to end the wide fluctuation in commodity prices that has plagued developing countries dependent on their commodity exports.

In 1980, the Agreement Establishing the Common Fund for Commodities was adopted by the UN Negotiating Conference on a Common Fund. International agreements have also been concluded for seven commodities—cocoa, coffee, tin, olive oil, sugar, natural rubber, and wheat.

Other multilateral agreements in the field of international trade negotiated by UNCTAD include (1) the Convention on a Code of Conduct for Liner Conferences (1974), which establishes rules concerning the operation of liner shipping, in particular as regards the loading rights of national shipping lines in respect of liner cargoes generated by their countries' foreign trade; (2) the Set of Multilaterally Agreed Equitable Principles and Rules for the Control of Restrictive Business Practices (1980), which establishes, for the first time, international means for the control of restrictive business practices, including those of transnational corporations, adversely affecting international trade, in particular the trade and economic development of developing countries; and (3) the UN Convention on International Multimodal Transport of Goods (1980), which establishes an international legal regime for the contract for the international multimodal transport of goods.

Negotiations have been in progress since 1978 on an International Code of Conduct on the Transfer of Technology. The provisions of the proposed code fall into two broad groups: those concerning the regulation of the transfer of technology transactions and of the conduct of parties to them; and those relating to steps to be taken by governments to meet their commitments to the code.

At the sixth session of UNCTAD, held in Belgrade in June 1983, with more than 3,000 delegates from 164 countries attending, the developing countries called for an "immediate-action program" designed to pump an additional $70 billion into the poorer countries over a two-year period, and for measures to stabilize raw material prices, including a rollback of protectionist trade measures under UNCTAD supervision, foreign debt relief through postponement of debt payments, and more aid for developing countries, in particular through a new $30 billion issue of IMF special drawing rights. Without such assistance, the developing countries insisted that the economic recovery under way in the industrialized countries would peter out because the developing countries would not have the means to sustain their imports from those countries.

At its conclusion, however, the conference did not impose any specific new obligations on the industrialized countries, but called on them to redouble their efforts to achieve by 1985 the UN aid target to developing countries and to respond "in a positive manner" to requests from individual poor countries for debt relief. It also called for early ratification of the agreement establishing the Common Fund for Commodities, and decided to establish a group to study financing of shortages in earnings from commodity exports.

UN INDUSTRIAL DEVELOPMENT ORGANIZATION (UNIDO)

The UN Industrial Development Organization (UNIDO) was established as an organ of the General Assembly in January 1967 to promote industrial development and help accelerate the industrialization of developing countries. UNIDO was also assigned the task of coordinating all activities of the UN system in this field. Its policy is formulated by an Industrial Development Board, which is made up of 45 countries elected by the Assembly on the basis of equitable geographical distribution. An executive director heads UNIDO's secretariat. Headquarters are in Vienna.

In 1971, at the first international conference of UNIDO, held in Vienna, 108 member countries examined the organization's program and made recommendations on finances and the future development of its activities. The second general conference of UNIDO met in Lima in March 1975 and approved a declaration and a plan of action setting the goal that the share of developing countries in world industrial production should be increased from 7% to 25% by the year 2000. The conference also proposed the conversion of UNIDO into a UN specialized agency and the establishment of an industrial development fund.

The seventh special session of the General Assembly, held in September 1975, endorsed the Lima declaration and plan of action. It decided that a system of consultations should be established at global, regional, interregional, and sectoral levels within UNIDO and other appropriate international bodies. By these means, UNIDO was to serve as a forum for negotiation in the field of industry between developing and developed countries and among developing countries, at the request of the countries concerned.

In 1976 the General Assembly decided to establish the UN Industrial Development Fund (UNIDF) to enable UNIDO to meet more promptly and flexibly the needs of developing countries. The industrial development board recommended a desirable funding level of $50 million annually.

The constitution for UNIDO as a specialized agency was adopted by consensus in 1979. By July 1983, 132 states had signed and 102 had ratified the constitution.

The third general conference of UNIDO, held in New Delhi in January-February 1980, adopted a declaration and a plan of action outlining measures to promote industrial development. The plan of action called for transformation of the system of consultations into negotiations that would seek "definite commitments" on the redeployment of industry to the developing countries; disaggregation of the Lima target into midterm, sectoral and regional targets; and establishment of an intergovernmental committee within UNIDO to consider "ways and means of increasing the share of developing countries in world trade in industrial products to the target of 30% by the year 2000" and to set targets for increasing the trade of developing countries in industrial products. The plan of action also outlined measures for cooperation among developing countries and assistance by developed countries in regard to promotion of training, transfer of technology, industrial production, development of energy resources, and special measures for least-developed countries.

UNIDO provides assistance to developing countries wishing to formulate industrial policies, establish new industries, or improve existing ones. In 1982 more than 1,500 projects in some 1~ countries were being carried out under UNIDO auspices. UNIDO also cooperates in a number of projects for which other organizations of the UN system have the principal responsibility.

By the end of 1982, nearly $635 million had been expended on UNIDO projects since the start of its activities. UNIDO receives funds from a variety of sources, including the UN regular budget, UNDP, UNIDF, several trust funds, and contributions from recipient countries in the form of land, buildings, services, staff, or cash. By far the largest share of UNIDO's field activities, some 70% of the total, is financed by UNDP.

Operational activities of UNIDO include the Special Industrial Services (SIS) program, which is designed to supplement other assistance by helping to solve urgent industrial problems at short notice and on flexible terms. During 1982 some 200 requests for assistance of this type were received from 95 countries. Technical cooperation activities during the year covered the fields of agro-metallurgical, engineering, and chemical industries, as well as industrial planning, development of institutional infrastructure, establishment and management of factories, industrial training, feasibility studies, program formulation and direction, development and transfer of technology, and advisory services in technology.

UNIDO supports its operational activities by a program of studies and research. It conducts symposia, seminars, and training programs dealing with specific industries and industrial techniques. In addition, it helps to stimulate the flow of foreign resources to industries in the developing countries by sponsoring meetings at which representatives of countries wishing to promote specific industrial projects can meet potential investors and suppliers of financial and technical resources.

WORLD FOOD COUNCIL (WFC)

The world food situation in the early 1970s was marked by extreme food shortages in many developing countries in Africa and parts of Southeast Asia, by a general lack of progress in the world fight against hunger and malnutrition, and by very slow progress in the creation of a system of internationally coordinated cereal reserves to meet crop shortfalls and other abnormal situations.

It was against this background that the nonaligned countries meeting in Algeria in September 1973 called for the convening of a conference to deal with global food problems. The General Assembly acted on the proposal in December of that year, and the World Food Conference was held in Rome in November 1974. One of the recommendations of the conference called for the creation of a 36-member ministerial-level World Food Council (WFC) to review annually major problems and policy issues affecting the world food situation and to bring its political influence to bear on governments and UN bodies and agencies alike.

The WFC's approach to solving world food problems and eliminating hunger is to encourage the adoption—by developing countries where most of the world's one billion hungry people live—of

national food strategies. Under this plan, each country assesses its present food situation—needs, supply, potential for increased production, storage, processing, transport, distribution, marketing, research, training and manpower, and the ability to meet food emergencies. It then works out a plan to improve its food situation so that enough food of sufficient nutritional value reaches all the people of the country. The aim of the food strategies is to build a greater degree of food self-reliance in the countries where the need is greatest and to assure that the peoples' consumption needs are met.

Some 30 countries, with a total population exceeding 500 million, have decided to adopt food strategies, and most have requested assistance from WFC for their preparation. Official development assistance from donor countries needed to support the food strategies and programs of developing countries in the period 1982–87 has been estimated at $8–12 billion a year.

In addition to its efforts to increase food production in developing countries, WFC seeks to promote an effective system of world food security through more open trade and assurances of continuity of food supplies for developing countries, as well as reserve programs in support of greater food self-sufficiency.

Other UN programs concerned with food aid include the World Food Program (which the UN sponsors jointly with FAO), and the IFAD.

UN FUND FOR POPULATION ACTIVITIES (UNFPA)

The UN has been concerned with population questions since its earliest years, establishing the Population Commission in 1947 as one of the functional commissions of ECOSOC. The early work of the UN on population questions concentrated on the improvement of demographic statistics, which were lacking for large parts of the world, and then began to focus on the application of statistical data in analytical studies and in the preparation of worldwide population estimates and projections. The first *Demographic Yearbook* was published by the UN Statistical Office in 1948.

In the 1960s, however, the extraordinarily rapid rate at which the world's population was growing became an urgent concern (between 1950 and 1960, world population increased from 2.5 billion to over 3 billion, and it was projected to more than double by the year 2000). In a resolution adopted in 1966, the General Assembly authorized the UN to provide technical assistance in population matters, and the following year the Assembly established a Trust Fund for Population Activities, renamed in 1969 the UN Fund for Population Activities (UNFPA), to provide additional resources to the UN system for technical cooperation activities in the population field. In 1972 the fund was placed under the authority of the General Assembly, which designated the governing council of UNDP as its governing body.

The World Population Conference, held in Bucharest in 1974, adopted a world population plan of action which stressed the relationship between population factors and overall economic and social development. The General Assembly affirmed that the plan was "an instrument of the international community for the promotion of economic development," and urged that assistance in the population field should be expanded, particularly to UNFPA, for the proper implementation of the plan.

To enable UNFPA to respond quickly and effectively to the most urgent needs, a "core program" of activities was established, setting out the main areas of UNFPA involvement in development assistance. At the same time, it was agreed that high priority should be given to countries especially in need of population assistance, taking into account the demographic situation, major population problems, and approaches to dealing with them. Using per capita income and certain demographic criteria, UNFPA determined those "priority countries" most in need of population assistance. At the end of 1982, 53 countries were given priority status—30 in Africa, 16 in Asia and the Pacific,

5 in the Middle East and Mediterranean, and 2 in Latin America and the Caribbean. Of the total resources allocated to country programs, 69% went to these 53 countries.

UNFPA's role is to build up the capacity to respond to needs in population and family planning, promote understanding of population factors (population growth, fertility, mortality, spatial distribution, and migration), assist governments to develop population goals and programs, and provide financial assistance to implement them.

UNFPA works in eight main areas: (1) family planning, including delivery systems, program management, and fertility-regulation techniques; (2) communication and education, including communication for family-planning motivation, population education in schools, and out-of-school programs; (3) basic data collection, including population censuses, vital statistics registration, and surveys; (4) population dynamics, including analyses of demographic data, the determinants and consequences of population trends, and the interaction of demographic and socio-economic variables; (5) formulation of population policies and programs, including evaluation of policies, and integration of demographic factors into social and economic plans; (6) implementation of policies and programs, including "beyond family planning" programs and programs to influence demographic trends; (7) special programs for women, children and youth, the aged, the poorest of the poor, the handicapped; and (8) multisector activities, including population conferences, documentation centers, clearinghouses, and interdisciplinary training.

UNFA is now the largest internationally funded source of assistance to population programs in developing countries. Virtually all of UNFPA's resources come from governments, the majority of which make annual pledges. In 1982, income totaled $130.9 million from 89 donor countries.

At year's end, UNFPA was assisting 1,659 projects, including 1,257 country projects and 170 regional projects. UNFPA itself executes almost one-third of its projects; other executing agencies are the UN, UNICEF, UNESCO, ILO, WHO, and FAO. The major portion of UNFPA's funds are allocated to family-planning projects.

In 1981, the General Assembly established a UN Population Award to be presented annually to an individual or individuals, or to an institution, for the most outstanding contribution to the awareness of population questions or to their solution. The winners of the first UN Population Award, announced in March 1983 by a committee set up for the purpose, were Indira Gandhi, prime minister of India, and Qian Xinzhong, minister in charge of the State Family Planning Commission of the People's Republic of China.

UN ENVIRONMENT PROGRAM (UNEP)

In the course of the twentieth century, and especially after World War II, the increase in the earth's population and the advance of technology, with concomitant changes in patterns of production and consumption, led to pressure on the environment and threats to its stability that were new in human history. For a long time, the implications of these phenomena were largely ignored. In the decade of the 1960s, however, problems such as soil erosion, air, water, and marine pollution, the need for conservation of limited resources, and desiccation of once-fertile zones became acute enough to awaken the consciousness of governments and people in all parts of the world, but especially in the industrialized countries, to the urgency of the situation. The UN responded with the decision of the 1968 General Assembly to convoke a world conference on the human environment.

The first UN Conference on the Human Environment was held in Stockholm in June 1972. The conference was a focus for, rather than the start of, action on environmental problems. At its conclusion, the participants, representing over 90% of the world's population, adopted a declaration and a 109-point action plan

for the human environment which became the blueprint for a wide range of subsequent national and international programs. The broad intent of the action plan was to define and mobilize "common effort for the preservation and improvement of the human environment." The preamble to the declaration conveys the urgency, magnitude, and complexity of that task.

Later in 1972, on the basis of the conference's recommendations, the General Assembly created the UN Environment Program (UNEP), with headquarters in Nairobi, to monitor significant changes in the environment and to encourage and coordinate sound environmental practices. UNEP is the first global UN agency to be headquarted in a developing country.

The UNEP secretariat is headed by an executive director. Its Governing Council, composed of 58 states elected by the General Assembly for staggered three-year terms on the basis of equitable geographic representation, meets annually. The council's functions and responsibilities include: promoting international cooperation in the field of environment and recommending policies to that end; providing general policy guidance for environmental programs within the UN system; keeping the world environmental situation under review so as to ensure that emerging problems requiring international assistance receive adequate consideration by governments; promoting the contribution by international scientific and other professional communities to knowledge about the environment and the technical aspects of UN environmental programs; keeping under review the impact of national and international development policies; and reviewing and approving the utilization of the resources of the Environment Fund.

UNEP's key programs include "Earthwatch," an international surveillance network which is carried out by three services: the Global Environmental Monitoring System (GEMS); the International Register of Potentially Toxic Chemicals (IRPTC); and the International Referral System (INFOTERRA). Other major programs include implementation, in the Sudano-Sahelian region of Africa, of the plan of action to combat the spread of deserts adopted by the 1977 UN Conference on Desertification. The plan comprises integrated national and international programs of land reclamation and management.

UNEP's efforts against marine pollution, begun with a pilot program in the Mediterranean, now also include programs to combat marine pollution in the Kuwait region, the Red Sea and the Gulf of Aden, the wider Caribbean, east, west, and central Africa, the east Asian seas, and the southern Pacific.

In the field of environmental law, UNEP's activities include the development of guidelines or principles regarding the harmonious utilization by states of shared natural resources, offshore mining and drilling, and the preparation of an international convention on the ozone layer and of regional conventions for the protection of the marine environment and related technical protocols.

In the field of energy, UNEP has supported pilot projects designed to produce energy from the sun and wind and from household and agricultural wastes.

UNEP's voluntary Environment Fund has financed over 600 projects concerned with marine pollution, soil degradation and desertification, the ecology of rural and urban settlements, the environmental impact of alternate energy sources, and similar questions. Its expenditures on projects for the 1984–85 biennium were estimated at $70 million. Slightly more than half of UNEP's activities are carried out in cooperation with other UN agencies, the remainder with organizations and individuals outside the UN system.

In May 1982, at a special session of the UNEP governing council held in Nairobi, over 100 governments reviewed the environmental achievements and shortcomings of the international community since the 1972 Stockholm conference and charted the main lines of action for UNEP in the 1980s.

UN CENTER FOR HUMAN SETTLEMENTS (HABITAT)

UN concern with the problems of human settlements, particularly with the deteriorating quality of living conditions in developing countries and the need to link urban and regional development programs with national development plans, led to the convening of the first international conference on the question in Vancouver, British Columbia, in May–June 1976. The declaration and plan of action adopted by Habitat: UN Conference on Human Settlements represented an important commitment on the part of governments and the international community to improve the quality of life for all people through human settlements development. The plan of action contained 64 recommendations for national action concerning settlement policies, settlement planning, provision of shelter, infrastructure and services, land use and land tenure, the role of popular participation, and effective institutions and management.

The conference also recommended the strengthening and consolidation of UN activities in a single organization concerned exclusively with human settlements. Acting on this recommendation, the General Assembly in 1978 established the UN Center for Human Settlements (Habitat), with headquarters in Nairobi, to serve as a focal point for human settlements action and to coordinate human settlements activities within the UN system.

The center's work program, based on the Vancouver plan of action, includes provision of technical assistance to government programs, organization of expert meetings, workshops, and training seminars, publication of technical documents, and dissemination of information through the establishment of a global information network. Technical cooperation projects in all developing regions of the world cover such fields as national settlement policies and programs, urban and regional planning, rural and urban housing and infrastructure development, slum upgrading and sites-and-services schemes, low-cost building technology, technologies for urban and rural water supply and sanitation systems, and the establishment and strengthening of government institutions concerned with human settlements.

In 1982, the General Assembly proclaimed 1987 as the International Year of Shelter for the Homeless and decided that the objectives of the year would be to improve the shelter situation of the poor and disadvantaged at both individual and community levels, particularly in developing countries, both before and during 1987, and to demonstrate means of continuing those efforts as ongoing national programs beyond 1987.

UN INSTITUTE FOR TRAINING AND RESEARCH (UNITAR)

In 1963 the General Assembly requested the secretary-general to establish a UN Institute for Training and Research as an autonomous body within the framework of the UN. UNITAR commenced functioning in March 1965. It is headed by an executive director and has its own board of trustees. UNITAR has its headquarters in New York and a European office in Geneva.

The mandate of UNITAR is to enhance the effectiveness of the UN in attaining its major objectives—particularly the maintenance of peace and the promotion of economic and social development—through training and research. The UN calls upon the institute to provide training, especially to individuals from developing countries, for assignments within the UN system or in the national services connected with the work of the system or the work of other institutions with related concerns.

UNITAR conducts a program of seminars and short courses for member states' new delegates and officers of their permanent missions to the UN. The program emphasizes the mechanics of conference diplomacy and negotiating procedures in the General Assembly and other UN organs.

The institute's research program studies problems of immediate concern to the international community and the UN. These include studies on peaceful settlement of disputes; decolonization; coordination within the UN system; relations between the UN and intergovernmental organizations; cooperation between different social systems; the situation of women in the UN; international youth organizations and the UN; and the "brain drain."

UNITAR's "Project on the Future," a continuous program, launched in 1975, includes work on devising a global model of economic development, a series of studies on alternative development strategies and the future of Asia and Africa, and studies on the supply aspects of energy and natural resources. A series of conferences on different aspects of energy supplies have been held since 1976. More recently, studies on the impact of energy on the global world economy have been undertaken as part of a continuing examination of North-South trade and development.

UNITAR is supported by voluntary contributions from governments and, in much smaller measure, from foundations and individuals. In 1982 its income was $2.5 million from 41 countries.

UN UNIVERSITY (UNU)

In 1969 U Thant, then secretary-general, proposed that a UN university be established. The Founding Committee was set up two years later, and in December 1973 the General Assembly approved a charter for the UN University (UNU). The following spring the UNU Council, composed of 24 academic leaders plus prominent persons from 24 countries, was appointed. Members of the university council serve in their individual capacities rather than as representatives of governments. UNU commenced operations in September 1975. Its headquarters are in Tokyo, with a liaison office in New York.

UNU is an autonomous organ of the General Assembly. It is jointly sponsored by the UN and UNESCO, whose secretary-general and director-general together appoint the rector and members of the university council. Its charter guarantees academic freedom and emphasizes the primacy of scholarly excellence over any other considerations—for example, choices of programs and personnel—in determining its activities.

Like traditional universities, UNU is concerned with the advancement of knowledge. Unlike traditional universities, however, it has no students of its own, no faculty, no campus. It is a completely new institution: an international community of scholars engaged in research, postgraduate training, and the dissemination of knowledge to help solve, in the words of its charter, "pressing global problems of human survival, development and welfare." It operates through worldwide networks of academic and research institutions and individual scholars who work together on projects concerned with such problems as peace; food, nutrition, and poverty; energy systems and policy; and resources policy and management.

UNU is supported by voluntary contributions from governments, foundations, and individuals. Its principal source of support is an endowment fund which assures academic freedom by providing financial independence. The endowment required was set at about $500 million, of which Japan pledged $100 million.

UN RESEARCH INSTITUTE FOR SOCIAL DEVELOPMENT (UNRISD)

Created in 1963 as an autonomous UN organ, the UN Research Institute for Social Development (UNRISD) conducts research into problems and policies of social development, based on two themes: improving the livelihood of the world's poor and increasing their participation in development. The institute's research programs, usually carried out in collaboration with national research institutions, include studies of food systems and society; the impact of socioeconomic changes on women; the social effects of developmental and environmental measures; and the social and economic implications of the large-scale introduction of new varieties of food grain (the "green revolution").

The institute, which has its headquarters in Geneva, is financed entirely by voluntary contributions.

SOCIAL AND HUMANITARIAN ASSISTANCE

UN CHILDREN'S FUND (UNICEF)

The UN International Children's Emergency Fund (UNICEF) was established by the General Assembly on 11 December 1946 to provide emergency relief assistance in the form of food, drugs, and clothing to the children of postwar Europe and China. In December 1950, the Assembly extended the life of the fund for three years, changing its mandate to emphasize health and nutrition programs of long-range benefit to children of developing countries. In October 1953, the Assembly decided to continue the fund indefinitely; its name was changed to the UN Children's Fund, although the acronym "UNICEF" was retained.

Following the global study of the needs of children in 1961, UNICEF increased the scope and flexibility of its approach to children to include projects that promote the role of children as an invaluable "human resource" in national development, thus making it possible to provide aid for education.

UNICEF was awarded the Nobel Peace Prize in 1965.

Purposes and Scope of Work

Combining humanitarian and development objectives, UNICEF's primary goal is to help children of the poorest and least-developed countries. It helps them directly, by supporting government programs to improve child health, nutrition, education, and social services, and indirectly, by serving as child advocate, appealing to governments and to the consciences of individuals worldwide to find and commit the resources required to protect and prepare children adequately.

UNICEF's mandate from the General Assembly's 1946 resolution for "strengthening . . . the permanent child health and welfare programs of the countries receiving assistance" has been developed and continuously adapted to current conditions. UNICEF advocates special attention to the needs of children within international and national development strategies, and promotes humanitarian as well as developmental objectives. As an intermediate-size organization with a highly decentralized structure, UNICEF plays the role of catalyst in focusing attention on needs and priorities of children, especially in low-income communities. It places strong emphasis on community participation in the development and operation of services for children and has increasingly focused on community-based action. As a funding agency—as distinct from a specialized agency—UNICEF is able to work with various ministries and nongovernmental organizations, maintaining an intersectoral approach to community action in meeting the needs of children.

In 1976, UNICEF adopted an approach to the provision of basic health and welfare services, the key element of which was community participation. This resulted from experiences in a number of economically and politically diverse developing countries showing that services are likely to be not only cheaper but more effective when community members are involved, because they mobilize hitherto unused abilities within the community and they can be run at recurrent costs that the country and community can afford. Integration of women into the establishment of community-based services is especially important, as their participation can have a significant impact on the quality of life for their children.

UNICEF gives priority to cooperation with the least-developed countries and the establishment of long-term programs, places special emphasis on the use of national expertise wherever feasible, and encourages innovative approaches to the problems of children.

UNICEF cooperates with developing countries in several ways: it assists in the planning and extension of services benefiting children and in the exchange of experience between countries; it provides funds to strengthen the training and orientation of national personnel, complementing, wherever possible, the work of specialized agencies; and it delivers technical supplies, equipment, and other aid for extending services. The specialized agencies collaborate with UNICEF from time to time in preparing joint reports on particular program areas. In particular, there is a UNICEF/WHO Joint Committee on Health Policy which advises on policies of cooperation in health programs and undertakes periodic reviews.

Organization

UNICEF is an integral part of the UN, with semiautonomous status provided by a 41-nation Executive Board elected by ECOSOC. The board meets annually to review the work of UNICEF, determine policy, consider requests, and commit funds for program cooperation and for administrative and program support costs. The executive director of UNICEF is appointed by the secretary-general in consultation with the executive board and is responsible for the execution of programs and policies, as well as for the appointment and direction of UNICEF staff.

UNICEF field offices are its key operational units. In 1983 UNICEF maintained 87 field offices serving 115 countries, with over 1,800 staff members. UNICEF's headquarters are in New York. Geneva is the headquarters for its network of 33 national committees around the world, and Copenhagen is the administrative headquarters of its supply operation.

Cooperation with Other Agencies

UNICEF collaborates closely with the specialized agencies, including the ILO, FAO, UNESCO, and WHO, as well as with the units of the UN Secretariat having technical competence relevant to services benefiting children. It has working relationships with the funding agencies of the UN system—such as the UNDP, UNFPA, WFP, World Bank, IFAD, and UNCDF—to exchange information, discuss policies of cooperation affecting the situation of children, and explore potential program collaboration. Some cooperative relations are also developing with UNEP, and working relations are maintained with UNDRO and with UNHCR in emergency relief and aid to refugees, respectively. UNICEF also works with regional development banks and the regional economic and social commissions and with bilateral aid agencies.

Of particular importance is UNICEF's cooperation and collaboration in programs with nongovernmental organizations, both national and international. The NGO Committee on UNICEF comprises 134 international professional and voluntary groups involved either directly with children or indirectly through concern with aspects of social development. A roster of international and national correspondent organizations is growing, particularly from developing countries. In all, some 400 organizations participate in activities and share information through UNICEF/NGO liaison offices in New York and Geneva. Many of these organizations have become important supporters of UNICEF by providing a channel for advocacy on behalf of children and by participating in fund-raising. In certain situations, NGOs are designated by governments to carry out part of the program with which UNICEF is cooperating.

The 33 national committees for UNICEF, primarily in industrialized countries, help generate a better understanding of the needs of children in developing countries and of the work of UNICEF. The committees are concerned with increasing financial support, either indirectly through advocacy, education, and information, or directly through the sale of greeting cards and other fundraising activities. The long-standing "trick or treat" Halloween program in the US and Canada provides one example of such activities.

Financing

UNICEF's work is accomplished with voluntary contributions both from governments and from nongovernmental sources. Total income in 1982 was $378 million. Of this total, almost 80% ($298 million) came from 134 governments, including those of most countries where UNICEF is cooperating in development programs, and from intergovernmental organizations; private sources raised 16% ($62 million) through fund-raising campaigns, greeting-card sales, and individual donations; and a further 4–5% came from the UN ($8 million) and miscellaneous sources ($10 million).

GOVERNMENT CONTRIBUTIONS TO UNICEF
AMOUNTING TO $1 MILLION OR MORE IN 1982

COUNTRY	CONTRIBUTION
US	$41,481,300
Sweden	20,958,000
Italy	17,475,700
Norway	14,642,800
UK	10,280,100
Canada	9,799,400
Netherlands	8,423,800
Japan	8,219,800
Denmark	5,207,400
FRG	4,936,200
Switzerland	3,791,200
Australia	3,672,600
Finland	2,278,800
India	1,748,600
France	1,740,600
Sa'udi Arabia	1,000,000

UNICEF's income is divided between contributions for general resources and contributions for specific purposes. General resources are the funds available to fulfill commitments for cooperation in country programs approved by the executive board and to meet administrative and program support expenditures. These funds in 1982 totaled $243 million. Contributions for specific purposes are those sought by UNICEF from governments and intergovernmental organizations as supplementary funds to support projects for which general resources are insufficient, or for relief and rehabilitation programs in emergency situations. Supplementary fundings in 1982, including $41 million for Lebanon relief operations, totaled $135 million. In addition to income, UNICEF received $7 million of donations-in-kind and $19 million in funds-in-trust (mainly for reimbursable procurement of goods and services) in 1982.

In 1983, the executive board approved in principle new or extended multiyear support totaling $245.5 million for programs affecting children and women in 54 of the 115 countries in which UNICEF now operates, and for several regional and interregional projects. Of that amount, $109.4 million was to be financed from general resources and $136.1 million from specific-purpose contributions.

UNICEF cooperates in a program on the basis of a government request and in accordance with a "plan of operations" which sets down working arrangements to be undertaken by the government ministries concerned. After review, these requests are submitted to the annual session of the executive board for funding approval.

MAIN TYPES OF UNICEF-ASSISTED PROJECTS

The major fields of UNICEF cooperation, as the table on the left shows, are: child health, including the extension of maternal and child health services, mainly at the local level and within the framework of primary health care; water supply for drinking and household use, and environmental sanitation; child and maternal nutrition; social welfare services; primary and nonformal education; and emergency relief and rehabilitation.

Primary Health Care

Since 1975, working with WHO, UNICEF has promoted primary health care (PHC) services in the developing countries as a means of extending health-service coverage nationwide. PHC uses health workers chosen by the community for curative, preventive, and promotional tasks. Properly trained, supported, and supervised, such health workers are able to diagnose and treat four-fifths of children's ailments.

Oral Rehydration Therapy. Prevention of diarrhea, which causes 5 million deaths a year from dehydration and is the greatest single cause of death among the developing world's children, has long been a WHO/UNICEF priority. Prevention is largely a matter of public health measures—clean water, better sanitation, and health education—programs which UNICEF supports widely but the results of which are not quickly realized. Oral rehydration therapy offers a simple, low-cost method of treating dehydration. Some 49 countries have now embarked on national diarrheal disease control programs. In 1982 UNICEF supplied 15 million sachets of oral rehydration salts and supported local production of another 20 million sachets. Equally important are home remedies using boiled water and a little salt and sugar; these, however, depend on adequate instruction for mothers on preparation of the treatment.

Immunization. Measles, diphtheria, tetanus, whooping cough, poliomyelitis, and tuberculosis kill an estimated 5 million children a year in the developing world and contribute significantly to the incidence and severity of childhood disabilities. UNICEF has been associated with WHO's Expanded Program of Immunization (EPI) for a number of years and is the main supplier of vaccines to some 80 countries in Asia, Africa, and the Middle East. UNICEF also provides "cold chain" equipment—refrigerators, cold boxes, transport—to enable vaccines to be kept active up to the moment of use. UNICEF participated in national EPI evaluations in eight countries in 1981 and 1982 and has been helping countries tackle organizational problems by support to workshops. By the end of 1981, more than 4,500 national and international personnel had participated in intensive EPI-related courses. UNICEF is also supporting mass mobilization drives to strengthen child vaccination in several countries.

Breast-feeding. The advantages of breast-feeding are associated with improved nutrition and hygiene. Bottle-feeding is especially hazardous in poor communities where it is impossible for mothers to properly sterilize the bottles and unlikely that they will correctly dilute the commercial formula. In recent years, the immunological properties of breast milk have been more widely appreciated.

The decline in breast-feeding in many developing countries has caused considerable alarm, and UNICEF is giving its fullest moral and material support to the campaign to halt and reverse this trend. In 1982, 24 countries with which UNICEF cooperates reported activities for the promotion of breast-feeding, and 16 countries reported information, education, and training activities in support of breast-feeding.

Growth Charts. UNICEF advocates the mass use of simple cardboard child-growth charts which mothers can keep in their homes as a stimulus and guide to proper child feeding. Such usage could have the effect of substantially reducing child malnutrition. Consistent undernutrition, successive infections, and bouts of diarrheal disease can hold back a child's growth over weeks and months in a way that may pass unnoticed by the mother but will be clearly visible from a properly kept chart.

In 1982, UNICEF cooperated in child-health programs in 107 countries (46 in Africa, 30 in Asia, 23 in the Americas, and 8 in the Middle East region); provided grants for training, orientation, and refresher courses for 69,000 health workers (doctors, nurses, public health workers, medical assistants, midwives, and traditional birth attendants); provided technical supplies and equipment for 44,800 health centers of various kinds, especially rural health centers and subcenters; and supplied medicines and vaccines against tuberculosis, diphtheria, tetanus, typhoid, measles, polio, and other diseases.

feeding in the first months of life; the treatment of diarrheal diseases by oral rehydration; and the extension of immunization programs.

Support in the field of nutrition is also given for community-based day care for young children and for more appropriate household technology designed to reduce women's domestic burden and improve family food production and conservation. Food and nutrition surveys have been supported in a number of countries. Nutrition education and training for mothers and community workers continues to be a prominent feature of many health and nutrition-related programs. UNICEF has also expanded its support for nutritional monitoring and surveillance. Cooperation in campaigns against specific problems resulting from nutritional

SUMMARY OF EXPENDITURES IN 1982
(in thousands of US dollars)

	AFRICA	AMERICAS	ASIA	EASTERN MEDITERRANEAN	EUROPE AND INTERREGIONAL	TOTAL	PERCENT
Child health	17,808	1,471	25,283	5,360	1,031	50,953	23.9
Water supply/sanitation	14,565	1,011	33,497	10,979	23	60,075	28.2
Child nutrition	2,621	1,250	14,745	227	170	19,013	8.9
Social welfare services	2,834	2,702	8,960	1,118	33	15,647	7.4
Primary education	6,235	392	8,921	5,002	10	20,560	9.7
Nonformal education	3,659	761	3,597	255	299	8,571	4.0
Emergency relief	2,667	94	8,024	5,371	107	16,263	7.6
General	5,809	3,440	7,751	2,670	2,344	22,014	10.3
SUBTOTAL	56,198	11,121	110,778	30,982	4,017	213,096	100.0
Program support services						39,551	
TOTAL ASSISTANCE						252,647	
Administrative services						36,752	
TOTAL EXPENDITURE						289,399	

Clean Water and Sanitation

Waterborne and water-related diseases are said to be responsible for 80% of the health problems of infants and children in the developing countries, and lack of adequate water supply and sanitation is a major cause of the high infant and child mortality in the spreading slums, shantytowns, and infested tenements of the developing world. For these reasons, water and sanitation projects are a part of UNICEF-assisted programs in 45 urban communities. In planning these efforts, care is taken to include education in personal cleanliness and food hygiene, as well as to locate water points close to bath and laundry facilities.

Since water supply and sanitation projects cannot be effective in isolation from other programs, an important trend in 1982 was to integrate them into health programs and other basic services. To minimize problems with operation, maintenance, and the replacement of parts, emphasis was on the installation of simple, low-cost water supply and excreta-disposal systems and on the training of village pump operators and caretakers, sanitation and health promoters, and well diggers and drillers.

In 1982, UNICEF cooperated in programs to supply safe water and improved sanitation in 93 countries (41 in Africa, 27 in Asia, 18 in the Americas, and 7 in the Middle East region); completed 76,824 water-supply systems, including 71,011 open/dug wells with hand pumps, 566 piped systems with 359 motor-driven pumps, and 4,888 other systems; benefited some 13.6 million people (40% of them children) from its rural water-supply systems; and completed 126,819 excreta-disposal installations benefiting some 934,600 people.

Child Nutrition

In 1982 UNICEF's executive board approved a five-year joint WHO/UNICEF Nutrition Support Program in selected countries, designed to support a wide range of activities related to expanded primary health care services. These include: emphasis on better weaning and child feeding practices; the importance of breast-

deficiencies, such as goiter and keratomalacia, are under way in several countries, particularly in the Asian subcontinent.

UNICEF's cooperation in programs of nutrition education and dietary supplements and the expansion of mother and child health services, together with immunization, are important in helping to reduce preventable childhood disabilities, such as those caused by poliomyelitis and measles. Support is now growing for the early detection and treatment of impairments through existing community-based health, welfare, and education services.

In 1982, UNICEF cooperated in nutrition programs in 90 countries (41 in Africa, 22 in Asia, 21 in the Americas, and 6 in the Middle East region); helped expand nutrition programs in 94,600 villages, equipping nutrition centers and demonstration areas, community and school orchards and gardens, and fish and poultry hatcheries; provided stipends to train 36,100 village-level nutrition workers; and delivered 24,438 metric tons of donated foods (including wheat flour, nonfat dry milk, special weaning foods, and nutrition supplements) for distribution through nutrition and emergency feeding programs.

Social Services

At its 1982 session, UNICEF's executive board reviewed a report entitled *Reaching Children and Women of the Urban Poor*, based on information solicited during 1981 from 70 countries and on detailed case studies from 9 countries. The report recognized the need to attach a higher priority to the problems of the urban poor in UNICEF program cooperation, in view of the fact that the developing world's urban population is expected to reach 2.1 billion by the year 2000.

UNICEF has continued to expand its urban activities in all the developing regions, with emphasis on childhood malnutrition, the situation of women, preschool and day-care services, responsible parenthood and family planning, abandoned and disabled children, and, as already noted, the provision of adequate water and sanitation facilities.

In collaboration with governments and private organizations, UNICEF is searching for low-cost methods of dealing with the problem of abandoned children, a special concern in the Americas. There are thought to be as many as 30 million children eking out an existence in city streets without support from their families, and 5 million living entirely in the streets by day and night.

UNICEF has also been active in promoting women's participation at every level in programs of country cooperation. Based on the primary role of mothers in child-rearing, UNICEF's early involvement in efforts for women revolved around pregnant and nursing mothers in their nurturing capacity. This was later extended to activities connected with improved child care, better home management, and the relief of daily drudgery. It was increasingly recognized that women had an important role to play in community development.

Since 1980, UNICEF has given more emphasis to the training of women in skills for income-generation, to help establish women's economic activities on a sounder and more entrepreneurial basis. At the same time, since working mothers still must look after their small children, attention is given to the provision of day care and to guidance for mothers on sound child-rearing practices.

In addition, UNICEF has been concerned with the promotion of appropriate technology at the village level, particularly the use of low-cost devices manufactured from locally available materials using local skills, which help relieve women's domestic burdens and allow them to make improvements in their family life-style. UNICEF is helping some 45 countries to develop low-cost technologies focused on the social rather than the economic aspects of life, including water supply, food conservation and storage, and energy and fuel saving.

In 1982, UNICEF cooperated in social services programs in 99 countries (44 in Africa, 27 in the Americas, 20 in Asia, and 8 in the Middle East region); supplied equipment to more than 32,500 child welfare and day-care centers, 7,100 youth centers and clubs, and 6,600 women's centers; provided stipends to more than 53,100 women and girls for training in child care, homecrafts, food preservation, and income-earning skills; provided stipends to train some 48,800 local leaders to help organize activities in their own villages and communities; and provided equipment and supplies to 700 training institutions for social workers and training stipends for 5,600 child-welfare workers.

Primary and Nonformal Education

Poor enrollment levels, high dropout rates, and low learning achievement still bedevil the school education system in all parts of the developing world. In parts of sub-Saharan Africa and south Asia, only 2 out of every 10 children complete primary education and illiteracy among women exceeds 90%. Given the link between female literacy and the use of health and social service amenities, these factors seriously impede the effective spread of basic services. For this reason, both primary and nonformal education remain high priorities in UNICEF country cooperation.

UNICEF cooperates with countries in education in four main areas: the upbringing, care, and education of the preschool child; primary school education; the development of nonformal educational opportunities for children whom the school system has passed by and for older girls and women; and the educational components of basic-services programs.

In primary education, UNICEF focuses on qualitative improvement and on reaching those in remote or deprived areas where the standard of education or the availability of school equipment and teaching services is comparatively low. Besides the training of professionals and para-professional workers, most basic-services programs include general consciousness-raising and community education in health, nutrition, sanitation, and child care.

In 1982, UNICEF cooperated in primary and nonformal education in 102 countries (46 in Africa, 26 in Asia, 22 in the Americas,

and 8 in the Middle East region); provided stipends for refresher training of some 96,400 teachers, including 66,800 primary-school teachers; helped equip more than 82,000 primary schools, teacher-training institutions, and vocational-training centers with teaching aids; and assisted many countries to prepare textbooks locally by funding printing units, bookbinding, and paper.

Emergency Relief and Rehabilitation

Although its main emphasis since the 1950s has been on long-range programs, UNICEF aid has continued to be needed for emergency and special situations in which children are usually among the worst affected and which often prevent the implementation of long-term programs. The general policy of UNICEF in emergency relief is to help meet the particular needs of children, which are not always understood, or are neglected, in the rush of providing basic relief in disaster situations.

After the emergency period, UNICEF's help is directed to longer-term rehabilitation of health, education, and other services for children. Resources and involvement are generally greater for medium-term reconstruction and rehabilitation than for emergency relief as such.

In its emergency relief operations, UNICEF works cooperatively with UNDP, UNDRO, UNHCR, WFP, WHO, and other agencies of the UN system, with bilateral aid agencies and the EEC, and with the ICRC, the League of Red Cross Societies, and other voluntary agencies.

In 1982, UNICEF expended a total of $2.5 million for emergency relief on medicaments, water-supply equipment, food supplements, tents and other relief essentials for 42 countries hit by disasters—21 in Africa, 11 in Asia, 7 in the Americas, and 3 in the Middle East.

THE ELDERLY AND AGING

The question of the elderly, a rapidly growing sector of the world's population, was first discussed by the General Assembly in 1969. Since then, the UN has given increasing attention to the needs of older persons and to the question of the aging of populations worldwide.

In 1973, the Assembly considered a comprehensive report that noted the demographic increase in the absolute and relative size of the older populations of the world (a trend that was expected to continue because of medical advances and decreases in birth and death rates) and estimated that the number of persons 60 years of age or over throughout the world would increase by 100% between 1970 and the year 2000. The Assembly recommended guidelines to governments in formulating policies for the elderly, including development of programs for the welfare, health, and protection of older people and their retraining in accordance with their needs, in order to maximize their economic independence and their social integration with other segments of the population.

In 1978, the Assembly decided to convene a world assembly for the purpose of launching "an international action program aimed at guaranteeing economic and social security to older persons," as well as opportunities for them to contribute to national development. The Assembly later decided that the conference should also consider the interrelated issue of the aging of whole populations.

The World Assembly on Aging, held in Vienna in July-August 1982, was attended by representatives of more than 120 countries. It adopted an international plan of action, both to help the aging as individuals and to deal with the long-term social and economic effects of aging populations. Recommendations contained in the plan of action covered (1) the need to help the elderly lead independent lives in their own family and community for as long as possible, instead of being excluded and cut off from all activities of society; (2) the importance of giving the elderly a choice as to the kind of health care they receive, and the importance of preventive care, including nutrition and exercise; (3) the need to provide support services to assist families, particularly low-income families, to continue to care for elderly relatives; and (4) the need to provide social-security schemes, to assist the elderly in finding (or returning to) employment, and to provide appropriate housing. The plan of action also included recommendations for meeting the needs of particularly vulnerable persons, such as elderly refugees and migrant workers.

DISABLED PERSONS

Under the Charter principles of the dignity and worth of the human being and the promotion of social justice, the General Assembly has acted to protect the rights of disabled persons. In 1971 it adopted the Declaration on the Rights of Mentally Retarded Persons and in 1975, the Declaration on the Rights of Disabled Persons (see the section on declarations in the chapter on Human Rights). In 1976 the Assembly decided to proclaim 1981 as International Year of Disabled Persons, and called for a plan of action for the year at the national, regional, and international levels.

The year's purpose, and its theme, was the promotion of "full participation and equality," defined as the right of disabled persons to take part fully in the life and development of their societies, to enjoy living conditions equal to those of other citizens, and to have an equal share in improved conditions resulting from socio-economic development. Other objectives of the year included increasing public understanding of disability and encouraging disabled persons to organize themselves to express their views effectively.

During the year, national committees were set up in more than 140 countries to map out plans of action to implement the objectives of the year. Regional seminars—for Asia and the Pacific, Africa, Latin America, Western Asia, and Europe—held during the year discussed regional cooperation on behalf of disabled persons. At the international level, organizations of the UN system and other intergovernmental organizations, as well as non-governmental organizations, discussed ways in which the world community could aid the disabled through technical cooperation and other means.

The year's activities were followed by the Assembly's adoption, in 1982, of a World Program of Action Concerning Disabled Persons, aimed at continuing long-term programs at the national, regional, and international levels. To provide the necessary timeframe for implementation of the program, the Assembly proclaimed the period 1983–92 as the UN Decade of Disabled Persons.

OFFICE OF UN HIGH COMMISSIONER FOR REFUGEES (UNHCR)

The UN Relief and Rehabilitation Administration (UNRRA) was established on 9 November 1943, to bring material aid to war-stricken areas of the world. Through its services, some 6 million displaced persons were repatriated. The constitution of a successor agency, broader in scope, the International Refugee Organization (IRO), was approved by the General Assembly on 15 December 1946. In addition to the assistance provided by UNRRA in the fields of relief and repatriation, IRO was charged with the protection of refugees and displaced persons and with resettlement responsibilities. The IRO Preparatory Commission became operative on 30 June 1947; by 31 December 1951, when IRO's operational activities ceased, more than 1 million persons had been resettled.

As part of a series of initiatives designed to address refugee problems following the dissolution of the IRO, the General Assembly agreed, in December 1949, on the necessity of setting up a body primarily responsible for the international protection of refugees. As a consequence, the Office of the UN High Commissioner for Refugees (UNHCR) was established as of 1 January 1951 for a limited period of three years. It was soon evident, however, that international assistance was needed and, as new situations which created refugees continued to arise, UNHCR's mandate was renewed by the Assembly for successive periods of five years, most recently until the end of 1988.

UNHCR was awarded the Nobel Peace Prize in 1954 and again in 1981.

Organization

The High Commissioner is elected by the General Assembly on the nomination of the secretary-general and is responsible to the Assembly. The 41-nation Executive Committee of UNHCR meets annually to review activities in the fields of protection and material assistance; approve assistance projects to be included in the next year's annual program; and provide overall guidance. The high commissioner reports to the executive committee on the implementation of special tasks that he may have been called upon to carry out—often at the request of the secretary-general—and on the administration of special trust funds.

UNHCR headquarters are in Geneva. At the end of 1982, it had offices in over 60 countries in Africa, Asia, Europe, Latin America, North America, and Oceania, and a worldwide staff of some 1,600, of whom over 1,100 were in the field.

Financing

The financial arrangements made at the creation of UNHCR reflected the fundamental difference between it and the IRO. IRO's budget was separate from that of the UN, while part of the basic administrative costs of UNHCR are covered by the regular UN budget, as UNHCR is an integral part of the Secretariat, rather than a specialized agency. Its substantive activities in the field of protection and material assistance, however, depend entirely on voluntary contributions.

At the outset, UNHCR was not allowed to appeal to governments for funds without the express authorization of the General Assembly. The first funds of any magnitude put at the high commissioner's disposal came from the Ford Foundation in 1952 in the form of a grant of $2.9 million (later increased to $3.1 million) for a pilot program of projects intended to promote the local settlement of some 100,000 refugees in Europe through measures such as low-rent housing, small loans, vocational training, and rehabilitation of the handicapped. Subsequently, in 1954, the Assembly authorized the high commissioner to appeal to governments for a 4-year $16 million program oriented toward permanent solutions and modeled on the Ford experimental undertaking. The target was eventually reached through $14.5 million in contributions by governments and over $2 million by private organizations.

Clearing refugee camps in Europe was the main objective of UNHCR at this time, and the funds needed to finish this task were raised to a large extent through World Refugee Year (1959/60), a campaign which extended to 100 countries and areas.

In 1957 UNHCR's capacity to react effectively to unexpected situations was enhanced when the Assembly authorized the high commissioner to establish an emergency fund not to exceed $500,000. This innovation grew out of the experience of 1956 when some 200,000 refugees from Hungary crossed into Austria and Yugoslavia within a matter of weeks, prompting the high commissioner to appeal for funds for the emergency. In 1974 the Assembly raised the emergency fund's ceiling to $2 million and in 1980 to $10 million, with the provision that no more than $4 million be spent for a single emergency in any one year.

The annual, or general, program continues to be the main ongoing vehicle for UNHCR's material assistance activities, which have been greatly expanded in recent years. In 1982 expenditures under the general program totaled $318.8 million, as compared with $14.1 million in 1975. Estimated requirements for 1983 were $348 million. Eighty-four governments contributed to UNHCR in 1982.

Since 1971, UNHCR has also been called upon to undertake a series of special tasks, usually at the request of the secretary-general, which have gone beyond the scope of the usual terms of

UNHCR's action and have involved appeals for funds outside the general program. In 1982 over $88 million was spent for such special programs as assistance to returnees to Chad, Ethiopia, and Kampuchea, orderly departure from Viet-Nam, and language training for Indochinese refugees in southeast Asia.

The High Commissioner's Responsibilities

The high commissioner's primary responsibility is international protection. In addition, he promotes durable solutions to the problems of refugees through voluntary repatriation, local integration, or resettlement in another country of asylum, according to the wishes of the individual refugee and available possibilities. Whatever the field of activity, he and his staff always are guided by humanitarian and strictly nonpolitical considerations. UNHCR's ability to adhere to this policy over the years since its inception in 1951 has led the General Assembly to extend the scope of its material assistance activities, in many cases to persons who do not necessarily meet the terms of the definition of a refugee which is contained in the high commissioner's statute. This describes a refugee as someone who, owing to well-founded fear of being persecuted for reasons of race, religion, nationality, or political opinion, is outside his country of nationality and is unable or unwilling, because of such fear, to avail himself of the protection of that country. In recent years, UNHCR has increasingly been called on to help not only refugees but also persons uprooted by man-made disasters and displaced either outside or within their country of origin. However, UNHCR's competence does not extend to refugees already receiving help from another UN organization, notably the Arab refugees from Palestine who are cared for by UNRWA (see separate section below).

In the implementation of programs of material assistance which it has helped to draw up and finance, UNHCR relies on operational partners in the field. These may be services of the government which has requested UNHCR's aid or private organizations. Especially in its work of settling refugees in developing countries, UNHCR cooperates closely with other members of the UN system and benefits from their expertise in such matters as agriculture (FAO), health (WHO), education (UNESCO), child welfare (UNICEF), and training (ILO). The participation of the World Food Program is particularly important in supplying food for settlements until such time as the refugees are able to grow their own crops.

International Protection

Since refugees no longer enjoy the protection of the countries they have fled, they must rely on the international community to provide it. The main vehicle for international protection is the 1951 Convention Relating to the Status of Refugees, which lays down minimum standards for the treatment of refugees by countries that have acceded to it. As of mid-1983, 93 countries had done so.

One of the most important provisions of the 1951 convention is that a refugee must not be sent back to a country where he may face persecution on grounds of race or political opinion, religion, nationality, or membership in a particular social group. The convention also defines a refugee's rights in the country of asylum with respect to such matters as, for example, the right to work, education, access to courts, and social security. It provides, moreover, for the issue of travel documents by the country of residence, to offset the fact that a refugee is not in a position to use his national passport.

By its statute and under the 1951 convention, UNHCR is given specific responsibility for supervising the application of the provisions of this instrument. UNHCR is also available to supply technical advice to governments on appropriate legal and administrative measures to give effect to the stipulations of the convention.

The 1951 convention originally covered only persons who became refugees as a result of events occurring before 1951. In 1967 a protocol was adopted which removed the dateline, making the convention applicable in all refugee situations, present and future. As of August 1983, 92 countries had acceded to that protocol.

Another important legal instrument concerning refugees is the 1969 OAU Convention Governing the Specific Aspects of Refugee Problems in Africa. This convention, which came into force on 20 June 1974, emphasizes that the granting of asylum is a peaceful and humanitarian act which should not be regarded as unfriendly by any member state. A similar provision can be found in the Declaration on Territorial Asylum adopted by the General Assembly in December 1967 (see the section on declarations in the chapter on Human Rights).

Asylum is the key aspect of the protection work of the high commissioner's office. A conference of plenipotentiaries convened by the General Assembly in 1977 "to consider and adopt a convention on territorial asylum" failed to achieve its objectives, and the absence of such a convention remains a gap in the legal basis for the protection of asylum-seekers.

In 1975 UNHCR undertook new duties in the field of protection on a provisional basis following the entry into force on 13 December of the 1961 Convention on the Reduction of Statelessness. Under the terms of the convention, stateless persons may apply to national authorities to have nationality accorded to themselves or to their children or may ask UNHCR's assistance in presenting a claim.

In the same year, UNHCR's executive committee established a Subcommittee on International Protection to study in greater detail some of the more technical aspects of the legal protection of refugees. A recent major preoccupation of the subcommittee has been the problem of large-scale influxes of refugees and displaced persons and the responses of the international community to such mass movements. The subcommittee has also addressed such questions as the rescue and safety of asylum-seekers at sea, the reunion of refugee families, various legal aspects of the granting of asylum and refugee status, and security from military attack of refugee camps and settlements.

MATERIAL ASSISTANCE ACTIVITIES

UNHCR's material assistance activities include emergency relief, assistance in voluntary repatriation or local integration, and resettlement through migration to other countries, as well as counseling and education.

Africa

UNHCR's involvement in Africa dates from 1957, when thousands of people fled from the fighting in Algeria to Morocco and Tunisia. Working in conjunction with the League of Red Cross Societies, UNHCR provided both immediate and long-term assistance and helped to organize the repatriation of some 200,000 refugees in 1962, after the cessation of hostilities.

By 1967 there were an estimated 750,000 refugees in Africa, many of them victims of the struggles for independence in Guinea-Bissau, Angola, and Mozambique. In 1974–75 UNHCR assisted in repatriating many of these refugees to their newly independent homelands. A large-scale repatriation and rehabilitation program involving some 200,000 refugees and displaced persons in Zimbabwe was coordinated by UNHCR in 1980, and a major repatriation to Chad was completed in 1982.

In the Horn of Africa, which has one of the largest concentrations of refugees on the continent, developments in early 1983 gave rise to hopes for voluntary repatriation of refugees from Djibouti to Ethiopia. The high commissioner launched an appeal to the international community in June 1983 for support for a $6-million program for the rehabilitation of such returnees.

By the early 1980s, however, with Africa thought to be harboring half of the world's estimated 10 million refugees, many of the upheavals which produce refugees remained without solution, and large concentrations of refugees persisted, particularly in the

Horn of Africa, the Sudan, Zaire, and Angola. In addition, thousands of South Africans and Namibians continued to seek refuge in neighboring countries. Where voluntary repatriation has not been feasible in the short term, UNHCR has, wherever possible, shifted the emphasis of its assistance programs from emergency relief to longer-term self-help measures designed to assist the refugees and relieve the burden on both host countries and the international community. Such measures have frequently taken the form of the establishment of rural settlements as, for example, in the Sudan, which hosts over 600,000 refugees and where UNHCR spent over $20 million in 1982 on this kind of assistance. A similar emphasis was being given to assistance to Somalia's large refugee population.

The refugee situation in Africa has imposed an increasing social and economic burden on African countries of asylum, thus hampering their development efforts. To address this problem and following a General Assembly resolution in November 1980, an International Conference on Assistance to Refugees in Africa was convened in Geneva in April 1981, attended by representatives of 92 states. As a result of the conference, a total of $566.9 million was pledged in bilateral and multilateral assistance by over 49 countries and the EEC. A second conference was scheduled to meet in July 1984 to consider additional aid required by refugees and returnees, and measures necessary to strengthen the socioeconomic infrastructure of affected countries.

UNHCR assistance in Africa in 1982 totaled $137.8 million.

The Middle East and Southwest Asia
In May 1971, the high commissioner was appointed "focal point" for UN assistance to millions of Bengali refugees from East Pakistan (later Bangladesh) in India. More than $180 million in cash, kind, or services was channeled through this focal point, mainly for emergency relief in India but also for the repatriation operation that began early in 1972, following the creation of Bangladesh. The operation involved the transfer of non-Bengalis from Bangladesh to Pakistan and of Bengalis from Pakistan to Bangladesh. By the time it was concluded in July 1974, 241,300 people had been moved, nearly all by air, across the subcontinent in either direction.

In August 1974, following events in Cyprus, the high commissioner was designated to coordinate humanitarian relief for 241,300 people who had been uprooted and displaced. In the absence of a political settlement, aid was still being channeled to the island in 1983.

Another major crisis erupted in mid-1978 when nearly 200,000 refugees from the Arakan state of Burma flooded into Bangladesh. UNHCR was again designated as coordinator of UN assistance. Following an agreement concluded with the Burmese government in July 1978, repatriation began in November of that year. The UNHCR program included assistance to the returnees once they were back in their country of origin.

As a result of events in Afghanistan, almost 1 million refugees crossed into the Northwest Frontier and Baluchistan province of Pakistan between January 1979 and mid-1980. By the end of 1982, the Pakistan government estimated the total to have risen to some 3 million. UNHCR began large-scale assistance to cope with this massive influx in the second half of 1979 with an allocation of $190,000 from the emergency fund. By 1983 assistance was being extended to some 2.3 million beneficiaries in 340 refugee villages, and covered provision of immediate relief assistance, as well as health care, education, and the promotion of income-generating and self-help programs. On the basis of recommendations by the ILO, projects were being launched involving vocational training and wage-earning activities, while, at the request of UNHCR, the World Bank was formulating a project which would provide employment opportunities to refugees and local people and help repair the ecological and infrastructural damage caused by the massive influx of refugees and their livestock.

UNHCR contributions to the Afghan refugee program in Pakistan between August 1979 and mid-1983, both in cash and kind, totaled just over $300 million. Another major contributor was WFP, which was supplying basic food rations.

UNHCR assistance in the Middle East and southwest Asia in 1982 totaled $108.3 million.

East and South Asia
Early in 1975, the conflict that for almost three decades had involved Viet-Nam, Cambodia, Laos, and extracontinental forces, notably those from France and the US, came to an end with changes of regime in the three countries of Indochina. Since that time, well over 1 million Kampucheans, Laotians, and Vietnamese have left their homes and sought asylum in neighboring countries. These mass movements reached their peak in 1979, when some 393,560 people arrived by boat or overland in various asylum countries throughout the region, and in early 1980, when additional large numbers of Kampucheans moved into the border area with Thailand to escape hostilities in their own country.

UNHCR has undertaken to provide temporary assistance for Indochinese in various countries of southeast Asia, to ask governments to extend permanent resettlement opportunities, and to facilitate voluntary repatriation where feasible. In addition, large numbers of displaced persons in the Thai-Kampuchean border area have been assisted by other UN agencies and the ICRC. Since countries in the region, with the exception of the People's Republic of China, have been able to provide only temporary asylum and since voluntary repatriation has been feasible only for limited groups, UNHCR was obliged to launch a massive resettlement operation which, by mid-1983, had seen over 1 million Indochinese resettled in over 30 countries throughout the world, with the greatest numbers in Australia, Canada, France, and the US. There remained some 200,000 refugees in camps throughout the region, the majority in Thailand.

Meanwhile, UNHCR has assisted in the local integration on state farms of some 263,000 refugees who crossed from Viet-Nam into the People's Republic of China, mostly in 1979. Assistance has also been given toward the reintegration of returnees from Thailand, Laos, and Viet-Nam to Kampuchea.

Under the terms of a memorandum of understanding concluded with the Vietnamese government in May 1979, UNHCR has been coordinating a program of orderly departure from Viet-Nam which recently averaged well over 1,000 departures a month. A further coordinating role played by UNHCR has been in the funding of a major program to combat piracy against refugee boats and other vessels in the South China Sea.

UNHCR assistance in east and south Asia and Oceania in 1982 totaled $103.4 million.

The Americas
Originally, Latin America was a primary resettlement area for European refugees. However, the events in Chile in September 1973 involved UNHCR in major assistance measures for Latin American refugees. UNHCR had to contend first with the problem of several thousand refugees of various nationalities in Chile, providing relief, care, and maintenance and helping to establish "safe havens" where they could live until their departure and resettlement could be arranged.

In addition to ongoing assistance to Chilean refugees, UNHCR was called on to assist an increasing number of Nicaraguans in Costa Rica, Honduras, and Panama in late 1978. By 1979 the number of Nicaraguan refugees receiving such assistance had risen to 100,000. Following the change of government in Nicaragua in July 1979, however, voluntary repatriation began, and UNHCR launched a special program to facilitate both the return itself and the rehabilitation of returnees through assistance in such areas as agriculture, health, and housing.

Since the early 1980s, Central America has become an area of increasingly grave concern to UNHCR. By the end of 1980, 80,000 refugees from El Salvador had sought refuge in neighboring countries. By June 1983, the total refugee population of the area had reached 326,500, composed mainly of Salvadorans but with increasing numbers of refugees from Guatemala and Nicaragua.

Recent UNHCR assistance has concentrated largely on emergency relief to destitute new arrivals, the consolidation of care and maintenance measures for the largely rural refugee populations living in camps in Honduras and Mexico or spontaneously settled in Costa Rica and Nicaragua, and the development of self-sufficiency through rural settlements.

UNHCR assistance in the Americas in 1982 totaled $31 million.

Europe

When UNHCR came into existence in 1951, it inherited responsibility for some 120,000 persons still living precariously, and often in squalor, in refugee and displaced persons' camps, mainly in the Federal Republic of Germany, Austria, Italy, and Greece. The great majority of these persons had been uprooted during World War II, primarily through the Nazi policies of removing people from occupied territories for forced labor and forcibly shifting populations for racial reasons. Particularly deplorable was the situation of the children born in the camps. Clearance of those camps was long delayed, mainly for lack of funds. Eventually, some 100,000 people, refugees since World War II, were settled as a result of UNHCR's programs.

New movements of refugees have, however, continued to occur. One of the largest of these was the result of the Hungarian crisis in 1956. The high commissioner was called on, in October 1956, to coordinate the activities of governments and voluntary organizations on behalf of the 200,000 Hungarians who sought refuge in Austria and Yugoslavia. From October 1956 until the end of 1959, about 180,000 Hungarian refugees arrived in Austria and 19,000 in Yugoslavia. The total movement involved 203,100 persons. Of these, 18,000 eventually chose to return to Hungary, 9,600 elected to remain in Austria, 65,400 went to other European countries, and 107,400 emigrated overseas; the whereabouts of 2,700 are unknown.

UNHCR's material assistance activities in Europe have, in recent years, been limited in scale, as assistance is in most cases provided by governments and private organizations. In 1977, however, a UNHCR branch office was opened in Portugal to assist large numbers of refugees from former Portuguese territories in Africa. In late 1981 a large number of Polish asylum-seekers began arriving in Austria, prompting the high commissioner to make an allocation from his emergency fund to provide for local integration measures. Assistance was also given with resettlement overseas. There were more than 23,000 asylum-seekers under the care of the Austrian government at the end of 1981, most of them Poles. Resettlement had reduced the caseload to some 6,000, including 2,663 Poles, by April 1983.

Resettlement in Europe, particularly of large numbers of Indochinese refugees since the late 1970s, has required increased material assistance from UNHCR in such fields as local integration and counseling. Increasing levels of assistance have also been required by asylum-seekers whose requests for refugee status are pending in various European countries.

UNHCR assistance in Europe in 1982 totaled $14.1 million.

UN RELIEF AND WORKS AGENCY FOR PALESTINE REFUGEES IN THE NEAR EAST (UNRWA)

The plight of Palestine refugees has been a serious concern of the UN ever since the Arab-Israeli War of 1948. When a cease-fire came into effect early in 1949, hundreds of thousands of Arabs who lived in the territory which is now Israel were stranded on the other side of the armistice line from their homes. The Arab states claim that the refugees were driven out by the Israelis or fled in fear of reprisals. Israel, on the other hand, asserts that Arab states ordered the Arab population to evacuate the area

temporarily so that their armies could more easily drive the Israelis into the sea. (For the political background, see the section on the Middle East in the chapter on Maintaining Peace and Security.)

Emergency relief was given the refugees at first by the International Committee of the Red Cross, the League of Red Cross Societies, and the American Friends Service Committee, using money and supplies provided by the temporary UN Relief for Palestine Refugees, established in December 1948. In December 1949, the General Assembly created a special agency, the United Nations Relief and Works Agency for Palestine Refugees in the Near East (UNRWA), to provide relief and works projects in collaboration with the local governments. The following year, the Assembly extended UNRWA's mandate to June 1952 and instructed it to carry out development projects that would enable the refugees to be absorbed into the economy of the region. As originally conceived, UNRWA was a large-scale but definitely temporary operation to be terminated by the end of 1952. The Assembly accordingly asked Israel and its neighbors to secure "the permanent reestablishment of the refugees and their removal from relief." In carrying out programs of resettlement, however, all parties concerned, including UNRWA, were to act without prejudice to the rights of those refugees who "wished to return to their homes and live in peace with their neighbors." These were to "be permitted to do so at the earliest practicable date"; those who chose not to do so were to be compensated for their losses.

These goals were not achieved by 1952 and have not been met since then. Large-scale development projects to induce the refugees to leave the camps and enable them to become self-supporting in their host countries were approved by the Assembly but never realized. Since 1952, UNRWA's mandate has been extended ten times, most recently until 30 June 1984.

UNRWA extends its activities over an area of more than 100,000 sq mi. It deals with four host governments: Jordan, Lebanon, Syria, and Egypt; and with the government of Israel as occupying power on the West Bank of the Jordan River and in the Gaza Strip since June 1967. In 1983 there were 1.9 million Palestine refugees, 80.8% of whom were eligible for some or all of UNRWA's services.

Organization

UNRWA is a subsidiary organ of the General Assembly and its policy and functions are determined by the Assembly. It is headed by a commissioner-general, who is assisted by a 10-nation Advisory Commission composed of Belgium, Egypt, France, Japan, Jordan, Lebanon, Syria, Turkey, the UK, and the US. The commissioner-general is appointed by the secretary-general in consultation with the governments of the advisory commission.

Headquarters are in Vienna and in 'Amman, Jordan, and field offices are located in Jerusalem, Gaza, 'Amman, Beirut, and Damascus. UNRWA has liaison offices at UN headquarters in New York and in Cairo. Each field office is headed by a representative of the commissioner-general, who is responsible for UNRWA activities in each area. UNRWA's staff consists of some 120 international officials and over 17,000 locally recruited persons, almost all of them refugees.

Financing

UNRWA depends almost entirely on voluntary contributions. Total expenditure on the regular program for 1982 was $183 million, with additional expenditures for emergency relief to refugees in Lebanon amounting to $52 million.

Most of UNRWA's income is contributed by governments. The leading donor, the US, contributed a total of $67 million to the regular program in 1983. Numerous private organizations and individuals throughout the world also contribute to UNRWA. Successive commissioners-general have stated that some more certain remedy than appeals for increased contributions is required.

In recent years, UNRWA has faced cash crises which have been resolved by budget reductions, early payment of pledges by donor countries, and special contributions. The ongoing strife in Lebanon since 1975 and the Israeli invasions of 1978 and 1982 have seriously affected the agency's operations. In June 1982, UNRWA mounted an emergency relief operation to continue into 1984.

Number and Geographic Distribution of Refugees

On 30 June 1983, 1,957,061 refugees were registered with UNRWA. Of this total, approximately 244,000 were registered in Lebanon, 226,000 in Syria, 759,000 in east Jordan, 344,000 on the West Bank, and 383,000 in the Gaza Strip. The largest concentrations of refugees were in the occupied territories and east Jordan, with smaller numbers in Lebanon and Syria. Of the 759,000 refugees in east Jordan, about 40% fled there from the West Bank and Gaza during and immediately following the June 1967 war.

For relief purposes, UNRWA defines a "Palestine refugee" as a person whose normal residence was Palestine for a minimum of two years immediately before the outbreak of the Arab-Israeli conflict in 1948 and who, as a result of this conflict, lost both his home and his means of livelihood. To be eligible for UNRWA assistance he must be registered and in need, and must have taken refuge in Jordan, Lebanon, Syria, or the Gaza Strip, the areas contiguous to Israel in which the agency operates. Children and grandchildren of registered refugees are also generally eligible for assistance.

Services Provided by UNRWA

Food. Once a major part of UNRWA's program, the general distribution of food rations has ceased except in Lebanon, where it is still needed. Since 1982, UNRWA has distributed food only to special hardship cases, which include widows, orphans, the aged, the physically and mentally handicapped, and the chronically ill. In June 1983, such persons numbered 89,000. These persons also receive other assistance such as blankets, clothing, and token cash grants.

Under a supplementary feeding program, UNRWA provides milk for pregnant women and nursing mothers and for infants and children.

Shelter. When the agency first began its work, some 30,000 tents provided the principal shelter for the 30% of the refugees living in the camps. As funds and the availability of suitable sites permitted, the agency gradually replaced the tents with huts. At first, many refugees objected to using a shelter that they regarded as permanent, but this objection was gradually overcome. By the end of 1959, all the tents in UNRWA camps had been replaced by huts. In 1967, 10 emergency tent camps were established in east Jordan and Syria for some 110,000 of the refugees and other persons displaced as a result of the Six-Day War. The tents have since been replaced by shelters. There were 733,271 registered refugees (35.06% of the total) accommodated in 63 camps in June 1983.

Health Services. Under an agreement with UNRWA, WHO has been responsible since 1949 for the technical direction of the agency's health services. WHO also provides certain senior medical staff, including the agency's chief medical officer. The preventive and curative health services, as well as the health education and environmental sanitation programs, are very extensive. In 1983, 98 health centers were operated directly by UNRWA, which also subsidizes clinics and outpatient facilities of hospitals in the host countries. A total of 1,432 hospital beds were maintained or reserved by the agency in 1983.

Educational and Vocational Services. UNRWA–UNESCO schools for refugee children have been in operation in Jordan, Lebanon, Syria, and the Gaza Strip since 1951. Eventually, UNRWA, after building hundreds of schools and fostering teacher training, was able to offer six years of elementary education to all refugee children and three years of preparatory education to all elementary school graduates. As UNRWA has reported, "The refugee child today has considerably greater educational opportunities than his parents had."

In 1982–83, 336,207 pupils were enrolled in UNRWA–UNESCO elementary and preparatory schools and another 92,403 refugee children attended state and private schools.

UNRWA constantly endeavors to place job-seeking refugees, particularly those graduating from its eight vocational and training centers. Close consultation with employers has also made it possible to adjust courses to requirements.

OFFICE OF THE UN DISASTER RELIEF COORDINATOR (UNDRO)

Beginning in 1965, proposals were put forward in the General Assembly to increase the UN's ability to help people stricken by disasters, but the disasters of 1970 brought international concern for emergency relief to a head. The Assembly that year requested the secretary-general to conduct a study, and this led to the 1971 Assembly's creation of the Office of the United Nations Disaster Relief Coordinator (UNDRO), with headquarters in Geneva.

UNDRO was not designed to assume all the responsibilities of meeting disasters from its own resources. Its principal function is that of catalyst and coordinator of donors of aid and services. Its data bank and independent telecommunications system, supplemented by the worldwide UN system, give it the capacity to define the specific needs arising from a disaster and respond rapidly to it by identifying potential sources of relief. It directs and mobilizes aid emanating from the UN system and coordinates aid from without.

UNDRO's mandate also includes assisting governments in preventing disasters or mitigating their effects by contingency planning, in association with similarly concerned voluntary organizations. It promotes the study, prevention, control, and prediction of natural disasters, and gathers and disseminates all kinds of information relevant to disaster relief.

During the first ten years of its existence, UNDRO was involved in more than 215 major disasters, and $1,200 million worth of international assistance were reported to it, mobilized by UNDRO or channeled through it.

UNITED NATIONS SAHELIAN OFFICE (UNSO)

Another UN undertaking in disaster relief developed in response to the desiccation of the Sudano-Sahelian zone of West Africa. Many years of drought in Chad, Mali, Mauritania, Niger, Senegal, and Upper Volta had, by 1973, resulted in a crisis and the threat of mass starvation in the region. In May, the secretary-general, acting under Assembly and ECOSOC resolutions, designated FAO as the "focal point" of an emergency operation of the UN system to provide and transport rations, seeds for sowing, animal feed, and vaccines to victims in the six countries. The following month, the UN Sahelian Office (UNSO) was created to promote medium- and long-term recovery in cooperation with the Permanent Interstate Committee on Drought Control in the Sahel, known by its French acronym CILSS, and composed of affected states. UNSO is established in Ouagadougou, Upper Volta, with a liaison office in New York. It works closely with CILSS to mobilize additional resources for the CILSS program, and coordinates and monitors the efforts of the UN family for recovery and rehabilitation.

ASSISTANCE TO LEAST-DEVELOPED COUNTRIES AND LEBANON

The UN also provides special assistance to more than 20 countries, mostly in Africa, facing severe economic and financial difficulties and requiring aid for reconstruction, rehabilitation, and development. Many of these countries are among the least-developed in the world and some are geographically handicapped—that is, landlocked or island countries.

For Lebanon, which has borne the brunt of successive Middle East conflicts, the General Assembly in 1978 established a special committee to coordinate assistance efforts relating to the reconstruction and development of the country. Following the June 1982 Israeli invasion of Lebanon, the problem became even more acute because of the mass destruction of property as well as extensive damage to the economic and social structure of Lebanon. The secretary-general made a special appeal for international assistance, and the General Assembly, in December 1982, called on all organs, organizations, and bodies within the UN system to expand and intensify programs of assistance in response to the country's needs.

NARCOTIC DRUGS CONTROL

In the first issue of the *United Nations Bulletin on Narcotics* (October 1949), Trygve Lie, then secretary-general of the UN, summarized the importance of international narcotics control:

"The problem of narcotic drugs is in no sense a problem confined to one continent or civilization.

"In themselves narcotic drugs are neither dangerous nor harmful. Indispensable to modern medicine, they are used the world over to alleviate pain and restore health. Thus used they bring a great benefit to mankind. But abused they cause havoc and misery. The social dangers of drug addiction are well known.

"This dual nature of narcotic drugs has made it necessary to submit them to the most stringent international control. . . . This control, functioning now under the auspices of the United Nations and expanding rapidly to the field of newly discovered synthetic drugs, ensures the limitation of their manufacture, trade, and consumption to legitimate needs only."

Until the end of the 19th century, trade in narcotics was considered a legitimate business. Misuse of addiction-producing substances—opium, coca leaf, Indian hemp—was considered the result of ingrained habits in particular areas of the world.

Early in the 19th century, a number of bilateral treaties curbed the import of narcotics into some Asian countries. The problem was considered a domestic one. However, modern technology and the expansion of transport and world trade introduced a new dimension. An increasing number of alkaloids and derivatives were being produced from opium and coca leaves and easily distributed.

In addition, a large number of psychotropic substances (depressors of the central nervous system such as barbiturates, stimulants of the central nervous system such as amphetamines, and hallucinogens such as LSD) have been developed and their consumption has increased enormously; hence problems once considered local are now global.

The UN exercises functions and powers relating to the worldwide control of narcotic drugs in accordance with a number of international treaties concluded between 1912 and 1972. By 1983 the majority of countries were parties to one or more of the treaties. The international control system is based on the cooperation of the states that are bound by these treaties in controlling the manufacture and sale of drugs within their jurisdiction. The treaties stipulate that these states are bound to adopt appropriate legislation, introduce necessary administrative and enforcement measures, and cooperate with international control organs as well as with each other.

Narcotics Control under the League of Nations

The League of Nations Covenant provided that League members should "entrust the League with the general supervision over agreements with regard . . . to the traffic in opium and other dangerous drugs." The first League Assembly created an Advisory Committee on Traffic in Opium and Other Dangerous Drugs to assist the League's Council in its supervisory tasks in the field. The Permanent Central Opium Board was composed at first of eight independent experts, to which League members were required to submit annual statistics on the production of opium and coca leaves, the manufacture, consumption, and stocks of narcotic drugs, and quarterly reports on the import and export of narcotic drugs. Specific governmental authorizations were required for every import and export of narcotic drugs. The Convention for Limiting the Manufacture and Regulating the Distribution of [Narcotic] Drugs, signed at Geneva in 1931, created a new technical organ composed of independent experts, the Drug Supervisory Body. The aim of the 1931 convention was to limit world manufacture of drugs to the amount actually needed for medical and scientific purposes.

The Convention for the Suppression of Illicit Traffic in Narcotic Drugs, signed at Geneva in 1936, called for severe punishment of illicit traffickers in narcotics and extradition for drug offenses.

Developments under the UN

A protocol signed on 11 December 1946 transferred to the UN the functions previously exercised by the League of Nations under the pre–World War II narcotics treaties.

Drug-control functions in the UN system are exercised by several bodies, either in implementation of the international drug treaties or of the UN Charter. The main bodies are the General Assembly, ECOSOC, the Commission on Narcotic Drugs, the International Narcotics Control Board, the UN Secretariat, especially the Division of Narcotic Drugs and the UN Fund for Drug Abuse Control, and the specialized agencies, particularly WHO. Organizations outside the UN system also play a part, especially the International Criminal Police Organization (INTERPOL).

The General Assembly plays a role when important questions are debated such as appeals to states to become parties to relevant international treaties or the establishment of new bodies, one outstanding example being the establishment of the UN Fund for Drug Abuse Control.

In 1981, faced with the increasing seriousness of the drug problem in the world, the Assembly called for an international campaign against traffic in drugs. It also adopted an International Drug Abuse Control Strategy and a five-year program which called for integrated action at the national, regional, and international levels, coordinated through the UN.

The Economic and Social Council considers the reports of the Commission on Narcotic Drugs and the resolutions which that body directs to it for adoption. Two of its main functions in that respect are to take decisions for any proposal with financial implications and ensure coordination in the field.

The Commission on Narcotic Drugs, one of the functional commissions of ECOSOC, has three main purposes: to prepare such draft international conventions as may be necessary; assist ECOSOC in exercising such powers of supervision over the application of international conventions and agreements dealing with narcotic drugs as may be assumed by or conferred on ECOSOC; and consider what changes may be required in the existing machinery for the international control of narcotic drugs and submit proposals thereon to ECOSOC. In addition, the commission has special functions under the Single Convention, such as to place drugs under international control and make recommendations for the implementation of the aims and provisions of the Convention, including programs of scientific research and the exchange of information of a scientific or technical nature. The commission meets annually either in regular or in special sessions.

The International Narcotics Control Board was created by the 1961 Single Convention on Narcotic Drugs as a successor to the Permanent Central Opium Board and Drug Supervisory Body. The 13 members of the board are not government representatives but experts acting in their private, individual capacities. The board has very important functions to perform under the treaties, especially by providing for quantitative control extending throughout the world. It watches over statistics of drug production, manufacture, trade, and consumption; and over the estimates needed for the coming year that states are required to furnish to it (if a state does not send estimates, the board makes them itself).

The board may request any state to explain a condition which in its view indicates an improper accumulation of narcotic drugs. It may even recommend, in case of difficulties created by a country for the international control, that other states stop the shipment of drugs to that country. A most effective means of ensuring compliance is publicity: the reports of the board (and of other international bodies) ensure that public opinion is made aware of any situation which may contribute to the spread of drug abuse.

The Division of Narcotic Drugs is part of the UN Secretariat. Its functions stem from international treaties, resolutions, and decisions of the General Assembly, ECOSOC, and the Commission on Narcotic Drugs, and instructions from the secretary-general. It has a number of duties to fulfill as secretariat to the commission and in terms of the implementation of the international drug control system. It has a wide range of activities as executive agency for a number of technical cooperation projects. These operational activities may cover legislation, law enforcement and administration, public information, etc. The UN Narcotics Laboratory is part of the division; it conducts original research, coordinates the work of scientists the world over in the drug field, and administers many fellowships in technical and scientific matters.

The UN Fund for Drug Abuse Control (UNFDAC) is also part of the UN Secretariat. It was established in April 1971 by the secretary-general, an action which had been called for by the General Assembly, ECOSOC, and the Commission on Narcotic Drugs.

The fund assists governments by helping to finance projects aimed at reducing the illicit supply and demand for drugs—for example, projects to replace illicit opium cultivation, treat and rehabilitate drug addicts, strengthen control measures, and organize information and education programs. The fund relies entirely on voluntary contributions, mainly from governments but also from private sources.

The specialized agencies of the UN may have a part to play in drug control but only WHO is given a role by the international drug treaties. WHO advises on placing drugs under control and on questions related to drug demand. In addition, WHO as well as UNESCO, ILO, and FAO execute a number of projects related to the suppression of drug abuse, financed by their regular budgets or, mainly, by UNFDAC.

The Treaty System

One of the tasks of the UN in drug control is to adapt international treaty machinery to changing conditions. Five agreements have been drawn up under UN auspices:

The Paris Protocol of 1948. The prewar international conventions on narcotics applied to all addictive products of three plants—the opium poppy, the coca bush, and the cannabis plant—and to products belonging to certain chemical groups known to have addictive properties. By the end of World War II, however, a number of synthetic narcotics not belonging to the defined chemical groups had been developed. A protocol signed in Paris on 19 November 1948 authorized WHO to place under international control any new drug not covered by the previous conventions that was or could be addictive. The Paris protocol came into force on 1 December 1949.

The Opium Protocol of 1953. Opium production continued and found its way into illicit channels. The Commission on Narcotic Drugs first proposed an international opium monopoly, with production quotas and a system of international inspection. It was impossible, however, to obtain agreement on such important questions as the price of opium and inspection rights.

A compromise was worked out by the UN Opium Conference held in New York in May–June 1953 and embodied in a Protocol for Limiting and Regulating the Cultivation of the Poppy Plant, the Production of, International Trade in, and Use of Opium. Under this protocol only seven states—Bulgaria, Greece, India,

Iran, Turkey, the USSR, and Yugoslavia—were authorized to produce opium for export. Producing states were required to set up a government agency to license opium poppy cultivators and designate the areas to be cultivated. Cultivators were to deliver all opium immediately after harvesting to this agency, the only body with the legal right to trade in opium. The Permanent Central Narcotics Board, under the protocol, was empowered to employ certain supervisory and enforcement measures and, with the consent of the government concerned, to carry out local inquiries. The protocol came into force in December 1964.

The Single Convention on Narcotic Drugs, 1961. On 30 March 1961, a conference at UN headquarters adopted and opened for signature the Single Convention on Narcotic Drugs, 1961. This convention, which entered into force on 13 December 1964, was a milestone in international narcotics control.

The first objective of the convention—codification of existing multilateral treaty law in this field—was almost completely achieved. The second goal—simplification of the international control machinery—was achieved: the Permanent Central Opium Board and the Drug Supervisory Body were combined as the International Narcotics Control Board. The third goal was extension of control to cover cultivation of plants grown for narcotics. The treaty continued controls on opium, including national opium monopolies and the obligation of governments to limit production to medical and scientific purposes. Provisions dealing with medical treatment and rehabilitation of addicts were quite new as treaty obligations. Opium smoking, opium eating, coca-leaf chewing, hashish (cannabis) smoking, and the use of cannabis for nonmedical purposes are prohibited. The convention requires parties to take special control measures for particularly dangerous drugs, such as heroin and ketobemidone. Earlier treaty provisions, requiring (1) that exports and imports of narcotic drugs be made only on government authorization from both sides, (2) that governments report on the working of the treaty, and (3) that they exchange, through the secretary-general, laws and regulations passed to implement the treaty, were retained. Provisions for controlling the manufacture of narcotic drugs and the trade and distribution of narcotic substances were also continued, along with measures for controlling new synthetic drugs.

The Convention on Psychotropic Substances, 1971. During the 1960s, there was increasing concern over the harmful effects of such drugs as barbiturates, amphetamines, LSD, and tranquilizers. WHO and the Commission on Narcotic Drugs recommended that governments take appropriate legislative and administrative measures for their control.

On the basis of a draft drawn up by the Commission on Narcotic Drugs—in close collaboration with WHO—a plenipotentiary conference for the adoption of a protocol on psychotropic substances met in Vienna in 1971 with 71 states represented. On 21 February 1971, it adopted and opened for signature the Convention on Psychotropic Substances, 1971. The convention has been in force since 1976.

The 1971 convention is a major step in the extension of international drug control. It contains a number of prohibitive measures for hallucinogens which present a high risk of abuse and have no therapeutic application. Special provisions regarding substances such as LSD prescribe, among other things, prohibition of their use except for research authorized and supervised by governments.

The requirement of licenses for manufacture, trade, and distribution; the supervision of these activities; and the repression of acts contrary to laws and regulations are applied to all of the drugs enumerated in the 1971 convention. Governments may limit or prohibit the import (and export) of any psychotropic drug. With this regulatory system, governments can protect themselves against unwanted drugs. Psychotropic drugs used in therapy but with great abuse potential, such as sleeping pills, are controlled by requiring medical prescriptions and by supervision of export-import activity. International trade in the most dangerous stimulants—the amphetamines—is subject to a more stringent authorization system. Strict record-keeping of drug movements and statistical reports to the International Narcotics Control Board are also required.

A humane provision in the treaty requires "all practicable measures for the prevention of abuse, the early identification, treatment, education, after-care, rehabilitation, and social reintegration of persons involved. . . . Either as an alternative to conviction or punishment or in addition to conviction or punishment, such abusers shall undergo measures of treatment, education, after-care, rehabilitation, and social reintegration."

The Protocol Amending the 1961 Single Convention on Narcotic Drugs, 1972. A plenipotentiary conference adopted on 25 March 1972 amendments to strengthen the international narcotics control system and to include new concepts and means.

The International Narcotics Control Board was increased from 11 to 13 members, to serve for five years instead of three. Technical measures concern limitation of the production of opium, seizure and destruction of illicitly cultivated opium poppies, and the option of the Board to recommend technical or financial assistance to governments. The Protocol, like the 1971 Convention, provides for after-care and rehabilitation of drug abusers. Also, drug offenders are made extraditable in any extradition treaty. The protocol came into force on 8 August 1975.

Narcotic Drugs under International Control

Opium and Its Derivatives. Opium, the coagulated juice of the poppy plant *Papaver somniferum L.,* was known to the Sumerians living in Lower Mesopotamia in 5000 BC. It was used by the Greeks and Arabs for medicinal purposes and was probably introduced into China by the Arabs in the 9th or 10th century. The opium poppy can be grown in most of the habitable parts of the world and is often cultivated for its beautiful flowers or its seeds, which are a valuable food. As an addictive drug, opium was originally eaten or drunk as an infusion. The practice of smoking opium is only a few hundred years old.

The best-known derivatives of opium are morphine, codeine, and diacetylmorphine, more commonly called heroin. While morphine and codeine have valuable medicinal properties, heroin has no medical uses for which less dangerous analgesics cannot be substituted, and upon the recommendation of the Commission on Narcotic Drugs its manufacture has been banned in most countries. A number of drugs are derived from morphine, or are compounded with it, including ethylmorphine and benzylmorphine. Some morphine derivatives, such as apomorphine, are not addictive in themselves.

The most important drugs in national and international illicit traffic are still opium and its derivatives, in particular morphine and heroin. As a result of effective international controls, there has been little diversion of opium or opiates from legitimate channels into the illicit trade. There is, however, illicit production of opium in some countries. From these supplies, clandestine factories manufacture morphine which is converted into heroin. Opium contains as an average 10% of morphine, which is made into diacetylmorphine or heroin in equal weight by relatively simple methods. Clandestine factories have been moving closer to the opium-producing areas. Morphine can be extracted from poppy capsules whether or not the opium has been extracted—at least 30% of licit morphine comes from this process. When Turkey in 1974 resumed cultivation of the opium poppy, which had been stopped two years earlier, it decided not to produce opium but to use the "poppy-straw method" for extraction of morphine. About 90% of the licit morphine is used to make codeine, whereas 90% of illicit morphine is used to make heroin. An effective way of eradicating heroin is to cut off illicit poppy cultivation. This is the intent of the international treaties, and also of crop substitution undertaken in several countries with the support of UNFDAC.

Coca Leaf and Cocaine. Coca leaves grow on an evergreen shrub, *Erythroxylon coca,* native to western South America. The leaves are the raw material for the manufacture of cocaine. The leaves themselves for centuries have been chewed by some of the Andean peoples. When the leaves are chewed, cocaine enters the bloodstream. This has a stimulating effect on the user, but it leads to physical exhaustion and reduces appetite.

The Commission on Narcotic Drugs concluded that coca-leaf chewing is a dangerous habit and constitutes a form of addiction. In 1954, ECOSOC recommended that the countries concerned should gradually limit the cultivation and export of coca leaf to medical, scientific, and other legitimate purposes and should progressively abolish the habit of coca-leaf chewing. At the same time it was recognized that there was little chance of eliminating coca-leaf addiction unless the living conditions of those among whom the habit was widespread could be improved and that the problem must be attacked on this front as well.

Coca leaves are used to make licit cocaine, whose production has declined to about one ton a year, but also for the illicit market which supplies increasing quantities of this dangerous drug to North America, Western Europe, and other regions.

Cannabis (Marijuana). The plant *Cannabis sativa,* or the crude drug derived from it, is known under almost 200 different names —marijuana, hashish, Indian hemp, charas, ganji, kif, bhang, and maconha, to name a few. Widely used as an intoxicant by millions of people for at least 4,000 years, it can be grown in most parts of the inhabited world. Depending on the soil and cultivation, the plant grows to a height of 1 to 20 feet. The narcotic resin is found in the flowering tops.

Cannabis is used as a narcotic in great parts of Africa, the Middle East, and the Americas. Because the plant grows wild and is easy to cultivate illicitly, traffickers have little difficulty in obtaining cannabis. Statistics on users are not available, but their number must run well in the millions

Synthetic Narcotic Drugs. A number of synthetic substitutes, especially for morphine, are widely used. They were placed under control by the 1948 protocol. They may and do give rise to abuse but in a relatively limited way, and there is little, if any, illicit traffic in these drugs. The most widely known are pethidine and methadone.

Psychotropic Substances. Psychotropic substances placed under international control by the 1971 convention are listed, like narcotic drugs, in treaty schedules which may be modified from time to time by the Commission on Narcotic Drugs. They have widely different characteristics, and, according to complex criteria having to do with the dangers they present to the individual and society, they have been placed in four schedules with decreasing severity of control. In Schedule I are found mainly hallucinogens such as LSD, mescaline, and psilocine. All are made by synthesis, but the last two are also found in plants, respectively the peyotl cactus and the hallucinatory mushroom. Schedule II contains mainly drugs of the amphetamine type that stimulate the central nervous system. They have limited therapeutic value but are widely abused, especially by young people who inject them intravenously, possibly causing psychoses. In Schedule III are found mainly the most powerful depressants of the central nervous system —barbiturates used as hypnotics (sleeping pills) by a very large number of consumers everywhere. These drugs, if used without therapeutic necessity, produce a form of addiction which can be extremely dangerous. Barbiturates are often used in association with heroin, with alcohol (with an especially dangerous interaction) and even with stimulants. Schedule IV has some barbiturate depressants and a number of tranquilizers. These constitute a very large body of medicaments supposed to eliminate anxiety and nervousness. Large quantities of such drugs as meprobamate and diazepan are consumed without therapeutic need and may alter mood and behavior.

HUMAN RIGHTS

In the preamble to the Charter, "the peoples of the United Nations" express their determination "to reaffirm faith in fundamental human rights, in the dignity and worth of the human person, in the equal rights of men and women and of nations large and small." One of the purposes of the UN is that of "promoting and encouraging respect for human rights and for fundamental freedoms for all without distinction as to race, sex, language, or religion" (Article 1). In Articles 55 and 56, "all Members pledge themselves to take joint and separate action in cooperation with the Organization for the achievement" of this purpose. The Charter vests responsibility for assisting in the realization of human rights and fundamental freedoms in the General Assembly, on which all member states are represented; under the authority of the General Assembly, in the 54-member Economic and Social Council; and in the Trusteeship Council, another principal organ the importance of which, however, has declined as almost all former trust territories have become independent. The Charter also provides for the establishment of commissions for the promotion of human rights as subsidiary bodies of ECOSOC. Early in the history of the organization two such commissions were created: the Commission on Human Rights and the Commission on the Status of Women.

THE INTERNATIONAL BILL OF RIGHTS

At the San Francisco Conference, a proposal to embody an international bill of rights in the Charter itself was put forward but not proceeded with because it required more detailed consideration. The idea of establishing an international bill of rights, however, was regarded as inherent in the Charter. Even before the Charter was ratified and entered into force, and before the UN as an organization was established, steps were taken toward this goal. The Preparatory Commission of the UN and its Executive Committee, meeting in the fall of 1945, both recommended that the work of the Commission on Human Rights should be directed, in the first place, toward the "formulation of an international bill of rights." The General Assembly agreed with these recommendations in January 1946. Accordingly, when the terms of reference of the Commission on Human Rights were laid down in February 1946, "an international bill of rights" was the first item on its work program.

When the Commission on Human Rights and the drafting committee started their work on this ambitious project, it turned out that there was doubt and disagreement among the members about the form that the draft bill of rights should take. Some members thought the bill should be a "declaration" or "manifesto" that would be proclaimed by a resolution of the General Assembly. Others urged that it should take the form of an international treaty, which, in addition to being approved by the General Assembly, would have to be opened for signature, ratification, or accession by governments and would be binding only on those governments which had ratified it or acceded to it. The relevant report of the drafting committee records that it was agreed by those who favored the declaration form that the declaration should be accompanied or followed by one or more conventions. It was also agreed by those who favored the convention form that the General Assembly, in recommending a convention to member nations, might make a declaration wider in content or more general in expression. As a consequence, drafts of a "declaration"

and of a "convention" were prepared, and studies were undertaken for the creation of international supervisory and enforcement machinery, called "measures of implementation."

Eventually the decision emerged that the international bill of rights should not be produced by one single, comprehensive, and final act but should consist of two or more international instruments, namely a declaration and a convention (covenant), plus measures of implementation. Later it was decided that there should be not one but two covenants and that the provisions on the measures of implementation should be embodied in the texts of the covenants. The latter decision was modified somewhat in 1966, when the provisions regulating one specific aspect of the implementation arrangements, the right of petition (communication), were included in a separate optional protocol.

The first part of this International Bill of Rights was adopted by the General Assembly in the form of a resolution entitled the *Universal Declaration of Human Rights,* on 10 December 1948. The remaining parts—namely, the *International Covenant on Economic, Social and Cultural Rights,* the *International Covenant on Civil and Political Rights,* and the *Optional Protocol to the International Covenant on Civil and Political Rights*—were adopted and opened for signature, ratification, and accession on 16 December 1966, the two Covenants unanimously, the Optional Protocol by majority vote. They entered into force in 1976.

THE UNIVERSAL DECLARATION OF HUMAN RIGHTS

The Universal Declaration of Human Rights was prepared by the Commission on Human Rights in 1947 and 1948 and adopted and proclaimed by the General Assembly on 10 December 1948 by a vote of 48 in favor, none against, with 6 abstentions. Two representatives were absent. One of them stated later that, if he had been present, he would have voted in favor.

The Universal Declaration proclaims—and in this regard it differs from the traditional catalogues of the rights of man that are contained in various constitutions and fundamental laws of the 18th and 19th centuries and of the first decades of the 20th century—not only civil and political rights but also rights which were eventually regulated in the International Covenant on Economic, Social and Cultural Rights.

The Declaration proclaims that all human beings are born free and equal in dignity and rights (Article 1). It states further that "everyone is entitled to all the rights and freedoms set forth in this Declaration, without distinction of any kind, such as race, color, sex, language, religion, political or other opinion, national or social origin, property, birth or other status" and that "no distinction shall be made on the basis of the political, jurisdictional or international status of the country or territory to which a person belongs, whether it be independent, trust, non-self-governing or under any other limitation of sovereignty" (Article 2).

In Articles 3 to 21, the Declaration deals with the traditional civil and political rights: the right to life, liberty, and security of person; freedom from slavery and servitude; freedom from torture and from cruel, inhuman, or degrading treatment or punishment; equality before the law and equal protection of the law; freedom from arbitrary arrest, detention, or exile; the right to be presumed innocent until proved guilty; the right to protection against arbitrary interference with one's privacy, family, home or correspondence and to protection against attacks upon one's honor and reputation; freedom of movement and residence; everyone's right to leave any country, including his own; the right to seek and enjoy in other countries asylum from persecution (but not the right to be granted asylum); the right to a nationality and to change one's nationality; the right of men and women of full age to marry, without any limitation due to race, nationality, or religion; freedom of thought, conscience, and religion; the right to own property and not to be arbitrarily deprived of it; freedom of opinion and expression; the right to peaceful assembly and association; the right to vote and to take part in the government of one's country, and to equal access to public service.

Economic, social, and cultural rights (Articles 22 to 27) are introduced by Article 22, which states generally that "everyone, as a member of society, has the right to social security" and is entitled to the realization of "economic, social and cultural rights indispensable for his dignity and the free development of his personality." The article implies, however, that those economic, social, and cultural rights are not everywhere and immediately achievable. It states that the "realization" of these rights is to be brought about "through national effort and international cooperation and in accordance with the organization and resources of each state."

The Declaration affirms everyone's right to work, to free choice of employment, to just and favorable conditions of work, and to protection against unemployment. It affirms the right of everyone to equal pay for equal work; to "just and favorable remuneration"; to form and join trade unions; to "a standard of living adequate for the health and well-being of himself and of his family"; and to "rest and leisure, including reasonable limitation of working hours and periodic holidays with pay." It also proclaims "the right to security in the event of unemployment, sickness, disability, widowhood, old age or other lack of livelihood in circumstances beyond [one's] control." Everyone has the right to education, which shall be free "at least in the elementary and fundamental stages" and be compulsory on the elementary level. The Declaration affirms everyone's right "freely to participate in the cultural life of the community, to enjoy the arts and to share in scientific advancement and its benefits."

Article 28 asserts that "everyone is entitled to a social and international order in which the rights and freedoms set forth in this Declaration can be fully realized." In the exercise of his rights and freedoms, everyone shall be subject only to such limitations as are determined by law. The law must provide for limitations solely for the purpose of securing due recognition and respect for the rights and freedoms of others and of meeting the just requirements of morality, public order, and the general welfare in a democratic society (Article 29). In order to protect a democratic society against totalitarian movements, Article 30 states that nothing in the Declaration may be interpreted as implying for any state, group, or person any right to engage in any activity or to perform any act aimed at the destruction of any of the rights and freedoms set forth in the Declaration.

The Universal Declaration of Human Rights was adopted, not in the form of an international convention which, when ratified, is legally binding on the states that are parties to it, but in the form of a resolution of the General Assembly, as "a common understanding" of the rights and freedoms to the respect for and observance of which member states have pledged themselves and as "a common standard of achievement for all peoples and all nations." In the view of most of those who were instrumental in its preparation and adoption, the Declaration was not meant to be a "binding" instrument. However, as soon as the Declaration was adopted, it began to be used as a code of conduct and as a yardstick to measure the compliance by governments with the international standards of human rights.

The first instance occurred in April 1949, when a complaint was brought before the General Assembly that the USSR had violated fundamental human rights by preventing Soviet wives of citizens of other nationalities from leaving their country with their husbands or joining them abroad. The General Assembly invoked the articles of the Declaration which provide that everyone has the right to leave any country including his own and that men and women of full age have the right to marry without any limitation due to race, nationality, or religion. The Assembly declared that measures taken by the USSR were not in conformity with the UN Charter and it called upon the USSR government to withdraw them.

Another human rights conflict that came before the General Assembly early in its history was the treatment of people of Indian and Pakistani origin in South Africa. In repeated resolutions, the General Assembly exhorted the parties to resolve the dispute on the basis of the provisions of the Charter and of the Declaration. On the question of the racial situation in southern Africa, a perennial issue before the UN, the Assembly repeatedly invoked the Declaration in its endeavor to have South Africa and the other authorities in southern Africa abandon the policy of racial discrimination.

In countless other disputes and controversies that it was called upon to examine, the UN and its various organs have had recourse to the Declaration, whether they were dealing with allegations of forced labor, with discrimination in non-self-governing and trust territories, with customs and practices inconsistent with the physical integrity and dignity of women, or with other blemishes on our civilization. The Declaration has played an important role also in the activities of specialized agencies such as the ILO, UNESCO, and ITU, in regional organizations such as the OAS, the Council of Europe, and the OAU. The All African Charter of Unity of 1963, which is the constitution of the OAU, lists among the purposes of the organization "to promote international cooperation, with due regard for the United Nations Charter and the Universal Declaration of Human Rights."

From these examples alone it is clear that the Declaration has acquired a purpose different from that which was contemplated by many of the governments that brought it into being in 1948. The international community, the states that had been instrumental in its creation as well as those that later acceded to independence, used the Declaration for the purpose of fulfilling an assignment greater and more far-reaching than that which had been originally carved out for it. In the decades following 1948, the process of creating a comprehensive international law of human rights by the traditional method of concluding international treaties, by establishing and putting into force the International Covenants on Human Rights, slowed down. As a consequence the Declaration, temporarily at least, filled the void. It took over the function originally contemplated for the International Bill of Rights as a whole.

THE INTERNATIONAL COVENANTS ON HUMAN RIGHTS

The Commission on Human Rights, the Economic and Social Council, and the General Assembly devoted 19 years (1947–66) to the preparation and adoption of the International Covenants on Human Rights. One problem that created a considerable amount of controversy, particularly in the first years, was whether the treaty that would give effect in law to the rights and freedoms set forth in the Universal Declaration of Human Rights should regulate only those rights that traditionally had been guaranteed in national constitutions or catalogues of rights, and are known as "civil and political rights," or whether the treaty should set forth also "economic, social and cultural rights."

As already indicated, it was eventually decided that there should be two covenants dealing with the two sets of provisions, respectively. The principal reason for having two separate instruments regulating the two groups of rights was the fundamentally different character of the rights concerned, which led some even to question whether "economic, social and cultural rights" are, technically, rights at all—in the sense of subjective, enforceable, and justiciable rights. The different character of these rights made it necessary to provide for a difference in the type of international obligations to be undertaken by states parties that accept one or the other, or both, of the two covenants. Another reason for establishing two different covenants was thought to be the necessity to adjust the arrangements for international supervision —the "measures of implementation"—to the different character of the rights.

In the International Covenant on Civil and Political Rights, each state party undertakes to *respect* and to *ensure* to all individuals within its territory and subject to its jurisdiction the rights recognized in that covenant. In the International Covenant on Economic, Social and Cultural Rights, each state party only undertakes to *take steps,* individually and through international assistance and cooperation, to the maximum of its available resources, *with a view to achieving progressively* the full realization of the rights recognized in that covenant by all appropriate means. Subject to certain exceptions and modifications, the Civil and Political Rights Covenant imposes upon states parties the obligation to maintain defined standards. The states parties to the International Covenant on Economic, Social and Cultural Rights assume the obligation to promote an objective—the achievement of human rights.

By and large, the two covenants between them cover the rights proclaimed in the Universal Declaration of Human Rights as they have been described above. However, there are considerable differences between the Universal Declaration and the covenants in regard to the coverage of rights.

The provisions of the Universal Declaration proclaiming that everyone has a right to own property and that everyone has the right to seek and to enjoy in other countries asylum from persecution have no counterpart in the covenants. On the other hand, the covenants deal with a number of questions in regard to which the Declaration contains no provision. Examples are the provisions of both covenants that all peoples have the right to self-determination by virtue of which they freely determine their political status and freely pursue their economic, social, and cultural development.

The International Covenant on Civil and Political Rights, but not the Declaration, protects aliens against expulsion, entitles everyone not to be compelled to testify against himself or to confess guilt, provides for a right to compensation for miscarriage of justice, and also provides that no one shall be liable to be tried or punished again for an offense for which he has already been finally convicted or acquitted. The Covenant prohibits any propaganda for war and any advocacy of national, racial, or religious hatred. It provides for the protection of ethnic, religious, or linguistic minorities. The Declaration does not contain corresponding provisions. While the Declaration proclaims *everyone's* right to a nationality, the Civil and Political Rights Covenant provides that *every child* has the right to acquire a nationality.

The International Covenant on Economic, Social and Cultural Rights sets forth the right to work, including the right of everyone to the opportunity to gain his living by work that he freely chooses or accepts; the right of everyone to the enjoyment of just and favorable conditions of work; the right of everyone to form and to join trade unions and, subject to the law of the land, the right to strike; the right of everyone to social security, including social insurance and the protection of the family; the right to an adequate standard of living and freedom from hunger; the right to the enjoyment of the highest attainable standards of physical and mental health; the right to education; and the right to take part in cultural life.

The International Covenant on Economic, Social and Cultural Rights entered into force on 3 January 1976. By 31 December 1982, 75 states had ratified or acceded to it.

The International Covenant on Civil and Political Rights and the Optional Protocol entered into force on 23 March 1976. By 31 December 1982, 72 states had ratified or acceded to the Covenant and 28 states to the Optional Protocol.

Measures of Implementation

The states parties to the Covenant on Economic, Social and Cultural Rights undertake to submit to ECOSOC reports on the measures they have adopted and the progress made in achieving the observance of the rights recognized in that covenant. These reports are studied by ECOSOC and, if the Council so decides, by the Commission on Human Rights. Both are expected to make recommendations of a general nature.

Under the International Covenant on Civil and Political Rights, an 18-member Human Rights Committee was established to consider reports submitted by states parties on measures taken to implement the covenant's provisions and also to consider communications alleging violations under the optional protocol. The optional protocol provides for consideration of communications from individuals who claim to be victims of violations of any rights set forth in the covenant. However, only claims against states parties to the protocol can be considered.

Apart from the right of individual complaint under the specific procedure of the optional protocol, thousands of letters and reports are received each year by the UN alleging human rights violations. Communications containing complaints of violations of human rights are summarized and sent confidentially to the members of the Commission on Human Rights and its Subcommission on Prevention of Discrimination and Protection of Minorities; copies of the complaint are also sent to the member states named. The identity of the writers is not disclosed unless they have consented to disclosure. Any replies from the government are forwarded to the commission and subcommission.

The subcommission, if it finds the communications appear to reveal "a consistent pattern of gross and reliably attested violations" of human rights, may refer the situation to the commission which, in turn, can decide to carry out a thorough study of the situation or to name an ad hoc committee to investigate it. All these procedures are confidential and are dealt with in private meetings until a report, if any, is made by the commission to ECOSOC.

The Commission on Human Rights and its subcommission also consider in public session each year the question of violations of human rights and fundamental freedoms, including racial discrimination and apartheid, in various countries and territories. For example, since 1967, an ad hoc working group of experts of the commission has reported regularly on allegations of ill-treatment of opponents of apartheid and other racist policies, and on the treatment of political prisoners and detainees, in South Africa and Namibia. The commission has also kept under continuous review the question of the adverse consequences for human rights of political, military, economic, and other forms of assistance given to colonial and racist regimes in southern Africa.

Since 1968, the commission has been considering the question of the violation of human rights in the territories occupied by Israel as a result of the 1967 hostilities in the Middle East, including Israel's violation of the 1949 Geneva Convention relative to the protection of civilian persons in time of war.

In 1975, the commission established a five-member working group to study the human rights situation in Chile. The group visited Chile in 1978 and submitted a report to the General Assembly and the commission. After the completion of the group's mandate, the commission appointed a special rapporteur in 1979 to continue to study the situation. The commission has also decided to request that studies or reports be prepared by special rapporteurs or by the secretary-general on the human rights situation in Bolivia, El Salvador, Equatorial Guinea, Guatemala, Iran, and Poland. The human rights situation, and especially the question of the exercise of the right to self-determination, in Afghanistan and Kampuchea has also been considered by the commission.

In addition, the commission and its subcommission have studied specific phenomena of particularly serious violations of human rights. Thus two working groups have been established—one to study slavery and the exploitation of child labor, and the other to examine the question of enforced or involuntary disappearances —and special rapporteurs have been appointed to examine the question of human rights and mass exoduses, and the question of summary or arbitrary executions.

OTHER INTERNATIONAL CONVENTIONS IN THE FIELD OF HUMAN RIGHTS

The UN and two of the specialized agencies, the ILO and UNESCO, have prepared and put into force a number of conventions in the human rights field which, while not as comprehensive as the International Bill of Human Rights, deal with important specific rights. (Conventions on racial discrimination and on the status of women are discussed in separate sections below.)

Prevention and Punishment of Genocide
In 1948 the General Assembly adopted the Convention on the Prevention and Punishment of the Crime of Genocide (in force since 1951). Genocide means any of the following acts committed with intent to destroy in whole or in part a national, ethnical, racial, or religious group as such: (a) killing members of the group; (b) causing serious bodily or mental harm to members of the group; (c) deliberately inflicting on the group conditions of life calculated to bring about its physical destruction in whole or in part; (d) imposing measures intended to prevent births within the group; (e) forcibly transferring children of the group to another group. One result of this convention is that the states parties place it beyond doubt that genocide (and conspiracy, incitement, and attempt to commit it, and complicity in it), even if perpetrated by a government in its own territory against its own citizens, is not a matter essentially within the domestic jurisdiction of states but one of international concern. States parties confirm that genocide, whether committed in time of peace or in time of war, is a crime under international law which they undertake to prevent and to punish. Any contracting party can call upon UN organs to intervene.

Freedom of Association
The Freedom of Association Convention of 1948 (in force since 1950) was the first major achievement of the joint efforts of the UN and the ILO in the field of international legislation on human rights problems. By this convention, states parties undertake to give effect to the right of workers and employers, without distinction whatsoever, to establish and join organizations of their own choosing without previous authorization. In exercising the rights provided for in the convention, workers and employers and their respective organizations, like other persons or organized collectives, shall respect the law of the land. However, the law of the land shall not be such as to impair, not shall it be so applied as to impair, the guarantees provided in the convention.

Under the Right to Organize and Collective Bargaining Convention of 1949 (in force since 1951), workers shall enjoy adequate protection against acts of anti-union discrimination in their employment, particularly in respect to acts calculated to make the employment of a worker subject to the condition that he shall not join a union or shall relinquish trade union membership.

Freedom of Information
Out of the very ambitious legislative program of the UN and the specialized agencies to guarantee through international instruments the right set forth in Article 19 of the Universal Declaration of Human Rights to seek, receive, and impart information and ideas through any medium and regardless of frontiers, only the Convention on the International Right of Correction has been adopted. At a UN Conference on Freedom of Information held in 1948, two additional conventions in this field were drafted—a general Convention on Freedom of Information and a Convention on the International Transmission of News—but these have not yet been opened for signature and ratification, although the General Assembly has approved the latter convention.

The idea underlying the Convention on the International Right of Correction, which was opened for signature in 1952 and has been in force since 1962, is the attempt to transfer to the international level an institution that has been part of national law in a great number of countries. In the convention the contracting states agree that in cases where a contracting state contends that a news dispatch capable of injuring its relations with other states, or its national prestige or dignity, transmitted from one country to another by correspondents or information agencies and published or disseminated abroad, is false or distorted, it may submit its version of the facts (called communiqué) to the contracting states within whose territories such dispatch has been published or disseminated. The receiving state has the obligation to release the communiqué to the correspondents and information agencies operating in its territory through the channels customarily used for the release of news concerning international affairs for publication.

Protection of Refugees and Stateless Persons
In the Convention Relating to the Status of Refugees of 1951 (in force since 1954, with a Protocol of 1967) and the Convention Relating to the Status of Stateless Persons of 1954 (in force since 1960), far-reaching provisions for the protection of refugees and stateless persons were enacted. Two principles are the basis of both conventions: (1) there shall be as little discrimination as possible between nationals on the one hand and refugees or stateless persons on the other; and (2) there shall be no discrimination based on race, religion, or country of origin at all among refugees and stateless persons.

In 1961 a conference of plenipotentiaries adopted the Convention on the Reduction of Statelessness, which entered into force in 1975. (See also the section on UNHCR in the chapter on Social and Humanitarian Assistance.)

Abolition of Slavery, the Slave Trade, and Forced Labor
The fight against slavery has been an international concern since the beginning of the 19th century. In more recent times, under the auspices of the League of Nations, the Slavery Convention of 1926 was enacted by which the contracting parties undertook to prevent and suppress the slave trade and to bring about "progressively and as soon as possible" the complete abolition of slavery in all its forms. Under UN auspices, the Supplementary Convention on the Abolition of Slavery, the Slave Trade and Institutions and Practices Similar to Slavery was adopted in 1956 (in force since 1957). Under it states parties undertake to bring about, also only "progressively and as soon as possible," the complete abolition or abandonment not only of slavery but also of other objectionable practices such as debt bondage and serfdom.

By the Convention Concerning the Abolition of Forced Labor, adopted by the International Labor Conference in 1957 and in force since 1959, states parties undertake to suppress and not to make use of any form of forced or compulsory labor, inter alia, as a means of political coercion or education or as a punishment for holding or expressing political views or views ideologically opposed to the established political, social, or economic system; as a punishment for having participated in strikes; or as means of racial, social, national, or religious discrimination.

Equality in Employment and Occupation
By the Discrimination (Employment and Occupation) Convention, adopted by the International Labor Conference in 1958 (in force

since 1960), each state party undertakes to declare and pursue a national policy designed to promote, by methods appropriate to national conditions and practices, equality of opportunity and treatment with respect to employment and occupation, with a view to eliminating discrimination. The fulfillment of the obligations undertaken by this convention is subject to the supervisory arrangements that apply under the constitution of the ILO.

Equality in Education

In 1960 the General Conference of UNESCO adopted the Convention Against Discrimination in Education (in force since 1962). Like the Discrimination (Employment and Occupation) Convention, the Convention Against Discrimination in Education prohibits any distinction, exclusion, limitation, or preference based on race, color, sex, language, religion, political or other opinion, national or social origin, or economic condition or birth having the purpose or effect of impairing equality of treatment in education. The establishment or maintenance of separate educational systems or institutions for pupils of the two sexes is not prohibited, provided that these systems or institutions offer equivalent access to education and provide a teaching staff meeting the same standard of qualification. A special protocol adopted in 1962 institutes a Conciliation and Good Offices Commission to be responsible for seeking a settlement of any disputes that may arise between the states parties to the Convention Against Discrimination in Education.

Non-Applicability of Statutory Limitations to War Crimes and Crimes Against Humanity

In 1968, the General Assembly adopted the Convention on the Non-Applicability of Statutory Limitations to War Crimes and Crimes Against Humanity. The convention, in force since 1970, provides that no statutory limitation shall apply to war crimes and crimes against humanity irrespective of the date of their commission. It also revises and extends the concepts of war crimes and crimes against humanity as they were defined in 1945 in the Charter of the International Military Tribunal and were applied and interpreted by the tribunal. The states parties to the 1968 convention undertake to adopt all necessary domestic measures with a view to making possible the extradition of persons who have committed such crimes.

In the International Convention on the Suppression and Punishment of the Crime of Apartheid, adopted in 1973, the states parties declare that apartheid is a crime against humanity and undertake to punish persons guilty of that crime. (See also under Racial Discrimination below.)

Prevention and Punishment of Crimes Against Internationally Protected Persons

In 1973, the General Assembly adopted the Convention on the Prevention and Punishment of Crimes Against Internationally Protected Persons, Including Diplomatic Agents. The convention, in force since 1977, aims at preventing the commission of acts of terrorism against heads of state, heads of government, ministers of foreign affairs, representatives of states, and officials of international organizations, as well as members of their families who accompany them or form part of their households. Each state party to the convention agrees to make murder, kidnapping, or other attacks upon the person or liberty of an internationally protected person and a violent attack upon his official premises, private accommodations, or means of transport a punishable crime. States agree to cooperate in the prevention of these crimes and in the prosecution and punishment of offenders.

REGIONAL HUMAN RIGHTS INSTRUMENTS

The work of the UN in the human rights field, for which the provisions of the Charter have been the point of departure, has inspired important developments for the protection of human rights also on the regional level by the Council of Europe and the Organization of American States.

The European Convention on Human Rights

Under the auspices of the Council of Europe, the European Convention on Human Rights was signed in 1950 and entered into force in 1953. The convention is based on an early draft of what is now the International Covenant on Civil and Political Rights. It was concluded by the governments of European countries "to take the first steps for the collective enforcement of certain of the rights stated in the Universal Declaration of Human Rights." It was subsequently supplemented by five additional protocols. As far as the substantive provisions are concerned, the European Convention and the International Covenant on Civil and Political Rights cover, more or less, the same ground, although there are a number of important differences between the two instruments.

The European Convention established two internal organs "to ensure the observance of the engagements undertaken by the High Contracting Parties in the present Convention"—that is, the European Commission on Human Rights and the European Court of Human Rights. Any party to the convention has the right to refer to the commission any alleged breach of the convention by another party. The commission may also receive petitions from any person, nongovernmental organization, or group of individuals claiming to be the victim of a violation by one of the parties of the rights set forth in the convention and in the relevant protocols. The exercise of this power by the commission is subject to the condition that the state against which the complaint is directed has recognized this competence of the commission.

If the commission does not succeed in securing a friendly settlement on the basis of respect for human rights as defined in the convention, it draws up a report on the facts and states its opinion as to whether the facts found disclose a breach by the state concerned of its obligations under the convention. The final decision is taken either by the Committee of Ministers of the Council of Europe, a political organ, or, if it has jurisdiction and the matter is referred to it, by the European Court of Human Rights.

The European Social Charter

The European Social Charter is the European counterpart to the International Covenant on Economic, Social and Cultural Rights. The provisions of the European Social Charter, however, are more specific and detailed. It has established a reporting procedure. The reports are examined by a committee of independent experts, which submits its conclusions to a governmental social subcommittee. The Consultative Assembly of the Council of Europe is consulted. In the final stage, the Committee of Ministers may make to any contracting party any recommendation it considers necessary in the areas of economic, social, and cultural rights.

The American Convention on Human Rights

In 1948, several months before the adoption by the General Assembly of the Universal Declaration of Human Rights, the Ninth International Conference of American States adopted at Bogotá the American Declaration of the Rights and Duties of Man. This declaration was followed in 1969 by the signing of the "Pact of San José, Costa Rica," the American Convention on Human Rights. The convention, in force since 1978, is a very comprehensive instrument, similar both to the European Convention on Human Rights and to the International Covenant on Civil and Political Rights. The organs of implementation of the Pact of San José are the Inter-American Commission on Human Rights (corresponding to the European Commission and to the Human Rights Committee under the International Covenant on Civil and Political Rights) and the Inter-American Court of Human Rights. While under the European Convention and the International Covenant on Civil and Political Rights and its Optional Protocol, the right of petition of individuals is optional, in the Inter-American system every state party accepts the right of petition automatically. The provisions of the American Convention are progressive also in other respects.

THE FIGHT AGAINST RACIAL DISCRIMINATION

The idea of the equality of races emerged as the one which, more than any other, has dominated the thoughts and actions of the post–World War II period. The aim of racial equality has permeated the lawmaking and the standard-setting activities of the UN family of organizations and also the day-to-day work of many of its organs. The Charter, the Universal Declaration of Human Rights, and the two International Covenants on Human Rights prohibit discrimination on the grounds of race or color, as do also the conventions against discrimination in employment and occupation and in education that have already been described.

The Declaration on the Elimination of All Forms of Racial Discrimination

In 1963, the General Assembly proclaimed the Declaration on the Elimination of All Forms of Racial Discrimination, which affirms that discrimination between human beings on the grounds of race, color, or ethnic origin is an offense to human dignity, a denial of Charter principles, a violation of the rights proclaimed in the Universal Declaration of Human Rights, and an obstacle to friendly and peaceful relations among peoples.

The International Convention on the Elimination of All Forms of Racial Discrimination

In 1965, the General Assembly adopted the International Convention on the Elimination of All Forms of Racial Discrimination (in force since 1969). States parties undertake not only to condemn racial discrimination, and to pursue a policy of eliminating it in all its forms, but also to prohibit and bring to an end, by all appropriate means including legislation as required by circumstances, racial discrimination by any persons, group, or organization. States parties undertake to declare it an offense punishable by law to disseminate ideas based on racial superiority or hatred, and incitement to racial discrimination. They also commit themselves to declare illegal and prohibit organizations which promote and incite racial discrimination and to recognize participation in such organizations as an offense punishable by law. The convention provides for the establishment of international supervisory machinery similar to that laid down in the International Covenant on Civil and Political Rights but contains tighter provisions.

Under the convention, a Committee on the Elimination of Racial Discrimination was established, which, like the Human Rights Committee provided for in the covenant, has the function of considering reports by states and allegations by a state party that another state party is not giving effect to the provisions of the convention. States parties to the convention may also recognize the competence of the Committee on the Elimination of Racial Discrimination to receive and consider petitions (communications) from individuals or groups of individuals. In the last instance, the International Court of Justice can be apprised of disputes with respect to the interpretation and application of the convention.

The International Convention on the Suppression and Punishment of the Crime of Apartheid

The International Convention on the Suppression and Punishment of the Crime of Apartheid, adopted by the General Assembly in 1973 and in force since 1976, provides that international responsibility for the crime of apartheid shall apply to individuals, members of organizations and institutions, and representatives of a state, whether residing in the state in which the acts are perpetrated or elsewhere. Persons charged can be tried by any state party to the convention. A three-member group of the Commission on Human Rights meets each year to review progress in implementing the convention.

The International Declaration Against Apartheid in Sports

The International Declaration Against Apartheid in Sports, adopted by the General Assembly in 1977, calls on states to take all appropriate action to cease sporting contacts with any country practicing apartheid and toward the exclusion or expulsion of any such country from international and regional sports bodies. The Assembly has called for the preparation of an international convention against apartheid in sports.

Decade for Action to Combat Racism and Racial Discrimination

In 1972 the General Assembly decided to launch a Decade for Action to Combat Racism and Racial Discrimination and to inaugurate its activities on 10 December 1973, the 25th anniversary of the Universal Declaration of Human Rights. In 1973 the Assembly approved a comprehensive and ambitious program for the Decade. Among its goals were to promote human rights for all without distinction of any kind on grounds of race, color, descent, or national or ethnic origin, especially by eradicating racial prejudice, racism, and racial discrimination; to arrest any expansion of racist policies; to identify, isolate and dispel the fallacious and mythical beliefs, policies and practices that contribute to racism and racial discrimination; and to put an end to racist regimes.

While there was not necessarily complete unanimity in the General Assembly on every phrase and formulation of the relevant decisions on the Decade adopted in 1972, 1973 and 1974, there was a general consensus in support of its goals. However, at the 1975 session of the Assembly, a resolution was adopted by which the Assembly "determines that Zionism is a form of racism and racial discrimination." The resolution was adopted by 72 votes to 35, with 32 abstentions. Among those strongly opposed were the nine members of the European Common Market, as well as the US, Canada, Australia and New Zealand, and other states of Western Europe, Latin America, and Africa. Many of these states declared that the resolution radically changed the concept of the Decade and would therefore change their attitude towards it.

The midpoint of the Decade was marked by a world conference held in Geneva in August 1978. The conference adopted a new program of action, including recommendations for comprehensive mandatory sanctions against the racist regimes of southern Africa, elimination of all discriminatory laws and practices, adoption of laws to punish dissemination of ideas based on racial superiority or hatred, and promotion of the rights of indigenous peoples and migrant workers. The Assembly adopted a program in 1979 for the remaining four years of the Decade, and in 1982 decided that a second world conference would be held in 1983.

The Second World Conference to Combat Racism and Racial Discrimination, held in Geneva in August 1983, was attended by representatives of 128 states, as well as of UN organs and specialized agencies and of intergovernmental and nongovernmental organizations. The conference adopted a declaration and a program of action in which it noted that "in spite of the efforts of the international community during the Decade, at the national, regional and international levels, racism, racial discrimination and apartheid continue unabated and have shown no sign of diminishing." The program of action contained practical suggestions on matters such as action to combat apartheid; education, teaching, and training; dissemination of information and the role of the mass media in combating racism and racial discrimination; measures for the promotion and protection of the human rights of persons belonging to minority groups, indigenous populations and peoples, and migrant workers who are subject to racial discrimination; recourse procedures for victims of racial discrimination; implementation of the International Convention on the Elimination of All Forms of Racial Discrimination and other related international instruments; national legislation and institutions; seminars and studies; action by nongovernmental organizations; and international cooperation. The conference called on the General Assembly to declare a second Decade for Action to Combat Racism and Racial Discrimination beginning in 1984.

THE WORK OF THE UN RELATING TO THE STATUS OF WOMEN

The work relating to the status of women, aimed at achieving equal rights for men and women, is an important part of the UN's efforts to promote and to encourage respect for human rights and fundamental freedoms. The organ given the main responsibility in this field is the Commission on the Status of Women, a functional commission of ECOSOC. Almost all the achievements of the UN in this matter are due to the initiative and work of the commission.

The Convention on the Political Rights of Women

The Convention on the Political Rights of Women, adopted in 1952 and in force since 1954, represents the culmination of the endeavors of generations of fighters for women's rights. It provides that women shall be entitled to vote in all elections, that they shall be eligible for election to all publicly elected bodies, and that they shall be entitled to hold public office and to exercise all public functions on equal terms with men and without any discrimination.

The Convention on the Nationality of Married Women

The Convention on the Nationality of Married Women, adopted in 1957 and in force since 1958, provides that neither the celebration nor the dissolution of marriage between a national and an alien, nor the change of nationality by the husband during marriage, shall automatically affect the nationality of the wife.

The Convention on Consent to Marriage, Minimum Age for Marriage, and Registration of Marriages

The Convention on Consent to Marriage, Minimum Age for Marriage, and Registration of Marriages, adopted in 1962 and in force since 1964, provides that no marriage shall be legally entered into without the full free consent of both parties, such consent to be expressed by them in person after due publicity and in the presence of the authority competent to solemnize the marriage. States parties to the convention are committed to take legislative action to specify a minimum age for marriage. All marriages shall be registered in an official register by a competent authority.

In a recommendation on the same subjects as those of this convention, adopted in 1965, the General Assembly stated that the minimum age shall be not less than 15 years.

The Declaration on the Elimination of Discrimination Against Women

In 1967, the General Assembly solemnly proclaimed the Declaration on the Elimination of Discrimination Against Women. The declaration states that discrimination against women, denying or limiting as it does their equality of rights with men, is fundamentally unjust and constitutes an offense against human dignity. Work was started on a convention to put the principles of the declaration into binding legal form.

The Convention on the Elimination of All Forms of Discrimination Against Women

On 18 December 1979, the General Assembly adopted the Convention on the Elimination of All Forms of Discrimination Against Women. The convention came into force in September 1981; by the end of 1982, 45 states had become parties to it.

Under the convention, states parties undertake to adopt all appropriate measures to abolish existing laws, regulations, customs, and practices that are discriminatory against women and to establish legal protection of the rights of women on an equal basis with men. The convention contains detailed provisions concerning equal rights for women in voting and holding public office and in education, employment, and health care. It provides for equality before the law and for the elimination of discrimination against women in all matters relating to marriage and family relations. The convention established a Committee on the Elimination of Discrimination Against Women to periodically examine reports by states parties on measures they have taken to implement the convention.

International Women's Year

In 1972, the General Assembly decided to proclaim the year 1975 International Women's Year, and ECOSOC in 1974 decided to convene in 1975 an international conference to examine to what extent the organizations of the UN system have implemented the recommendations for the elimination of discrimination against women made by the Commission on the Status of Women since its establishment, and to launch an international action program aimed at achieving the integration of women as full and equal partners with men in the total development effort, eliminating discrimination on grounds of sex, and achieving the widest possible involvement of women in strengthening international peace and eliminating racism and racial discrimination.

The World Conference of the International Women's Year took place in June/July 1975 in Mexico City. It was the most representative meeting on women's issues ever held, bringing together more than 1,000 representatives, about 70% of them women, from more than 130 countries. The conference adopted the "Declaration of Mexico on the Equality of Women and Their Contribution to Development and Peace, 1975"; a world plan of action for implementation of the objectives of the International Women's Year; regional plans of action; and a great number of decisions on concrete problems. In the Declaration of Mexico, the conference affirmed its faith in the objectives of the International Women's Year—equality, development, and peace.

The world plan of action set 14 minimum objectives, including: a marked increase in literacy and civic education of women; extension of coeducational technical and vocational training in industry and agriculture; equal access to education at every level, and compulsory primary school education; increased employment opportunities, and reduction of unemployment and of discrimination in the terms and conditions of employment; equal eligibility to vote and to seek elected office; greater participation of women in policy-making positions, locally, nationally, and internationally; increased welfare services in health education, sanitation, nutrition, and family-planning education; parity in the exercise of civil, social, and political rights; and recognition of the value of women's work in the home, in domestic food production, in marketing, and in other nonremunerated activities.

UN Decade for Women

Later in 1975, the General Assembly endorsed the proposals of the Mexico conference and proclaimed the period 1976–85 as the UN Decade for Women: Equality, Development, and Peace. The Assembly called for the decade to be devoted to effective and sustained action to implement the world plan of action, and it decided to convene in 1980, at the midterm of the decade, another world conference to review and evaluate the progress made. At the same time, the Assembly established a voluntary fund for the decade and also approved the creation of an International Research and Training Institute for the Advancement of Women, which began operations in 1979.

The second world conference, held in Copenhagen in July 1980, adopted a program of action for the second half of the decade, 1980–85, to promote the three objectives of equality, development, and peace, with special emphasis on the subtheme—employment, health, and education. It called for specific action to ensure that the objectives of the world plan were met by the end of the decade.

The Copenhagen conference provided an occasion for assessing the condition of women against the objectives established in the world plan of action and also against the conditions then prevailing in the world. In so doing, it served to advance international understanding of the fact that women, far from being simply a social welfare sector or a disadvantaged group, were an integral part of every global concern.

The program of action was endorsed later in 1980 by the General Assembly, which decided to convene in 1985 a world conference to review and appraise the achievements of the Decade.

The Declaration on the Participation of Women in Promoting International Peace and Cooperation

The Declaration on the Participation of Women in Promoting International Peace and Cooperation was adopted by the General Assembly in 1982. It states that women and men have an equal and vital interest in contributing to international peace and cooperation and, to this end, women must be enabled to exercise their right to participate in the economic, social, cultural, civil, and political affairs of society on an equal footing with men.

OTHER DECLARATIONS IN THE HUMAN RIGHTS FIELD

Between the action taken on the basis of the authority vested in UN organs by the Charter and the preparation, opening for signature, and putting into force of international conventions adding to the obligations deriving from the Charter, there is an intermediate stage of acts and developments that do not fully belong within either of these two categories. As a consequence of the political and technical obstacles that have delayed concluding international treaties on human rights and making them operative, the international community has had recourse to the proclamation of declarations that emanante from UN organs, are not subject to ratification by states, and do not intend to create obligations in the strict legal sense, but that nevertheless have had a great impact on developments. The first and best-known example is the Universal Declaration of Human Rights, described and analyzed at the beginning of this chapter.

The Declaration of the Rights of the Child

In 1959, the General Assembly adopted the Declaration of the Rights of the Child, which proclaims that every child, without distinction or discrimination on account of race, color, sex, language, religion, political or other opinion, national or social origin, property, birth, or other status, whether of himself or of his family, shall enjoy special protection and be given opportunities and facilities to enable him to develop physically, mentally, morally, spiritually, and socially in a healthy and normal manner and in conditions of freedom and dignity. Every child shall be entitled from birth to a name and nationality and shall enjoy the benefits of social security. The child who is physically, mentally, or socially handicapped shall be given the special treatment, education, and care required by his or her particular condition. Every child is entitled to receive education that shall be free and compulsory, at least in the elementary stages. Every child shall be protected against all forms of neglect, cruelty, and exploitation and from practices that may foster racial, religious, and any other form of discrimination.

The General Assembly has called for the preparation by the Commission on Human Rights of a convention on the rights of the child.

The Declaration on the Granting of Independence to Colonial Countries and Peoples

The Declaration on the Granting of Independence to Colonial Countries and Peoples, adopted by the General Assembly in 1960, declares that the subjection of peoples to alien subjugation, domination, and exploitation constitutes a denial of fundamental human rights, is contrary to the Charter, and is an impediment to the promotion of world peace and cooperation. The declaration proclaims that all peoples have the right to self-determination.

In 1961, the Assembly established a Special Committee on the Situation with Regard to the Implementation of the Declaration (see also the chapter on the Independence of Colonial Peoples).

The Declaration on Territorial Asylum

The Declaration on Territorial Asylum, adopted by the General Assembly in 1967, supplements Article 14 of the Universal Declaration of Human Rights and provides that asylum granted by a state in the exercise of its sovereignty to persons entitled to invoke Article 14 of the Universal Declaration, including persons struggling against colonization, shall be respected by all other states. It rests with the state granting asylum to evaluate the grounds for asylum. Where a state finds difficulty in granting or continuing to grant asylum, states individually or jointly or through the UN shall consider, in the spirit of international solidarity, appropriate measures to lighten the burden on that state. No person entitled to invoke Article 14 of the Universal Declaration shall be subjected to measures such as retention at the frontier or, if he has already entered the territory in which he seeks asylum, expulsion or compulsory return to any state where he may be subjected to persecution. (See also the section on UNHCR in the chapter on Social and Humanitarian Assistance.)

The Declaration on Social Progress and Development

In 1969, the General Assembly solemnly proclaimed the Declaration on Social Progress and Development, which sets forth the principals, objectives, means, and methods to eliminate from the life of society all evils and obstacles to social progress, particularly such evils as inequality, exploitation, war, colonialism, and racism. The declaration shows the close connections between social development policies and endeavors to promote respect for human rights. Article 1 provides that all peoples and all human beings, without distinction as to race, color, sex, language, religion, nationality, ethnic origin, family or social status, or political or other conviction, shall have the right to live in dignity and freedom and to enjoy the fruits of social progress and should, on their part, contribute to it.

The Declaration on Principles of International Law Concerning Friendly Relations and Cooperation Among States

On 24 October 1970, the 25th anniversary of the entry into force of the Charter, the General Assembly adopted the Declaration on Principles of International Law Concerning Friendly Relations and Cooperation among States in Accordance with the Charter of the United Nations. One of the principles thus proclaimed reads as follows:

"States shall cooperate in the promotion of universal respect for, and observance of, human rights, and fundamental freedoms for all, and in the elimination of all forms of racial discrimination and all forms of religious intolerance."

The Declaration on the Rights of Mentally Retarded Persons

The Declaration on the Rights of Mentally Retarded Persons of 1971 proclaims that the mentally retarded person has, to the maximum degree of feasibility, the same rights as other human beings: the right to proper medical care and physical therapy, education, training, rehabilitation, and guidance; the right to economic security and to perform productive work; and the right, when this is required, to a qualified guardian and to protection from exploitation, abuse, and degrading treatment. Whenever mentally retarded persons are unable to exercise all their rights in a meaningful way or it should become necessary to restrict or deny them, the procedure used must contain proper legal safeguards against abuse.

The Declaration on the Protection of Women and Children in Emergency and Armed Conflicts

In 1974, the General Assembly proclaimed the Declaration on the Protection of Women and Children in Emergency and Armed Conflicts. The declaration states that attacks on civilians, "especially on women and children, who are the most vulnerable members of the population," shall be prohibited and condemned, and that states involved in armed conflicts shall make all efforts "to spare women and children from the ravages of war."

The Declaration on the Rights of Disabled Persons

In 1975, the Declaration on the Rights of Mentally Retarded Persons was confirmed and expanded by the Declaration on the Rights of Disabled Persons. The term "disabled person" means any person unable to ensure by himself or herself wholly or partly the necessities of a normal individual and/or social life, as a result of a deficiency in his or her physical or mental capacities. While the formulation of some of the rights set forth in the Declaration on the Rights of Disabled Persons occasionally differs from that contained in the earlier instrument, there are no differences as regards the principles and purposes, except that the later Declaration applies also to persons who are physically, not mentally, handicapped.

The Declaration on the Use of Scientific and Technical Progress

In 1975, the General Assembly adopted the Declaration on the Use of Scientific and Technological Progress in the Interests of Peace and for the Benefit of Mankind. The declaration provides that all states shall promote international cooperation to ensure that the results of scientific and technological developments are used in the interests of strengthening international peace and security, freedom and independence, and also for the purpose of the economic and social development of peoples and the realization of human rights and freedoms. All states shall take appropriate measures to prevent the use of scientific and technological developments to limit or interfere with the enjoyment of the human rights of the individual.

All states shall take effective measures to prevent and preclude the utilization of scientific and technological achievements to the detriment of human rights.

The Declaration on the Protection Against Torture and Other Cruel, Inhuman or Degrading Treatment or Punishment

In 1975, the General Assembly proclaimed the Declaration on the Protection of All Persons from Being Subjected to Torture and Other Cruel, Inhuman or Degrading Treatment or Punishment. The Universal Declaration of Human Rights (Article 5) and the International Covenant on Civil and Political Rights (Article 7) both provide that no one may be subjected to torture, or cruel, inhuman or degrading treatment or punishment. The Declaration of 1975 spells the prohibition out in greater detail. It gives a definition of torture (Article 1) and states (Article 2) that any act of torture, etc., is an offense to human dignity and shall be condemned as a violation of human rights and fundamental freedoms proclaimed in the Universal Declaration of Human Rights. Exceptional circumstances such as a state of war or a threat of war, internal political instability, or any other public emergency may not be invoked as a justification of torture, etc. (Article 3). If an investigation establishes that an act of torture appears to have been committed, criminal proceedings shall be instituted against the alleged offender, in accordance with national law. If the allegation of other forms of cruel treatment (other than torture) is considered to be well founded, the alleged offender shall be subject to criminal, disciplinary, or other appropriate proceedings (Article 10). Where the act has been committed by or at the instigation of a public official, the victim shall be afforded redress and compensation, in accordance with national law (Article 11). A statement made as a result of torture or other cruel, inhuman, or degrading treatment may not be invoked as evidence (Article 12).

Declaration on the Elimination of All Forms of Religious Intolerance

The Declaration on the Elimination of All Forms of Intolerance and of Discrimination Based on Religion and Belief, prepared by the Commission on Human Rights and adopted by the General Assembly in 1981, states that everyone shall have the right of freedom of thought, conscience, and religion, and that no one shall be subject to discrimination on the grounds of religion or other beliefs.

INDEPENDENCE OF COLONIAL PEOPLES

Since the creation of the UN, more than 75 territories that were formerly under foreign rule have become sovereign states and members of the UN. In this radical transformation of the world's political map, the UN has played a significant role that stems from the basic precepts of its Charter as laid down in Article 1, which states that one of the purposes of the UN is to "develop friendly relations among nations based on respect for the principle of equal rights and self-determination of peoples. . . ." Chapters XI, XII, and XIII of the Charter are devoted specifically to

measures that are designed to promote the welfare of dependent peoples.

In its efforts to implement these measures, the UN has dealt with two types of territories: (1) former colonial territories administered by designated member states as UN Trust Territories pending independence, and (2) non-self-governing dependencies or colonies of UN member states. Since the UN powers and responsibilities differ considerably in regard to the two categories of territories, this chapter has been divided into two sections.

A. TRUST TERRITORIES

The main features of the trusteeship system are outlined in the chapter on the Trusteeship Council. What follows here is a brief description of the territories originally placed under UN trusteeship in 1946.

TRUST TERRITORIES THAT HAVE ACHIEVED INDEPENDENCE

Of the 11 territories that were placed under the trusteeship system in 1946, 10 have since achieved the goals of the Charter, either as independent states or as parts of independent states.

Togoland under UK Administration. To ascertain the freely expressed wishes of the people as to their political future, the UN, in agreement with the UK, conducted a plebiscite in 1956. As a result of the plebiscite, the territory united in March 1957 with the former Gold Coast to form the independent state of Ghana.

Togoland under French Administration. In 1958, with the agreement of France, the UN supervised elections, and the territory became the independent state of Togo on 27 April 1960.

Cameroons under French Administration. Following a notification in 1958 by its legislative assembly of the desire of the territory to become independent, and acting upon the recommendation of the Trusteeship Council, the Assembly, in agreement with France, resolved that on 1 January 1960 trusteeship status would end and the territory would become independent as Cameroon.

Cameroons under UK Administration. Both the northern and southern sectors of the territory were administered as part of the federation of Nigeria, a British dependency. Following a plebiscite held under UN supervision in March 1961, the northern sector became part of newly independent Nigeria on 1 June 1961. Following a similar plebiscite, the peoples of the southern sector joined the newly independent state of Cameroon on 1 October 1961.

Somaliland under Italian Administration. In union with the dependency of British Somaliland, the territory became the sovereign state of Somalia on 1 July 1960.

Tanganyika under UK Administration. Following negotiations between the UK and African leaders, the territory attained independence on 9 December 1961. It united with Zanzibar in 1964 to become Tanzania.

Ruanda-Urundi under Belgian Administration. In a special session convened in June 1962, the General Assembly approved separate independence for the two territories, which were estab-

lished on 1 July 1962 as the Republic of Rwanda and the Kingdom of Burundi.

Western Samoa under New Zealand Administration. In agreement with the administering authority, the UN conducted a plebiscite in May 1961, following which the territory attained independence on 1 January 1962.

Nauru Administered by Australia on behalf of a joint administering authority comprising Australia, New Zealand, and the UK. The territory became independent on 31 January 1968, in accordance with a 1965 Assembly resolution setting this date as the target for accession to independence.

New Guinea under Australian Administration. The trust territory of New Guinea was administered by Australia together with the non-self-governing territory of Papua until the two were united and became the independent state of Papua New Guinea in 1975.

TERRITORY STILL UNDER UN TRUSTEESHIP

By 1983, only the Trust Territory of the Pacific Islands remained under the UN trusteeship system. It is administered by the US under an agreement approved by the Security Council. Because it is a "strategic" trust territory, it is under the ultimate authority of the Security Council rather than the Assembly. (See the chapter on the Trusteeship Council.)

The Pacific Islands, collectively known as Micronesia, include the former Japanese-mandated islands of the Marshalls, the Carolines, and the Northern Marianas (the entire group except for Guam, which was ceded to the US by Spain in 1898). In 1975, a covenant for political union with the US was approved by a majority of 78.8% in a vote taken in the Northern Marianas. In February 1976, the US Congress gave final approval for granting commonwealth status to the Northern Marianas.

In a referendum held on 12 July 1978, Kosrae, Ponape, Truk, and Yap—in the Caroline archipelago—approved and ratified a draft constitution for a proposed Federated States of Micronesia. The four districts subsequently held elections, and the Congress of the Federated States of Micronesia was inaugurated on 10 May 1979.

The Marshall Islands and Palau rejected the draft constitution and continued drafting their own constitutions. On 21 December 1978, the Marshall Islands Constitutional Convention approved a draft constitution and, in a referendum held on 1 March 1979, the voters of those islands adopted it by a substantial majority.

Legislative power in the Marshall Islands was vested in the *Nitijela* (legislature); the first general election under the new constitution took place on 10 April 1979. On 2 April 1979, the Constitutional Convention of Palau adopted a draft constitution, approved by referendum on 9 July. Elections were held on 4 November 1980, and the new constitution came into force on 1 January 1981.

As of June 1983, constitutional governments were fully functioning in Palau, the Marshall Islands, the Northern Marianas, and the Federated States of Micronesia. The US retained the necessary authority to comply with its responsibilities under the Trusteeship Agreement, the UN Charter, and the applicable US laws and treaties.

B. NON-SELF-GOVERNING TERRITORIES

Delegates attending the 1945 San Francisco Conference, at which the UN was founded, included many spokesmen for anticolonialist sentiment. Due to their efforts and to generous proposals by Australia and the UK (which possessed the world's largest colonial empire at the time), the Charter incorporates a pledge on the part of the colonial powers to assume certain obligations toward the peoples of their dependencies.

CHARTER DECLARATION ON NON-SELF-GOVERNING TERRITORIES

The pledge takes the form of a declaration regarding non-self-governing territories that is embodied in Article 73, Chapter XI. Under Article 73, all UN members "which have or assume responsibilities for the administration of territories whose peoples have not yet attained a full measure of self-government recognize the principle that the interests of the inhabitants of these territories are paramount, and accept as a sacred trust the obligation to promote to the utmost, within the system of international peace and security established by the present Charter, the well-being of the inhabitants of these territories. . . . " This general obligation is then broken down into five specific obligations: (a) to "ensure, with due respect for the culture of the peoples concerned, their political, economic, social, and educational advancement, their just treatment, and their protection against abuses"; (b) to "develop self-government, to take due account of the political aspirations of the peoples, and to assist them in the progressive development of their free political institutions, according to the particular circumstances of each territory and its peoples . . . "; (c) to "further international peace and security"; (d) to "promote constructive measures of development . . . "; and (e) to "transmit regularly to the Secretary-General for information purposes, subject to such limitations as security and constitutional considerations may require, statistical and other information of a technical nature relating to economic, social, and educational conditions in the territories for which they are respectively responsible. . . . "

Today, when so many of these dependent peoples have claimed and won their independence, the obligations contained in the declaration may not seem very far-reaching. For example, nothing is said about preparing non-self-governing territories for actual independence—indeed, the word "independence" nowhere appears in the declaration. Although due account is to be taken of the "political aspirations of the peoples," all that is explicitly acknowledged is the obligation to develop "self-government," which does not necessarily imply independence. But the validity of the declaration must be considered in the context of its era. Few people at the San Francisco Conference foresaw how intense or universal the desire of colonial peoples for full political sovereignty would be. All told, the obligations included in the declaration probably represented the maximum that reasonably could be expected from colonial countries at that time. Moreover, in the circumstances then prevailing, the colonial nations' agreement, under paragraph (e) of Article 73, to submit information to an international body concerning their own territories—in effect to yield up a degree of their sovereignty—was a considerable concession.

Territories Covered by the Declaration

The somewhat unwieldy term "non-self-governing territory" was chosen primarily because it was broad enough to include the various constitutional designations given by administering powers to their dependencies—colony, protectorate, and so on—as well as all stages of political development short of actual self-government or independence. The declaration includes all those territories "whose peoples have not yet attained a full measure of self-government." However, the precise meaning of the phrase "a full measure of self-government" was not specified in the Charter, an omission that left the door open for subsequent dispute and controversy.

At the outset, it was considered the responsibility of the eight colonial powers that were UN members to identify the dependencies they regarded as non-self-governing within the meaning of Article 73 of the Charter. At its first working session, in 1946, the General Assembly adopted a resolution enumerating 74 non-self-governing territories that the administering countries had identified as falling within the provisions of the declaration. The eight colonial countries were Australia, Belgium, Denmark, France, the Netherlands, New Zealand, the UK, and the US. The combined population of their dependencies, which ranged from tiny Pitcairn Island with a population of 100 persons to the Netherlands Indies with 73 million, was estimated at 215 million. (The dependencies of Spain and Portugal could not be included in the 1946 list, since these two colonial powers were not UN members at the time.)

THE ROLE OF THE UN

The Charter does not assign any particular task to the UN with respect to non-self-governing territories. It does not even specify what should be done with the information transmitted to the secretary-general. Hence, the General Assembly has considered itself free to define its own functions.

Since even in the very beginning the majority of UN members were vehemently anticolonial, the immediate task the Assembly set for itself was to induce the colonial countries by every means in its power to fulfill their obligations under the Charter declaration. Judging from the disputes and controversies that arose even as early as 1946, it seems safe to assume that this development was totally unforeseen by the colonial countries at the time of the San Francisco Conference.

Although the Assembly lacks the power to enforce its recommendations, the colonial powers had no wish to see themselves recorded as being in constant opposition in majority decisions. Consequently, they fought from the start to maintain the right to take the initiative in affairs concerning their own territories and to prevent the UN from expanding its role in colonial matters. However, they were fighting a losing battle against an irreversible trend of world opinion; in effect, the story of the UN's role essentially has been one of increasing involvement in the process of decolonization.

Disputes over the Transmission of Information

The first dispute that arose between the colonial powers and the other UN members concerned the Assembly's desire to discuss the reports that had been submitted on the various territories. Some of the colonial governments, particularly Belgium, contended that the mere submission of reports fulfilled the Charter's requirements under paragraph (e) of Article 73. Disregarding these protests, the 1947 Assembly set up a special committee to report on the information received. In 1949 this committee was established as the Committee on Information from Non-Self-Governing Territories, composed of an equal number of administering and nonadministering countries. In the same year, the Assembly adopted a standard questionnaire, which the administering powers were expected to answer in annual reports. The questionnaire covered virtually every aspect of the social, economic, and educational conditions in the territories. However, due to the controversies discussed below, the committee received reports on only 56 of the 74 territories.

Cessation of Information

By 1949 some of the administering powers had unilaterally interpreted paragraph (e) of Article 73 as meaning that when they themselves considered that a territory had attained self-government, they no longer needed to submit reports on it to the UN. On this basis, the UK had ceased sending information on Malta after its first report in 1946. Likewise France, after 1946, stopped sending reports on certain of its territories that it regarded as overseas departments with rights equal to those of the metropolitan departments of France or as having reached a requisite stage of "internal autonomy." Nor had the US sent reports on the Panama Canal Zone after 1946 (though this was possibly because Panama itself contested classification of the Zone as a non-self-governing territory). Concerned at these developments, the 1949 Assembly, over the opposition of the colonial powers (the US abstaining), decided that it was "within the responsibility of the General Assembly to express its opinion on the principles which have guided or which may in future guide the members concerned in enumerating the territories for which the obligation exists to transmit information under Article 73(e) of the Charter."

The Assembly in 1952 established a special committee to draw up a list of criteria of self-government and at its next session voted itself competent to decide on the basis of this list whether reports were due on a given territory. Since that time, the Assembly has formally approved the cessation of reports on a number of territories, finding that they had "attained a full measure of self-government." However, in each case the administering power in question had already announced, prior to the Assembly action, that it would no longer transmit information on these territories. These territories and the dates of Assembly approval were: from 1953 to 1955, Puerto Rico (US), Greenland (Denmark), Suriname and Curaçao (Netherlands); in 1959, Alaska and Hawaii (US); and in 1965, the Cook Islands and 1974, Niue (New Zealand).

It should be noted, however, that so long as a territory is not actually independent, the Assembly considers it has the right to reopen the question of the territory's status at any time.

In 1967, the UK announced that as a number of its small Caribbean dependencies—namely, Antigua, Dominica, Grenada, St. Kitts-Nevis-Anguilla, and St. Lucia—had achieved the status of associated states with a "full measure of self-government," it would no longer submit reports on those territories. The Assembly did not, however, approve the territories' new status as constituting full self-government and continued to consider them as non-self-governing. (All the associated states except Anguilla subsequently attained independence.) A similar situation arose in 1972 with respect to Brunei when the UK informed the secretary-general that the territory had attained full internal self-government and that, consequently, the UK considered the transmission of information about it no longer appropriate.

Refusal to Transmit Information

Until the General Assembly began to assert a competence in the matter, the inclusion of a territory in the list of non-self-governing territories to which Article 73 applies was at the discretion of the administering power concerned. For instance, in 1946 the UK did not include Southern Rhodesia in the list of dependent territories under its administration because the territory was self-governing, but subsequently changed its position on this after the unilateral declaration of independence by the white-majority regime in 1965.

When Spain and Portugal became UN members in 1955, they also refused to transmit information on their overseas territories, maintaining that these were not colonial possessions but "overseas provinces." Spain retreated from this position in 1960, to the "satisfaction" of the Assembly, and began to submit reports. But Portugal maintained its stand until 1974, when an internal upheaval brought about a change of government.

These differences concerning the obligation to transmit information under Article 73(e) led the Assembly in 1960 to adopt a resolution that unequivocally defined a "full measure of self-government" to mean one of three specific conditions: (a) emergence of the territory as a sovereign independent state; (b) free association with an independent state; or (c) integration with an independent state—both (b) and (c) to be the result of a free and voluntary choice of the people concerned, and the people to possess certain specified rights and safeguards in their new status. Unless one of these three conditions pertained, the Assembly asserted, the administering power had an obligation to transmit information on any territory that is "geographically separate and ethnically and culturally distinct from itself."

THE 1960 ASSEMBLY DECLARATION ON THE ENDING OF COLONIALISM

Throughout the 1950s, the various disputes with colonial powers over the transmission of information on non-self-governing territories took place against a background of steady decolonization. Whether gracefully granted or bitterly fought for, sovereignty was achieved by a growing number of former colonial dependencies. In 1946, at the first working session of the Assembly, only a handful of members had memories of recent foreign rule: India, the Philippines, and the four Arab countries that had been League of Nations mandate territories (Iraq, Jordan, Lebanon, and Syria). By 1959, eight Asian countries (Burma, Cambodia, Ceylon, Indonesia, Laos, Malaya, Nepal, and Pakistan) and two African countries (Ghana and Guinea) had become sovereign independent states. As these nations joined the UN, many of them after years of struggle against their former masters or with humiliating memories of the indignities of foreign rule, anticolonialist sentiment became increasingly bitter and significantly influenced the tone of the debates in the Assembly. Wholeheartedly supported by the Soviet-bloc nations, the newly independent nations began a drive to put a speedy end to colonialism altogether, thus going far beyond anything specifically spelled out in the Charter.

The 1960 Assembly proved to be decisive for the triumph of the anticolonialist forces in the UN. At the opening of that session, 16 new African states and Cyprus became members, thereby bringing the total number of African and Asian nations to 44 out of a total UN membership of 100. In addition, the Afro-Asian Group, as it is called, knew that they could count on the support of the Soviet bloc, many Latin American countries, and the Scandinavian countries. By the end of the session, they had drafted the text of a Declaration on the Granting of Independence to Colonial Countries and Peoples that was designed, to all intents, to replace the Charter declaration as the UN's basic terms of reference for its work in colonial matters.

Main Provisions of the Declaration

Whereas the Charter declaration had been a gentlemanly agreement among masters to look after the welfare of their subjects, the Assembly declaration in effect was an assertion of the right of these subject peoples to be subjects no longer. Written entirely from the viewpoint of the colonial peoples themselves, the declaration in its preamble unequivocally recognizes "the passionate yearning for freedom in all dependent peoples"; the existence of "increasing conflicts resulting from the denial . . . of the freedom of such peoples, which constitute a serious threat to world peace"; and "the important role of the United Nations in assisting the movement for independence in Trust and Non-Self-Governing Territories." In commanding tones, the declaration then lists seven provisions: (1) the subjection of peoples to alien domination "is contrary to the Charter of the United Nations and is an impediment to the promotion of world peace and cooperation"; (2) "all peoples have the right to self-determination"; (3) inadequacy of preparedness "should never serve as a pretext for delaying independence"; (4) all armed action or repressive measures against dependent peoples "shall cease in order to enable them to exercise peacefully and freely their right to complete independence"; (5) "immediate steps shall be taken . . . to transfer all powers to the peoples of those territories, without any conditions or reservations"; (6) any attempt to disrupt the national unity and territorial integrity of a country "is incompatible with the purposes and principles of the Charter"; (7) all states "shall observe faithfully and strictly" the provisions of the Charter, the Universal Declaration of Human Rights, and "the present Declaration" on the basis of equality, noninterference in the internal affairs of states, and respect for the sovereign rights of all peoples.

Although the phrase "colonial powers" does not appear, the declaration was clearly and firmly directed against those countries. Nevertheless, such was the force of anticolonial sentiment that no colonial power cared to record a negative vote. Accordingly, on 14 December 1960 the Declaration on the Granting of Independence to Colonial Countries and Peoples was adopted 89–0, with only 9 abstentions (Australia, Belgium, the Dominican Republic, France, Portugal, South Africa, Spain, the UK, and the US).

Establishment of the Committee of 24
A year after the adoption of the Assembly declaration, the USSR took the initiative by asking the Assembly to discuss the problem of implementing the declaration. The ensuing debate led to the creation of a 17-member Special Committee on the Situation with Regard to the Implementation of the Declaration on the Granting of Independence to Colonial Countries and Peoples. Due to the importance attached to its work, seven additional members were added the following year. Since that time, the composition of the Committee of 24—as it came to be known—has changed slightly when certain countries have withdrawn for various reasons, to be replaced by countries representing the same geopolitical grouping as the outgoing members. Originally, the committee included three colonial or administering powers—Australia, the UK, and the US—but France, Spain, and the two most recalcitrant administering countries, Portugal and South Africa, were never members. Thus the committee's deliberations have always been unambiguously anticolonialist in tone.

In 1963 the committee's functions were expanded to include the work of the 1947 Committee on Information from Non-Self-Governing Territories, which was dissolved. At the same time, the Assembly gave the Committee of 24 the right to apprise the Security Council of any developments in any territory that it examined that might threaten international peace and security. (Normally, subsidiary bodies do not have this right, but must act through the Assembly.) In addition, the Assembly empowered the committee to examine information on the trust territories as well as on non-self-governing territories—though the Trusteeship Council continued to exercise its normal functions. The committee is also empowered to send visiting missions to dependent territories. Hence, since 1963, the Committee of 24 has been the Assembly's chief executive arm in colonial matters.

Besides considering problems connected with individual colonial territories, the committee, which is in session for about nine months of every year, debates topics of a more general nature assigned to it by the Assembly: for example, the role played by foreign economic and military interests in preventing the granting of independence or exploiting the natural resources of the territories that rightfully belong to the indigenous inhabitants. The Committee of 24 has been particularly active in the dissemination of information on colonial problems and in mobilizing international support and assistance for the colonial peoples and their national liberation movements in their efforts to achieve self-determination and independence.

The 1970 Program for Implementing the Declaration
In the 10 years following the adoption of the declaration on the ending of colonialism, 27 territories (with a total population of over 53 million) attained independence. Some 44 territories (with a population of approximately 28 million) remained under foreign rule or control, however, and the Assembly's work in hastening the process of decolonization was far from completed. As the 1970 Assembly's commemorative session celebrating the UN's 25th anniversary happened to coincide with the 10th anniversary of the declaration, the leaders of the drive to end colonialism deemed this an appropriate occasion to reaffirm the aims of the declaration and set forth a program for its implementation. Actually, the nine-point program ceremonially adopted on 12 October 1970 consists for the most part of measures that had been recommended in several Assembly resolutions adopted throughout the 1960s.

Because some of the program's provisions amounted to an open invitation to the UN membership to take hostile action against the colonial or administering powers, however, the latter group of countries, together with their supporters, strongly opposed its formulation. And though the majority view, led by the Afro-Asian Group, finally won out, the program was adopted by only 86 votes in favor—three less than the number of votes that had been cast in favor of the 1960 declaration when the Assembly had a considerably smaller membership. Moreover, whereas no country had cared to vote against the declaration, five countries —Australia, New Zealand, South Africa, the UK, and the US —voted against the 1970 program.

PROGRESS OF DECOLONIZATION IN THE 1970s
The adoption by the Assembly of the 1970 program of action was an expression of the growing sense of frustration felt by many UN members, especially the African and Asian states, at what they considered the painfully slow pace of decolonization. In southern Africa an ever-widening confrontation had emerged between the colonial and white-minority regimes on the one hand, and on the other the roughly 18 million Africans in Portuguese Angola, Portuguese Guinea (now Guinea-Bissau), and Mozambique; Southern Rhodesia, which was legally still a British possession; and the old League of Nations mandate territory of South West Africa, officially renamed Namibia by the UN. Resisting all efforts by the UN to bring an end to white-minority rule by peaceful means, these regimes had reacted to pressures brought upon them both by the international community and by the demands of the African peoples of the territories with an adamant refusal to agree to change.

This had led to the emergence of African national liberation movements within the territories and to an ever-widening series of armed conflicts that were seen by independent African states as a menace to peace and stability and as the potential cause of a bloody racial war engulfing the whole of Africa. Armed conflict, beginning in 1960 in Angola, had in fact spread to all the Portuguese-controlled territories on the African mainland and, as the African liberation movements gained strength and support, had developed into full-scale warfare in Angola, Portuguese Guinea, and Mozambique, engaging large Portuguese armies and putting a serious strain on Portugal's economy.

In Southern Rhodesia and Namibia, armed struggle for liberation was slower to develop, but despite the essential differences of the problems presented by these territories, the Assembly —partly in response to a growing collaboration between South Africa, Portugal, and the white-minority regime in Southern Rhodesia—had come to view them as aspects of a single consuming issue of white-minority rule versus black-majority rights.

The strategy advocated by the Afro-Asian Group, supported by the Soviet-bloc countries and many others, for rectifying the situation in these territories was essentially to obtain recognition and support for their African national liberation movements and to seek the application, through a Security Council decision made under Chapter VII of the Charter, of mandatory enforcement measures, including full economic sanctions and military force as circumstances warranted. In each case, except partially in that of Southern Rhodesia, however, the use of mandatory enforcement measures was decisively resisted by two permanent members of the Security Council, the UK and the US, which, together with several other Western nations, felt that they could not afford to embark upon a policy of confrontation against the economically wealthy white-minority regimes of southern Africa.

Despite this resistance, the African and Asian nations continued to maintain the spotlight of attention on issues of decolonization. Year after year, one or another of the cases mentioned above was brought before the Security Council. Each session of the Assembly, and of the Special Committee on decolonization, was the scene of lengthy and often acrimonious debates. This constant pressure produced significant results. It led to greater recognition and status for the African national liberation movements of the territories in southern Africa and brought about widespread condemnation and isolation of the white regimes. In 1971, for the first time, a mission of the Special Committee visited the liberated areas of Guinea-Bissau at the invitation of the African liberation movement concerned, and found that the liberation movement had established an effective administration. Following the return of the mission, the Special Committee recognized the liberation movement as "the only and authentic" representative of the people, thereby anticipating the proclamation of Guinea-Bissau and Cape Verde as independent states in 1974 and 1975, respectively.

In 1972, at the request of the OAU, the Security Council held meetings in Addis Ababa, Ethiopia, devoted to the consideration of questions relating to Africa. Later the same year, the General Assembly affirmed for the first time that "the national liberation movements of Angola, Guinea-Bissau and Cape Verde, and Mozambique are the authentic representatives of the true aspirations of the peoples of these territories" and recommended that, pending the independence of those territories, all governments and UN bodies should, when dealing with matters pertaining to the territories, ensure the representation of those territories by the liberation movements concerned. The following year, the Assembly extended similar recognition to the national liberation movements of Southern Rhodesia and Namibia.

On 25 April 1974, largely as a result of internal and external pressures resulting from its colonial wars, there occurred in Portugal a change of regime which had major repercussions on the situation in southern Africa. The new regime pledged itself to ending the colonial wars and began negotiations with the national liberation movements. By the end of 1974, Portuguese troops had been withdrawn from Guinea-Bissau and the latter became a UN member. This was followed in 1975 by the independence and UN membership of all the former Portuguese-administered territories in Africa.

Southern Rhodesia. The problem of Southern Rhodesia, which in 1977 had a population of almost 7 million, of whom 6.5 million were Africans, was not resolved until the end of the decade.

Southern Rhodesia had been given full internal self-government in 1923—although under a constitution that vested political power exclusively in the hands of the white settlers. Hence, the UK did not include this dependency in its original 1946 list of non-self-governing territories and did not transmit information on it to the UN. Although by the terms of the 1923 constitution the UK retained residual power to veto any legislation contrary to African interests, this power was never used, and no attempt was made to interfere with the white settlers' domination of the territorial government.

UN involvement in the question of Southern Rhodesia began in 1961, when African and Asian members tried, without success, to bring pressure to bear upon the UK not to permit a new territorial constitution to come into effect. While giving Africans their first representation in the Southern Rhodesian parliament, the 1961 constitution restricted their franchise through a two-tier electoral system heavily weighted in favor of the European community.

In June 1962, acting on the recommendation of its special committee on the ending of colonialism, the General Assembly adopted a resolution declaring Southern Rhodesia to be a non-self-governing territory in the sense of Article 73 of the Charter, on the grounds that the vast majority of the African population had no voting rights and had exercised no voice in drawing up the new constitution. The Assembly also requested the UK to submit information on the territory and to convene a conference of all political parties in Rhodesia for the purpose of drawing up a new constitution that would ensure the rights of the majority on the basis of "one-man, one-vote." However, the UK continued to maintain that it could not interfere in Rhodesia's domestic affairs. The 1961 constitution duly came into effect in November 1962.

On 11 November 1965, the government of Ian Smith unilaterally declared Southern Rhodesia independent. The UK, after branding the declaration an "illegal act," brought the matter to the Security Council the following day, and a resolution was adopted condemning the declaration and calling upon all states to refrain from recognition and from giving assistance to the "rebel" regime. On 20 November, the Council adopted a resolution condemning the "usurpation of power," calling upon the UK to bring the regime to an immediate end, and requesting all states, among other things, to sever economic relations and institute an embargo on oil and petroleum products. The Council imposed wider mandatory sanctions against Southern Rhodesia and established a committee to oversee the application of the sanctions in 1968. The General Assembly urged countries to render moral and material assistance to the national liberation movements of Zimbabwe, the African name for the territory. On 2 March 1970, Southern Rhodesia proclaimed itself a republic, thus severing its ties with the UK.

After Mozambique became independent in 1975, guerrilla activity along the border intensified; the border was then closed, further threatening the economy of Southern Rhodesia, already hurt by UN-imposed sanctions.

In 1977, Anglo-American proposals for the settlement of the Southern Rhodesian problem were communicated to the Security Council by the UK. The proposals called for the surrender of power by the illegal regime, free elections on the basis of universal suffrage, the establishment by the UK of a transitional administration, the presence of a UN force during the transitional period, and the drawing up of an independence constitution. The proposals were to be discussed at a conference of all political parties in Southern Rhodesia, white and African. However, the regime rejected the idea of such a conference. Attempts by the regime in 1978 and early 1979 to draft a new constitution giving some political power to Africans but maintaining effective control by the white minority failed, and the struggle by forces of the liberation movement, called the Patriotic Front, intensified.

In August 1979, British Prime Minister Margaret Thatcher stated at the Conference of Commonwealth Heads of State and Government that her government intended to bring Southern Rhodesia to legal independence on a basis acceptable to the international community. To this end, a constitutional conference was convened in London on 10 September, to which representatives of the Patriotic Front and the Rhodesian administration in Salisbury were invited. On 21 December, an agreement was signed on a draft independence constitution and on transitional arrangements for its implementation, as well as on a cease-fire to take effect on 28 December. Lord Soames was appointed governor of the territory until elections, which took place in February 1980 in the presence of UN observers. On 11 March, Lord Soames formally appointed Robert G. Mugabe, whose party had received the majority of seats in the House of Assembly, as prime minister. The independence of Zimbabwe was proclaimed on 18 April 1980 and, on 25 August, Zimbabwe became a member of the UN.

REMAINING COLONIAL ISSUES

Apart from Namibia, most of the 20 remaining dependent territories are small islands scattered about the globe. Their tiny populations and minimal economic resources render it almost impossible for them to survive as viable, fully independent states. Most of these small territories belong to the UK, the remainder to the US and other Western nations. Although the administering powers join with the rest of the UN membership in asserting that the peoples of these small territories have an inalienable right to the exercise of self-determination, the leaders of the drive to end colonialism have doubted the genuineness of the preparations for achieving this goal. As evidence to justify their skepticism, the African and Asian nations point out that military bases have been established in many of the small territories, which they declare "is incompatible with the purposes and principles of the Charter." Moreover, in the case of territories which the administering powers have declared their intention of preparing for self-governing status rather than for full independence, the majority of UN members feel that the Assembly should be granted an active role in ascertaining the wishes of the inhabitants and furnished with more comprehensive information on conditions prevailing in the territories. The refusal of some of the administering powers to supply this information or to permit visits by UN missions has tended to reinforce the skepticism of the anticolonialist nations.

Other small or sparsely populated territories that have been brought under the Assembly's surveillance through the Committee of 24 include two UK possessions where the issue of decolonization is complicated by conflicting claims of sovereignty by other nations—the Falkland Islands claimed by Argentina, and Gibraltar claimed by Spain. In regard to two other territories, East Timor and Western Sahara, the administering powers—Portugal and Spain, respectively—informed the General Assembly that developments in the territories have prevented them from carrying out their responsibilities or exercising their authority.

The Problem of Namibia (South West Africa)

The status of South West Africa (officially designated as Namibia by the Assembly in June 1968), a pre–World War I German colony that beginning in 1920 was administered by South Africa under a League of Nations mandate, has preoccupied the General Assembly almost from the first moment of the UN's existence. In 1946 South Africa proposed that the Assembly approve its annexation of the territory. Fearing that the South African government would seek to extend its apartheid system to South West Africa, the Assembly did not approve the proposal and recommended instead that the territory be placed under the UN trusteeship system. The following year, South Africa informed the Assembly that while it agreed not to annex the territory, it would

not place it under trusteeship. Although South Africa had reported to the Assembly on conditions in the territory in 1946, it declined to submit further reports, despite repeated requests from the Assembly.

In 1950 the International Court of Justice, in an advisory opinion requested by the General Assembly, held that South Africa continued to have international obligations for the territory to promote to the utmost the material and moral well-being and social progress of the inhabitants as a sacred trust of civilization, and that the UN should exercise the supervisory functions of the League of Nations over the administration of the territory. South Africa refused to accept the Court's opinion and continued, over the ensuing 15 years, to oppose any form of UN supervision over the territory's affairs.

In October 1966, the General Assembly decided to terminate the League of Nations mandate exercised by South Africa, declaring that South Africa had failed to fulfill its obligations under the mandate and to ensure the well-being of the people of the territory, and that it had, in fact, disavowed the mandate. The Assembly decided that the mandate was therefore terminated, that South Africa had no other right to administer the territory, and that thenceforth the territory came under the direct responsibility of the UN. In May 1967, the Assembly established the UN Council for South West Africa (later renamed the UN Council for Namibia) to administer the territory until independence "with the maximum possible participation of the people of the territory." It also decided to establish the post of UN Commissioner for Namibia to assist the council in carrying out its mandate. Later the same year, in the face of South Africa's refusal to accept the Assembly's decision and to cooperate with the Council for Namibia, the Assembly recommended that the Security Council take measures to enable the Council for Namibia to carry out its mandate.

In its first resolution on the question, in 1969, the Security Council recognized the termination of the mandate by the Assembly, described the continued presence of South Africa in Namibia as illegal, and called on South Africa to withdraw its administration from the territory immediately. The following year, the Security Council explicitly declared for the first time that "all acts taken by the government of South Africa on behalf of or concerning Namibia after the termination of the mandate are illegal and invalid." This view was upheld in 1971 by the International Court of Justice, which stated, in an advisory opinion requested by the Security Council, that "the continued presence of South Africa in Namibia being illegal, South Africa is under obligation to withdraw its administration from Namibia immediately and thus put an end to its occupation of the territory." South Africa, however, continued to refuse to comply with UN resolutions on the question of Namibia, and it continued to administer the territory.

To secure for the Namibians "adequate protection of the natural wealth and resources of the territory which is rightfully theirs," the UN Council for Namibia enacted in September 1974 a Decree for the Protection of the Natural Resources of Namibia. Under the decree, no person or entity may search for, take, or distribute any natural resource found in Namibia without the council's permission, and any person or entity contravening the decree "may be held liable in damages by the future government of an independent Namibia." The council also established, in the same year, the Institute for Namibia (located in Lusaka, Zambia, until South Africa's withdrawal from Namibia) to provide Namibians with education and training and equip them to administer a future independent Namibia.

In 1976, the Security Council for the first time demanded that South Africa accept elections for the territory as a whole under UN supervision and control so that the people of Namibia might freely determine their own future. It condemned South Africa's "illegal and arbitrary application . . . of racially discriminatory and repressive laws and practices in Namibia," its military buildup, and its use of the territory "as a base for attacks on neighboring countries."

In the same year, the General Assembly condemned South Africa "for organizing the so-called constitutional talks at Windhoek, which seek to perpetuate the apartheid and home-lands policies as well as the colonial oppression and exploitation of the people and resources of Namibia." It decided that "any independence talks regarding Namibia must be between the representatives of South Africa and the South West Africa People's Organization," which the Assembly recognized as "the sole and authentic representative of the Namibian people." The Assembly declared in 1977 that South Africa's decision to annex Walvis Bay, Namibia's main port, was "illegal, null, and void" and "an act of colonial expansion." It condemned the annexation as an attempt "to undermine the territorial integrity and unity of Namibia."

At a special session on Namibia in May 1978, the Assembly adopted a Declaration on Namibia and a program of action in support of self-determination and national independence for Namibia. Expressing "full support for the armed liberation struggle of the Namibian people under the leadership of the SWAPO," it stated that any negotiated settlement must be arrived at with the agreement of SWAPO and within the framework of UN resolutions.

The UN Plan for Namibian Independence. In July 1978, the Security Council met to consider a proposal by the five Western members of the Council—Canada, France, the FRG, the UK, and the US—for a settlement of the Namibian question. The proposal comprised a plan for free elections to a constituent assembly under the supervision and control of a UN representative, assisted by a UN transition assistance group which would include both civilian and military components. The Council took note of the Western proposal and requested the secretary-general to appoint a special representative for Namibia. In September 1978, after approving a report by the secretary-general based on his special representative's findings, the Council, in resolution 435 (1978), endorsed the UN plan for the independence of Namibia and decided to establish, under its authority, the UN Transition Assistance Group (UNTAG) to assist the special representative to carry out his mandate—namely, to ensure the early independence of Namibia through free and fair elections under UN supervision and control.

The secretary-general's report stated that the implementation of the UN plan would be carried out in three stages: (1) cessation of all hostile acts by all parties; (2) the repeal of discriminatory or restrictive laws and the release of political prisoners, and voluntary return of exiles and refugees; and (3) the holding of elections after a seven-month preelectoral period, to be followed by the entry into force of the newly adopted constitution and the consequent achievement of independence by Namibia.

Since 1978, the General Assembly has continually reaffirmed that Security Council resolution 435 (1978), in which the Council endorsed the UN plan for the independence of Namibia, is the only basis for a peaceful settlement. It has condemned South Africa for obstructing the implementation of that resolution and other UN resolutions, and for "its maneuvres, in contravention of those resolutions, designed to consolidate its colonial and neo-colonial interests at the expense of the legitimate aspirations of the Namibian people." In furtherance of the objective of bringing to an end South Africa's occupation of Namibia, the Assembly has called upon all states to sever all relations with South Africa, and it has urged the Security Council to impose mandatory comprehensive sanctions against South Africa. The Assembly has also continued to authorize the Council for Namibia, as the legal administering authority for Namibia, to continue to mo-

bilize international support in order to press for the withdrawal of the illegal South African administration from Namibia; counter South Africa's policies against the Namibian people and against the UN; denounce and seek the rejection by all states of South Africa's attempts to perpetuate its presence in Namibia; and ensure the nonrecognition of any administration or political entity installed in Namibia that is not the result of free elections held under UN supervision and control.

TABLE I
Non-self-governing territories, listed by the General Assembly in 1946 and subsequent years, that have become independent states or joined neighboring independent states

Australia
Papua (now part of Papua New Ginea)

Belgium
Belgian Congo (now Zaire)

France
Comoros
French Equatorial Africa (now Central African Rep., Chad, Congo, and Gabon)
French Somaliland (later called the Territory of the Afars and the Issas; now Djibouti)
French West Africa (now Dahomey, Guinea, Ivory Coast, Mali, Mauritania, Niger, Senegal, and Upper Volta)
Indochina (now Kampuchea, Laos, and Viet-Nam)
Madagascar
Morocco
New Hebrides (Anglo-French condominium; now Vanuatu)
Tunisia

Netherlands
Netherlands Indies (now Indonesia)
Suriname
West New Guinea (West Irian; now part of Indonesia)

Portugal
Angola
Cape Verde
Mozambique
Portuguese Guinea (now Guinea-Bissau)
São Tomé and Príncipe

Spain
Fernando Póo and Río Muni (now Equatorial Guinea)

United Kingdom
Aden (now the People's Dem. Rep. of Yemen)
Antigua (now Antigua and Barbuda)
Bahamas
Barbados
Basutoland (now Lesotho)
Bechuanaland (now Botswana)
British Guiana (now Guyana)
British Honduras (now Belize)
British Somaliland (now Somalia)
Cyprus
Dominica
Ellice Islands (now Tuvalu)
Fiji
Gambia
Gilbert Islands (now Kiribati)
Gold Coast (now Ghana)

Grenada
Jamaica
Kenya
Malaya (now Malaysia)
Malta
Mauritius
Nigeria
New Hebrides (Anglo-French condominium; now Vanuatu)
North Borneo (now part of Malaysia)
Northern Rhodesia (now Zambia)
Nyasaland (now Malawi)
St. Christopher and Nevis
St. Lucia
St. Vincent and the Grenadines
Sarawak (now part of Malaysia)
Seychelles
Sierra Leone
Singapore
Solomon Islands
Southern Rhodesia (now Zimbabwe)
Swaziland
Trinidad and Tobago
Uganda
Zanzibar (now part of Tanzania)

TABLE II
Non-self-governing territories, listed by the General Assembly in 1946 and subsequent years, that were taken off the list by the administering power with or without the Assembly's assent

Denmark
Greenland

France
French establishments in India
French establishments in Oceania
French Guiana
Guadeloupe
Martinique
New Caledonia
Réunion
St. Pierre and Miquelon

Netherlands
Curaçao

New Zealand
Cook Islands
Niue

Portugal
Goa
Macau
São João Batista de Ajuda

Spain
Ifni

United Kingdom
Hong Kong

United States
Alaska
Hawaii
Panama Canal Zone
Puerto Rico

TABLE III
Remaining non-self-governing territories listed by the General Assembly, as of 30 September 1983

Australia
Cocos (Keeling Islands)

New Zealand
Tokelau Islands

Portugal
East Timor[1]

Spain
Western Sahara[2]

United Kingdom
Anguilla
Bermuda
British Virgin Islands
Brunei
Cayman Islands
Falkland Islands (Islas Malvinas)
Gibraltar
Montserrat
Pitcairn Island
St. Helena
Turks and Caicos Islands

United Nations
Namibia (formerly South West Africa)[3]

United States
American Samoa
Guam
Trust Territory of the Pacific Islands
US Virgin Islands

1. On 20 April 1977, Portugal informed the secretary-general that effective exercise of its sovereignty of the territory had ceased in August 1975 and that the only information that could be transmitted would concern the first months of 1975. In subsequent years, Portugal further informed the secretary-general that conditions prevailing in East Timor continued to prevent it from assuming its responsibilities for the administration of the territory and that it had nothing to add to the information already given.
2. Spain informed the secretary-general on 26 February 1976 that as of that date it had terminated its presence in the territory of the Sahara and deemed it necessary to place the following on record: "Spain considers itself henceforth exempt from any responsibility of an international nature in connection with the administration of the territory in view of the cessation of its participation in the temporary administration established for the territory."
3. In 1966, the General Assembly terminated South Africa's mandate over South West Africa and placed the territory under the direct responsibility of the UN. In 1968, the Assembly declared that the territory would henceforth be called Namibia, in accordance with its people's wishes.

INTERNATIONAL LAW

Article 13 of the UN Charter requires the General Assembly to "initiate studies and make recommendations for the purpose of . . . encouraging the progressive development of international law and its codification." To help it fulfill this mandate, the Assembly has set up two law commissions. The International Law Commission was established in 1947 as a permanent subsidiary organ with its own separate statute. It began meeting in 1949 and since that time has completed a significant body of work. At its 1966 session, the Assembly established another commission with the specific object of promoting the harmonization and unification of international law in the field of trade. The UN Commission on International Trade Law held its first meeting in 1968.

INTERNATIONAL LAW COMMISSION

Like the judges of the International Court of Justice, the 34 (originally 15) members of the International Law Commission (ILC) are not representatives of governments. Instead, they are chosen in their individual capacity "as persons of recognized competence in international law" and with due consideration to representation of "the main forms of civilization" and "the principal legal systems of the world." No two members of the commission may be nationals of the same country. They are elected for five-year terms by the General Assembly, from a list of candidates nominated by UN member states.

Unlike the judges of the World Court, the legal experts do not serve in a full-time capacity on the International Law Commission and need not give up their other professional activities. Many of them are law school professors. They meet each year, normally in Geneva, for a session of approximately 12 weeks. The various topics under consideration are usually assigned to individual members, who then serve as special rapporteurs on the item concerned, carry out the necessary studies between sessions, and submit reports to the commission at its annual sessions.

Functions

Development of New International Law. The Charter does not lay down any principles for determining a desirable "progressive development" of international law. Nevertheless, from the outset the discussions in the International Law Commission and the General Assembly have made very clear the main considerations involved. The traditional legal norms prevailing at the time of the San Francisco Conference were inherited from an era when world politics was dominated by a handful of Western European nations. As a consequence, international law itself reflected the values and interests of those nations. In essence, therefore, what has been required is an adjustment of the entire international legal order so as to take account of the interests and traditions of a much broader community of nations.

As prescribed by the decision of the 1947 Assembly, the International Law Commission is to give effect to the Charter provision for the progressive development of international law by preparing "draft conventions on subjects which have not yet been regulated by international law or in regard to which the law has not been sufficiently developed in the practice of States."

Since the filling of any gap in international law directly affects the behavior and obligations of states, it is for the UN member nations acting through the Assembly to decide the subjects on which the commission may prepare draft conventions. In one instance, a subject was presented to the commission through ECOSOC and later incorporated into one which had previously been forwarded to it by the Assembly.

Preparing an international convention is a complex and often lengthy business. After appointing a rapporteur, the commission formulates a plan of work and circulates a questionnaire to governments, inviting them to supply relevant information. It may also consult with scientific institutions and individual experts in law and other fields. If the rapporteur's draft is satisfactory to the commission, it is sent by the secretary-general of the UN to governments for comment. The draft is then reconsidered by the commission in the light of these comments, and the final version is submitted to the General Assembly. When the Assembly has discussed and approved the draft—which may not occur until the commission has responded to requests for further modifications—it usually convokes a special international conference of plenipotentiaries for the purpose of adopting the actual convention, which subsequently has to be ratified by a given number of states (as specified in the articles of the convention itself) before it can come into force as a legal instrument.

Codification of Existing International Law. To give effect to the Charter request for the codification of law, the 1949 Assembly charged the commission with providing "more precise formulation and systemization of [existing] rules of international law in fields where there already has been extensive State practice, precedent and doctrine." In this respect, the commission may act on its own initiative, and it is authorized to "survey the whole field of international law with a view to selecting topics for codification."

Scope of the Commission's Work

The Assembly does not assign all legal issues with which it is concerned to the International Law Commission. Thus the legal aspect of an agenda item that relates to another sphere of the Assembly's work is often handled by a subcommittee of the special committee that was set up to study that particular subject. This is the case, for example, with the legal aspects of the peaceful uses of outer space and with many matters of human rights and economic and social development (see the chapters on these subjects). On occasion, too, the Assembly has established a special committee to consider certain legal topics that directly affect the conduct of nations in international peace and security and are therefore highly political. Thus the agenda item on the Consideration of Principles of International Law Concerning Friendly Relations and Cooperation Among States in Accordance with the Charter of the United Nations was assigned to a special 31-member committee. After eight years of contentious discussion, the committee completed a draft declaration, as requested, in time for the commemorative session to celebrate the UN's 25th anniversary in 1970. The declaration embodies seven principles: the nonuse of force; peaceful settlement of disputes; nonintervention; sovereign equality; duty to cooperate; equal rights and self-determination; and fulfillment of obligations under the Charter.

Another example of a legal topic having a strongly political character is the definition of aggression. The International Law Commission originally was asked to draw up a definition of aggression. The task was taken over by the Assembly only after the commission had failed to reach agreement. A special committee of the Assembly drafted the text of the Definition of Aggression, which was adopted by the Assembly in 1974. Another special committee of the Assembly drafted the International Convention on the Taking of Hostages, which was adopted by the Assembly in 1979, and in 1980 the Assembly established an ad hoc committee to draft an international convention against the recruitment, use, financing, and training of mercenaries.

The International Law Commission has been requested to consider other topics relating to peace and security and has presented texts on them to the Assembly, but for the most part its work has been confined to topics that affect the day-to-day relationship of nations, such as the conclusion and observance of treaties and the exchange of envoys at various levels.

Topics Selected for Codification
At its first session, in 1949, the commission considered 25 topics for possible study. It selected 14 of these for codification. The list was only provisional, and it was understood that changes might be made after further study by the commission or in compliance with the wishes of the Assembly. The list, however, still constitutes the commission's basic long-term program of work.

Topics on which the commission has completed its work and submitted final drafts or reports to the General Assembly include: extended participation in multilateral treaties concluded under the auspices of the League of Nations; law of treaties; law of the sea; nationality, including statelessness; diplomatic and consular relations; special missions; protection of diplomats; relations between states and international organizations; and succession of states.

Extended Participation in Multilateral Treaties Concluded Under the Auspices of the League of Nations
The commission's conclusions on this question were submitted to the Assembly in 1963. On the basis of these conclusions, the Assembly decided that it was the appropriate organ of the UN to exercise the functions of the League Council with respect to 21 general multilateral treaties of a technical and nonpolitical character concluded under the auspices of the former world body.

Law of Treaties
The most far-reaching task undertaken by the International Law Commission has been its work on the law of treaties—the laws governing the way in which treaties are to be negotiated, adopted, altered, and abrogated. The commission, which began work on this project in 1949, finally completed it in 1966, after 18 sessions. Throughout this period, the commission regularly submitted provisional draft articles to the Assembly's Sixth Committee and to individual governments for comment. Accordingly, the final draft of 75 articles adopted by the commission and submitted to the Assembly's 1966 session included many revisions. At a conference which met in two sessions in Vienna in 1968 and 1969, the Vienna Convention on the Law of Treaties was adopted. It entered into force in 1980.

Law of the Sea
In accordance with its 1949 program, the commission worked for a number of years on the codification of the law of the sea, frequently revising draft articles in the light of comments received from governments. Following a request of the 1954 Assembly, the commission grouped together the articles it had previously adopted and submitted a final draft on the law of the sea in 1956. The Assembly called a special conference on the law of the sea at Geneva in 1958. At that conference, four conventions were adopted: (1) the Convention on the High Seas, which came into force on 30 September 1962; (2) the Convention on the Continental Shelf, on 24 April 1964; (3) the Convention on the Territorial Sea and the Contiguous Zone, on 10 September 1964; and (4) the Convention on Fishing and Conservation of the Living Resources of the High Seas, on 20 March 1966. (See also the chapter on the Law of the Sea.)

Reduction of Statelessness
In 1954 the commission prepared two drafts, one for a convention on the elimination of statelessness, and another, which would impose fewer obligations on states, on the reduction of statelessness. General Assembly discussions showed that the first and more sweeping draft had no chance of acceptance. Even the measures on which countries would have to agree in order to reduce the number of stateless persons raised so many problems that it eventually required two special conferences, one in 1959 and one in 1961, to arrive at a Convention on the Reduction of Statelessness. It came into force in 1975.

Diplomatic and Consular Relations
In 1959, the commission adopted final draft articles on diplomatic intercourse and immunities. The Assembly endorsed the drafts and convoked an international conference which met in Vienna in 1961 and adopted the Vienna Convention on Diplomatic Relations and two optional protocols—one concerning acquisition of nationality, the other compulsory settlement of disputes. The convention adapts to 20th-century requirements the rules for diplomatic intercourse formulated by the 1815 Congress of Vienna, which since that time have essentially governed diplomatic relations. It came into force in 1964.

Final draft articles on consular relations were submitted by the commission to the Assembly in 1961. On the basis of these drafts, an international conference, held in Vienna in 1963, adopted the Vienna Convention on Consular Relations and two protocols. It came into force in 1967.

Special Missions
In 1968 and 1969 the General Assembly considered the question of a draft convention on special missions on the basis of draft articles prepared by the commission. On 8 December 1969, the Assembly adopted the Convention on Special Missions and an optional protocol concerning the compulsory settlement of disputes. The convention, not yet in force, provides rules applying to forms of ad hoc diplomacy—itinerant envoys, diplomatic conferences, and special missions sent to a state for limited purposes—that are not covered by the Vienna conventions of 1961 and 1963 relating to diplomatic and consular relations among states.

Protection of Diplomats
In 1973 the General Assembly adopted the Convention on the Prevention and Punishment of Crimes Against Internationally Protected Persons, Including Diplomatic Agents, on the basis of draft articles prepared by the commission. The convention's preamble states that crimes against diplomatic agents and other internationally protected persons, jeopardizing their safety, create a serious threat to the maintenance of normal international relations necessary for cooperation among states. It came into force in 1977.

Relations Between States and International Organizations
On the basis of draft articles prepared by the commission, the Vienna Convention on the Representation of States in Their Relations with International Organizations of a Universal Character was adopted in 1975 by an international conference. It is not yet in force.

Succession of States
Another conference convened by the General Assembly met in April 1977 and again in August 1978 and adopted the Vienna Convention on Succession of States in Respect of Treaties. It is not yet in force. The commission has also completed draft articles for a convention on succession of states in respect of state property, archives, and debts.

Other Topics
Other topics on which the commission has completed work include: the draft Declaration on the Rights and Duties of States; ways and means of making the evidence of customary international law more readily available; formulation of the Nürnberg Principles; the question of international criminal jurisdiction; reservations to multilateral conventions; arbitral procedure; most-favored-

nation clauses; and the question of treaties concluded between states and international organizations or between two or more international organizations.

Topics on which the commission is currently working include: draft code of offenses against the peace and security of mankind; jurisdictional immunities of states and their property; state responsibility; status of the diplomatic courier and the diplomatic bag not accompanied by diplomatic courier; the law of the non-navigational uses of international watercourses; relations between states and international organizations (second part of the topic); and international liability for injurious consequences arising out of acts not prohibited by international law.

UN COMMISSION ON INTERNATIONAL TRADE LAW (UNCITRAL)

In contrast to the International Court of Justice and the International Law Commission, whose members serve in their individual capacities, the UN Commission on International Trade Law is composed of the representatives of 36 (originally 29) states. Like the International Law Commission, UNCITRAL is a permanent subsidiary organ of the General Assembly, which elects its members, observing the principle of balance among the geographical regions and the main economic and legal systems of the world. Members serve six-year terms and are eligible for reelection. The commission holds one regular session a year. Between sessions, working groups designated by the commission meet on specific topics.

Functions

A clear understanding of the respective rights and obligations of buyer and seller facilitates the flow of trade from one country to another. When the laws of countries in this field are at variance, impediments may arise. In creating UNCITRAL, the UN recognized a need that it play a more active role in removing or reducing legal obstacles to international trade.

The trade law of medieval Europe was exercised by the merchants and their guilds. Upon the emergence of strong centralized states, the autonomous merchants' courts were superseded by royal courts. The process of the unification of commercial law on a multilateral basis was only begun during the past century.

UNCITRAL is charged with the task of seeking to resolve differences in national laws by providing texts which may become the basis of international conventions or other agreements. The 1966 Assembly resolution establishing UNCITRAL invests it with seven specific functions in the furtherance of "progressive harmonization and unification of the law of international trade." They are: coordinating the work of international organizations active in this field; the promotion of wider participation in existing international conventions; the preparation of new ones; the promotion of means of ensuring their uniform interpretation and application; collecting and disseminating information on national legislation and legal development in the field of international law; maintaining a close collaboration with UNCTAD; and maintaining liaison with other concerned UN organs and specialized agencies.

The Work of UNCITRAL

The commission draws up its own program of work, subject to the approval of the Assembly. It selects topics which are both intrinsically capable of unification and ripe for final settlement by virtue of a sufficiently close convergence in their treatment among bodies of national law. At its first session, the commission chose nine such topics. International sale of goods, international payments, and commercial arbitration were given priority. Other subjects listed by the commission for its consideration included transportation, insurance, intellectual property, and elimination of discrimination in laws affecting international trade. Product liability and multinational enterprises were later added to the program of work.

The first treaty elaborated under the auspices of UNCITRAL fixes at four years the period of time in which parties to a contract for the international sale of goods may sue under contract. The length of this period has been the subject of conflicting national rules. In 1972, the commission prepared a draft Convention on the Limitation Period in the International Sale of Goods. It was the subject of substantive comments by 24 governments and two international organizations and was adopted in its final form at the UN Conference on Prescription (Limitation) in the International Sale of Goods, held at New York in 1974. Similar international conferences adopted the Convention on the Carriage of Goods by Sea in 1978 and the Convention on Contracts for the International Sale of Goods in 1980. None of the conventions has entered into force.

A working group of the commission has adopted two draft conventions—on international bills of exchange and international promissory notes, and on international checks—for consideration by UNCITRAL. Another working group, on the new international economic order, has recommended for the commission's consideration legal issues involving developing countries.

BIBLIOGRAPHY

General
Annual Report of the Secretary-General on the Work of the Organization.
Basic Facts About the United Nations, 1983.
Charter of the United Nations and Statute of the International Court of Justice.
Everyone's United Nations. 9th ed., 1979.
UN Chronicle. Issued 11 times a year.
Yearbook of the United Nations.
Your United Nations: The Official Guidebook, 1982.

Disarmament
The Arms Race or the Human Race?, 1981.
Comprehensive Study of the Question of Nuclear-Weapon-Free Zones in All Its Aspects, 1976.
Disarmament: A Periodic Review by the United Nations.
Economic and Social Consequences of the Arms Race and of Military Expenditures, 1978.
Ionizing Radiation: Sources and Biological Effects, 1982.
The United Nations and Disarmament, 1976.
The United Nations Disarmament Yearbook.

Outer Space
Space Activities and Resources: A Review of the Activities and Resources of the United Nations, Its Specialized Agencies and Other Competent International Bodies Relating to the Peaceful Uses of Outer Space, 1977.
The United Nations and Outer Space, 1977.

Law of the Sea
The Law of the Sea, 1983. Text of the UN Convention on the Law of the Sea and the Final Act of the Third UN Conference on the Law of the Sea. Also contains supplementary information.

Economic Development
GENERAL:
International Development Strategy for the Third United Nations Development Decade, 1981.
Interrelations: Resources, Environment, Population and Development, 1980.
Monthly Bulletin of Statistics.
Statistical Yearbook.
Towards the New International Economic Order. Report of the Director-General for Development and International Economic Cooperation, 1982.
World Economic Survey 1981–1982—Current Trends in the World Economy, 1982.
World Statistics in Brief. Issued annually.
SCIENCE AND TECHNOLOGY:
Science and Technology for Development, 1979.
Technology Assessment for Development, 1980.
TRANSNATIONAL CORPORATIONS:
The CTC Reporter. Issued periodically by the UN Center on Transnational Corporations.
The Impact of Multinational Corporations on Development and on International Relations, 1974.
Survey of Research on Transnational Corporations, 1977.
INDUSTRIAL DEVELOPMENT AND INTERNATIONAL TRADE:
Handbook of International Trade and Development Statistics. Issued periodically.
Industry and Development. Bulletin issued periodically.
Restructuring of World Industry. New Dimensions for Trade Cooperation, 1977.

World Industry in 1980, 1981.
Yearbook of Industrial Statistics.
Yearbook of International Trade Statistics.
Yearbook of World Energy Statistics.

Regional Development
CEPAL Review. Economic bulletin for Latin America. Issued periodically.
Economic and Social Survey for Asia and the Pacific. Issued annually.
Economic Bulletin for Africa. Issued periodically.
Economic Bulletin for Asia and the Pacific. Issued periodically.
Economic Bulletin for Europe. Issued periodically.
Economic Survey of Europe. Issued annually.
Economic Survey of Latin America. Issued annually.
Statistical Yearbook for Asia and the Pacific.
Statistical Yearbook for Latin America.
Survey of Economic Conditions in Africa, 1974.

Social Development
POPULATION:
Demographic Yearbook.
Population and Vital Statistics. Issued quarterly.
Population Bulletin of the United Nations. Issued periodically.
Population Policy and Development Planning: Aspects of Technical Cooperation, 1981.
World Population Trends and Policies, 1982.
SOCIAL WELFARE AND OTHER QUESTIONS:
Bulletin on Narcotics. Issued quarterly.
Integration of Disabled Persons into Community Life, 1981.
Model Rules for Disaster Relief Operations, 1982.
Poverty and Self-Reliance: A Social Welfare Perspective, 1982.
Report of the International Narcotics Control Board on Its Work in 1982, 1983.
Report on the World Social Situation, 1982.
Social Services in Rural Development: Issues Concerning Their Design and Delivery, 1979.
Social Welfare and Family Planning: Concepts, Strategies and Methods, 1979.
The State of the World's Children, 1982–83, 1983.
UNICEF: Annual Report.

Human Rights
The International Bill of Human Rights.
United Nations Action in the Field of Human Rights, 1979.
The United Nations and Human Rights, 1978.
Universal Declaration of Human Rights.
Yearbook on Human Rights.

Decolonization
The Right to Self-Determination: Historical and Current Development on the Basis of United Nations Instruments, 1980.
The United Nations and Decolonization, 1980.

International Law
Multilateral Treaties in Respect of Which the Secretary-General Performs Depositary Functions: List of Signatures, Ratifications, etc. Issued annually.
United Nations Commission on International Trade Law Yearbook.
United Nations Juridical Yearbook.
United Nations Treaty Series. Treaties and international agreements entered into by UN member states.
Yearbook of the International Law Commission.
(A complete list of UN publications appears in *United Nations Publications in Print, 1983/84.*)

THE UNITED NATIONS

RELATED AGENCIES

Guide to Related Agencies

The arrangement of articles on the United Nations related agencies follows the order of the chart on the Structure of the United Nations System. All information contained in each article is uniformly keyed by means of small superior numerals to the left of the subject headings, as follows:

1 Background
2 Creation
3 Purposes
4 Membership
5 Structure
6 Budget
7 Activities
8 Bibliography

THE INTERNATIONAL ATOMIC ENERGY AGENCY (IAEA)

[1]**BACKGROUND:** The UN came into existence at the beginning of the atomic age. Man's success in harnessing atomic energy has made the UN's objectives not only vital but absolutely indispensable. The primary purpose of the UN is to prevent war. A major war involving the use of atomic weapons would be not simply catastrophic but very probably suicidal. The second objective of the UN is to promote the economic and social welfare of peoples throughout the world. Atomic energy promises to contribute greatly to worldwide prosperity. Although "atoms for peace" has been a continuing concern of the UN itself, and although a number of organizations of the UN family, such as the FAO and WHO, have been concerned with specific aspects of peaceful uses of atomic energy, it was not until 1957 that a special organization, the International Atomic Energy Agency, came into being for the express purpose of accelerating and enlarging the contribution of atomic energy to peace, health, and prosperity throughout the world.

[2]CREATION

Addressing the UN General Assembly in December 1953, US President Dwight D. Eisenhower called for the establishment of an international atomic energy organization to "serve the peaceful pursuits of mankind." The President said that he hoped the atomic powers, through such an organization, would dedicate "some of their strength to serve the needs rather than the fears of mankind."

President Eisenhower stated that the USSR "must, of course, be one" of the countries principally involved in the proposed organization. Accordingly, as a first step, the US State Department in the spring and summer of 1954 submitted a series of memoranda to the USSR suggesting the principles that should be incorporated in the statute of such an agency. It was, however, impossible for the two powers to reach agreement at that time. The USSR maintained that the issues of disarmament and peaceful uses of atomic energy were inseparable and that agreement on a general prohibition of nuclear weapons would have to precede the creation of the agency. The US countered with the argument that effective international control of nuclear weapons would have to precede their prohibition, and announced that it was prepared to go ahead with international negotiations even without the participation of the USSR.

In the summer of 1954, the US issued invitations to seven other countries, including both "atomic powers" and important uranium-producing states—Australia, Belgium, Canada, France, Portugal, South Africa, and the UK—to meet with it in Washington to prepare a draft statute for the proposed agency. In September the USSR reversed its previous position. It announced its willingness to separate the issues of disarmament and peaceful uses of atomic energy and to accept the eight-power draft statute as a basis for further negotiations and guidance.

In December 1954, the General Assembly unanimously adopted an "Atoms for Peace" resolution expressing the hope that the International Atomic Energy Agency would be established "without delay" in order to assist "in lifting the burdens of hunger, poverty and disease." An international conference on the statute was convened at UN headquarters in New York on 20 September 1956, with the participation of 81 nations, including some, such as the Federal Republic of Germany, that were not members of the UN itself. After adopting a number of amendments, proposed for the most part by the atomic "have not" powers, the conference unanimously adopted the statute as a whole on 26 October 1956.

On 29 July 1957, the statute entered into force after 26 states had deposited instruments of ratification, and the International Atomic Energy Agency officially came into existence. The first General Conference of the IAEA was held in Vienna in October 1957, at which time it was decided to make Vienna the permanent headquarters site of the agency. The address of the IAEA is: Kärntner Ring 11, A-1011 Vienna.

[3]PURPOSES

According to the statute of the IAEA, the agency "shall seek to accelerate and enlarge the contribution of atomic energy to peace, health and prosperity throughout the world. It shall ensure, so far as it is able, that assistance provided by it or at its request or under its supervision and control is not used in such a way as to further any military purpose."

The IAEA acts as a clearinghouse for the pooling and coordination of experience and research in the peaceful uses of nuclear power and radioisotopes. It helps its member countries acquire the necessary skills and materials to share in the benefits of the atomic age. In practice, the IAEA has been particularly concerned with bringing the advantages of atomic energy to underdeveloped regions.

The IAEA is obliged under its statute to "ensure, so far as it is able," that all the activities in which it takes part are directed exclusively to civilian uses. A second important task of the IAEA, then, is to establish a system of supervision and control to make certain that none of the assistance programs it fosters, none of the materials whose distribution it supervises, is used for military purposes. This aspect of the work has assumed significance far beyond its primary objective, with the entry into force in March 1970 of the Treaty on the Non-Proliferation of Nuclear Weapons (NPT), since the IAEA is the body responsible for the necessary control system. By July 1983, 121 states had become parties to the NPT.

[4]MEMBERSHIP

Any member of the UN or of any of the specialized agencies that signed the statute within 90 days after 26 October 1956 thereby became a charter member of the IAEA upon ratification of the statute. Other countries, even if not members of the UN or any of the specialized agencies, may be admitted by the General Conference of the IAEA upon recommendation of the Board of Governors.

As of 1 March 1983, the IAEA had 111 members:

Afghanistan
Albania
Algeria
Argentina
Australia
Austria
Bangladesh
Belgium
Bolivia
Brazil
Bulgaria
Burma
Byelorussia
Cameroon
Canada
Chile
Colombia
Costa Rica
Cuba
Cyprus
Czechoslovakia
Denmark
Dominican Republic
Ecuador
Egypt
El Salvador
Ethiopia
Finland
France
Gabon
German Dem. Rep.
Germany, Fed. Rep.
Ghana
Greece
Guatemala
Haiti
Hungary
Iceland
India
Indonesia
Iran
Iraq
Ireland
Israel
Italy
Ivory Coast
Jamaica
Japan
Jordan
Kampuchea
Kenya
Korea, Dem. People's Rep.
Korea, Rep.
Kuwait
Lebanon
Liberia
Libya
Liechtenstein
Luxembourg
Madagascar
Malaysia
Mali
Mauritius
Mexico
Monaco
Mongolia
Morocco

Namibia
Netherlands
New Zealand
Nicaragua
Niger
Nigeria
Norway
Pakistan
Panama
Paraguay
Peru
Philippines
Poland
Portugal
Qatar
Romania
Sa'udi Arabia
Senegal
Sierra Leone
Singapore
South Africa
Spain
Sri Lanka
Sudan
Sweden
Switzerland
Syria
Tanzania
Thailand
Tunisia
Turkey
Uganda
Ukraine
USSR
United Arab Emirates
UK
US
Uruguay
Vatican
Venezuela
Viet-Nam
Yugoslavia
Zaire
Zambia

[5]STRUCTURE

The three organs of the IAEA are the General Conference, the Board of Governors, and the Secretariat, headed by a director-general.

General Conference

The General Conference consists of all members, each having one vote. It meets once a year at IAEA headquarters in Vienna. Special sessions may be convened by the director-general at the request of the Board of Governors or a majority of the IAEA members. The General Conference elects 22 of the 34 members of the Board of Governors. It considers the board's annual report and approves reports for submission to the UN and agreements with the UN and other organizations. It approves the budget recommended by the board and the appointment of the director-general. The General Conference may discuss any matter concerning the IAEA and may make recommendations to the Board of Governors or to any of the member states.

The *Scientific Advisory Committee* of the IAEA was established by the Board of Governors in September 1958. It is "a standing scientific advisory council composed of scientists of international eminence." The committee meets periodically—about twice a year—to advise the director-general and through him the Board of Governors on specific scientific and technical questions arising out of the IAEA's program.

The 15 members of the committee, appointed by the director-general with the concurrence of the board for the period 1982–85, were scientists from Algeria, Argentina, Canada, France, the FRG, India, Japan, Mexico, Poland, Romania, Spain, the USSR, the UK, the US, and Zaire. They serve not as representatives of their governments but "in their individual capacity." The committee, it should be noted, is independent of the IAEA secretariat.

Board of Governors
The Board of Governors is the body actually vested with "the authority to carry out the functions of the Agency in accordance with (the) Statute." It is composed as follows: the outgoing Board of Governors designates for membership on the board the nine members most advanced in the technology of atomic energy, including the production of source materials, and the member most advanced in technology of atomic energy and production of source materials in each of the following areas in which none of the aforesaid nine is located—North America, Latin America, Western Europe, Eastern Europe, Africa, Middle East and South Asia, Southeast Asia and the Pacific, and the Far East.

The General Conference elects to membership of the Board of Governors: (1) 20 members, with due regard to geographical representation, so that the board at all times will include in this category 5 representatives of Latin America, 4 representatives of Western Europe, 3 representatives of Eastern Europe, 4 representatives of Africa, 2 representatives of the Middle East and South Asia, 1 representative of Southeast Asia and the Pacific, and 1 representative of the Far East; (2) in addition, 1 further member from among the members of the following areas: Middle East and South Asia, Southeast Asia and the Pacific, and Far East; (3) and 1 further member from among the members in the following areas: Africa, Middle East and South Asia, and Southeast Asia and the Pacific.

The Board of Governors for 1982–83 was composed of Algeria, Argentina, Australia, Bangladesh, Brazil, Bulgaria, Canada, Colombia, Czechoslovakia, Denmark, Egypt, France, FRG, India, Indonesia, Italy, Japan, Kenya, Korea (ROK), Libya, Mexico, Netherlands, Pakistan, Panama, Portugal, Romania, Spain, Thailand, USSR, UK, US, Venezuela, Zaire, and Zambia.

Director-General and Staff
The staff of the IAEA is headed by a director general. He is appointed by the Board of Governors with the approval of the General Conference for a term of four years. The statute describes the director-general as "the chief administrative officer of the Agency," but it closely limits his independent powers by providing that he "shall be under the authority and subject to the control of the Board of Governors." The director-general is responsible for "the appointment, organization, and functioning of the staff."

The first director-general, who held the post from 1957 to 1961, was Sterling Cole of the US, a former congressman. In 1961, Dr. Sigvard Eklund, Swedish physicist and administrator, was elected director-general, to serve until 1965. He was reelected unanimously until 1981, when Dr. Hans Blix of Sweden, former foreign minister, was elected for a four-year term.

The staff includes qualified scientific and technical and other personnel as may be required to fulfill the objectives and functions of the agency. The statute requires that the IAEA's "permanent staff shall be kept to a minimum." At the end of 1982, its staff numbered 1,718, of whom 617 were in professional categories. The statute provides that the first consideration in recruiting should be "to secure employees of the highest standards of efficiency, technical competence, and integrity. Subject to this consideration due regard shall be paid to the contributions of members to the agency and to the importance of recruiting the staff on as wide a geographical basis as possible." By 1983, 86 nationalities were represented.

POSITION IN THE UN SYSTEM
The IAEA is an autonomous international organization occupying its own position in the UN family of organizations. Under the relationship agreement between the UN and the IAEA, the IAEA is recognized as being "responsible for international activities concerned with the peaceful uses of atomic energy." One of the statutory objectives of the IAEA is to ensure that none of the assistance it gives to member states is "used in such a way as to further any military purpose," and the IAEA shall establish a staff of inspectors to report violations of this rule. In case of noncompliance the agency's Board of Governors shall report to the Security Council and the General Assembly of the UN.

The agency has relationship agreements with seven specialized agencies of the UN (UNESCO, ILO, WHO, WMO, ICAO, FAO, IMO). Cooperation agreements have also been concluded with organizations not a part of the UN system that are concerned with the peaceful uses of atomic energy, such as the Inter-American Nuclear Energy Commission, the Agency for the Prohibition of Nuclear Weapons in Latin America, the League of Arab States, the OAU, the Nuclear Energy Agency of the OECD, the CMEA, and the European Atomic Energy Community (EURATOM). Finally, the IAEA maintains contact and has working relations with 19 nongovernmental organizations which have consultative status with the agency.

⁶BUDGET
The IAEA is financed by regular and voluntary contributions from member states. The regular budget for 1982 amounted to $86,369,000 and for 1983, $92,821,000. The target for voluntary contributions to finance the IAEA program of technical cooperation was $16 million for 1982, $19 million for 1983, $22.5 million for 1984, $26 million for 1985, and $30 million for 1986.

⁷ACTIVITIES
A. ASSISTANCE TO MEMBER STATES
The initial program of the IAEA, unanimously adopted by the 1957 General Conference, emphasized activities that could be undertaken while the IAEA's experience and resources were still relatively limited. High priority was given "to those activities which will give the maximum possible benefit from the peaceful applications of atomic energy in improving the conditions and raising the standard of living of the peoples in the underdeveloped areas."

In the light of these considerations, two of the IAEA's major objectives are to help member states prepare for the eventual use of nuclear power and to encourage them in the wider use of radioisotopes. Although it cannot undertake actual programs of development for its members, it can assist them in initiating and carrying out such programs.

Technical Assistance and Cooperation
Since 1959, numerous fact-finding, advisory services, and programming missions have been sent to countries desiring assistance. The findings of these missions are taken into account in providing technical assistance.

In 1982, 86 countries received technical assistance, mainly related to nuclear engineering and technology; the application of isotopes and radiation in agriculture; uranium prospecting; the use of isotopes in industry, medicine, and hydrology; and nuclear safety.

Assistance was provided through the services of 417 experts and 224 lecturers; equipment valued at $11.5 million; and training for 419 fellows and for 851 participants in study tours and specialized training courses.

Provision of Materials

Under the IAEA statute, any member desiring to set up an atomic energy project for peaceful purposes "may request the assistance of the Agency in securing special fissionable and other materials."

The IAEA acts, on request, as an intermediary in arranging the supply of reactor fuel and specialized equipment from one member state to another. Argentina, Finland, Japan, Mexico, Norway, Pakistan, Uruguay, and Zaire, among other countries, have been beneficiaries of such arrangements. Small quantities of special fissionable materials have also been supplied to a number of countries for research purposes.

Training of Technical Personnel

IAEA's training program has retained its importance, not only because of the pressing needs for trained staff but also because less elaborate preparations are required for assistance of this kind than for technical assistance operations involving the provision of expert services and demonstration equipment.

To meet the shortage of scientific and technical workers that is a major obstacle to "atoms for peace" progress, the IAEA has initiated a fivefold program:

1. *Fellowships.* Fellowships are awarded in all subjects involving the peaceful uses of atomic energy, such as in nuclear physics; the production, handling, and application of isotopes in agriculture, industry, medicine, biology, and hydrology; nuclear chemistry; the planning, construction, and operation of research and power reactors; health physics; and radiological protection. Fellows receive a monthly stipend to cover room, board, and incidentals, the amount of which varies according to the local cost of living.

2. *Assignment of experts and consultants.* The program provides for scientists and engineers to advise and provide in-service training to the developing countries on various subjects.

3. *Survey of available facilities in member states.* The IAEA collects detailed information from its member states about their training and research programs, training facilities, and the experts they are prepared to make available to the IAEA. It is thus in a position to act as an international clearinghouse for training in atomic energy and to promote technical cooperation among developing countries.

4. *Training courses.* The organization of these courses for participants from various countries requires elaborate preparations and cooperation with other organizations, national governments, universities, and scientific institutions. Such courses, which are given in different parts of the world, vary in duration from a few weeks to several months. In 1982, 35 regional and interregional courses were organized on such subjects as the application of isotopes and radiation in medicine, nuclear instrumentation for laboratory technicians, the use and maintenance of nuclear and related electronic equipment, radiological and safety protection, the utilization of research reactors, nuclear-power projects and other high-technology subjects, the preparation and control of radiopharmaceuticals, physics, and uranium prospecting and ore analysis.

5. *Expanded manpower training programs.* A number of developing countries, faced with the need to introduce nuclear power, require special assistance in the training of their key staff; therefore the agency has initiated an expanded training program on nuclear-power project planning, implementation, and operation. Special training courses contribute to the development of efficient legal and organizational infrastructures for nuclear-power programs, including instruction in quality assurance and safety aspects. In addition, on-the-job training is arranged on subjects for which no formal courses are available.

B. EXCHANGE OF INFORMATION

While its assistance programs are directed primarily to the needs of economically developing areas, the IAEA's program of conferences and exchange of information is designed to benefit all of its members—even the most technically advanced.

The International Nuclear Information System (INIS), set up by the agency in 1970, provides worldwide coverage of the literature dealing with all aspects of peaceful uses of atomic energy and is the first fully decentralized computer-based information system. Countries and organizations participating in INIS collect and process all the relevant literature within their geographic areas and send it to the IAEA. In Vienna, the information is checked, merged, and further processed, and the resulting output is distributed to individuals and organizations around the world. The major products of the system are the magnetic tape service, the *INIS Atomindex,* and the direct availability of the INIS database online from the IAEA computer in Vienna. The magnetic tapes and the online service, available to member states and participating organizations only, contain bibliographic descriptions, subject indexing, and abstracts, and are utilized for current selective dissemination of information and retrospective searching. The *INIS Atomindex,* an international nuclear abstract journal, is published twice a month and is available to the public on a subscription basis. An additional service is the provision on microfiche of texts of all nonconventional literature submitted to the system. In 1982 INIS membership included 67 countries and 14 international organizations; it reported on over 72,000 documents.

The IAEA also cooperates with FAO in the provision of a similar information system for agriculture, known as *AGRIS.*

A second important information service of the IAEA concerns nuclear data—numerical and associated information on neutron cross-sections, related fission, capture, and scattering parameters of neutron-induced reactions, as well as other nuclear physical constants. The IAEA maintains an efficient system for collection of these data and, together with three other regional centers in France, the USSR, and the US, issues *CINDA,* an index to the literature on microscopic neutron data. It also compiles *WRENDA,* the world request list for nuclear-data measurements needed for both the development of fission and fusion reactors and for nuclear-materials safeguards.

The IAEA also plays a leading role in promoting the dissemination of scientific and technical information by organizing each year 15 to 20 conferences, symposia, and seminars, and a large number of smaller technical meetings. The IAEA was entrusted with the scientific aspects of the International Conference on the Peaceful Uses of Atomic Energy, held in Geneva in 1971, and has organized major international conferences dealing with more specific aspects of the peaceful uses of nuclear energy, including conferences on nuclear power and its fuel cycle (Salzburg, 1977), on current nuclear-power safety issues (Stockholm, 1981), on nuclear-power experience (Vienna, 1982), and on waste management (Seattle, 1983).

C. RESEARCH

In 1964, the IAEA set up the International Center for Theoretical Physics, in Trieste, which brings together specialists from developing and developed countries to carry out research and to enable scientists from developing countries to keep abreast of progress without having to leave their own countries permanently or for long periods. Fellowships from developing countries are awarded for training and research and an international forum is provided for personal contacts. Associate memberships are awarded by election to enable distinguished physicists to spend one to three months every year at the center. Senior and junior positions are offered by invitation, and a federation scheme is designed to forge a partnership with institutions in developing countries. Assistance has been given by Italy and by the university and city of Trieste. Further aid has come from the Ford Foundation and UNESCO, which in 1970 undertook joint management of the center.

Many of the IAEA's technical assistance activities involve work with isotopes and radiation sources. The development of the practical uses of atomic energy, rather than fundamental research, is the statutory task of the IAEA. Nevertheless, it very soon became clear that in order to develop a practical "atoms for peace" program the IAEA would have to concern itself with certain serious gaps in existing knowledge concerning the use of radioisotopes. In particular, additional research was required concerning safeguards, radiation safety and protection, and radiation health problems. Accordingly, the IAEA allocates funds for research to be carried out at IAEA headquarters or to be contracted out to research institutions in member states.

The IAEA has three laboratories: a small one at its headquarters in Vienna, the main laboratory at Seibersdorf (20 miles from Vienna), and one at Monaco for research on the effects of radioactivity in the sea. The laboratories undertake work in agriculture, hydrology, medicine, physics, chemistry, and low-level radioactivity.

A research contract program has been established with various institutions in member states. The subjects include nuclear power and reactors, waste treatment, physics, and chemistry; radioisotope and radiation applications in agriculture, food technology, industry, and medicine; water resources development; protection of humans against ionizing radiation; radiation biology; medical and biological radiation dosimetry; health physics and radiation protection; environmental contamination; and waste disposal.

To keep abreast of scientific developments, members of the IAEA's scientific staff visit institutions in member states and conduct various studies. The IAEA has made a survey of research trends in the sterilization of food and drugs by ionizing radiation, a problem of considerable interest to both developed and developing countries.

D. NUCLEAR POWER

Nuclear power is already an important source of electricity generation, particularly in industrialized countries, and technically and economically ripe for an even larger application worldwide. As a result, many developing countries are taking an interest in nuclear power. In response to this interest, the IAEA has played an increasing role in objective nuclear-power planning studies for individual member states. Energy planning methodologies have been developed and made available. The IAEA has cooperated with interested member states in applying these methodologies to specific country cases. The methodology for assessing the economic role of nuclear power in meeting increasing electricity requirements has been made available to 45 member states and several international organizations, including the World Bank. The Agency has assisted a number of countries by making preliminary assessments of nuclear-power requirements. In creating an awareness of preconditions for and requirements of nuclear power, the IAEA has published a number of guidebooks focusing on important issues and special demands of nuclear technology for the use of its developing member states. Recognizing the importance of qualified personnel to supervise program development, the IAEA launched in 1975 a Nuclear Power Training Program, which is offering training courses in problem areas related to program planning and execution, siting and safety assessments, operational safety, and other important subjects. By the end of 1982, the program had been used by more than 1,300 trainees from some 60 developing countries in 47 courses.

The IAEA started to collect operating experience data from nuclear power plants in the late 1960s and has now established a Power Reactor Information System which monitors the performance of the 294 nuclear power plants in operation in 25 countries of the world. Beyond the performance indices and energy production, the system also contains information about some 10,000 full and partial plant outages affecting 3.6 million hours of plant operation, and covers nearly 2,000 years of power-reactor operating experience in the world (to the end of 1982). Periodic publications by the IAEA make this information available to planners and operators in member states.

As an increasing number of countries are interested in the use of nuclear plants for heat-only production and co-generation (for example, desalination combined with electricity generation), the IAEA is periodically reviewing progress in this direction. In addition, a number of scientific meetings on nuclear power have been organized to discuss such matters as economic competitiveness of nuclear power, integration of nuclear power plants in electric grids, operating experience, introduction of small and medium power reactors, development of fast-breeder and high-temperature reactors, and fusion technology.

E. RADIOLOGICAL AND NUCLEAR SAFETY

Since the basic raw materials of atomic energy are radioactive and since all ionizing radiation is dangerous, a very important duty of the IAEA is to establish standards of safe practice for activities carried out under its auspices or with its assistance. The statute specifically authorizes the IAEA to establish and adopt "standards of safety for protection of health and minimization of danger to life and property (including such standards for labor conditions)" and to provide for the application of these standards to its own operations and operations carried out with its assistance. If required, the IAEA may also provide for the application of these standards to a state's own nuclear activities or to any bilateral or multilateral arrangement between states.

The IAEA has formulated basic safety standards for radiation protection which take account of the recommendations of the International Commission on Radiological Protection (ICRP) and are revised, when necessary, to conform with new recommendations of the ICRP. It has also issued regulations and technical guidance on specific types of operations, including in particular the safe transport of radioactive materials. Such standards have proved to be a useful basis for international regulations and national legislation. Many manuals of guidance on radiological safety practices have been issued by the IAEA in its *Safety Series*.

A system has been established by the IAEA for facilitating the provision of emergency assistance to member states in the event of radiation accidents. This is intended mainly to help those countries that have not sufficient experience or resources to deal with the consequences of such accidents.

The projected rapid growth of nuclear power both in industrialized and developing countries has led the IAEA to establish a program to formulate safety criteria in the form of safety codes, guides, and users' manuals. This Nuclear Safety Standards Program will assist the authorities of the various countries to ensure that basic safety requirements are understood and met in their nuclear power development. Codes of practice and safety guides have been prepared in the areas of governmental organization, siting, design, operation, and quality control.

F. WASTE MANAGEMENT AND ENVIRONMENTAL PROTECTION

Safe management of radioactive wastes produced in all the stages of the nuclear fuel cycle is essential for the growth of nuclear power. The IAEA has been active since its establishment in all aspects of this field, including the publication of *Safety Series* and *Technical Reports* giving guidelines and recommendations; the holding of seminars, symposia, and conferences; and the arranging of study tours for the benefit of member states. Major areas currently being pursued by the IAEA are in the fields of underground disposal, waste handling and treatment, and environmental aspects of waste disposal.

Safety Standards and Codes of Practice have been, or are planned to be, prepared on the management of wastes produced by users of radioactive materials; on the management of wastes from the mining and milling of uranium and thorium ores; on the disposal of wastes in shallow ground, rock cavities, and deep geological formations; and on criteria for underground disposal of wastes.

G. NUCLEAR LAW

From its inception, the IAEA has been faced with the need for international coordination and harmonization of the principles governing third-party liability in the event of nuclear damage. The absence of special legislation might leave injured victims without redress. Great difficulties might arise if different nations were to incorporate different principles and procedures in their legislation concerning third-party liability.

Some steps toward worldwide harmonization of compensation for damage arising from nuclear operations have been taken through the adoption of two international conventions: the Brussels Convention on the Liability of Operators of Nuclear Ships (1962) and the Vienna Convention on Civil Liability for Nuclear Damage (1963). These two conventions set the minimum standards concerning the liability of the operator of a nuclear installation or a nuclear ship in the event of accidents that occur during the operation of nuclear ships and installations or during transport of nuclear materials.

Another convention was adopted in December 1971 by an international conference held in Brussels under the joint auspices of the IMO, the Nuclear Energy Agency of the OECD, and the IAEA: the Convention on Civil Liability in the Field of Maritime Carriage of Nuclear Matter, which entered into force on 15 July 1975. This convention exonerates shipowners from liability under international maritime law in the case of nuclear damage falling within the purview of the Paris Convention on Third Party Liability in the Field of Nuclear Energy (1960), which entered into force on 1 April 1968, or the Vienna Convention on Civil Liability for Nuclear Damage (1963) whenever the carriage of nuclear material is involved; it thus eliminates what had been a serious impediment to sea transport of such material.

The Convention on the Physical Protection of Nuclear Material was adopted on 26 October 1979 at a meeting of governmental representatives held at IAEA headquarters. The convention is designed to ensure that the prescribed levels of physical protection be applied to potentially hazardous nuclear materials during international transport. As of 24 March 1983, the convention had been signed by 33 states and EURATOM and ratified by 6 states; it will enter into force on the 30th day following the date of deposit of the 21st instrument of ratification, acceptance, or approval with the director-general of the IAEA.

In conjunction with the increasing number of states embarking on nuclear programs, there has also been a growing awareness of the necessity for establishing both a proper legislative framework and specialized regulations for the licensing and control of nuclear installations. The IAEA has provided advisory services to several developing countries in the framing of statutory and regulatory provisions in such areas as the establishment of competent bodies on atomic energy; radiation and environmental protection; transport of radioactive materials; licensing of nuclear installations; nuclear liability; and nuclear merchant ships. In-service training on various legal aspects of atomic energy at IAEA headquarters has also been provided to a number of officials nominated by member states under the IAEA fellowships program or through other arrangements.

H. SAFEGUARDS ON THE PEACEFUL USES OF NUCLEAR ENERGY

The basic science and technology of nuclear energy are the same for both peaceful and military purposes. Therefore, the IAEA statute requires the agency "to establish and administer safeguards" to ensure that no materials, services, equipment, facilities, or information that the IAEA makes available are used "in such a way as to further any military purpose." Such safeguards may also be applied, "at the request of the parties, to any bilateral or multilateral arrangement, or, at the request of a state, to any of that state's activities in the field of atomic energy."

Under the IAEA safeguards system, which was first developed by the Board of Governors on the basis of these statutory provisions in 1961, and continuously revised to cover all major aspects of the fuel cycle, the IAEA exercises its control either over assistance provided directly by it or under its auspices, or over items placed voluntarily under IAEA safeguards by any state or group of states—for instance, over reactors, their fuel, and fuel-reprocessing plants. Safeguards based on this system were being applied in 14 countries in 1982.

The Non-Proliferation Treaty. A major development greatly affecting the significance of the IAEA's work was the coming into force in 1970 of the Treaty on the Non-Proliferation of Nuclear Weapons (NPT), under which states without nuclear weapons and party thereto agreed to accept IAEA safeguards on all their peaceful nuclear activities. By early 1983, 82 of the states party to the NPT had concluded the required safeguards agreements with IAEA for the purpose of preventing diversion of nuclear energy from peaceful uses to nuclear weapons or other nuclear explosive devices. Two of the nuclear-weapon states party to the treaty, the UK and the US, have concluded safeguards agreements with the IAEA, permitting the Agency to apply its safeguards to all their nuclear activities, excluding only those having direct national security significance. Such an agreement has also been concluded with France (which is not a party to the NPT), and a similar accord is under negotiation with the USSR, the third nuclear-weapon state party to the NPT.

IAEA's Safeguards System. The objective of safeguards applied under agreements concluded in connection with the NPT is the timely detection of diversion of significant quantities of nuclear material from peaceful nuclear activities to the manufacture of nuclear weapons or of other nuclear explosive devices or for purposes unknown, and the deterrence of such diversion by the risk of early detection.

This objective is achieved by the independent verification of the findings of the national system of accountancy and control of nuclear materials which a state without nuclear weapons must establish and maintain under the agreement. IAEA verification is accomplished by material accountancy, containment, and surveillance, including inspections, whose number, intensity and duration must be kept to the minimum consistent with the effective implementation of safeguards. Considerable effort continues to be made to improve the safeguarding techniques and to increase their efficiency with the greatest economy in cost and manpower. A number of research contracts have been placed for this purpose.

Upon the report by the director-general, the Board of Governors may call upon a state with a safeguards agreement to take the necessary action if this is essential and urgent in order to ensure verification that safeguarded nuclear material is not diverted. Further, the board may report noncompliance to all members of the IAEA and to the Security Council and the General Assembly of the UN. In the event of failure of that state to take fully corrective action within a reasonable time, the board may take one or both of the following measures: direct curtailment or suspension of assistance being provided by the agency or by a member state, and call for the return of materials and equipment made available to the noncomplying member state. IAEA may also suspend any noncomplying member state from the privileges and rights of membership.

The Treaty of Tlatelolco. In February 1967, 21 states adopted the Treaty for the Prohibition of Nuclear Weapons in Latin America (Treaty of Tlatelolco). The treaty provides for the establishment of a control system and the parties agree to conclude with the IAEA multilateral or bilateral agreements for the application of safeguards. Nineteen states had concluded such agreements with the IAEA by the end of 1982, either in connection with the Treaty of Tlatelolco alone or in connection with the NPT and the Treaty of Tlatelolco.

⁸BIBLIOGRAPHY

INIS Atomindex. Twice a month.

International Atomic Energy Agency Bulletin. Six times a year, with information written for the lay reader.

Meetings on Atomic Energy. Quarterly, with exhaustive listings of major meetings, plus two computerized indices.

Nuclear Fusion. Quarterly.

Safety Series. Manuals on the safe handling and transport of radioactive materials, monitoring of personnel, and disposal of radioactive wastes.

(The IAEA also publishes proceedings of scientific meetings covering an extensive range of nuclear-related subjects, including life sciences, nuclear safety and environmental protection, physics, chemistry, geology and raw materials, reactors and nuclear power, industrial applications, and nuclear law and safeguards.)

THE GENERAL AGREEMENT ON TARIFFS AND TRADE (GATT)

[1]**BACKGROUND:** Efforts to foster international trade go back to antiquity; so do national efforts to expand exports to the detriment of competitors and to restrict or even prohibit imports. Wars have been fought over such issues, and for long periods of time in many countries controversy between protectionists and free traders has dominated the political scene. In the 1930s, when the world was suffering from an intense economic depression, many governments attempted to find shelter behind protective trade barriers: high tariff walls, quota restrictions on imports, exchange controls, and the like. If anything, these uncoordinated and mutually antagonistic policies prolonged the international economic crisis. During World War II, serious thought was given to ways and means of preventing such restrictive trade practices from becoming permanently fastened upon the world. Postwar attempts to create a full-fledged international agency to foster and liberalize world trade failed. The General Agreement on Tariffs and Trade (GATT) is today the major result of the efforts that were made in this direction. In the absence of a true international trade organization, it serves as the only intergovernmental instrument that lays down rules for trade and harmonizes trading relations among the nations of the international community.

[2]CREATION

The starting point for the General Agreement on Tariffs and Trade can be traced to the Atlantic Charter and to the lend-lease agreements in which the wartime allies bound themselves to seek a world trading system based on nondiscrimination and aimed at higher standards of living to be achieved through fair, full, and free exchange of goods and services.

Three agencies to operate in the specialized field of economic affairs were contemplated: an International Monetary Fund (IMF), an International Bank for Reconstruction and Development (IBRD), and an International Trade Organization (ITO). The IMF and the IBRD were duly established at the Bretton Woods Conference of 1944, but for various reasons, including the complexity of the problems involved, the drafting of the ITO charter was delayed. The UN Economic and Social Council took the matter up at its first session, in February 1946, and appointed a 17-nation preparatory committee to draft such a charter. The committee's draft was submitted to a 56-nation conference that met in Havana from 21 November 1947 to 24 March 1948 and, after considering some 800 separate amendments, hammered out a document known as the Havana Charter to serve as the constitution of the ITO.

The Havana Charter dealt not only with the reduction of trade barriers but with a number of other complex (and sometimes controversial) matters, including employment and investment policies, mutual cooperation for economic development, commodity control agreements, and the control of international cartels. In view of the preponderant economic position of the US at that time, US participation in the proposed agency was indispensable. The US government favored ratification, but opinion in the country and in Congress was sharply divided. Some opponents argued that the Havana Charter contained too many escape clauses to be effective; others argued that it was too strong and would stifle private enterprise. In December 1950, the US president decided not to submit the Havana Charter to the US Senate for ratification, since it was evident that the requisite two-thirds majority could not be obtained. After it became clear that the US would not join the ITO, the plan to create the agency was quietly buried; however, some of it survived.

While the draft charter of the ITO was being worked out prior to the Havana Conference, the governments of the 17-member preparatory committee had agreed to sponsor negotiations for an interim agreement aimed at lowering customs tariffs and reducing the other trade restrictions among themselves. The first tariff negotiating conference was held in Geneva in 1947. The tariff concessions resulting from these special negotiating sessions were embodied in a multilateral agreement called the General Agreement on Tariffs and Trade (GATT), which included a set of rules designed to prevent the tariff concessions from being frustrated by other protective devices. The agreement was signed on 30 October 1947 and came into force on 1 January 1948. GATT was originally intended as no more than a stopgap arrangement pending the creation of the ITO, but as events have worked out, it has functioned since 1948, in fact if not in name, as an agency fulfilling some of the proposed ITO's most important functions.

[3]PURPOSES

The General Agreement on Tariffs and Trade is a multilateral trade treaty embodying reciprocal rights and duties. It contains the world's first common code of commercial conduct and fair trading, the objective of which is to expand the production and exchange of goods and so to promote economic development, full employment, and higher standards of living. Under the agreement, all parties are to accord to one another the same "most-favored-nation" treatment in the application of import and export duties and charges and in their administration. Protection is to be afforded to domestic industries exclusively through customs tariffs, import quotas being specifically outlawed as a protectionist device (though they may be used for certain other purposes, such as redressing a country's balance of payments). Countries adhering to GATT agree to avoid, through consultations, damage to the trading interests of any of the contracting parties. GATT itself provides a framework within which negotiations can be held for the reduction of tariffs and other barriers to trade and within which the results of such negotiations can be embodied in a legal instrument. The importance of this "fair trading" code can be measured by the fact that it is accepted and applied by countries accounting for well over 80% of world exports.

[4]MEMBERSHIP

Since GATT is a treaty rather than an organization, adhering governments are designated as "contracting parties." When the agreement was brought into operation on 1 January 1948, it was applied by eight governments only. As of 1 July 1983, there were

89 contracting parties to the General Agreement, and one country (Tunisia) had acceded provisionally. In addition, there were 29 other countries to whose territories GATT had been applied and which, as independent states in 1983, maintained a de facto application of GATT pending final decisions as to their future commercial policy.

CONTRACTING PARTIES TO GATT

Argentina	Haiti	Philippines
Australia	Hungary	Poland
Austria	Iceland	Portugal
Bangladesh	India	Romania
Barbados	Indonesia	Rwanda
Belgium	Ireland	Senegal
Benin	Israel	Sierra Leone
Brazil	Italy	Singapore
Burma	Ivory Coast	South Africa
Burundi	Jamaica	Spain
Cameroon	Japan	Sri Lanka
Canada	Kenya	Suriname
Central African Rep.	Korea, Rep.	Sweden
Chad	Kuwait	Switzerland
Chile	Luxembourg	Tanzania
Colombia	Madagascar	Thailand
Congo	Malawi	Togo
Cuba	Malaysia	Trinidad
Cyprus	Maldives	and Tobago
Czechoslovakia	Malta	Tunisia (prov.)
Denmark	Mauritania	Turkey
Dominican Republic	Mauritius	Uganda
Egypt	Netherlands	UK
Finland	New Zealand	US
France	Nicaragua	Upper Volta
Gabon	Niger	Uruguay
Gambia	Nigeria	Yugoslavia
Germany, Fed. Rep.	Norway	Zaire
Ghana	Pakistan	Zambia
Greece	Peru	Zimbabwe
Guyana		

DE FACTO ADHERENTS OF GATT

Algeria	Guinea-Bissau	São Tomé and
Angola	Kampuchea	Príncipe
Bahamas	Kiribati	Seychelles
Bahrain	Lesotho	Solomon Islands
Belize	Mali	Swaziland
Botswana	Mozambique	Tonga
Cape Verde	Papua New Guinea	Tuvalu
Dominica	Qatar	United Arab
Equatorial Guinea	St. Lucia	Emirates
Fiji	St. Vincent and the	Yemen, People's
Grenada	Grenadines	Dem.Rep.

New adherents to the General Agreement are welcomed. Countries that are former dependencies of existing contracting parties may, on achieving independence, themselves adhere to GATT by stating that they accept the obligations of membership. Other applicants must negotiate the terms of their adherence with the existing members, offering trade concessions to balance those they will enjoy as a result of accession. Normally this is done in a working group. The proposed terms of accession are submitted to a vote, and must be approved by two-thirds of all GATT members. Developing countries are not expected to make concessions inconsistent with their developmental, financial, and trade needs. A number of Eastern European countries have negotiated their accession, even though many lack meaningful tariff systems and therefore cannot offer tariff concessions, on the basis of assurances regarding the expected evolution of their trade with GATT members.

Under a special provision (Article XXXV) of the General Agreement, a GATT country that has not yet entered into tariff negotiations with another GATT country is permitted to declare that the GATT obligations will not apply between the two of them.

[5]STRUCTURE

Sessions of the Contracting Parties and the Council
The central forum in which the GATT countries act collectively is the usually annual "Session of the Contracting Parties to the General Agreement on Tariffs and Trade." The sessions, usually held in Geneva, provide an opportunity to review developments and trends in international trade, and in the operations of the General Agreement itself.

Between sessions, the work of GATT is largely carried on by a 65-nation council of representatives, established in 1960. Capable of being called together at a few days' notice, it can deal with both routine and urgent matters. Although it cannot make decisions where these require a vote by the contracting parties as a whole, it can and frequently does submit such decisions to a postal ballot. The council can as necessary set up committees, working groups, or panels of experts to assist it in its work. The questions that come before it are extremely varied: they may range from routine reports of standing committees to urgent complaints by governments alleging violation of GATT obligations by other countries.

In 1975, the GATT council set up the Consultative Group of Eighteen, consisting of 18 high-level representatives nominated by governments, so chosen as to provide a balanced representation of the membership of GATT. Its meetings assist GATT by following international trade developments, dealing with sudden disturbances that threaten multilateral trade relations, and coordinating with the IMF. Apart from the Consultative Group of Eighteen and the Committee on Trade and Development, which has the duty to follow all activities of GATT, ensuring that problems of concern to developing countries are given priority attention, a number of standing committees deal with, respectively, the situation of countries using trade restrictions to protect their balance of payments; textiles; tariff concessions; antidumping practices; customs valuation; government procurement; subsidies and countervailing measures; import licensing; technical barriers to trade; agriculture; trade in meat; trade in dairy products; trade in civil aircraft; quantitative restrictions and other nontariff measures; and budget, financial, and administrative questions.

Director-General and Secretariat
GATT is administered by a secretariat of about 290 people under Director-General Arthur Dunkel of Switzerland. The headquarters address is: Centre William Rappard, CH 1211 Geneva 21, Switzerland.

[6]BUDGET

Governments party to GATT are assessed for its administrative expenses according to their share in the total trade of the contracting governments. Contributions for 1983 totaled 49,637,000 Swiss francs (approximately $22.5 million).

[7]ACTIVITIES

The General Agreement on Tariffs and Trade is a multilateral treaty consisting of 38 articles.

Articles I and II deal directly with tariffs. The first article is the mutual guarantee of most-favored-nation treatment among all contracting parties. It states that any "advantage, favor, privilege or immunity" in regard to duties, payments, and formalities in connection with imports and exports granted by a GATT country to another must automatically be extended to all other GATT countries. Article II provides detailed schedules for tariff reductions agreed to as a result of GATT negotiations.

Article III prohibits the use of internal taxes to protect domestic products against imports.

Articles IV to X—known as the technical articles—provide

general rules and principles relating to transit trade, antidumping duties, customs valuation, customs formalities, and marks of origin. For example, all countries adhering to GATT are required to grant freedom of transit to goods en route to or from other GATT countries; and if a country can prove that another country is injuring its industry by dumping a product on its markets at less than normal value, it may levy a special duty on the product in question.

Articles XI to XIV include a general prohibition of quantitive import restrictions except to safeguard balance of payments, while Article XV deals with relations between contracting parties and the IMF.

Subsequent articles deal with the progressive elimination of export subsidies (XVI), and with state trading (XVII), emergency measures (XIX), and general and security exceptions (XX and XXI). Article XVIII recognizes that the less-developed countries need to maintain a special degree of tariff flexibility to protect vulnerable new industries, and may need to apply some import quotas in order to have sufficient foreign exchange for imports that are vital.

The important provisions for action by contracting parties to settle differences arising out of the application of the General Agreement are contained in Articles XXII and XXIII. Article XXIV, which has assumed great importance, lays down conditions under which a customs union or free-trade area is accepted as a basis for an exception to the most-favored-nation principle.

Article XXVIII deals with the general principles of tariff negotiation and sets forth the arrangements under which contracting parties can, by negotiation, modify existing tariff concessions. Other articles deal with technical matters relating to the agreement, such as acceptance, accession, and withdrawal.

One of the most important provisions is that in Article XXV, which provides for joint action by the contracting parties. This is the legal basis that has allowed GATT, as a collective enterprise, rather than just a treaty, to work toward the expansion of international trade and serve as a forum for the discussion of international trade problems.

In 1965 a chapter on trade and development, consisting of Articles XXXVI to XXXVIII, was added to the General Agreement. These articles provide a legal basis for collective action on the part of the contracting parties aimed at enlarging the export earnings of developing countries.

A. TRADE NEGOTIATIONS

"The substantial reduction of tariffs and other barriers to trade" is laid down in the General Agreement as one of the principal means of obtaining its broad objectives. Before this agreement, tariffs were generally established by simple unilateral action, each government acting independently or through bilateral negotiations, in which one government would trade reciprocal concessions with another. The General Agreement provided the first machinery for multilateral tariff negotiations, aimed at reducing tariffs simultaneously among all the contracting parties, in accordance with the most-favored-nation principle. There have been several long series of such negotiations, the most ambitious of which was the Tokyo Round, so-called because it was launched in Tokyo in September 1973 with a ministerial meeting.

During GATT's first 35 years, it held seven major trade negotiations: 1947 (Geneva), 1949 (Annecy, France), 1951 (Torquay, England), 1956 (Geneva), 1960–61 (Geneva, the "Dillon Round"), 1964–67 (Geneva, the "Kennedy Round"), and 1973–79 (Geneva, the "Tokyo Round"). Smaller-scale negotiations preceded the accession to GATT of countries such as Japan, Switzerland, and Hungary. As a result, the tariff rates for thousands of items entering into world commerce were reduced or frozen ("bound," in GATT parlance) to prevent their being increased.

The tariff and nontariff concessions agreed upon in these nego-tiations have affected a high proportion of the trade of GATT countries and, indirectly, the trade of many nonmembers as well. GATT has thus contributed greatly to the spectacular growth in world trade since 1948.

B. THE "TOKYO ROUND" OF TRADE NEGOTIATIONS

Agreement to open a new round of trade negotiations, more ambitious in scope than ever previously attempted, was reached at the Tokyo ministerial meeting in September 1973, and embodied in a document known as the Tokyo Declaration. The Declaration defined the scope of the negotiations as covering both tariff and nontariff obstacles to trade in the whole range of industrial and agricultural products, including tropical products and raw materials, whether in primary form or at any stage of processing, and including in particular products and measures of importance to the trade of developing countries. The Declaration also called for review of the basic trading rules embodied in the General Agreement itself. Developed countries negotiated on a basis of reciprocity—to make trade concessions balancing those they received. Reciprocity was not expected from developing countries. Ninety-nine countries participated in the Tokyo Round.

The negotiations were concluded in November 1979 with agreements that covered an improved legal framework for the conduct of world trade (including recognition of tariff and nontariff treatment in favor of and among developing countries as a permanent legal feature of the world trading system); nontariff measures (subsidies and countervailing measures); technical barriers to trade; government procurement; customs valuation; import licensing procedures; a revision of the 1967 GATT Antidumping Code; bovine meat; dairy products; tropical products; and civil aircraft. The agreements contain provisions for special and more favorable treatment for developing countries. Participating countries also agreed to reduce tariffs on thousands of industrial and agricultural products, the cuts to be gradually implemented, for the most part over a period of seven years beginning on 1 January 1980.

The agreements improving the framework for the conduct of world trade took effect in November 1979. The other agreements took effect on 1 January 1980, except for those covering government procurement and customs valuation, which took effect on 1 January 1981, and the concessions on tropical products, which entered into force as early as 1977. Committees or councils supervise implementation of the agreements.

Tariffs

The tariff reductions agreed to in the Tokyo Round began on 1 January 1980, and are continuing with equal annual cuts, the total reduction to become effective not later than 1 January 1987. The total value of trade affected by the Tokyo Round most-favored-nation tariff reductions, and by bindings of prevailing tariff rates, amounts to more than $155 billion, measured on most-favored-nation imports in 1977. As a result of these cuts, the weighted average tariff (that is, the average tariff measured against actual trade flows) on manufactured products in the world's nine major industrial markets will decline from 7% to 4.7%, representing a one-third reduction of customs collection, a cut comparable to that achieved in the Kennedy Round (1964–67). Since the tariff-cutting formula adopted by most industrialized countries results in the largest reductions generally being made in the highest duties, the customs duties of different countries will be brought closer together, or "harmonized." Developing countries made tariff-cutting commitments, in the form of tariff bindings or reductions, on $3.9 billion of their imports in 1977.

Nontariff Measures

As the general level of tariff protection declined in the post–World War II period, the distorting effects on world trade of nontariff measures became more pervasive. The complex and often very difficult negotiations to counter the negative effects of these measures distinguished the Tokyo Round from the earlier GATT trade negotiations. The core of the Tokyo Round results consists of the binding agreements, or codes, aimed at reducing, and bringing under more effective international discipline, these nontariff measures. All the agreements provide for consultation and dispute settlement; they also provide for special and more favorable treatment for developing countries. The following are agreements on nontariff measures.

The agreement on *subsidies and countervailing measures* commits signatory governments to ensuring that any use of subsidies by them does not harm the trading interests of another signatory, and that countervailing measures do not unjustifiably impede international trade; these measures may only be applied if it can be shown that the subsidized imports in question are in fact responsible for causing material injury, or threatening such injury, to the domestic industry which has lodged the complaint.

The agreement on *technical barriers to trade* (also known as the Standards Code) commits signatories to making sure that when governments or other bodies adopt technical regulations or standards, for reasons of safety, health, consumer or environmental protection, among others, these regulations or standards, and the testing and certification schemes related to them, shall not create unnecessary obstacles to trade.

The agreement on *import licensing procedures* recognizes that these procedures can have acceptable uses, but also that their inappropriate use may hamper international trade; it aims at ensuring that they do not in themselves act as restrictions on imports. By becoming parties to the agreement, governments commit themselves to simple import licensing procedures and to administering them in a neutral and fair way.

The agreement on *government procurement* aims to secure greater international competition in the bidding for government procurement contracts. It contains detailed rules on the way in which tenders for government purchasing contracts should be invited and awarded. It is designed to make laws, regulations, procedures, and practices regarding government procurement more transparent, and to ensure that they do not protect domestic products or suppliers, or discriminate among foreign products or suppliers. The agreement's provisions will apply to individual government contracts worth more than SDR 150,000 (about $170,000). Listed in an annex to the agreement are all the government agencies in each signatory country whose purchases are covered by the agreement.

The agreement on *customs valuation* sets a fair, uniform, and neutral system for the valuation of goods for customs purposes, a system that conforms to commercial realities and that outlaws the use of arbitrary or fictitious customs values. The code provides a revised set of valuation rules, expanding and giving greater precision to the provisions on customs valuation already found in GATT. Developing countries may delay applying the code for five years, and are given greater powers to counter potentially unfair valuation practices.

Under the *revised GATT Antidumping Code,* "dumped" goods are broadly defined as imports which are sold at prices below those charged by the producer in his domestic market. Participants in the Tokyo Round agreed on a revision of the earlier GATT Antidumping Code negotiated by a group of major industrialized countries during the Kennedy Round (1964–67). The new code interprets the provisions of GATT's Article VI, which lays down the conditions under which antidumping duties may be imposed as a defense against dumped imports, and brings certain of its provisions into line with the relevant provisions of the Code on Subsidies and Countervailing Measures.

Agreement on Trade in Civil Aircraft
Several industrialized participants agreed in the Tokyo Round to eliminate, by 1 January 1980, all customs duties and similar charges of any kind on civil aircraft, aircraft parts, and repairs on civil aircraft. These zero duties are legally "bound" under GATT and, according to the most-favored-nation rule, apply to all GATT member countries. The agreement contains an annex listing all the products covered, ranging from passenger airliners, helicopters, and ground flight simulators to food warmers and oxygen masks.

The Multilateral Safeguard System and Adjustment Assistance
The Tokyo Declaration provided that "with a view to furthering trade liberalization and preserving its results," the negotiations would include an examination of the adequacy of the multilateral safeguard system and in particular of the way in which Article XIX of the General Agreement is applied. This issue was not resolved during the Tokyo Round, and a committee was established within GATT to continue the safeguards negotiations.

Article XIX is the main GATT "escape clause." It allows member countries to take emergency action of a nondiscriminatory character to restrict imports of particular products when they "cause or threaten serious injury to domestic producers." The question of internal adjustment policies is closely linked with that of safeguards.

Agricultural Products
Many countries that depend on farm exports felt that agriculture had been left out of earlier negotiating rounds, and that liberalization of agricultural trade had been limited. The Tokyo Declaration therefore put equal stress on agricultural negotiations along with those on industrial products. The agreements on tariff and nontariff concessions, and all the multilateral agreements reached in the Tokyo Round, apply to world trade in farm products, as well as to industrial products. Participating countries also drew up multilateral agreements on bovine meat and on dairy products, which entered into force on 1 January 1980.

The *Arrangement Regarding Bovine Meat* aims to promote expansion, liberalization, and stabilization of international trade in meat and livestock, as well as to improve international cooperation in this sector. The arrangement covers beef and veal, as well as live cattle. The International Meat Council within GATT reviews the functioning of the arrangement, evaluates the world supply and demand situation for meat, and provides a forum for regular consultation on all matters affecting international trade in bovine meat.

The *International Dairy Arrangement* aims to expand and liberalize world trade in dairy products; to achieve greater stability in this trade and, therefore, in the interests of exporters and importers, to avoid surpluses and shortages, undue fluctuations in prices, and serious disturbances in international trade; to further the economic and social development of developing countries; and to improve international cooperation in the dairy products sector. The arrangement covers all dairy products. Annexed to the arrangement are three protocols setting specific provisions, including minimum prices, for international trade in certain milk powders, milk fats (including butter), and certain cheeses. The International Dairy Products Council within GATT reviews the functioning of the arrangement and evaluates the situation in, and future outlook for, the world dairy market.

Tropical Products
Concessions and contributions by industrialized countries reducing import duties and other trade barriers facing exports of tropical products from developing countries were the first concrete results of the Tokyo Round; most were implemented in 1976 and 1977. Further concessions offered during the later stages of the negotiations took effect from 1980 onward. The concessions cover such products as coffee, cocoa, tea, spices, and a variety of other goods in raw, processed, and semiprocessed forms.

C. GATT AND DEVELOPING COUNTRIES
About two-thirds of the member countries of GATT are in the

responsibility, as the organization under whose rules the greater part of world trade moves, to assist their economic growth.

The developing countries take full part in GATT's work. Their presence underlines not only their determination to promote their own trading interests but also their recognition that the success of their own efforts to promote their economic development is closely linked with the continued expansion of world trade. This expansion of trade in turn is largely dependent on GATT's success in its efforts to maintain an open world trading system. Promotion of the trade interests of the developing countries was a priority aim of the Tokyo Round, while a number of provisions of the General Agreement have for many years permitted flexibility to these countries in their application of some GATT rules.

Part IV of the General Agreement

In 1965 a new chapter—Part IV—on trade and development was added to the General Agreement, committing developed countries to assist the developing countries "as a matter of conscious and purposeful effort." Part IV laid down the important principle, subsequently elaborated in the Tokyo Round "framework" agreements, that developed countries would not expect developing countries, in the course of trade negotiations, to make contributions inconsistent with their individual development, financial, and trade needs. Developed countries also agreed that, except when compelling reasons made it impossible, they would refrain from increasing barriers to exports of primary and other products of special interest to developing countries, and would give high priority to reducing existing barriers, including fiscal taxes. Consultation procedures were also established, and the Committee on Trade and Development was set up. The committee has the duty to follow all activities of GATT, ensuring that problems of concern to developing countries are given priority attention. The committee's role was strengthened following the Tokyo Round by the creation of two new subcommittees, one to examine any new protective measures taken by developed countries against imports from developing countries, and the other to consider the trade problems of the least-developed countries.

One of the most important issues agreed upon for developing countries during the Tokyo Round was the differential and more favorable treatment, reciprocity, and fuller participation of developing countries which marked a turning point in international trade relations by recognizing tariff and nontariff preferential treatment in favor of and among developing countries as a permanent legal feature of the world trading system. This "enabling clause" includes provision of a permanent legal basis for the extension of the generalized system of preferences by developed countries to developing countries (previously authorized by a temporary waiver from the provisions of Article I). It also permits special trade treatment for the least-developed countries.

Developed countries state that they do not expect reciprocity for commitments made by them in trade negotiations to reduce or remove tariffs and other barriers to the trade of developing countries, while developing countries recognize that, as their economies grow stronger, they would expect to participate more fully in the GATT framework of rights and obligations.

Three other important agreements emerged from negotiations on the framework for the conduct of world trade:

The agreement on *trade measures taken for balance-of-payments purposes* states principles and codifies practices and procedures regarding the use of trade measures by governments to safeguard their external financial position and their balance of payments.

The agreement on *safeguard action for development purposes* concerns facilities accorded to developing countries under Article XVIII of the General Agreement, giving them greater flexibility in applying trade measures to meet their development needs.

The *understanding on notification, consultation, dispute settlement, and surveillance* in GATT provides for improvements in the existing mechanisms concerning notification of trade measures,

consultations, dispute settlement, and surveillance of developments in the international trading system.

Preferential Agreement Among Developing Countries

An agreement embodying the exchange of preferential tariff concessions among developing countries (18 in 1983) entered into force in February 1973. This first multilateral effort by these countries to expand their mutual trade had been successfully concluded in November 1971, when the agreement was approved by the GATT contracting parties. The participants exchanged concessions on some 500 tariff headings or subheadings, 30% of which concern agricultural products and raw materials. The concessions granted are generally in the form of a preferential duty rate or the binding of a margin of preference expressed either as a percentage of the most-favored-nation rate or, in some cases, as a reduction of that rate. The arrangement provides a framework for further efforts aimed at extending the scope of the concessions to cover more products and more developing countries.

Technical Assistance and Training

Since 1955, GATT has provided training in commercial policy for over 800 officials from 109 developing countries at its headquarters in Geneva. Assistance to developing countries is also provided through a Technical Cooperation Division within the GATT secretariat in all fields of GATT's work, including in particular follow-up action of the Tokyo Round of multilateral trade negotiations, and results of the November 1982 ministerial meeting (see below).

International Trade Center

In 1964, GATT established the International Trade Center to provide trade information and trade promotion advisory services for developing countries. Since January 1968, the center has been jointly operated by GATT and UNCTAD.

D. OTHER GATT ACTIVITIES
The 1982 Ministerial Session

In November 1981, at the annual session of the GATT member governments, it was agreed unanimously that the 1982 session should be held at ministerial level in order to examine "the implementation of the results of the Multilateral Trade Negotiations, problems affecting the trading system, the position of developing countries in world trade, and future prospects for the development of trade," and to "determine future priorities for cooperation among contracting parties."

The session was held in Geneva in November 1982, with 88 GATT member countries attending. The meeting agreed upon a declaration which opened with a diagnosis of the problems facing the world trading system. It affirmed a basic commitment against protectionism and in support of the GATT system, and agreed to abide by GATT obligations and to support and improve the GATT trading system, preserve the system's unity and consistency, and ensure that GATT provides a continuing forum for negotiation and consultation. The declaration also set out undertakings on which contracting parties have agreed in drawing up their work program and priorities for the 1980s. The practical consequences for GATT's future work of these political commitments were then spelled out in separate decisions, which constituted the bulk of the declaration. Each dealt with a specific issue, starting with safeguards, GATT rules and activities relating to developing countries, dispute settlement, trade in agriculture, and continuing through various other decisions, including tropical products, quantitative restrictions and nontariff measures, tariffs, structural adjustment and trade policy, trade in counterfeit goods, exports of domestically prohibited goods, textiles, and services.

The GATT Council subsequently established procedural arrangements for action on the topics identified by the ministers.

Settlement of Differences

Among the matters that are referred to the GATT Council are trade disputes over the application of Articles XXII and XXIII of the agreement. If a GATT country considers that a benefit that should accrue to it is being nullified or impaired (or that the attainment of any objective of the agreement is being impeded), it is first expected to seek redress through diplomatic channels. If no satisfactory adjustment can be reached through bilateral consultations, the country may lodge a complaint with GATT. The contracting parties are then required to carry out prompt investigations and to make recommendations or rulings. Such trade differences as are not settled through bilateral consultations are submitted to a group of experts from countries that have no direct interest in the matter. These panels, as they are called, have frequently succeeded in bringing about an agreement.

Improvements in the procedures for dispute settlement, especially to take into account problems of developing countries, were adopted during the Tokyo Round in the "Understanding and Notification, Consultation, Dispute Settlement and Surveillance."

The 1982 Ministerial Declaration strengthened the responsibilities of the Council for dispute settlement.

Textiles

Trade in textiles has long been a major concern of GATT. From 1962 until 1973, world trade in cotton textiles was largely regulated by the so-called Long-Term Arrangement, which was drawn up to ensure the orderly development of this trade. World trade in textiles and clothing has largely been regulated since 1974 by the Arrangement Regarding International Trade in Textiles, otherwise known as the Multi-Fiber Arrangement. Negotiated under GATT auspices, the arrangement took effect on 1 January 1974 for a period of four years. It was extended for a further four years, from 1 January 1978 to 31 December 1981, and then for another period of four years and seven months, from 1 January 1982 to 31 July 1986. The arrangement is intended to reconcile the interests of importing and exporting countries in the sensitive and difficult field of textiles by permitting the expansion of trade while avoiding disruption of markets. The safeguard provisions of the arrangement may be invoked by participants if their domestic market is disrupted, or threatened with disruption, as a result of imports; any restrictions imposed must permit exports from an affected supplying country to expand in an orderly and equitable manner. Most safeguard measures under the arrangement have taken the form of bilateral agreements. Supervision of the arrangement is entrusted to the Textiles Surveillance Body, consisting of an independent chairman and eight members so chosen as to provide balanced representation of the countries participating in the Multi-Fiber Arrangement.

There is no precedent in international trade relations for a multilateral surveillance group of this kind. The Textiles Surveillance Body reports to the Textiles Committee, which reviews the operation of the arrangement once a year.

Regional Arrangements

If two or more countries form a customs union or free-trade area, goods moving between them are liberated from import and export duties and other trade barriers. Under a free-trade-area arrangement, the participating countries maintain their right to determine separate customs tariffs toward the outside. Under a customs union, the participating countries go further; they set up a common customs tariff for trade with the outside. Clearly, both arrangements affect the commercial interests of third countries.

The EEC and EFTA are the two regional arrangements that have posed the greatest problems in respect to the most-favored-nation principles of the General Agreement, since the countries belonging to EEC and EFTA are all parties to the agreement and since their combined foreign commerce accounts for a very high proportion of total world trade.

On 1 January 1973, the position of the EEC as the world's largest trading entity was further reinforced by the accession of Denmark, Ireland, and the UK to membership, and in 1981 by the accession of Greece. All 10 member countries of the community are GATT contracting parties. Careful scrutiny of the trade effects of the community's enlargement was therefore necessary.

The rules in the General Agreement relating to customs unions and free-trade areas are contained in Article XXIV. This article states that integration of national economies is conceived of as a means of contributing to the objectives of GATT. It lays down the conditions under which a customs union or free-trade area is accepted as a basis for an exception to the most-favored-nation clause. It sets out a series of rules designed to ensure that a customs union or a free-trade area shall in effect lead to the reduction and elimination of barriers within the area without raising new barriers to trade with the outside.

Since its enlargement, the EEC has signed trade agreements with all remaining countries of EFTA (Austria, Iceland, Norway, Portugal, Sweden, and Switzerland), as well as with Finland. This means that a high proportion of trade between West European countries takes place on a tariff-free basis.

The compatibility of these agreements with Article XXIV of the General Agreement was examined by special working groups, but no unanimous conclusions were reached. The parties to the agreements, supported by some other countries, maintain that these agreements are fully compatible with the rules of GATT, which specifically allow the formation of free-trade areas as these encourage the growth and liberalization of world trade. Against this, other countries consider that the agreements are preferential trade arrangements for industrial products rather than instruments of free trade, since the agricultural sector as a whole is excluded. The many agreements which have been negotiated between the EEC and a number of Mediterranean and developing countries have given rise to similar controversy.

Other regional trading arrangements are examined regularly by the contracting parties within the framework of Article XXIV of the General Agreement.

[8]BIBLIOGRAPHY

GATT: What It Is, What It Does. Information brochure.
GATT Activities. Annual report on the work of GATT and account of developments of the year under review.
GATT Focus. Newsletter published 10 times a year.
International Trade. Annual. Report on developments in world trade.

THE INTERNATIONAL LABOR ORGANIZATION (ILO)

BACKGROUND: The ILO is the only major organization originally part of the League of Nations system that has existed from the founding of the League in 1919 down to the present day. Its name is actually too narrow, for it is an organization neither of nor for labor alone. As the late James T. Shotwell, president emeritus of the Carnegie Endowment for International Peace, pointed out long ago, the ILO might more accurately have been termed an International Organization for Social Justice. Furthermore, as the organization's responsibilities have widened, it has given increasing attention to measures designed to help raise general standards of living, and its work now includes activities as remote from the traditional field of labor relations as training courses for management personnel and high government officials in modern methods to improve productivity and efficiency.

CREATION

The ILO was created by the 1919 Peace Conference that followed World War I. Its original constitution, which formed part of the Treaty of Versailles, established it as an autonomous organization associated with the League of Nations.

The statement in the constitution's preamble, "Conditions of labor exist involving such injustice, hardship, and privation to large numbers of people as to produce unrest so great that the peace and harmony of the world are imperilled," was not mere rhetoric. World War I had shaken many countries to their foundations. The revolution in Russia had succeeded. All over the world there was labor unrest, and the conviction of the need to improve the lot of working people was by no means limited to labor itself. Organized labor, however, had been especially active during the war in demanding that the peace treaty include recognition of the rights of labor and that labor be given a voice in international matters. The American Federation of Labor (AFL) and other powerful trade-union bodies demanded in particular an international organization of labor that would wield "tremendous authority."

At the 1919 Paris Peace Conference, the president of the AFL, Samuel Gompers, was chairman of the conference's Commission on Labor Legislation. The Peace Conference, instead of establishing an international organization of labor, created an organization in which labor, employers, and governments were to be represented on an equal footing. As so constituted, the ILO was, and still is, unique among international governmental organizations in that it is the only one in which private citizens, namely representatives of labor and of employers, have the same voting and other rights as possessed by governments.

The ILO's principal function was to establish international labor and social standards through the drafting and adoption of international labor conventions. Prior to the existence of the ILO, only two international labor conventions had been adopted: one, designed to protect the health of workers in match factories, prohibited the use of white phosphorus, a poison, in the manufacture of matches; the other prescribed modest restrictions on night work by women. Neither of these had been widely ratified. By contrast, 159 international labor conventions were adopted by the ILO between 1919 and 1983, and many of them have been ratified.

PURPOSES

The aims and objectives of the ILO were originally set forth in the preamble to its constitution, written in 1919. The preamble declares that "universal and lasting peace can be established only if it is based upon social justice." Hence, the basic objective of

the organization is to help improve social conditions throughout the world. The following examples of concrete measures "urgently required" are specifically mentioned in the preamble:

Regulation of the hours of work, including the establishment of a maximum working day and week.

Regulation of the labor supply.

Prevention of unemployment.

Provision of an adequate living wage.

Protection of the worker against sickness, disease, and injury arising out of his employment.

Protection of children, young persons, and women.

Provision for old age and injury.

Protection of the interests of workers when employed in countries other than their own.

Recognition of the principle of equal remuneration for work of equal value.

Recognition of the principle of freedon of association.

The organization of vocational and technical education, and other measures.

International action in these matters is required, the preamble makes clear, because "the failure of any nation to adopt humane conditions of labor is an obstacle in the way of other nations which desire to improve the conditions in their own countries." Finally, in agreeing to the ILO constitution, the member governments declare in the preamble that they are "moved by sentiments of justice and humanity as well as by the desire to secure the permanent peace of the world."

The Declaration of Philadelphia, adopted by the 1944 International Labor Conference, rephrased and broadened the "aims and purposes" of the ILO and "the principles which should inspire the policy of its members." President Roosevelt stated that the declaration summed up the aspirations of an epoch that had known two world wars and that it might well acquire a historical significance comparable to that of the US Declaration of Independence. The declaration, which was incorporated into the amended constitution of the ILO, affirms that labor is not a commodity; that freedom of expression and association are essential to sustained progress; that poverty anywhere constitutes a danger to prosperity everywhere; and that the war against want must be carried on, not only with unrelenting vigor within each nation, but also by "continuous and concerted international effort in which the representatives of workers and employers, enjoying equal status with those of Governments, join with them in free discussion and democratic decision with a view to the promotion of the common welfare."

The Declaration of Philadelphia recognizes the "solemn

obligation" of the ILO to further among nations of the world programs that will achieve:

a. Full employment and the raising of standards of living.

b. Employment of workers in the occupations for which they are best suited and where they can make their greatest contribution to the common well-being.

c. Facilities for training and the transfer of labor, including migration for employment and settlement.

d. Policies in regard to wages and earnings, hours, and other conditions of work calculated to ensure a just share of the fruits of progress to all, and a minimum living wage to all employed and in need of such protection.

e. Effective recognition of the right of collective bargaining, the cooperation of management and labor in the continuous improvement of productive efficiency, and the collaboration of workers and employers in the preparation and application of social and economic measures.

f. Extension of social security measures to provide a basic income to all in need of such protection, and comprehensive medical care.

g. Adequate protection for the life and health of workers in all occupations.

h. Child welfare and maternity protection.

i. Adequate nutrition, housing, and facilities for recreation and culture.

j. Assurance of equality of educational and vocational opportunity.

[4]MEMBERSHIP

Originally, ILO membership was identical with League of Nations membership, since adherence to the League carried with it participation in ILO. However, several countries not members of the League were admitted to the ILO, notably the US, which joined in 1934. In 1946 the ILO became the first specialized agency associated with the UN. The constitution of the ILO now provides that any nation that is a member of the UN can become a member of the ILO by unilaterally notifying the director-general that it accepts the obligations of the ILO constitution. Other nations may be admitted to ILO membership by a two-thirds vote of the International Labor Conference.

The ILO constitution originally made no provision for the expulsion of a member. However, two amendments adopted by the International Labor Conference in 1964 and still open for ratification would empower the ILO membership, by a two-thirds vote, to expel or suspend any member that had been expelled or suspended by the UN or that had been found by the UN to be flagrantly and persistently pursuing by its legislation a policy of racial discrimination. The amendments were adopted in response to South Africa's policy of apartheid. They will take effect when they have been ratified or accepted by two-thirds of the member nations, including five of the ten that are represented on the Governing Body as "states of chief industrial importance."

A state may withdraw from the ILO by formal notification of its intent to do so, such withdrawal to be effective two years after ILO receives the notification. South Africa notified the organization of its intent to withdraw before the amendments that could have led to its expulsion were adopted. Its withdrawal became effective on 11 March 1966. Albania withdrew in 1967. Germany, which was one of the original members, withdrew in 1935. Fourteen other countries withdrew their membership at various times (11 of them during the World War II period), but all sooner or later rejoined the organization. Readmission is governed by the same rules that govern original admission to membership. In November 1975, the US filed a two-year notice of intent to withdraw, stating at the same time that it did not desire or expect to leave the ILO, but hoped to help the ILO "return to basic principles." US Secretary of State Henry Kissinger said the ILO had been

"falling back" in four fundamental areas: workers' and employers' groups in the ILO falling under the domination of governments; "an appallingly selective" concern for human rights; "disregard of due process" in condemning member states "which happen to be the political target of the moment"; and "increasing politicization of the organization." The notice of intent to withdraw was allowed to run its course, thereby ending US membership in the ILO in November 1977. On the return of the US to membership in February 1980, President Jimmy Carter said: "As a member of the ILO and with the support of other countries, the United States will seek to ensure that the ILO continues to serve the interests of the world's working men and women by promoting more and better jobs while protecting human rights and dignity."

On 1 January 1983, the ILO had 150 members:

Afghanistan
Algeria
Angola
Antigua and Barbuda
Argentina
Australia
Austria
Bahamas
Bahrain
Bangladesh
Barbados
Belgium
Belize
Benin
Bolivia
Botswana
Brazil
Bulgaria
Burma
Burundi
Byelorussia
Cameroon
Canada
Cape Verde
Central African Republic
Chad
Chile
China
Colombia
Comoros
Congo
Costa Rica
Cuba
Cyprus
Czechoslovakia
Denmark
Djibouti
Dominica
Dominican Republic
Ecuador
Egypt
El Salvador
Equatorial Guinea
Ethiopia
Fiji
Finland
France
Gabon
German Dem. Rep.
Germany, Fed. Rep.
Ghana
Greece
Grenada
Guatemala
Guinea
Guinea-Bissau
Guyana
Haiti

Honduras
Hungary
Iceland
India
Indonesia
Iran
Iraq
Ireland
Israel
Italy
Ivory Coast
Jamaica
Japan
Jordan
Kampuchea
Kenya
Kuwait
Laos
Lebanon
Lesotho
Liberia
Libya
Luxembourg
Madagascar
Malawi
Malaysia
Mali
Malta
Mauritania
Mauritius
Mexico
Mongolia
Morocco
Mozambique
Namibia
Nepal
Netherlands
New Zealand
Nicaragua
Niger
Nigeria
Norway
Pakistan
Panama
Papua New Guinea
Paraguay
Peru
Philippines
Poland
Portugal
Qatar
Romania
Rwanda
St. Lucia
San Marino
São Tomé and Príncipe
Sa'udi Arabia
Senegal
Seychelles
Sierra Leone
Singapore
Somalia
Spain
Sri Lanka
Sudan
Suriname
Swaziland
Sweden
Switzerland
Syria
Tanzania
Thailand
Togo
Trinidad and Tobago

Tunisia
Turkey
Uganda
Ukraine
USSR
United Arab Emirates
UK
US
Upper Volta
Uruguay
Venezuela
Viet-Nam
Yemen, People's Dem. Rep.
Yemen Arab Rep.
Yugoslavia
Zaire
Zambia
Zimbabwe

⁵STRUCTURE

The principal organs of the ILO are the International Labor Conference, the Governing Body, and the International Labor Office.

International Labor Conference

The International Labor Conference is the organization's policymaking and legislative body, in which every member state is represented. It meets once a year at ILO headquarters in Geneva.

Tripartite Representation. Each member country sends a national delegation consisting of four delegates to the International Labor Conference. Two represent the government, one represents the country's employers, and one represents the country's workers. Alternates and advisers may be sent as well. Each delegate has one independent vote. Discussing this system of tripartite representation in 1959, the director-general noted that the ILO is "the only intergovernmental agency in whose work nongovernment delegates take part on an equal footing with government representatives as a matter of constitutional right. Representatives of employers' and workers' organizations are included in its policy-making, standard-setting, and executive machinery and participate, with full voting rights, in all these aspects of its work."

The government, employers', and workers' representatives to the conference act in many respects as three separate groups, functioning somewhat as political parties function in a national legislature: the three groups meet separately for informal discussions of strategy; they hold caucuses; and, voting separately, they elect the government, the employers', and the workers' delegates to the Governing Body and to tripartite committees. If the tripartite system is to function as intended, it is essential that employers' and workers' delegates be true spokesmen for their respective points of view. The ILO constitution provides that governments must appoint these delegates in agreement with the "most representative" organizations of employers or workers, "if such organizations exist."

Governing Body

The Governing Body is the executive council of the ILO. It is composed of 56 members, 14 representing employers. 14 representing workers, and 28 representing governments.

Members of the Governing Body are elected by the corresponding groups in the International Labor Conference, except that ten of the government representatives are appointed by countries that do not participate in the election of the other government representatives since these ten countries are entitled to permanent seats as "states of chief industrial importance." The ten governments permanently represented on the Governing Body are Brazil, China, France, the FRG, India, Italy, Japan, the USSR, the UK, and the US. The remaining government members, elected in 1981 for three years, were from Australia, Bahrain, Bangladesh, Barbados, Bulgaria, Colombia, Ecuador, Egypt, the GDR, Kenya, Mali, Mexico, Mozambique, the Netherlands, Nigeria, the Philippines, Senegal, and Venezuela.

Employers' representatives on the Governing Body, elected for three years by the 1981 conference, included leading industrialists or ranking employers' association officers from Argentina, Australia, Belgium, France, the FRG, Ghana, India, Japan, Lebanon, Morocco, Niger, the UK, the US, and Venezuela.

The 14 members of the workers' group were ranking trade union officials from Australia, Canada, Denmark, the FRG, Ghana, India, Japan, Mauritania, Mexico, Tanzania, the USSR, the UK, the US, and Venezuela.

Meeting several times a year, the Governing Body coordinates and in many ways shapes the work of the organization. It draws up the agenda for each session of the International Labor Conference; while the conference is empowered to change this agenda, it rarely does. The Governing Body appoints the director-general of the International Labor Office. It examines the proposed budget submitted to it each year by the director-general and approves it for adoption by the conference. The Governing Body is also responsible for convening the scores of other conference and committee meetings held under ILO auspices every year in various parts of the world and decides what action ought to be taken on their resolutions and reports.

International Labor Office and Director-General

The International Labor Office in Geneva, headed by the director-general, is ILO's headquarters and its permanent secretariat. Its staff consists of about 3,000 persons from more than 100 countries. During World War II, when for a time Switzerland was entirely surrounded by Axis forces, the International Labor Office and a skeleton staff were temporarily moved to Montreal where, thanks to the hospitality of the Canadian government and McGill University, the office was able to continue its more urgent work.

The International Labor Office services the sessions of the conference, the Governing Body, and the various subsidiary organs and committees. It prepares the documents for these meetings; publishes periodicals, studies, and reports; and collects and distributes information on all subjects within ILO's competence. As directed by the Conference and the Governing Body, it carries out ILO operational programs that have been decided on in various fields.

The ILO has had five directors-general—Albert Thomas, France: 1919–32; Harold Butler, UK: 1932–38; John G. Winant, US: 1938–41; Edward J. Phelan, Ireland: 1941–48; David A. Morse, US: 1948–70; Wilfred Jenks, UK: 1970–73; and Francis Blanchard, France, since 1974.

Regional, Branch, and Field Offices. The ILO has three regional offices—in Addis Ababa for Africa, Lima for the Americas, and Bangkok for Asia; 8 branch offices—in Washington, Ottawa, Tokyo, Paris, Bonn, Rome, Moscow, and London; and 37 other field offices.

THE ISSUE OF INDEPENDENT WORKER AND EMPLOYER REPRESENTATION

Since its early days, the ILO has been troubled by a basic constitutional issue: can the organization, without violating its own principles, countenance the seating of workers' and employers' delegates from countries where workers' and employers' organizations are not free from domination or control by the government?

Challenges to the Credentials of Workers' Delegates

When in the early 1920s a member of the Italian Fascist labor corporations appeared at Geneva to take his seat as the workers' member of the Italian delegation to the ILO, his credentials were challenged, though unsuccessfully, by the workers' group, which maintained that he was not a true spokesman for Italian labor.

Every session of the conference from 1923 to 1938 saw the credentials of one or more workers' delegates challenged on the grounds that these delegates did not represent an independent labor point of view. Among them were workers' delegates from Austria, Bulgaria, Germany, Greece, Italy, Latvia, Lithuania, and Poland. In all cases, however, the delegates were seated.

Since World War II, the conference has on several occasions actually refused to seat a workers' delegate whose credentials had been challenged. In 1945 it refused to seat the workers' delegate chosen by the Perón regime in Argentina on the ground that workers' organizations in Argentina did not at that time enjoy freedom of association, action, or speech. In 1950 it refused to seat the workers' delegate appointed by the government of Venezuela on the ground that the delegate could not have been nominated in agreement with the country's most representative workers' associations since the government had at that time dissolved all trade unions. Challenges to the credentials of Argentinian and Venezuelan workers' delegates on other occasions were overruled by the credentials committee, however, as was a 1955 challenge to the credentials of the Chilean workers' delegate.

The Question of Employers' Delegates from Communist Countries

Much greater difficulties have arisen over the seating of employers' delegates from Communist countries. When the first employers' delegate from the USSR, Mr. Kaoulin of the People's Commissariat of Water Transport, appeared at the 1936 maritime conference, the employers' group acquiesced in his seating but requested an examination of the constitutional questions involved. A study duly carried out by the International Labor Office concluded that the ILO constitution did not require an employer to be a private person, and that in countries where the state was the chief employer it was for the state to choose the employers' delegate. The employers' group at the conference voted unanimously to reject this interpretation.

At the 1945 ILO Conference, held in Paris shortly after the end of World War II, two constitutional amendments were proposed that aimed at increasing the size of the national delegations so as to give representation to both the public and private sectors of the economy. Both proposed amendments were, for a variety of reasons, rejected by the conference. The employers' group, however, issued a declaration stating that in the event that the USSR, which had withdrawn from the ILO in 1940, were to resume membership, "it would naturally appoint as employers' delegates a representative of the socialized management of the USSR."

At the 1953 conference, the employers' group challenged the credentials of the Czechoslovakian employers' delegate and, when the USSR did rejoin the organization in 1954, challenged those of the Soviet employers' delegate as well. On both occasions, the group was overruled by the credentials committee, which held that the delegates in question performed executive and managerial functions corresponding to those normally exercised by employers under other economic systems.

The McNair Report

When the Governing Board met in November 1954, it was sharply divided on the question of employers' delegates from countries with nationalized economies. In hopes of facilitating a compromise, it appointed a special fact-finding committee, headed by Sir Arnold McNair, former president of the International Court of Justice, to report on the "extent of the freedom of employers' and workers' organizations" in ILO member countries "from government domination or control." The lengthy report, which the committee submitted in February 1956, was based on a study of the situation in 59 countries, including 5 in the Soviet bloc.

The report recognized at the outset that the unique feature of the ILO—cooperation among government, employers', and workers' spokesmen—could only be meaningful if the latter represented their constituents in the true sense of the word and had the right "to speak and vote freely without government control." On the other hand, the report noted, major changes had occurred in the economic structure of many countries since 1919, with governments participating in their countries' economic and social life in a wide variety of new ways. The ILO had long maintained that the principle of freedom of association is violated if the right to organize is subject to government authorization. Yet, the report found, the constitutions of no less than 21 ILO countries subjected the right of association to statutory regulation. No attempt was made to minimize the difficulty of reconciling the principle of universality of ILO membership, regardless of political and economic differences, and the principle that workers' and employers' representatives should be independent of government control; but the report at least made it clear that the problem was not limited to countries of the Soviet bloc. For example, it was found that in the less developed non-Communist countries trade unions and employers' associations were generally "not strong vis-à-vis their governments as in the leading industrial countries" and that many opportunities existed for government domination.

A possible line of compromise was suggested in the committee's discussion of the role of management in the socialist economies. "The difference in function between the employing class in the majority of countries and the managerial class in the USSR and similar countries is that, while both are concerned with ensuring efficient management and development of industry, the latter are not concerned with the protection of the interests of private capital because there is no private capital to protect." Yet, the report noted, the managers of socialist enterprises "have extensive powers and discretions and responsibilities" and by reason of their experience should be capable of making "a distinct contribution" to the deliberations of the ILO.

If anything, the controversy over the right of certain workers' and employers' delegates to be seated sharpened after the McNair Committee submitted its fact-finding report. At the 1956 ILO Conference, the employers' group proposed a constitutional amendment requiring all employers' and workers' delegates to the ILO to be designated by organizations independent of their governments. The government and workers' groups opposed the move. An Italian government delegate, Roberto Ago, noted that a good third of the ILO member states could not appoint workers' and employers' delegates if the proposed amendment were strictly enforced. The proposed amendment was rejected by the Governing Body in November 1956 by a vote of 29 to 11.

ILO and the Hungarian Uprising

The Hungarian uprising of 1956 had sharp repercussions in the ILO, which were reflected in the credentials dispute. The Governing Body expressed solidarity with the Hungarian workers "who were struggling to secure their fundamental rights," and the 1957 conference rejected the credentials of the employers' and workers' delegates appointed by the Kádár government, which had, in effect, restored the Hungarian *status quo ante*. In 1958 and 1959, the ILO conference took the unprecedented step of not only rejecting the credentials of the Hungarian workers' and employers' delegates, but also of refusing admission to the Hungarian government delegates.

In the meantime, various attempts were made to find a general solution to the problem that would satisfy all concerned, including the Western employers' delegates. Involved in the problem was the fact that, under the conference rules, each group —government, employers, and workers—could refuse to seat delegates whose credentials it did not accept. In 1959, acting on a plan proposed by a tripartite committee headed by Robert Ago of Italy, the ILO established a five-man Appeals Board composed of persons of "internationally recognized independence and impartiality" to rule on such matters. However, when the Appeals Board decided at the 1959 Conference to seat the employers'

delegates from the Soviet bloc countries on certain technical committees, the chairman of the employers' group, Pierre Waline of France, announced "on behalf of the free employers of the Conference" that he and his colleagues could no longer take part in the work of those committees. Later, the free employers' group resumed participation in these technical committees under protest.

An uneasy truce developed over the seating of workers' and employers' representatives from Eastern Europe. Their credentials are usually challenged by one or more of the Western groups, but increasingly these challenges are becoming a kind of opening-day formality, for it is becoming clear that if the ILO is to operate as a world organization, it cannot bar representatives from states with centrally directed economies. In a sense, the truce was broken at the 1966 session of the International Labor Conference, when the workers' group from the US staged an informal boycott of the proceedings to protest the election of a representative of a Communist country, Leon Chajn of Poland, as president of the conference. The boycott was not official, however, and ended before the conclusion of the conference.

⁶BUDGET

ILO's activities are financed by a biennial budget fixed by the International Labor Conference and raised from the governments of member states according to a scale of contributions approved by the Conference. The scale ranges from 0.01% for a number of smaller countries to 11.02% for the USSR and 25% for the US. In addition, the ILO receives for its technical assistance programs a share of the funds raised from voluntary government contributions to the UNDP.

A net expenditure budget of $254.7 million for 1984–85 was adopted by the 1983 Conference.

⁷ACTIVITIES

A. INTERNATIONAL LABOR CODE

One of the principal achievements of the ILO in its first 64 years of existence has been the formulation of an extensive international labor code through the drafting and adoption of various standard-setting conventions and recommendations. The first international convention adopted was the 1919 Hours of Work Convention establishing the eight-hour day and the six-day week in industry. By 1983 the various sessions of the International Labor Conference had built up the edifice of the international labor code through the adoption of 159 conventions and 168 recommendations, covering such questions as the following:

Employment and unemployment: employment services, national development programs, provisions for unemployment.

Various aspects of conditions of work: wages, hours, weekly rest periods, annual holidays with pay, and allied topics.

Employment of children and young persons: minimum age of admission to employment, medical examination for fitness for employment, vocational training and apprenticeship, and night work.

Employment of women: maternity protection, night work, and employment in unhealthy work.

Industrial health, safety, and welfare.

Social security.

Industrial (i.e., management-labor) relations.

Labor inspection.

Social policy in nonmetropolitan areas and concerning indigenous and tribal populations.

Protection of migrants.

Trade unionism and collective bargaining.

At first the effort to build up minimum labor and social standards that would be internationally valid was considered by many as utopian. In these fields, international action used to be virtually unknown. But the freely accepted conventions and recommendations and the ILO machinery of mutual supervision have helped to improve working conditions and management–labor relations, protect the fundamental rights of labor, promote social security, and lessen the frequency and intensity of labor conflicts.

The international labor code is continually being revised and extended, not only to broaden its scope but to keep pace with advancing concepts of social and economic welfare. In 1960, for example, the Conference adopted a convention and a recommendation on the protection of workers against ionizing radiations. These instruments, in essence, provide for the establishment of maximum permissible doses and amounts of radioactive substances that may be taken into the body. Appropriate radiation levels are fixed for workers over 16 years of age. Under these international instruments, workers under 16 years of age are prohibited from working in direct contact with ionizing radiations.

In pursuit of ILO efforts to help extend the scope of social security coverage throughout the world and eliminate discrimination based upon nationality, the 1962 Conference adopted a convention on the equal treatment of nationals and nonnationals in social security. Under this convention, a ratifying country shall give to nationals of other ratifying countries, within its territory, equal treatment with its own nationals under its social security legislation. Countries may accept the obligations of the convention in any or all of the following types of social security: medical care; sickness benefits; maternity benefits; unemployment benefits; and family allowances. The International Labor Code includes 25 conventions and 17 recommendations concerning various aspects of social security provisions.

The adoption of protective standard measures against occupational cancer was taken up at the 1974 session of the Conference. Two international agreements were drawn up aimed at limiting the use and the adverse effects of carcinogenic (cancer-causing) substances, and strengthening protective measures to be used against them.

The 1982 Conference adopted a convention and a recommendation concerning termination of employment at the initiative of the employer. Under the terms of the convention, employees would have greater protection from dismissal and would have recourse to rights of appeal and severance allowance.

The rights of handicapped people were addressed by the 1983 Conference. The resulting convention strengthened the 1955 recommendation on this subject, aiming at increased employment opportunities for the disabled.

B. OBLIGATION OF MEMBER GOVERNMENTS AFTER ADOPTION OF INTERNATIONAL LABOR STANDARDS

The ILO, it should be borne in mind, is not a world lawgiver. The International Labor Conference cannot pass legislation that by itself is binding on any country. However, ingenious arrangements have been written in the ILO constitution to make sure that conventions and recommendations adopted by the International Labor Conference are not regarded as mere pious pronouncements. Member governments must report back to the ILO on the measures they have taken to bring the ILO convention or recommendation before their competent legislative authorities, and they must also keep the ILO informed of decisions made by the latter.

Supervision of Application of Ratified Conventions

Once a convention has been ratified and has come into force, every country that has ratified it is obligated to take all necessary measures to make its provisions effective.

By ratifying a convention, a country automatically agrees to report every year to the International Labor Office on how the convention is being applied in its territory. These reports are much more than a formality. For each convention, the Governing Body formulates a number of questions. They always include requests for information on the results of labor inspection, relevant court decisions, and statistics on the number of persons covered. Copies of each annual report prepared by a government are to be sent to the country's most representative employers' and workers' organizations, and the report as finally submitted to the ILO has to state whether the government has received any comments from them on the practical implementation of the convention in question.

These annual reports on the application of ratified conventions are first considered by a committee of independent experts and then by an employer-worker-government committee, which in turn reports to the full International Labor Conference. The object of this whole system of supervision is to enable the conference to determine what progress has been made from one year to the next by various countries in implementing the standards set forth in the conventions. On the basis of the intelligence it receives, the conference may, if it feels this to be necessary, make "observations" to governments, that is, suggest to them ways in which they may overcome discrepancies between the provisions of the conventions they have ratified and existing national laws or practices.

The effectiveness of this supervisory machinery depends naturally on the cooperation of member governments in submitting their annual reports. On the whole, an increasing percentage of governments have been living up to their obligations in this respect. If required reports are not forthcoming or if the reports submitted by certain countries are not really informative, the ILO supervisory committees express their dissatisfaction in polite but quite unmistakable terms. These criticisms are included in the printed reports of the committees and may occasion debates in the conference itself, thus giving the matter further publicity.

The ILO constitution provides two other procedures that may be followed to induce governments to carry out the provisions of conventions they have ratified. First, workers' or employers' organizations may make representations to the International Labor Office if they believe that any government, even their own, has failed to live up to a convention it has ratified. If the government concerned fails to provide a satisfactory answer to the allegation, the Governing Body may decide to publish the allegation and, if one has been submitted, the government reply. Second, any ILO member government may file a complaint against any other member for alleged noncompliance with a ratified convention. The ILO constitution provides that in this event a commission of inquiry shall examine the matter, report on its findings, and recommend such remedial steps as it thinks proper. The fact that the ILO constitution provides for specific machinery to take up such complaints itself has contributed to the observance of ratified international labor conventions on the part of member governments.

Reports on Recommendations and Unratified Conventions

Recommendations adopted by the International Labor Conference, unlike the conventions it adopts, are not international treaties and are not subject to ratification. Hence these recommendations can never be binding on a member government in the sense that the provisions of a ratified convention are binding. Nevertheless, the recommendations constitute an important part of the International Labor Code; and since 1948 the Governing Body of the ILO has had the right periodically to ask member governments to what extent they have given or intend to give effect to conventions not ratified and to recommendations. In such case, the governments also have to state the reasons that have so far prevented or delayed the ratification of conventions and the modification of national law and practices according to recommendations.

Ratifications

By January 1983, there were more than 5,000 ratifications, as shown below. In 1960, only about 1,900 conventions had been ratified.

NUMBER OF INTERNATIONAL LABOR CONVENTIONS RATIFIED BY ILO MEMBER STATES, 1 JANUARY 1983

Afghanistan	15	Liberia	20
Albania	17	Libya	27
Algeria	48	Luxembourg	55
Angola	30	Madagascar	30
Argentina	60	Malawi	19
Australia	43	Malaysia	11
Austria	46	Malta	27
Bahamas	26	Mauritania	37
Bahrain	4	Mauritius	31
Bangladesh	31	Mexico	62
Barbados	34	Mongolia	8
Belgium	79	Morocco	40
Benin	18	Mozambique	11
Bolivia	39	Nepal	3
Brazil	56	Netherlands	85
Bulgaria	80	New Zealand	53
Burma	21	Nicaragua	58
Burundi	23	Niger	27
Byelorussia	35	Nigeria	28
Cameroon	43	Norway	90
Canada	26	Pakistan	30
Cape Verde	7	Panama	69
Central African Republic	35	Papua New Guinea	19
Chad	19	Paraguay	33
Chile	40	Peru	62
China	37	Philippines	21
Colombia	45	Poland	74
Comoros	29	Portugal	46
Congo	14	Qatar	2
Costa Rica	40	Romania	39
Cuba	86	Rwanda	20
Cyprus	34	St. Lucia	23
Czechoslovakia	52	São Tomé and Príncipe	7
Denmark	56	Sa'udi Arabia	13
Djibouti	62	Senegal	34
Dominican Republic	26	Seychelles	18
Ecuador	52	Sierra Leone	32
Egypt	53	Singapore	21
El Salvador	4	Somalia	12
Ethiopia	8	former Br. Somaliland	2
Fiji	17	South Africa	12
Finland	70	Spain	107
France	104	Sri Lanka	25
Gabon	31	Sudan	12
German Dem. Rep.	24	Suriname	26
Germany, Fed. Rep.	66	Swaziland	30
Ghana	40	Sweden	72
Greece	49	Switzerland	42
Grenada	25	Syria	45
Guatemala	39	Tanzania	18
Guinea	53	Tanganyika	6
Guinea-Bissau	30	Zanzibar	4
Guyana	28	Thailand	11
Haiti	23	Togo	12
Honduras	19	Trinidad and Tobago	12
Hungary	45	Tunisia	52
Iceland	14	Turkey	27
India	34	Uganda	21
Indonesia	8	Ukraine	43
Iran	11	USSR	43
Iraq	49	United Arab Emirates	4
Ireland	55	UK	77
Israel	44	US	7
Italy	97	Upper Volta	30
Ivory Coast	28	Uruguay	82
Jamaica	23	Venezuela	35
Japan	36	Viet-Nam	22
Jordan	17	Yemen, People's Dem. Rep.	13
Kampuchea	5	Yemen Arab Rep.	11
Kenya	42	Yugoslavia	64
Kuwait	14	Zaire	27
Laos	4	Zambia	35
Lebanon	28	Zimbabwe	7
Lesotho	11		

The relative number of ratifications a given convention has received is not, in itself, an accurate measure of its acceptance or impact. The fact that a convention has not been ratified by a particular country does not necessarily mean that that country has not met the standards prescribed in the convention. The UK, for example, advised the ILO that it did not intend to propose parliamentary ratification of the convention requiring a minimum 24-hour weekly rest period for commercial and office workers. It explained that such workers in the UK were already assured a rest period of at least that length through established custom, and that it was not the policy of the government to intervene in matters that had already been satisfactorily settled by the parties concerned themselves. New Zealand, which in many ways has pioneered in labor legislation, waited until 1938 to ratify the eight-hour-day, six-day-week convention of 1919. On the same day, New Zealand also ratified the more restrictive 40-hour-week convention of 1935 and, in fact, remained for 18 years the only country ratifying it. Ratifications may be withheld for various reasons by a country for a number of years, after which a number of ratifications may be approved at once. Thus, in 1962 alone, Peru ratified 31 different international labor conventions.

Very often countries do not ratify conventions on subjects that they feel do not concern them. The various maritime conventions, for example, are primarily of interest to nations with sizable merchant marine fleets. Occasionally, however, countries as a matter of principle ratify conventions on conditions quite alien to them. Thus Switzerland ratified the 1957 Convention on the Abolition of Forced Labor on the recommendation of the Swiss Federal Council, which called for the convention's ratification because of its great humanitarian significance, although "forced labor in any of the forms mentioned in the Convention has never existed in Switzerland."

For a growing number of workers in an increasing number of countries, wages, working conditions, vacations, and so-called fringe benefits are being determined, not through government legislation, but through collective bargaining. The international standards embodied in the ILO's conventions, even though they may not show on the statute books, frequently serve as guides for labor-management agreements. The widening impact of ILO standards owes much to the various arrangements that have been worked out to make the provisions of the International Labor Code more widely known to employers' and workers' organizations.

The significance of the sharply increased rate at which governments have been ratifying ILO conventions since 1960 is very great. Ratification, particularly in a developing country, regularly signifies a step forward.

C. THE ILO AS PROMOTER OF HUMAN RIGHTS

Freedom of Association

World War II stimulated the growth of trade unions and increased their responsibilities. In many countries labor was recognized as an equal partner in the effort that won the war. Nevertheless, in various parts of the world the position of unions was far from secure, and in many countries such a basic freedom as the worker's right to join a union of his choice was respected neither in law nor in practice.

In 1948 the International Labor Conference adopted the Convention on Freedom of Association and the Right to Organize, and in 1949 it adopted the Convention on the Right to Organize and Collective Bargaining. These conventions stipulate that all workers and employers shall possess the right to establish and join organizations of their own choosing without having to obtain government authorization. Such organizations shall have the right to function freely and without interference from public authorities; they may be dissolved or suspended only by normal judicial procedure and never by administrative authority. Workers must be

protected against discrimination on the grounds of union membership or activities; thus a worker may not be discharged because he joins or is active in a union. Employers and workers must not interfere in the establishment or operation of one another's organizations, a provision that outlaws such devices as employer-dominated unions.

By 1 January 1983, the first of the two conventions had been ratified by 94 countries and the second by 110.

The ILO has been particularly concerned with safeguarding the rights enumerated in these two conventions. It has made full use of its regular procedure to ascertain whether all member states have presented the conventions to the appropriate domestic authorities for ratification and to supervise the implementation of the conventions by states that have ratified them. In addition, the International Labor Conference has conducted reviews concerning the extent to which member states, whether bound by the conventions or not, have given effect to their provisions. In 1969 a special review was made, in connection with the 50th anniversary of the ILO, of the problems and prospects of ratification of 17 key conventions. Special bodies were set up to deal with complaints against governments for violation of trade-union rights: a committee of the Governing Body, known as the Committee on Freedom of Association, composed of government, employer, and worker representatives; and the quasi-judicial Fact-Finding and Conciliation Commission, composed of nine independent persons serving as individuals. The Fact-Finding and Conciliation Commission is authorized to make on-the-scene investigations, but it cannot consider a case unless the government concerned gives its consent. Japan in 1964 was the first to do so; Greece was the second, in 1965. The government-employer-worker Committee on Freedom of Association, however, not being a semijudicial body, may consider complaints whether or not the government concerned gives its consent.

Feeling that fuller factual information was needed about conditions in various countries affecting freedom of association, the ILO Governing Body decided in 1958 to inaugurate a worldwide survey to be carried out through on-the-spot studies. The first country to invite such a survey was the US, the second was the USSR. An ILO survey mission visited both countries in 1959. At the invitation of the governments of Sweden, the UK, Burma, and Malaya, surveys on freedom of association in those countries were made in 1960 and 1961.

Forced Labor

Before World War II, ILO's efforts in this field, including the adoption of the 1930 Convention on Forced Labor and the 1936 Convention on Recruiting of Indigenous Workers, were directed primarily toward stamping out abuses in non-self-governing territories. A convention adopted in 1939 prescribed that contracts for the employment of indigenous labor must always be made in writing, and an accompanying recommendation called for regulation of the maximum period of time for which a native worker could bind himself under contract. Another convention adopted in 1939 required all penal sanctions exacted against indigenous labor for breach of contract to be progressively abolished "as soon as possible"; when applicable to juvenile workers, the sanctions against breach of contract were to be abolished without delay.

After World War II, emphasis shifted from protection against exploitation in colonial areas to the abolition of systems of forced labor wherever they occur, as part of the promotion of human rights. The first step in this broader attack was an impartial inquiry into the nature and extent of forced labor, including prison labor, gang labor, labor service, and the like. A joint UN-ILO committee studied the existence in the world of systems of forced or "corrective" labor as means of political coercion or as punishment for political views. In 1953, the committee reported that it had found two principal forms of forced labor existing in fully self-governing countries: one used mainly as a means of political coercion or political punishment, the other used mainly for economic reasons.

In 1957, the International Labor Conference, by a vote of 240 to 0, with 1 abstention, adopted the Abolition of Forced Labor Convention. The convention outlaws any form of forced or compulsory labor (a) as a means of political coercion or education or as punishment for political or ideological views, (b) as a means of obtaining labor for economic development, (c) as a means of labor discipline, (d) as punishment for participation in strikes, or (e) as a means of racial, social, national, or religious discrimination. The convention, one of the farthest-reaching adopted by the ILO, has been in force since 17 January 1959 and had been ratified by 107 states by 1 January 1983.

Discrimination in Employment and Occupation

The Convention on Discrimination in Employment and Occupation, adopted by the International Labor Conference in 1958, constitutes another effort to promote the principle of equal rights. The convention defines such discrimination as any distinction, exclusion, or preference based on race, color, sex, religion, political opinion, national extraction, or social origin that impairs equal access to vocational training, equal access to employment and to certain occupations, or equal terms and conditions of employment. Measures affecting a person justifiably suspected of being engaged in activities prejudicial to the security of the state are not to be deemed discrimination, provided such a person is guaranteed the right of appeal. Furthermore, special measures of protection or assistance required because of sex, age, disablement, family responsibility, or social or cultural status are not to be considered discriminatory, but workers' and employers' organizations must in certain cases be consulted on such measures.

Every state ratifying the convention thereby undertakes to declare and pursue a national policy designed to promote, by methods appropriate to national conditions and practice, equality of opportunity and treatment in respect of employment and occupation, with a view to eliminating discrimination. This is to be done through cooperation with employers' and workers' organizations, through legislation, and through educational programs. Ratifying states also agree to pursue nondiscriminatory public employment policies and to ensure the observance of such policies by public vocational guidance, training, and placement services. By 1 January 1983, the convention had been ratified by 102 states.

A worldwide survey of the effect given to the convention was made by the ILO in 1963. Commenting on the broad degree of acceptance by member states of the convention, the survey report concluded that in the majority of countries the principle of equality had become a fundamental element of public law. But it was recognized that equality before the law was not enough and that the convention required the application of a positive policy to promote equal opportunity and treatment for all social groups, not only in law but also in practice. Particular emphasis was placed on the need to guarantee to all categories of persons the means of obtaining the vocational education and training that open the way to all levels of employment.

D. MARITIME QUESTIONS

The problems of merchant sailors differ in many respects from those of other workers. When plans for an international labor organization were being worked out in 1919, world seamen's organizations urged the creation of a separate "permanent general conference for the international regulation of maritime labor" and of a separate "supervisory office for maritime labor." Although it was eventually decided to include maritime questions as falling within the purview of ILO, special ILO machinery was established to deal with them, including special maritime sessions of the International Labor Conference and a Joint Maritime Commission.

Maritime sessions of the International Labor Conference are periodic full-scale sessions of the conference devoted exclusively to maritime questions. The first such conference was held in 1920. Since then, some 50 conventions and recommendations concerning seafarers have been adopted pertaining to conditions of employment, health and safety, welfare, and social security. Together, these conventions and recommendations form the International Seafarers' Code, which is binding on all subscribing countries.

The Joint Maritime Commission keeps questions regarding the merchant marine under review on a year-to-year basis. Since it began its work in 1920, the commission has been enlarged several times, mainly to provide wider geographical representation.

Conditions of Employment

The first of the ILO's maritime conventions, adopted in 1920 and ratified by 50 countries by 1 January 1983, forbids the employment of children under 14 at sea, except on family-operated vessels. A convention adopted in 1936 and by 1983 in force in 49 countries raises the minimum age to 15. A convention adopted in 1926 and by 1 January 1983 ratified by 49 countries prescribes the standard form and content of seafarers' articles of agreement or employment contracts, signing procedures, and the conditions under which such contracts may be terminated. A 1926 convention subsequently ratified by 35 countries guarantees that no seafarer shall be abandoned in a foreign port and provides that a seafarer put ashore through no fault of his own must be repatriated at no expense to himself. A 1920 convention, designed to abolish many abuses and as of 1983 in force in 32 countries, stipulates that seafarers must be hired not through private fee-charging agencies but through free public employment offices operated either jointly and under public control by shipowners' and seafarers' organizations or, in the absence of such machinery, by the government itself.

Social Security for Seafarers and Their Families

The first step toward social insurance for seafarers was taken by a 1920 convention, by 1983 in force in 48 countries, which required a shipowner to pay two months' wages to crew members of a lost or foundered vessel. Two conventions of much wider scope were adopted 16 years later. The 1936 Shipowners' Liability Convention, ratified by 15 states, entitles a sick or injured seafarer to medical care and maintenance up to a maximum of 16 weeks. The Sickness Insurance Convention, ratified by 13 countries, gives a sick seafarer who is incapable of work and deprived of wages a cash benefit and, with certain exceptions, medical treatment for at least the first 26 weeks of such physical incapacity.

The 1946 Social Security (Seafarers) Convention has not received enough ratifications to enter into force. The Seafarers' Pensions Convention, ratified by nine states, has entered into force.

Three conventions affecting seafarers were adopted at the 1976 ILO Conference: continuity of employment; annual leave with pay; and merchant shipping (minimum standards). The third convention provides that a state which has ratified the convention and in whose port a ship calls may take account of a complaint or evidence that the ship does not conform to the standards of the convention.

The standards set by these conventions, even when not ratified by many countries, have an influence on collective agreements, national statutes, and regulations.

E. TECHNICAL COOPERATION

Member states have always been able to count on the direct cooperation of the ILO. The expression "technical assistance" is to be found in an ILO report as early as 1930. ILO officials who were then sent on consultative missions to governments were the precursors of today's experts.

Depending on priority programs established by governments, the activities of consultants have become an increasingly integral feature of national development plans. Among these priorities are the development of human resources, raising of living standards, and promotion of full employment. The ILO works actively with the authorities to set up and put into effect concrete cooperative projects. These tasks range from brief preliminary missions to major projects such as the setting up of networks of vocational training or management development centers, to the establishment of full-scale rural development programs.

A cooperative project is deemed a success when it can be fully taken over by the national counterparts of the country concerned, after the ILO experts have left. To encourage this trend, the ILO has made it possible for some 20,000 national officials to complete their training overseas. Many cooperative projects also provide for study grants and the organization of training courses and seminars. The supply of specialized equipment for certain services is another form of ILO aid—for example, equipment to set up vocational training centers.

The international technical cooperation effort is financed in part by UNDP. Some of the industrialized countries also make funds available to the ILO for cooperative projects, among them Belgium, Canada, Denmark, the FRG, Finland, Japan, the Netherlands, Norway, Sweden, and Switzerland.

In all, about $125 million a year is allocated to ILO technical cooperation activities, a modest figure when compared with the enormous need in this area. The ILO, therefore, concentrates its efforts on activities that produce maximum long-term results, such as the creation of institutions of various kinds, or of training centers for trainers. It also seeks to enlist the aid of employers and workers in the technical cooperation effort.

Technical cooperation is linked to action promoting adherence to international labor standards, such as aid in the area of labor legislation and administration. This policy improves workers' conditions while taking into account the realities of the situation in the country concerned.

The ILO considers help to member states in the struggle against unemployment to be one of its major responsibilities. Much work has been carried out in this area. Guided by international labor standards, and often with the practical aid of the ILO, many countries have taken steps to ease the lot of the unemployed, to organize employment bureaus, and to develop vocational training facilities. But these measures are far from enough to solve the immense unemployment problem facing the world today.

A coherent set of measures is needed to solve the unemployment and underemployment problem: development of rural areas as well as urban industrialization; training of citizens in modern employment techniques; taking a census of the active population and concentrating the development effort on sectors and techniques calculated to absorb the maximum manpower. In short, employment does not automatically flow from economic expansion unless it is geared to a policy designed to promote employment systematically. The International Labor Conference recognized this when, in 1964, it adopted a convention and a recommendation on unemployment policy; the promotion and planning of employment are now an integral part of the development effort.

Faced with the unemployment crisis, the ILO in 1969 launched the World Employment Program. This was the starting point for the ILO's efforts to help combat unemployment and underemployment.

During the 1960s, per capita income grew exceptionally fast by historical standards in most developing countries. However, growth often tended to be concentrated in relatively limited parts of the economy, mostly those using capital-intensive techniques and having few linkages with the traditional rural sector or the informal urban sector, which between them account for by far the greater part of total employment in most developing countries. As a result, the benefits of growth, and in particular opportunities for produc-

tive employment, have mainly gone to a very small part of the population.

It was in keeping with the recognition that growing world poverty required new initiatives that the World Employment Conference was held in 1976. The resulting declaration of principles and program of action called the world's attention to the need for full employment and an adequate income to every inhabitant in the shortest possible time.

The ILO-developed concept of basic needs is paramount to the effort to get to the root of poverty. Basic needs include two elements: certain minimum requirements of a family for private consumption—adequate food, shelter, and clothing are obviously included, as would be certain household equipment and furniture; and essential services provided for the community at large, such as safe drinking water, sanitation, public transport, and health and education facilities.

The program of the 1976 conference emphasized that strategies and national development plans and policies should include explicitly, as a priority objective, the promotion of employment and the satisfaction of basic needs of each country's population. The people should participate in making the decisions which affect them through organizations of their own choice. The concept of freely chosen employment is an integral part of a basic needs strategy. Among measures to be taken by governments to meet the target of creating sufficient jobs for all in developing countries by the year 2000 are: ratification of selected ILO conventions; selection of development projects with a view to their employment and income distribution potential; and implementation of active labor market policies and consideration given to social policies designed to increase the welfare of working people, especially women, the young, and the aged.

ILO operational activities and advisory missions remain important elements of the program. Regional employment teams in Asia, Africa, and Latin America provide technical advisory services and training courses in response to requests from a large number of countries. They have completed several country and intercountry studies of important issues and factors influencing manpower, employment, and basic needs policies and programs. For example, a mission of high-level experts to Arab countries in 1982 laid the foundation for developing a project to provide the region with longer-term manpower and employment promotion programs.

Technical cooperation projects in the fields of employment planning, manpower planning, and labor-market information range from multi-expert, long-term projects to short-term consultancies and special advisory missions. In Sudan, for example, a major UNHCR/ILO project on income-generating activities for refugees was launched in 1982. The aim of the project is to provide concrete proposals for income-generating activities to help refugees achieve self-reliance and, to the extent possible, help the local population in refugee-affected areas. The project includes a socioeconomic and skill survey for the refugee population in settlements in the urban areas (1,600 households); a study of the labor markets in the Sudan; and identification of self-help and income-generating activities for refugees in eastern and central Sudan, including the economic viability and marketability of these activities. Another example is a long-term rural development project in the Congo aimed at employment promotion in order to increase the incomes of small farmers and encourage their participation in development activities.

ILO technical advisory missions for special public works programs in Africa, Asia, and Central America not only help the governments to define and, where appropriate, expand the scope of special public works programs and determine the technical feasibility of projects and organizational and staffing needs, but also assist in the preparation of technical cooperation components and in management reviews of ongoing programs.

There has been an increased demand from Central American countries for ILO consultancy assistance in the planning of labor-intensive public works schemes, as elements of national rural development programs. In India, ILO technical advisory services have been requested to help improve the monitoring and evaluation procedures of a nationwide rural development program. Other advisory missions—in Sri Lanka and Togo, for example—have focused on preparatory assistance to special youth employment and training programs, which constitute an important element of ILO's rural employment policies.

Development of Human Resources

In an age when production techniques and structures are changing at bewildering speed, simultaneously with a rapid increase in the world's active population, the entire concept of labor and vocational training must be viewed in a new light.

Many new trades for which young people are now being prepared will have undergone radical transformation before the end of their working lives, and the qualifications they hold today will be obsolete without frequent refresher courses. Moreover, there will be a steady increase in the number of workers switching from one sector to another—for example, from agriculture to industry, or from industry to commerce.

Any modern conception for developing human resources must take these factors into account by extending and diversifying vocational training facilities: apprenticeships, technical training and education, advanced training, and refresher courses. Vocational guidance must be developed, not only to aid young people to make a wise choice of a career, but also to retrain adult workers for different jobs. A coherent policy aimed at utilizing human resources must, therefore, include measures which make it possible for the worker to continue his education and training throughout his active life, depending on his aptitudes and the opportunities in the labor market.

Vocational training is one of the key elements of ILO's technical cooperation program. Hundreds of projects have been mounted on all continents, some designed to create or strengthen national vocational training systems, others aimed at specific sectors of the economy: specialized industries, agriculture, handicrafts, commerce, the hotel trade, and tourism, among others. A total of 80 vocational training projects were operational in 1982, and 25 projects were completed—11 in industrial training, 8 in rural training, and 6 in commercial and clerical training. In Bangladesh, for example, assistance was provided to the Bangladesh Agricultural Development Corporation regarding training in the operation, maintenance, and repair of low-lift pumps used for irrigation purposes. In Algeria, a pre-investment study on training needs in hydraulics was completed. The study recommended the formulation of a training policy for water resources development and a plan for the setting up of new training facilities for skilled workers, technicians, and foremen. Short-term technical missions have been carried out in Djibouti, Equatorial Guinea, the Philippines, and other countries to assist the government ministries concerned in the formulation of training plans and proposals in connection with industrial training in heavy equipment, energy, construction, and other industries.

There has been an increasing utilization of UN Volunteers in ILO-assisted rural vocational training projects. In 1982, eight UN Volunteers were assigned in Pacific countries, nine in Upper Volta, and two in Haiti.

The ILO also cooperates in projects for management development. A total of 96 management development projects were in operation in 1982, of which 35 were completed and 30 new projects started. A project in Sri Lanka, for example, included assistance to that country's National Institute of Business Management in developing a strong consulting division, a computer services division, and a six-month diploma course in computer systems design. A computerized management information system for public enterprises was also designed and became operational. On completion of ILO assistance, the institute was virtually self-financing through the consultancy, training, and advisory services it supplies to industry.

The ILO is also active in the field of vocational rehabilitation. Its long-standing interest in the handicapped person was expressed anew in 1983 with the adoption of a recommendation and a convention recognizing the importance it attaches to the formulation and implementation of coherent national policies. The convention emphasizes collective participation—notably that of the representatives of employers' and workers' organizations and of the disabled themselves—in determining needs and developing vocational rehabilitation services at national as well as community levels. In Indonesia, for example, a three-year project, completed in 1982, resulted in the establishment of a national network of community-based rehabilitation facilities to serve disabled people in rural areas of the country. In Fiji, another three-year project led to the establishment of vocational training, sheltered employment, and placement services for the disabled. These services will serve as subregional focal points for the training of rehabilitation staff from neighboring islands.

Social Institutions

The ILO's efforts to foster social justice in order to improve working and living conditions and to encourage balanced economic and social development would be wasted if there were no social structures promoting large-scale participation.

To assist governments, employers' associations, and trade unions in building or consolidating the necessary institutions and mechanisms, the ILO is active in such fields as labor law and administration, labor relations, workers' education, promotion of cooperatives, and rural institutions.

The ILO's work in standard-setting has had a formative effect on social legislation and labor law throughout the world. The ILO has also supplied expert advice to countries requesting it on the measures needed to bring their legislation up to the level of international labor standards, or to solve certain social problems. Many developing countries have sought ILO help in establishing or codifying their labor and social legislation. To ensure that the legislation is effectively applied, a country must have a labor administration comprising the necessary services. To meet this need and to help labor ministries play an active role in designing a development policy, the ILO has mounted an increasing number of projects in this field.

The ILO has always been keenly concerned with labor-management relations and with the relations among trade unions, employers' organizations, and governments. When such relations are cordial, they foster a climate conducive to economic and social progress. When they are unsatisfactory, they can impede united national development. The ILO considers labor relations to be good when they are based on the full recognition of freedom of association, in law and in practice, and when they permit labor, management, and government representatives to tackle various problems of common concern.

Here again, technical cooperation is an extension of the action designed to set up standards and guidelines. ILO help is increasingly being sought in the field of industrial relations. Bipartite ILO missions comprising trade-union and management experts from industrialized countries have been sent to developing nations to encourage the establishment of a healthy working relationship between workers and employers. Study courses and seminars have been organized in various parts of the world.

Adequate training of workers' representatives is a prerequisite if they are to play an effective role in economic and social life. The trade unions themselves are aware of this fact and are increasing their own training programs accordingly. To assist them in this task, the ILO has established a workers' education program to enable trade unions and workers' education bodies to develop their services and to provide workers and their representatives with the social and economic training they need. ILO efforts have been directed to such objectives as the training of unionists to help them take part in the planning and execution of development policies; cooperative action; and the organization of union research and information services.

As part of this program, the ILO has organized seminars, study courses, and technical discussions, often on a regional basis. An average of 50 courses of this type, including discussions on such matters as population and family planning, are held each year in different parts of the world. There is also a publications program consisting of handbooks, booklets, bulletins, and educational material, plus a film and filmstrip lending library.

Since its earliest days, the ILO has played an important role in developing the cooperative movement. Its range of activities in this field has grown with the introduction of the cooperative system in many developing countries. The governments of these countries recognize that cooperatives provide an instrument which can facilitate social and economic advancement. With their built-in system of controls and internal management, their freely elected councils, and public discussion of their programs, cooperatives can be compared to grass-roots civics classes, giving their members a true sense of responsibility and involvement in national development. They are a unifying agent in bringing men and women together for constructive tasks, and they contribute to training for leadership. Above all, cooperatives are a key factor in rural development, for both production and marketing. The creation of processing cooperatives in rural areas for handling produce, as well as the organization of cooperatives for small enterprises and handicraft workshops, can aid progress toward industrialization. Whatever form they take, cooperatives raise living standards and increase employment opportunities. At the request of the governments, and with the financial support of UNDP, ILO experts are helping countries set up or develop cooperative movements.

F. PROBLEMS OF CERTAIN KEY INDUSTRIES

During World War II, and even earlier, it was felt that a gap existed in the structure of the ILO: special machinery was needed for the detailed and continuing study of specific industries by persons with thorough practical knowledge of their particular problems. Acting on a plan prepared by British Minister of Labor and National Services Ernest Bevin, submitted in 1943 by the UK government, the Governing Body in 1945 established seven ILO industrial committees "to provide machinery through which the special circumstances of the principal international industries [could] receive special and detailed consideration." By 1946 industrial committees had been created to deal with problems of the following key industries: inland transport; coal mines; iron and steel; textiles; petroleum; building, civil engineering, and public works; and chemical industries.

Other ILO committees that deal with special problems of international significance include the Advisory Committee on Salaried Employees and Professional Workers, the Permanent Agricultural Committee, and the Committee on Work on Plantations. The ILO has also established the Asian Advisory Committee, the African Advisory Committee, and the Inter-American Advisory Committee, which provide information on special regional problems. The ILO industrial committees are, in effect, small-scale specialized international labor conferences.

Resolutions adopted by these committees may call for further action on the part of the ILO. They may also be designed for the guidance of employers' associations and trade unions in their collective bargaining; and they may contain suggestions addressed to the UN, to other specialized agencies, or to governments. The following are a few examples of subjects concerning which important resolutions or recommendations have been adopted.

Inland Transport Committee: prevention of accidents involving dock labor; inland transport working conditions in Asia and Africa; automatic coupling of railway cars; transport and handling of dangerous goods; limitation of loads carried by one man; marking of weights on loads; interport competition.

Coal Mines Committee: principles for incorporation in a coal miners' charter; coal miners' housing; productivity in coal mines; safety in coal mines; social consequences of fuel and power consumption trends.

Iron and Steel Committee: regularization of production and employment at a high level; dismissal pay and payment for public holidays; cooperation at the industry level.

Metal Trades Committee: regularization of production and employment at a high level; long-term estimates of raw material requirements.

Textiles Committee: disparities in wages in the textile industries of different countries.

Building, Civil Engineering, and Public Works Committee: reduction of seasonal unemployment in the construction industry; social aspects of the world timber situation and outlook; national housing programs.

Committee on Work on Plantations: the place of the plantation in the general economy of the countries concerned; living and working conditions as related to plantation productivity; the need for international action on commodity regulation.

Advisory Committee on Salaried Employees and Professional Workers: rights of the inventor who is an employed person; migration of salaried and professional workers; hygiene in shops and offices; employment problems of musicians, actors, and other public performers; employment conditions of teachers; professional problems of journalists; problems involved in collective bargaining for white-collar and professional workers; wages and working conditions of hospital and health-service staff; wages and working conditions of civil servants.

G. NEW INITIATIVES TO DEAL WITH THE CHANGING WORLD OF WORK

International Program for the Improvement of Working Conditions and Environment

Launched in 1976, the ILO's International Program for the Improvement of Working Conditions and Environment (PIACT) aims to give governments and employers' and workers' organizations the necessary help in drawing up and implementing programs for the improvement of working conditions and environment. The various means of action include: standard-setting; technical cooperation, including the sending of multidisciplinary teams to member states at their request; tripartite meetings, particularly meetings of industrial committees, regional meetings, and meetings of experts; action-oriented research and studies; and gathering and dissemination of information, particularly through the International Occupational Safety and Health Information Center.

The conditions in which men and women work are at the very heart of ILO's mandate. Despite the progress achieved over the past 64 years, the working conditions of a great many workers remain arduous or give rise to new problems as a result of technological developments. PIACT's concerns are: the safety and healthiness of the working environment; working time; organization and content of work; working conditions and choice of technology; and working and living environment.

There is a complementary factor between the ILO's Employment Program and PIACT: the former concentrates on the creation of jobs, the latter on the quality of the jobs created by endeavoring to improve the working conditions of those employed.

International Health Hazard Alert System

A new approach to dealing with the many newly discovered or suspected occupational hazards which spread so quickly around the world is the ILO's International Health Hazard Alert System.

Established in 1977, the system is now fully operational, with 100 countries participating—30 in Africa, 28 in Europe, 21 in the Americas, 14 in Asia, and 7 in the Middle East. When a new hazard is discovered, an alert is sent out by the ILO to the participating countries for their assessment and reply.

Tripartite consultations concerning communications circulated within the system were carried out, for example, in Australia, Finland, the FRG, New Zealand, Norway, and Sweden. Substantial arrangements for the dissemination of information at the national level have been made in several countries, including to employers' and workers' organizations. Among them are Canada and India, where 2,000 and 5,000 copies, respectively, have been distributed of the alert on 2-Nitropropane. The communication concerning carbonless copy papers has been widely disseminated in several countries, notably Australia, Belgium, the FRG, Indonesia, Italy, New Zealand, Norway, and the US. This alert concerned possible health hazards in the use of carbonless copy papers and was signaled by Sweden and circulated by the Alert System in November 1981. By April 1982, 21 replies had been received and a summary of them had been sent to all the designated bodies in the system as well as to international organizations concerned.

Tripartite Declaration concerning Multinational Enterprises and Social Policy

The 1977 Tripartite Declaration concerning Multinational Enterprises and Social Policy applies to the fields of employment, training, conditions of work and life, and industrial relations. While already operational in the ILO, where it will continue to affect its purposes, it is foreseen as the employment and labor chapter of the UN Code of Conduct on Transnational Corporations. The declaration stresses the positive contributions that multinational enterprises can make to economic and social progress and at minimizing and resolving the difficulties which their various operations may create. The principles are commended to governments and employers' and workers' organizations of home and host countries and to the multinational enterprises themselves for their voluntary observance.

The subject areas covered by the declaration conform to the areas of substantive competence of the ILO within the overall program of the UN. Fifteen ILO conventions and 19 recommendations are referenced in the declaration. The declaration is universal in scope; it is addressed to all of the parties of the ILO's tripartite structure; it ascribes a leading role to multinational enterprises when they operate in developing countries; and finally, it is voluntary.

A 1980 follow-up on implementation of the declaration resulted in replies from 56 governments and reflected a good degree of acceptance of the declaration. As a result of the survey, the ILO Governing Body created a standing committee on multinational enterprises. It also decided to undertake a new survey covering the years 1980–82.

[8]BIBLIOGRAPHY

The Cost of Social Security, 1975–77, 1981.

International Labor Review. Articles on economic and social topics of international interest affecting labor, research notes, notices of new books received by ILO. Six issues per year.

Legislative Series. A collection of reprints or translations into English of the most important national laws on labor and social security. Two issues and index per year.

Official Bulletin. Contains documents, information, and articles concerning ILO. Two or three issues per year.

Social and Labor Bulletin. Notes on current significant events, national and international, in the social and labor field; brief descriptions of major legislation, collective agreements, experiments in improving the work environment, etc. Four issues and index per year.

Year Book of Labor Statistics. Includes statistics on population, employment, hours of work, consumer price indices, family living costs, industrial injuries, unemployment, wages and labor income, social security, and industrial disputes, as well as migration.

(The ILO also issues special publications—codes of practice and illustrated guides on safety and health, major reference works and international comparative studies, research monographs and reports on particular countries or issues, specialized bibliographies and directories, training and workers' education materials, and specialized statistical handbooks.)

THE FOOD AND AGRICULTURE ORGANIZATION OF THE UNITED NATIONS (FAO)

"To the millions who have to go without two meals a day the only acceptable form in which God dare appear is food."
Mahatma Gandhi

[1]**BACKGROUND:** Hunger is still the most urgent problem confronting the greater part of the human race. Hundreds of millions of the world's inhabitants are seriously and chronically undernourished. Not only is their diet quantitatively insufficient, it is qualitatively insufficient as well, lacking the protein essential to health and vigor. Only about one person in four in the world is really well fed and adequately nourished.

From the mid-19th century, reflecting a growing recognition of the interdependence of nations in agriculture and associated sciences, international conferences were held at which there were exchanges of knowledge relating to biology, biochemistry, crop diversification, and animal health. But it was not until 1905 that these individually valuable but unrelated efforts were coordinated with the founding of the International Institute of Agriculture (IIA).

One of the institute's aims, which were necessarily modest because of public and governmental apathy, was "to get the farmer a square deal." The words were those of David Lubin, a prosperous California dry-goods dealer, ghetto-born in Poland, who almost singlehandedly founded the institute. Depressed by the plight of his farmer customers during the agricultural crisis of the 1890s, he bought and managed his own fruit farm in order to study their problems. Rebuffed in his adopted country, he toured the chancelleries of Europe, preaching the importance of a healthy agriculture as a requisite of a healthy international society. Finally, Lubin found a sympathetic listener in King Victor Emmanuel III of Italy. Under his patronage the institute started functioning in Rome in 1908 as a center for the dissemination of farming news, trends, prices, statistics, and techniques. Though lacking the capacity to initiate or directly assist projects in the field, IIA's experience as a "head office" for the collection, collation, analysis, and redissemination of data formed a useful platform for the launching, later, of FAO's similar but much larger activities in agriculture.

The League of Nations did not directly concern itself with agriculture, but work done under its auspices in the relatively new field of nutrition proved of great practical significance. Ironically, Nazi Germany, although a sardonic critic of the League, was the first country to base its wartime rationing system on the scientific standards of diet drawn up by the League for heavy workers, expectant mothers, children, and others. Soon other countries did the same, often with striking results. In the UK, for example, the meager, often uninteresting but balanced diet dictated by the ration card actually led to an improvement in the nation's nutritional health.

[2]CREATION

FAO was the end product of a series of conferences held during World War II. In 1941 the US Nutrition Conference for Defense, attended by 900 delegates, resolved that it should be a goal of the democracies to conquer hunger, " . . . not only the obvious hunger that man has always known, but the hidden hunger revealed by modern knowledge of nutrition."

The UN Conference on Food and Agriculture, called by President Franklin D. Roosevelt at Hot Springs, Virginia, in May and June 1943, was the first full UN conference, antedating the Charter Conference itself by two years. Roosevelt felt that a conference on food, a relatively noncontroversial topic, offered a good opportunity for testing whether the Allies would be able to cooperate on postwar problems.

The conference, convened in Quebec and attended by 44 nations, agreed that a permanent international organization should be set up, and an interim commission, headed by Lester B. Pearson of Canada, drew up a draft constitution for FAO. This constitution was accepted by more than 20 governments, and FAO came into being on 16 October 1945.

[3]PURPOSES

As expressed in the preamble to the FAO constitution, member states are pledged to promote the common welfare through separate and collective action to raise the levels of nutrition and standards of living, to improve the efficiency of the production and distribution of all food and agricultural products, to better the conditions of rural populations, and thus to contribute toward an expanding world economy and ensure humanity's freedom from hunger. Specifically, FAO is charged with collecting, evaluating, and disseminating information relating to nutrition, food, and agriculture and its derivatives, including fisheries, marine products, forestry, and primary forestry products.

FAO is committed to promote and, where appropriate, to recommend national and international action with respect to:

(a) scientific, technological, social, and economic research relating to nutrition, food, and agriculture;

(b) the improvement of education and administration relating to nutrition, food, and agriculture and the spread of public knowledge of nutritional and agricultural science and practice;

(c) the conservation of natural resources and the adoption of improved methods of agricultural production;

(d) the improvement of the processing, marketing, and distribution of food and agricultural products;

(e) the adoption of policies for the provision of adequate agricultural credit, national and international;

(f) the adoption of international policies on agricultural commodity arrangements.

It is also the function of FAO: to furnish such technical assistance as governments may request; to organize, in cooperation with the governments concerned, such missions as may be needed to assist them to fulfill the obligations arising from their acceptance of the recommendations of the UN Conference on Food and Agriculture and of its constitution; and generally, to take all necessary and appropriate action to implement the purposes of the organization as set forth in the preamble.

4MEMBERSHIP

The 45 countries represented on the interim commission were entitled to original membership. One of these, the USSR, had not taken up its membership by January 1983 but could do so at any time by ratification of FAO's constitution. There is, however, an unofficial exchange of publications and statistical data, and FAO, as an executing agency for UNDP, receives funds from the USSR and employs some Soviet experts.

Any nation may withdraw after four years. Czechoslovakia did so in December 1950 but rejoined in November 1969. Poland withdrew in April 1951 but rejoined in November 1957. Hungary withdrew in January 1952 but rejoined in November 1967. Nationalist China withdrew in July 1952 and South Africa in December 1964. Indonesia gave notice of withdrawal in 1965 but later decided to remain a member.

By January 1983, FAO had 152 members:

Afghanistan
Albania
Algeria
Angola
Argentina
Australia
Austria
Bahamas
Bahrain
Bangladesh
Barbados
Belgium
Benin
Bhutan
Bolivia
Botswana
Brazil
Bulgaria
Burma
Burundi
Cameroon
Canada
Cape Verde
Central African Rep.
Chad
Chile
China
Colombia
Comoros
Congo
Costa Rica
Cuba
Cyprus
Czechoslovakia
Denmark
Djibouti
Dominica
Dominican Republic
Ecuador
Egypt
El Salvador
Equatorial Guinea
Ethiopia
Fiji

Finland
France
Gabon
Gambia
Germany, Fed. Rep.
Ghana
Greece
Grenada
Guatemala
Guinea
Guinea-Bissau
Guyana
Haiti
Honduras
Hungary
Iceland
India
Indonesia
Iran
Iraq
Ireland
Israel
Italy
Ivory Coast
Jamaica
Japan
Jordan
Kampuchea
Kenya
Korea, Dem. People's Rep.
Korea, Rep.
Kuwait
Laos
Lebanon
Lesotho
Liberia
Libya
Luxembourg
Madagascar
Malawi
Malaysia
Maldives
Mali
Malta
Mauritania
Mauritius
Mexico
Mongolia
Morocco
Mozambique
Namibia
Nepal
Netherlands
New Zealand
Nicaragua
Niger
Nigeria
Norway
Oman
Pakistan
Panama
Papua New Guinea
Paraguay
Peru
Philippines
Poland
Portugal
Qatar
Romania
Rwanda
St. Lucia
St. Vincent and the Grenadines
São Tomé and Príncipe
Sa'udi Arabia

Senegal
Seychelles
Sierra Leone
Somalia
Spain
Sri Lanka
Sudan
Suriname
Swaziland
Sweden
Switzerland
Syria
Tanzania
Thailand
Togo
Tonga
Trinidad and Tobago
Tunisia
Turkey
Uganda
United Arab Emirates
UK
US
Upper Volta
Uruguay
Venezuela
Viet-Nam
Western Samoa
Yemen, People's Dem. Rep.
Yemen Arab Rep.
Yugoslavia
Zaire
Zambia
Zimbabwe

5STRUCTURE

The principal organs of FAO are the FAO Conference, the FAO Council, and the Secretariat.

FAO Conference

The supreme body of FAO is the all-member FAO Conference, which holds its regular biennial sessions in Rome in odd-numbered years. The conference determines the policy of FAO and adopts its budget. It makes recommendations relating to food, agriculture, fisheries, forestry, and associated matters to member nations and to other international organizations. It approves conventions and agreements for submission to member governments. It may establish commissions, working parties, and consultative groups and may convene special conferences. It periodically elects the director-general as well as the member nations to be represented on the FAO Council. Each FAO member has one vote in the conference.

FAO Council

The FAO Council, consisting of 49 member nations elected by the FAO Conference for three-year terms on a rotating basis, meets at least once a year, under an independent chairman, as an interim governing body between meetings of the conference. The committees of the council include the Program and Finance Committees and the Committees on Commodity Problems, Fisheries, Agriculture, and Forestry.

Director-General and Secretariat

Under the supervision of the conference and the council, the director-general has full power and authority to direct the work of the FAO. Edouard Saouma, of Lebanon, was elected in 1975 for a six-year term; he was reelected for a further six-year term in 1982. In November 1982, FAO had a total staff of 7,248, including 5,000 staff members working in various development projects in the field.

Headquarters and Regional Offices. FAO headquarters were in Washington until 1951. Since then they have been located in Rome on extraterritorial grounds near the Colosseum and the Baths of Caracalla. The building was planned originally by the govern-

ment of Mussolini, but construction was halted by World War II. Completed after the war, it was leased by the Italian government for the "permanent use and occupancy" of FAO at an annual rental of $1. With the increase in FAO's operations, extra office space has been rented.

There are regional offices for Africa, in Accra, Ghana; for Asia and the Pacific, in Bangkok, Thailand; for Latin America, in Santiago, Chile; and a liaison office for North America, in Washington, D.C. Headquarters in Rome serves also as the regional office for Europe and the Near East.

6BUDGET

FAO's internal budget, or Regular Program, which is financed by contributions from member governments, covers the cost of the organization's secretariat, its Technical Cooperation Program, and part of the cost of several Special Action Programs. The 21st session of the FAO Conference, in November 1981, approved a budget of $366.6 million for 1982–83.

FAO's Field Program is funded largely from external sources such as UNDP and various trust funds provided by donor governments. In 1981, FAO disbursed some $182.6 million in UNDP funds in more than 120 countries. An increasing amount of money comes from donor countries which ask FAO to carry out part of their aid activities for them. Many of these countries also assign and finance young technicians to work as associate experts in FAO projects. During 1981, FAO trust fund activities accounted for total spending of about $120.1 million.

FAO's Technical Cooperation Program, financed from its own Regular Program budget, had resources amounting to just over $47 million for the 1982–83 biennium.

7ACTIVITIES

Of the more than 4,000 million people in the world, hundreds of millions are seriously undernourished. The consequences are human misery, chronic illness, and death. Nobody knows how many people die from starvation every year, but countless millions are known to die from illnesses which they are too weak to resist as a result of malnutrition and undernourishment. In some Latin American countries, for example, more than half of all deaths of children under five years of age are attributable to nutritional deficiencies.

The problem of widespread hunger and malnutrition is not simply a problem of inadequate food production; it is the most critical and cruel element of the overall problem of poverty. Farmers in the developing world are discouraged from increasing food production by the lack of purchasing power among rural and urban populations as much as by a lack of technical assistance or inputs such as improved seeds and fertilizers. People go hungry because they do not have the money to buy food rather than because local farmers cannot produce more. The fight against world hunger is a major part of the battle against world poverty. Building up a country's agriculture provides both food for the hungry and jobs for the rural populace; it contributes to the overall prosperity of the nation.

World Food Program

FAO is a sponsor, with the UN, of the World Food Program (WFP), which began operations in 1963. WFP uses food commodities, cash, and services contributed by UN member states to back programs of social and economic development, as well as for relief in emergency situations. In 1981, WFP shipped about 1.5 million tons of food from its own resources and from other international and national sources, mainly to the least developed countries and those most seriously affected.

WFP supplies for development purposes are used in a variety of ways. There are, for example, "food-for-work" projects where the food is provided as part-payment to men and women planting trees, digging irrigation canals, building roads, houses, schools, or bridges, or working on a wide variety of other community improvement programs. Food is given to settlers on new land until they can harvest their own first crops. Food is supplied to industrial workers to help build up their productivity.

WFP food is distributed through hospitals, child-care centers, and schools in many countries, where it helps vulnerable groups of the national population. It encourages school attendance and almost invariably improves the children's health, thus enabling them to get the most out of their lessons. By the end of 1982, WFP had committed resources totaling $6,146 million to 1,150 economic and social projects, and 600 operations for emergency relief in 96 countries.

A. INCREASING FOOD PRODUCTION

FAO devotes a large share of the resources of its Field and Regular Programs each year to work aimed directly at increasing output of crops, livestock, and food fish. Activities range from supporting applied research to giving direct practical help to farmers in the developing world, with emphasis on assisting countries to plan and carry out their own programs and on encouraging technical and economic cooperation among developing countries.

Crops

FAO's work in crop production includes collecting, conserving, and evaluating genetic resources; improving seed quality, production, and distribution; increasing crop output; and preventing losses before harvest. Particularly important in developing countries is the supply of high-quality food-crop seed to small farmers, who are often responsible for more than 90% of domestic food production. National seed services and centers are often crucial for the supply of seeds to farmers, and much of FAO's seed development work is concerned with building up these national institutions.

Information on seed development has been improved with a new International Seed Information System, and FAO's ability to respond to requests for the supply of seed and planting material has been strengthened with the creation in Rome of a new seed laboratory, which sent out more than 20,000 seed samples in 1982.

Priority has been given to increasing production of food legumes, roots, and tubers—important staples for much of the developing world. Surveys and evaluation of food legume production have been completed for Central America, the Caribbean, the Andean Region, Rio de la Plata Basin countries, Chile, Mexico, and Brazil. The emphasis in the Pacific countries has been on increasing the production of tropical root crops, a basic element in rural diets.

FAO has helped to develop varieties of wheat and barley suited to arid conditions. Work to develop more nutritive varieties of wheat and barley has been undertaken in Egypt, Ethiopia, India, Iran, Pakistan, and Turkey. In African countries, the emphasis has been on maize, sorghum, millet, and rice.

FAO is helping more than 20 national rice or rice-based programs, covering a wide range of environmental and growing conditions: upland rice in Gabon, Upper Volta, and Zanzibar; lowland rainfed rice in the Comoros, Laos, Mozambique, Sierra Leone, and Viet-Nam; irrigated rice in Mauritania, Senegal, Zambia, and Zanzibar; mangrove rice in Guinea-Bissau. FAO is also assisting the West Africa Rice Development Association with its special projects on irrigated and mangrove rice. New varieties of cold-tolerant rice adapted to high altitudes in East Africa are being bred, and work is under way to intensify production on small irrigated rice farms.

Requests for technical assistance in horticulture have continued to increase. The production of fruit and vegetables in arid areas is particularly important. FAO is involved in some 100 projects, including: citrus production in the Mediterranean; date palm production in the Near East and the Mediterranean; protected cultivation of vegetables in the Near East and North Africa; promotion of tropical fruit-tree production in humid and subhumid

areas; and improved vegetable production in tropical semiarid and humid regions.

FAO has updated and published the state of research on sesame, an ancient crop which produces very high quality oil and is considered to have great potential for increased cultivation. Despite the fact that it is the only source of edible oil in many areas of Africa and the Near East, sesame has received little international research support. Research is now under way on an international basis to improve the low yield of existing varieties.

Plant diseases remain one of the major checks on crop production. The easiest and most economical way of coping with plant parasites is to breed varieties that are resistant to them. FAO-supported research has been aimed at breeding varieties with durable or long-term resistance.

Since the early 1950s, FAO has coordinated the campaign against the destructive desert locust, which intermittently swarms in the Middle East and North African regions. Campaigns were almost continuous until 1963, when the pest was brought under control. There have, however, been serious outbreaks of swarms since then, particularly between 1967 and 1970, and in 1978 in desert areas in India. The pest is particularly difficult to monitor, as initial infestations usually occur in remote desert regions. FAO is now using remote sensing techniques with satellite images in its efforts to keep the locust under control.

Livestock

Livestock often forms a key component of the "production systems approach" promoted by FAO in agricultural development schemes. The approach is based on the principle that the production of different commodities is often linked and that increased production of one may result in increased output of another. In India, for example, the production of food grain has increased markedly in villages where dairy cooperatives are functioning well. Milk sales provide the small farmer with the cash income to purchase inputs such as fertilizers, improved seeds, and irrigation water essential for increased grain yields. Thus, increased milk production has led to significant improvements in farm output and living standards. The production systems approach is also being applied to sheep, goat, poultry, and rabbit production.

A large number of developing countries are enhancing the genetic potential of indigenous dairy herds with support from FAO's Artificial Insemination and Breeding Development Program. Milk yields can be improved by crossbreeding the cows of unimproved breeds with bulls of specialized dairy breeds, using artificial insemination. FAO has been supporting the use of artificial insemination, mainly on small farms in areas where a market is available for milk and where the genetically improved animals can be adequately provided with feed, health care, and management. Originally, the program emphasized assistance to countries setting up their own artificial insemination programs. Many of these have been established, and activities are now directed mainly at solving specific problems met by established artificial insemination services. The provision of semen continues to be a major activity: in 1982, for example, some 50,000 doses were supplied in 15 countries. The exchange of semen between developing countries is also being encouraged.

Improvement of the genetic potential of livestock must be accompanied by simultaneous improvement of feeding and management standards. FAO's work on improved animal feeding is intended to reduce to a minimum the amount of grain consumed by animals, and to make maximum use of pasture and fodder, crop residues, and agro-industrial by-products.

Planning assistance for livestock production is provided through the International Scheme for the Coordination of Dairy Development and the International Meat Development Scheme. FAO technical assistance missions review and survey the livestock sector of a country, identify impediments to its progress and ways of overcoming them, and formulate development projects. Later, potential sources of funding are identified. Some $25 million were generated in 1982 by missions carried out in 1981–82. Gambia, for example, has received assistance to improve animal health, livestock marketing, and meat processing.

While disease continues to check animal production in most developing countries, substantial gains have been made in improving methods of control. FAO is involved in both the laboratory and the field. A global network of reference laboratories for major infectious diseases is being developed. FAO has already identified centers for foot-and-mouth disease, rinderpest, African swine fever, classical swine fever, and Newcastle disease. These, together with centers for diseases transmissible from animals to man which have been recognized jointly by FAO and WHO, are able to provide diagnostic services for both developed and developing countries.

Efforts are continuing to improve the control of African swine fever, which posed a worldwide threat to pig production when it spread in the Mediterranean Basin and to Latin America and the Caribbean in 1978. Preparations were begun in 1982 for a long-term campaign to eradicate the cattle plague, rinderpest, from Africa, following successful emergency control measures over the previous two years supported by FAO's Technical Cooperation Program. For the control of ticks, FAO has supplied insecticide-resistance test kits, organized a workshop on dip management, and prepared a field manual on tick control.

Through the European Commission for the Control of Foot-and-Mouth Disease, which was created at the 1953 FAO Conference, FAO is involved in efforts to control the disease in Europe and to prevent its entry from areas outside Europe where foot-and-mouth disease regularly affects cattle. Through the commission, countries exchange information on outbreaks, determine what viruses are involved, inform each other on available vaccines, and coordinate research. Work to control African animal trypanosomiasis—spread by the tsetse fly—in the Ivory Coast, Mozambique, Senegal, and Zambia, has contributed to the development of more economical and environmentally acceptable methods of control, especially for the prevention of the reinvasion of areas cleared of the fly, and for the rearing of trypanotolerant livestock. One such method, involving the use of traps, has been found to be particularly useful in preventing the reinvasion of areas.

Fisheries

In 1982 the total world fishery catch was 72 million tons, more than double the catch of 20 years earlier. The increase has been brought about by widespread introduction of technological change in the fishing industry. Substantial changes have also taken place in the international laws governing marine resources, particularly the introduction of the 200-mi exclusive economic zones, which have replaced the former 6- or 12-mi zones. The problems and opportunities presented to developing coastal states by the establishment of exclusive economic zones are an important focus for FAO's work in fisheries. Priorities include advice to developing countries on policies and programs for fisheries development, management, and training.

The migratory nature of many marine species creates special problems for resource management. The South China Sea Fisheries Development and Coordination Program has established a permanent regional coordinating body with the support of the countries concerned. The program has channeled some $15 million from a wide range of sources and has identified and assisted almost all the foreign fishery projects in the region, with a total value of $38 million.

Small-scale fisherfolk still supply much of the fish for human consumption, but they remain the least privileged members of the world fishing community. It is estimated that small-scale fisheries involving more than 8 million fisherfolk produce about 20 million tons of food fish annually.

The Bay of Bengal Program concentrates on developing small-scale fisheries in the region. A recent achievement has been the successful testing and operation of new designs of beach landing craft in India and Sri Lanka, countries which, with their long stretches of sandy beaches, lack suitable sites for fishing harbors and jetties and where the higher surf often hinders the use of conventional fishing boats.

An important task for FAO's Fisheries Department is evaluation of data on world aquatic resources. In 1972, for example, the department produced a comprehensive atlas of the living resources of the sea. Every year, FAO presents a review of world fish resources and their exploitation to FAO member governments.

Promotion of aquatic animal and plant farming is an important part of FAO's work. Inland fisheries and systematic aquaculture in inland waters also provide an opportunity for increased food supplies, particularly in inland areas where there is often a shortage of high-protein food supplies. FAO's Aquaculture Development and Coordination Program, supported by UNDP, helps identify and prepare aquaculture projects. The program has established seven aquaculture centers, and there are plans for an eighth center in the Caribbean. The centers trained 75 candidates as senior aquaculturists and 20 as senior technicians in 1982.

Food Instead of Meal. The need for increased food production has prompted efforts to make direct use, for human consumption, of the large quantities of fish at present converted to fish meal for animal feeding. The potential is great but has not been realized to date because of a lack of suitable handling and processing technology. Almost 40% of the present world fish catch—mostly of small pelagic species such as sardines—is converted into meal and oil. The potential exists for present catches of small pelagic species to be doubled, to 25 million tons. If processed for human consumption, this would add greatly to the supply of fish for food.

FAO is helping to develop and test the technology for converting small fish into commercially acceptable food. Trials and demonstrations of better on-board handling techniques for these species have been carried out in several countries, including India, Mexico, Morocco, Senegal, Tanzania, and Thailand. New products have been developed and are being introduced in India and Thailand. Early results have been encouraging, but no short-term solutions are expected. More work is needed, much of it in association with technical institutions in the developing countries themselves.

As a parallel activity, attempts are being made to increase the fish component—at present less than 1%—of food aid. The purchase in developing countries of fish products, for aid to food-deficient countries, would encourage the establishment of fish-processing industries.

B. MORE RESOURCES FOR AGRICULTURE

Land and Water Development

The rising cost of bringing new land under cultivation has increased pressure to intensify production on land already under cultivation. This emphasis on vertical rather than horizontal expansion of production requires better management of land for sustained agricultural production. FAO has advised and assisted farmers, governments, and nongovernmental organizations on how to overcome soil and land degradation and increase the productivity of land.

Soil and Water Conservation. Field projects to help countries develop the administrative and institutional capacity to tackle problems of land degradation are now in operation in several countries. In Ethiopia, for example, the government's watershed management program is being supported by various multilateral and bilateral agencies. FAO is carrying out a UNDP-funded project which is training technicians and helping to train some 8,000 leaders of the country's peasant associations. Severe soil erosion affects more than half of Ethiopia and is leading to accelerated desertification in the highlands, where about 70% of the country's population are farmers. The government's soil and water conservation campaign aims to arrest erosion of fertile soils, minimize sedimentation, floods, and droughts in the mountain catchments, and build up the country's forest resources. A feature of the campaign is the involvement of the peasants' associations, the work of which is being assisted through WFP's "food-for-work" scheme.

In addition to training, the FAO/UNDP project is helping the Ethiopian Ministry of Agriculture to select demonstration sites, prepare action plans, and implement the WFP project. The project is also advising on the introduction and propagation of fodder trees, legumes, and improved varieties of grasses, together with improved grazing systems.

FAO has also assisted national soil conservation projects in Bolivia, Dominica, Kenya, Portugal, and Togo. These projects are designed to establish pilot demonstration areas and provide information for extension workers and farmers. A project in Portugal is testing and demonstrating alternative technology and management practices for drainage, soil conservation, soil preparation, and agricultural mechanization in the Alentejo, the largest of the seven agricultural regions of Portugal. A major regional soil conservation project for Africa is under way, and FAO is supporting a smaller subregional project involving the five countries of the Rio de la Plata basin in South America.

WFP provides assistance for land and water development throughout the developing world, particularly in the poorest countries. The aid, in the form of "food-for-work," contributes to the construction of irrigation works; terracing, reforestation, or other measures of erosion control; and water resources development. An example of such a project is in Pakistan. It is one of a series which aims to slow the rate of deforestation in a country with very small forest resources. The watershed management project will help reduce Pakistan's reliance on imported industrial wood through reforestation, but more important is its effect on food production. The Indus River and its tributaries provide irrigation water for about 80% of Pakistan's crop production. Dams built to conserve water for irrigation are in danger of silting up because of soil erosion resulting from overgrazing and deforestation. The project approved for Pakistan will cover reforestation, soil and water conservation, and pasture management over a period of five years. Wheat, vegetable oil, pulses, dried skim milk, sugar, and tea worth $15 million will be supplied by WFP as payment to workers for about 17 million man-days of work. In addition, the government of Pakistan has agreed to provide goods and services worth $14 million. FAO will provide technical support and advice to ensure the economic and ecological viability of the project.

Water Management
Effective management of available farm water is as important as the provision of water itself. A Bangladesh government project, supported by FAO and UNDP, illustrates the importance of good water management if full use is to be made of irrigation water. In the northwest of Bangladesh, a large number of tube wells have been sunk over the past decade to extend the irrigable area and to allow crop production during the dry season. Unfortunately, the use of the wells has proved disappointing. Inadequate farm irrigation systems and poor management—combined with social constraints, such as the prevailing land tenure system—have allowed the use of only a third of the potential irrigable areas of the tube wells. Following an earlier phase of the project, when various techniques and methods were tested and demonstrated, field officers are now being trained. Some 400 officers will receive training during the three years of the project. Their task, in turn, is to build up teams of village-based technicians who can encourage and help farmers improve their field irrigation systems and water management.

Concern over the critical food situation in Africa has increased the attention being given to the development of small-scale irrigation in that region. FAO is assisting countries to plan, execute, and manage systems which can be run by farmers and which generally use simple technology and involve relatively small investment.

Fertilizer Supply
After land and water, fertilizers are the most important input for increasing agricultural yield. Increased fertilizer use probably accounted for half the increase in yields in developing countries between 1965 and 1976. The Fertilizer Program—one of FAO's Special Action Programs—encourages the efficient use of fertilizers. It works in direct contact with many small farmers through local extension services.

In 1982, fertilizer distribution and credit pilot schemes in 16 countries supplied fertilizers and established optimum conditions for farmers to buy them. Contributions from UNDP, donor governments, and the fertilizer industry to the fertilizer program amounted to $8.5 million in 1982.

Investment
The agricultural sectors of the developing countries rely heavily on external investment. FAO helps countries formulate investment projects that will attract external financing to increase food production, raise farmers' incomes, and strengthen rural economies. In addition to helping developing countries obtain badly needed foreign exchange, the investment assistance also helps promote local investment in agriculture, because the projects must, in large part, be supported by the countries themselves. From its establishment in 1964 to the end of 1982, FAO's Investment Center had helped to channel $22,000 million of foreign and domestic capital to developing countries. FAO technical assistance missions work closely with national staff in the preparation of projects; this, in turn, increases the capacity of countries to prepare investment projects themselves.

The World Bank is the single most important financing institution for investment projects prepared by FAO. Much investment work with the Bank is concentrated on those countries which qualify for loans from its concessional "lending window," the IDA. FAO also helps prepare projects for financing by IFAD, which lends for food production and agricultural development on concessional terms, concentrating on the poorest developing countries. Since IFAD was established in 1978, FAO has prepared six out of every ten projects financed entirely by the fund. The Investment Center also works closely with the three regional development banks—the African Development Bank, the Asian Development Bank, and the Inter-American Development Bank—and has an active program involving national and commercial banks interested in agricultural investment.

Information for Agriculture
FAO has a major role in monitoring the state of natural resources: it supports research efforts in developing countries; provides technical information for specialists through an active publishing program which includes the compilation of statistical yearbooks, international catalogs and scientific monographs, and advanced data-processing facilities; and prepares training material for use in developing countries. Every decade, FAO has sponsored a worldwide agricultural census, continuing and expanding the first world census carried out by the International Institute of Agriculture in 1930.

FAO has made considerable efforts to identify future demands on agriculture, and how these demands might be met, based on the results of data collection and analysis, policy reviews, and practical knowledge of agricultural development. In 1969, FAO published the Provisional World Plan for Agricultural Development, an attempt to analyze the major issues that would confront world agriculture in the 1970s and early 1980s. Building on this base, FAO produced in 1981 a study entitled *Agriculture: To-*

ward 2000. The study's main purpose is to provide a framework for the analysis of options and consideration of policy issues relevant to the development of world agriculture until the end of the century. The study is global in scope, but the major emphasis is on developing countries. Approximately 90 developing countries which, excluding China, together account for over 98% of the population of the developing countries, are studied individually. The study was intended as a major contribution by FAO to the formulation of the development strategy of the UN within the context of the new international economic order. It also offered individual developing countries a framework in which to devise national plans and policies, and assisted in the preparation of international economic programs, including bilateral programs of developed countries. The study did not attempt to provide a precise forecast of developments. Rather, the emphasis was on the possible outcomes in production, consumption, trade, nutrition, agricultural incomes, and other relevant variables if alternative sets of national and international policies and policy objectives were pursued.

Monitoring the Environment. The threat of desertification to fragile ecosystems is widely acknowledged but, until recently, little was known about its exact extent or causes. The Desertification Assessment and Mapping Project was set up to improve and refine methods used to assess desertification; it is being undertaken by FAO and UNEP, in association with UNESCO and WMO. The project, the result of a recommendation of the UN Conference on Desertification in 1977, became operational in 1980 and was largely completed in 1982. With the involvement of many governmental and nongovernmental bodies, a methodology was prepared to assess and map the causes and dynamics of desertification, and was discussed at a meeting of experts in Rome in 1982, following tests in the US, Mexico, Upper Volta, Sudan, Tunisia, Syria, the USSR, Pakistan, and Australia.

That many areas in the developing world could support greater populations than they do at present is one of the main findings of another major study completed by FAO during 1982. The study, which had its origins in the Soil Map of the World published in 1978 by FAO and UNESCO, was carried out jointly with the International Institute for Applied Systems Analysis and UNFPA. The report, *Land Resources for Populations of the Future,* was issued early in 1983.

UNISPACE '82, the Second UN Conference on the Exploration and Peaceful Uses of Outer Space, held in Vienna in August 1982, confirmed that FAO has the responsibility within the UN system for the application of remote sensing to renewable resources. FAO's Remote Sensing Center has helped more than 70 developing countries apply remote sensing to natural resources such as land, water, forests, grassland, and fishery resources and to the monitoring of crops, pests, drought, and soil degradation. UNISPACE '82 urged FAO to continue to help countries train technicians and develop remote-sensing programs in renewable resources. Current FAO projects funded by UNDP involve the strengthening of the Argentine national space institute, and assisting in the establishment of a national space agency in Bangladesh and a national training and application center for agricultural remote sensing in China.

The growing demand for information on forest resources has led to the development by FAO of a computer software package for the analysis of forest resources data in developing countries. The program was developed to fill a need of many forestry institutions in the tropics that have not been able to take full advantage of available data-processing facilities because of the lack of suitable programming or adequately trained staff. FAO's program places a minimal demand on the type and size of computer and on programming staff, who can learn to use it in two or three weeks. Although designed for the tropics, it has general application and can be used anywhere.

Other forestry projects include the computerization of information collected as part of the joint FAO/UNEP Tropical Forests Resources Assessment Program, and the completion of special surveys to assess fuel-wood consumption in Bangladesh and Upper Volta. The survey results will be used in the development of standard methods for assessing fuel wood consumption.

Research and Technical Information. The FAO Conference, at its 21st session in 1981, stressed the importance of agricultural research in developing countries. Accordingly, much attention has been given to increasing research capacity in the developing world. The shortage of trained manpower for research remains a major problem in developing countries. This is unlikely to change significantly in the near future: the need for trained staff is expected to increase by 10% or more per year.

The International Information System for the Agricultural Sciences and Technology (AGRIS) and the Current Agricultural Research Information System (CARIS) are two worldwide networks coordinated by FAO in support of research and development programs in food and agriculture. In 1982, 110 national centers and 13 multinational centers reported more than 130,000 documents to AGRIS, bringing the total references available in the data base to 840,000. CARIS linked 71 developing countries, allowing them to exchange information on their current research activities.

A new and unique multilingual thesaurus, AGROVOC, jointly developed by FAO and the Commission of the European Community, has been published in English, French, Spanish, German, and Italian. More than 100 documentalists in 50 countries have been trained to use the system, which allows publications indexed in one language to be sought in another.

The computerized facilities of FAO's David Lubin Memorial Library, at its Rome headquarters, supplies 2,000 on-demand bibliographies, in many instances to field projects and institutions in FAO member countries.

FAO is also active in the preparation of audiovisual materials for use in village-level training schemes. It has organized and funded courses in the use of video equipment, particularly in China.

Fisheries Information. FAO provides advice and information to member countries on the state of the world's fish stocks and techniques for their evaluation. Increasing emphasis has been given to the stock information needs of developing countries.

To provide information on science and technology of marine and freshwater environments, FAO, the Intergovernmental Oceanographic Commission, and the Ocean Economics and Technology Branch of the UN jointly operate the Aquatic Sciences and Fisheries Information System (ASFIS), in collaboration with a number of national centers. ASFIS links data bases with complementary information sources. A coordinating center at FAO headquarters collects and processes information from the national centers, and makes it available to users worldwide.

The computerization of statistical data bases covering information on fish catches, production, and trade was completed in 1982. This new Fisheries Data Base, which contains information received from member governments, is being used to generate yearbooks and ad hoc tables to meet the data needs of the global fisheries community.

Two new marketing and information projects are improving distribution and trade in food-fish products in Latin America and Asia by providing regular information on product development, fish availability, and prices. Similar services are planned for the Near East and Africa.

Reaching Rural People. Filmstrips offer one of the most effective ways of reaching illiterate and semiliterate rural people. FAO uses filmstrips extensively for rural communications and has some 90 titles available in its filmstrip catalog, two-thirds of which deal with specific agricultural and development topics. Filmstrip production by FAO is funded externally for the most part. Governments and development agencies, for instance, sponsor filmstrips on specific topics. They are relatively cheap to produce and can be shown anywhere on inexpensive and simple projectors, powered if necessary by batteries.

C. IMPROVING DISTRIBUTION AND FOOD SECURITY

Inadequate distribution of agricultural products wastes output and hinders agricultural development by denying farmers the economic returns they need to produce more. FAO is involved at every stage in the distribution chain, from the prevention of food losses to attempts to bring about a more equitable regime of international trade. Programs are being mounted for the prevention of post-harvest losses, to assist the development of marketing skills in developing countries, to bolster food security, and to help producers and exporters to obtain a fair return.

Storage and the Prevention of Losses

National plans for increasing food production very often overlook the need for complementary storage facilities, with the result that short-term and expensive solutions may become necessary when the harvest is brought in. FAO's Special Action Program for the Prevention of Food Losses (PFL), established in 1977, is specifically concerned with assisting countries to prevent losses because of poor storage. Post-harvest food losses were estimated to have accounted for 70 million tons of grains, or 10% of the food production of developing countries in 1982.

The lack of dry, pest-free storage facilities is a major contributor to food losses. As a result, recent PFL assistance has emphasized the drying of food grains before storage. In the Comoros, for example, a combination of natural and artificial drying has been recommended for maize. In production areas, storage cribs are used to reduce the moisture content of maize on the cob to about 18%, the lowest level possible in the humid climate. At a central storage depot, the maize is shelled and then dried in a simple tray drier, the heat for which is supplied by burning the stripped maize cobs. In PFL projects in Malaysia and Indonesia, driers for paddy rice have been supplied to groups of farmers. These driers, which were originally developed by the International Rice Research Institute, can be heated by either kerosene burners or rice husk furnaces. PFL projects in Latin America are introducing improved cribs for maize drying and simple solar driers for grains and legumes.

Processing and Marketing

Faced with wheat imports growing at more than 10% annually, African countries are anxious to develop food products made from locally produced grains, roots, tubers, and legumes. FAO's Composite Flour Program is encouraging the replacement, wherever possible, of imported wheat flour with flour made from locally grown cereals and other local foods. Such an approach not only helps local production by absorbing seasonal gluts, but also contributes to rural development. The program has assisted Sierra Leone and Nigeria in processing local foods, such as cassava and yams, and advised on the economic viability of these products and the implications of consumer preferences.

Poor marketing of local agricultural products often seriously impedes distribution and trade. FAO is studying the effect of increased energy costs on the transport component of marketing in order to advise member countries. A program to promote technical cooperation among developing countries through the formation of associations of marketing enterprises has been launched in Asia and Africa. Assistance is being given to train people involved in marketing, from the "grassroots" level to the senior management of marketing boards, as well as officials responsible for marketing policy, legislation, and marketing infrastructure.

Commodities and Trade

The 1949 FAO conference turned down a plan for an international commodity clearinghouse, but established more modest machinery to deal with commodity issues. The Committee on Commodity Problems, with representatives from producing and consuming countries, was thus formed. Since then, it has set up 12 subsidiary intergovernmental bodies to deal with problems of particular commodities. Six are concerned with foodstuffs (grains; rice; meat; oilseeds, oils, and fats; bananas; and citrus fruits), three with beverage crops (cocoa, tea, and wine and vine products), and two with agricultural raw materials (jute, kenaf, and allied fibers, and hard fibers). The twelfth body is the Consultative Committee on Surplus Disposal. FAO services these groups with an intelligence system covering the prices, production, trade, and consumption of about 80 food and agricultural products. Concern over the competition between natural products and synthetics has prompted increased monitoring of costs and prices of various raw materials, particularly jute. A major research study is being undertaken on the impact on natural products of competition from synthetics. A joint FAO/World Bank study is assessing the prospects for jute in the 1980s.

Recent commodity policy studies include several on agricultural trade barriers and protectionism in relation to rice, grains, bananas, jute, and hides and skins. Other studies involve analysis of support prices as an incentive for production with respect to wheat, rice, and oilseeds; the scope for increased cooperation and trade in rice and meat among developing countries; national commodity policies on rice and oilseeds; and bilateral contracts and futures trading in grains.

Strengthening Food Security

Following the serious depletion of world grain reserves caused by the poor harvests of 1972, FAO proposed a system to maintain minimum world food security. Under this system, all countries, developed and developing alike, would cooperate in building up national food reserves to be used under a system of international coordination to offset the effects of future crop failures. Special efforts would also be made to increase the self-reliance of developing countries. The World Food Conference, held in Rome in November 1974, endorsed these proposals and requested FAO to prepare an International Undertaking on World Food Security. In 1976, FAO established the Food Security Assistance Scheme to carry through the work of the International Undertaking. By the end of 1981, more than 80 countries, accounting for over 95% of world cereal exports and over half of all imports, had subscribed to the scheme.

After the failure of negotiations in 1979 on a new international wheat agreement, the FAO Council adopted a five-point plan to strengthen world food security through a voluntary system of nationally held food stocks under international coordination. The plan called for the adoption of grain stock policies, agreed criteria for release of supplies to meet large-scale food shortages, measures to help poor countries meet import needs, more aid for reserves in developing countries, and increased collective self-reliance among developing countries.

Regional projects are absorbing an increasing share of FAO efforts to enhance world food security—a level of food production and distribution that would assure all countries access to adequate food supplies when and where needed. In 1982, FAO's Committee on Food Security agreed that there was considerable scope for regional cooperation to supplement national and global arrangements for strengthening food security.

The most advanced regional plan is in the Sahel, an area particularly vulnerable to food shortages. In 1981, at the request of the eight Sahelian countries, FAO prepared a feasibility study which recommended a coordinated system of national and regional cereal reserves, and coordinated grain procurement policies. The study recommended that the existing storage capacity in the region be doubled to 465,000 tons and be widely dispersed. The Food Security Assistance Scheme (FSAS) has since assisted the Permanent Inter-State Committee for Drought Control in the

Sahelian Zone and governments with projects resulting from the feasibility study. Trust fund contributions to FSAS since the scheme's inception in 1976 amounted to $50.4 million.

FAO's Global Information and Early Warning System for Food and Agriculture was established in 1975 to monitor developments in food demand and supply. The system prepares monthly, quarterly, and annual reports, as well as emergency warnings, which provide comprehensive up-to-date analyses of the world food situation and identify countries threatened by shortages, as a guide to potential donors. Monitoring by the system of production prospects and the food-supply situation has helped avert food crises in several developing countries, particularly in Africa, where widespread drought has resulted in serious shortfalls in the cereal production of some countries. In 1982, for example, the system issued early warnings of potential food shortages for 22 developing countries.

FAO is helping to set up national and regional early-warning systems linked to the global system. Projects to establish national systems are now under way in Tanzania and Zambia. Governments and FAO are examining the feasibility of a regional early-warning system and improved national systems for the nine member countries of the Southern Africa Development Coordination Conference.

Emergency Assistance for Agriculture
When severe flooding struck much of Nicaragua in May 1982, it destroyed more than 80% of the country's maize crop. Less than two weeks later, FAO had approved emergency assistance worth $250,000 to help rehabilitate Nicaragua's food crop sector. The emergency project supplied 137 tons of maize seed, 48 tons of bean seed, and 1,000 tons of fertilizers to aid the planting of more than 20,000 ha of crops for the next harvest. The operation was one of 72 emergency projects with a total budget of $47 million under way in 1982 through FAO's Office for Special Relief Operations (OSRO).

OSRO began operations in 1973 as the Office for Sahelian Relief Operation, as FAO's response to the disastrous drought in 1972/73 in the semiarid countries on the southern edge of the Sahara Desert. In 1975, following an improvement in the Sahel situation, its work extended to cover emergencies elsewhere. The emphasis in these operations is on speedy approval and delivery of assistance. When disaster strikes a country, the FAO representative assesses needs in close collaboration with local authorities and other UN agencies. At the request of the government, emergency missions are organized by FAO to assess in detail the damages and losses and to prepare assistance projects for consideration by multilateral and bilateral agencies. Most emergency projects are funded by governments, nongovernmental organizations, and UN agencies. In many cases FAO, through its Technical Cooperation Program, offers an immediate source of funding for special relief operations. Supplies and equipment provided include seeds, fertilizers, pesticides, and livestock supplies and equipment, as well as logistic support. Disaster-prone countries may also receive preventive assistance to cope with calamities.

In Kampuchea, victim of war and drought, FAO has been channeling emergency assistance for agriculture and fisheries since 1979. The entire program has been funded by 26 donors at a cost of $68 million. The rehabilitation of Kampuchea's agricultural sector has prevented massive starvation and substantially reduced the number of people fleeing to neighboring countries.

D. PROMOTING RURAL DEVELOPMENT
FAO is the UN's lead agency for the implementation of the Program of Action of the World Conference on Agrarian Reform and Rural Development, which met in 1979 under FAO auspices. FAO assistance to countries ranges from high-level missions on agrarian reform to ensuring that the principles of the conference's action program are embodied in field projects. Much of the work involves field projects to promote agrarian reform, land tenure

improvement, production structure improvement, and land settlement. Since 1975, for instance, FAO has helped train almost 2,000 officials, mainly field staff, of the Philippines Ministry of Agrarian Reform. A major task of the newly trained staff is to assist tenant farmers cultivating rice and maize to buy, over a period of 15 years, the land they work. In 1982, FAO began an exercise to evaluate the impact of agrarian reform on the social and economic situation of the farmers. The evaluation also covered rice and maize production, which has increased dramatically since the start of the government's program.

FAO has reviewed the agrarian reform and rural development policies of many countries and identified potential field projects. In addition, numerous technical missions have assisted countries to plan agrarian reform and land settlement projects.

Other FAO activities are helping the rural poor to organize in order to increase agricultural production. The aim is to improve wherever possible the access of the smallest and poorest farmers to the resources needed to increase food production and incomes. For example, the objective of the Community Action Program for Disadvantaged Rural Women is to increase opportunities for women in food production and income-producing work.

Forestry for Rural Development
FAO gives priority to the potential of trees and forests to supply food, energy, income, and employment in the rural community. An Action Program on Forestry and Rural Energy has been started to mobilize resources for large-scale forestry projects in developing countries with major fuel-wood deficits, a situation which affected some 1,150 million people by 1980. The program's first project became operational in Peru in 1982. A second special action program, Forestry for Local Community Development, completed in 1982 its first three-year phase, during which 50 countries requested assistance and 37 projects became operational. The program encourages and supports forestry activities that contribute to basic needs such as food, fuel, and housing materials, and increase the incomes and quality of life of rural people.

Community-level forestry is an important part of FAO's Forestry Program. For example, a project in the Philippines, financed by UNDP, is helping farmers rehabilitate areas used for shifting cultivation. Five hundred farmers have volunteered to undertake work to protect farmlands while increasing food production. Land has been fenced off, forage grasses sown, and a large number of trees planted for fruit production and erosion control.

Participation by farmers is crucial to the success of community forestry projects. An experiment in village forestry in Senegal, funded by Finland, is tackling most of the familiar problems of the Sahel region—desertification, soil erosion, loss of soil fertility, and scarcity of fuel wood (in 1982, 94% of the population faced an acute fuel-wood scarcity). One solution is to plant trees such as acacia, which provide shelter, fodder, and forage for animals, and renewable supplies of firewood and small-building timber. They also increase soil fertility and prevent soil erosion.

Nutrition
Increased food production and better distribution are essential but not sufficient for raising general standards of nutrition of poor peoples. In 1982, FAO began a long-term program to raise nutrition standards in the poorest countries by applying nutrition guidelines to development projects. Twenty-six developing countries were helped to assess the effects on nutrition of local development projects, to select complementary nutrition activities, and to establish nutrition evaluation or surveillance systems. The guidelines, which have been developed over a number of years, can be applied to all development and investment projects, irrespective of the funding source.

FAO has undertaken training programs to improve national skills in nutrition assessment and planning. An important feature of this work involves monitoring the effects of national food and agricultural strategies on the nutrition of underprivileged groups.

FAO work in nutrition involves community education projects. Training was provided in 1982, for example, to Benin, Fiji, Lesotho, Malawi, and Sudan. Nutrition education for women, and for people working in agriculture generally, formed a major part of the programs. A course has been developed which deals with the relationships between food and agricultural production and supply, and the health and well-being of rural women. Regional workshops to introduce this subject into the curricula of agricultural training institutions have been held in Latin America and Africa.

FAO helps to ensure food quality and safety with activities at both national and international levels. Assistance is provided to developing countries through national seminars on food-quality control. Detailed studies on the identification and control of potential food contamination and on quality-control problems were organized in 13 countries in Africa and Asia during 1982. Assistance was given to 30 countries to improve national food-control systems, while two international courses in food contaminant analysis were organized with the support of UNEP. The Joint FAO/WHO Codex Alimentarius Commission, which develops and recommends international standards and codes of practice for foods, is giving greater emphasis to problems of developing countries and to nutrition.

Popular Participation

The participation by people in the provision of their own food is stressed in FAO development activities. World Food Day and the Freedom from Hunger Campaign/Action for Development program (FFHC/AD) endeavor to involve people in food and agriculture issues on the broadest possible level in both developing and developed countries.

FAO launched World Food Day on 16 October 1981, the 36th anniversary of its founding. FAO member governments had decided that this day should be observed each year to increase public awareness of the nature of world food and agricultural problems and the steps necessary to overcome them.

Individuals and nongovernmental organizations in the developing and developed worlds have been linked for more than 20 years by FFHC/AD in a common effort for development. The program identifies national and rural-based nongovernmental organizations in developing countries which are working directly with the poorer sections of the rural population. The aim is to assist these organizations, through workshops and other activities, to improve their capacity to carry out projects that will increase the self-reliance of rural communities. The program also aims to assist organizations in developed countries to channel funds for development to organizations and institutions in the developing world. During 1982, some 90 projects with a total value of $6.3 million were under way. Of this amount, $4.6 million had been donated by nongovernmental organizations.

[8]BIBLIOGRAPHY

Agrindex—International Information System for the Agricultural Sciences and Technology.
Animal Health Yearbook.
Annual Fertilizer Review.
Ceres—FAO Review on Development. Bimonthly.
Commodity Review and Outlook. Annual.
Fertilizer Yearbook.
Food and Agricultural Legislation. Semiannual.
Food and Nutrition—A Quarterly Review Devoted to World Development in Food Policies and Nutrition.
Monthly Bulletin of Agricultural Economics and Statistics.
Plant Protection Bulletin. Quarterly.
Production Yearbook.
The State of Food and Agriculture. Annual world survey.
Trade Yearbook.
Unasylva: An International Journal of Forestry and Forest Products. Quarterly.
World Animal Review. Quarterly.
World Food Report. Annual.
World Grain Trade Statistics: Exports by Source and Destination. Annual.
Yearbook of Fishery Statistics.
Yearbook of Forest Products Statistics.

THE UNITED NATIONS EDUCATIONAL, SCIENTIFIC AND CULTURAL ORGANIZATION (UNESCO)

[1]BACKGROUND:

"Since wars begin in the minds of men," the preamble to the UNESCO constitution states, "it is in the minds of men that the defenses of peace must be constructed." As also stated in the preamble, "the great and terrible war which has just ended was a war made possible by the denial of the democratic principles of the dignity, equality and mutual respect of men, and by the propagation, in their place, through ignorance and prejudice, of the doctrine of the inequality of men and races." World War II was too recent an event when UNESCO was created for its founders to forget that. UNESCO's purpose as a member of the UN family of organizations is "to contribute to peace and security by promoting collaboration among the nations through education, science and culture in order to further universal respect for justice, for the rule of law and for the human rights and fundamental freedoms which are affirmed for the peoples of the world, without distinction of race, sex, language or religion, by the Charter of the United Nations."

Occasional attempts at international cooperation in educational, scientific, and cultural matters were made before World War I, but no machinery existed to promote these efforts on a worldwide scale. Even the League of Nations Covenant, when it was drawn up after the war, failed to mention international cooperation in these matters. However, thanks in great part to the efforts of the Belgian delegate Henri La Fontaine, a League of Nations Committee on Intellectual Cooperation was formed. Composed of 12 eminent persons, the committee met for the first time in the summer of 1922 under the chairmanship of the French philosopher Henri Bergson. Among those who served on the Committee were Marie Curie, Gilbert Murray, and Albert Einstein. The intellectual atmosphere that prevailed in the committee was a lofty one, but at the same time the committee established precedents in practical matters that have proved useful to UNESCO. Thus, the 40-odd national committees on intellectual cooperation whose creation it promoted were a precedent for the national commissions operating as of 1983 in 147 countries to further the work of UNESCO. The International Institute of Intellectual Cooperation, established with the aid of the French government, and located in Paris, began work early in 1926 and provided a permanent secretariat for the committee.

The League was thus provided with a technical body to promote international activity, and was active in many fields, especially those of interest to scholars, professional men, learned societies, librarians, and the like. Numerous conferences and symposia were held under the auspices of the International Institute in Paris. Among the topics taken up by these conferences as the world situation became more menacing were the psychological causes of war and methods of promoting peaceful change as a substitute for war.

[2]CREATION

More intensive international cooperation in the field of educational problems began during World War II itself. A Conference of Allied Ministers of Education (CAME) was convened in London in November 1942 to consider how the devastated educational systems of the countries under Nazi occupation could be restored after the war. The first meeting of the conference was attended by representatives of eight governments in exile and the French National Committee of Liberation. CAME met at frequent intervals throughout the war, with the participation of a growing number of representatives of other allied governments. The US delegation to the April 1944 meeting of the conference included J. William Fulbright, then congressman and later senator from Arkansas, and the poet Archibald MacLeish, at that time Librarian of Congress, who was later to participate in the drafting of UNESCO's constitution.

It was decided at San Francisco that one of the objectives of the UN should be to promote international cultural and educational cooperation. Addressing the closing plenary session, President Harry Truman declared: "We must set up an effective agency for constant and thorough interchange of thoughts and ideas. For there lies the road to a better and more tolerant understanding among nations and among peoples."

The conference creating UNESCO was convened by the UK and France in London in November 1945. It was decided that the new organization should deal not only with the transmission of existing knowledge, but with the pursuit of new knowledge as well. Hence, the encouragement of natural and social sciences through international cooperation was one of the principal tasks assigned UNESCO. UNESCO's constitution was adopted by the London conference after only two weeks of discussion, and entered into effect on 4 November 1946, when 20 states had deposited instruments of acceptance with the UK government.

[3]PURPOSES

UNESCO's functions as prescribed in its constitution are:

(a) "to collaborate in the work of advancing the mutual knowledge and understanding of peoples, through all means of mass communication. . . .

(b) "to give fresh impulse to popular education and to the spread of culture by collaborating with members, at their request, in the development of educational activities; by instituting collaboration among the nations to advance the ideal of equality of educational opportunities without regard to race, sex, or any distinction, economic or social; by suggesting educational methods best suited to prepare the children of the world for the responsibilities of freedom;

(c) "to maintain, increase, and diffuse knowledge . . . by assuring the conservation and protection of the world's inheritance of books, works of art, and monuments of history and science . . . ;

by encouraging cooperation among the nations in all branches of intellectual activities, including the international exchange of persons active in the fields of education, science, and culture, and the exchange of publications, objects of artistic and scientific interest, and other materials of information; by initiating methods of international cooperation calculated to give the people of all countries access to the printed and published materials produced by any of them."

In short, UNESCO is to promote on the one hand the democratization of education, science, and the arts, and on the other hand the progress of all sciences and all branches of intellectual activity, aiming to improve material as well as spiritual life.

Since UNESCO's constitution specifically emphasizes the need to preserve "the independence, integrity and fruitful diversity of the cultures and educational systems" of the member states, the organization cannot impose any particular standard either on all its members or on any of them, and it is "prohibited from intervening in matters . . . within their domestic jurisdiction."

4MEMBERSHIP

Any UN member may join UNESCO. Other states may be admitted to UNESCO membership upon the recommendation of the organization's Executive Board and the approval of its General Conference by a two-thirds majority. Austria, Hungary, and Japan joined UNESCO years before entering the UN.

A state may withdraw from UNESCO by notifying the organization's director-general of its intention to do so; the withdrawal takes effect as of the end of the respective calendar year. South Africa so withdrew as of 31 December 1956. Czechoslovakia, Hungary, and Poland suspended their participation in UNESCO activities in 1952, but returned as active participants in 1954. Portugal withdrew in 1972, but returned in 1974. In November 1974 a vote dominated by Arab and Communist delegations excluded Israel from UNESCO's European regional group and withheld aid from it on the ground that it persists "in altering the historic features" of Jerusalem during excavations—an allegation not sustained by UNESCO's archaeological expert. On 29 December 1983, the US formally gave notice of its intention to withdraw from UNESCO within a year.

Under a UK-proposed amendment to the constitution adopted in 1951, territories or groups of territories not responsible for their international relations can be admitted as associate members upon application of member states or other authorities responsible for their international relations. Associate members do not have the right to vote. At the end of 1946, UNESCO had 27 members; in July 1983, 160 members and 1 associate member:

Afghanistan
Albania
Algeria
Angola
Antigua and Barbuda
Argentina
Australia
Austria
Bahamas
Bahrain
Bangladesh
Barbados
Belgium
Belize
Benin
Bhutan
Bolivia
Botswana
Brazil
Bulgaria
Burma
Burundi

Byelorussia
Cameroon
Canada
Cape Verde
Central African Republic
Chad
Chile
China
Colombia
Comoros
Congo
Costa Rica
Cuba
Cyprus
Czechoslovakia
Denmark
Dominica
Dominican Republic
Ecuador
Egypt
El Salvador
Equatorial Guinea
Ethiopia
Fiji
Finland
France
Gabon
Gambia
German Dem. Rep.
Germany, Fed. Rep.
Ghana
Greece
Grenada
Guatemala
Guinea
Guinea-Bissau
Guyana
Haiti
Honduras
Hungary
Iceland
India
Indonesia
Iran
Iraq
Ireland
Israel
Italy
Ivory Coast
Jamaica
Japan
Jordan
Kampuchea
Kenya
Korea, Dem. People's Rep.
Korea, Rep.
Kuwait
Laos
Lebanon
Lesotho
Liberia
Libya
Luxembourg
Madagascar
Malawi
Malaysia
Maldives
Mali
Malta
Mauritania
Mauritius
Mexico
Monaco
Mongolia

Morocco
Mozambique
Namibia
Nepal
Netherlands
New Zealand
Nicaragua
Niger
Nigeria
Norway
Oman
Pakistan
Panama
Papua New Guinea
Paraguay
Peru
Philippines
Poland
Portugal
Qatar
Romania
Rwanda
St. Lucia
St. Vincent and the Grenadines
San Marino
São Tomé and Príncipe
Sa'udi Arabia
Senegal
Seychelles
Sierra Leone
Singapore
Somalia
Spain
Sri Lanka
Sudan
Suriname
Swaziland
Sweden
Switzerland
Syria
Tanzania
Thailand
Togo
Tonga
Trinidad and Tobago
Tunisia
Turkey
Uganda
Ukraine
USSR
United Arab Emirates
UK
US
Upper Volta
Uruguay
Venezuela
Viet-Nam
Western Samoa
Yemen, People's Dem. Rep.
Yemen Arab Rep.
Yugoslavia
Zaire
Zambia
Zimbabwe

Associate Member
  Br. Eastern Caribbean Group

⁵STRUCTURE

UNESCO is an autonomous organization affiliated with the UN through a relationship agreement signed in 1946. Its three principal organs are the General Conference, the Executive Board, and the Secretariat, headed by the Director-General.

General Conference

All UNESCO members have the right to be represented in the General Conference, which determines UNESCO's policies and decides on its major undertakings. Each member state has one vote in the conference but may be represented by five delegates. UNESCO's constitution requires that member governments are to consult with national educational, scientific, and cultural bodies before selecting these delegates; in countries where national UNESCO commissions have been established, these too are to be consulted.

From 1946 through 1952, the General Conference met every year, and then met in alternate even-numbered years only. It now meets in odd-numbered years. As a rule, the conference takes place in Paris, but it has also met in Mexico City, Beirut, Florence, Montevideo, and New Delhi.

Decisions of the General Conference are made by a simple majority vote except for certain constitutionally specified matters that require a two-thirds majority, such as to amend the UNESCO constitution or to adopt an international convention. Member nations are not automatically bound by conventions adopted by the General Conference, but the UNESCO constitution requires them to submit such conventions to their appropriate national authority for ratification within one year. The same applies to recommendations, which the General Conference is empowered to adopt by simple majority vote.

Executive Board

The 51-member Executive Board, elected by the General Conference, supervises the execution of UNESCO's program. It meets at least twice a year. Before the General Conference convenes, the Executive Board reviews the budget estimates and work program for the following two-year period as prepared by the Director-General. It submits these with its recommendations to the General Conference, and prepares the agenda for the conference.

The UNESCO constitution provides that "Although the members of the Executive Board are representatives of their respective governments, they shall exercise the powers delegated to them by the General Conference on behalf of the Conference as a whole." The members of the board are not states but personalities designated by name. In electing the individuals who are to sit on the board, the General Conference shall, as stated in UNESCO's constitution, "endeavor to include persons competent in the arts, the humanities, the sciences, education and the diffusion of ideas" and shall also "have regard to the diversity of cultures and a balanced geographical distribution."

Following a constitutional amendment adopted by the General Conference in 1972, board members are elected for four years and are not immediately eligible for a second term. At each session the General Conference elects members to succeed those whose terms end with that session. A system of electoral groups of member states, governing only elections to the Executive Board, was established in 1968.

Director-General and Secretariat

The Secretariat carries out UNESCO's program of action. It is headed by a Director-General, nominated by the Executive Board and appointed by the General Conference. The staff are appointed by the Director-General. Julian Huxley of the UK was UNESCO's first Director-General. Amadou Mahtar M'bow of Senegal was appointed to the position in 1974 and was reelected for a seven-year term of office in 1980.

Headquarters. UNESCO's first headquarters were in the Hotel Majestic, in Paris, a building which, ironically, had served as headquarters for the German army during its occupation of France. In 1958, the organization's headquarters were transferred to a 3-hectare (7.5-acre) site, located at 7 place de Fontenoy, donated to UNESCO by the government of France.

UNESCO headquarters originally consisted of a conference

building, a secretariat building, and a building for the permanent delegations assigned to UNESCO. In 1965 a new building constructed around underground patios was added, and in 1970 and 1977, two supplementary buildings. The buildings were designed and approved by several leading architects. Works by contemporary artists are an integral part of the headquarters.

National Commissions for UNESCO

The UNESCO constitution requests every member state to associate "its principal bodies interested in educational, scientific, and cultural matters with the work of the Organization, preferably by the formation of a National Commission. . . . " By July 1983, 146 member states had established such broadly representative national commissions to collaborate with UNESCO in attaining its objectives. These commissions are not official UNESCO organs, but they provide a vital link between UNESCO and the public at large. They advise their governments and the delegations that attend the UNESCO General Conference on pertinent matters and serve as liaison agencies and information outlets.

The various national commissions vary greatly in size and composition. Often the country's minister of education is the commission's president, and its members may include high government officials, leaders in the fields of education, science, and the arts, and representatives of professional organizations. Through meetings, publications, broadcasts, contests, and exhibitions, the commissions stimulate public interest in specific UNESCO projects. National UNESCO commissions of several countries often meet for regional conferences. National commissions are frequently given contracts to translate UNESCO publications and to handle printing and distribution of these translations.

Cooperation with Nongovernmental Organizations

The constitution of UNESCO states that "a peace based exclusively upon the political and economic arrangements of governments would not be a peace which could secure the unanimous, lasting and sincere support of the peoples of the world, and that peace must therefore be founded, if it is not to fail, upon the intellectual and moral solidarity of mankind."

In order to attain that objective, the founders of UNESCO sought ways of associating the peoples of the world as closely as possible in the preparation and implementation of the organization's aims and programs. Thus, from its inception, UNESCO has sought the collaboration of international nongovernmental organizations (NGO's). The NGO's with which UNESCO cooperates, now numbering over 500, have activities and interests paralleling those of the organization, ranging from specialized or scholarly organizations (of teachers, scientific researchers, philosophers, sociologists, journalists, writers, legal experts) to mass organizations (trade unions, cooperatives, women's associations, youth movements) and denominational organizations.

UNESCO consults and cooperates with NGO's so as to receive the broadest possible assistance from them in the preparation and implementation of its programs, thus strengthening international cooperation in the fields of education, science, and culture.

6 BUDGET

For the three-year period 1981–83, the 1980 session of the General Conference voted a regular budget of $625,374,000, of which $104,564,100 was for program services and operations in education; $68,441,200 for natural sciences and their application to development; $50,289,600 for culture and communication; $27,745,300 for the social sciences and their applications; and $20,360,800 for copyright, information systems, and statistics.

UNESCO's budget is financed through contributions assessed against member states on a sliding scale. For the 1981–83 period, these assessments ranged from a minimum of 0.01% of the total amount, as in the cases of Afghanistan and Zambia, to 25% in the case of the US.

Like other UN specialized agencies, UNESCO receives UNDP funds for operational assistance to member states. In 1981–83, UNDP funds amounted to $260,493,000, which, when added to $118,890,100 from other sources, made a grand total of $1,004,757,100.

7 ACTIVITIES

UNESCO's work is carried out principally in the fields of education, the natural sciences, the social and human sciences, culture, and communication.

A. EDUCATION

UNESCO's largest sectoral activity, education, is the field for constant but changing endeavor. From at first helping to reconstruct war-torn educational systems in Europe and carrying out isolated, modest projects elsewhere, UNESCO has progressed to large-scale undertakings such as literacy campaigns, rural development, science teaching, educational planning and administration, and teacher training.

UNESCO's work in the struggle against illiteracy combines literacy programs with a drive to make primary education universal and thus eliminate illiteracy's root causes. At present rates, the number of illiterates in the world will reach 1,000 million by the end of the century. UNESCO assists member states in carrying out literacy drives to suit their needs. Examples are a campaign in Ethiopia, launched in 1981, and a major project in Latin America and the Caribbean, designed to ensure education for the entire population by the year 2000.

In developing countries the bulk of the population is often rural. To meet their needs, pilot projects are being carried out to develop teaching materials that will improve science teaching in rural areas. Other activities aim at integrating an educational component into rural development programs. UNESCO is also encouraging innovation in rural development.

UNESCO stresses general scientific and technological education, for the problem is not only to train specialists but to give to populations at large the scientific attitudes without which development cannot take place. UNESCO is helping to set up national machinery for science teaching and national centers for producing teaching materials, as well as pilot projects exploring the link between learning and work.

UNESCO also works to increase access to education for disadvantaged groups, particularly women, who are discriminated against in many countries, and the handicapped, who suffer from discrimination almost everywhere. UNESCO's objectives are to open to women careers traditionally reserved for men, and to give handicapped children the opportunity for ordinary schooling. UNESCO cooperates with UNRWA to provide schooling for 314,000 Palestinian refugee children, and during 1981–83, it aided the Azania Institute, in the Sudan, for exiles from South Africa.

In the field of educational planning and administration, UNESCO projects include the training of educational planners and administrators and the encouragement of local building and furniture industries to construct and equip needed schools. UNESCO also helps developing countries that are launching educational systems to devise and apply their own educational policies and to assess the results of such policies.

Among UNESCO's other activities is teacher training, with 91 projects under way. UNESCO also continues to carry out studies and promote teaching in the still new fields of drugs, population, and the environment, and has tried to translate into concrete educational action the fostering of certain basic goals, including respect for human rights, especially the right to education.

B. THE NATURAL SCIENCES

One of the tasks assigned to UNESCO by its constitution is to "maintain, increase and diffuse knowledge . . . by encouraging cooperation among the nations in all branches of intellectual activity," including the natural sciences.

Scientists themselves appear to have always had an instinct as well as a need for cooperation. The founders of UNESCO gave a high-priority role to science and to international cooperation in science. Various steps have been taken to ensure effective international cooperation in science. One of these steps has been the development of "mechanisms" designed to further cooperation at the international level. For example, since its very beginning UNESCO has been instrumental in establishing autonomous intergovernmental organizations such as the European Organization for Nuclear Research (Geneva) and the Latin American Center for Physics (Rio de Janeiro). An outstanding example of a semiautonomous body supported by UNESCO is the International Center for Theoretical Physics (Trieste). This center, jointly sponsored by the IAEA and a member state (Italy), furthers close collaboration among the world's scientists. UNESCO serves as an international meeting place where scientists from all parts of the world come together for an open exchange of information and views. These meetings range from small groups of experts to ministerial conferences such as those of ministers responsible for science policy, organized for Europe in 1970 and 1978, for Asia in 1972, for Africa in 1974, and for Latin America in 1981.

UNESCO has developed its own programs in science. These programs are largely formulated by the UNESCO Secretariat, discussed and approved by UNESCO's member states, and administered and guided by the organization's staff, both at headquarters and in the field. There is probably no single answer to why UNESCO's program in science has taken the form it has. On the one hand, UNESCO is a "development organization" which aims to help developing member states in their economic and social development plans. From this naturally springs "development programs" that include the training of technicians, engineering education, science policy studies, the sending of experts and teams of experts in different fields to developing countries on missions, the establishment of training and information centers in developing countries, and the examination of the science component of agricultural education. On the other hand, UNESCO's mandate in science requires that fundamental research be initiated and carried out. Thus, UNESCO supports programs and projects in the life sciences, in ecology and natural resources research, in surveys of technological innovations, in marine sciences, and in hydrology.

Under its science and technology policy program, UNESCO is responsible for standard-setting and methodological works concerning the responsibilities and rights of scientific workers; selection of objectives of scientific research and experimental development with regard to human values and ethical criteria; multilingual terminology, planning, and budgetary techniques used in science and technology policy-making; the preparation and organization of regional ministerial conferences and experts' meetings in the field of science and technological policies; international comparative studies such as ones on the organization and performance of research units and on the construction of meaningful indicators of scientific and technological development; development and promotion of information exchange in the field of science and technology policies; and the training of qualified personnel in science policy matters.

UNESCO has also developed programs and created special mechanisms to coordinate and stimulate scientific programs of national governments as well as of other organizations in the environmental and natural resources fields. The prime example is the Intergovernmental Oceanographic Commission (IOC) that was set up in 1960 under UNESCO auspices. The Assembly of IOC, which now includes members from 110 nations, meets every two years. IOC participates with other international organizations in developing programs and projects through the Inter-Secretariat Committee on Scientific Programs Relating to Oceanography (ICSPRO). Created in 1969 and composed of the

executive heads of several UN organizations (FAO, IMO, UNESCO, and WMO, as well as the UN itself) having interests in marine sciences, ICSPRO serves as a committee on interagency cooperation in marine sciences and the development of scientific programs in oceanography.

Another intergovernmental program, launched by UNESCO in 1965, was the International Hydrological Decade, which aimed to seek the scientific information needed for rational management of water resources. In 1975 it became a long-term endeavor, the International Hydrological Program (IHP). Now in its third phase (1984–89), IHP–III is actively involved with more than 130 countries in the development of scientific bases for the rational management of water resources and the implementation of an education and training program which includes the transfer of knowledge and technical skills. The ultimate goal of IHP–III is to help solve socioeconomic development problems related to water resources.

In view of the importance of ecology and the earth sciences, UNESCO has also prompted scientific research in these areas and has trained specialists in related disciplines through the creation of research institutions, postgraduate training courses, and the development of centers of integrated studies. In addition, UNESCO has prepared earth science maps, launched the International Geological Correlation Program, and studied the causes of natural disasters.

In 1971, UNESCO launched "Man and the Biosphere" (MAB) as an international program of applied research on the interactions between man and his environment. Its aim is to provide the scientific knowledge and trained personnel to manage natural resources in a rational and sustained manner. The MAB program gives priority to work in the field at the local level, within general frameworks for scientific cooperation at the international level. Based on a network of over 100 MAB national committees, in early 1983 the MAB program covered 1,030 field research projects associating over 10,000 researchers in 79 countries, with 215 biosphere reserves in 58 countries as sites for genetic conservation, research, training, and education. MAB information materials include state-of-knowledge reports, slide-tape shows, and a 36-poster exhibit on the theme "Ecology in Action."

A large part of UNESCO's program is carried out under contract or through subvention to various nongovernmental organizations such as the International Council of Scientific Unions (ICSU), the International Cell Research Organization (ICRO), the International Brain Research Organization (IBRO), and the World Federation of Engineering Organizations. UNESCO funds many of these organizations.

UNESCO also works closely with other UN specialized agencies —with WHO in matters concerning cell and brain research and microbiology; with WMO concerning hydrology and climatology; with FAO concerning agricultural and forestry education and research, soil science, marine sciences, and nature conservation; with UNEP on activities relating to the use and conservation of the biosphere and its resources and on environmental education and information; and with the UN itself concerning the application of science and technology to development.

C. THE SOCIAL AND HUMAN SCIENCES

UNESCO encourages the development of the social and human sciences in all regions at the international level, particularly through professional nongovernmental organizations, and at the regional level, through its continued support of the European Coordination Center for Social Science Research and Documentation, in Vienna; the Latin American Council for the Social Sciences, in Buenos Aires; the Center for Social Science Research and Documentation for Africa South of the Sahara, in Kinshasa; and the Arab Regional Center for the Social Sciences, in Cairo. UNESCO also promotes social and human sciences training and research activities as well as international exchanges through information and documentation services and through publications, with special emphasis on a number of key disciplines such as history, anthropology, geography, linguistics, and management sciences.

UNESCO studies relating to development are concerned with economic theories and the functioning of the world economy; new styles of development and participation of populations in the development process; rural development and food self-sufficiency; the sociocultural impact of the activities of transnational corporations; cooperation among developing countries and sociocultural factors enhancing regional and subregional integration; and practical experience in endogenous development.

Its activities concerning development planning and evaluation are aimed at elaboration and application of social science methods with a view to strengthening national capacity in these skills. They deal with the practical use of socioeconomic indicators to illuminate problems of rapid socioeconomic change, in particular through training, research on planning methods, and studies on evaluation methods and their use in different countries. Several projects to train planners in developing countries are being implemented.

In the field of population, UNESCO is concerned with the demographic, sociocultural, and economic aspects of internal and international migration; the interrelationship between population, environment, and technological progress in the perspective of development; training of personnel in social communication techniques; and training of journalists in population-related problems.

UNESCO has continued its work for human rights, in particular the elimination of racial discrimination and apartheid. It promotes the setting up of specialized courses in human rights for university students and concerned socio-professional organizations, and the creation of networks of institutions and the improvement of information and documentation for human rights teaching, including regional training seminars for university teachers and the publication of teaching materials.

UNESCO's program concerning the status of women and the participation of women in development aims at analyzing sociocultural obstacles to the exercise by women of their fundamental rights, and at promoting the development of multidisciplinary research and teaching programs related to women.

Its youth program deals with the analysis of problems and dissemination of information concerning youth; enrollment of young people in the service of international cooperation, development, and peace; and action on behalf of disadvantaged young people. UNESCO planned to further strengthen its cooperation with member states and nongovernmental organizations in preparation for the International Youth Year (1985).

D. CULTURE

UNESCO's action in the field of culture has four main objectives: (1) safeguarding of cultural heritage; (2) study of the nonphysical aspects of culture such as history, languages, oral traditions, and promotion of cultural values; (3) dissemination of cultures; and (4) cultural development.

Safeguarding of Cultural Heritage

Under the terms of its constitution, UNESCO was entrusted with the task of "ensuring the preservation and protection of the world heritage of works of art and monuments of historic or scientific interest." The organization has therefore endeavored to promote and foster international action in this field.

UNESCO's activities in the safeguarding of cultural heritage are best known through its campaigns to mobilize international support. The first such campaign was devoted to safeguarding the monuments of Nubia, in Egypt, and led to the successful reconstruction of the Temple of Abu Simbel, a $40-million undertaking. Another undertaking, successfully brought to a conclusion in 1983, was the restoration of Borobudur in Indonesia. A second Egyptian campaign was devoted to the creation of museums in Aswan and Cairo. Today there are 27 such international campaigns.

The growing determination of member states to preserve and present their national cultural heritage has led to an increase in museum development and in activities to preserve historical monuments and sites, works of art, and other cultural property. UNESCO's contribution in this field has consisted mainly in the provision of consultant services, equipment, supplies, and financial assistance to individual projects throughout the world. Improving the training of specialists in the conservation, preservation, and presentation of the cultural heritage has involved the provision of lecturers and fellowships for international, regional, and subregional training projects.

UNESCO's activities have also resulted in the adoption of a number of conventions and recommendations, such as the International Convention Concerning the Protection of the World Cultural and National Heritage—the World Heritage Convention—adopted by the General Conference in 1972. The convention provides, for the first time, a permanent legal, administrative, and financial framework for international cooperation. It also relates sectors which had previously been considered very different —the protection of the cultural heritage and that of the natural heritage—and introduces the concept of "world heritage," which transcends all political or geographic boundaries. The convention aims to foster a greater awareness among all peoples of the irreplaceable value of the world heritage and the perils to which it is exposed. It is intended to complement, assist, and stimulate national endeavors without either competing with or replacing them. By 1 July 1983, the convention had been ratified or accepted by 74 member states. The World Heritage Committee has thus far included 136 properties on the World Heritage List and has regularly approved financial support for technical cooperation through the World Heritage Fund.

Under its research, study, and information exchange activities, UNESCO has contributed to the advancement and spread of specialized knowledge concerning heritage preservation. It has issued a series of technical manuals on such subjects as museums, underwater archaeology, preserving and restoring monuments and historic buildings, the man-made landscape, conservation standards for works of art in transit and on exhibition, and conservation of stone. In response to the need for more elementary and accessible practical guidance, particularly in developing countries, a new series of technical handbooks was launched in 1975. The quarterly *Museum*, published since 1948 in English, French, Spanish, and Russian, is an international forum of information and reflection on museums of all kinds.

Study and Promotion of Cultures

At the second World Conference on Cultural Policies, held in Mexico City in 1982 and attended by representatives of 127 member states, emphasis was placed on the necessity to continue and intensify research and activities focusing on cultural identity. An important part of this program consists of the preparation of general histories and works on various geocultural areas, such as the *General History of Africa,* of which two volumes have already been published in several languages, the *General History of Latin America,* the *General History of Central Asia,* and studies on various aspects of Islamic culture. At the same time, work has continued on a revision of the *History of the Scientific and Cultural Development of Mankind* to reflect changes in the world during the last decades and the accession to independence of many former colonial countries.

Matching these activities, in which history is uppermost, more emphasis has been put on cultural values in studies and research. UNESCO also continues its support for cultural events and regional festivals, which embody the most vital aspects of cultural distinctiveness.

Finally, greater importance has been given to the promotion of national and regional languages, including the languages of Africa, Latin America, the Caribbean, Asia, and the Pacific, as well as Slavic and Arctic languages. In addition to these regional studies, an attempt has been made to systematize research activities on two phenomena of general interest: the impact of technical and industrial progress on culture, and the process of encounter and interaction between cultures.

Dissemination of Cultures
The catalog of the UNESCO *Collection of Representative Works* by 1983 listed nearly 800 titles. Most are translations into widely spoken languages—English and French—of the classics of more than 60 different literatures in some 45 Asian and 20 European languages, and the literature of Africa and Oceania.

UNESCO has published two catalogs of color reproductions of paintings, one devoted to works before 1860, the other to works painted since that time. The plates for these catalogs are chosen by international experts. UNESCO has organized 13 traveling exhibitions of reproductions, which have circulated or are circulating in most of the organization's member states.

The UNESCO World Art Series aims at drawing attention to works still too little known despite their importance to the history of art and existing, for example, in Australia, Egypt, Ethiopia, Mexico, Poland, and Sri Lanka. Recent art albums have been devoted to Central Asia, Latin America, Bulgaria, and India.

Cultural Development
The Universal Declaration of Human Rights asserts that everybody has the right to participate freely in the cultural life of society. From this follows the right to share in the cultural heritage of the world community, and it implies that culture cannot be the privilege of an elite few but must be regarded as a dimension of human life. In this spirit, since the end of the 1960s, UNESCO has attached increased importance to cultural policies and activities related to cultural development. In 1970, for example, the Intergovernmental Conference on Institutional, Administrative, and Financial Aspects of Cultural Policies, held in Venice, examined the role of public authorities in defining and achieving the objectives of cultural development, and acknowledged for the first time the responsibility of governments to provide and plan for the cultural needs of society by implementing appropriate cultural policies.

The Venice conference was followed by a series of regional conferences on cultural policies—for Europe (in Helsinki, 1972), for Asia (Jakarta, 1973), for Africa (Accra, 1975), and for Latin America and the Caribbean (Bogotá, 1978). Discussions at these meetings reflected a need to locate man and culture at the heart of the development process, rather than considering development as only economic progress. With this central idea as a starting point, UNESCO has defined the objectives and guidelines that are now giving direction to the organization's cultural activities, such as the strengthening of cultural identities, the safeguarding and promotion of cultural heritage, the enlargement of access to culture and participation in cultural life, the stimulation of artistic creativity, and the promotion of cultural cooperation. The principles governing UNESCO's activities in the field of culture include strengthening the cultural dimension of development, that is, viewing culture not only in itself but in relation to certain key areas of development—educational systems (including the cultural content of education and adaptation of teaching models to local culture), the environment, science, and communications.

The World Conference on Cultural Policies, held in Mexico City in 1982, took stock of the experience acquired in policies and practices in the field of culture and gave new impetus to the worldwide action carried out under UNESCO's auspices since the end of the 1960s aimed at promoting international consideration of the problems of culture in the contemporary world. The conference unanimously adopted the Mexico City Declaration on Cultural Policies, which proclaimed the guiding principles for promoting culture and strengthening the cultural dimension of development.

E. COMMUNICATION
UNESCO is enjoined by its constitution to "collaborate in the work of advancing the mutual knowledge and understanding of peoples, through all means of mass communication. . . . " It is also authorized to recommend international agreements to facilitate "the free flow of ideas by word and image" and to encourage the international exchange of persons active in intellectual affairs and the exchange of "publications, objects of scientific interest, and other materials of information." UNESCO considers all these activities part of its work in the field of mass communications.

In recent years, particular emphasis has been given to the problem of disparities in communication in and among developing countries as compared with industrialized states. The great strides in communication technologies, notably in space communication, have only served to emphasize these disparities.

In UNESCO's view, its constitutional responsibilities, and especially those pertaining to communication itself, call upon it to contribute to the removal of imbalances and inequalities in the capacity to produce, disseminate, and receive messages and to eliminate the obstacles to a wider and better balanced flow of information.

New World Information and Communication Order
In 1976, following a decision of the General Conference inviting UNESCO to undertake a review of all the problems of communication in contemporary society in the context of technological progress and recent developments in international relations, an International Commission was appointed to study communication problems. The commission's recommendations were published by UNESCO in 1980 under the title *Many Voices, One World*. The General Conference considered the commission's report in 1980 and proposed 11 considerations on which a New World Information and Communication Order could be based. It also urged UNESCO "to contribute to the clarification, elaboration and application of the concept of a New World Information and Communication Order."

An important landmark in UNESCO's program in the field of communication was the adoption by the General Conference in 1978, after eight years of studies, consultations, and meetings, of the Declaration on Fundamental Principles Concerning the Contribution of the Mass Media to Strengthening Peace and International Understanding, to the Promotion of Human Rights and to Countering Racialism, Apartheid and Incitement to War.

Increased Exchange of News and Programs
In the belief that high tariffs are an obstacle to the free flow of information, a UNESCO Working Group on Telecommunication Tariffs, established in 1979, has recommended special tariffs under a Development Press Bulletin Service and a Conventional Press Bulletin Service to be applied to developing and developed countries, respectively.

In collaboration with the regional broadcasting unions, UNESCO has also been engaged in operational experiments using the international satellite systems INTELSAT and INTERSPUTNIK. The purpose of these experiments is to demonstrate not only the advantages of such exchanges but also the increased flow of information which would be possible if concessionary rate structures were applied.

Since the first World Conference of the International Women's Year, in 1975, UNESCO has continued to promote the use of media to accelerate women's participation in society and encourage their equal integration in development. A series of regional seminars has been organized to focus on the need to promote the access of women to the decision-making levels of media organizations.

Development of Communication

UNESCO's wide range of field programs includes assistance for the development or establishment of radio and television systems, newspapers (mainly rural press), news agencies, book production, distribution infrastructures, film and cinema organizations, and communication training institutions. These projects, financed by UNESCO's regular program and by UNDP, have been increasingly supported by funds-in-trust arrangements with sponsoring countries and regional institutions. The training of production and technical personnel accounts for the major share of project expenditure, with provision of equipment an important component.

Recently, in collaboration with ECA and ITU, UNESCO embarked on a program for the development of communication technologies adapted to the needs and manufacturing capacities of developing countries. These include rural radio stations and solar-powered receivers.

UNESCO identifies and recruits communication specialists for developing countries, particularly specialists who have a background in development. More than 60% of the organization's communication consultants now come from developing countries.

In 1980, the General Conference decided to set up the International Program for the Development of Communication (IPDC) and to establish an Intergovernmental Council composed of 35 members responsible to the General Conference for the implementation of the activities of IPDC. The aim of the program is to mobilize international support to strengthen the infrastructures of developing countries both in manpower and equipment, so as to enable them to produce and disseminate news and programs and thereby do away with the imbalances which exist in the flow of information.

Among the principal regional mechanisms which have recently benefited from IPDC assistance are the Pan-African News Agency (PANA), the Arab project for communication planning and exchange, the Asia-Pacific News Network, the Latin American Special Information Services Agency, and the Caribbean regional project for broadcasting, training, and program exchange. In addition to these regional projects, several interregional proposals, such as the feasibility study on facilities for international dissemination and exchange of information by global satellite systems, and the center for the study of communication, energy, and space technologies, as well as some national projects in many areas in the field of communication, have benefited from IPDC assistance.

F. AGREEMENT ON THE IMPORTATION OF EDUCATIONAL, SCIENTIFIC, AND CULTURAL MATERIALS

The states parties to the Agreement on the Importation of Educational, Scientific, and Cultural Materials and its protocol, adopted by the General Conference of UNESCO at Florence in 1950 and at Nairobi in 1976, respectively, exempt all the following materials from customs duties and any other importation charges: books, newspapers, periodicals; various other categories of printed or duplicated matter; manuscripts including typescripts; music; geographic, hydrographic, and astronomical maps and charts, etc., all irrespective of language and destination; works of art (paintings, drawings, sculpture, etc.) and antiques, defined as articles more than 100 years old; visual and auditory materials such as films, filmstrips, microfilms, sound recordings, glass slides, models, wall charts, posters of an educational, scientific, or cultural character; scientific instruments and apparatus, under condition (a) that they be intended exclusively for educational purposes or pure scientific research; (b) that they be consigned to public or private institutions approved by the importing country as entitled to exemption from customs duty; and (c) that instruments or apparatus of equivalent scientific value not be manufactured in the importing country. Books and other publications for the blind, and other materials of an educational, scientific, or cultural character for the use of the blind are also exempt.

In other words, any individual living in a country where the agreement is in force may import duty free books, works of art, or antiques from any other country where the agreement is in force, in accordance with the provisions of the agreement and protocol.

G. THE UNESCO COUPON PROGRAM

UNESCO coupons are a type of international money order permitting persons living in countries with foreign-exchange restrictions to purchase from abroad books and many other articles of a scientific or cultural nature.

A person living in a country that participates in the UNESCO coupon plan who wishes to obtain from another participating country an item covered by the plan buys the required UNESCO coupons, pays for them in local currency at the official UN rate, and mails them abroad without having to go through any formalities. To redeem the coupons, the seller sends them to Bankers Trust Company in New York (for the Americas), the Japan Society for the Promotion of Science in Tokyo (for Asia and the Far East), or to UNESCO's headquarters in Paris (for Europe and Africa). They are redeemed in the seller's national currency at the official UN exchange rate, after the deduction of a handling charge. In September 1983, 95 countries were participating in the UNESCO coupon plan, and about $230 million in coupons had been redeemed since the project was launched in 1948.

H. ENCOURAGEMENT OF INTERNATIONAL EXCHANGES

As a means of promoting education, research, and international understanding, UNESCO aids and encourages various forms of exchange between its member states. It acts as a clearinghouse for governments as well as international organizations on all questions of exchange, administers its own program of fellowships and exchange of experts, and promotes study, training, and teaching abroad with the cooperation of governments and organizations. The principal publication issued by the exchange service is *Study Abroad*, a trilingual publication issued every two years, listing more than 200,000 individual opportunities for subsidized higher education and training abroad through a wide variety of fellowships, scholarships, and educational exchange programs of some 2,600 awarding agencies in 130 different countries and territories.

I. COOPERATIVE ACTION PROGRAM

UNESCO's Cooperative Action Program (Co-Action) enables individuals and groups to make direct contributions to community development projects in developing countries, such as schools, libraries, and vocational institutions for the disabled. An illustrated catalog of selected Co-Action projects describing some of the priority needs and estimated costs is issued by UNESCO's Public Liaison Division.

Contributions through the Co-Action program have totaled more than $7 million, but its significance is more than a matter of money. Direct "people-to-people" relationships are established between donors and recipients that have often developed into lasting friendships. In addition, the program has a special appeal for school groups.

Within the framework of the UN Decade for Women (1976–85), the Co-Action program has sponsored projects for the advancement of women run under the direct responsibility of local women's groups in developing countries.

[8]BIBLIOGRAPHY

The ABC of Copyright.
Copyright Bulletin. Quarterly.
Cultures. Quarterly review.
Educational Documentation and Information. Quarterly bulletin.
General History of Africa.

Impact of Science on Society. Quarterly.
Index Translationum. International bibliography of translations.
International Marine Science Newsletter. Quarterly.
International Social Science Journal. Quarterly.
Museum. Illustrated quarterly.
The International Yearbook of Education.
New UNESCO Source Book for Science Teaching.
Prospects. Quarterly review of education.
Study Abroad.
The UNESCO Courier. Illustrated monthly magazine.

UNESCO's Standard-Setting Instruments. Texts of UNESCO conventions, agreements, recommendations, declarations.
UNESCO Statistical Digest.
UNESCO Statistical Yearbook.
UNESCO Thesaurus.
(UNESCO also issues publications on such topics as education and rural development, educational buildings and equipment, agricultural education, technical and vocational training, earth sciences, hydrology, oceanography, natural resources, social sciences, and communications.)

THE WORLD HEALTH ORGANIZATION (WHO)

¹BACKGROUND: In taking the pulse of global health in 1974, WHO member states concluded that despite vaccines, antibiotic drugs, and a host of extraordinary advances in medical technology, the world was far from healthy. There was a "signal failure," the 27th World Health Assembly concluded, to provide basic services to two-thirds of the world's population, particularly to rural inhabitants and the urban poor, who, despite being the most needy and in the majority, were the most neglected.

That assessment—made two dozen years after WHO's establishment—led to a reorientation of WHO's outlook and to the adoption of the goal of "Health for All by the Year 2000" through the approach of primary health care. The main task of WHO through the end of this century is to work to ensure that people everywhere have access to health services that will enable them to lead socially and economically productive lives.

During the 19th century, waves of communicable diseases swept Europe, accompanying the growth of railways and steam navigation. Yet the first international sanitary conference, attended by 12 governments, was not held until 1851. An international convention on quarantine was drawn up, but it was ratified by only three states. Progress was slow.

The limited objectives of the nations participating in these early conferences also militated against the success of international health efforts. International public health did not come of age until the 20th century. The first international health bureau with its own secretariat was established by the republics of the Americas in 1902—the International Sanitary Bureau. The name was changed in 1923 to the Pan American Sanitary Bureau.

The idea of a permanent international agency to deal with health questions was seriously discussed for the first time at the 4th conference (1874), but it was not until the 11th conference (1903) that the establishment of such an agency was recommended. By that time, scientific discoveries concerning cholera, plague, and yellow fever had been generally accepted. The agency, known as the Office International d'Hygiène Publique (OIHP), was created in December 1907 by an agreement signed by 12 states (Belgium, Brazil, Egypt, France, Italy, Netherlands, Portugal, Russia, Spain, Switzerland, the UK, and the US). The OIHP was located in Paris, and its first staff consisted of nine persons. Originally a predominantly European institution, OIHP grew to include nearly 60 countries and colonies before the outbreak of World War I.

World War I left in its wake disastrous pandemics. The influenza wave of 1918–19 was estimated to have killed 15 to 20 million people, and in 1919 almost 250,000 cases of typhus were reported in Poland and more than 1.6 million in the USSR. Other disasters also made heavy demands on OIHP.

OIHP found itself overburdened with work. Early in 1920 a plan for a permanent international health organization was approved by the League of Nations. United official action to combat the typhus epidemic then raging in Poland was urged by the League council. OIHP, however, was unable to participate in an interim combined League-OIHP committee. This was partly because the US, which was not a member of the League, wished to remain in OIHP but could not if OIHP were absorbed into a League-connected agency. OIHP existed for another generation, maintaining a formal relationship with the League of Nations.

OIHP's main concern continued to be supervision and improvement of international quarantine measures. Smallpox and typhus were added to the quarantinable diseases by the International Sanitary Convention in 1926. Also adopted were measures requiring governments to notify OIHP immediately of any outbreak of plague, cholera, or yellow fever, or of the appearance of smallpox or typhus in epidemic form.

The League of Nations established a permanent epidemiological intelligence service to collect and disseminate worldwide data on the status of epidemic diseases of international significance. The Malaria Commission was founded, and adopted a new international approach: to study and advise on control of the disease in regions where it exists rather than to work out the conventional precautions to prevent its spread from country to country. The annual reports of the League's Cancer Commission on such matters as results of radiotherapy in cancer of the uterus became an important source of international information on that disease. Other technical commissions included those on typhus, leprosy, and biological standardization.

Most of the work of OIHP and the League's health units was cut short by World War II, although the *Weekly Epidemiological Record* continued. Fear of new postwar epidemics prompted the Allies to draw up plans for action. At its first meeting in 1943, the newly created United Nations Relief and Rehabilitation Administration (UNRRA) put health work among its "primary and fundamental responsibilities."

²CREATION

At its first meeting, in 1946, the UN Economic and Social Council decided to call an international conference to consider the establishment of a single health organization of the UN. The conference met in New York and on 22 July adopted a constitution for the World Health Organization, which would carry on the functions previously performed by the League and OIHP.

WHO did not come into existence until April 1948, when its constitution was ratified by the required 26 UN member states. In the meantime, UNRRA was dissolved and a WHO Interim Commission carried out the most indispensable of UNRRA's health functions. The first WHO assembly convened in June 1948.

Among the severe problems that beset the Interim Commission was a cholera epidemic in Egypt in 1947. Three cases were reported on 22 September; by October, 33,000 cases were reported in widely separated areas on both sides of the Red Sea and the Suez Canal. Urgent calls for vaccine were sent out by the Interim Commission within hours after the first three cases were reported, and by means of a history-making cholera airlift, 20 million doses of vaccine were flown to Cairo from the US, the USSR, India, and elsewhere, one-third of them outright gifts.

The cholera epidemic claimed 20,472 lives in Egypt by February 1948. During the epidemic the number of countries ratifying WHO's constitution increased by almost 50%.

³PURPOSES

WHO's main functions can be summed up as follows: to act as directing and coordinating authority on international health work; to ensure valid and productive technical cooperation; and to promote research.

WHO establishes norms and standards in a variety of fields, including food, biological and pharmaceutical matters, diagnostic procedures, environmental health, and the international nomenclature and classification of diseases. An important WHO function is the generation and international transfer of valid information on health matters. WHO serves as a clearinghouse for health information of many kinds.

Besides providing technical cooperation for individual member states, WHO facilitates technical cooperation between them, whether they are developed or developing countries. It helps countries reinforce their health systems by building up infrastructure, which includes services for the individual, family, and community; health institutions and manpower; systems for referring complex problems to more specialized services; and the provision of essential drugs and other supplies and equipment.

WHO promotes the research required to develop appropriate health technologies and to identify social and behavioral approaches that could lead to healthier lifestyles in both industrialized and developing societies. These technical, social, and behavioral investigations relate to all aspects of health, including nutrition, safety of the environment, water quality and sanitation, mental health, the control of specific diseases, accident prevention, medical care, and rehabilitation.

⁴MEMBERSHIP

UN members can join WHO by unilateral, formal notification to the UN secretary-general that they accept the WHO constitution. A non-UN member may be admitted if its application is approved by a simple majority vote of the World Health Assembly. Territories or groups of territories "not responsible for the conduct of their international relations" may be admitted as associate members upon application by the authority responsible for their international relations.

As of March 1983, WHO had 160 member states and 1 associate member:

Afghanistan
Albania
Algeria
Angola
Argentina
Australia
Austria
Bahamas
Bahrain
Bangladesh
Barbados
Belgium
Benin
Bhutan
Bolivia
Botswana
Brazil
Bulgaria
Burma
Burundi
Byelorussia
Cameroon
Canada
Cape Verde

Central African Rep.
Chad
Chile
China
Colombia
Comoros
Congo
Costa Rica
Cuba
Cyprus
Czechoslovakia
Denmark
Djibouti
Dominica
Dominican Republic
Ecuador
Egypt
El Salvador
Equatorial Guinea
Ethiopia
Fiji
Finland
France
Gabon
Gambia
German Dem. Rep.
Germany, Fed. Rep.
Ghana
Greece
Grenada
Guatemala
Guinea
Guinea-Bissau
Guyana
Haiti
Honduras
Hungary
Iceland
India
Indonesia
Iran
Iraq
Ireland
Israel
Italy
Ivory Coast
Jamaica
Japan
Jordan
Kampuchea
Kenya
Korea, Dem. People's Rep.
Korea, Rep.
Kuwait
Laos
Lebanon
Lesotho
Liberia
Libya
Luxembourg
Madagascar
Malawi
Malaysia
Maldives
Mali
Malta
Mauritania
Mauritius
Mexico
Monaco
Mongolia
Morocco
Mozambique
Nepal

Netherlands
New Zealand
Nicaragua
Niger
Nigeria
Norway
Oman
Pakistan
Panama
Papua New Guinea
Paraguay
Peru
Philippines
Poland
Portugal
Qatar
Romania
Rwanda
St. Lucia
San Marino
São Tomé and Príncipe
Sa'udi Arabia
Senegal
Seychelles
Sierra Leone
Singapore
Solomon Islands
Somalia
South Africa
Spain
Sri Lanka
Sudan
Suriname
Swaziland
Sweden
Switzerland
Syria
Tanzania
Thailand
Togo
Tonga
Trinidad and Tobago
Tunisia
Turkey
Uganda
Ukraine
USSR
United Arab Emirates
UK
US
Upper Volta
Uruguay
Vanuatu
Venezuela
Viet-Nam
Western Samoa
Yemen, People's Dem. Rep.
Yemen Arab Rep.
Yugoslavia
Zaire
Zambia
Zimbabwe

Associate Member
   Namibia

⁵STRUCTURE

The principal organs of WHO are the World Health Assembly, the Executive Board, and the Secretariat.

World Health Assembly

All WHO members are represented in the World Health Assembly. Each member has one vote but may send three delegates. According to the WHO constitution, the delegates are to be chosen for their technical competence and preferably should represent national health administrations. Delegations may include alternates and advisers. The assembly meets annually, usually in May, for approximately three weeks. Most assemblies have been held at WHO headquarters in Geneva. A president is elected by each assembly.

The World Health Assembly determines the policies of the organization and deals with budgetary, administrative, and similar questions. By a two-thirds vote the assembly may adopt conventions or agreements. While these are not binding on member governments until accepted by them, WHO members have to "take action" leading to their acceptance within 18 months. Thus each member government, even if its delegation voted against a convention in assembly, must act: for example, it must submit the convention to its legislature for ratification. It must then notify WHO of the action taken. If the action is unsuccessful, it must notify WHO of the reasons for nonacceptance.

In addition, the assembly has quasi-legislative powers to adopt regulations on important technical matters specified in the WHO constitution. Once such a regulation is adopted by the assembly, it applies to all WHO member countries (including those whose delegates voted against it) except those whose governments specifically notify WHO that they reject the regulation or accept it only with certain reservations.

WHO is empowered to introduce uniform technical regulations on the following matters: (1) sanitary and quarantine requirements and other procedures designed to prevent international epidemics; (2) nomenclature with respect to disease, causes of death, and public health practices; (3) standards with respect to diagnostic procedures for international use; (4) standards with respect to safety, purity, and potency of biological, pharmaceutical, and similar products in international commerce; (5) advertising and labeling of biological, pharmaceutical, and similar products in international commerce.

The assembly at its first session, in 1948, adopted World Health Regulation No. 1, *Nomenclature with Respect to Diseases and Causes of Death*. This regulation guides member countries in compiling statistics on disease and death and, by providing for a standardized nomenclature, facilitates their comparison. World Health Regulation No. 2 deals with quarantinable diseases.

Each year, the assembly doubles as a scientific conference on a specific topic of worldwide health interest, selected in advance. These technical discussions are held in addition to other business. They enable the delegates, who as a rule are top-ranking public health experts, to discuss common problems more thoroughly than formal committee debates would permit. Governments are asked to contribute special working papers and studies to these discussions and, if practicable, to send experts on the matters to be discussed with their delegations.

Executive Board

The World Health Assembly may elect any 30 member countries (the only rule being equitable geographic distribution) for three-year terms, and each of the countries elected designates one person "technically qualified in the field of health" to the WHO Executive Board. The countries are elected by rotation, eight every year, and may succeed themselves. Board members serve as individuals and not as representatives of their governments.

The Executive Board is the executive organ of the World Health Assembly. One of its important functions is to prepare the assembly's agenda. It meets twice a year, for sessions of a few days to several weeks, but it may convene a special meeting at any time. The WHO constitution authorizes the board "to take emergency measures within the functions and financial resources of the Organization to deal with events requiring immediate action. In particular, it may authorize the director-general to take the necessary steps to combat epidemics and to participate in the organization of health relief to victims of a calamity."

Director-General and Secretariat

The Secretariat comprises the technical and administrative personnel of the organization. It is headed by a director-general, appointed by the assembly. The first director-general of WHO was Dr. Brock Chisholm of Canada. He was succeeded in 1953 by Dr. Marcolino G. Candau of Brazil, and in 1973 by Dr. Halfdan T. Mahler of Denmark.

At the end of March 1983, WHO had a total staff of 4,437, including those employed at headquarters (Geneva) and in the field, those financed by voluntary funds, and those employed by the International Agency for Research on Cancer (Lyon, France).

WHO's activities have been progressively decentralized. There are six regional offices, each covering a major geographic region of the world. These are located in Alexandria for the Eastern Mediterranean area, in Manila for the Western Pacific area, in New Delhi for the Southeast Asia area, in Copenhagen for Europe, in Brazzaville for the African area, and in Washington, where the directing council of the Pan American Health Organization acts as the regional committee of WHO in the Americas.

While all work of direct assistance to individual member governments is decentralized to the regional offices, the Geneva headquarters is where the work of the regions is coordinated and worldwide technical services are organized, including collection and dissemination of information. Headquarters cooperates with the UN, specialized agencies, and voluntary organizations, and is responsible for medical research.

WHO assistance is given in response to a request from a government. Member governments meet annually in regional committees to review and plan WHO activities for their areas. Requests are consolidated by the regional directors and forwarded to the director-general, who incorporates regional programs and their estimated costs into the overall WHO draft program and budget. The program and budget, after review by the Executive Board, are submitted to the World Health Assembly.

6BUDGET

For 1949, the first year of WHO's existence, its regular budget amounted to $5 million. A budget of $520.1 million was approved by the World Health Assembly for 1984–85.

7ACTIVITIES

Under the global "Health for All" strategy, WHO and its member states have resolved to place special emphasis on the developing countries. Nevertheless, the benefits of WHO's international health work are reaped by all countries, including the most developed. For example, all nations have benefited from their contributions to the WHO programs that led to the global eradication of smallpox and to better and cheaper ways of controlling tuberculosis.

Prevention is a key word in WHO. It believes that immunization, which prevents the six major communicable diseases of childhood —diphtheria, measles, poliomyelitis, tetanus, tuberculosis, and whooping cough—should be available to all children who need it. WHO is leading a worldwide campaign to provide effective immunization for all children by 1990.

Provision of safe drinking water and adequate excreta disposal for all are the objectives of the International Drinking Water Supply and Sanitation Decade proclaimed by the UN in 1981 and supported by WHO.

WHO is also active in international efforts to combat the diarrheal diseases, killers of infants and young children. The widespread introduction of oral rehydration salts, together with improved drinking water supply and sanitation, will, it is hoped, greatly reduce childhood mortality from diarrhea.

WHO's program for primary health care contains eight essential elements: (1) education concerning prevalent health problems and the methods of preventing and controlling them; (2)

promotion of food supply and proper nutrition; (3) maintenance of an adequate supply of safe water and basic sanitation; (4) provision of maternal and child health care, including family planning; (5) immunization against the major infectious diseases; (6) prevention and control of locally endemic diseases; (7) appropriate treatment of common diseases and injuries; and (8) provision of essential drugs. These eight elements were defined in the Declaration of Alma-Ata, which emerged from the International Conference on Primary Health Care, held in Alma-Ata, USSR, in 1978.

A. COMMUNICABLE DISEASES
Cholera

Since 1961, cholera caused by the *El Tor vibrio* has spread from its endemic foci and gradually invaded practically all countries in the Western Pacific and Southeast Asia regions, most of which had been free from cholera for many years. Cholera continued to spread westward, reaching West Pakistan, Afghanistan, Iran, and Uzbekistan (USSR) in 1965 and Iraq in 1966. The spread of cholera in 1969 and 1970 created great problems in the Middle East, North and West Africa, and Europe. Furthermore, it was shown that most of the persons who come in contact with *El Tor vibrio* become mild cases or carriers of the disease, thus spreading infection.

Numerous field and laboratory studies, organized mostly by WHO, showed that current control measures are rather ineffective. The anticholera vaccines in use, when tested in controlled field trials, were shown to protect at most about half the persons vaccinated and for less than six months. Some vaccines provided no protection at all.

In view of these findings, WHO has intensified its research activities in improving treatment and vaccines; it is also trying to reinforce the ability of governments to face the problem of cholera within the framework of control programs directed against diarrheal diseases in general. With modern treatment, case fatalities should be no more than 1% to 3%.

A simple and inexpensive oral-rehydration treatment, proved effective in the 1970s for all acute diarrhea, has made cholera treatment substantially easier. As most of the cases of *El Tor* cholera cannot be differentiated from other diarrheal diseases on clinical grounds, WHO has developed a comprehensive and expanded program for the control of *all* diarrheal diseases, including cholera.

Leprosy

Leprosy is a serious public health problem in the developing countries, particularly because the populations exposed to the risk of contracting the disease are very large (about 1.4 billion), and more than one-third of leprosy patients face the threat of permanent and progressive physical and social disability. WHO's global estimate of leprosy patients is 10.6 million cases, but the problem of leprosy is far more serious than the numbers alone indicate, especially because of the suffering that results from the social problems related to the disease.

More than 5 million patients are now registered, an increase of over 2 million during the past decade. During the same period, it is estimated that approximately 1.5 million leprosy cases have been cured and released from control. In a few places, where it was possible to implement well-organized control programs over long periods of time, the prevalence of leprosy was reduced by up to 80%.

The establishment by WHO in 1974 of an international program of research into the immunology of leprosy was followed in 1976 by a research program on the therapy of leprosy. When the Special Program for Research and Training in Tropical Diseases, sponsored by UNDP, the World Bank, and WHO, became operational in 1976, leprosy was one of the six tropical diseases chosen for intensified research.

A major problem which threatened the progress made in control during the past three decades was the growing resistance of *Mycobacterium leprae* to dapsone. Cases of both secondary and primary resistance have been proven in many countries and their prevalence appears to be on the increase. A WHO study group was convened in 1981 to define chemotherapy suitable for the control of leprosy under field conditions. As a direct result of the knowledge accumulated under WHO's program on the therapy of leprosy, the study group was able to recommend multidrug regimens designed to deal with the problem of resistance and also to reduce significantly the periods of time previously required to treat patients effectively. These regimens are being increasingly adopted by the governments of endemic countries.

Vaccines have proved to be potent weapons in the control of communicable diseases, and one of the main aims of WHO's program of research on the immunology of leprosy is the production of an anti-leprosy vaccine. Considerable progress has been made, and for the first time a batch of purified, killed *M. leprae* has been produced on licensed premises for human use. Much work still remains to be done in testing the vaccine, and it will be at least a decade before scientists can be sure of the value of the trial vaccine.

Trachoma

Trachoma, a communicable eye disease that is the leading cause of preventable blindness, is endemic in many regions. Trachoma can be prevented and cured by various antibiotics and sulfonamides. Large-scale campaigns to prevent blindness from trachoma have been successfully undertaken in several countries, utilizing the intermittent application of antibiotic eye ointment or drops. Such campaigns have to be conducted over a sufficient time period, and must be linked with the provision of facilities for treatment of complications due to trachoma, especially surgery for deformation of the eyelids. An essential factor for control of trachoma is health education aimed at changing local factors relevant to transmission of the infection.

Increased understanding of the natural history of the disease has been obtained through epidemiological studies based on comparable criteria and to a certain extent on the utilization of new methods for the laboratory diagnosis of the infection. The existence of a "pool" of causative organisms in women and children in many communities in trachoma-endemic areas is receiving increasing attention, as it serves as a source of reinfection. This aspect, together with recent evidence that several general disorders may be caused by strains of the same agent as trachoma, has led to more frequent use of systemic antibiotic treatment to control trachoma.

Smallpox

WHO's program to eradicate smallpox from the world marks the first time a human malady has ever been totally eliminated. This became feasible because the virus causing the disease is transmitted only by direct human contagion; there are no animal reservoirs or human "carriers." Victims of the disease are immune to further attacks, while successful vaccination at three-year intervals gives essentially complete protection.

Eradication was based on a two-fold strategy of surveillance-containment and vaccination. Rapid detection of cases, their immediate isolation, and the vaccination of anyone with whom the patient could have come in contact during the infective period, lasting about three weeks after the onset of rash, prevents further transmission. Implementation of these procedures, coupled with the basic immunity level attributable to routine immunization, resulted in the eradication of smallpox everywhere in the world.

Although a global program of eradication was initiated in 1959, it was not until 1967, when a special WHO budget with increased bilateral and multilateral support was prepared, that a definitive target date of 10 years was set for global eradication. By the end of 1977, this goal was achieved.

In 1967, 131,418 cases of smallpox were reported from 43 countries, but the actual number of cases was estimated to have been more than 2.5 million. Since that time, WHO has convened many international commissions which certified smallpox eradication in 79 recently endemic countries. The global eradication of the disease was declared by the World Health Assembly in 1980. Consequently, by the beginning of 1983 almost all countries of the world had discontinued routine smallpox vaccination.

Diseases Transmissible Between Animals and Man (Zoonoses) and Related Problems

Since its inception, WHO has been developing veterinary public health programs in cooperation with its member states. In the 1970s, WHO's veterinary public health program was reoriented toward more direct collaboration with member states in the development of national and intercountry programs in which zoonoses and food-borne diseases control receive the highest priority. This was justified because these diseases have become increasingly prevalent in many countries mainly as a result of: the greatly expanded international and national trade in live animals, animal products, and animal feedstuffs, which facilitates the spread of infection; the growth of urbanization, coupled with the increased numbers of domestic and half-wild animals living in close association with city populations, which exposes more people to zoonoses; and changing patterns of land use, such as irrigation, and new systems of animal farming, which may lead to changes in the ecology that disseminate and increase animal reservoirs of zoonoses.

The 1978 World Health Assembly adopted a resolution on "prevention and control of zoonoses and food-borne diseases due to animal products" in which member states were invited to formulate and implement appropriate countrywide programs for the control of zoonoses; to strengthen cooperation between national veterinary and public health services in improving the surveillance, prevention, and control of these diseases; and to collaborate further in ensuring the appropriate development of zoonoses centers. The resolution also requested the director-general to continue development of national, regional, and global strategies and of methods for the surveillance, prevention, and control of zoonoses, and to promote the extension of the network of zoonoses centers in all regions so that the necessary support could be provided to country health programs dealing with these diseases.

WHO cooperates with member states in planning, implementing, and evaluating their national zoonoses and food-borne diseases control programs. WHO centers, such as those in Athens (Mediterranean Zoonoses Control Center) and Buenos Aires (Pan-American Zoonoses Control Center), play an increasing role in the direct collaboration with countries and in organizing intercountry technical cooperation. A network of such centers has been planned.

After the eradication of smallpox and with the introduction of efficient preventive measures against six diseases covered by the WHO Expanded Program on Immunization (diphtheria, measles, tetanus, poliomyelitis, pertussis, and tuberculosis), zoonoses remains the most serious communicable disease.

Influenza

The wave of influenza that swept over the world in 1918–19 was the greatest epidemic in history. Approximately 1 billion persons were affected, of whom perhaps as many as 1 out of 50 died. Epidemic influenza often attacks 30% to 40% of a country's population, and is frequently accompanied by secondary complications such as bacterial pneumonia.

There are several types of influenza viruses. The virus of human influenza A was discovered in 1933, and that of influenza B in 1940. Each influenza virus has many subtypes and variants. No variant immunizes against any other, and new ones may appear at any time. For effective vaccination, the virus causing a specific epidemic must be known. Hence, science must constantly be on the alert for new strains and their possible epidemiological impact on influenza, including reliable and internationally comparable virus tests, which must be continuously exchanged.

Because reports on influenza outbreaks can be interpreted correctly only through laboratory studies of the virus responsible, WHO set up a network of national influenza laboratories, with international centers in London and Atlanta. National laboratories report with all speed the occurrence of influenza and isolate and identify the virus. The viruses are dispatched by air to London or Atlanta for further study and for comparison with strains isolated elsewhere. Strains that show unusual characteristics are exchanged without delay so that they are available in both hemispheres for vaccine production if required. The WHO network of 108 collaborating laboratories keeps track of influenza epidemics. Both epidemiological information from the national collaborating laboratories and virological information from London and Atlanta are disseminated weekly by WHO from Geneva to all health administrations throughout the world.

Global Epidemiological Surveillance
In the Weekly Epidemiological Record (WER), WHO publishes notes on communicable diseases of international importance and information concerning the application of the International Health Regulations. In the past the publication was chiefly a summary of the weekly or daily notifications of diseases under the regulations, with declarations of infected areas or of freedom from infection when attained. It then became the vehicle for timely reports, narrative summaries, and interpretative comments on a variety of communicable disease topics. Annual, semiannual, or quarterly summaries are published on major trends in diseases receiving special attention, such as malaria and smallpox. Data from special surveillance programs, such as smallpox eradication, the global influenza program, the European program for salmonella, and dengue-hemorrhagic fever surveillance, are summarized and published at appropriate intervals. The WER also communicates important changes in the International Health Regulations or the changing policies of the member states.

B. NONCOMMUNICABLE HEALTH PROBLEMS

Cancer
Cancer, a noncommunicable disease, has recently been ranked as the second or third of the main causes of death globally among persons who survive the first five years of life. Contrary to the general belief that cancer occurs mainly in the industrialized world, it is estimated that more than half of all cancer patients today are in developing countries.

In May 1982, the World Health Assembly endorsed the WHO cancer program, which urges countries to take, without delay, positive control measures that are already known, such as the cessation of tobacco smoking and chewing, vaccination against virus B hepatitis, and early detection of cancers of the mouth, skin, and cervix uteri. Such measures, if implemented, would have an important effect on cancer globally.

The International Agency for Research on Cancer, as part of WHO, continues research on identification of carcinogenic factors in the environment, as well as lifestyle factors in cancer development.

Cigarette Smoking
Cigarette smoking is one of the largest preventable causes of premature mortality and ill health, particularly in industrialized countries but also in developing countries, where it is spreading. Cigarette smoking is estimated to be responsible for about 90% of lung cancer deaths, 75% of bronchitis deaths, and 25% of coronary heart disease deaths. It is estimated that, worldwide, at least 1 million premature deaths annually are caused by cigarette smoking. It may bring about circulatory complications in women using oral contraceptives, cause lower body weight in newborns of smoking mothers, and be associated with cancers of organs other than the lungs.

Tobacco use is considered as a dependence disorder in WHO's 9th International Classification of Diseases. WHO has taken the lead in international action to stem the spread of smoking and its harmful health consequences. It collaborates with numerous national smoking and health associations around the world, as well as with nongovernmental organizations and other UN agencies. WHO collaborating reference centers assist in analyses of toxic components of cigarettes from developing countries. Seminars and conferences muster scientific knowledge and political support.

Occupational Health
WHO's Occupational Health Program has four main aims: (1) health protection of the underserved working populations who constitute the bulk of the economically productive manpower in developing countries; (2) strengthening of general health services through the application of occupational health technologies and approaches; (3) workers' participation in their health care delivery systems; and (4) development of occupational health science, technology, and practice.

The program incorporates identification and control of "work-related diseases," recognition of neuro-behavioral changes in occupational exposure to health hazards, control of occupational impairment in reproductive functions and other delayed effects and of adverse occupational psychosocial hazards, and the application of ergonomics as a factor in health promotion. WHO cooperates with countries in the development of their institutional framework for the health care of working people. Special attention is given to occupational health aspects of employed women, children, the elderly, migrant workers, and other groups.

C. EXPANDED PROGRAM ON IMMUNIZATION
Immunization, one of the most powerful and cost-effective weapons of disease prevention, remains tragically underutilized. In the developing world today, 10 children die and another 10 become disabled with each passing minute because of the unavailability of immunizations. Diseases such as neonatal tetanus and poliomyelitis, which have been virtually eliminated in most of the developed world, continue to take a heavy toll in developing countries. Measles, which kills only some 2 per 10,000 cases in the US, kills 2 per 100 cases in the developing world, the figure rising to 10 or more in malnourished populations. Whooping cough is another major killer, particularly in infants less than six months old; diphtheria and tuberculosis are other serious problems. During the course of a year, 5 million children will die and another 5 million will become crippled, deaf, blind, or mentally retarded because of these six vaccine-preventable diseases.

With the help of UNICEF, UNDP, national donor agencies, and voluntary agencies, WHO is sponsoring a global Expanded Program on Immunization, with the goal of providing immunizations for all children of the world by 1990. An estimated $72 million was invested in the program in 1981, two-thirds from developing countries themselves. But at an estimated cost of $5 per fully immunized child, some $500 million will be required each year by the end of the decade to reach the 100 million children needing coverage in the developing world.

Since its inception in 1974, the Expanded Program on Immunization has grown to the point that all developing countries are now taking active measures to increase immunization, particularly of infants under 1 year of age. By 1982, coverage of children in developing countries in their first year of life with one dose of BCG and measles vaccines and with three doses of DPT and poliomyelitis vaccines was estimated at about 20%.

In its coordinating role, WHO has given priority to the managerial training of health workers and the development of cold-chain systems in order to provide for the establishment of vaccine delivery mechanisms capable of achieving high coverage of susceptible populations with vaccines known to be safe and potent at the time of use.

D. FAMILY HEALTH

Since 1970 WHO has developed a program in family health covering maternal and child health and nutrition. The program is systematically identifying the special health needs and problems of the family as the basic social unit, particularly during the critical phases of reproduction, growth, and development. Stress is placed on an epidemiological and educational approach to the interrelationships of the various components. A priority of the program is the development of comprehensive care, particularly for the vulnerable and high-risk groups; maternal and child health, nutrition, and health education form priority core elements of primary health care. This is in the context of the high rates of human wastage resulting from malnutrition, infection, and unregulated fertility, which mainly affect mothers and children. This approach necessitates the cooperation of many disciplines as well as the development of soundly based country health programming to ensure that family health care is fully integrated within the total health care system. The development of appropriate health manpower is an essential part of the program. WHO gives direct assistance to some 80 countries in the development of maternal and child health care, family planning, nutrition, and health education.

Maternal and Child Health

From the beginning of WHO activities, maternal and child health was included as a priority program. WHO assists governments in their efforts to reduce maternal, perinatal, infant, and childhood mortality and morbidity and to stimulate and facilitate the systematic and expanded application of preventive, curative, and rehabilitative measures in maternal and child care through the provision of health and other social services, in order to promote optimum physical growth and psychosocial development of the child, improve reproductive health, and enhance the quality of human life. The approaches adopted in this program are as follows:

(a) identifying the extent and nature of the main health needs of mothers and children during stages of rapid change and of increased psychobiological and social demands—the periods of fetal and child growth and development, and the reproductive period;

(b) developing methods, and formulating technical principles and guidelines, for activities in maternal and child care (including family planning), and disseminating relevant information to health or other authorities concerned and to training and research institutions;

(c) providing technical guidance on the systematic planning of alternative strategies for the implementation, management, and evaluation of maternal and child health and family-planning programs, as part of the strengthening of health services;

(d) promoting the development of health manpower (including auxiliaries, volunteer aides, and community workers) for the delivery of maternal and child care at various levels;

(e) identifying and giving support in priority areas to collaborative research in basic, clinical, and applied aspects of pediatrics, obstetrics, and maternal and child health in general, including research to facilitate and evaluate the application of the risk approach in the delivery of maternal and child health and family-planning care;

(f) collaborating at national and international levels with various organizations and agencies actively concerned with maternal and child health activities, and coordinating and contributing to the development of intersectoral policies and programs.

Nutrition

Formal international interest in human nutrition dates only from the 1930s, following reports of the health organization of the League of Nations. Food shortages during World War II focused attention on the subject, and in 1948 the first World Health Assembly gave priority to nutrition in the program of WHO. Studies carried out since then showing the magnitude and severity of malnutrition, particularly in the developing countries, and a serious deterioration of the world food supplies, analyzed in the first UN World Food Conference held in 1974, have given a greater urgency to the problem.

The work of WHO, in cooperation with other UN specialized agencies, particularly FAO and UNICEF, as well as with interested bilateral and nongovernmental agencies, has been devoted primarily to the following areas: nutrition requirements; assessment of nutritional status; interrelation of nutrition with other health problems; nutrition activities in the primary health care system; prevention, care, and rehabilitation of the common nutritional deficiencies in developing countries; protein-energy malnutrition, vitamin A deficiency, nutritional anemias, and endemic goiter; and food and nutrition planning. WHO also cooperates with member governments in the development of applied research and services in the field of human nutrition, as well as in the training of health-related personnel in this field.

E. MENTAL HEALTH

The objectives of the program in mental health are the reduction of psychiatric and neurologic morbidity, the utilization of mental health skills in the improvement of general health services, and an increased awareness of mental health aspects of social action. Activities, involving governments and institutions in some 80 countries, range from improvement of mental health services delivery, manpower development, and information exchange to research into the epidemiology and biology of mental disorders.

A number of international collaborative studies have been sponsored and coordinated by WHO. These have focused on the form and course of mental disorders in different cultures, on the development of prevention and treatment methods, on the operation of mental health services, and on psychosocial aspects of health and health care. International exchange of information is fostered through publications, training courses, seminars, and networks of collaborating research and training centers in some 40 countries.

The mental health program also includes projects concerned with the development of standardized procedures, diagnostic classifications, and statistics necessary for an improved mental health information system and collaboration in mental health research, and a major program concerned with the prevention and treatment of alcohol and drug dependence.

In all its activities in the field of mental health, WHO fosters the integration of mental health care into the variety of human services aimed at the reduction of morbidity and distress wherever they may arise.

F. DIAGNOSTIC, THERAPEUTIC, AND REHABILITATIVE TECHNOLOGY

Pharmaceutical Products Moving in International Commerce

Since 1964, WHO has studied ways of ensuring that all drugs exported from a country comply with its domestic drug quality requirements. In 1969 a Certification Scheme on the Quality of Pharmaceutical Products Moving in International Commerce was adopted by the World Health Assembly; in 1975 the assembly adopted a revised version. According to the scheme, the health authorities of the exporting countries would provide a certificate that the product is authorized for sale in the exporting country, and that the plant in which the product is produced is subject to regular inspection to ensure that it conforms to good practices of manufacture and quality control as recommended by WHO. Also under the scheme, the importing country may request from the authorities of the exporting country additional information on the controls exercised on the product. If, in addition to the product certificate issued by the competent authority of the exporting country, batch certificates are required, the latter may be issued either by the competent authority of the exporting country or by the manufacturer stating that the quality of the batch complies with quality specifications and indicating the expiration date and storage conditions.

International Biological Standardization

Biological substances cannot be characterized entirely by physical or chemical means. In order to measure their activity (potency) it is therefore necessary to use a biological test using animals, microorganisms, or ligand assays. In such assays the national or working standards are calibrated in international units by the inclusion of appropriate international reference material.

Much work in this field was done under League of Nations auspices. By 1945, 34 international biological standards had been established for such substances as antibiotics, antibodies, antigens, blood products, and related substances and hormones. Since then, WHO has enlisted the collaboration of more than 100 laboratories to conduct international collaborative biological assays, and there are now more than 200 International Reference Materials calibrated in international units.

The work on biological standardization has expanded considerably and comprises a number of new activities, including the establishment of international reference reagents for the purpose of diagnosis and identification. The biological standardization program has responsibility also for ensuring that vaccines are produced and controlled satisfactorily throughout the world. In order to achieve this, requirements have been written on the production and control of specific vaccines and these are published in the *Technical Report Series*. Such requirements are kept up to date in the light of developing technology. By the end of 1982, 35 sets of requirements had been published. In addition, guidelines have been published on such subjects as the setting up of a standard, the testing of an assay kit, and interferon therapy.

A complete list of International Standards, International Reference Preparations, and International Reagents is published in *Biological Substances*, which is kept up to date.

Pharmaceutical Quality Control

International Pharmacopoeia. Attempts to establish internationally agreed-upon specifications for therapeutic agents have been made since the 1850s. By 1910, limited agreements were reached concerning certain potent drugs. Since 1951, WHO has published the *International Pharmacopoeia,* which provides internationally acceptable standards for the purity and potency of pharmaceutical products moving in international commerce that are available for adoption by member states in accordance with the WHO constitution and resolutions of the World Health Assembly.

The first edition, consisting of two volumes and a supplement, was issued between 1951 and 1959. The second edition was published in 1967; a supplement was added in 1971 and additional monographs in 1972. Work on the third edition, started in 1975, aims to accommodate the needs of developing countries by offering sound standards for the essential drugs. The first two volumes were issued in 1979 and 1981, respectively.

International Nonproprietary Names for Drugs. Many pharmaceutical substances are known not only by their nonproprietary, generic, or scientific names, but by various trade names as well. In order to identify each pharmaceutical substance by a unique, universally available nonproprietary name, WHO has set up a procedure to select international nonproprietary names for pharmaceutical substances. Such names are published regularly in the *WHO Chronicle.* By the end of 1982 over 4,600 names had been proposed and published in 48 lists. A sixth cumulative list was published in 1982.

WHO Collaborating Center for Chemical Reference Substances. As a further service in the area of drug quality control, the WHO Collaborating Center for Chemical Reference Substances was established in Solna, Sweden, at the Apotekens Centrallaboratorium in 1955. Its function is to collect, assay, and store chemical reference substances and to make them available free to national and nonprofit laboratories and institutes and, for a nominal fee, to commercial firms. About 110 chemical reference substances needed for tests and assays described in the *International Pharmacopoeia* were available in 1982.

Good Practices in the Manufacture and Quality Control of Drugs. To assist member states with technical advice on adequate control processes in drug manufacture, the World Health Assembly recommended, in 1969, the requirements in a publication entitled *Good Practices in the Manufacture and Quality Control of Drugs.* A revised text was adopted in 1975 by the assembly. The text contains requirements pertaining to personnel, premises, and equipment of manufacturing establishments and to general hygienic and sanitation measures. Special requirements pertain to raw materials, manufacturing operations, and labeling and packaging of products. The organization and duties of a quality-control department and a quality-control laboratory are specified. There is also a recommendation concerning the maintenance of distribution records.

Rehabilitation of the Disabled

Since the early 1950s, WHO has had a program for rehabilitation of the disabled. The program was initially set up to increase awareness of the problems faced by war veterans and to stimulate governments to provide increased services for this group.

During the 1970s, the program was reoriented to promote rehabilitation in developing countries. A new policy was accepted by the World Health Assembly in 1976, making rehabilitation part of primary health care services. WHO then developed a whole series of teaching-training materials to be used at the community level. All of this material has been published in a manual entitled *Training the Disabled in the Community.*

The basic idea governing the program is that training for disabled people can be successfully given by family members, under the guidance and supervision of a local health worker. Referral services are needed for some 30%, mostly for short-term interventions. The program stresses the importance of involving the family and community in rehabilitation.

The WHO program is developing rapidly. Future plans include efforts to provide leadership training for disabled persons so that they can better participate in the planning, implementation, and control of community-based rehabilitation programs.

G. RESEARCH PROMOTION AND DEVELOPMENT

WHO, through its advisory committees on medical research—one for each of the six WHO regions and one at the global level —provides guidelines for research planning, execution, and implementation in health programs directly linked to national priorities. The committees also offer an appropriate forum for the discussion of national and regional experiences and for the detailed formulation of scientific and technological policies in the field of health. Research programs and activities are developed in close coordination with medical research councils or analogous bodies, with particular emphasis on the strengthening of managerial capacities at all levels.

WHO's coordinating role in research calls for the development of a system for the exchange of scientific information and the enlistment of the collaboration of groups of scientists and research workers in various areas for solving key problems and developing methods for most effectively combining their efforts.

WHO has been instrumental in maximizing the utilization of technological resources in the health sector, particularly in respect of disease prevention and control, as well as fertility regulation. Following the confirmation of the worldwide eradication of smallpox, an expanded program of immunization is under way to vaccinate all children against diphtheria, tetanus, pertussis, tuberculosis, poliomyelitis, and measles. In addition, the diagnostic capabilities of microbiological laboratories in developing countries have been strengthened and support has been given in the pharmacological sector and in the field of medicinal plants.

Major breakthroughs have been achieved in the fight against tropical diseases and in the control of infantile diarrhea by means of inexpensive oral rehydration procedures.

Over the years nearly 700 institutions with the necessary expertise and facilities have been designated by WHO as "WHO Collaborating Centers." Another 400 institutions are nationally designated to provide specific technical services. Financial assistance is sometimes provided by WHO through technical services agreements, partially offsetting the much larger expenses borne by the centers themselves.

In order to increase the research potential of member countries, WHO has developed a program to train research workers. The duration of grants varies, but as far as possible they are made sufficiently long to permit the candidate to gain an adequate knowledge of methods and techniques and, very often, to carry out under supervision a specific piece of research.

Communication among scientists is also promoted. A scientist from one country is enabled to visit scientists in other countries for a period of up to three months, thus facilitating personal contact and the exchange of ideas.

WHO promotes meetings, symposia, seminars, and training courses in special techniques, bringing scientists together from various parts of the world. Reports of such meetings are circulated, when appropriate, to the scientific community, as are the reports of expert committees and scientific and consultant groups.

Tropical Disease Research

In response to the immense and growing burden of disease borne by people living in the tropics and in recognition of the need for research to solve the problems impeding disease control, WHO, with the cosponsorship of UNDP and the World Bank, has initiated a Special Program for Research and Training in Tropical Diseases. The program has two interdependent objectives: research on and development of new and improved tools to control six major tropical diseases—malaria, schistosomiasis, filariasis, trypanosomiasis (both African sleeping sickness and Chagas' disease), leishmaniasis, and leprosy; and strengthening of national institutions, including training, to increase the research capabilities of the tropical countries affected by these diseases.

Early results of the special program include progress in drug treatment for malaria, schistosomiasis, and filariasis; biological control of the disease vectors of onchocerciasis and malaria; and development and testing of a possible vaccine against leprosy. There has also been progress in developing the fundamental knowledge required for a vaccine against malaria, and the simple and accurate field tests needed for the diagnosis of malaria, leprosy, and African trypanosomiasis.

The program makes a deliberate effort to have research carried out in those countries which face the problems of tropical diseases, and by their own scientists. This is done by working with the affected countries within the context of national programs of research and development. The percentage of program project support going to tropical developing countries rose from 29% in 1977 to 54% in 1982, primarily through institution strengthening and training support, awarded exclusively to institutions and scientists of developing endemic countries. Since 1977, over 350 individual training grants have been awarded, and in 1982, 63 national institutions were being strengthened.

From the beginning of technical activities in 1977 until the end of 1982, the program had supported 1,655 projects in 88 WHO member countries, and over 2,850 scientists from 126 WHO member countries had participated in the planning, implementation, operation, and evaluation of the program. In total, more than $88 million has been spent in direct support to national scientists and institutions.

Malaria. The main thrusts of malaria research are in drugs and vaccine development. The rapid spread of drug-resistant parasites has created an emergency need for new drugs, and program-

supported scientists have been moving forward on four levels:

(a) field application—completion of the clinical testing of a new and effective drug, mefloquine;

(b) development—clinical testing of mefloquine, alone and in combination with other drugs, to delay the onset of parasite resistance;

(c) new drugs—synthesis and testing of compounds based on totally different chemical formulations, in particular the traditional Chinese medicine qinghaosu;

(d) field evaluation—widespread testing of new microkits for monitoring parasite resistance.

Since 1976 there has been more progress toward a vaccine against malaria than during the previous 50 years, and the possibility of an effective vaccine has moved from a concept viewed with skepticism to a real possibility. Genetic engineering technology has provided the means through which the antigens responsible for stimulating immunity can now be produced on a large enough scale to enable scientists to move ahead rapidly toward the actual development of possible vaccines.

Schistosomiasis. This disease, also known as bilharziasis ("snail fever"), is caused by trematode worms that live in human veins. The disease is endemic in many tropical and subtropical regions of Africa, South America, and the Caribbean. The parasite spends part of its life cycle in freshwater snails, and human beings contract the debilitating disease through wading or swimming in contaminated water.

The tools available for the control of schistosomiasis have changed dramatically in recent years. A number of new, effective drugs are now at the stage of application, and their effectiveness at the village level needs to be assessed.

Filariasis. The most urgent need concerning this family of diseases is for new drugs to treat river blindness (onchocerciasis). Through an international network of collaborating laboratories, the possibilities of developing such drugs have increased in recent years. The discovery of effective animal screens revealed a number of promising new groups of chemical compounds. This, along with the active collaboration of the Onchocerciasis Control Program and the resurgence of interest by pharmaceutical companies in the development of drugs against this disease, has created the opportunities and the environment for success.

Leprosy. The control of leprosy continues to pose difficulties —for example, the increasing incidence of resistance of the leprosy bacillus to dapsone, the standard method of treatment. With major support from WHO's tropical disease program, scientists have developed a possible vaccine against the disease. However, because the disease takes a very long time before revealing itself in man, trials of a possible vaccine are expected to take at least 5 and probably closer to 10 years to complete. Preliminary work is under way to determine whether the vaccine does indeed prevent leprosy.

All components of the WHO Special Program are linked together to enable progress in one part to be applied to others whenever and wherever possible. This interaction occurs most frequently through research in epidemiology, the social and economic sciences, the basic biomedical sciences, and the biological control of vectors. Program-supported efforts in vector control have resulted in the large-scale field application of *Bacillus thuringiensis,* serotype H-14 to control the vectors of both onchocerciasis and malaria. This agent will continue to be improved and readied for large-scale production and widespread application. Other agents, especially those which recycle themselves in their natural environment, will also be evaluated. A five-minute diagnostic test for African sleeping sickness (trypanosomiasis) has been developed and is ready for wide application in the field.

In concert with these efforts, WHO's program will continue to stimulate the tropical countries afflicted by these diseases to assume a leading role in the research required to identify and solve their health problems. This is being done in conjunction with national authorities, through training of nationals and the strengthening of national institutions.

The Special Program depends entirely upon voluntary contributions. From 1975 to the end of 1982, 27 governments (including those of 11 developing countries) and 8 other organizations, together with UNDP, the World Bank, and WHO, contributed over $117 million.

H. HEALTH MANPOWER DEVELOPMENT

WHO's role in health manpower development is to collaborate with its member states in their efforts to plan, train, deploy, and manage teams of health personnel made up of the numbers and types required (and that they can afford), and to help ensure that such personnel are socially responsible and possess appropriate technical, scientific, and management competence.

WHO's program for the development of health manpower concentrates on two main areas: the managerial process for health manpower development and the formation of health personnel. The program's activities aim at fostering national and international action so that: all countries will have health manpower policies formulated as an integral part of national health policy and the majority of countries will have health manpower plans based on these policies and will take steps to implement and monitor them; all countries will have developed the training programs required by their national health manpower plans and will have strengthened the institutions responsible for implementing these programs and for maintaining and/or improving the competence of personnel; and all countries will have developed the managerial capability to assure optimal utilization of available human resources.

The fundamental approach to achieve these targets is that of promoting the functional integration of health services and manpower development in countries so as to improve the planning and deployment of health personnel and ensure the relevance of training programs to community health needs. This involves supporting the development of manpower policies and strategies as part of national strategies for health development and ensuring that qualitative and quantitative health manpower requirements are taken into account during the development and application of the managerial process for national health development. Efforts are made to enlist the support of decision-makers as well as health professionals to strengthen national commitment to health services and manpower development and to improve the planning, distribution, and functioning of health personnel. WHO supports the establishment and/or strengthening of mechanisms for coordination of health services and manpower development. It also supports countries in their efforts to strengthen the capacity of the educational system to respond to the rapidly changing needs for certain types of health personnel. In so doing, it helps to ensure appropriate staffing for primary health care and supporting levels of the health system, including practitioners of traditional medicine, where relevant, and such innovative categories as health generalists, as well as the monitoring and evaluation of manpower deployment.

WHO is attempting to raise the political, economic, and social status of women as health care providers in the formal and nonformal health care system and in the community, and to ensure that they receive the education, training, and orientation to enable them to expand the scope and improve the quality of the health care they provide to themselves, to each other, to their families, and to other members of the community.

Promotion of community-oriented educational programs with team and problem-based methods of teaching/learning is the second main approach. The programs are designed to prepare personnel to perform tasks directly related to identified service requirements of specific concern to the country. This demands cooperation at all levels between decision-makers in health and education, as well as in other sectors that are concerned directly or indirectly with health development. Support is given to national educational institutions and programs, especially those involved in the training of front-line workers and their supervisors, teacher training being emphasized in this context. The training requirements identified by other programs—infrastructure, scientific, technical, or managerial—are analyzed on the basis of primary health care and the specific programs concerned to arrive at an agreed distribution of responsibilities for the development of training programs and career possibilities for different types of manpower contributing to health development, taking into account the repercussions of self-care and community care. Curricula are drawn up according to the tasks to be performed and to the agreed distribution of responsibilities for the development programs. WHO encourages teachers in the health professions, including those for middle-level and primary health care workers, to define the learning objectives of their programs based on the health needs of their country and to develop competence in the planning, implementation, and evaluation of curricula.

Appropriate teaching and learning materials, including those for self-teaching and audiovisual purposes, adapted to different cultures and languages, are promoted for all categories of health manpower contributing to health development, particularly primary health workers and their teachers and supervisors.

WHO fosters cooperation between ministries of health and education, as well as other ministries concerned, for the orientation and training of workers, leaders, and decision-makers concerned with health development in other sectors, such as teachers, magistrates, police, engineers, agronomists, agricultural extension workers, and civic and religious leaders.

Universities are being encouraged not only to reshape their educational programs in light of these principles, but also to become involved in the different types of research required to support the movement for health for all and to consider appropriate ways of creating a sense of social responsibility among all students and faculty who could contribute to the development and implementation of a national strategy for health for all.

WHO's third approach is to cooperate with countries, other UN agencies, and nongovernmental organizations to improve living and working conditions, job security, labor relations, job satisfaction, and social motivation, particularly for front-line health workers, in order to attract and retain needed health manpower and reduce undesirable migration of trained staff. Such cooperation will include the study of methods of providing incentives for service in primary health care, particularly in remote areas, and of analyzing those which have proved successful as well as those that have not, in different national circumstances. This requires support for the planning and implementation of national career development schemes, supervision practices, and continuing education systems for all categories of health manpower as part of broader manpower policies. WHO is collaborating with countries in their efforts to develop and strengthen national capabilities in the management of their health systems, and in planning and monitoring the use of fellowships.

Fellowships occupy an important place in WHO's program as one of the ways to provide opportunities for training and study in health matters which are not available in the fellow's own country and for the international exchange of scientific knowledge and techniques relating to health. WHO encourages the nomination, selection, and evaluation of fellows based on and determined by a member state's manpower development policy, in line with its national policy for health development, so that fellowships can contribute to the training of the type and amount of manpower needed to achieve the global target of health for all. WHO awards fellowships preferably to candidates who will be directly involved in primary health care programs, and tries to ensure that the program of studies is relevant to the long-term goals of a country's health policy.

In all of these activities, technical cooperation among countries is especially important, particularly for the training of teachers and for the production and exchange of learning materials. There is a drive to strengthen national political commitment to health manpower development reform, as well as to create awareness among policy-makers and health personnel, and in particular teaching personnel, of the social responsibilities of all health workers. The support of health professionals is needed to effect the necessary increase in the relevance of training so as to attain the goal of health for all by the year 2000. The health manpower component of health systems research is being promoted and coordinated in order to enhance the abilities of staff to perform better in health services, as well as to identify and assess appropriate technologies for application as educational instruments by various categories of manpower. WHO is promoting the development of networks of institutions and programs that will be responsible for trying out innovative methods of health manpower development and resource pooling, carrying out research on common problems, and exchanging staff and students as well as information on accumulated experience and views on various aspects of health manpower development.

I. PUBLIC INFORMATION AND EDUCATION FOR HEALTH

To integrate health education and information for health, WHO established the Division of Public Information and Education for Health. Its major tasks, in close cooperation with all regions, are to work with governments in developing coordinated information/education programs aimed at promoting healthy behavior and at increasing self-reliance among individuals and communities, and to work with technical units in planning, developing, and implementing an information/education component in their programs.

The need for promotion, advocacy, and greater public awareness of health issues is a recurring theme in virtually all WHO programs. WHO considers health education as the sum of activities that will encourage people who want to be healthy, to know how to stay healthy, to do what they can individually and collectively to maintain health, and to seek help whenever it may be needed.

[8]BIBLIOGRAPHY

Bulletin of the World Health Organization. The principal scientific periodical of WHO; 2 vols. (12 nos.) annually.

Chronicle of the World Health Organization. Monthly. Describes all public health activities undertaken under WHO auspices or with WHO participation. Also reviews all WHO technical publications.

WHO Offset Publications (a series begun in 1974 for wider distribution of otherwise internal documents), for example, Nos. 12-16: "Health Project Management"; "Manual on Practical Entomology in Malaria"; "Understanding Research in Nursing"; "Community Water Supply and Excreta Disposal Situation in the Developing Countries"; "First WHO Seminar on Expansion of the Use of Immunization in Developing Countries."

Weekly Epidemiological Record. Contains notifications and other information relating to diseases designated as "quarantinable" in the International Sanitary Regulations. For the guidance of national health administrations and quarantine services.

World Directory of Medical Schools.

World Health. Illustrated WHO periodical for the nontechnical reader.

World Health Statistics Report. Monthly. Statistics on notifiable infectious diseases, natality, mortality, causes of death, etc.

THE INTERNATIONAL MONETARY FUND (IMF)

[1]BACKGROUND: The 1930s saw a decade not only of great political upheavals but also of grave financial and economic difficulties. There was widespread abandonment of the gold standard. There were sudden changes in currency exchange rates. Economic chaos was aggravated by lack of coordination between governments imposing controls over international financial transactions and by ruthless economic warfare.

During World War II, more and more countries knew that they would emerge from the conflict with their economic resources depleted at a time when they would be confronted by a reconstruction effort of staggering dimensions. It was also known that the UK would emerge from the war as the world's principal debtor nation and the US, the only major power whose productive capacity had greatly increased during the war, as the world's principal creditor nation.

[2]CREATION

The UK, the US, and their allies were convinced that international economic and financial cooperation through intergovernmental institutions expressly established for that purpose was required to prevent a more serious recurrence of the economic and monetary chaos of the 1930s. Two plans were proposed almost simultaneously in 1943: a US plan for an International Stabilization Fund, frequently referred to as the White plan, after H. D. White, then assistant to the US secretary of the treasury, and a British plan for an International Clearing Union, frequently referred to as the Keynes plan, after the British economist John Maynard Keynes. Both plans called for international machinery to stabilize currencies and—a radical innovation—a prohibition against altering exchange rates beyond narrow limits without international approval. Both would have introduced a new international currency unit defined in terms of gold. The American plan called for participating nations to contribute to a relatively limited stabilization fund of about $5 billion, on which they would be permitted to draw in order to bridge balance-of-payments deficits. The British plan would have established a system of international clearing accounts, under which each member country could borrow up to its own quota limit, while its creditors would be credited with corresponding amounts, expressed in international currency units. Both plans were discussed with financial experts of other powers, including the Republic of China, the French Committee for Liberation, and the USSR. The IMF as finally constituted resembled the US-suggested stabilization fund. The proposal to establish a new international monetary unit was dropped.

THE 1944 BRETTON WOODS CONFERENCE

A conference called by President Franklin D. Roosevelt and attended by delegates from all 44 of the United and Associated Nations was held from 1 to 22 July 1944 at Bretton Woods, New Hampshire. The Bretton Woods Conference produced the constitutions, or Articles of Agreement, of two agencies conceived as sister institutions: the International Monetary Fund (IMF) and the International Bank for Reconstruction and Development (IBRD, or World Bank).

The IMF came into existence on 27 December 1945, when 29 governments representing 80% of the quotas to be contributed to the Fund signed the IMF Articles of Agreement in Washington. An agreement with the UN, under which the IMF became an agency related to the UN, entered into force on 15 November 1947.

[3]PURPOSES

The purposes of the IMF are:

1. To promote international monetary cooperation.

2. To facilitate the expansion and balanced growth of international trade and contribute thereby to the promotion and maintenance of high levels of employment and real income.

3. To promote exchange stability, maintain orderly exchange arrangements among member states, and avoid competitive currency depreciations.

4. To assist in establishing a multilateral system of payments of current transactions among members and in eliminating foreign-exchange restrictions that hamper world trade.

5. To alleviate serious disequilibrium in members' international balance of payments by making the resources of the Fund available under adequate safeguards, so as to avoid their resort to measures endangering national or international prosperity.

[4]MEMBERSHIP

The original members of the IMF were the 29 nations whose governments ratified the Articles of Agreement by 31 December 1945. Any other state, whether or not a member of the UN, may become a member of the IMF in accordance with terms prescribed by the Board of Governors. IMF membership reached 146 by 1 March 1983. Switzerland is the only important free-market nation that does not belong. Membership in the IMF is a prerequisite to membership in the World Bank. A member may withdraw from the IMF at any time, and its withdrawal becomes effective on the day a written notice to that effect is received by the Fund.

If a member state fails to fulfill its obligations under the IMF Articles of Agreement, the Fund may declare that country ineligible to use its resources. If, after a reasonable period has elapsed, the member state persists in its failure to live up to its obligations, the Board of Governors may require it to withdraw from membership.

The full membership of the IMF is listed in section D below.

[5]STRUCTURE

The Fund has a Board of Governors, composed of as many governors as there are member states; 22 Executive Directors; and a Managing Director and staff.

Board of Governors

All powers of the IMF are vested in its Board of Governors, on which all member states are represented. Each member state appoints one governor and one alternate governor, who may vote when the principal governor is absent. A government customarily appoints its minister of finance, the president of its central bank, or other high-ranking official as its governor. For example, in March 1983, the US governor was Secretary of the Treasury Donald T. Regan, and the alternate, Federal Reserve Board Chairman Paul A. Volcker.

The principle that applies in most international bodies, one nation one vote, does not apply in the IMF Board of Governors. Multiple votes are assigned IMF member states, more votes being assigned those subscribing larger quotas to the Fund's resources. Each member has 250 votes plus one additional vote for each SDR 100,000 of its quota. The total number of votes of all IMF members was 643,098 on 1 March 1983; of these the US held about 20% and the UK about 7%.

Each governor is entitled to cast all the votes allotted to his country as a unit. On certain matters, however, voting power varies according to the use made of the Fund's resources by the respective member. IMF decisions are made by a simple majority of the votes cast, unless otherwise stipulated in the constitution. The Board of Governors regularly meets once a year. The board may also be convened for other than annual meetings.

Except for such basic matters as admission of new members, quota changes, and the like, the Board of Governors delegates most of its powers to the Executive Directors of the Fund.

The Articles, as amended effective 1 April 1978, provide that the Board of Governors may decide to establish a new council at the ministerial level which would "supervise the management and adaptation of the international monetary system." Pending establishment of the council, a 22-member Interim Committee on the International Monetary System, established in 1974, advises the Board of Governors.

Executive Directors

The 22 Executive Directors of the IMF are responsible for the Fund's general operations and exercise for this purpose all the powers delegated to them by the Board of Governors. They "function in continuous session" at the Fund's headquarters and meet as often as business may require.

Each of the five member nations having the largest quotas —the US, the UK, France, the FRG, and Japan—is entitled to appoint one Executive Director; Sa'udi Arabia, as one of the Fund's two largest net creditors over the previous two-year period, appoints an additional director. Each of these six directors casts only the votes of the country that appointed him. The 16 other Executive Directors are elected by the governors of the other IMF member countries. Each elected director casts as a unit all the votes of the countries that elected him.

Managing Director and Staff

The Managing Director, who is chosen by the Executive Directors, is responsible for the conduct of the ordinary business of the Fund. He is appointed for a five-year term and may not serve concurrently as a governor or executive director of the IMF. The Managing Director chairs meetings of the Executive Directors but may vote only in case of a tie. Jacques de Larosière of France has held this post since June 1978.

Permanent headquarters of the IMF are at 700 19th Street, N.W., Washington, D.C. 20431. As of March 1983, the staff consisted of about 1,600 persons from 100 countries.

⁶BUDGET

The approved budget for the fiscal year ended April 1983 was SDR 159,232,009. The Fund's income considerably exceeds its administrative expenditures. This income is derived principally from charges on the Fund's transactions.

⁷ACTIVITIES

A. RESOURCES OF IMF

The Fund obtains its necessary financial resources from the accumulated subscriptions made by its members. How much a mem-

ber government subscribes to the Fund's resources is determined by the quota assigned that country. As mentioned, the quota also determines the country's voting strength in the IMF. Furthermore, the quota, which is expressed in SDRs (see section F below), determines the amounts the country may draw from the Fund's currency pool as well as the country's allocations of SDRs.

In determining a member's quota, the IMF considers appropriate economic data, including the country's national income, its international reserves, and the volume of the country's imports and exports.

The method of payment for initial quota subscriptions or increases in quotas was modified with the entry into effect of the Second Amendment of the Articles of Agreement in 1978. Under the original Articles, members were required to pay 25% of their quota in gold and the remainder in their own currencies. Following the Second Amendment, an amount not exceeding 25% of new members' initial quotas, or existing members' increases in quotas, is paid in reserve assets, while the remainder is paid in members' own currencies.

The Fund is required by its constitution to review its members' quotas every five years and to propose called-for adjustments in quotas. All quota changes must be approved by an 85% majority of the total voting power.

Several reviews of the adequacy of members' quotas have led to general and selective increases of Fund quotas. A special review in 1958/59 resulted in a 50% increase in quotas; it was followed by a 25% general increase in 1965 and a further 25% general increase in 1970. The 1976 review of quotas was affected by developments in the international monetary system, including the quadrupling of oil prices. As a result of that review, total quotas were increased by 32.5%, to SDR 39 billion, reflecting a doubling of the collective share in total quotas of the major oil-exporting countries. The share of all other developing countries was maintained at its then existing level. The 1978 review provided for a 50% general quota increase for most members and additional special increases for 11 members. Consents to increases under this review raised total quotas to SDR 59.6 billion; in addition, Sa'udi Arabia's quota was increased in 1981 from SDR 1,040.1 million to SDR 2,100 million.

Agreement was reached at a meeting of the Interim Committee in February 1983 that the overall total of Fund quotas be increased by 47.5%, to SDR 90 billion.

Quotas in effect on 1 March 1983 are listed in the table in section D below.

The Fund is authorized under its Articles to supplement its resources by borrowing. In January 1962, a four-year agreement was concluded with 10 industrial members (the Group of 10)—subsequently joined by Switzerland as an associate—which undertook to lend to the Fund to finance drawings by participants of the General Arrangements to Borrow (GAB) "if this should be needed to forestall or cope with an impairment of the international monetary system." These General Arrangements to Borrow have been extended several times; the most recent five-year renewal ends in October 1985.

On 19 January 1983, the ministers of the Group of 10 agreed in principle to enlarge the GAB to SDR 17 billion, from approximately SDR 6.4 billion, and to permit the Fund to borrow under the enlarged credit arrangements to finance exchange transactions with members that are not GAB participants. In addition, the ministers agreed to authorize Swiss participation in the agreement. The changes will become effective when all participants have notified the Fund that they concur in the amendments and in the increased credit commitments. Once the increases become effective, the amounts of credit arrangements will be (in millions of SDRs): US, 4,250; FRG, 2,380; Japan, 2,125; France, 1,700; UK, 1,700; Italy, 1,105; Canada, 892.5; Netherlands, 850; Belgium, 595; Norway, 382.5; Switzerland, 1,020.

The Fund also supplemented its resources by borrowing for the oil facility for 1974 and 1975 and for the supplementary financing facility, whose resouces of SDR 7,784 billion were borrowed from 14 members or institutions.

At its meeting in Hamburg in April 1980, the Interim Committee encouraged the managing director to start discussions with potential lenders on the terms and conditions under which the Fund could borrow to increase its resources, if the need arose. The Interim Committee's encouragement was made in light of the size and the distribution of payments imbalances and the necessity to phase adjustment over a reasonable period of time. These discussions led to an agreement between the Fund and the Sa'udi Arabian Monetary Agency (SAMA), which came into effect on 7 May 1981 and under which SAMA made a lending commitment to the Fund of SDR 4 billion in the first year of the agreement and a further SDR 4 billion in the second year. The Sa'udi Arabian authorities also indicated their intention to enter into another commitment for the third year if their balance-of-payments and reserve position so permits. Borrowing agreements amounting to about SDR 1.3 billion have been made between the Fund and the Bank for International Settlements and a number of other countries in a strong balance-of-payments and reserve position.

The Interim Committee has also held open the possibility of recourse to the private markets if need be, but only as a last resort.

B. GENERAL OBLIGATIONS OF IMF MEMBERS

The economic philosophy of the Bretton Woods Agreement holds that monetary stability and cooperation, and the unhampered movement of money, especially in payment of current international transactions, will promote national and international prosperity. This principle is reflected in certain general obligations that countries undertake by accepting the IMF's Articles of Agreement. The Articles favor stabilization measures to help overcome short-term balance-of-payments difficulties and they discourage exchange controls under normal conditions. The Agreement also enables the Fund to help governments in short-term payments difficulties.

C. CONSULTATIONS

Consultations with members, although modified in focus and content under the amended Articles of Agreement, remain more than ever an essential component of the Fund's work, and they also provide a major instrument for Fund surveillance of members' policies in several key areas.

Article IV, entitled "Obligations Regarding Exchange Arrangements," allows individual members considerable freedom in the selection of their specific arrangements but stipulates required general obligations and specific undertakings.

In order to help the Fund to ensure observance of these obligations and to exercise "firm surveillance" over exchange rate policies, members are required to consult with the Fund regularly under Article IV, in principle on an annual basis. These consultations provide an opportunity for detailed review of the economic and financial situation and the policies of members from both the national and international viewpoints. They also help the Fund to deal expeditiously with members' requests for the use of Fund resources and proposed changes in policies or practices that are subject to Fund approval. For the individual member, regular consultations provide the occasion for an external appraisal of policies and for discussion of any special difficulties that may arise from actions of other members.

Members availing themselves of the transitional arrangements permitted under Article XIV to maintain restrictions on current international payments or multiple exchange rates are required to consult annually with the Fund. For Article VIII countries —those which have accepted the obligation to avoid such practices

—the consultations were held regularly on a voluntary basis prior to the Second Amendment of the Articles. The new consultations under Article IV include the regular consultations under Article VIII and Article XIV, and are required for all members.

Between annual consultations, there is a supplemental surveillance procedure under which the managing director initiates an informal and confidential discussion with a member whenever he considers that a modification in the member's exchange arrangements or exchange-rate policies or the behavior of the exchange rate of its currency may be important or may have important effects on other members.

Special consultations with selected countries also supplement the regular consultations in connection with the periodic reviews of the world economic outlook undertaken by the Executive Board. The purpose of these special consultations is to provide up-to-date knowledge of the economic situation in countries whose external policies are regarded as being of major importance to the world economy.

D. TRANSACTIONS BETWEEN THE FUND AND ITS MEMBERS
Use of Resources

Members of the Fund may draw on its financial resources to meet their balance-of-payments needs. They may use the reserve tranche and, under tranche policies, the four credit tranches (see below). In addition, there are three permanent facilities for specific purposes—the facility for compensatory financing of export fluctuations (established in 1963, liberalized in 1975 and 1979, and expanded in 1981 to compensate for fluctuations in cereal import costs), the buffer stock financing facility (established in 1969), and the extended Fund facility (established in 1974).

Furthermore, members may make use of temporary facilities established by the Fund with borrowed resources. For 1974 and 1975, for example, following the sharp rise in oil prices, the Fund provided assistance under a temporary oil facility designed to help members meet the increased cost of imports of petroleum and petroleum products. In 1978, a supplementary financing facility was established with borrowed resources amounting to SDR 7,784 billion from 13 member countries or their institutions and the Swiss National Bank. In March 1981, a policy of enlarged access to the Fund's resources was adopted, allowing the Fund to continue to provide assistance on a scale similar to that under the supplementary financing facility.

For any drawing, a member is required to represent to the Fund that the desired purchase is needed because of its balance-of-payments or reserve position or developments in its reserves.

When a member draws on the Fund, it uses its own currency to purchase the currencies of other member countries or SDRs held by the General Resources Account. Thus a drawing results in an increase in the Fund's holdings of the purchasing member's currency and a corresponding decrease in the Fund's holdings of other currencies or SDRs that are sold. Within a prescribed time, a member must reverse the transaction (unless it is a reserve tranche purchase) by buying back its own currency with SDRs or currencies specified by the Fund. Usually, repurchases are required to be made within three to five years after the date of purchase. However, under the extended Fund facility, the period for repurchases is within four and a half to ten years; under the oil facility, within three and a quarter to seven years; and under the supplementary financing facility and the enlarged access policy, within three and a half to seven years. In addition, a member is expected normally to repurchase as its balance-of-payments and reserve position improves.

Reserve Tranche. If the Fund's holdings of a member's currency are less than its quota, the difference is called the reserve tranche. A member using Fund resources in the credit tranches has the option either to use or to retain a reserve tranche position. Purchases in the reserve tranche—a reserve asset that can be mobilized by the member with minimum delay—are subject to balance-of-payments need but not to prior challenge, economic policy conditions, or repurchase requirements.

Credit Tranches. Further purchases are made in four credit tranches, each of 25% of the member's quota. In the past, the total of purchases under credit tranche policies was normally limited to 100% of the member's quota, an amount that would raise the Fund's holdings of the member's currency to 200% of its quota. However, in response to the structural and deep-rooted nature of the payments imbalance currently confronting many members, the Fund is placing greater emphasis on programs involving adjustment periods of longer duration, and provision has been made for a larger access above these limits.

All requests for the use of the Fund's resources other than use of the reserve tranche are examined by the Fund to determine whether the proposed use would be consistent with the provisions of the Articles and with Fund policies.

The criteria used by the Fund in determining whether its assistance should be made available are more liberal when the request is in the first credit tranche (Fund holdings of a member's currency rising from 100% but not above 125% of the member's quota) than when it is in the higher credit tranches (that is, when the Fund's holdings following the drawing exceed 125% of quota).

A member requesting a direct purchase expects to draw the full amount immediately after approval of the request; under a standby arrangement, a member may make the agreed drawing at any time during the period of the standby arrangement.

Requests for purchases in the higher credit tranches require substantial justification. Such purchases are almost always made under standby or similar arrangements. The amount available under a standby arrangement in the upper credit tranches is phased to be available in portions at specified intervals during the standby period, and the member's right to draw is always subject to the observance of certain key policy objectives described in the program or to a further review of the situation.

Compensatory Financing. The compensatory financing facility was designed to extend the Fund's financial support to member countries—particularly primary-commodity exporting countries—encountering payments difficulties caused by temporary shortfalls in export proceeds. Members having a balance-of-payments need may draw on the Fund under this facility to compensate for such shortfalls, if the Fund is satisfied that the shortfall is temporary and is largely attributable to circumstances beyond the member's control, and that the member will cooperate with the Fund in an effort to solve its balance-of-payments difficulties.

Members may draw up to 100% of quota under the compensatory financing facility. Requests for drawings beyond 50% of quota are met only if the Fund is satisfied that the member has been cooperating in an effort to solve its balance-of-payments problems. Export shortfalls may include, at the option of the member, receipts from travel and workers' remittances.

The Fund decided in May 1981 to extend financial assistance to members that encounter a balance-of-payments difficulty caused by an excess in the cost of their cereal imports and presumed to be reversible within a few years. An excess in cereal import costs is calculated as the cost of such imports in a given year less their average cost for the five-year period centered on that year. The decision integrates this assistance with that for shortfalls in export receipts under the compensatory financing facility, so that compensation, subject to quota limits, is given for the net shortfall, which is the sum of the export shortfall and the excess in cereal import costs. The limit on drawings in respect of cereal import excesses is 100% of quota, but there is a joint limit of 125% of quota in respect of cereal import excesses and export shortfalls together. The facility relating to cereal imports is operative for an initial period of four years from 13 May 1981.

Drawings under the compensatory financing facility, whether for export shortfalls or for excesses in cereal import costs, are additional to those which members may make under tranche policies.

The Fund has, to date, authorized the use of Fund resources in connection with tin, cocoa, and sugar buffer stocks, but drawings have been made only with respect to sugar.

Extended Facility. Under the extended facility, the Fund may provide assistance to members to meet their balance-of-payments deficits for longer periods and in amounts larger in relation to quotas than under the credit tranche policies. For example, a member might apply for assistance under the facility if it has serious payments imbalances relating to structural maladjustments in production, trade, and prices and if it intends to implement a comprehensive set of corrective policies for two or three years. Or, use of the facility might be indicated by an inherently weak balance-of-payments position that prevents the pursuit of an active development policy.

Drawings under extended arrangements may take place over periods of up to three years. Purchases outstanding under the extended facility may not exceed 140% of the member's quota, nor raise Fund holdings of a member's currency above 265% of the member's quota (excluding holdings relating to compensatory financing, buffer stock financing, and the oil facility). Purchases under the extended facility are additional to those a member may make under the first credit tranche.

Enlarged Access Policy. The enlarged access policy replaced the supplementary financing facility following the full commitment of the resources available under the latter. The purpose of this policy is to enable the Fund to provide supplementary financing in conjunction with the use of the Fund's ordinary resources to all members of the Fund facing serious payments imbalances that are large in relation to their quotas. The enlarged access policy, like its predecessor the supplementary financing facility, is used only in support of economic programs under standby arrangements reaching into the upper credit tranches or under extended arrangements. The period of such standby arrangements will normally exceed one year and may extend up to three years.

The amount of assistance under this policy is determined according to guidelines adopted by the Fund from time to time. Present guidelines specify limits of 150% of quota annually or 450% over a three-year period; at the same time, a limit of 600% of quota, net of scheduled repurchases, applies on the cumulative use of Fund resources. These limits, which may be exceeded in exceptional circumstances, exclude drawings under the compensatory and buffer-stock financing facilities or outstanding drawings under the oil facility.

The Fund may approve a standby or an extended arrangement that provides for enlarged access until the current (Eighth) General Review of Quotas becomes effective.

QUOTAS, VOTING POWER, AND PURCHASES
(as of 1 March 1983, in millions of SDRs)

MEMBER	QUOTA	VOTING POWER (%)	CUMULATIVE PURCHASES
Afghanistan	67.50	0.14	66.3
Algeria	427.50	0.70	—
Antigua and Barbuda	3.60	0.04	0.7
Argentina	802.50	1.28	2,344.3
Australia	1,185.00	1.87	864.9
Austria	495.00	0.80	—
Bahamas	49.50	0.12	—
Bahrain	30.00	0.08	5.0
Bangladesh	228.00	0.39	726.6
Barbados	25.50	0.08	36.5
Belgium	1,335.00	2.10	129.5
Belize	7.20	0.05	—
Benin	24.00	0.08	1.9
Bhutan	1.70	0.04	—
Bolivia	67.50	0.14	196.4

Botswana	13.50	0.06	—		Netherlands	1,422.00	2.24	524.5
Brazil	997.50	1.58	1,077.2		New Zealand	348.00	0.58	676.6
Burma	109.50	0.21	223.1		Nicaragua	51.00	0.12	164.9
Burundi	34.50	0.09	36.3		Niger	24.00	0.08	—
Cameroon	67.50	0.14	40.8		Nigeria	540.00	0.87	328.2
Canada	2,035.50	3.18	691.0		Norway	442.50	0.72	9.6
Cape Verde	3.00	0.04	—		Oman	30.00	0.08	—
Central African Rep.	24.00	0.08	38.2		Pakistan	427.50	0.70	1,864.3
Chad	24.00	0.08	22.4		Panama	67.50	0.14	154.0
Chile	325.50	0.54	1,375.8		Papua New Guinea	45.00	0.11	83.5
China	1,800.00	2.82	818.1		Paraguay	34.50	0.09	8.1
Colombia	289.50	0.49	404.9		Peru	246.00	0.42	1,080.4
Comoros	3.50	0.04	1.3		Philippines	315.00	0.53	1,506.2
Congo	25.50	0.08	18.5		Portugal	258.00	0.44	292.2
Costa Rica	61.50	0.13	203.3		Qatar	66.20	0.14	—
Cyprus	51.00	0.12	77.0		Romania	367.50	0.61	1,226.1
Denmark	465.00	0.76	199.5		Rwanda	34.50	0.09	14.1
Djibouti	5.70	0.05	—		St. Lucia	5.40	0.05	5.2
Dominica	2.90	0.04	9.9		St. Vincent and the			
Dominican Republic	82.50	0.17	325.2		Grenadines	2.60	0.04	2.1
Ecuador	105.00	0.20	128.4		São Tomé and Príncipe	3.00	0.04	—
Egypt	342.00	0.57	765.9		Sa'udi Arabia	2,100.00	3.28	—
El Salvador	64.50	0.14	220.7		Senegal	63.00	0.14	220.1
Equatorial Guinea	15.00	0.06	20.8		Seychelles	2.00	0.04	—
Ethiopia	54.00	0.12	133.5		Sierra Leone	46.50	0.11	98.3
Fiji	27.00	0.08	24.6		Singapore	92.40	0.18	—
Finland	393.00	0.65	353.4		Solomon Islands	3.20	0.04	4.2
France	2,878.50	4.49	2,465.9		Somalia	34.50	0.09	98.3
Gabon	45.00	0.11	17.5		South Africa	636.00	1.02	1,882.3
Gambia	13.50	0.06	39.8		Spain	835.50	1.33	1,004.3
Germany, Fed. Rep.	3,234.00	5.04	762.9		Sri Lanka	178.50	0.31	777.1
Ghana	159.00	0.28	213.4		Sudan	132.00	0.24	747.3
Greece	277.50	0.47	282.3		Suriname	37.50	0.10	
Grenada	4.50	0.05	7.6		Swaziland	18.00	0.07	7.2
Guatemala	76.50	0.16	152.7		Sweden	675.00	1.08	
Guinea	45.00	0.11	49.3		Syria	94.50	0.18	121.5
Guinea-Bissau	5.90	0.05	4.3		Tanzania	82.50	0.17	196.2
Guyana	37.50	0.10	125.5		Thailand	271.50	0.46	811.1
Haiti	34.50	0.09	102.6		Togo	28.50	0.08	31.3
Honduras	51.00	0.12	166.0		Trinidad and Tobago	123.00	0.23	16.1
Hungary	375.00	0.62	295.9		Tunisia	94.50	0.18	78.2
Iceland	43.50	0.11	114.5		Turkey	300.00	0.50	2,258.9
India	1,717.50	2.69	3,930.5		Uganda	75.00	0.15	311.3
Indonesia	720.00	1.15	471.9		United Arab Emirates	202.60	0.35	—
Iran	660.00	1.06	184.2		UK	4,387.50	6.82	12,517.6
Iraq	234.10	0.40	179.2		US	12,607.50	19.52	5,827.1
Ireland	232.50	0.40	62.5		Upper Volta	24.00	0.08	0.8
Israel	307.50	0.51	528.6		Uruguay	126.00	0.23	411.2
Italy	1,860.00	2.91	3,171.0		Vanuatu	6.90	0.05	—
Ivory Coast	114.00	0.21	553.1		Venezuela	990.00	1.57	—
Jamaica	111.00	0.21	760.3		Viet-Nam	135.00	0.25	102.4
Japan	2,488.50	3.88	249.0		Western Samoa	4.50	0.05	8.0
Jordan	45.00	0.11	7.4		Yemen, People's Dem.			
Kampuchea	25.00	0.08	18.3		Rep.	61.50	0.13	67.9
Kenya	103.50	0.20	453.3		Yemen Arab Rep.	19.50	0.07	11.3
Korea, Rep.	255.90	0.43	1,542.7		Yugoslavia	415.50	0.68	2,482.9
Kuwait	393.30	0.65	—		Zaire	228.00	0.39	689.4
Laos	24.00	0.08	28.2		Zambia	211.50	0.37	889.8
Lebanon	27.90	0.08	—		Zimbabwe	150.00	0.27	70.0
Lesotho	10.50	0.05	2.6					
Liberia	55.50	0.12	196.0					
Libya	298.40	0.50	—					
Luxembourg	46.50	0.11	—					
Madagascar	51.00	0.12	164.7					
Malawi	28.50	0.08	105.0					
Malaysia	379.50	0.63	352.9					
Maldives	1.40	0.04	—					
Mali	40.50	0.10	65.9					
Malta	30.00	0.08	—					
Mauritania	25.50	0.08	69.1					
Mauritius	40.50	0.10	188.6					
Mexico	802.50	1.28	1,091.4					
Morocco	225.00	0.39	1,101.6					
Nepal	28.50	0.08	27.6					

Conditionality

A country making use of the Fund's resources is generally required to carry out an economic policy program aimed at achieving a viable balance-of-payments position over an appropriate period of time. This requirement is known as "conditionality," and it reflects the principle that balance-of-payments financing and adjustment must go hand in hand.

Executive directors have, on several occasions, reviewed and amended the policies and practices relating to the conditional use of Fund resources. The first general review was undertaken in 1968 and was followed by a second comprehensive review in 1979. Revised conditionality guidelines include the use of consultation clauses in Fund-supported programs, the phasing of purchases, and the injunction that objective indicators for monitoring performance be limited only to those variables necessary to ensure achievement of the objectives of the programs. In addition, the guidelines emphasize the need to encourage members to adopt corrective measures at an early stage of their balance-of-payments difficulties, recognize that in many cases adjustment will take longer than the period associated with standby arrangements, provide for the adoption of a flexible approach for the treatment of external borrowing in adjustment programs, and stress the necessity to pay due regard to the domestic social and political objectives, economic priorities, and the circumstances of members, including the causes of their payments problems.

Within the context of the guidelines, Fund-supported programs emphasize a number of major economic variables, including certain financial aggregates such as domestic credit, public sector financial needs, and external debt, as well as some key elements of the price system, including the exchange rate, interest rates, and, in exceptional cases, the prices of commodities that bear significantly upon the public finances and foreign trade.

The Fund-supported corrective strategy provides for a reorientation of the economy toward sustained growth and avoids purely deflationary policies that may have a deleterious effect on investment and fail to encourage the required shift of resources to the external sector.

Charges for Use of Resources and Remuneration on Creditor Positions

The Fund applies charges for the use of its resources, except for reserve tranche purchases. A service charge of 0.5% is payable on purchases other than reserve tranche purchases. In addition, the Fund levies charges on balances of members' currencies resulting from purchases. The rate of charge on purchases in the four credit tranches and under the extended Fund facility, the compensatory financing facility, and the buffer-stock financing facility is determined at the beginning of each financial year on the basis of the estimated income and expense of the Fund during the year and a target amount of net income. The rate of charge calculated for the financial year 1983 is 6.6% a year. Charges on balances in excess of 200% of members' quotas resulting from purchases under standby arrangements or in excess of 140% of quota under extended arrangements granted not later than 23 February 1979, when the supplementary financing facility became effective, are the average yield on US government securities determined on the basis of a constant maturity of five years over the six months preceding the determination of the rate of charge, rounded upward to the nearest one quarter of 1% per annum.

There are separate charges for the use of the supplementary financing facility and of borrowed resources under the enlarged access policy, under which charges are equal to the cost of borrowing by the Fund plus a margin of 0.2% a year. The margin charged on the use of supplementary financing is increased to 0.325% after the first three and a half years.

When the Fund's holdings of a member's currency are reduced below a specified level, the member acquires a creditor position in the Fund on which it earns remuneration (i.e., interest). The Fund pays remuneration on creditor positions at a rate determined by a formula based on short-term market interest rates in the US, the FRG, the UK, France, and Japan. A weighted average of daily interest rates in the five countries is calculated for the three-week period ending two business days before the start of each calendar quarter. Since 1 May 1981, the rate of remuneration for a calendar quarter is 85% of the interest rate on the SDR, which, in turn, is 100% of the combined market rate.

E. TECHNICAL ASSISTANCE

Technical assistance is a major activity of the Fund. Staff officials are sent to member countries, sometimes for extended periods, to give advice on stabilization programs or on the simplification of exchange systems, the modification of central banking machinery, the reform of fiscal systems and budgetary controls, or the preparation of financial statistics. The Fund collects and publishes a considerable amount of statistics supplied by members. As part of its technical cooperation the Fund established the IMF Institute in May 1964 to coordinate and expand its training program for staff members of finance ministries and central banks.

F. SPECIAL DRAWING RIGHTS

The SDR is an international reserve asset created by the Fund and allocated to its members as a supplement to existing reserve assets. The Fund has allocated a total of SDR 21.4 billion in six allocations, and holdings of SDRs by member countries amounted to some 5% of total non-gold reserves in August 1982.

The last allocation of SDRs in the third basic period was made on 1 January 1981, when a total of SDR 4,052 million was allocated to the 141 countries that were members of the Fund at that time. Similar amounts were allocated in each of the two previous years. The Fund allocates SDRs to its members in proportion to their quotas at the time of allocation. In deciding on the timing and amount of SDR allocations, the Fund considers whether there exists a global need to supplement existing reserve assets, and it takes into account the objectives of the Fund's Articles of Agreement, which call upon Fund members to collaborate with each other and with the Fund with a view to making SDR the principal reserve asset of the international monetary system.

All 146 member countries of the Fund are participants in the Special Drawing Rights Department and are eligible to receive allocations. They may use SDRs in transactions and operations among themselves, with prescribed "other holders," of which there are now 12, and with the Fund itself. The SDR is the Fund's unit of account and, increasingly, commercial transactions and private financial obligations are being denominated in SDRs.

Members with a balance-of-payments need may use SDRs to acquire foreign exchange in a transaction with designation—that is, where another member, designated by the Fund, provides currency in exchange for SDRs. The Fund designates members to provide currency on the basis of the strength of their balance-of-payments and reserve positions. However, a member's obligation to provide currency does not extend beyond the point at which its holdings are three times the net cumulative allocation it has received. Fund members and "other holders" may also use SDRs in a variety of voluntary transactions and operations by agreement. They may buy and sell SDRs both spot and forward; use SDRs in swaps and in settlement of financial obligations; or make donations (grants) with SDRs.

The valuation of the SDR is determined on the basis of a basket of five currencies—the US dollar, the deutsche mark, the French franc, the Japanese yen, and the pound sterling. The value of the SDR is calculated daily by the Fund as the sum of the values in US dollars, based on market exchange rates, of specified amounts of the five currencies in the basket. These amounts, or "currency units," are derived from agreed percentage weights for the currencies in the basket, using average exchange rates for the three months ended 31 December 1980. The agreed weights—42% for the US dollar, 19% for the deutsche mark, and 13% each for the French franc, the Japanese yen, and the pound sterling—broadly reflect the relative importance of the currencies in international trade and payments, based on the value of the exports of goods and services of the member countries issuing these currencies and the balances of these currencies held as reserves by members of the Fund over the five-year period 1975–79. The SDR interest rate is based on the short-term obligations in the money markets of the same five countries whose currencies are used in valuation.

G. GOLD SALES BY THE FUND

In May 1980, the Fund completed a four-year gold sales program, through which 50 million oz, or one-third of the Fund's gold holdings at the beginning of the period, were sold.

The program was derived from agreements by the Interim Committee in 1975 on the future role of gold. As part of these agreements, one-sixth of the Fund's gold (25 million oz) was sold at the former official price of SDR 35 an ounce directly to the 127 countries that were members of the Fund on 31 August 1975, and one-sixth was sold at public auction for the benefit of developing member countries. The proportion of the profits from the sale of gold that corresponded to the share of quotas of these countries on 31 August 1975 was transferred directly to each developing country in proportion to its quota, and the balance was used to finance loans by the Trust Fund, which was established in May 1976 under the Fund's administration and was terminated in April 1981. The Trust Fund provided highly concessional balance-of-payments assistance to eligible developing member countries. An eligible member qualified for a Trust Fund loan if the Fund, as trustee, was satisfied that the member had a need for balance-of-payments assistance, and that it was making a reasonable effort to strengthen its balance-of-payments position.

The Trust Fund's assistance was made in the form of loans to support programs of balance-of-payments adjustment and was provided in two periods, each of two years' duration. A total of SDR 2,991 million was disbursed over the four years to 55 member countries.

[8]BIBLIOGRAPHY

Annual Report of the Executive Board. Reviews the Fund's activities and surveys the world economy.

Annual Report on Exchange Restrictions.

Balance of Payments Yearbook. Published as a series of looseleaf sections.

Direction of Trade. Monthly. Trade-by-country statistics of some 100 countries and summaries by geographic and monetary areas. Compiled by the IMF and the IBRD, and published jointly by the Fund, the Bank, and the UN.

Government Finance Statistics Yearbook.

IMF Survey. Twice a month.

International Financial Statistics. Monthly. Statistics on all aspects of domestic and international finance (exchange rates, gold and foreign exchange holdings, money supply, bank assets, international trade, prices, production, interest rates, etc.).

THE INTERNATIONAL BANK FOR RECONSTRUCTION AND DEVELOPMENT (IBRD)

[1]**BACKGROUND:** The World Bank, formally known as the International Bank for Reconstruction and Development (IBRD), like its sister institution, the International Monetary Fund (IMF), was born of the realization by the Allies during World War II that tremendous difficulties in reconstruction and development would face them in the postwar transition period, necessitating international economic and financial cooperation on a vast scale. As early as February 1943, US Undersecretary of State Sumner B. Welles urged preparatory consultation aimed at the establishment of agencies to finance such reconstruction and development. The US and the UK took leading roles in the negotiations that were to result in the formation of the World Bank and the IMF.

[2]CREATION

The World Bank, or IBRD, emerged from the 1944 Bretton Woods Conference as the sister organization to the IMF. They came into existence on 27 December 1945, when the constitutions, or Articles of Agreement, of the two organizations were signed in Washington. The Bank and the Fund both have their headquarters in Washington. Membership in the Fund is a prerequisite to membership in the Bank.

[3]PURPOSES

The principal purposes of the World Bank, as set forth in its Articles of Agreement, are to assist in the reconstruction and development of member territories by facilitating the investment of capital for productive purposes, thus promoting the long-range balanced growth of international trade, increased productivity, higher standards of living, and better conditions for labor. It is to supplement private investment when private capital is not available on reasonable terms by providing financing out of its own resources. It is to coordinate its own lending with other international loans so that the most urgent and useful projects will receive priority, with due regard for the effect its investments may have on business conditions in member territories. One of the Bank's early functions was to assist in bringing about a smooth transition from wartime to peaceful economies. But economic development soon became its main object.

[4]MEMBERSHIP

Membership in the World Bank rose gradually from 41 governments in 1946 to 144 as of 30 June 1983. Some that attended the 1944 Bretton Woods Conference waited a long time to join—New Zealand until August 1961, Liberia until March 1962—and the USSR did not join at all. The Bank's membership in 1983 included almost all developing countries and all the major or financial powers except Switzerland.

A government may withdraw from membership at any time by giving notice of withdrawal. Poland did so in March 1950, Cuba in November 1960, and Indonesia in August 1965. Indonesia rejoined in April 1967. Membership also ceases for a member suspended by a majority of the governors for failure to fulfill an obligation, if that member has not been restored to good standing by a similar majority within a year after the suspension. Czechoslovakia ceased to be a member in December 1954. The Dominican Republic, which had ceased to be a member, rejoined in 1961.

Members of the Bank are listed in section A below.

[5]STRUCTURE

Board of Governors

All powers of the Bank are vested in its Board of Governors, composed of one governor and one alternate from each member state. Ministers of finance, central-bank presidents, or persons of comparable status usually represent member states on the Bank's board of governors. The board meets annually.

The World Bank is organized somewhat like a corporation. According to an agreed-upon formula, member countries subscribe to shares of the Bank's capital stock. Each governor is entitled to cast 250 votes plus one vote for each share of capital stock subscribed by his country. Maldives, with 6 shares of the Bank's capital stock, is the smallest shareholder; the US, with 102,239 shares, is the largest.

Executive Directors

The Bank's Board of Governors has delegated most of its authority to 21 Executive Directors. Five are appointed by the five largest shareholders—the US, the FRG, Japan, the UK, and France. The other directors are elected for two-year terms by the governors of the remaining states. Each director from the five largest shareholders casts his nation's total votes; each of the other directors casts the combined votes of the countries he is elected to represent. Thus, for example, a Canadian elected as director by Bahamas, Barbados, Belize, Canada, Dominica, Grenada, Guyana, Ireland, Jamaica, St. Lucia, and St. Vincent and the Grenadines casts the votes to which those 11 countries are entitled.

President and Staff

The President of the Bank, elected by the Executive Directors, is also their chairman, although he is not entitled to a vote, except in case of an equal division. Subject to their general direction, the President is responsible for the conduct of the ordinary business of the Bank. Action on Bank loans is initiated by the President and the staff of the Bank. The amount, terms, and conditions of a loan are recommended by the president to the executive directors; and the loan is made if his recommendation is approved by them.

Robert S. McNamara was president of the Bank from 1968 to 1981. A. W. Clausen has been president since 1 July 1981. He heads a staff of about 5,500 persons from some 106 countries.

Headquarters. The IBRD's headquarters are at 1818 H Street, N.W., Washington, D.C. Most annual meetings of the Board of Governors have been held at headquarters; others have taken place in London, Paris, Mexico City, Istanbul, New Delhi, Vienna, Tokyo, Rio de Janeiro, Manila, Belgrade, and Toronto. The Bank's New York office, which helps in the execution of programs for the marketing of World Bank bonds and arranges sales from the Bank's portfolio securities, is located at 747 Third Avenue, New York.

The European office of the Bank is in Paris, and there are offices in Geneva and Tokyo. The Bank maintains regional missions in Nairobi, Abidjan, and Bangkok. There are resident missions or staff in 28 other countries of Asia, Africa, and Latin' Amerca.

⁶BUDGET

The World Bank's administrative budget rose from $2.1 million in fiscal year 1947 (ending 30 June 1947) to $345.4 million in fiscal 1983. Administrative expenses are paid from the Bank's income.

⁷ACTIVITIES

A. FINANCIAL RESOURCES
Authorized Capital

At its establishment, the Bank had an authorized capital of $10 billion. Countries subscribing shares were required to pay in only one-fifth of their subscription on joining, the remainder being available on call, but only to meet the Bank's liabilities if it got into difficulties. Moreover, not even the one-fifth had to be paid over in hard cash at that time. The sole cash requirement was the payment in gold or US dollars of 2% of each country's subscription. A further 18% of the subscription was payable in the currency of the member country concerned, and although this sum was technically paid in, in the form of notes bearing no interest, it could not be used without the member's permission. Only the US and Canada were in a position for some time after the war to allow these notes to be cashed. Most of the other industrialized countries have since freed the national currency part of their subscriptions on a convertible basis, but the subscriptions of many of the less-developed members of the Bank are still largely frozen in this way.

In 1959, each member was given an opportunity to double its subscription without any payment. Thus, for countries joining the Bank after the 1959 capital increase and for those subscribing to additional capital stock, the statutory provisions affecting the 2% and 18% portions have been applied to only one-half of these countries' total subscriptions, so that 1% of each subscription which is freely usable in the Bank's operations has been payable in gold or US dollars, and 9% which is usable only with the consent of the member is in the member's currency. The remaining 90% is not paid in but may be called by the Bank.

SUBSCRIPTIONS TO CAPITAL STOCK
AS OF 30 JUNE 1983
(in thousands of US dollars)

MEMBER	AMOUNT PAID IN	AMOUNT SUBJECT TO CALL
Afghanistan	3,205	28,845
Algeria	42,312	465,688
Argentina	50,223	452,008
Australia	117,281	1,243,477
Austria	49,019	535,263
Bahamas	1,827	16,442
Bahrain	2,967	57,501
Bangladesh	13,269	119,420
Barbados	2,527	52,921
Belgium	101,686	1,022,005
Belize	417	3,750
Benin	1,068	9,615
Bhutan	96	865
Bolivia	2,820	25,834
Botswana	764	34,599
Brazil	98,205	1,045,570
Burma	6,314	56,826
Burundi	1,603	14,423
Cameroon	2,137	19,230
Canada	139,575	1,352,056
Cape Verde	171	1,538
Central African Rep.	1,068	9,615
Chad	1,068	9,615
Chile	13,248	119,228
China	218,200	2,290,500
Colombia	12,553	112,978
Comoros	171	1,538
Congo	1,068	9,615
Costa Rica	1,400	12,596
Cyprus	5,053	79,133
Denmark	45,891	502,814
Djibouti	331	2,981
Dominica	171	1,538
Dominican Republic	3,184	59,742
Ecuador	3,932	35,384
Egypt	29,999	337,940
El Salvador	1,282	11,538
Equatorial Guinea	684	6,154
Ethiopia	1,218	10,961
Fiji	1,795	43,610
Finland	30,891	331,493
France	233,750	2,284,031
Gabon	1,282	11,538
Gambia	566	5,096
Germany, Fed. Rep.	320,246	3,349,216
Ghana	9,145	82,306
Greece	10,096	90,863
Grenada	182	1,635
Guatemala	1,784	16,057
Guinea	2,137	19,230
Guinea-Bissau	288	2,596
Guyana	3,093	58,765
Haiti	1,603	14,423
Honduras	897	8,077
Hungary	21,816	196,341
Iceland	2,372	21,346
India	209,616	2,208,381
Indonesia	41,537	373,837
Iran	16,880	151,919
Iraq	10,213	91,921
Ireland	23,020	266,541
Israel	11,837	106,536
Italy	184,013	1,909,099
Ivory Coast	6,239	56,152
Jamaica	4,765	42,884
Japan	318,921	3,335,477
Jordan	2,489	22,403
Kampuchea	2,286	20,576
Kenya	4,273	38,461
Korea, Rep.	25,331	289,512
Kuwait	58,241	630,951
Laos	1,068	9,615
Lebanon	961	8,654
Lesotho	459	4,135
Liberia	2,276	20,480
Libya	20,843	187,592
Luxembourg	4,511	71,769
Madagascar	2,340	21,057
Malawi	1,603	14,423
Malaysia	22,072	198,649
Maldives	64	577
Mali	1,848	16,634
Mauritania	1,068	9,615
Mauritius	2,361	21,249
Mexico	33,717	303,454
Morocco	22,184	256,869
Nepal	2,658	54,286
Netherlands	139,633	1,475,391
New Zealand	24,871	266,254
Nicaragua	972	8,750
Niger	1,068	9,615

Nigeria	31,420	282,782
Norway	25,747	231,725
Oman	2,051	18,461
Pakistan	26,912	242,206
Panama	2,308	20,769
Papua New Guinea	2,628	23,653
Paraguay	1,277	39,962
Peru	10,021	90,190
Philippines	31,407	352,985
Portugal	14,145	127,305
Qatar	3,493	31,442
Romania	21,378	192,399
Rwanda	1,859	16,730
St. Lucia	310	2,788
St. Vincent and the Grenadines	139	1,250
São Tomé and Príncipe	150	1,346
Sa'udi Arabia	52,338	471,046
Senegal	3,867	34,807
Seychelles	118	1,058
Sierra Leone	1,603	14,423
Singapore	3,419	30,768
Solomon Islands	182	1,635
Somalia	2,019	18,173
South Africa	36,997	332,973
Spain	48,621	437,585
Sri Lanka	10,267	92,402
Sudan	6,410	57,691
Suriname	1,731	15,577
Swaziland	1,784	45,223
Sweden	66,844	720,209
Syria	9,233	122,494
Tanzania	3,739	33,653
Thailand	26,872	305,492
Togo	1,603	14,423
Trinidad and Tobago	5,716	51,441
Tunisia	3,985	35,864
Turkey	29,660	334,434
Uganda	3,558	32,018
United Arab Emirates	10,470	94,228
UK	277,771	2,499,939
US	1,024,820	9,897,883
Upper Volta	1,068	9,615
Uruguay	4,391	39,518
Vanuatu	686	33,821
Venezuela	21,068	189,611
Viet-Nam	5,801	52,210
Western Samoa	182	1,635
Yemen, People's Dem. Rep.	1,132	10,192
Yemen Arab Rep.	2,649	23,846
Yugoslavia	16,121	145,093
Zaire	10,256	92,305
Zambia	12,297	110,670
Zimbabwe	8,728	78,556

Financial Resources for Lending Purposes

The subscriptions of the Bank's members constitute the basic element in the financial resources of the Bank. Altogether, the paid-in portion of the subscriptions was a little over $4.7 billion on 30 June 1983. But the Bank draws much more money from borrowings in the market and from earnings. The Bank's outstanding borrowings as of 30 June 1983 were 37.9 billion, raised in the capital markets of the world. These obligations were denominated in 19 different currencies and were placed with investors, including central banks and government institutions, in more than 100 countries. Four-fifths of the total debt is owed to non-US investors. The Bank has raised this large sum, at interest rates little or no higher than are paid by governments, because of confidence in the Bank engendered by its record of reliability since 1947, and the investors' knowledge that should the Bank ever be in difficulty, it can call in unpaid portions of member countries' subscriptions.

B. LENDING OPERATIONS

Under the Bank's declared purposes, its main function is to make loans according to specific principles: first, on condition that private capital is not available on reasonable terms; second, that the borrower will be able to repay the loan; third, that the project or program to be financed will benefit the economy sufficiently to justify borrowing the foreign exchange; and fourth, that the program or project is well designed and feasible.

The World Bank lends to member governments, or, with government guarantee, to political subdivisions, or to public or private enterprises.

The Bank's first loan, $250 million for postwar reconstruction, was made in the latter part of 1947. Altogether it lent $497 million for postwar reconstruction, all to European countries. The Bank's first development loans were made in the first half of 1948. As of 30 June 1983, the total of loans and credits made by the World Bank was nearly $120 billion, of which $89.6 billion represented IBRD loans and $30 billion IDA credits.

Loan Terms and Interest Rates

The Bank normally makes long-term loans, with repayment commencing after a certain period. The length of the loan is generally related to the estimated useful life of the equipment or plant being financed. For example, the cost of a hydroelectric power plant consists partly of installations that last a very long time and partly of generating equipment that has a shorter economic life. The terms for such loans may be 15 to 20 years. On the other hand, loans for the purchase of less durable goods, such as farm machinery, could be for shorter terms.

Since in the long run the Bank must raise money in order to lend money, it uses as a basis for determining its own standard interest charge the estimated rate the Bank itself would have to pay as a borrower at the time of the loan. Hence, the level of the Bank's interest rate reflects rather closely the fluctuations in the main capital markets of the world. The Bank's standard rate was 10.97% as of 1 April 1983.

TOTAL IBRD LOANS AND IDA CREDITS
AS OF 30 JUNE 1983
(in millions of US dollars)

COUNTRY	IBRD LOANS	IDA CREDITS
Afghanistan	—	230.1
Algeria	1,201.0	—
Argentina	1,918.3	—
Australia	417.7	—
Austria	106.4	—
Bahamas	22.8	—
Bangladesh	46.1	2,546.5
Barbados	46.2	—
Belgium	76.0	—
Belize	5.3	—
Benin	—	173.2
Bolivia	299.3	104.8
Botswana	176.2	15.8
Brazil	87,337.3	—
Burma	33.4	610.0
Burundi	4.8	178.2
Cameroon	538.1	253.0
Cape Verde	—	7.2
Caribbean Region	43.0	14.0
Central African Rep.	—	79.2
Chad	—	78.5
Chile	605.2	19.0
China	563.1	310.4
Colombia	3,681.1	19.5
Comoros	—	24.8
Congo	111.7	74.6
Costa Rica	407.4	5.5
Cyprus	196.0	—

Denmark	85.0	—	Somalia	—	195.4
Djibouti	—	9.4	South Africa	241.8	—
Dominica	—	5.0	Spain	478.7	—
Dominican Republic	292.5	22.0	Sri Lanka	136.6	654.6
E. African Community	244.8	—	Sudan	166.0	781.5
Ecuador	694.4	36.9	Swaziland	61.6	7.8
Egypt	2,029.0	981.2	Syria	505.7	47.3
El Salvador	216.1	25.6	Tanzania	318.2	753.3
Equatorial Guinea	—	4.4	Thailand	3,313.5	125.1
Ethiopia	108.6	500.1	Togo	20.0	197.3
Fiji	83.7	—	Trinidad and Tobago	124.8	—
Finland	316.8	—	Tunisia	1,211.7	74.6
France	250.0	—	Turkey	4,446.6	178.5
Gabon	69.3	—	Uganda	8.4	366.8
Gambia	—	35.4	Upper Volta	1.9	246.2
Ghana	207.0	281.3	Uruguay	456.4	—
Greece	490.8	—	Venezuela	383.3	—
Guatemala	296.0	—	Viet-Nam	—	60.0
Guinea	75.2	155.0	W. African Region	6.1	17.0
Guinea-Bissau	—	44.9	Western Samoa	—	14.4
Guyana	80.0	38.5	Yemen, People's Dem. Rep.	—	153.1
Haiti	2.6	205.2	Yemen Arab Rep.	—	338.8
Honduras	484.0	83.2	Yugoslavia	3,781.7	—
Hungary	239.4	—	Zaire	220.0	495.6
Iceland	47.1	—	Zambia	604.1	108.1
India	5,553.3	11,529.2	Zimbabwe	381.0	53.9
Indonesia	5,985.0	931.8	Other	329.4	15.3
Iran	1,210.7	—			
Iraq	156.2	—			
Ireland	152.5	—			
Israel	284.5	—			
Italy	399.6	—			
Ivory Coast	1,088.3	7.5			
Jamaica	597.5	—			
Japan	862.9	—			
Jordan	220.8	85.3			
Kenya	1,022.4	632.3			
Korea, Rep.	4,480.5	110.8			
Laos	—	53.2			
Lebanon	116.6	—			
Lesotho	—	70.2			
Liberia	156.0	88.8			
Luxembourg	12.0	—			
Madagascar	32.9	395.7			
Malawi	75.2	325.5			
Malaysia	1,610.0	—			
Maldives	—	8.2			
Mali	1.9	248.3			
Malta	7.5	—			
Mauritania	126.0	78.8			
Mauritius	128.5	20.2			
Mexico	6,739.8	—			
Morocco	2,244.5	50.8			
Nepal	—	355.9			
Netherlands	244.0	—			
New Zealand	126.8	—			
Nicaragua	233.6	60.0			
Niger	—	214.6			
Nigeria	2,135.7	35.5			
Norway	145.0	—			
Oman	62.0	—			
Pakistan	1,097.7	1,846.7			
Panama	471.1	—			
Papua New Guinea	145.1	113.2			
Paraguay	428.1	45.5			
Peru	1,544.9	—			
Philippines	3,878.5	122.2			
Portugal	943.2	—			
Romania	2,184.3	—			
Rwanda	—	209.4			
Senegal	164.9	286.5			
Sierra Leone	18.7	89.3			
Singapore	181.3	—			
Solomon Islands	—	6.5			

WORLD BANK TOTAL LENDING BY REGION
AS OF 30 JUNE 1983
(in millions of US dollars)

REGION	IBRD LOANS	IDA CREDITS	TOTALS
East Africa	3,794.5	5,144.0	8,938.5
West Africa	4,720.8	2,696.5	7,417.3
East Asia and Pacific	21,977.5	1,862.9	23,840.4
South Asia	6,867.1	17,551.1	24,418.2
Europe, Middle East, and North Africa	23,845.3	2,139.7	25,985.0
Latin America and Caribbean	28,411.0	684.7	29,095.7
TOTALS	89,616.2	30,078.9	119.695.1

C. PURPOSES OF THE LOANS

The main purpose of the World Bank's operations, including IDA operations, is to lend to developing member countries for productive projects in such sectors as agriculture, industry, and tourism, and to help improve basic services considered essential for development. From 1948 through the 1960s, much of the Bank's lending went to power and transportation projects. Lending also supported large-scale irrigation and flood-control projects. Since 1963, the Bank has been increasing its lending to agriculture. In 1982, agriculture absorbed the highest proportion of the Bank's disbursements (23%), followed by transportation (15%), power (13%), and industry (10%).

The main criterion for assistance is that it should be provided where it can be most effective in the context of the country's specific lending programs developed by the Bank in consultation with its borrowers.

Agriculture and Rural Development

In recent years the largest share of Bank lending has gone to help finance agriculture and rural development projects. The reasons are compelling. Approximately six out of every ten people in developing countries depend on agriculture and related pursuits for their livelihood. Equally important, agricultural production is a key factor in the development of most countries. In the poorest countries it is critical. Bank projects help developing countries expand irrigation, provide more effective extension services, make credit easier to get, adapt technology, increase storage capacity, and improve their domestic marketing and distribution facilities.

In Brazil's Bahia state, for example, a $68-million rural development project financed by the Bank sought to raise the incomes and living standards of 45,000 small-farm families through improved land tenure and redistribution of land, improvements in research and extension activities, and expansion and upgrading of social services and physical infrastructure throughout the region affected.

In northeast China, a $35-million project to develop about 200,000 hectares (494,000 acres) of virgin land was expected to help produce more than 440,000 tons of grain and soybeans. Principal features of the project include provisions for drainage, agricultural machinery and construction equipment, housing, and supporting infrastructure.

WORLD BANK CUMULATIVE LENDING BY PURPOSE
AS OF 30 JUNE 1983
(in millions of US dollars)

PURPOSE	IBRD LOANS	IDA CREDITS	TOTALS
Agriculture and rural development	18,950.1	11,263.9	30,214.0
Development finance companies	9,163.6	723.1	9,886.7
Education	3,197.8	1,771.2	4,969.0
Energy	19,197.0	3,833.8	23,030.8
Industry	6,672.2	1,135.5	7,807.7
Nonproject	5,470.5	3,166.1	8,636.6
Population, health, and nutrition	312.8	365.0	677.8
Small-scale enterprises	1,577.1	292.5	1,869.6
Technical assistance	141.6	263.7	405.3
Telecommunications	1,602.1	1,046.2	2,648.3
Tourism	363.6	86.7	450.3
Transportation	16,470.5	4,190.7	20,661.2
Urbanization	2,249.5	703.0	2,952.5
Water supply and sewerage	4,247.8	1,237.5	5,485.3
TOTAL	89,616.2	30,078.9	119,695.1

Energy

The Bank's lending for energy has risen sharply since the 1970s. Nearly two-thirds of its program is in electric power, helping to tap the immense hydroelectric potential in many developing countries. The Bank also aids in the development of coal resources, which requires large-scale investments in infrastructure as well as in mines, and in forestry, where investments are needed in conservation and reforestation to renew the world's rapidly dwindling sources of firewood. In developing oil and gas resources, the Bank helps to develop data which countries can use to attract private investment for exploration and development, and assists in financing the infrastructure necessary for the development of oil and gas fields. In the Philippines, for example, a $36-million loan aimed to provide seismic surveys, studies, exploratory drilling, and technical assistance in energy development and oil exploration to help extend exploration activities to relatively unexplored onshore areas and attract foreign investment in the sector. In India, a $156-million project involved the building of a hydroelectric plant in the eastern region to help increase the power-generating capacity of Orissa state. Roads, bridges, sewerage facilities, and other related facilities were also to be constructed as part of the project.

Transportation

Bank assistance has been provided for the expansion and improvement of all major modes of transport. Most important since the mid-1960s has been lending for roads and highways. Hun-

dreds of thousands of kilometers of main, secondary, feeder, and rural access roads have been built and hundreds of thousands more have been improved. Financing has also been provided for improving railway track, purchasing locomotives and rolling stock, modernizing signaling and communications systems, and creating supporting facilities for maintenance and operations. Lending for ports and shipping has encompassed construction and expansion of seaports and river-ports, improvement of inland waterways and port-access channels, and procurement of vessels, principally for port operations or for transport among islands or through inland waterways. A lesser number of loans has been made for projects relating to domestic or international airports. In Cameroon, for example, a project financed by a $22-million Bank loan assisted the National Port Authority to expand the Douala port capacity, mainly through extension of general cargo facilities and provision of fruit-handling equipment, data-processing facilities, and technical assistance. In a $100-million project in Thailand about 1,000 km (620 mi) of provincial roads were to be constructed and improved, and another 1,000 km (620 mi) of paved national and provincial roads were to be strengthened and rehabilitated.

Industry and Mining

The Bank's direct lending for industry has been largely confined to assisting large-scale undertakings. The Bank has supported projects in most of the basic industrial sectors such as steel, cement, textiles, chemicals, fertilizers, and mining. The project may be for import substitution or to produce goods for export. The largest share of direct industrial lending has been for fertilizer production and distribution projects. Chemical and synthetic-fuels projects, particularly those designed to produce energy economically from domestic resources such as coal, natural gas, and biomass, are becoming an important area of direct lending by the Bank.

A $165-million project in Egypt, for example, assisted the construction and operation of an integrated reinforcing bar plant to help meet the needs of the domestic market for a stable supply of rebar, a vital input for the construction industry. In Senegal, a Bank loan of $7.7 million was aimed at financing studies and tests to help the phosphate mining and processing operations in the country maximize their overall efficiency. The project was also designed to help orient the country's development efforts to exploit its phosphate resources in the direction regarded as the one offering the most promise.

Development Finance Companies

While assistance to large-scale industrial projects is provided directly through Bank loans, support for medium-size and small-scale productive enterprises is largely channeled through local development finance companies, some of which are privately controlled, some government-owned. Most development finance companies lend to manufacturing enterprises. The Bank uses these companies to help small enterprises. In Jamaica, for example, foreign exchange and credit were provided by a $30-million loan, through the country's Export Development Fund, to exporters of nontraditional manufactured and agricultural products and to qualified domestic enterprises producing inputs for the export producers, and a second loan of $15 million encouraged industrial development, particularly for export-oriented industry, by providing the foreign-exchange component of subloans to manufacturing, agro-industrial, tourist, and mining enterprises. In the Comoros, the newly created Development Bank was strengthened by providing it with a $2.3-million IDA credit for lending to small and medium-scale enterprises functioning on the islands.

Urban Development

The Bank's approach to urban poverty aims to create productive employment opportunities and to develop programs to deliver basic services to the urban poor on a large scale, at standards they and the economy can afford. Urban projects usually contain as major components the upgrading of slums and squatter settlements or the creation of serviced sites for additional low-income housing. In such projects the emphasis is on self-help; finance is supplied only for those basic services that people cannot provide for themselves. A project in Haiti, for example, funded by $21 million in IDA credits, included rehabilitation and upgrading of the Port-au-Prince central-market area, a sites-and-services scheme for families displaced by that upgrading, sites-and-services schemes in both Cap-Haïtien and Les Cayes, and measures aimed at institutional development. In Mexico, a $9.2-million Bank loan provided consultant services to support the preinvestment stage of a deconcentration program for the Mexico City region. In the Dominican Republic, technical assistance was furnished through a $7-million Bank loan to the Municipality of Santo Domingo to handle complex issues of city management planning and of development arising from rapid growth.

Water Supply and Sewerage

The Bank's lending for water supply and sanitation has broadened greatly since it started in 1963. At first it was concentrated in major cities, but subsequently it has encompassed smaller cities, towns, and villages. In Pakistan, for example, a project to expand the water supply system in Karachi, financed by a $25-million Bank loan, was expected to provide as many as half a million low-income consumers with additional supplies of safe water. In Ghana, technical assistance was provided through $13 million in IDA credits to the Ghana Water and Sewerage Corp. to improve its management, operating, and financial performance.

Education

The Bank has helped to build or improve a wide variety of educational institutions, from primary schools to universities and teacher-training colleges. Primary and nonformal basic education, including literacy training, has received increasing support in recent years. The Bank has also supported projects for nonformal vocational and agricultural training. Assistance has been provided for curriculum development, educational radio and television broadcasting, mobile educational units, and the production and distribution of textbooks, learning materials, and equipment. In Colombia, a $15-million Bank project that is part of the government's ten-year program for strengthening rural basic education was expected to help increase the coverage, quality, and efficiency of primary education and to bring about institutional improvements by training teachers; introducing new curricula; supplying educational materials, furniture, and equipment; financing civil works for repair and upgrading of existing buildings; and developing a computerized management-information system. In Uganda, a project financed by $32 million in IDA credits aimed to assist the country's educational system, from primary schools to technical schools and Makerere University, with texts and library books, teachers' guides and classroom equipment, roofing materials, and spare parts and tools.

D. OTHER ACTIVITIES
Technical Assistance
The Bank renders its members a wide variety of technical assistance, much of it financed under its lending program. It conducts full-scale surveys of their economic potential, undertakes economic studies in depth, and advises on individual sectors in the economy or on specific projects. The Bank pays continuous attention to the economic performance of its borrowers. Each proposal for a loan or a credit is considered in the context of the Bank's assessment of the economic position, policies, and prospects of the borrowing country. The Bank's technical assistance activities are directed not only toward assuring sound lending but also toward assisting developing countries to maximize their resource utilization. Many of the Bank's loans have been instrumental in the establishment of more efficient management and better administrative methods.

Interorganizational Cooperation

The Bank is executing agency for preinvestment projects financed by the UNDP, the main UN source of technical assistance funds. In fiscal 1983, the Bank was executing agency for 127 projects for which UNDP had committed more than $160 million. Some 33 new projects involving commitments of $33.1 million were approved during the year. Although these activities related to a number of sectors, energy was particularly prominent. In addition to the diagnosis of major energy problems in some 60 developing countries, carried out under the UNDP/Bank Energy Assessment Program that was launched in 1980, the Bank and UNDP reached agreement in 1983 on an Energy Sector Management Program expected to cost $47 million over a span of four years.

The Bank also cooperates with other UN agencies, including FAO, in agriculture and rural development; WHO, in disease control; UNESCO, in education; and UNIDO, in industrial development. With FAO and UNDP, the Bank sponsors the Consultative Group on International Agricultural Research (CGIAR), the aim of which is to develop technologies that farmers in developing countries can use to grow more food. Through its 36 donor members, CGIAR provided grants amounting to some $165 million in 1983 to assist 13 international agricultural research institutions which carry out research on all important food crops, on livestock, and on farming systems. These institutions also fulfill an important training function.

Training

The Economic Development Institute (EDI) was established by the Bank in 1955 to provide training in practical techniques of development programming and project analysis for officials in developing countries. Since its inception, EDI has trained some 10,000 such officials. In fiscal 1983, EDI offered 17 seminars at Bank headquarters in Washington and conducted 52 activities overseas, attended by a total of some 1,500 participants. The preponderance of overseas courses reflects the fact that the institute cannot alone meet the constantly growing demand for training. It maximizes its scarce resources by building up training capabilities in member countries themselves, either by working through existing institutions or by organizing nuclear courses for indigenous training programs.

Economic Research and Studies

The Bank's economic and social research program, inaugurated in 1972, is undertaken by the Bank's own research staff and is funded out of its administrative budget. The research program is shaped by the Bank's own needs as a lending institution and as a source of policy advice to member governments, and by the needs of member countries. Its main purpose is to gain new insights into the development process and the policies affecting it, to introduce new techniques or methodologies into country, sectoral, and project analyses, to provide the analytical bases for major Bank documents such as the *World Development Report*, and to help strengthen indigenous research capacity in member developing countries.

Mediation

Developing countries depend heavily on foreign private capital to finance development. Such capital flows are sensitive to legal and political conditions in developing countries. The International Center for Settlement of Investment Disputes (ICSID) was founded in 1966 by the Bank to improve the investment climate in developing countries, under the Convention on the Settlement of Investment Disputes between States and Nationals of Other States. Subject to the consent of both parties, a state and a foreign investor can settle any legal dispute that might arise out of an investment through conciliation and/or arbitration before an impartial international forum. By 30 June 1983, 83 states had ratified the convention; 5 more had signed it but not yet completed the ratification process.

[8]BIBLIOGRAPHY

Making the Most of Business Opportunities from World Bank Projects.
Policies and Operations: The World Bank Group.
Questions and Answers: World Bank and IDA.
The World Bank and International Finance Corporation.
World Bank Annual Reports.
World Bank Atlas.
(The Bank also publishes many economic reports on countries; survey reports on such subjects as agriculture, natural resources, and energy; and books on development economics and policy.)

THE INTERNATIONAL DEVELOPMENT ASSOCIATION (IDA)

¹BACKGROUND: The world's poorer countries have gone heavily into debt to finance their development. The total outstanding debt of 97 such countries rose from an estimated $59 billion in 1970 to $465 billion in 1981. Annual interest and amortization charges on this debt had, by 1981, reached a level of $99 billion. Many countries have long since arrived at the point where they can no longer afford to raise all the development capital they are in a position to make good use of at ordinary rates of interest and in the time span of conventional loans, World Bank loans included. The function of the International Development Association, an affiliate of the Bank and the youngest member of the World Bank Group (IBRD, IFC, and IDA), is to supply financing for high-priority purposes on terms that will permit such countries to pursue their development without adding excessively to their debt-servicing burden. IDA's loans are interest-free and repayable over very long terms, with extended grace periods. As a result, IDA's resources, unlike the resources of a regular lending institution, must be regularly replenished through contributions if the agency is to continue in business.

²CREATION

The creation of an international agency such as IDA was discussed in the UN at various times during the 1950s. A report drawn up by a group of experts on financing and economic development in 1951 referred to the need for an "international development authority." Although such proposals were at first opposed by the US, IDA as it was finally launched was largely the result of US initiative. In 1958 the US Senate passed a resolution introduced by Senator A. S. ("Mike") Monroney calling for cooperative international action along these lines. Eventually, on 1 October 1959, the World Bank's Board of Governors approved, without objections, a motion of US Secretary of the Treasury Robert Anderson that a new agency, under the name International Development Association, be established as an affiliate of the World Bank.

The debate that preceded the Board's action revealed potential disagreements among members of the Bank on a number of points, such as the terms IDA should set for its loans, permissible restrictions that countries subscribing to IDA's capital could place on the use of funds supplied in their national currencies, and related matters. Rather than decide these matters itself, the Board of Governors asked the Executive Directors of the World Bank to draw up a constitution ("Articles of Agreement") for IDA, which would then be submitted to the Bank's member governments.

IDA's Articles of Agreement were accordingly drafted by the Executive Directors of the World Bank and early in 1960 transmitted to the member governments of the Bank. The next step was for those governments desiring to join IDA to take whatever legislative or other action might be required to accept membership and to subscribe funds. The new lending association came into existence in September 1960, when governments whose subscriptions to its capital aggregated $650 million, or 65% of the projected $1-billion goal, had accepted membership. IDA started operations in November of that year.

³PURPOSES

In the preamble to the Articles of Agreement, the signatory governments declare their conviction that mutual cooperation for constructive economic purposes, healthy development of the world economy, and balanced growth of international trade foster peace and world prosperity; that higher standards of living and economic and social progress in the less-developed countries are desirable, not only in the interest of the latter, but also for the international community as a whole; and that achievement of these objectives would be facilitated by an increase in the international flow of capital, public and private, to assist in the development of the resources of less-developed countries. Hence, as stated in its Articles of Agreement, the purposes of IDA are "to promote economic development, increase productivity and thus raise standards of living in the less-developed areas of the world included within the Association's membership, in particular by providing finance to meet their important developmental requirements on terms which are more flexible and bear less heavily on the balance of payments than those of conventional loans, thereby furthering the developmental objectives of the [World Bank] and supplementing its activities."

⁴MEMBERSHIP

For the purposes of IDA, members are divided into two categories. Part I members, of which there are 22, are economically advanced countries. These countries pay their subscriptions in convertible currency and have made further agreed contributions to replenish the Association's resources. Part II members, 109 in 1983, are the less-developed countries, which pay 10% of their subscriptions in convertible currencies and the remaining 90%, and any additional subscriptions, in their own currency. A list of members, with their subscriptions, is given in section 7A below.

⁵STRUCTURE

IDA is administered by the same officers and staff who administer the affairs of the World Bank. The president of the Bank also serves as the president of IDA, and the governors and executive directors of the Bank serve in the same capacity in IDA.

As in the World Bank, a government's voting power in IDA is roughly proportionate to its capital subscription. As of 30 June 1983, the 22 Part I countries had 63.02% of the total votes, including 18.51% for the US, 7.26% for the FRG, 7.18% for Japan, and 7.13% for the UK. The 109 Part II countries had 36.98% of the total votes.

[6]BUDGET

Since IDA relies entirely on the World Bank's staff and facilities for all its activities, it reimburses the bank through a management fee for administrative expenses incurred on its behalf. The management fee was established at $213.7 million for the fiscal year ending 30 June 1983.

[7]ACTIVITIES

A. FINANCIAL RESOURCES

IDA's funds are obtained from three main sources: members' subscriptions; periodic "replenishments" provided by richer members and certain special contributions; and transfer of income from the IBRD and repayments on IDA credits. As of 30 June 1983, members' subscriptions and supplementary resources totaled $28.2 billion. Of this total, $27 billion represented subscriptions and supplementary resources by Part I members, including the US ($9.6 billion), Japan ($3.4 billion), the FRG ($3.2 billion), and the UK ($2.9 billion), and $1.2 billion represented subscriptions and supplementary resources by Part II members.

Initial subscriptions alone were never envisaged as the sole source of IDA's lending funds, but by the early 1960s it became clear that more funding would be needed much earlier than expected. Thus IDA members began the practice of replenishments, of which there have been six since 1964, the first totaling $750 million and the latest, for the three-year period from 1 July 1980 to 30 June 1983, totaling $12 billion.

Aside from their contributions under replenishment agreements, a number of countries have agreed over the years to make voluntary increases and special contributions in excess of their normal shares. Under IDA's second replenishment, for example, Canada, Denmark, Finland, the Netherlands, and Sweden offered supplementary contributions totaling $17.5 million. Also, a growing share has been taken up by several of the more advanced developing countries and by oil-exporting developing countries.

Since 1964, IDA has received regular support from the IBRD through the transfer of some of its net income not needed for the Bank's own purposes. In fiscal 1983, the Bank authorized transfers to IDA of $1.6 billion.

IDA's income in fiscal 1983, including income from development credits and from investments, was $145 million.

SUBSCRIPTIONS TO THE CAPITAL OF IDA
AS OF 30 JUNE 1983
(In thousands of US dollars)

Part I Members' Subscriptions Payable in Convertible Currencies

Australia	528,378
Austria	189,914
Belgium	398,245
Canada	1,493,460
Denmark	285,069
Finland	132,012
France	1,355,329
Germany, Fed. Rep.	3,232,701
Iceland	2,282
Ireland	30,688
Italy	809,633
Japan	3,488,684
Kuwait	446,704
Luxembourg	12,865
Netherlands	782,504
New Zealand	27,304
Norway	279,218
South Africa	47,274
Sweden	819,851
United Arab Emirates	136,464
UK	2,918,660
US	9,642,646

Part II Members' Subscriptions Payable 10% in Convertible Currencies and 90% in the Nation's Own Currency

Afghanistan	1,210
Algeria	4,698
Argentina	46,656
Bangladesh	6,238
Belize	216
Benin	541
Bhutan	54
Bolivia	1,199
Botswana	188
Brazil	52,658
Burma	2,380
Burundi	907
Cameroon	1,161
Cape Verde	87
Central African Rep.	578
Chad	562
Chile	3,979
China	35,173
Colombia	10,427
Comoros	92
Congo	572
Costa Rica	230
Cyprus	893
Djibouti	175
Dominica	88
Dominican Republic	548
Ecuador	902
Egypt	5,966
El Salvador	369
Equatorial Guinea	359
Ethiopia	620
Fiji	629
Gabon	565
Gambia	314
Ghana	2,740
Greece	5,811
Grenada	107
Guatemala	479
Guinea	1,200
Guinea-Bissau	152
Guyana	957
Haiti	910
Honduras	361
India	50,859
Indonesia	12,875
Iran	5,822
Iraq	893
Israel	2,392
Ivory Coast	1,155
Jordan	393
Kampuchea	1,152
Kenya	1,966
Korea, Rep.	4,014
Laos	568
Lebanon	521
Lesotho	188
Liberia	910
Libya	1,171
Madagascar	1,093
Malawi	896
Malaysia	3,015
Maldives	35
Mali	1,014
Mauritania	577
Mauritius	1,035
Mexico	13,684
Morocco	4,124
Nepal	591
Nicaragua	396
Niger	585
Nigeria	3,836
Oman	383

Pakistan	12,010
Panama	26
Papua New Guinea	1,020
Paraguay	353
Peru	1,915
Philippines	5,913
Rwanda	907
St. Lucia	167
St. Vincent and the Grenadines	75
São Tomé and Príncipe	76
Sa'udi Arabia	774,004
Senegal	1,958
Sierra Leone	898
Solomon Islands	98
Somalia	872
Spain	61,140
Sri Lanka	3,495
Sudan	1,174
Swaziland	376
Syria	1,101
Tanzania	1,965
Thailand	3,601
Togo	886
Trinidad and Tobago	1,461
Tunisia	1,697
Turkey	6,609
Uganda	1,894
Upper Volta	578
Vanuatu	205
Viet-Nam	1,703
Western Samoa	103
Yemen, People's Dem. Rep.	1,388
Yemen Arab Rep.	515
Yugoslavia	21,004
Zaire	3,403
Zambia	2,911
Zimbabwe	4,507

B. TERMS OF IDA LENDING

The terms of IDA's development credits are discretionary. Credits have a 50-year maturity, and repayments begin 10 years after the credit is signed. After this grace period, 1% of the credit is repaid in each of the next 10 years and then 3% in each of the remaining 30 years. The loans carry no interest rate, although there is a service charge of 0.75% a year on the disbursed balance.

In January 1982, a commitment fee of 0.5% a year on the undisbursed balance was introduced to bring the timing of IDA's income from credits more into line with its administrative expenses.

C. IDA'S OPERATIONS

While IDA's financial terms are liberal, its economic and technical criteria for development credits are exactly the same as those applied by the IBRD in lending on conventional terms. Each credit must be justified by the borrowing country's economic position, prospects, and policies. Credits are extended only for high-priority purposes that, in the words of IDA's Articles of Agreement, will "promote economic development, increase productivity and thus raise standards of living in the less developed areas of the world."

Since IDA's resources have been considerably less than the need of developing countries for additional external finance on easy terms, they must be carefully rationed on the basis of need and prospects for their most effective use. On a cumulative basis, 81% of IDA's commitments were to countries that in 1980 had per capita incomes of $410 or less; 98% went to countries with incomes of $730 or less.

By 30 June 1983, IDA had committed a total of $30 billion for development projects in over 80 countries. Of the total, $17.5 billion had been lent to countries of South Asia; $7.8 billion to countries of Africa other than North Africa; $2.1 billion to countries of Europe, the Middle East, and North Africa; and $684 million to countries of Latin America and the Caribbean.

Most of IDA's credits have been for agriculture and rural development ($11.2 billion), transportation ($4.1 billion), and energy ($3.8 billion). (See sections 7A and 7B in the article on the IBRD for IDA credits to individual countries and by region and purpose.)

Since the IDA is managed and directed as an affiliate of the World Bank, all its operations are closely coordinated with those of the Bank, and a joint annual report is issued covering the work of the two institutions.

[8]BIBLIOGRAPHY

Policies and Operations: The World Bank Group.
Questions and Answers: World Bank and IDA.
The World Bank and International Finance Corporation.
World Bank Annual Reports.
World Bank Atlas.

THE INTERNATIONAL FINANCE CORPORATION (IFC)

[1]**BACKGROUND:** The International Finance Corporation is the member of the World Bank Group that promotes the growth of the private sector in less-developed member countries. IFC's principal activity is helping to finance individual private enterprise projects that contribute to the economic development of the country or region where the project is located. The Corporation is one of the very few international development organizations that can supply equity financing as well as provide loans and make underwriting and standby commitments. In addition, IFC helps identify and promote promising projects; encourages the flow of domestic and foreign capital in productive investments in developing countries; assists development finance companies and other institutions with goals similar to IFC's; helps improve investment conditions in the developing countries by assisting in establishment of institutions that marshal funds for investments or provide a liquid market for investments; and assists banks and companies that have difficulty in making viable plans for sound projects by offering the needed finance.

[2]CREATION

Within a few years of the founding of the World Bank (IBRD), it became evident that sufficient provision had not been made for financing the development of the private sector in countries looking to the UN system for aid. The Bank's charter restrained it from making equity (capital stock) investments or from lending money, directly or indirectly, to a private company without a governmental guarantee. Yet "venture capital" was the very thing needed in many developing countries to get a variety of productive enterprises under way, and the amount of venture capital available through private banking and investment channels was inadequate.

The first public suggestion for an international institution to close this gap appeared in a report, "Partners and Progress," which Nelson Rockefeller (then chairman of the advisory board of the Point 4 Program) had submitted to President Harry S Truman in 1951. The matter was taken up by the staff of the World Bank, and in 1952 the Bank submitted proposals for such an institution to the UN Economic and Social Council. Some members of the council, including the UK and the US, voiced the fear that the proposed institution might deter the flow of private capital to the developing countries. They also objected in principle to an intergovernmental organization's having the right to purchase shares in private companies.

The majority of ECOSOC members, however, strongly endorsed the idea of an international financial institution to aid the private sector of development, and by late 1954 a compromise was worked out. The International Finance Corporation, as originally established, could lend money to private enterprises without government guarantees, but it was not empowered to make equity investments, though loans with certain equity features, such as stock options, were allowed. The 31 countries necessary to launch the IFC pledged their consent over the next 18 months, and IFC formally came into existence on 24 July 1956 as a separate legal entity affiliated with the World Bank.

The IFC's early investments often included such features as stock options and other profit-sharing devices in lieu of direct equity financing, but the terms were complex and difficult to negotiate, and it soon became apparent to all concerned that the IFC's effectiveness was severely circumscribed by the restriction on equity investment. Proposals to amend the charter so as to permit IFC to hold shares were put to the Board of Directors and the Board of Governors, and approved in 1961—with the support, this time, of both the UK and the US. The revision of IFC's charter in 1961 to permit investment in equities made it possible to broaden and diversify operations as well as to simplify the terms of investment. With the demand for IFC's services steadily expanding, the Board of Directors amended the charter again in 1965 to permit IFC to borrow from the World Bank up to four times its unimpaired subscribed capital and surplus.

[3]PURPOSES

In its simplest form, IFC's purpose is to assist its less-developed member countries by promoting the growth of the private sector of their economies. It does this by providing venture capital for productive private enterprises in association with local investors and management, by encouraging the development of local capital markets, and by stimulating flow of private capital. The Corporation is designed to supplement, rather than replace, private capital. It provides financial and technical assistance to privately controlled development finance companies. IFC attempts to recruit foreign capital for a project and encourages the participation of other private investors in its own commitments.

[4]MEMBERSHIP

Membership in IFC is open to all members of the World Bank. On 30 June 1983, IFC had 124 member states. For the list of members, see section 7A below.

[5]STRUCTURE

The structure of IFC is similar to that of the World Bank. The IFC's Board of Governors consists of those governors of the World Bank whose countries are also members of IFC. Its Board of Directors is now composed of all the Executive Directors of the World Bank. IFC headquarters, like those of the World Bank, are at 1818 H Street N.W., Washington, D.C. The Corporation also has offices in Paris, London, New York, and Tokyo, and regional missions in Abidjan, Cairo, Manila, Nairobi, and New Delhi. The annual meeting of the IFC Board of Governors is held in conjunction with the annual meeting of the Board of Governors of the World Bank.

The first president of IFC was Robert L. Garner, formerly vice-president of the World Bank. Since 1961, the president of the World Bank also has been the president of the Corporation. The immediate direction of the Corporation is the responsibility of the executive vice-president, Hans A. Wuttke, who has served in that post since January 1981.

IFC had a staff of 410, from 68 countries, in fiscal 1983.

[6]BUDGET

The administrative expenses of IFC, which are met from income, totaled $43 million in 1983.

[7]ACTIVITIES

A. FINANCIAL RESOURCES

Capital Subscriptions

The authorized capital of IFC is $650 million. Each member country subscribes to it, and the amount of the subscription determines voting power. As of 30 June 1983, $543.7 million had been subscribed by 124 members. The largest subscriptions were by the US ($146.6 million), the UK ($37.9 million), the FRG ($33.2 million), France ($29.5 million), Japan ($25.5 million), Canada ($20.9 million), India ($19.7 million), Italy ($19.1 million), the Netherlands ($14.4 million), Belgium ($13.7 million), and Australia ($12.1 million).

SUBSCRIPTIONS TO CAPITAL STOCK
AS OF 30 JUNE 1983
(in thousands of US dollars)

MEMBER	SUBSCRIPTION
Afghanistan	111
Argentina	9,821
Australia	12,191
Austria	5,085
Bangladesh	2,328
Barbados	93
Belgium	13,723
Belize	26
Bolivia	490
Botswana	29
Brazil	10,169
Burma	666
Burundi	100
Cameroon	490
Canada	20,952
Chile	2,328
China	4,154
Colombia	2,083
Congo	67
Costa Rica	245
Cyprus	551
Denmark	4,779
Djibouti	21
Dominica	11
Dominican Republic	306
Ecuador	674
Egypt	3,124
El Salvador	11
Ethiopia	33
Fiji	74
Finland	4,043
France	29,528
Gabon	429
Germany, Fed. Rep.	33,204
Ghana	1,306
Greece	1,777
Grenada	21
Guatemala	306
Guinea	134
Guinea-Bissau	18
Guyana	368
Haiti	306
Honduras	184
Iceland	11
India	19,788
Indonesia	7,351
Iran	372
Iraq	67
Ireland	332
Israel	550
Italy	19,114
Ivory Coast	913
Jamaica	1,103
Japan	25,546
Jordan	429
Kenya	1,041
Korea, Rep.	2,450
Kuwait	4,533
Lebanon	50
Lesotho	18
Liberia	83
Libya	55
Luxembourg	551
Madagascar	111
Malawi	368
Malaysia	3,921
Maldives	4
Mali	116
Mauritania	55
Mauritius	429
Mexico	6,004
Morocco	2,328
Nepal	306
Netherlands	14,458
New Zealand	923
Nicaragua	184
Niger	67
Nigeria	5,575
Norway	4,533
Oman	306
Pakistan	4,411
Panama	344
Papua New Guinea	490
Paraguay	123
Peru	1,777
Philippines	3,247
Portugal	2,144
Rwanda	306
St. Lucia	19
Sa'udi Arabia	9,251
Senegal	707
Seychelles	7
Sierra Leone	83
Singapore	177
Solomon Islands	11
Somalia	83
South Africa	4,108
Spain	6,004
Sri Lanka	1,838
Sudan	111
Swaziland	184
Sweden	6,923
Syria	72
Tanzania	724
Thailand	2,818
Togo	368
Trinidad and Tobago	1,059
Tunisia	919
Turkey	3,063
Uganda	735
United Arab Emirates	1,838
UK	37,900
US	146,661
Upper Volta	245
Uruguay	919
Vanuatu	25
Venezuela	7,106
Viet-Nam	166
Western Samoa	9
Yemen Arab Rep.	184
Yugoslavia	2,422
Zaire	1,929
Zambia	1,286
Zimbabwe	546

Earnings and Borrowings

IFC's operating income in fiscal 1983 was $137.4 million. Net income, after deducting operating and administrative expenses, was $23 million. With paid-in capital of $543.8 million, total paid-in capital and accumulated earnings amounted to $747.6 million.

IFC may borrow from the World Bank for use in its lending operations as long as the Corporation's total borrowings do not exceed four times its unimpaired subscribed capital and surplus. During 1983, IFC borrowed the equivalent of $145 million from the Bank. Total borrowings at the end of the year were $1,012 million.

Disbursements

During 1983, approximately $228.1 million was disbursed against committed loans and equity investments, and an additional $146.3 million was disbursed for participants in IFC financing managed by the Corporation. Repayments and sales of $124.6 million were received during the year, so that net disbursements were $249.8 million.

At the end of fiscal 1983, IFC's investment portfolio, including undisbursed balances, held for its own account was $1,881.9 million. Of this, $1,587.8 million was in the form of loans and $294.1 million in equity. In addition, $1,122.7 million was held and managed for participants in IFC financing. IFC had equity investments in 230 companies in 62 developing countries.

B. INVESTMENT POLICIES

IFC provides risk capital for a wide variety of productive private enterprises and will consider investments in utilities, agriculture, mining, tourism, and other fields, as well as manufacturing. IFC is prepared to assist companies to expand, modernize, or diversify their operations as well as to help finance new projects. Generally, the Corporation will invest only in the less developed of its member countries and will finance only ventures in which there is room for local participation. IFC will not invest in undertakings that are government owned or controlled, though it may be prepared to help an enterprise in which the government has a minority interest. IFC does, however, advise the government concerned of any proposed investment in a country and will not proceed if that government objects.

Every venture in which IFC invests must hold out the prospect of earning a profit and must benefit the economy of the country in which it is made. IFC never invests alone. It expects to mobilize and supplement private capital, not to replace it. IFC attaches great importance to the extent of the sponsor's participation in the share capital of an enterprise. IFC will never be a majority shareholder.

IFC investments generally are no more than 25% of the project cost, and it normally provides between $1 million and $30 million. However, it can raise substantial funds in addition to its own investment for larger projects; it may also invest less than $1 million, especially in ventures in small and least-developed countries.

Periodic progress reports, other information as may be necessary, and the right to visit plants and other property and consult with management are required by IFC. In this, as in the provision of its regular investment agreements, IFC carries on its business in the manner of a private investor. It neither seeks nor accepts government guarantees for its investments.

IFC will provide loan capital, equity capital, or a combination of the two. IFC financing may be used to acquire fixed assets or for working capital and is available for foreign exchange as well as local currencies. Funds are not tied to procurement from specific countries, except to the extent that goods and services must be procured in a member country of the World Bank or in Switzerland. IFC's direct investments are made in association with local or foreign investors, and the Corporation welcomes projects combining both.

IFC loans normally run for a term of 7–12 years. Amortization is usually payable semiannually or quarterly after the expiration of an agreed-upon grace period. A commitment fee of 1% per year is payable on the undisbursed part of the loan. Interest rates vary according to the circumstances of particular transactions.

Through its Capital Markets Department, IFC provides advice and financial support for the establishment of institutions in the developing countries to mobilize and allocate domestic savings and to make possible the sale and purchase of securities by local investors. In fiscal 1983, the Capital Markets Department carried out 11 projects in 9 countries.

Development Finance Companies

The principal contribution of the World Bank Group to the building of financial institutions in the developing countries has been its support of development finance companies. These institutions can perform many important services, such as providing medium- and long-term capital to local private enterprises, mobilizing domestic private savings for investment purposes, acting as a channel for foreign capital, identifying and promoting new investment opportunities, carrying out underwritings, and selling their more seasoned portfolio securities to local investors.

IFC has played a key role in creating or substantially reorganizing a number of privately owned development finance companies. It is a shareholder of many such companies, and it has engaged in a wide range of activities designed to improve their management, staff, policies, and operations.

There are many kinds of investment companies. Some operate in a single country, others regionally, and still others worldwide. Some are locally owned and controlled, while others are owned and controlled by private interests in capital exporting countries. All are eligible for IFC support if they need it, are well managed, contribute to the development of the countries in which they are doing business, and follow policies generally consistent with those of IFC.

C. IFC INVESTMENTS

IFC's history has been marked by growth in the number and size of investments and by a continued search for new ways to assist its member countries. During its first five years, IFC approved $51.2 million for 46 projects with a total cost of $231 million. During the five-year period 1979–83, the Board of Directors approved $3,374 million for 282 ventures with a total cost of $13,261 million.

In fiscal 1983, 58 investments in 36 countries were approved, totaling $844.5 million. Of these, 19 were in Latin America, 16 each in Africa and Asia, and 7 in the Middle East and Europe. By sector, 38% was for manufacturing, 24% for agribusiness, and the remainder for financial institutions in developing countries and for mining and other enterprises.

In Africa, of the 16 projects approved, 6 were in agribusiness and 4 in mining and metals. In Guinea, for example, IFC participated with a number of international investors and banks in putting together the financing for a diamond mine. The project was expected to have a major impact on Guinea's balance of payments and to serve as a model for other potential investors to undertake projects in the country.

In Asia, IFC projects included aid to develop an integrated tin and tantalum processing industry in Thailand and to double the production capacity of the nation's glass industry. In Fiji, IFC is helping to finance the expansion and rehabilitation of the sugar mills, which are a major source of foreign exchange and employment in the country.

In Europe and the Middle East, examples of IFC investments include assistance in establishing Turkey's first modern abbatoir, which is designed to serve a growing domestic market and to increase the export of chilled beef and lamb to growing Middle East markets. Promotional efforts in the Yemen Arab Republic resulted in the completion of a $4-million investment in a dry batteries company and the building up of the project inventory of potential investments to include several agribusiness and mineral projects.

IFC projects in Latin America and the Caribbean included agro-industrial, manufacturing, mining, and capital markets ventures. In Brazil and Uruguay, for example, IFC played an important part in ensuring that projects that faced serious difficulties or delays were able to proceed. In Brazil, the start-up of a ferro-nickel project in Goiás and a fertilizer project in the Amazon region were set back, respectively, because of delays in completion of a power line and because of market conditions. IFC led the efforts to complete the financial plans for the two projects, participated in capital increases, and arranged with other banks to refinance long-term loans so as to provide for secure financial structures during the extended start-up phase. In Uruguay, IFC similarly helped to put together a financial package which enabled an integrated fishing company to overcome a liquidity crisis and proceed on schedule.

D. TECHNICAL ASSISTANCE

IFC's project-related technical assistance involves more than just minor improvements designed to enhance project operability. On an increasing number of occasions, assistance has resulted in technical restructuring. A technical evaluation of a tin mining project, for example, indicated the need for a major revamping of the operating parameters in order to improve the project's viability. In the energy sector, the technical appraisal of a gas recovery project led the sponsors to reassess the field development priorities. In an agribusiness project to process malting barley, it was demonstrated that the location of the plant should be changed to the farming area.

Greater emphasis is being placed on the use of technology especially suited for small-size industrial units in developing countries characterized by limited markets and scarcity of skills. These units would be aimed especially at using available natural resources and at promoting import substitution.

[8]BIBLIOGRAPHY

IFC—Annual Report.
IFC—General Policies.
IFC—International Finance Corporation (information sheet).
IFC—Preliminary Project Information Required.
Capital Markets: Mobilizing Resources for Development.
The World Bank and International Finance Corporation.

THE INTERNATIONAL CIVIL AVIATION ORGANIZATION (ICAO)

[1]**BACKGROUND:** In December 1903, the first heavier-than-air craft, designed by the Wright brothers, managed to fly 37 m (120 ft) under its own power carrying one person. In 1981, scheduled airlines alone flew 694 billion passenger-mi, carrying 749 million passengers. Total operating revenues (passenger, cargo, mail) of the world's airlines had reached $3.7 billion a year by 1958 and $93 billion by 1981. Although in a number of countries regulation of domestic flights was established fairly soon, little was accomplished until 1944 to solve the multifarious technical, economic, and legal problems posed by international civil aviation.

[2]CREATION

The first international civil aviation conference, held in 1910 and attended by European governments only, since transocean flight was then regarded as no more than a wild dream, was a failure. Almost another decade elapsed before an international convention, signed in Paris in 1919, created the International Commission for Air Navigation. The commission was to meet at least once a year and concern itself with technical matters. An international committee of jurists was also established, to concern itself with the intricate legal questions created by cross-border aviation. In 1928 a Pan American convention on commercial aviation was adopted at a conference held in Havana to deal with problems then emerging as international flights became more frequent in the Western Hemisphere. Although some progress in obtaining agreement on international flight regulations had been made by the end of the 1930s, most nations still granted very few concessions to each other's airlines, and no agreement existed permitting foreign planes to fly nonstop over the territory of one country en route to another country.

THE CHICAGO CONFERENCE OF 1944

The tremendous development of aviation during World War II demonstrated the need for an international organization to assist and regulate international flight for peaceful purposes, covering all aspects of flying, including problems in the technical, economic, and legal fields. For these reasons, in early 1944 the US conducted exploratory discussions with its allies of World War II on the basis of which invitations were sent to 55 allied and neutral states to meet in Chicago in November 1944.

In November and December 1944, delegates of 52 nations met at the International Civil Aviation Conference in Chicago to plan for international cooperation in the field of air navigation in the postwar era. It was this conference that framed the constitution of ICAO, called the Convention on International Civil Aviation. This convention provided that ICAO would come into being after the convention was ratified by 26 nations. To respond to the immediate needs of civil aviation, a provisional organization was created and functioned for 20 months until, on 4 April 1947, ICAO officially came into existence.

In essence, the conference was faced with two questions: (1) whether universally recognized navigational signals and other navigational and technical standards could be agreed upon; and (2) whether international rules concerning the economics of air transport could be established. One group of countries, led by the US, wanted an international organization empowered only to make recommendations regarding standard technical procedures and equipment. In its economic aspects, these countries believed, air transport should be freely competitive. This would also best serve the interests of the "consumer nations" that had no international

airlines of their own. Another group of countries, led by the UK, favored a stronger organization, which would have a great deal to say about the economics of civil aviation. It would be empowered to allocate the international routes that the airlines of different countries would be allowed to fly, regulate the frequency of flights, and fix rates. A radical proposal, advanced by New Zealand and supported by Australia, called for international ownership and operation of international air transport.

The Convention on International Civil Aviation finally adopted by the conference was something of a compromise between the American and British positions. The convention established for the first time an independent international body, the International Civil Aviation Organization, to supervise "order in the air," obtain maximum technical standardization for international aviation, recommend certain practices that member countries should follow, and carry out other functions. Countries ratifying or acceding to the convention thereby agreed in advance to conform to the greatest possible extent to ICAO-adopted civil aviation standards and to endeavor to conform to ICAO-adopted recommendations.

In the economic field, ICAO has no regulatory powers, but one of its constitutional objectives is to "prevent economic waste caused by unreasonable competition." Furthermore, under the convention member states undertake to have their international airlines furnish ICAO with traffic reports, cost statistics, and financial statements showing, among other things, all receipts from operations and the sources of such revenues.

The Chicago convention affirms every state's "complete and exclusive sovereignty over the airspace above its territory." It provides that nonscheduled flights may, subject to certain permissible conditions and limitations, be made by the civil aircraft of one country into or over the territory of another. Scheduled international air service, however, may be operated from one country into or over the territory of another country only with the latter's authorization. Furthermore, member states are permitted to establish areas prohibited to foreign aircraft as long as these regulations are nondiscriminatory. Pilotless aircraft as well as conventional aircraft are covered by these provisions. The term "airspace" is not precisely defined, however, and with the development of rockets and long-range missiles the problem of deciding where a country's airspace ends and where outer space begins has become a matter of practical concern. This problem has come under study by the UN Committee on the Peaceful Uses of Outer Space.

An important matter considered by the Chicago conference was the question of the exchange of commercial rights in international civil aviation. It was not possible to reach an agreement satisfactory to all states attending the conference. Hence, the question was covered, not in the Convention on International Civil Aviation that serves as ICAO's constitution, but in two supplementary agreements adopted by the conference: the International Air Services Transit Agreement and the International Air Transport Agreement. These two treaties do not form part of the ICAO constitution and are binding only on the ICAO member states that have ratified them.

The International Air Services Transit Agreement guarantees (1) the freedom of civil aircraft to fly over foreign countries and territories as long as they do not land, and (2) the freedom of civil aircraft to make nontraffic landings, for refueling or overhaul only, in foreign territory. The agreement, which thus established for the first time the principle of automatic right of transit and of emergency landing, had come into force between 96 countries by March 1983.

The International Air Transport Agreement, also known as the Five Freedoms Agreement, affirms, in addition to the two freedoms covered by the transit agreement, three other freedoms of the air: (3) freedom to transport passengers and cargo from an aircraft's homeland to other countries, (4) freedom to transport passengers and cargo from other countries to an aircraft's homeland, and (5) freedom to carry air traffic between countries other than the aircraft's homeland.

Because the Chicago convention was adopted in December 1944, ICAO possesses a constitution older than the UN Charter. Countries were much slower in ratifying the Chicago convention, however, than they were in ratifying the UN Charter. For this reason, ICAO did not come into being until 4 April 1947, 30 days after the convention had been ratified by the required 26 states.

³PURPOSES

ICAO's aims and objectives, as stated in the Chicago convention, are to foster the planning and development of international air transport so as to ensure the safe and orderly growth of international civil aviation throughout the world; encourage the arts of aircraft design and operation for peaceful purposes; encourage the development of airways, airports, and air navigation facilities for international civil aviation; meet the needs of the peoples of the world for safe, regular, efficient, and economical air transport; prevent economic waste caused by unreasonable competition; ensure that the rights of contracting states are fully respected and that every contracting state has a fair opportunity to operate international airlines; avoid discrimination between contracting states; promote safety of flight in international air navigation; and promote generally the development of all aspects of international civil aeronautics.

⁴MEMBERSHIP

As of March 1983, ICAO had 150 member states:
Afghanistan
Algeria
Angola
Antigua and Barbuda
Argentina
Australia
Austria
Bahamas
Bahrain
Bangladesh
Barbados
Belgium
Benin
Bolivia
Botswana
Brazil
Bulgaria
Burma
Burundi
Cameroon

Canada
Cape Verde
Central African Rep.
Chad
Chile
China
Colombia
Congo
Costa Rica
Cuba
Cyprus
Czechoslovakia
Denmark
Djibouti
Dominican Republic
Ecuador
Egypt
El Salvador
Equatorial Guinea
Ethiopia
Fiji
Finland
France
Gabon
Gambia
Germany, Fed. Rep.
Ghana
Greece
Grenada
Guatemala
Guinea
Guinea-Bissau
Guyana
Haiti
Honduras
Hungary
Iceland
India
Indonesia
Iran
Iraq
Ireland
Israel
Italy
Ivory Coast
Jamaica
Japan
Jordan
Kampuchea
Kenya
Kiribati
Korea, Dem. People's Rep.
Korea, Rep.
Kuwait
Laos
Lebanon
Lesotho
Liberia
Libya
Luxembourg
Madagascar
Malawi
Malaysia
Maldives
Mali
Malta
Mauritania

Mauritius
Mexico
Monaco
Morocco
Mozambique
Nauru
Nepal
Netherlands
New Zealand
Nicaragua
Niger
Nigeria
Norway
Oman
Pakistan
Panama
Papua New Guinea
Paraguay
Peru
Philippines
Poland
Portugal
Qatar
Romania
Rwanda
St. Lucia
São Tomé and Príncipe
Sa'udi Arabia
Senegal
Seychelles
Sierra Leone
Singapore
Somalia
South Africa
Spain
Sri Lanka
Sudan
Suriname
Swaziland
Sweden
Switzerland
Syria
Tanzania
Thailand
Togo
Trinidad and Tobago
Tunisia
Turkey
Uganda
USSR
United Arab Emirates
UK
US
Upper Volta
Uruguay
Venezuela
Viet-Nam
Yemen, People's Dem. Rep.
Yemen Arab Rep.
Yugoslavia
Zaire
Zambia
Zimbabwe

⁵STRUCTURE

The three main organs of ICAO are the Assembly, the Council, and the Secretariat, headed by the secretary-general.

The Assembly

The all-member Assembly meets every three years. Every member state has one vote in the Assembly and decisions are made by a simple majority vote unless otherwise specified by the Chicago convention. Sessions have been held in many different cities.

The Assembly makes policy recommendations, reviews the work of ICAO, offers guidance to other ICAO bodies, elects the council, and determines the budget. The Assembly may amend the ICAO constitution by a two-thirds majority vote, and it has done so on several occasions. But amendments come into force for the states that ratify them only after they have been ratified by at least two-thirds of the ICAO member states as specified by the Assembly. In other words, the Assembly may feel that it would not be fair to introduce a particular innovation in international civil aviation unless certain states would abide by it. On the other hand, the Assembly possesses a rather unusual prerogative to induce wide ratification of an amendment it has adopted: if a member state does not ratify a particular amendment within a given period of time, the assembly has the right to revoke that country's membership in ICAO. However, this provision (Article 94[b]) has never been invoked.

The Council

The Council is a permanent body, composed of 33 member states elected by the Assembly for three-year terms. In selecting the membership of the Council, the Assembly is required by the Chicago convention to give adequate representation to nations of major importance in air transport, to nations that provide the largest share of facilities for international civil air navigation, and to nations whose inclusion on the Council will ensure broad geographical representation. The following countries were elected by the 1980 assembly to be represented on the Council until 1983:

Algeria
Argentina
Australia
Brazil
Cameroon
Canada
China
Colombia
Czechoslovakia
Denmark
Egypt
El Salvador
France
Germany, Fed. Rep.
India
Indonesia
Iraq
Italy
Jamaica
Japan
Lebanon
Madagascar
Mexico
Netherlands
Nigeria
Pakistan
Senegal
Spain
Uganda
USSR
UK
US
Venezuela

Since August 1976, Dr. Assad Kotaite of Lebanon has been president of the Council.

The Council's powers are unusually broad, as compared with those of the executive councils of most other specialized agencies. It adopts international standards and recommended practices regarding civil air navigation and transport. It may act as arbiter between member states on disputes relating to the interpretation or application of the Chicago convention and its annexes. It may investigate any situation that presents avoidable obstacles to the development of international air navigation. In general, it may take whatever steps are necessary to maintain the safety and regularity of operation of international air transport.

The Secretary-General and the Secretariat
The ICAO Secretariat is headed by a secretary-general, who is appointed by the Council. The secretary-general appoints the staff of the ICAO secretariat and supervises and directs its activities. Yves Lambert of France has been secretary-general since 1976.

Headquarters and Regional Offices. ICAO headquarters are at International Aviation Square, 1000 Sherbrooke Street West, in the center of Montreal, occupying 18 floors of a 27-story building as well as a complete conference complex adjacent to it. ICAO maintains regional offices in Paris, Bangkok, Cairo, Mexico City, Nairobi, Lima, and Dakar. The regional offices assist member states in providing the aeronautical services expected of them.

⁶BUDGET
The 1980 Assembly voted the following net budgets: 1981, $27,806,000; 1982, $29,382,000; 1983, $31,679,000. Contributions by member states are assessed on a sliding scale determined by the Assembly.

⁷ACTIVITIES

A. ESTABLISHMENT OF INTERNATIONAL STANDARDS AND RECOMMENDED PRACTICES
By joining ICAO—that is, accepting the Chicago Convention—states undertake to collaborate in securing the highest practicable degree of uniformity in regulations, standards, procedures, and organization in all matters in which such uniformity will facilitate and improve air navigation. Hence, one of ICAO's chief tasks is to adopt such international standards and recommendations and to keep them up to date through modifications and amendments.

A standard, as defined by the first ICAO Assembly, is "any specification for physical characteristics, configuration, material, performance, personnel, or procedures, the uniform application of which is recognized as *necessary* for the safety or regularity of international air navigation and to which Member States *will conform.*" Standards may thus include specifications for such matters as the length of runways, the materials to be used in aircraft construction, and the qualifications to be required of a pilot flying an international route. A recommendation is any such specification, uniform application of which is recognized as "*desirable* in the interest of safety, regularity, or efficiency of international air navigation and to which Member States will *endeavor to conform.*"

Preparing and revising these standards and recommendations is largely the responsibility of ICAO's Air Navigation Commission, which plans, coordinates, and examines all of ICAO's activities in the field of air navigation. The commission consists of 15 persons, appointed by the Council from among persons nominated by member states. If the council approves the text, it is submitted to the member states. While recommendations are not binding, standards automatically become binding on all member states, except for those who find it impracticable to comply and file a difference under Article 38 of the convention.

Annexes to the ICAO Convention on International Civil Aviation
The various standards and recommendations that have been adopted by ICAO are grouped into 18 annexes to the Chicago Convention. The aim of most of the annexes is to promote progress in flight safety, particularly by guaranteeing satisfactory minimum standards of training and safety procedures and by assuring uniform international practices.

1. Personnel Licensing—licensing of flight crews, air traffic controllers, and aircraft maintenance personnel.
2. Rules of the Air—rules relating to the conduct of visual and instrument flights.
3. Meteorological Services—provision of meteorological services for international air navigation and reporting of meteorological observations from aircraft.
4. Aeronautical Charts—specifications for aeronautical charts for use in international aviation.
5. Units of Measurement—dimensional systems to be used in air-ground communications.
6. Operation of Aircraft. Part I: International Commercial Air Transport; Part II: International General Aviation—specifications which will ensure in similar operations throughout the world a level of safety above a prescribed minimum.
7. Aircraft Nationality and Registration Marks—requirements for registration and identification of aircraft.
8. Airworthiness of Aircraft—certification and inspection of aircraft according to uniform procedures.
9. Facilitation—simplification of customs, immigration, and health inspection regulations at international airports.
10. Aeronautical Telecommunications—standardization of communications equipment and systems and of communications procedures.
11. Air Traffic Services—establishment and operation of air traffic control, flight information, and alerting services.
12. Search and Rescue—organization and operation of facilities and services necessary for search and rescue.
13. Aircraft Accident Investigation—uniformity in the notification, investigation, and reporting of aircraft accidents.
14. Aerodromes—specifications for the design and equipment of aerodromes.
15. Aeronautical Information Services—methods for the collection and dissemination of aeronautical information required for flight operations.
16. Environmental Protection. Vol. I: Aircraft Noise—specifications for aircraft noise certification, noise monitoring, and noise exposure units for land-use planning. Vol. II: Aircraft Engine Emissions—standards relating to vented fuel and emissions certification requirements.
17. Security—specifications for safeguarding international civil aviation against acts of unlawful interference.
18. Safe Transport of Dangerous Goods by Air—specifications for the labeling, packing, and shipping of dangerous cargo.

B. AIR NAVIGATION
It is evident that air navigation covers an extremely broad spectrum of activities ranging from short take-off and landing airplanes to supersonic transports, from security questions to aviation's impact on the environment, from training and operating practices for pilots to the facilities required at airports.

The ICAO action program regarding the environment provides a case in point. Growing air traffic and increased use of jet engines have heightened public awareness of civil aviation's environmental impact. Therefore ICAO instituted activities in 1968 aimed at reducing aircraft noise. The first measures involved development of internationally agreed standards for the noise certification of aircraft (contained in Vol. I of Annex 16) which resulted in a quieter generation of jet aircraft.

Comparable studies of aviation's share in air pollution have resulted in the development of standards (Vol. II of Annex 16) relating to the control of fuel venting and of smoke and gaseous emissions from newly manufactured turbo jet and turbofan engines for subsonic airplanes.

As part of its continuing effort to improve air safety, ICAO has adopted standards for the safe transport of dangerous goods by air. These form a new Annex 18 to the Chicago Convention. ICAO studies many other important subjects such as all-weather operations, supersonic operations, application of space techniques to aviation, automated-data interchange systems, and visual aids.

C. REDUCING FORMALITIES AT AIRPORTS

Since its foundation, ICAO has had as an important objective the removal of unnecessary obstacles from the path of free and unimpeded passage of aircraft and has endeavored to facilitate customs, immigration, public health, and other procedures for passengers, crews, baggage, cargo, and mail across international boundaries and to provide certain related facilities and services at international airports. A comprehensive facilitation program is published in Annex 9 to the Chicago Convention. It covers all commercial and noncommercial international flights by civil aircraft. There has been a great decrease in the red tape involved when entering and leaving countries by air.

ICAO convenes international meetings, every four to five years, of representatives of the various governmental departments involved, as well as of airlines and airports, for the purpose of reviewing developments and recommending improvements. After such a meeting in Montreal in 1979, numerous amendments were made to Annex 9. That meeting also led to continuing studies on alleviation of airport congestion, electronic data-processing techniques in the handling of cargo, improved baggage delivery at arrival, and wider introduction of standard airport signs.

In order to assist states in complying with the provisions of Annex 9, members of the secretariat from ICAO headquarters and its seven regional offices visit a number of nations each year to discuss problems and suggest solutions. Meetings of groups of states in different regions are also held for this purpose.

D. REGIONAL PLANNING FOR AIR NAVIGATION

While worldwide uniformity is desirable for certain matters pertaining to civil aviation, others are best approached on a regional basis, since operating conditions vary a great deal from region to region. In the North Atlantic region, for example, long-range ocean flying predominates, whereas in Europe many international flights are short overland jumps. To deal with these different conditions and to facilitate detailed planning, ICAO has mapped out nine geographic regions. At meetings held for each of them, detailed plans are drawn up for the facilities, services, and procedures appropriate to that region. Altogether the nine regional plans specify the air navigation facilities and services that are required, and the locations where they are required: communications, air traffic control, search and rescue and meteorological facilities, and so on. The ICAO plans for the nine regions of the world are regularly revised or amended to meet the needs of increasing traffic and the never-ending technical developments in civil aviation.

The seven regional offices are ICAO's principal agents in advising and assisting states in implementation. The offices direct as much of their resources as possible to giving practical help, among other ways through frequent visits to states by members of the technical staff. In addition, ICAO has since 1960 budgeted funds for long-duration advisory implementation missions to help member countries overcome local deficiencies.

Shortcomings are taken up by the regional offices and the ICAO secretariat with the governments concerned. More complex ones may require study by the Air Navigation Commission and, if necessary, by the ICAO Council. The problem of eliminating deficiencies in navigational services and facilities is one that ICAO considers critical. The organization in 1956 set up a special implementation panel, which in 1960 was succeeded by the council's Standing Group on Implementation.

The major difficulties are lack of funds for facilities and services, a shortage of trained personnel, and administrative and organizational difficulties. ICAO has encouraged governments to upgrade their facilities through loans for capital expenditures, technical assistance, and other means. It has also produced manuals and other documentation to assist states in setting up aviation training programs for flight and ground personnel and offers advice on maintenance and improvement of technical standards.

E. JOINTLY OPERATED OR FINANCED SERVICES

Under the Chicago Convention, every ICAO member state is required to provide air navigation facilities and services on its own territory. Navigational facilities and services must also be provided for air routes traversing the high seas and regions of undetermined sovereignty. The ICAO Council is constitutionally authorized at the request of a member state to "provide, man, maintain, and administer any or all of the airports and other air navigation facilities, including radio and meteorological services, required in its territory for the safe, regular, efficient, and economical operation of the international air services of the other contracting states." The council may also act on its own initiative to resolve a situation that might impair the "safe, regular, efficient, and economical operation" of international air services. Although ICAO has not yet undertaken the actual supervision of any nation's international air navigation facilities and services, two international agreements are in effect to furnish such services and facilities in parts of the North Atlantic region through so-called "joint-support" programs.

Under these joint-support agreements, the nations concerned provide services, facilities, or cash payments based on the use by their own aircraft of the routes involved. The two existing agreements are the Agreement on the Joint Financing of Certain Air Navigation Services in Greenland and the Faroe Islands and the Agreement on the Joint Financing of Certain Air Navigation Services in Iceland.

The vast majority of aircraft that utilize the special traffic-control, navigational, and meteorological services furnished from Iceland and Greenland for transatlantic crossings are neither Icelandic nor Danish. Hence, 19 countries, including Iceland and Denmark, provide the funds necessary for the operation of these services.

ICAO administers these two agreements, the secretary-general having certain responsibilities and the ICAO Council others. A special standing body, the Committee on Joint Support of Air Navigation Services, advises the council in these matters. The operation and costs of the services are constantly reviewed and international conferences held. After the conference in 1973, charges were imposed on all civil aircraft crossing the North Atlantic, for the use of the aeronautical facilities and services. These "user charges" covered only 40% of the costs allocable to civil aviation but were increased to 50% for the years 1975 to 1978. Following a further conference in 1977, the user charges were increased to 60% for 1979 and 1980, 80% for 1981, and 100% thereafter.

F. TECHNICAL ASSISTANCE

Based on the recognition of the importance of the airplane for international and domestic transport in countries where road and railway services are lacking and to aid these countries' social and economic development, ICAO has, from its inception, operated technical assistance programs. These are conducted under the programs of UN organizations and UNDP.

Assistance programs executed by ICAO fall into three main categories. UNDP obtains its funds from donor countries and allocates these funds among recipient countries in the form of country, intercountry, and interregional projects. The Funds-in-Trust program provides financial assistance for specific projects in the country receiving the technical assistance. The Associate

Experts program provides experts from certain countries to work under ICAO guidance.

Each civil aviation project may include one or more of the following forms of assistance: experts to provide specialist advice to the civil aviation administration or national airline; fellowships to allow nationals to be trained abroad in civil aviation disciplines, often at civil aviation training centers that have been established through ICAO technical assistance; equipment such as radio navigational aids or communication facilities to ensure safe and regular air service.

Fellowships have been awarded in many fields, including training as pilots, aircraft maintenance technicians, air traffic controllers, radio and radar maintenance technicians, communication officers, airport engineers, electronics engineers, air transport economists, aeronautical information officers, aeronautical meteorologists, aviation medicine specialists, accident investigation experts, flight operations officers, airport fire officers, and instructors.

Major types of equipment provided include air traffic control, radar, and flight simulators; training aircraft; radio communication and radar systems; distance-measuring equipment; very high frequency omni radio ranges; instrument landing systems; nondirectional beacons; "navaid" flight-test units; airworthiness data-acquisition systems; language laboratories; audiovisual aids; visual approach slope indicator systems; and firefighting vehicles.

Major training institutions assisted by ICAO include civil aviation training centers in Egypt, Ethiopia, Gabon, Indonesia, Kenya, Mexico, Nigeria, Singapore, Thailand, Trinidad and Tobago, and Tunisia.

Expenditures for ICAO technical assistance programs in 1982 totaled nearly $65 million, of which more than half came from UNDP and the remainder from funds-in-trust. UNDP expenditures by region were: $11.7 million for Africa; $7.9 million for Asia and the Pacific; $5.39 million for the Americas; $4.74 million for Europe, the Mediterranean, and the Middle East; and $5.62 million for interregional projects.

G. SETTLEMENT OF DISPUTES BETWEEN ICAO MEMBER STATES

The Chicago Convention vests important semijudicial powers in the ICAO Council. In the event that a disagreement between ICAO member states concerning the interpretation or application of the Chicago Convention or its Annexes cannot be settled by negotiation, "it *shall,* on the application of any state concerned in the disagreement, be *decided*" by the ICAO Council. Thus once a particular party to a disagreement brings the matter before the council, the other state or states concerned cannot disclaim the council's jurisdiction. Under certain conditions, however, a member state may appeal the council's decision either to a special ad hoc tribunal (in agreement with the other party or parties) or to the International Court of Justice. If, once a decision is final, the council decides that a given airline is not complying with that decision, all ICAO members are pledged to deny the use of their air space to that airline. If a member state does not comply with a council decision, its voting rights shall be suspended.

While three disputes have been brought before the council, the council has not decided on the merits of any case because the disputes were eventually settled by direct negotiation between the states concerned.

H. INTERNATIONAL CONVENTIONS PREPARED UNDER ICAO AUSPICES

The increasing number of incidents of unlawful interference with civil aviation beginning in the 1960s—aircraft hijacking, the placing of bombs on board aircraft, the attacks at airports on aircraft, passengers, and crew members—led to the adoption of three conventions.

The Tokyo Convention of 1963. The Convention on Offenses and Certain Other Acts Committed on Board Aircraft does not define specific offenses, but it does have the virtue of ensuring that there will always be a jurisdiction (namely, that of the state of registry of the aircraft) in which a person who has committed an offense on board an aircraft can be tried. The convention also provides for the powers and duties of the aircraft commander and others respecting restraint and disembarkation of the suspected offender. It provides a detailed code of behavior for states in whose territory the suspected offender has disembarked and also stipulates the steps to be taken in case of hijacking of an aircraft. The convention entered into force in 1969.

The Hague Convention of 1970. The Convention for the Suppression of the Unlawful Seizure of Aircraft defines the offense of unlawful seizure and provides for universal jurisdiction over the suspected offender, arrest, and custody. It also provides that prosecution or extradition of the suspected offender take place without many restrictions. The Hague Convention entered into force in 1971.

The Montreal Convention of 1971. The Convention for the Suppression of Unlawful Acts Against the Safety of Civil Aviation defines a number of acts of unlawful interference directed against international civil aviation. It provides for universal jurisdiction over the offender and, in general, contains provisions on custody, extradition, and prosecution similar to those in the Hague Convention. The Montreal Convention entered into force in 1973.

All three conventions are concerned with the preservation of the means of international communication and provide specifically that in the case of the unlawful seizure of an aircraft any contracting state in which the aircraft or its passengers or crew are present shall facilitate the continuation of the journey of the passengers and crew as soon as practicable, and shall return the aircraft and its cargo to the person lawfully entitled to possession.

The cooperative international action contemplated by the Tokyo, Hague and Montreal conventions is intended to eliminate safe havens for hijackers and saboteurs.

Regime and Liability of Air Carriers

Much of ICAO's work has been devoted to keeping up to date the regime and limits of liability of air carriers in the case of death of, or injury to, passengers and in the carriage of cargo and postal items by air.

The Warsaw Convention of 1929. The Convention on the Unification of Certain Rules Relating to International Carriage by Air, adopted during the early days of aviation, dominated the field of aviation passenger liability for almost half a century. It limits the liability, except in cases of gross negligence on the part of the carrier, to a maximum of 125,000 Poincaré gold francs (about $10,000). The Hague Protocol of 1955 doubled the existing limits of liability. In 1971, by the Guatemala City Protocol, the rule of the Warsaw Convention based on presumption of fault, yielded to *strict* liability, irrespective of fault. However, it will be some time before the 1971 protocol comes into force because at least 30 ratifications, including those of five nations with major air traffic, must be deposited. An interesting feature of the Guatemala City Protocol is that, although it provides for a limit of about $100,000 per passenger, there is also provision for a domestic supplement if a state party to the protocol wishes to have a higher limit.

An International Conference on Air Law, convened under the auspices of ICAO, adopted in September 1975 new amendments to the Warsaw Convention, as amended by the Hague Protocol. Under the new provisions the carrier is responsible for cargo damage, irrespective of fault. Another major change concerns the method of cálculating the liability limits by turning from a solely gold monetary basis to a dual system, allowing countries that are members of the IMF to base passenger, baggage, and cargo liability on Special Drawing Rights, whereas countries not members of the IMF would declare liability limits in monetary units based on gold.

The Guadalajara Convention of 1961. The Guadalajara

Convention, supplementary to the Warsaw Convention, contains rules with regard to carriage performed by other than the contracting carrier, that is to say, by a carrier that had not issued the ticket to the passenger, or air waybill to the consignor. In this case, both the contracting carrier and the actual carrier would be held jointly and severally liable under the Warsaw Convention, or that convention as amended by the Hague Protocol.

As of March 1983, the Warsaw Convention had 116 parties, the Hague Protocol had 100, and the Guadalajara Convention had 61; however, only 4 states had taken action to ratify the Guatemala City Protocol.

The Rome Convention of 1952. The Convention on Damage Caused by Foreign Aircraft to Third Parties on the Surface includes the principle of absolute liability of the aircraft operator for damage caused to third parties on the surface but places a limitation on the amount of compensation, expressed in Poincaré gold francs and calculated in relation to the aircraft concerned. However, a diplomatic conference convened in 1978 under ICAO auspices adopted a protocol for the amendment of the Rome Convention. The basic feature of the protocol is a substantial increase in the limits of liability and the expression of the limits in the Special Drawings Rights of the IMF.

The Geneva Convention of 1948. The Convention on the International Recognition of Rights in Aircraft was prepared in order to promote the financing of the sale of aircraft by providing protection of the lender's rights in an aircraft whenever the aircraft was in the territory of a state party to the convention. As of March 1983, 47 states were parties to the convention.

Other legal subjects on ICAO's work program include liability of air traffic control agencies, aerial collisions, and study of the status of the instruments of the "Warsaw System."

[8]BIBLIOGRAPHY

Air Navigation Plans. For all 9 ICAO regions of the world.

ICAO Bulletin. Provides a concise account of the activities of ICAO and features additional information of interest to contracting states and the international aeronautical world. Monthly.

Memorandum on ICAO and Catalogue of ICAO Publications.

(ICAO also issues technical publications on international conventions, agreements, and arrangements; ICAO rules of procedure and administrative regulations; annexes to the Chicago Convention; procedures for air navigation services; and air navigation and air transport.)

THE UNIVERSAL POSTAL UNION (UPU)

[1]**BACKGROUND:** Every year over 290 billion pieces of mail are channeled into the inland stream of some 630,000 post offices around the globe, employing some 5 million persons. Of this mass, some 8 billion pieces cross international boundaries with a minimum of formalities and are swiftly and safely delivered to their destinations. The orderly and economical movement of international mail is made possible by the Constitution and Convention of the Universal Postal Union, the basic Acts under which the UPU operates. Since some 166 countries now come under these Acts, the provisions affect virtually the entire world population. Under the Constitution, UPU member countries form a single postal territory for the reciprocal exchange of letter-post items, and freedom of transit is guaranteed throughout the entire territory of the Union.

[2]CREATION

Although generally taken for granted, present-day postal service is of relatively recent origin. The use of postage stamps for prepayment of postage was not introduced until 1840, when the UK established a unified internal postage charge, the famous penny rate, to be paid by the sender of a letter regardless of the distance it had to travel. Until that year, the postal fee based on distance was often very high and was not paid by the sender but by the addressee. If the addressee could not pay, the letter was returned. Gradually, other countries introduced adhesive stamps, and their use spread to international mail. In 1863, on the initiative of the US, representatives of 15 postal administrations met in Paris to consider the problem of standardizing international postal practices.

The decisive development came 11 years later with the meeting of the first International Postal Congress at Bern in 1874 at the suggestion of the German government. The Bern Congress was attended by delegates from 22 countries: 20 European countries (including Russia), Egypt, and the US. The Congress adopted a treaty concerning the establishment of a General Postal Union —commonly known as the Bern Treaty—signed on 9 October 1874. This was the forerunner of the series of multilateral Universal Postal Union conventions and came into force the following year, when the Union was formally established to administer its operative regulations.

The 1874 Convention provided for subsequent postal congresses to revise the Convention in the light of economic and technical developments. The second Postal Congress, held in Paris in 1878, changed the name of the General Postal Union to the Universal Postal Union (UPU). Four more congresses were held prior to World War I: Lisbon, 1885; Vienna, 1891; Washington, 1897; and Rome, 1906. There were five congresses between the wars: Madrid, 1920; Stockholm, 1924; London, 1929; Cairo, 1934; and Buenos Aires, 1939. The first post–World War II Congress met in Paris in 1947 and arranged for the UPU to be recognized as a specialized agency of the UN family in 1948. Other congresses met at Brussels, 1952; Ottawa, 1957; Vienna, 1964; Tokyo, 1969; Lausanne, 1974; and Rio de Janeiro, 1979. The 19th congress was scheduled to take place in Hamburg in 1984.

[3]PURPOSES

The basic objective of the Union was stated in the 1874 Convention, reiterated in all successive revisions, and embodied in the Constitution adopted at Vienna in 1964. "The countries adopting this Constitution comprise, under the title of the Universal Postal Union, a single postal territory for the reciprocal exchange of letter-post items." The 1924 Congress added: "It is also the object of the Postal Union to secure the organization and improvement of the various international postal services." The 1947 Congress added another clause: "and to promote the development of international collaboration in this sphere."

In recognition of the Union's continued interest and newly assumed responsibilities in the field of development aid, the Congress held in Vienna in 1964 enlarged UPU's goals to include the provision of postal technical assistance to member states.

Under the single-territory principle, all the Union's member countries are bound by the Constitution and Convention to observe certain fundamental rules pertaining to ordinary mail. Ordinary mail (the letter post) under the Lausanne Convention includes letters, postcards, printed papers, small packets, and literature for the blind such as books in Braille. Although the Convention lays down basic postage rates for ordinary mail sent to addresses in UPU territory, variations are permitted within generous limits. Postal authorities of all member states are pledged to handle all mail with equal care, regardless of its origin and destination, and to expedite mail originating in other UPU countries on a level comparable to the best means of conveyance used for their own mail. In the past, foreign mail was delivered to destination without charge to the country where it was posted and each country retained the postage collected on international mail. As of 1 July 1971, however, where there is an imbalance between mail sent and received, the postal administration of the country receiving the larger quantity is authorized to ask for repayment at a standard rate (fixed by the Postal Congress) to offset its excess costs. However, each country reimburses, at standard rates fixed by the Postal Congress, all intermediary countries through which its mail passes in transit.

Freedom of transit—the basic principle of the Union—is guaranteed throughout UPU territory. Specific regulations provide for the dispatch of mail and for returning undeliverable mail to the sender. Certain articles such as opium and other drugs and inflammable or explosive agents are excluded from the international mails.

Eight optional postal agreements supplement the Convention. They cover parcel mail, insured letters, money orders, giro (postal checks), cash on delivery, settlement of personal debts, savings bank service, and subscriptions to periodicals.

[4]MEMBERSHIP

The original treaty allowed "overseas" countries to be admitted to the Union subject to the agreement of administrations having postal relations with them. The 1878 Congress decreed, however, that any country could accede directly to the Union merely by unilaterial declaration and communication of that declaration to the Swiss government. This system was revised by the Paris Congress of 1947, which ruled that applications for membership in the Union could be filed only by sovereign states and had to be channeled through the Swiss government. Approval is then required by at least two-thirds of the full membership. At the 1964 Vienna Congress, it was also decided that any member nation of the UN could accede directly to the UPU by a formal declaration addressed to the Swiss government. Dependent territories were granted collective membership by a special postal conference held in Bern in 1876.

Membership in the UPU as of 1 January 1983 had reached 166, including 164 independent states and two collective members of dependent territories:

Afghanistan
Albania
Algeria
Angola
Argentina
Australia and Australian territories
Austria
Bahamas
Bahrain
Bangladesh
Barbados
Belgium
Belize
Benin
Bhutan
Bolivia
Botswana
Brazil
Bulgaria
Burma
Burundi
Byelorussia
Cameroon
Canada
Cape Verde
Central African Rep.
Chad
Chile
China
Colombia
Comoros
Congo
Costa Rica
Cuba
Cyprus
Czechoslovakia
Denmark (including Faroe Islands and Greenland)
Djibouti
Dominica
Dominican Republic
Ecuador
Egypt
El Salvador
Equatorial Guinea
Ethiopia
Fiji
Finland
France and French overseas departments and territories
Gabon
Gambia
German Dem. Rep.

Germany, Fed. Rep.
Ghana
Greece
Grenada
Guatemala
Guinea
Guinea-Bissau
Guyana
Haiti
Honduras
Hungary
Iceland
India
Indonesia
Iran
Iraq
Ireland
Israel
Italy
Ivory Coast
Jamaica
Japan
Jordan
Kampuchea
Kenya
Korea, Dem. People's Rep.
Korea, Rep.
Kuwait
Laos
Lebanon
Lesotho
Liberia
Libya
Liechtenstein
Luxembourg
Madagascar
Malawi
Malaysia
Maldives
Mali
Malta
Mauritania
Mauritius
Mexico
Monaco
Mongolia
Morocco
Mozambique
Nauru
Nepal
Netherlands
Netherlands Antilles
New Zealand and New Zealand territories
Nicaragua
Niger
Nigeria
Norway
Oman
Pakistan
Panama
Papua New Guinea
Paraguay
Peru
Philippines
Poland
Portugal (and Macau)
Qatar

Romania
Rwanda
St. Lucia
St. Vincent and the Grenadines
San Marino
São Tomé and Príncipe
Sa'udi Arabia
Senegal
Seychelles
Sierra Leone
Singapore
Somalia
South Africa
Spain
Sri Lanka
Sudan
Suriname
Swaziland
Sweden
Switzerland
Syria
Tanzania
Thailand
Togo
Tonga
Trinidad and Tobago
Tunisia
Turkey
Tuvalu
Uganda
Ukraine
USSR
United Arab Emirates
UK
UK overseas territories
US and US territories
Upper Volta
Uruguay
Vanuatu
Vatican
Venezuela
Viet-Nam
Yemen, People's Dem. Rep.
Yemen Arab Rep.
Yugoslavia
Zaire
Zambia
Zimbabwe

Independent countries whose situation with regard to the UPU had not yet been settled:
Antigua and Barbuda
Kiribati
Solomon Islands

Country for which the UN is directly responsible:
Namibia

Territory in a special situation:
East Timor

RESTRICTED POSTAL UNIONS

Members of the UPU may establish restricted unions and make special agreements concerning the international postal service, provided always that they do not introduce provisions less favorable to the public than those provided for by the Acts of the UPU to which member countries concerned are parties. Restricted unions are the Asian-Pacific Postal Union (APPU), the African Posts and Telecommunications Union (APTU), the African Postal Union (APU), the European Conference of Postal and Telecommunications Administrations (CEPT), the Pan-African Postal Union (PAPU), the Postal Union of the Americas and Spain (PUAS), the Arab Postal Union (UPA), and the Nordic Postal Union (UPPN).

[5]STRUCTURE

The permanent organs of the UPU are the Universal Postal Congress, the Executive Council, the Consultative Council for Postal Studies, and the International Bureau.

Universal Postal Congress

The Universal Postal Congress, which meets in principle every five years, is the supreme body of the UPU. The Congress consists of representatives of member countries who are plenipotentiaries furnished by their governments with the necessary powers. Its main function is to study and revise the Acts of the Union on the basis of proposals submitted to it. In addition to this legislative activity, the Congress considers certain administrative matters, such as reports on the work of the Executive Council and the Consultative Council for Postal Studies (CCPS). It also fixes the annual expenditure ceiling for the succeeding five-year period, decides the study programs of the Executive Council and the CCPS, considers technical assistance matters, and elects the director-general and the deputy director-general.

Executive Council

The Executive Council was created under the title Executive and Liaison Committee by the 1947 Congress to ensure the continuity of the work of the UPU between congresses. Its name was changed by the 1964 Vienna Congress. The Executive Council consists of a chairman and 39 members. The chairmanship (Brazil from 1979 to 1984) devolves by right on the host country of each Congress; the 39 members are elected by the Congress on the basis of equitable geographical distribution. At least half the membership is renewed at each session of the Congress, and no member may be elected by three successive congresses.

Broadly speaking, the Executive Council maintains the closest working relations with the postal administrations of member countries with a view to improving international postal service, and coordinates and supervises all Union activities between congresses. It also studies administrative, legislative, and legal problems of interest to the postal service, draws up proposals, and makes recommendations to the Congress. It is also responsible, within the framework of international technical cooperation, for promoting, supervising, and coordinating all aspects of postal technical assistance, including vocational training.

To some extent, the Executive Council supervises the activities of the International Bureau, considering and approving the annual report of the Bureau. It also examines the annual report of the CCPS and makes contacts, for the purpose of studies, with the UN and the specialized agencies and other international bodies.

Consultative Council for Postal Studies

Originally, the Consultative Committee for Postal Studies (CCPS) was composed of all the member countries of the UPU, and it worked through a Management Council of 26 members meeting yearly. The 1969 Tokyo Congress abolished the Consultative Committee and replaced its Management Council by a Consultative Council for Postal Studies (CCPS) with the same function and a membership of 30, increased to 35 by the 1974 Lausanne Congress.

The CCPS exercises its functions during the period between congresses, and its members are elected by the Congress, in principle on the basis of as wide a geographical distribution as possible. The CCPS is responsible for carrying out studies of major problems affecting postal administration in all UPU member countries. CCPS reports, published as a "Collection of Postal Studies," comprised some 130 studies at the end of 1982.

Seven standing committees deal with, respectively, the future of the postal services; postal operations; postal mechanization, buildings, and motor transport; financial services and accounting; staff; postal management; and international post.

The chairman (UK from 1979 to 1984), the vice-chairman (Tunisia from 1979 to 1984), and the committee chairmen of the CCPS constitute the Steering Committee, which meets at the chairman's request and prepares and directs the work of each session of the CCPS.

In principle, the CCPS meets annually at UPU headquarters in Bern.

International Bureau

Since the establishment of the Union, a central office known as the International Bureau has functioned at Bern. The Bureau has five primary duties. (1) It serves as the UPU's permanent secretariat. (2) It acts as a clearinghouse for information concerning postal matters, being responsible, among other things, for the coordination, publication, and dissemination of all manner of information regarding the Union and the international postal service. (3) It functions as a clearinghouse for the settlement between postal administrations of debts relating to transit charges, terminal dues, and international reply coupons. (4) It acts as a conciliator and arbitrator in disputes over postal matters between administrations. (5) It promotes technical cooperation of all types. The Bureau is headed by a director-general, who serves also as the secretary-general of the Union's bodies; since 1974, the office has been held by M. I. Sobhi of Egypt.

⁶BUDGET

The Postal Congress sets a ceiling for the ordinary annual expenditure of the UPU. However, the ceiling may be exceeded, if circumstances so require, on the authority of the Executive Council and subject to certain conditions. The 1979 Rio de Janeiro Congress set the following ceilings: SwFr17.1 million for 1981, SwFr17.5 million for 1982, SwFr17.8 million for 1983, SwFr18.1 million for 1984, and SwFr18.5 million for 1985.

UPU's expenses are shared by all member countries, which, for this purpose, are divided into eight contributing classes. The 1979 Congress introduced a system of self-financing of the UPU; previously the funds needed for running the Union were advanced by the Swiss Confederation, and member countries settled their contribution afterward on the basis of actual expenditure. The Congress has authorized the Executive Council to exceed the ceilings of expenditure in order to deal with situations created by new and unforeseen circumstances entailing unavoidable expenditure.

⁷ACTIVITIES

A. CLEARING ACCOUNTS FOR INTERNATIONAL SERVICES

In this, as in certain other respects, the UPU acts as a central office for the international postal traffic carried on by its members. In principle, UPU member states retain the revenue they derive from the sale of postage stamps and from other fees and charges for foreign-bound mail. Administrations must however reimburse one another for the transportation of foreign mail in intermediate transit and for the imbalance between international mail sent and received (terminal dues). At the end of each year, the Bureau draws up an annual general clearing account for transit and terminal charges, stating the balances due. For 1982, 119 postal administrations settled their transit and terminal charges through the Bureau's clearing account, 36 paying and 83 receiving balances.

The Bureau publishes every two years a general clearing account for the international reply coupons that it supplies to facilitate payment of international correspondence. Some 155 countries now sell these coupons, and all countries must accept them as payment for postage.

B. INFORMATION SERVICES

The UPU acts as an international clearinghouse for postal information. At the request of postal administrations, the Inter-national Bureau circulates inquiries concerning the operation of the various postal systems and makes the replies available to all UPU members. Inquiries may concern domestic as well as international postal practices and cover subjects as diverse as the texts of propaganda permitted on letters and packages, mobile post offices on motorboats, opening of new offices of exchange, introduction of summer time, and national regulations covering the dispatch of radioactive substances.

The International Bureau publishes a number of useful and essential international postal handbooks, including the following: *Postal Statistics* (internal and international); *List of Prohibited Articles* (prohibited from the mails); *International List of Post Offices*; and *List of Kilometric Distances and Shipping Lines*. The Consultative Council for Postal Studies has prepared the *Multilingual Vocabulary of the International Postal Service*, an essential tool designed to ensure that terms used by different national postal services convey the identical meaning.

The Bureau also prepares an annotated edition of UPU legislation, which includes discussion of principles, opinions, decisions, and practices underlying current international postal procedures and the present organization of the Union. The *Genèses des Actes de l'UPU* (in French only) is a compendium of analytic data on the evolution of UPU's legislative texts from 1874 to 1979.

C. ARBITRATION AND INTERPRETATION OF INTERNATIONAL POSTAL RULES

If a difference of opinion on the interpretation of UPU legislation between two or more postal administrations cannot be resolved by direct negotiations, the matter is settled by in-house arbitration. The countries concerned may also designate a single arbitrator, such as the International Bureau of the UPU.

D. REVISION OF RULES GOVERNING INTERNATIONAL SERVICES

The main function of the Congress, as noted above, is to study and revise the Acts of the Union, on the basis of proposals put forward by member countries, the Executive Council, and the CCPS. At the 1979 Congress, which was attended by representatives of 143 countries, 1,351 proposals were considered. The main results were the following:

(a) *Postal rates and regulations*—a new general increase in charges and outward and inward rates to take account of inflation; a similar increase in terminal dues (compensation for imbalance of mails); the introduction of a single basic rate for the conveyance of all categories of mail; and the incorporation into the Universal Postal Convention of the Insured Letters Agreement;

(b) *Technical assistance*—specification of the plan and guidelines for technical assistance for the period 1980–84; strengthening of technical cooperation among developing countries; and a 50% increase in the credits provided in the annual budget for consultants' missions to developing countries;

(c) *UPU organization and functioning*—the introduction of a system of self-financing; the election of members of the Executive Council and the CCPS; the renewal of the term of office of the director-general and the deputy director-general of the International Bureau; the introduction of Special Drawing Rights (SDRs) in the Acts for accounting and clearing purposes; and the introduction of Chinese, Portuguese, and Russian as languages of documentation.

E. TECHNICAL ASSISTANCE

Aims and Fields of Activity

The principle of technical assistance is contained in Article 1 of the UPU Constitution; it was couched in general terms in order to give the Union flexibility in the use of all forms of technical cooperation, present and future.

Since direct technical assistance between the administrations of UPU member countries—sending officials abroad and exchanging information, documentation, and the results of tests—has been a traditional practice, technical cooperation activities conducted by the Union itself started only in relatively recent times. Beginning in 1963, the UPU has participated in the UN Expanded Program of Technical Assistance, which merged with the UN Special Fund in 1966 to become UNDP. The UNDP has, in fact, become the main source of financing for UPU assistance to developing countries.

Requests for UPU assistance in technical cooperation matters cover all sectors—planning, organization, management, operations, training, and financial services. The aid provided comes in three forms: recruiting and sending of experts, consultants, or volunteers; granting vocational training or further training fellowships for individual or group courses; and supplying equipment and training or demonstration aids. Its application serves four main objectives:

(1) To intensify, within available resources, UPU activities related to technical assistance;

(2) To give priority to the needs of postal administrations of countries that are disadvantaged and to newly independent countries;

(3) To recognize the urgency of (a) setting up means of postal training up to senior management level in developing regions; (b) improving postal management, including the utilization of personnel; (c) increasing the number of postal establishments and improving mail conveyance and delivery, particularly in rural areas, as well as in the international service; and (d) setting up postal financial services on a general basis and, in the first instance, money order services and postal savings banks; and

(4) To direct the efforts of the Union toward (a) priority allocation of UPU aid to the most needy countries and those which seem determined to put it to good use; (b) optimum programming of technical assistance activities, taking account of needs reported by postal administrations on a regular, multiannual basis; (c) optimum decentralization of UPU technical assistance activities through increased UPU presence in the field; (d) development of UPU collaboration with the restricted unions, taking account of the policies and procedures established by the UPU and UNDP and the resources at the disposal of these regional organizations; (e) expansion of evaluation exercises and of the forwarding of results to the countries concerned, as a form of feedback; (f) establishment of systematic follow-up procedures designed to consolidate results already achieved or to simplify the implementation of recommendations already formulated; and (g) active promotion of technical cooperation among developing countries.

Program of Activities

Within the framework of UNDP, the UPU executes country and intercountry projects covering all aspects of the postal services and the three components of experts, fellowships, and equipment. Projects common to several countries, which form a very important part of this program, make it possible to solve, economically and rationally, the problems which arise in a given region, especially by setting up intercountry postal training schools.

Funds from the UPU budget make it possible to provide additional assistance to that of UNDP—namely, in the form of short consultant missions of three months at most, at the request of the postal administration concerned. A noteworthy feature is that,

for many missions, the consultants' countries of origin also share the cost of this form of technical cooperation by continuing to pay all or part of the salaries of their officials during the mission. At the same time, since 1981 the UPU has also funded integrated projects incorporating short-term consultants' missions, vocational training fellowships, and items of minor equipment. The UPU Special Fund, set up in 1966 and maintained by voluntary contributions from member countries, is mainly designed to finance training and to further training activities in the form of fellowships, equipment, and training courses or study cycles.

Some developed countries provide the International Bureau with funds for the management of associate experts in order to supplement the staff of ongoing projects and to give young people with sufficient training the opportunity to improve their professional qualifications.

Lastly, under a resolution adopted by the Executive Council in 1967, governments may avail themselves of technical assistance against payment, which they finance themselves from funds in trust; the International Bureau then undertakes to manage the projects implemented in this way. Of course, the UPU through the International Bureau continues to act as an intermediary, wherever expedient, for supplying assistance in kind to developing countries on the basis of offers from developed countries. It has also made a special effort in the field of vocational training by assessing the needs to be met and listing the facilities available in the various member countries. This effort is reflected in the establishment or reinforcement of national or multinational schools and the organization of study cycles for the further training of senior staff and of instructor-training courses, with the aid of which a large number of postal administrations now have qualified postal instructors.

F. POSTAL STUDIES

The 1979 Postal Congress assigned the CCPS some 48 topics for consideration, while allowing it a certain latitude as to the program's content and the conduct of studies. These technical studies, in the fields of management, postal organization, postal operations, international post, financial services, and personnel, include issues as varied as the future of the postal services, the use of the postal network for nonpostal activities, the role of agency functions in improving the financial position of postal services, financial autonomy of postal services, postal monopoly, electronic mail, energy and raw materials, conservation, and postal mechanization in newly independent countries.

[8]BIBLIOGRAPHY

Annual Report of the Work of the Union. Résumé and general review of UPU activities.

Collection of Postal Studies. A series of publications concerning topics studied by the CCPS.

The Postal Service in the World. Features postal statistics.

Postal Technical Cooperation. Quarterly.

Union Postale. Bimonthly. Parallel text in the seven languages of the Union—Arabic, Chinese, English, French, German, Russian, and Spanish. Contains articles on postal services, information on UPU activities, and, in the French section, an illustrated feature listing new postage stamps.

The Universal Postal Union. A brief outline of UPU features.

THE INTERNATIONAL TELECOMMUNICATION UNION (ITU)

[1]**BACKGROUND:** The International Telecommunication Union is the oldest of the intergovernmental organizations that have become specialized agencies related to the UN. In 1865 a convention establishing an International Telegraph Union was signed in Paris by the plenipotentiaries of 20 continental European states, including two extending into Asia—Russia and Turkey. Three years later, a permanent international bureau for the Union was established in Bern, Switzerland. This bureau, which operated until 1948, was the forerunner of the present General Secretariat of the ITU. In 1885, at Berlin, the first regulations concerning international telephone services were added to the telegraph regulations annexed to the Paris Convention. By the end of the 19th century, radiotelegraphy, or "wireless," had been developed, and for the first time it was possible to communicate directly between shore stations and ships at sea. Rival wireless companies frequently refused to accept one another's messages, however. In 1903 an international conference was called to consider the problem, and in 1906, in Berlin, 29 maritime states signed the International Radiotelegraph Convention, establishing the principle of compulsory intercommunication between vessels at sea and the land. The International Radiotelegraph Conference, which met in Washington in 1927, drew up for the first time a table of frequency allocations.

[2]CREATION

Two plenipotentiary conferences were held in 1932 at Madrid: one covering telephone and telegraph and the other radiotelegraph communications. The two existing conventions were amalgamated into a single International Telecommunication Convention (the word "telecommunication" signifying "any transmission, emission or reception of signs, signals, writing, images and sounds, or intelligence of any nature by wire, radio, optical, or other electromagnetic systems"). The countries accepting the new convention, which came into force in 1934, formed the International Telecommunication Union.

The International Telecommunication Convention of 1932 has been revised six times. The Plenipotentiary Conference of the ITU, meeting in Atlantic City in 1947, radically changed the organization to keep up with developments in telecommunications; for example, a new permanent organ, the International Frequency Registration Board, was created to cope with the overcrowding of certain transmission frequencies; and an agreement was drawn up under which ITU was recognized by the UN as the specialized agency for telecommunications. The convention was further modified in certain respects by plenipotentiary conferences in 1952, 1959, 1965, 1973, and 1982.

[3]PURPOSES

ITU's objectives include maintaining and extending international cooperation between all members of the Union for the improvement and rational use of telecommunications; promoting and offering technical assistance to developing countries in the field of telecommunications; promoting the development of technical facilities and their most efficient operation; making telecommunications services, as far as possible, generally available to the public; and harmonizing the actions of nations in the attainment of these goals.

[4]MEMBERSHIP

As of 1 July 1983, the ITU had 158 members:
Afghanistan
Albania

Algeria
Angola
Argentina
Australia
Austria
Bahamas
Bahrain
Bangladesh
Barbados
Belgium
Belize
Benin
Bolivia
Botswana
Brazil
Bulgaria
Burma
Burundi
Byelorussia
Cameroon
Canada
Cape Verde
Central African Rep.
Chad
Chile
China
Colombia
Comoros
Congo
Costa Rica
Cuba
Cyprus
Czechoslovakia
Denmark
Djibouti
Dominican Republic
Ecuador
Egypt

El Salvador
Equatorial Guinea
Ethiopia
Fiji
Finland
France
Gabon
Gambia
German Dem. Rep.
Germany, Fed. Rep.
Ghana
Greece
Grenada
Guatemala
Guinea
Guinea-Bissau
Guyana
Haiti
Honduras
Hungary
Iceland
India
Indonesia
Iran
Iraq
Ireland
Israel
Italy
Ivory Coast
Jamaica
Japan
Jordan
Kampuchea
Kenya
Korea, Dem. People's Rep.
Korea, Rep.
Kuwait
Laos
Lebanon
Lesotho
Liberia
Libya
Liechtenstein
Luxembourg
Madagascar
Malawi
Malaysia
Maldives
Mali
Malta
Mauritania
Mauritius
Mexico
Monaco
Mongolia
Morocco
Mozambique
Nauru
Nepal
Netherlands
New Zealand
Nicaragua
Niger
Nigeria
Norway
Oman
Pakistan

Panama
Papua New Guinea
Paraguay
Peru
Philippines
Poland
Portugal
Qatar
Romania
Rwanda
St. Vincent and the Grenadines
San Marino
São Tomé and Príncipe
Sa'udi Arabia
Senegal
Sierra Leone
Singapore
Somalia
South Africa
Spain
Sri Lanka
Sudan
Suriname
Swaziland
Sweden
Switzerland
Syria
Tanzania
Thailand
Togo
Tonga
Trinidad and Tobago
Tunisia
Turkey
Uganda
Ukraine
USSR
United Arab Emirates
UK
US
Upper Volta
Uruguay
Vatican
Venezuela
Viet-Nam
Yemen, People's Dem. Rep.
Yemen Arab Rep.
Yugoslavia
Zaire
Zambia
Zimbabwe

[5]STRUCTURE

ITU carries out its work through the Plenipotentiary Conference, administrative conferences, the Administrative Council, the International Frequency Registration Board, international consultative committees, and the General Secretariat, headed by a secretary-general.

The Plenipotentiary Conference

The supreme body of the ITU is the Plenipotentiary Conference, in which each member has one vote. It meets at intervals of five or more years—in Atlantic City in 1947, Buenos Aires in 1952, Geneva in 1959, Montreux in 1965, Torremolinos in 1973, and Nairobi in 1982. The Conference governs the Union's activities and revises the International Telecommunication Convention as necessary. It establishes the general basis of the ITU's budget and approves the accounts of the ITU.

Administrative Conferences

ITU administrative conferences are convened to consider particular telecommunications matters of worldwide or regional import. There are two regular world administrative conferences: one for telegraph and telephone, the other for radio and other forms of wireless transmission. These conferences revise the telegraph, telephone, and radio regulations annexed to the International Telecommunication Convention and review the activities of the International Frequency Registration Board. Regional administrative conferences consider questions of restricted geographical scope, such as the assignment of television frequencies of limited radius.

Administrative Council

The Administrative Council, which normally meets once a year but may meet more frequently, facilitates implementation by member countries of provisions of the convention, of decisions of plenipotentiary conferences, and, where appropriate, of provisions of other conferences and meetings of the ITU. The Council was established by the Atlantic City conference of 1947. Since 1982, it has consisted of 41 members elected by the Plenipotentiary Conferences. The Council ensures efficient coordination within the Union and in its relations with other international organizations.

International Frequency Registration Board (IFRB)

The IFRB records all frequency assignments and advises members with a view to operating the maximum practicable number of radio channels in crowded portions of the radiofrequency spectrum. The IFRB is composed of five persons, each of a different nationality, elected by the Plenipotentiary Conference from candidates of ITU member states. IFRB members serve not as representatives of countries, but as individual custodians of an international public trust. They are experts in radio communications, with practical experience in the assignment and use of radio frequencies.

International Consultative Committees

The ITU has two permanent consultative committees, whose function is to study and draw up recommendations on telecommunication problems. The International Radio Consultative Committee (CCIR), in existence since the late 1920s, concerns itself with technical radio questions and resulting operational problems. The International Telegraph and Telephone Consultative Committee (CCITT) came into existence in 1957, replacing the separate telegraph and telephone consultative committees. Both the CCIR and the CCITT have their own secretariats and maintain laboratories.

At the head of each committee is a director, elected by the Plenipotentiary Conference. The two committees have a very large membership that includes member states, international organizations, scientific and industrial organizations, and private agencies active in international telecommunications.

The consultative committees hold plenary assemblies, usually at four-year intervals. Programs of study are carried out by specially constituted study groups. This work is revised by the plenary assemblies of the consultative committees, which finally draw up and publish recommendations. These recommendations are not binding, but governments, operating agencies, and private companies readily comply with the recommended rules, since no system of international telecommunications is practicable without agreement on technical means. Many of these recommendations are adopted by ITU administrative conferences to form a part of ITU regulations.

General Secretariat and Secretary-General

The General Secretariat is at ITU headquarters, Place des Nations, CH-1211 Geneva 20. It handles arrangements for ITU conferences and meetings and maintains liaison with member states and with the UN, the specialized agencies, and other international organizations. It also carries out the ITU's extensive publication program. It is headed by the secretary-general. Richard E. Butler of Australia was elected to the post by the Nairobi Plenipotentiary Conference in 1982.

⁶BUDGET

The ordinary expenses of the ITU are borne by all its members. Contributions roughly reflect the scale of telecommunications facilities of member states. Private agencies and international organizations contribute to the cost of the conferences in which they participate. The 1982 ITU budget was SwFr78,331,000 (approximately $35.6 million).

⁷ACTIVITIES

The ITU functions in five ways. (1) It allocates radio frequencies to different types of radiocommunication services, and it registers the assignment of frequencies to particular stations so as to achieve an orderly use of the radio-frequency spectrum and avoid, as far as possible, interference between radio stations in different countries. (2) It seeks to establish the lowest rates for telecommunication services that are consistent with efficient service and sound financial administration. (3) It promotes measures for ensuring the safety of life through the coordination of telecommunication services, a function of particular interest to maritime countries. (4) It carries out studies, makes recommendations, and collects and publishes information for the benefit of all its members. (5) It provides technical assistance to developing countries for the expansion of telecommunications and the training of personnel.

A. FREQUENCY ALLOCATIONS AND RADIO REGULATIONS

Although the range of radio frequencies (or wavelengths) is very great, it is limited. International traffic rules have become increasingly necessary. By 1947, the radio regulations drawn up by the conference at Cairo in 1938 were out of date. An administrative radio conference met concurrently with the Atlantic City Plenipotentiary Conference in 1947. It prepared a revised and expanded worldwide frequency allocation table covering frequencies from 10 kilohertz (KHz) up to the ultrashortwave channels ending at 10.5 gigahertz (GHz). The table adopted in 1938 extended only to 200 megahertz (MHz). Specific frequency bands were allocated to various essential radio services, such as maritime, air, coastal, and meteorological services. It was anticipated that operating frequencies would be assigned to individual radio stations throughout the world through a series of special international and regional conferences. Unforeseen difficulties arose, however, and in 1951 an extraordinary administrative radio conference was convened in Geneva to review the situation. The conference adopted frequency assignment plans and lists for stations operating up to 4,000 KHz and adopted plans for the aeronautical and maritime mobile services in worldwide exclusive frequency bands between 4 and 27.5 MHz. The 1959 radio conference in Geneva decided that the entire 1947 table of frequency allocations would come into force on 1 May 1961, together with all other parts of the revised radio regulations. The 1959 conference extended the table of frequency allocations from 10.5 GHz to 40 GHz.

In accordance with the radio regulations, the IFRB maintains a Master International Frequency Register of frequency assignments, including assignments for space communications and radioastronomy, reported to it by various countries. This register, whose contents are published as the *International Frequency List,* a service document of the ITU, includes information on some 1,300,000 frequency assignments to radio stations of various types. Summaries of monitoring information supplied by member countries are compiled by the IFRB and are published quarterly. The IFRB also does the technical planning for radio conferences and about every two years organizes seminars on the management of the radio-frequency spectrum.

The radio regulations, as revised by the Geneva radio conference in 1959, were also partially revised in 1963 by a space radio conference, in 1966 by an aeronautical radio conference, in 1967 by a maritime radio conference, in 1971 by the second space radio conference, in 1974 by a maritime conference, in 1977 by a satellite broadcasting conference, and in 1978 by an aeronautical mobile radio conference. An overall revision of the Radio Regulations was made by the World Administrative Conference in 1979, and the regulations were again partially revised by regional administrative medium-frequency broadcasting conferences in 1980, 1981, and 1982. The regulations are annexed to the International Telecommunication Convention and are binding on the member countries of the ITU.

B. TELEGRAPH AND TELEPHONE REGULATIONS

The ITU, through its Administrative Telephone and Telegraph Conference, draws up regulations for the conduct of international telegraph and telephone services. These regulations were considerably simplified by a conference held in Geneva in 1973.

C. TELECOMMUNICATIONS IN SPACE

As early as 1957, the ITU noted in its annual report to the UN that with the advent of artificial satellites new international problems had been raised, especially in connection with radio frequencies, to which the ITU would have to give its attention.

An extraordinary conference was convened by the ITU in 1963 in Geneva. It allocated over 6,000 MHz (about 15% of the entire radio-frequency spectrum) to the space radiocommunication services, and adopted regulations concerning the use of these frequencies. A second such conference, held in Geneva in 1971, made additional allocations to the space radiocommunication services and extended the table of frequency allocations from 40 GHz to 235 GHz. Owing to the need for sharing frequency bands between terrestrial and space radiocommunication services with equal rights, the conference drew up a series of regulations involving advance publication and coordination between members of the ITU for the use of frequencies on these bands. In 1977, a World Administrative Radio Conference for Planning of the Broadcasting-Satellite Service in frequency bands 11.7–12.2 GHz (Regions 2 and 3) and 11.7–12.5 GHz (Region 1) was held. A progress report is issued annually on space radio action by the ITU.

D. STUDY AND EXCHANGE OF INFORMATION

A large part of the regular activities of the ITU consists of continuous study of technical and administrative problems in telecommunications. The ITU functions as an international university of telecommunications. Study groups are composed of experts from governmental telecommunication administrations, private operators, and national scientific and industrial organizations. Most work under the two international consultative committees, the CCIR and the CCITT.

Each year study groups, subgroups, and working parties of the CCITT meet to discuss telegraph and telephone engineering, operating, and tariff problems. The plenary assemblies of the consultative committees review the findings of the study groups and draw up recommendations. Joint meetings of the CCIR and the CCITT discuss such problems as long-distance television transmission. Both also cooperate in the "Plan" committee, which, in conjunction with regional subcommittees, assembles data for the planning of international telecommunication networks. The CCIR is working out technical standards for all aspects of space telecommunications, involving aspects of microwave relay by satellites, positioning of satellites in geostationary orbit, maritime and aeronautical communications by satellites, and satellites for sound and television broadcasting.

One of the most important duties of the ITU headquarters is to collect and collate essential telecommunications data and to edit and publish the numerous documents essential for the day-to-day operation of the various telephone, telegraph, and broadcasting systems of the world. Among the documents regularly issued by the ITU are the *International Frequency List*; the quarterly *High Frequency Broadcasting Schedules*; yearly radio statistics; lists of coast, ship, and fixed stations; codes and abbreviations in general use; lists of radiolocation stations; an alphabetical list of call signs; summaries of international monitoring information; the *Telecommunication Journal*; and similar publications, all generally issued in separate English, French, and Spanish editions, or a single trilingual edition.

E. TECHNICAL COOPERATION

The ITU acts as a participating and executive agency for UNDP. While the major part of its technical cooperation activities are financed by UNDP, the ITU also administers a small program of trust-fund projects and an associate experts program.

The following subjects are included in the ITU's technical cooperation activities: development, organization, planning, operation, and maintenance of telecommunication equipment; traffic and tariffs; operating procedures; economic and technical studies of future requirements in telecommunications; radiocommunication techniques; frequency management and radio monitoring; switching and transmission; radio broadcasting and the technical aspects of television; rural and maritime telecommunications; space communications; data processing and computer applications for telecommunication administration; and establishment of testing, research, and development centers.

The ITU also cooperates in the training of personnel in all branches of telecommunications, the organization of seminars and group training, and the establishment or expansion of institutions for professional and vocational training in telecommunications.

The three main objectives of ITU's program of technical cooperation continue to be the development of regional telecommunication networks in Africa, Asia, and Latin America; the strengthening of telecommunication technical and administrative services in developing countries; and the training of telecommunications personnel.

In 1982, 612 expert missions were carried out, 739 fellows underwent training abroad, and 225 projects were assigned to the Union. Expenditure for equipment for various field projects was $5.5 million. Total expenditures for project implementation were $31.8 million, of which 82% ($26.2 million) was provided by UNDP and the remainder ($5.6 million) from trust funds, associate expert arrangements, and the ITU Special Fund.

Expenditure by region was as follows: $10.1 million for Africa, $5.4 million for the Americas, $7.6 million for Asia and the Pacific, $7.7 million for the Middle East, and $1 million for Europe and for interregional projects.

[8]BIBLIOGRAPHY

High Frequency Broadcasting Schedules. Quarterly.
International Frequency List.
Telecommunication Journal. Monthly.

THE WORLD METEOROLOGICAL ORGANIZATION (WMO)

[1]**BACKGROUND:** The practical uses of meteorology are to instruct, advise, and warn mankind about the weather. Thus it can help prevent devastation caused by flood, drought, and storm; and it can assist the peoples of the world in best adapting their agriculture and industry to the climatic conditions under which they live.

For meteorology, international cooperation is indispensable. In the words of President John F. Kennedy, " . . . there is the atmosphere itself, the atmosphere in which we live and breathe and which makes life on this planet possible. Scientists have studied the atmosphere for many decades, but its problems continue to defy us. The reasons for our limited progress are obvious. Weather cannot be easily reproduced and observed in the laboratory. It must, therefore, be studied in all of its violence wherever it has its way. Here, new scientific tools have become available. With modern computers, rockets and satellites, the time is ripe to harness a variety of disciplines for a concerted attack. . . . [The] atmospheric sciences require worldwide observation and, hence, international cooperation."

[2]CREATION

Beginning in 1853, many of the world's leading maritime countries tried to establish an international system for collecting meteorological observations made by ships at sea.

The first international meteorological congress was held in Vienna in 1873; it led to the founding of the International Meteorological Organization, composed of directors of meteorological services of various countries and territories throughout the world. This body carried out ambitious programs to perfect and standardize international meteorological practices.

As transport, communications, agriculture, and industry developed in the 20th century, they increasingly relied on meteorology. At the same time, meteorology itself relied to an increasing extent on advances in science and technology to perfect its methods of observing and predicting weather phenomena. Hence, the closest possible collaboration was called for between the International Meteorological Organization and other international bodies.

A conference of directors of national meteorological services met in Washington in 1947 under the auspices of the International Meteorological Organization and adopted the World Meteorological Convention, establishing the World Meteorological Organization as a UN specialized agency. On 23 March 1950, after 30 signers had ratified or acceded to the Convention, it came into force. The first WMO congress opened in Paris on 19 March 1951.

[3]PURPOSES

As set forth in the World Meteorological Convention, the purposes of the WMO are sixfold:

(1) To facilitate worldwide cooperation in the establishment of networks of stations for meteorological, hydrological, and other geophysical observations and to promote the establishment and maintenance of meteorological centers;

(2) To promote the establishment and maintenance of systems for rapid exchange of weather information;

(3) To promote standardization of meteorological observations and ensure uniform publication of observations and statistics;

(4) To further the application of meteorology to aviation, shipping, water problems, agriculture, and other human activities;

(5) To promote activities in operational hydrology and cooperation between meteorological and hydrological services;

(6) To encourage research and training in meteorology and to assist in coordinating them at the international level.

[4]MEMBERSHIP

Membership in WMO is not limited to sovereign states; it may include territories that maintain their own meteorological services. Membership is open to any of the 45 states and 30 territories attending the 1947 conference in Washington that signed the convention, or to any member of the UN with a meteorological service. Any of these automatically becomes a member of WMO upon ratifying or acceding to the Convention. Any other state, territory, or group of territories maintaining its own meteorological services may become eligible for membership upon approval of two-thirds of the WMO membership. As of 1 July 1983, WMO had 157 members, including 152 states and 5 territories:

Afghanistan
Albania
Algeria
Angola
Argentina
Australia
Austria
Bahamas
Bahrain
Bangladesh
Barbados
Belgium
Belize
Benin
Bolivia
Botswana
Brazil
Bulgaria
Burma
Burundi
Byelorussia
Cameroon
Canada
Cape Verde
Central African Rep.
Chad
Chile
China
Colombia

Comoros
Congo
Costa Rica
Cuba
Cyprus
Czechoslovakia
Denmark
Djibouti
Dominica
Dominican Republic
Ecuador
Egypt
El Salvador
Ethiopia
Fiji
Finland
France
Gabon
Gambia
German Dem. Rep.
Germany, Fed. Rep.
Ghana
Greece
Guatemala
Guinea
Guinea-Bissau
Guyana
Haiti
Honduras
Hungary
Iceland
India
Indonesia
Iran
Iraq
Ireland
Israel
Italy
Ivory Coast
Jamaica
Japan
Jordan
Kampuchea
Kenya
Korea, Dem. People's Rep.
Korea, Rep.
Kuwait
Laos
Lebanon
Lesotho
Liberia
Libya
Luxembourg
Madagascar
Malawi
Malaysia
Maldives
Mali
Malta
Mauritania
Mauritius
Mexico
Mongolia
Morocco
Mozambique
Nepal
Netherlands

New Zealand
Nicaragua
Niger
Nigeria
Norway
Oman
Pakistan
Panama
Papua New Guinea
Paraguay
Peru
Philippines
Poland
Portugal
Qatar
Romania
Rwanda
St. Lucia
São Tomé and Príncipe
Sa'udi Arabia
Senegal
Seychelles
Sierra Leone
Singapore
Somalia
South Africa
Spain
Sri Lanka
Sudan
Suriname
Swaziland
Sweden
Switzerland
Syria
Tanzania
Thailand
Togo
Trinidad and Tobago
Tunisia
Turkey
Uganda
Ukraine
USSR
UK
US
Upper Volta
Uruguay
Vanuatu
Venezuela
Viet-Nam
Yemen, People's Dem. Rep.
Yemen Arab Rep.
Yugoslavia
Zaire
Zambia
Zimbabwe

Territories:
British Caribbean territories
French Polynesia
Hong Kong
Netherlands Antilles
New Caledonia

5 STRUCTURE

The WMO is headed by a president and three vice-presidents, elected by the World Meteorological Congress.

World Meteorological Congress

The Congress is the supreme body of the organization, and is composed of the delegates representing its member states and territories. (According to the World Meteorological Convention, the principal delegate of each member "should be the director of its meteorological service.") The Congress, which is required to meet at least once every four years, determines regulations on the constitution and functions of the various WMO bodies, adopts regulations covering meteorological practices and procedures, and determines general policies to carry out the purposes of the organization and related matters. It established the regional associations and technical commissions.

Each member of the Congress has one vote. Election of individuals to serve in any capacity in the organization is by a simple majority of the votes cast: other questions are decided by two-thirds of the votes cast for and against. On certain subjects, only members that are states may vote.

Executive Committee

The Executive Committee has 29 members: the president and the 3 vice-presidents of the WMO; the presidents of the 6 regional associations; and 19 directors of meteorological services of its members selected by the Congress. Meeting at least once a year, the Committee carries out the activities of the organization and the decisions of the Congress. Its own decisions are reached by a two-thirds majority.

Regional Associations and Technical Commissions

There are six regional associations: one each for Africa, Asia, South America, North and Central America, the Southwest Pacific, and Europe. The regional associations are composed of the WMO members whose meteorological networks lie in or extend into the respective regions. They meet when necessary and examine from a regional point of view all questions referred to them by the executive committee. Each association has the responsibility of coordinating meteorological activity and promoting the execution of WMO resolutions within its region.

The technical commissions are composed of experts in meteorology. They study various meteorological problems and make recommendations to the executive committee and congress. The WMO has established eight commissions for, respectively, basic systems; instruments and methods of observation; atmospheric sciences; aeronautical meteorology; agricultural meteorology; marine meteorology; hydrology; and climatology and applications of meteorology.

Secretary-General and Secretariat

The Secretariat, in Geneva, completes the structure of the WMO. Its staff, under the direction of a secretary-general, undertakes studies, prepares publications, acts as Secretariat during meetings of the various WMO bodies, and provides liaison between the various meteorological services of the world. The president of the WMO, elected in 1979, is R. L. Kintana of the Philippines. The secretary-general is A. C. Winn-Nielsen of Denmark.

[6]BUDGET

Contributions to the WMO regular budget are assessed upon members by the congress. For 1980–83 the budget was $74.4 million. Estimates for 1983 approved by the Executive Committee amounted to $18.1 million. In addition, a budget of $2.4 million was approved for technical cooperation activities, the funds being obtained from extrabudgetary sources. Total extrabudgetary expenditures for 1983 were estimated at $20 million, funded through UNDP, the WMO Voluntary Cooperation Program, and funds-in-trust.

[7]ACTIVITIES

A. WORLD WEATHER WATCH

The World Weather Watch (WWW) was established by the Fifth World Meteorological Congress, held in Geneva in 1967.

The purpose of the WWW is to make available to each national meteorological service meteorological and related environmental information required in order to enjoy the most efficient and effective meteorological and related environmental services possible, both in applications and research. No other scientific discipline has such international interdependence. The WWW has three essential elements:

(1) *The Global Observing System* (GOS) provides information from observing stations in the regional basic synoptic networks, automatic weather stations, fixed sea stations, research and special-purpose vessels, mobile ships, automatic marine stations, aircraft, atmospheric detection system, weather radars, meteorological rockets, background pollution stations, radiation stations, near-polar orbiting satellites, and geostationary satellites.

(2) *The Global Data-Processing System* (GDPS) provides processed information to all meteorological services. It is composed of 3 world meteorological centers in Melbourne, Moscow, and Washington; 21 regional meteorological centers; and 148 national meteorological centers.

(3) *The Global Telecommunication System* (GTS) interconnects all GDPS centers for rapid and reliable interchange of information needed for world, regional, and national weather forecasting.

Every day about 4,000 land observing stations in the regional basic synoptic networks are taking 30,000 surface observations and 6,000 upper-air observations. Observations also come from 4,000 ships and 3,000 aircraft. Observations taken by meteorological radars, automatic weather stations, and the atmospheric detection system become more numerous every year. Data from meteorological satellites are increasing for daily use. These data as well as forecasts, analyses, and warnings are exchanged by the GTS in digital and pictorial forms; WMO developed a series of internationally agreed figure-codes, which is prescribed in the *WMO Manual on Codes*. Meteorological information in pictorial form is transmitted by analog facsimile. Details of international rules adopted by WMO regarding the GTS are prescribed in the *WMO Manual on the Global Telecommunication System,* which describes global and regional aspects of the organization, and procedures, technical characteristics, and specifications of meteorological telecommunications. WMO has issued the *Guide on the GDPS* and a number of *WWW Planning Reports*.

B. WORLD CLIMATE PROGRAM

The World Climate Program (WCP) was established by the eighth WMO Congress in 1979. Its objectives are to use existing climate information to benefit economic and social activities in every nation; to improve understanding of climate variability and change; and to predict changes in climate and warn of manmade climatic effects.

These objectives are being implemented through four major component programs: the World Climate Data Program, the World Climate Applications Program, the World Climate Impact Studies Program, and the World Climate Research Program. WMO is directly responsible for the first two programs and for the overall coordination of the WCP. WMO and the International Council of Scientific Unions (ICSU) are jointly responsible for the World Climate Research Program, and UNEP is responsible for the World Climate Impact Studies Program. Several other international organizations such as FAO, UNESCO, WHO, and UNRISD are also actively involved. The close cooperation required for the WCP, which is complex and multidisciplinary, is achieved through informal interagency meetings. Scientific and technical planning and guidance for the four component programs is provided by specially established bodies such as the WMO Advisory Committee for the World Climate Applications and Data Program, the WMO/ICSU Joint Scientific Committee (for the World Climate Research Program), and the UNEP Scientific Advisory Committee (for the World Climate Impact Studies Program).

C. RESEARCH AND DEVELOPMENT

WMO's Research and Development Program includes all activities related to promoting the understanding of atmospheric processes and to increasing skill in prediction of atmospheric circulation, and also includes activities related to environmental conditions important to human well-being. Activities include weather-prediction research, tropical meteorology, weather modification, and environmental prediction research.

Activities related to the Global Atmospheric Research Program (GARP), sponsored jointly by WMO and ICSU, also form an important component of the Research and Development Program. GARP is an international scientific effort involving a series of complex field experiments designed to promote studies of atmospheric processes, including those striving to improve the accuracy of weather forecasts and to acquire a better understanding of the physical basis of climate. The GARP Atlantic Tropical Experiment took place in 1974, and the first GARP Global Experiment was conducted in 1978–79. The main thrust of the weather modification program has been the Precipitation Enhancement Project, a field effort designed to demonstrate the scientific planning, execution, and evaluation of an experiment to increase precipitation by cloud seeding.

Within the Research and Development Program, the responsibility for promoting and coordinating research activities of WMO members and of arranging for the exchange of information lies with the Commission for Atmospheric Sciences. To accomplish this, the Commission in 1982, when reviewing the work accomplished, established seven working groups and seven groups of rapporteurs, and also appointed five individual rapporteurs to keep abreast of the latest developments in all fields of atmospheric research. Through this mechanism, the Commission also directs attention to outstanding research problems and facilitates the dissemination of scientific knowledge on topical issues to aid the application of research results to operational programs.

D. HYDROLOGY AND WATER RESOURCES

The purpose of WHO's Hydrology and Water Resources Program (HWRP) is to promote worldwide cooperation in the assessment of water resources and to assist in their development through the coordinated establishment of hydrological networks and services, including data collection and processing, hydrological forecasting and warnings, and the supply of meteorological and hydrological data for design of projects. The three components of this effort are the operational hydrology program; the hydrology in environmental management and development program; and cooperation with water-related programs of other international organizations.

The emphasis of the HWRP is on the operational hydrology program, and particularly its hydrological operational multipurpose subprogram, the main aim of which is to provide an efficient means and systematic institutional framework for transfer of operational hydrological technology to and between developing countries.

The hydrology in environmental management and development program includes technical support for WMO activities dealing with environmental problems, such as the Tropical Cyclone Program, the World Climate Program, and WMO activities relating to droughts and desertification.

The third program, cooperation with water-related programs of other international organizations, includes a wide range of activities undertaken jointly with other organizations, notably support by WMO to the International Hydrological Program of UNESCO.

E. REGIONAL PROGRAM

The main objectives of the Regional Program are to give the required support to the WMO regional associations to enable them to achieve their purposes as laid down in Article 18 of the Convention, and also to give the required support to the organization and implementation of WMO programs on a regional and subregional basis. Within the regional program, three regional offices have been established: for Africa, in Bujumbura, Burundi; for Asia and Latin America, in Geneva, Switzerland; and for Latin America, in Asunción, Paraguay.

F. TECHNICAL COOPERATION

WMO's technical cooperation activities—in the form of fellowships, expert missions, equipment, and assistance for group training, such as workshops and seminars—are carried out through UNDP, the Voluntary Cooperation Program, trust-fund arrangements, and the regular budget of the organization. Advice has been given on subjects ranging from the establishment, organization, and operation of meteorological and hydrological services to the application of meteorology in such fields as food production and alternative energy sources.

UNDP assistance is provided to individual countries to help in implementing development programs formulated by the countries themselves. WMO provides advice and assistance in the formulation and implementation of projects involving meteorology and operational hydrology. Over half the total funds for WMO's technical cooperation activities comes from UNDP, approximating $12 million in 1982.

WMO's Voluntary Cooperation Program is maintained by contributions from members to its two components: the Voluntary Cooperation Fund and the Equipment and Services Program. Intended primarily to implement the World Weather Watch, the Voluntary Cooperation Program also covers aspects of other WMO programs in such fields as agrometeorology, hydrology, and climate and the granting of fellowships to nationals of developing countries. Assistance totaling almost $5 million was provided through the program in 1982.

Under trust fund arrangements, countries make funds available through WMO for technical cooperation activities either in the country providing the funds or in another country. Trust fund arrangements accounted for approximately $5 million of total assistance rendered in 1982.

Activities under WMO's regular budget represent only a very small percentage of the total assistance, about $300,000 in 1982, and are confined mainly to the awarding of fellowships and participation in group training.

G. EDUCATION AND TRAINING

The Education and Training Program is designed to support the scientific and technical programs of WHO as well as to assist in the development of the required manpower of national meteorological and hydrological services of member countries. The program thus ensures that the full benefit of meteorological and hydrological skills and knowledge are obtained at national levels.

Activities under the program include surveys of personnel training requirements; the development of appropriate training programs; the establishment and improvement of regional training centers; the organization of training courses, seminars, and conferences; and the preparation of training materials in the form of compendia of lecture notes, problem workbooks, and visual and audiovisual aids. The program also undertakes the arrangement of individual training programs and the provision of fellowships. There are, on average, 470 WMO trainees a year, and about 225 fellowships are awarded annually from WMO's regular budget and from extrabudgetary resources such as UNDP, funds-in-trust, and the Voluntary Cooperation Program.

Another supporting activity of the program is the provision of advice on education and training in meteorology and operational hydrology and on the availability of suitable training facilities. A training library is maintained, and the training aids it contains also serve as the basis for advising WMO members on the availability of such material. Films are provided on a loan basis to members on request.

The Panel of Experts on Education and Training serves as the focal point of the program.

8BIBLIOGRAPHY

WMO Annual Report.

WMO Bulletin. Summarizes the work of WMO and of developments in international meteorology. Quarterly.

(WMO also publishes, in its *Basic Documents* series, *Technical Regulations* and *Agreements and Working Arrangements with Other International Organizations*. Scientific and technical publications include various guides, manuals, and technical notes, *WWW Planning Reports, WMO/IHD Projects Reports, Operational Hydrology Reports, Reports on Marine Science Affairs,* and *Special Environmental Reports.*)

THE INTERNATIONAL MARITIME ORGANIZATION (IMO)

¹BACKGROUND: The seven seas, accounting for about two-thirds of our planet's surface, are the only truly international part of our globe. Except for a marginal belt a very few miles wide, touching on the shores of countries, the greater part of the world's oceans and maritime resources are the common property of all nations. Since ancient times, however, "freedom of the seas" has too often been a theoretical ideal rather than a reality. In each historic era, the great maritime powers tended to use their naval might to dominate the sea. Some of those powers, while serving their own interests, served the world as a whole, as in the great explorations of unknown continents. Many sought to use the waters for purely national interests, particularly in matters affecting straits and other narrow waterways. Private shipping interests, often supported by their national governments, have been even more competitive, and international cooperation in maritime matters has been very limited.

The need for an international organization to develop and coordinate international maritime cooperation was best expressed by President Woodrow Wilson, who called for "universal association of the nations to maintain the inviolate security of the highway of the seas for the common and unhindered use of all the nations of the world." However, it was not until after the creation of the UN that such an organization came into being.

²CREATION

The Convention establishing the International Maritime Organization (originally called the Inter-Governmental Maritime Consultative Organization) was drawn up in 1948 by the UN Maritime Conference in Geneva, but it was ten years before the Convention came into effect. The conference decided that IMO's success depended on participation by most of the nations with large merchant navies and specified that the organization would come into being only when 21 states, including 7 having at least 1 million gross tons of shipping each, had become parties to the Convention. On 17 March 1958, the Convention came into effect. The first IMO Assembly met in London in January 1959. The relationship of IMO to the UN as a specialized agency was approved by the UN General Assembly on 18 November 1958 and by the IMO Assembly on 13 January 1959.

³PURPOSES

The purposes of IMO as set forth in the Convention are:

(1) To provide machinery for cooperation among governments in the field of governmental regulation and practices relating to technical matters of all kinds affecting shipping engaged in international trade;

(2) To encourage the general adoption of the highest practicable standards in matters concerning maritime safety, efficiency of navigation, and the prevention and control of marine pollution;

(3) To encourage the removal of discriminatory action and unnecessary restrictions by governments engaged in international trade, so as to promote the availability of shipping services to world commerce without discrimination;

(4) To consider matters concerning unfair restrictive practices by shipping concerns; and

(5) To consider any matters concerning shipping that may be referred to the IMO by any UN organ or specialized agency.

⁴MEMBERSHIP

Any state invited to the 1948 Maritime Conference or any member of the UN may become a member of IMO by accepting the 1948 Convention. Any other state whose application is approved by two-thirds of the IMO membership becomes a member by accepting the Convention. If an IMO member responsible for the international relations of a territory (or group of territories) declares the Convention to be applicable to that territory, the territory may became an associate member of IMO.

As of 1 July 1983, there were 124 IMO members and one associate member:

Algeria
Angola
Argentina
Australia
Austria
Bahamas
Bahrain
Bangladesh
Barbados
Belgium
Benin
Brazil
Bulgaria
Burma
Cameroon
Canada
Cape Verde
Chile
China
Colombia
Congo
Costa Rica
Cuba
Cyprus
Czechoslovakia
Denmark
Djibouti
Dominica
Dominican Republic
Ecuador

Egypt
El Salvador
Equatorial Guinea
Ethiopia
Fiji
Finland
France
Gabon
Gambia
German Dem. Rep.
Germany, Fed. Rep.
Ghana
Greece
Guatemala
Guinea
Guinea-Bissau
Guyana
Haiti
Honduras
Hungary
Iceland
India
Indonesia
Iran
Iraq
Ireland
Israel
Italy
Ivory Coast
Jamaica
Japan
Jordan
Kampuchea
Kenya
Korea, Rep.
Kuwait
Lebanon
Liberia
Libya
Madagascar
Malaysia
Maldives
Malta
Mauritania
Mauritius
Mexico
Morocco
Mozambique
Nepal
Netherlands
New Zealand
Nicaragua
Nigeria
Norway
Oman
Pakistan
Panama
Papua New Guinea
Peru
Philippines
Poland
Portugal
Qatar
Romania
St. Lucia
St. Vincent and the Grenadines
Sa'udi Arabia

Senegal
Seychelles
Sierra Leone
Singapore
Somalia
Spain
Sri Lanka
Sudan
Suriname
Sweden
Switzerland
Syria
Tanzania
Thailand
Trinidad and Tobago
Tunisia
Turkey
USSR
United Arab Emirates
UK
US
Uruguay
Venezuela
Yemen, People's Dem. Rep.
Yemen Arab Rep.
Yugoslavia
Zaire

Associate Member:
Hong Kong

5STRUCTURE

IMO's main organs are the Assembly, the Council, the Maritime Safety Committee, and the Secretariat, headed by a secretary-general.

The Assembly

The policy-making body of IMO is the Assembly, composed of all IMO members. The Assembly determines the work program, votes the budget to which all members contribute, and approves the appointment of the secretary-general. Meetings are held every two years.

Between sessions of the Assembly, the Council performs all functions of the organization except that of recommending the adoption of maritime safety regulations, a prerogative of the Maritime Safety Committee. The Council also has an important policy-making role. Drafts of international instruments and formal recommendations must be approved by the Council before they can be submitted to the Assembly.

The Council is made up of 24 members elected by the Assembly: 6 members represent states with the largest international shipping services; 6 represent states with the largest international seaborne trade; and 12 represent states, not elected under the foregoing categories, which have special interests in maritime transport or navigation and whose presence in the Council will ensure representation of the world's major geographic areas. The Council normally meets twice a year.

Maritime Safety Committee

The Maritime Safety Committee, the third major body of IMO, is made up of all member states. Its work is carried out mainly through subcommittees dealing with safety of navigation; radiocommunications; life-saving appliances; standards of training and watchkeeping; carriage of dangerous goods; ship design and equipment; fire protection; stability and load lines, and fishing vessel safety; containers and cargoes; bulk chemicals; and marine environment protection. IMO also has a Legal Committee and a Committee on Technical Cooperation.

Secretary-General and Secretariat

The Secretariat consists of a secretary-general appointed by the Council with the approval of the Assembly; the secretary of the Maritime Safety Committee; and an international staff. IMO headquarters are at 4 Albert Embankment, London, SE1, 7SR.

The secretary-general is C. P. Srivastava of India.

⁶BUDGET

A budget of $25.7 million was approved by the 12th IMO Assembly for the 1982–83 biennium.

⁷ACTIVITIES

IMO's general functions, as stipulated in its Convention, are "consultative and advisory." It thus serves as a forum where members can consult and exchange information on maritime matters. It discusses and makes recommendations on any maritime question submitted by member states or by other bodies of the UN, and advises other international bodies, including the UN itself, on maritime matters. Various other intergovernmental agencies deal with specialized maritime matters, such as atomic propulsion for ships (IAEA), health at sea (WHO), maritime labor standards (ILO), meteorology (WMO), oceanography (UNESCO), and ship-to-ship and ship-to-shore communications (ITU). One of the functions of IMO is to help coordinate the work in these different fields.

IMO is also authorized to convene international conferences when necessary and to draft international maritime conventions or agreements, for adoption by governments. These conferences, and the conventions resulting from them, have been mainly concerned with two subjects of primary concern to IMO: safety at sea and the prevention of marine pollution.

A. SAFETY AT SEA

A conference convened by IMO in 1960 adopted the International Convention on Safety of Life at Sea to replace an earlier (1948) instrument. The convention covers a wide range of measures designed to improve the safety of shipping, including subdivision and stability; machinery and electrical installations; fire protection, detection, and extinction; lifesaving appliances; radiotelegraphy and radiotelephony; safety of navigation; carriage of grain; carriage of dangerous goods; and nuclear ships. A new convention, incorporating amendments to the 1960 agreement, was adopted in 1974; it has been in force since 1980.

In 1966, an IMO conference adopted the International Convention on Load Lines (in force since 1968), which sets limitations on the draught to which a ship may be loaded, an important consideration in its safety. The 1969 International Convention on Tonnage Measurement of Ships, designed to establish a uniform system for tonnage measurement, has been in force since 1982.

Two conventions were adopted in 1972, following IMO conferences: the Convention on the International Regulations for Preventing Collisions at Sea, which concerns traffic separation schemes; and the Convention for Safe Containers, which provides uniform international regulations for maintaining a high level of safety in the carriage of containers by providing generally acceptable test procedures and related strength requirements. Both conventions have been in force since 1977.

The 1976 International Convention on the International Maritime Satellite Organization (INMARSAT), adopted in 1976 and in force since 1979, concerns the use of space satellites for improved communication, enabling distress messages to be conveyed much more effectively than by conventional radio.

Three additional conventions concerning safety at sea, not yet in force as of 1983, are the Torremolinos Convention for the Safety of Fishing Vessels, which applies to new fishing vessels of 24 m (79 ft) in length or longer; the Convention on Standards of Training, Certification, and Watchkeeping for Seafarers, which aims to establish internationally acceptable minimum standards for crews; and the International Convention on Maritime Search and Rescue, which is designed to improve existing arrangements for carrying out search and rescue operations following accidents at sea.

B. PREVENTION OF MARINE POLLUTION

The 1954 Oil Pollution Convention, for which IMO became depositary in 1959, was the first major attempt by the maritime nations to curb the impact of oil pollution. Since then the problem has become much more serious. The amount of oil carried by sea has risen 700% in 20 years, to around 1,700 million tons annually. At the same time, the world tanker fleet has increased from 37 million DWT in 1954 to around 340 million DWT, and the size of the tankers themselves has also grown. In 1954, the largest ship in the world was little more than 30,000 DWT; by 1983, several ships of more than 500,000 DWT were in service.

Following a conference convened by IMO, the 1954 convention was amended in 1962, but it was the wreck of the oil tanker *Torrey Canyon* in March 1967 which fully alerted the world to the great dangers which the transport of oil posed to the marine environment. In 1969, two new conventions were adopted: the Convention on Intervention on the High Seas in Cases of Oil Pollution Casualties, which gives states the right to intervene in incidents on the high seas which are likely to result in oil pollution; and the Convention on Civil Liability for Oil Pollution Damage, which is intended to ensure that adequate compensation is available to victims, and which places the liability for the damage on the shipowner.

Two years later, a conference convened by IMO led to the adoption of the Convention for the Establishment of an International Fund for Compensation for Oil Pollution Damage. The fund, with headquarters in London, is made up of contributions from oil importers. If an accident at sea results in pollution damage which exceeds the compensation available under the Civil Liability Convention, the fund is made available to pay an additional amount.

These three conventions all deal with the legal aspects of oil pollution, but the continuing boom in the transportation of oil showed that more work needed to be done on the technical side as well. The problem of oil pollution—not only as a result of accidents but through normal tanker operations, especially the cleaning of cargo tanks—was so great in some areas that there was serious concern for the marine environment. In 1973, a major conference was convened by IMO to discuss the whole problem of marine pollution from ships. The result of the conference was the International Convention for the Prevention of Pollution from Ships, which dealt not only with oil but also with other sources of pollution, including garbage, sewage, and chemicals. The convention greatly reduces the amount of oil which can be discharged into the sea by ships, and bans such discharges completely in certain areas, such as the Black Sea and the Red Sea. It gives statutory support for such operational procedures as "load on top," which greatly reduces the amount of mixtures to be disposed of after tank cleaning, and for segregated ballast tanks.

A series of tanker accidents which occurred in the winter of 1976/77 led to demands for further action and to the convening of the Conference on Tanker Safety and Pollution Prevention in February 1978. The most important measures adopted by the conference were incorporated in protocols to the 1974 Convention on the Safety of Life at Sea and the 1973 Marine Pollution Convention. In addition, IMO has been working on various other projects designed to reduce the threat of oil pollution—for example, the Regional Oil-Combating Center, established in Malta in 1976 in conjunction with UNEP. The Mediterranean is particularly vulnerable to pollution, and a massive oil pollution incident there could be catastrophic. The center's purpose is to coordinate antipollution activities in the region and to help develop contingency plans which could be put into effect should a disaster occur. IMO has also taken part in projects in other areas such as the Caribbean and West Africa.

C. OTHER MARITIME QUESTIONS

In 1965, IMO adopted the Convention on Facilitation of Maritime Traffic, the primary objectives of which are to prevent unnecessary delays in maritime traffic, to aid cooperation between states, and to secure the highest practicable degree of uniformity in formalities and procedures.

In association with the IAEA and the European Nuclear Energy Agency of the OECD, the IMO in 1971 convened a conference which adopted the Convention on Civil Liability in the Field of Maritime Carriage of Nuclear Matter.

The Convention on Carriage of Passengers and Their Luggage, adopted in 1974, establishes a regime of liability for damage suffered by passengers carried on seagoing vessels. It declares the carrier liable for damage or loss suffered by passengers if the incident is due to the fault or neglect of the carrier. The limit of liability is set at $55,000 per carriage.

Another convention on liability—the 1976 Convention on Limitation of Liability for Maritime Claims—covers two types of claims: (1) claims arising from loss of life or personal injury and (2) claims arising from damage to ships, harbor works, or other property.

In addition to such conventions, whose requirements are mandatory for nations which ratify them, IMO has produced numerous codes, recommendations, and other instruments dealing with maritime questions. These do not have the legal power of conventions, but can be used by governments as a basis for domestic legislation and as guidance. Some of these recommendations deal with bulk cargoes; safety of fishermen and fishing vessels; carriage of bulk chemicals, liquefied gases, or other dangerous goods; timber deck cargoes; mobile offshore drilling units; noise levels on board ships; and nuclear merchant ships.

D. TECHNICAL ASSISTANCE

While the adoption of conventions, codes, and recommendations has in the past been IMO's most important function, in recent years the agency has devoted increasing attention to securing the effective implementation of these measures throughout the world. As a result, IMO's technical assistance activities have become more important, and in 1975 it established the Committee on Technical Cooperation. The purpose of the technical assistance program is to help states, many of them developing countries, to ratify IMO conventions and to reach the standards contained in the conventions and other instruments.

Advisors and consultants employed by IMO, in the field and at headquarters, deal with such matters as maritime safety administration, maritime legislation, marine pollution, training for deck and engineering personnel, technical aspects of ports, and the carriage of dangerous goods.

Through its technical assistance program, IMO is able to offer advice in these and other areas and to assist in the acquisition of equipment and the provision of fellowships through which students can obtain abroad advanced training not available in their own countries. In some cases, financial aid can be provided through such other UN agencies as UNDP and UNEP, and by donor countries.

[8]BIBLIOGRAPHY

IMO—What It Is, What It Does. Descriptive leaflet.
IMO News. Quarterly.
(IMO publications also include a number of specialized manuals and guides, such as the *Manual on Oil Pollution*; *Regulations on Subdivision and Stability of Passenger Ships*; *Merchant Ship Search and Rescue Manual*; *International Maritime Dangerous Goods Code*; *Pocket Guide to Cold Water Survival*; *Noise Levels on Board Ships.*)

THE WORLD INTELLECTUAL PROPERTY ORGANIZATION (WIPO)

[1]**BACKGROUND:** Intellectual property includes industrial property such as inventions, trademarks, and designs on the one hand, and the objects of copyright and neighboring rights on the other. Until a century ago, there were no international instruments for the protection of intellectual property. Legislative provisions for the protection of inventors, writers, dramatists, and other creators of intellectual property varied from country to country and could be effective only within the borders of states adopting them. It came to be widely recognized that adequate protection of industrial property encourages industrialization, investment, and honest trade. That the arts would be advanced by legal safeguards in favor of their practitioners had long been argued, but such safeguards were difficult to devise and enact into law. The Paris Convention of 20 March 1883 and the Bern Convention of 9 September 1886 represented the initial steps toward systematic provision of the two sorts of international protection which led to the creation of WIPO more than eight decades later.

THE PARIS AND BERN UNIONS

The 1883 convention establishing the Paris Union, whose official name is the International Union for the Protection of Industrial Property, had its sixth revision in Stockholm in 1967, and a diplomatic conference began work on a seventh revision in 1980. It is open to all states and had 92 members by 15 March 1983. Its most important functions have to do with patents for inventions and marks for goods and services. The term industrial property is applied in its widest sense in the convention. In addition to inventions, industrial designs, trademarks, service marks, indications of source, and appellations of origin, it covers small patents called utility models in a few countries, trade names or the designations under which an industrial or commercial activity is carried on, and the suppression of unfair competition.

The convention states that members must provide the same protection of rights in industrial property to nationals of the other members as they provide to their own nationals. It permits foreigners to file for a patent which will apply in all member states within a year after first filing in the country of origin. Additionally, it defines conditions under which a state may license the use of a patent in its own territory, for example, if the owner of the patent does not exploit it there.

The convention which established the Bern Union in 1886 is open to all states. It had its fifth revision in Paris in 1971. The Union originally had 10 members; by 15 March 1983, it had 74. Its official name is the International Union for the Protection of Literary and Artistic Works, and its function is the protection of copyright. The main beneficiaries of copyright include authors of books and articles, publishers of books, newspapers, and periodicals, composers of music, painters, photographers, sculptors, film producers, and creators of certain television programs. Under the convention, each member state must accord the same protection to the copyright of the nationals of the other member states as it accords to that of its own nationals. The convention also prescribes some minimum standards of protection—for example, that copyright protection generally continues throughout the author's life and for 50 years thereafter. It includes special provisions for the benefit of developing countries.

In 1893 the secretariats of the Paris Union and the Bern Union were joined in the United International Bureaux for the Protection of Intellectual Property (BIRPI).

[2]CREATION

The World Intellectual Property Organization (WIPO) was established by a convention signed at Stockholm 14 July 1967 by 51 states. When the convention entered into force 26 April 1970, WIPO incorporated BIRPI and perpetuated its functions. BIRPI still has a function for members of the Paris or Bern unions that have not yet joined WIPO. WIPO became the fourteenth specialized UN agency, the first new once since 1961, when the General Assembly approved that status on 17 December 1974.

[3]PURPOSES

The purposes of WIPO are twofold: (1) to promote the protection of intellectual property throughout the world through cooperation among states and, where appropriate, in collaboration with any other international organization; and (2) to ensure administrative cooperation among the unions.

The WIPO Convention lists rights in intellectual property relating to literary, artistic, and scientific works; performances of artists; phonograms; broadcasts; inventions in all fields of human endeavor; scientific discoveries; industrial designs; trademarks; service marks; and commercial names and designations. The Convention also offers protection against unfair competition, and covers all other rights resulting from intellectual activity in the industrial, scientific, literary, or artistic fields.

WIPO administers the following unions or treaties, listed in the chronological order of their creation:

(1) *Industrial property:* the Paris Union (1883), for the protection of industrial property; the Madrid Agreement (1891), for the repression of false or deceptive indications of source on goods; the Madrid Union (1891), for the international registration of marks; the Hague Union (1925), for the international deposit of industrial designs; the Nice Union (1957), for the international classification of goods and services for the purpose of registration of marks; the Lisbon Union (1958), for the protection of appellations of origin and their international registration; the Locarno Union (1968), establishing an international classification for industrial designs; the International Patent Cooperation Union (1970), for the establishment of worldwide uniformity of patent classification; the Patent Cooperation Treaty (PCT Union, 1971), for cooperation in the filing, searching, and examination of international applications for the protection of inventions where such

protection is sought in several countries; the Trademark Registration Treaty (TRT Union, 1973), for the filing of international applications for the registration of trademarks where protection is sought in several countries; and the Budapest Union (1977), for the international recognition of the deposit of microorganisms for the purpose of patent procedure.

(2) *Copyright and neighboring rights*: the Bern Union (1886), for the protection of literary and artistic works; the Rome Convention (1961), for the protection of performers, producers of phonograms, and broadcasting organizations, jointly administered with ILO and UNESCO; the Geneva Convention (1971), for the protection of producers of phonograms against unauthorized duplication of their phonograms; and the Brussels Convention (1974), relating to the distribution of program-carrying signals transmitted by satellite. WIPO also administers the International Convention for the Protection of New Varieties of Plants (1961) and the Nairobi Treaty for the Protection of the Olympic Symbol (1981).

Four additional treaties are to be administered by WIPO when they come into effect: two Vienna agreements, one for the establishment of an international classification of the figurative elements of marks, the other for the protection of type faces and their international deposit; a Geneva treaty on the recording of scientific discoveries; and a Madrid multilateral convention on double taxation of copyright royalties.

⁴MEMBERSHIP

Membership in WIPO is open to any state that is a member of any of the unions, is a member of the UN or any of the specialized agencies or the IAEA, is party to the Statute of the International Court of Justice, or is invited by the General Assembly of WIPO to become a party to the WIPO Convention. The 101 members of WIPO (W), 92 members of the Paris Union (P), and 74 members of the Bern Union (B) as of 15 March 1983 are listed below:

Algeria	W,P
Argentina	W,P,B
Australia	W,P,B
Austria	W,P,B
Bahamas	W,P,B
Barbados	W
Belgium	W,P,B
Benin	W,P,B
Brazil	W,P,B
Bulgaria	W,P,B
Burundi	W,P
Byelorussia	W
Cameroon	W,P,B
Canada	W,P,B
Central African Rep.	W,P,B
Chad	W,P,B
Chile	W,B
China	W
Colombia	W
Congo	W,P,B
Costa Rica	W,B
Cuba	W,P
Cyprus	P,B
Czechoslovakia	W,P,B
Denmark	W,P,B
Dominican Republic	P
Egypt	W,P,B
El Salvador	W
Fiji	W,B
Finland	W,P,B
France	W,P,B
Gabon	W,P,B
Gambia	W
German Dem. Rep.	W,P,B
Germany, Fed. Rep.	W,P,B
Ghana	W,P

Greece	W,P,B
Guatemala	W
Guinea	W,P,B
Haiti	P
Hungary	W,P,B
Iceland	P,B
India	W,B
Indonesia	W,P
Iran	P
Iraq	W,P
Ireland	W,P,B
Israel	W,P,B
Italy	W,P,B
Ivory Coast	W,P,B
Jamaica	W
Japan	W,P,B
Jordan	W,P
Kenya	W,P
Korea, People's Dem. Rep.	W,P
Korea, Rep.	W,P
Lebanon	P,B
Libya	W,P,B
Liechtenstein	W,P,B
Luxembourg	W,P,B
Madagascar	P,B
Malawi	W,P
Mali	W,P,B
Malta	W,P,B
Mauritania	W,P,B
Mauritius	W,P
Mexico	W,P,B
Monaco	W,P,B
Mongolia	W
Morocco	W,P,B
Netherlands	W,P,B
New Zealand	P,B
Niger	W,P,B
Nigeria	P
Norway	W,P,B
Pakistan	W,B
Peru	W
Philippines	W,P,B
Poland	W,P,B
Portugal	W,P,B
Qatar	W
Romania	W,P,B
San Marino	P
Sa'udi Arabia	W
Senegal	W,P,B
Somalia	W
South Africa	W,P,B
Spain	W,P,B
Sri Lanka	W,P,B
Sudan	W
Suriname	W,P,B
Sweden	W,P,B
Switzerland	W,P,B
Syria	P
Tanzania	P
Thailand	B
Togo	W,P,B
Trinidad and Tobago	P
Tunisia	W,P,B
Turkey	W,P,B
Uganda	W,P
Ukraine	W
USSR	W,P
United Arab Emirates	W
UK	W,P,B
US	W,P
Upper Volta	W,P,B
Uruguay	W,P,B
Vatican	W,P,B
Venezuela	B
Viet-Nam	W,P

Yemen Arab Rep.	W
Yugoslavia	W,P,B
Zaire	W,P,B
Zambia	W,P
Zimbabwe	W,P,B

⁵STRUCTURE

The Paris and Bern unions each have an assembly consisting of the member states, meeting biennially. An executive committee elected by the assembly, consisting of one-fourth of the member states, meets annually. The other unions, in most cases, have an assembly but no executive committee.

WIPO itself has four organs: a General Assembly, a Conference, a Coordination Committee, and a secretariat called the International Bureau of Intellectual Property. The General Assembly consists of all states party to the WIPO Convention which are also members of any of the unions. It meets biennially and has the highest competence of the organs. The Conference consists of all states party to the WIPO Convention whether or not they are members of one or more of the unions. It also meets biennially and is competent for the discussion of matters of general interest in the field of intellectual property as well as for the establishment of WIPO's program of technical legal assistance and of the budget for that program. The Coordination Committee meets annually. It consists of executive committee members of the Paris Union or the Bern Union or both.

The International Bureau is headed by a Director-General, Arpad Bogsch.

⁶BUDGET

The budget is met from ordinary and special contributions of member states and income from international registration services and from publications. Total income in 1982 was approximately $20 million.

⁷ACTIVITIES

The activities of WIPO include encouragement of new international treaties and the harmonization of legislation; technical legal assistance to developing countries setting up patent and copyright laws and institutions; the compilation and dissemination of information; and cooperative administrative services such as international registration.

The WIPO secretariat centralizes information related to the protection of intellectual property and issues documents, periodicals, and other publications.

WIPO offers fellowships to nationals of developing countries, organizes seminars on their specific problems, and finances assistance by experts. Technical assistance is also given through administering projects within the framework of UNDP.

In pursuing one of its two aims, WIPO centralizes and supervises the administration of the unions in the WIPO secretariat at Geneva. This effects an economy for member states and the private sector concerned with intellectual property. Centralization is incomplete in the field of copyright, since the Universal Copyright Convention, concluded in Paris in 1952, is administered by UNESCO. In the field of neighboring rights, also, the Rome Convention of 1961 is administered in cooperation with UNESCO and the ILO.

⁸BIBLIOGRAPHY

Copyright. Monthly review of the Bern Union in English and French. State of ratifications, texts of laws, court decisions, studies.

Industrial Property. Monthly review of the Paris Union in English and French. State of ratifications, texts of laws, court decisions, studies.

Model Laws for Developing Countries on Inventions, on Marks, Trade Names and Acts of Unfair Competition and on Designs. In English, French, and Spanish.

THE INTERNATIONAL FUND FOR AGRICULTURAL DEVELOPMENT (IFAD)

[1]**BACKGROUND:** The International Fund for Agricultural Development (IFAD)—the newest UN specialized agency—is the first international institution established exclusively to provide additional resources for agricultural and rural development in developing countries and to channel those resources to the poorest rural populations in Africa, Asia, and Latin America, which suffer from chronic hunger and malnutrition.

[2]CREATION

IFAD was one of the major initiatives of the World Food Conference, held in Rome in 1974, following two years of negotiations. The agreement establishing the Fund was adopted by 91 governments on 13 June 1976 and was opened for signature or ratification on 20 December 1976, following attainment of the target of $1 billion in initial pledges. It came into force on 30 November 1977.

[3]PURPOSES

The objective of the Fund is to mobilize additional resources to be made available on concessional terms to help developing countries improve their food production and nutrition. The Fund is unique in that its projects are focused exclusively on agricultural development, and it concentrates on the poorest sections of the rural populations in developing countries. It deals with all aspects of agriculture, including crops, irrigation, agricultural credit, storage, livestock, and fisheries.

[4]MEMBERSHIP

IFAD had a total of 139 member nations in July 1983, compared to 90 at the time of its establishment. Of these, 20 were in Category I (developed countries), 12 in Category II (oil-exporting developing countries), and 107 in Category III (other developing countries).

CATEGORY I:
DEVELOPED COUNTRIES
Australia
Austria
Belgium
Canada
Denmark
Finland
France
Germany, Fed. Rep.
Ireland
Italy
Japan
Luxembourg
Netherlands
New Zealand
Norway
Spain
Sweden
Switzerland
UK
US

CATEGORY II: OIL-EXPORTING
DEVELOPING COUNTRIES
Algeria
Gabon
Indonesia
Iran
Iraq
Kuwait
Libya
Nigeria
Qatar
Sa'udi Arabia
United Arab Emirates
Venezuela

CATEGORY III: OTHER
DEVELOPING COUNTRIES
Afghanistan
Angola
Argentina
Bangladesh
Barbados
Belize
Benin
Bhutan
Bolivia
Botswana
Brazil
Burundi
Cameroon
Cape Verde
Central African Rep.
Chad
Chile
China
Colombia
Comoros
Congo
Costa Rica
Cuba
Cyprus
Djibouti
Dominica
Dominican Republic
Ecuador
Egypt
El Salvador
Equatorial Guinea
Ethiopia

Fiji
Gambia
Ghana
Greece
Grenada
Guatemala
Guinea
Guinea-Bissau
Guyana
Haiti
Honduras
India
Israel
Ivory Coast
Jamaica
Jordan
Kenya
Korea, Rep.
Laos
Lebanon
Lesotho
Liberia
Madagascar
Malawi
Maldives
Mali
Malta
Mauritania
Mauritius
Mexico
Morocco
Mozambique
Nepal
Nicaragua
Niger
Oman
Pakistan
Panama
Papua New Guinea
Paraguay
Peru
Philippines
Portugal
Romania
Rwanda
São Tomé and Príncipe
Senegal
Seychelles
Sierra Leone
Solomon Islands
Somalia
Sri Lanka
St. Lucia
St. Vincent and the Grenadines
Sudan
Suriname
Swaziland
Syria
Tanzania
Thailand
Toġo
Tonga
Tunisia
Turkey
Uganda
Upper Volta
Uruguay
Viet-Nam
Western Samoa
Yemen, People's Dem. Rep.
Yemen Arab Rep.
Yugoslavia
Zaire
Zambia
Zimbabwe

⁵STRUCTURE

IFAD is a new kind of institution in the UN system. The governing bodies which supervise its operations reflect an innovative formula bringing together the interests of industrialized countries, oil-exporting developing countries, and other developing countries, each of the three categories having the same number of votes (600). As an action-oriented organization, the Fund normally works by consensus rather than by voting.

The highest governing body of the Fund is the Governing Council, on which all members are represented. Current operations are overseen by an 18-member Executive Board, composed of six executive directors from each of the three constituent categories, and 17 alternates.

The president of the Fund, elected by the Governing Council for a three-year term, is responsible for the Fund's management, heads the Secretariat, and chairs the Executive Board. Abdelmuhsin Al-Sudeary of Sa'udi Arabia was elected to his second three-year term on 8 December 1980. IFAD had a staff of 167 persons from 41 countries in December 1982.

The Fund's headquarters are at Via del Serafico 107, 00142 Rome, Italy.

⁶BUDGET

Revenue, mainly income from investments, totaled $66.5 million during the 1982 budget period; expenses for the same year were $16.6 million.

⁷ACTIVITIES

The first project loans were approved by IFAD's Executive Board in April 1978. At the end of the three-year period 1978–80, the Fund's cumulative commitments amounted to nearly $900 million in loans and grants for some 70 of its developing member states.

For the period 1981–83, IFAD expanded its operational program. With the new projects approved in September 1982, IFAD's total financial commitments since April 1978 exceeded $1.4 billion. In four and a half years of operation, the Fund launched or approved projects and programs in some 80 member countries throughout the continents of Africa, Asia, and Latin America.

The replenishment of IFAD resources was unanimously approved by the Fund's Governing Council in January 1982, when final agreement was reached concerning the level of replenishment. Member countries offered to provide contributions totaling $1,100 million for the period 1981–83, including $620 million from the Category I (developed) countries, $450 million from Category II (oil-exporting developing) countries, and $40 million from Category III (other developing) countries.

A. LENDING ACTIVITIES

IFAD loan operations fall into two groups: projects initiated by the Fund, and projects cofinanced with other financial and development institutions. IFAD-initiated projects are those for which the Fund has taken the lead in project identification and preparation and in mobilizing additional resources from other financial agencies where necessary.

Three types of loans are made. Highly concessional loans entail a 1% service charge and 50-year maturity (including a 10-year grace period); intermediate loans, 4% interest, 20-year maturity (including a 5-year grace period); and ordinary loans, 8% interest, 15–18 year maturity (including a 3-year grace period).

IFAD loans represent only a part of the total project costs; the governments concerned contribute a share. In most of the projects approved so far, IFAD has also cooperated with the World Bank, the African, Asian, and Inter-American Development banks, the Islamic Development Bank, the Arab Fund for Economic and Social Development, and other multilateral and bilateral sources.

B. LEVEL OF LOAN COMMITMENTS

In 1978, its first year of operation, the Fund approved commitments of about $118 million in loans for projects in 10 developing countries. The following year, commitments more than tripled, reaching a level of over $370 million for 23 projects and $6 million for technical assistance grants. In 1980, IFAD approved 27 projects amounting to over $380 million and technical assistance grants totaling about $15 million.

During 1981, IFAD approved loans amounting to $350 million for 30 agricultural and rural development projects, as well as grants for technical assistance totaling $20 million. The Fund's total loan commitments over the period ending December 1982 exceeded $1,400 million for 114 projects and programs in more than 80 countries of Asia, Africa, and Latin America.

IFAD LOANS AND GRANTS, 1978–82

BY REGION	NO. OF PROJECTS	AMOUNT (MILLIONS OF US$)
Africa	35	338.7
Asia	35	607.9
Latin America	25	232.8
Near East and North Africa	19	235.2
TOTALS	114	1,414.6

BY SECTOR		
Agricultural production	23	258.2
Credit	16	179.0
Fisheries	6	25.4
Irrigation	17	288.4
Livestock	7	81.5
Program loan	3	59.2
Research, extension, training	4	32.9
Rural development	36	455.7
Settlement	2	34.3
TOTALS	114	1,414.6

C. TECHNICAL ASSISTANCE AND SPECIAL MISSIONS

IFAD provides grant financing for three broad categories of technical assistance—project preparation; institutional development and training as part of a project; and agricultural research and other activities which support the Fund's activities.

It also organizes special programming missions to selected countries to assist governments in obtaining a comprehensive view of their agricultural and rural poverty problems.

[8]BIBLIOGRAPHY

IFAD—What It Is and How It Works. Fact sheet.
IFAD Annual Report.

SUPPLEMENTS

THE POLAR REGIONS

ANTARCTICA

Antarctica, the coldest and second-smallest continent (after Australia), is centered on the South Pole and is situated almost entirely within the Antarctic Circle at 60°30′s. Some 98% of the total area of about 14,245,000 sq km (5,500,000 sq mi) is covered by ice, and the continent contains about 90% of the world's ice and 70% of the fresh water. Antarctica is bounded by the South Atlantic, Indian, and South Pacific oceans. The nearest points of land are the southern tip of South America and South Georgia, the South Sandwich Islands, the South Orkney Islands, and the South Shetland Islands. All of these UK island dependencies are located within the Antarctic Convergence, which encircles Antarctica at approximately 1,600 km (1,000 mi) from the coast and divides the cold Antarctic waters from the warmer waters of the three oceans, in a zone of perpetual turbulence.

Some 200 million years ago, Antarctica was joined to South America, Africa, India, and Australia in a large single continent, Gondwanaland; subsequent geological changes caused the breakup into separate continental masses. Recent geological studies and fossil finds indicate that Antarctica once had a tropical environment, but that its present ice cap is at least 20 million years old.

The Transantarctic Mountains divide the continent into two parts: the larger East Antarctic ice sheet, with land mostly below sea level; and the smaller West Antarctic ice sheet, with land mostly above sea level. The highest point is the Vinson Massif (5,140 m/16,864 ft), in the Ellsworth Mountains of West Antarctica. The South Pole lies at an altitude of about 3,000 m (9,800 ft). The Antarctic ice sheet averages 2,000 m (6,600 ft) in depth and is more than 4,500 m (14,750 ft) deep at its thickest point. Glaciers form ice shelves along nearly half the coastline. The larger ice shelves—the Amery in the east, Ross in the south, and Ronne in the northwest—move seaward at speeds of from 900 to 1,300 m (2,950–4,250 ft) per year. Sea ice up to 30 m (100 ft) thick forms a belt about 500 km (300 mi) wide that encircles the continent in winter. Ice-free areas are located generally along the coast and include the dry valleys in southern Victoria Land and the Bunger Oasis in Wilkes Land. Largely ice-free areas where much scientific activity takes place are Graham Land, on the eastern coast of the Antarctic Peninsula, and Ross Island in McMurdo Sound.

The severity of the Antarctic cold varies with location and altitude. East Antarctica has the coldest climate; the Antarctic Peninsula in the west has the mildest, with summer temperatures generally remaining above freezing. The mean annual temperature of the interior regions is −57°C (−71°F); mean temperatures at the coastal McMurdo station range from −28°C (−18°F) in August to −3°C (27°F) in January. The world's record low temperature of −88°C (−126°F) was registered at the Soviet Vostok station on 24 August 1960; highs of 15°C (59°F) have been measured on the northernmost Antarctic Peninsula. The interior is a vast desert, with annual precipitation averaging below 3 cm (1 in). The coastland is considerably more humid, with annual precipitation of about 25 cm (10 in) along the coasts of East Antarctica and the Antarctic Peninsula. Adélie Coast, in the southeast near the South Magnetic Pole, has recorded average wind speeds of 64 km/hr (40 mph), with gusts of nearly 320 km/hr (200 mph).

Because of its polar location, Antarctica has six months of continuous daylight from mid-September to mid-March, with the maximum 24 hours of light received at the summer solstice on 22 December; and six months of continuous darkness from mid-March to mid-September, with the winter solstice occurring 22 June. In summer, the continent receives more solar radiation than even the Equator at an equivalent period.

Although Antarctica has no native humans or large mammals, it does have a varied marine life ranging from microscopic plankton to the largest whales and including about 100 species of fish. Land life includes bacteria, lichens, mosses, two kinds of flowering plants (in the ice-free areas), penguins, and some flying birds. Five types of seal—the crabeater, Weddell, elephant, leopard, and Ross—thrive in Antarctica and together number about 32.7 million, with the crabeaters accounting for nearly 94% of the total. The once-numerous fur seals were reduced by uncontrolled slaughter (about 1 million were killed on South Georgia alone in 1820–22) to near extinction by 1870. This ended the Antarctic fur-sealing industry; since then, the number of fur seals has gradually increased, to an estimated 200,000, mostly on South Georgia. In 1972, the 12 nations active in the Antarctic signed the Convention for the Conservation of Antarctic Seals, which prohibits the killing of fur, elephant, and Ross seals, and sets annual quotas for the harvest of crabeater, leopard, and Weddell seals. The treaty entered into force in 1978, and as of 1983 had been ratified by 10 nations.

Destruction at the hands of humans threatens the survival of the Antarctic whales—the sperm, blue, humpback, fin, minke, and sei—which decreased in number from an estimated 1,830,000 at the beginning of the 20th century to about 870,000 by 1980. Since 1972, the International Whaling Commission (IWC) has set quotas by species on the taking of whales, and the survival of all species of Antarctic whales seemed assured by the early 1980s. In 1982, the IWC approved a moratorium on the commercial killing of all whales, to begin in 1985.

Exploration

The ancient Greeks reasoned that there must be an "Antarctic" (opposite the Arctic) to balance the large land mass in the Northern Hemisphere, but it was not until the 19th century that definite proof was found that the continent existed. British Capt. James Cook had crossed the Antarctic Circle and circumnavigated the continent without sighting land (1772–75). In 1820, however, two other British mariners, William Smith and James Bransfield, discovered and mapped the Antarctic Peninsula, which was also explored by the American sea captain Nathaniel Palmer and the Englishman James Weddell, who discovered the sea that bears his name. On 7 February 1821, US Capt. John Davis made the first known landing on the continent at Hughes Bay, in the northwest. Many other British and US sealers explored the area, including 11 shipwrecked Englishmen who spent the winter of 1821 on King George Island, in the South Shetlands. Palmer and Benjamin Pendleton led a pioneering expedition in 1828–30 that included James Eights, the first American scientist to visit Antarctica. A Russian expedition headed by Capt. Fabian Gottlieb von Bellingshausen found Queen Maud Land and Peter I Island, and a French expedition under J. S. C. Dumont d'Urville discovered the Adélie Coast (named for his wife) in eastern Antarctica. During the late 1830s, Lt. Charles Wilkes of the US Navy sailed along the coast of eastern Antarctica for about 2,400 km (1,500 mi), thereby definitely establishing that Antarctica was a continent, not a cluster of islands. British Capt. James C. Ross discovered Victoria Land and the sea and the ice shelf that were later named in his honor.

With the decline of the fur seal industry, Antarctic exploration was neglected for about 50 years, until Norwegian and Scottish whalers began operating in the area. A Norwegian whaling captain, Carl Anton Larsen, explored the east coast of the Antarctic Peninsula in 1892 and found the first fossils. Thus began a period of intensive exploration during which 9 countries sent 16 expeditions to Antarctica. Another Norwegian captain, Leonard Kristensen, landed at Cape Adare, on McMurdo Sound, in 1895. It was there that a British expedition, led by a Norwegian, Carsten Egeberg Borchgrevink, established a base in 1899; Borchgrevink became the first explorer to probe inland by sledge. Swedish, Scottish, Belgian, and French expeditions also arrived, and four British expeditions set up bases on Ross Island. From there, Sir Ernest Henry Shackleton sledged to within 156 km (97 mi) of the South Pole on 9 January 1909.

This feat encouraged five national expeditions to compete for the goal in 1911, and the competition narrowed to a "race to the pole" between Capt. Robert F. Scott and Roald Amundsen of Norway. Amundsen and four companions, with sledges and 52 dogs, left their base on the Ross Ice Shelf on 20 October, scaled 3,000-m (10,000-ft) glaciers in the Queen Maud Mountains, descended to the icy plateau, and located the South Pole by celestial observation on 14 December. They returned to their base by late January 1912. Meanwhile, Scott's party of five explorers, who had left McMurdo Sound on 1 November, reached the pole on 18 January 1912, only to find that Amundsen had beaten them there by more than a month. Disheartened, they met with mishaps on the return journey and, weakened by food shortages and exhausted from man-hauling their sledges, they all perished on the ice in late March. Another expedition that ended in tragedy was led in 1914–15 by Shackleton, who lost his ship *Endurance* in heavy pack ice in the Weddell Sea and, with five companions, made a perilous 1,300-km (800-mi) journey in an open whale boat to South Georgia Island, where he got help to rescue his stranded men. Shackleton died at South Georgia in 1922, while preparing another expedition.

Technological advances were applied to Antarctic exploration after World War I. An Australian, Sir Hubert Wilkins, in 1928 became the first man to fly an airplane along the Antarctic Peninsula. The following year, US Navy Adm. Richard Evelyn Byrd flew over the South Pole, with his Norwegian-American pilot Bernt Balchen; Byrd established the Little America base on the Ross Ice Shelf, and was the first explorer to coordinate airplanes, radios, aerial cameras, and other technological aids for the purpose of exploration. Another American, Lincoln Ellsworth, was the first to complete a transantarctic flight, from the Antarctic Peninsula to the Ross Ice Shelf, in 1935. American, British, German, and Norwegian scientific expeditions did considerable aerial mapping of the continent throughout the 1930s; research in oceanography and marine biology by a British expedition resulted in the discovery of the Antarctic Convergence. The US expedition of 1939–41, headed by Byrd, established two continuing bases in the Antarctic, but the program ended with the outbreak of World War II.

Scientific Research

After the war, the US took the lead in conducting scientific research in Antarctica. The Navy's Operation High Jump (1946–47), the largest expedition ever made to the continent, involved 4,700 men, 13 ships, and 25 airplanes to map extensive coastal areas by aerial photography. The Antarctic Research Expedition (1947–48),

headed by Finn Ronne, was the last privately sponsored US expedition to the continent. A major joint international expedition (1949–52), mounted by the UK, Norway, and Sweden, initiated the use of geophysical methods on a large scale to determine the thickness of ice caps. The USSR also mounted expeditions, in 1946–47 and 1951–52.

The greatest scientific undertaking involving the Antarctic was the International Geophysical Year (IGY) of 1957/58, in which 67 nations participated. The purpose of the IGY's Antarctic program was to study the effects of the continent's huge ice mass on global weather, the oceans, the aurora australis, and the ionosphere. More than 50 Antarctic stations were established by 12 countries: Argentina, Australia, Belgium, Chile, France, Japan, New Zealand, Norway, South Africa, the UK, the US, and the USSR. The US built a supply base and airfield on Ross Island, a station at the South Pole that was provisioned by air, and four other stations. The USSR had 4 bases, the UK 14, Argentina 8, and Chile 6. The South Pole was the terminus of three pole-to-pole observation chains along three meridians, and the US station at Little America analyzed meteorological reports from all over the world. Valuable information was gleaned from meteorological and seismic observations, studies of the upper atmosphere, magnetic measurements, and ice-sheet core drillings. The first surface transantarctic crossing, between the Weddell and Ross seas, was accomplished by the Commonwealth Transantarctic Expedition. After the IGY, very little of the continent remained to be explored or mapped.

An important result of the IGY's success was the continuation of significant research programs in Antarctica after 1958. Old stations were either closed or replaced with new buildings, and new stations were opened. The US constructed a year-round scientific village at McMurdo Sound, heated and lighted by a small atomic power plant that also used waste heat to distill seawater (the atomic reactor was replaced by thermal units in 1972). Besides McMurdo Station, the US as of 1983 maintained three other year-round stations, at the South Pole, in Ellsworth Land (temporarily closed in 1984–85), and on Anvers Island, off the Antarctic Peninsula. Other countries maintaining year-round stations as of 1983 were Argentina 8, the USSR 7, the UK 4, Chile 4, Australia 3, Japan 2, and 1 each by the Federal Republic of Germany (FRG), France, New Zealand, Poland, and South Africa.

Transportation services are essential to Antarctic operations; for example, transportation expenses accounted for about half the total expenditure of approximately $100 million for the US Antarctic program in 1983. The US, along with Argentina and New Zealand, routinely uses aircraft to carry both passengers and priority supplies to Antarctic stations. However, as of early 1984, only four airfields could handle wheeled aircraft, those of Argentina, Chile, the USSR, and the US, with France reportedly building a fully equipped airport on the Adélie Coast; air transport to other bases is by ski-equipped light aircraft. Transport between stations in the interior is provided mainly by tractor-trains and ski-equipped light aircraft. The longest surface supply route is from the Soviet Mirnyy station on the east coast to Vostok station in the interior, a distance of nearly 1,400 km (860 mi). Most nations operating in Antarctica rely on shipping for long-distance transportation and employ icebreakers to clear channels of pack ice. When conditions are favorable, ships offload cargo directly onto land or the ice shelf; when harbors are blocked by ice, tractors and helicopters carry passengers and cargo to shore.

Territorial Claims and
International Cooperation

Seven nations have made separate territorial claims in Antarctica. Five of the claims begin at 60°s latitude and continue in the shape of a pie wedge to the South Pole. The exceptions are the claims of the UK, which starts at 50°s in order to include the South Sandwich and South Georgia Islands of the Falkland chain; and

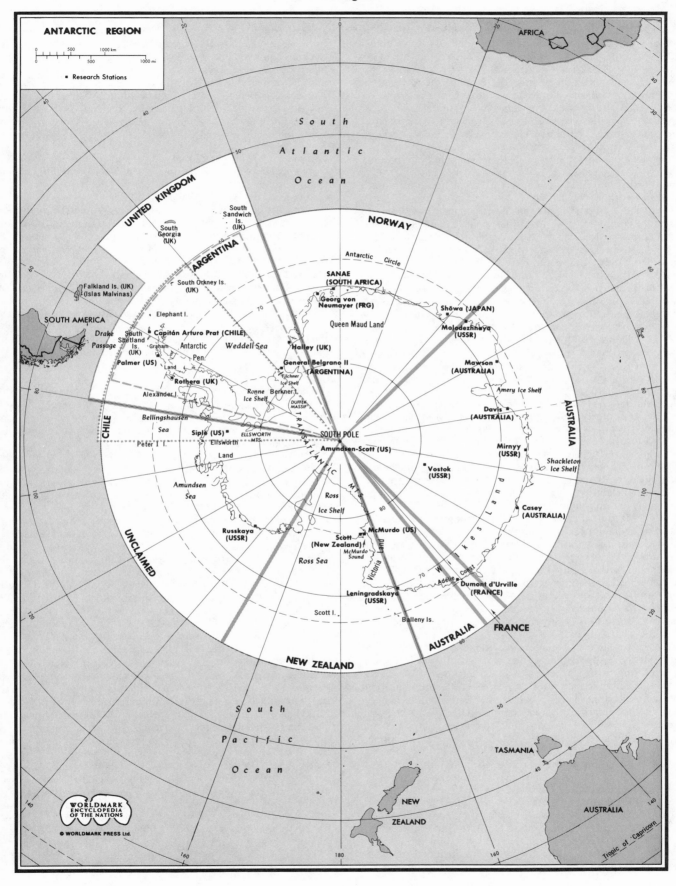

ANTARCTIC REGION

0 500 1000 km
0 500 1000 mi

■ Research Stations

AFRICA

South Atlantic Ocean

UNITED KINGDOM

NORWAY

Antarctic Circle

South Sandwich Is. (UK)

South Georgia (UK)

ARGENTINA

SANAE (SOUTH AFRICA)

Georg von Neumayer (FRG)

Shōwa (JAPAN)

Queen Maud Land

Molodezhnaya (USSR)

Falkland Is. (UK) (Islas Malvinas)

South Orkney Is. (UK)

SOUTH AMERICA

Elephant I.

Drake Passage

South Shetland Is. (UK)

Capitán Arturo Prat (CHILE)

Graham Land

Antarctic Pen.

Weddell Sea

Halley (UK)

General Belgrano II (ARGENTINA)

Filchner Ice Shelf

Mawson (AUSTRALIA)

Amery Ice Shelf

Palmer (US)

Rothera (UK)

Ronne Ice Shelf

Berkner I.

DUFEK MASSIF

Davis (AUSTRALIA)

AUSTRALIA

Alexander I.

CHILE

Bellingshausen Sea

Siple (US)

ELLSWORTH MTS.

TRANSATLANTIC

Mirnyy (USSR)

Shackleton Ice Shelf

Peter I I.

Ellsworth Land

SOUTH POLE

Amundsen-Scott (US)

Vostok (USSR)

Amundsen Sea

Ross Ice Shelf

MTS.

Casey (AUSTRALIA)

Wilkes Land

UNCLAIMED

Russkaya (USSR)

Scott (New Zealand)

McMurdo (US)

Victoria Land

Leningradskaya (USSR)

Adélie Coast

Dumont d'Urville (FRANCE)

Ross Sea

McMurdo Sound

Scott I.

Balleny Is.

AUSTRALIA

FRANCE

NEW ZEALAND

South Pacific Ocean

TASMANIA

WORLDMARK
ENCYCLOPEDIA
OF THE NATIONS

© WORLDMARK PRESS Ltd.

NEW ZEALAND

AUSTRALIA

Tropic of Capricorn

of Norway, the northern and southern boundaries of which are undefined. The UK, the first nation to claim a "slice" of the continent (in 1908), was followed by New Zealand (1923), France (1924), Australia (1933), Norway (1939), Chile (1940), and Argentina (1943). The claims of Argentina and Chile overlap with each other and with that of the UK. Neither the US nor the USSR has claimed any Antarctic territory, and neither recognizes the claims of other nations. Since international law requires "effective occupation" as the basis for ownership, and since no nation has met the criteria by sustaining such permanent occupation in Antarctica, these territorial claims have not been recognized by other countries, by the UN, or by any other international body.

In order to clarify the issue of territorial claims and to form a legal framework for the activities of nations in Antarctica, the 12 countries that had participated in the IGY signed the Antarctic Treaty on 1 December 1959: Argentina, Australia, Belgium, Chile, France, Japan, New Zealand, Norway, South Africa, the USSR, the UK, and the US. All 12 had ratified the treaty by 23 June 1961, when it duly entered into force. Other nations that conduct Antarctic research are entitled to consultative membership: as of 1983, four countries—Poland (1977), the FRG (1981), Brazil (1983), and India (1983)—had attained consultative status. By that year, 16 countries in addition to the signatory nations had acceded to the terms of the treaty: Poland (1961), Czechoslovakia (1962), Denmark (1965), the Netherlands (1967), Romania (1971), the German Democratic Republic (1974), Brazil (1975), Bulgaria (1978), the FRG (1979), Uruguay (1980), Papua New Guinea (1981), Italy (1981), Peru (1981), Spain (1982), China (1983), and India (1983).

The Antarctic Treaty provides that "Antarctica shall be used for peaceful purposes only," and prohibits military bases, weapons testing (including nuclear explosions), and disposal of radioactive wastes. It seeks to foster freedom of scientific investigation and cooperation between nations, with the free exchange of scientific programs, observations, results, and personnel guaranteed. The treaty neither recognizes nor nullifies any preexisting territorial claims but it does forbid any new claim or enlargement of any existing claim while the treaty remains in force (until 1991). The document specifies that contracting parties have the right to designate observers, and that such observers shall at all times have the right to inspect any station or installation. The treaty provides for the peaceful settlement of all disputes by the parties concerned or by the International Court of Justice. It also specifies periodic meetings between member states to exchange information and to enact measures in furtherance of treaty objectives; from 1961 to 1983, 12 consultative meetings were held. After 30 years, in 1991, any member may request a conference to review the treaty's operation.

Scientific research has continued under the provisions of the treaty, but the emphasis has shifted from short-term reconnaissance to long-term, large-scale investigations of Antarctic phenomena. Detailed study of the ice sheet has brought about increased understanding of global weather and climatic changes. The largest cooperative program completed to date has been the International Antarctic Glaciological Project (1971–81), conducted by Australia, France, the USSR, the UK, and the US. The principal objectives are to measure precisely the East Antarctic ice sheet by means of core drillings through the ice to bedrock at several coastal and interior locations, and to make extensive aerial surveys of the area. Another collaborative project, Polar Experiment (POLEX)–South (1975–85), mounted by Argentina, the USSR, and the US, expanded on existing national research programs on the atmosphere, ocean currents, and the ice sheet. The Dry Valley Drilling Project (1971–76), a joint project conducted by Japan, New Zealand, and the US, included geophysical exploration and bedrock drilling in the McMurdo Sound area.

The Ross Ice Shelf Project, an ongoing US endeavor begun in 1973, has incorporated contributions from at least 12 other nations to measure the surface and under-ice topography, ice thickness, gravity, and seismic activity of the Ross Ice Shelf. Another US project, inaugurated in November 1983, involved the most intensive study yet of the relationship between the West Antarctica ice sheet and the global climate. A Soviet exploration project (1975–80) in the Filchner Ice Shelf of West Antarctica used aerial photography and geological surveys to evaluate the area's mineral resources.

Resources

Estimates of Antarctica's mineral deposits are imprecise. A US Geological Survey study has concluded that the continent may contain some 900 major mineral deposits, but that only about 20 of these are likely to be found in ice-free areas. Two minerals, iron ore and coal, have been discovered in commercial quantities; small amounts of copper, chromium, platinum, nickel, gold, and hydrocarbons have also been found. Mineral exploration has been limited to comparatively small ice-free areas, but the Dufek Massif in the Pensacola Mountains of the Transantarctic Range shows the most potential for discovery of valuable metals. Offshore deposits of oil and natural gas show the greatest economic promise: traces of natural gas were discovered in a core taken from the Weddell Sea in 1972. However, the difficulty of operating in the harsh Antarctic climate, the inaccessibility of the deposits, and the high cost involved in mining and transportation make immediate mineral exploitation of Antarctica unlikely.

THE ARCTIC

The northernmost area of the earth's surface, the Arctic may be defined as all land and water within the Arctic Circle at 66°31′N. However, the regional boundary may also be considered the 10°C (50°F) atmospheric isotherm for the warmest month (July) that extends well below the Arctic Circle in some places and coincides roughly with the tree line. The region, centered around the North Pole, includes the ice-covered Arctic Ocean basin, which is surrounded by the northern mainland and islands of North America and Eurasia, with outlets to the Bering Sea and the North Atlantic Ocean. The Arctic Ocean, with an area of about 14 million sq km (5.4 million sq mi), comprises nearly two-thirds of the total area. Principal land masses are the northern reaches of the USSR, Scandinavia, Greenland, Canada, and Alaska.

Unlike Antarctica, the Arctic region has a year-round habitable climate at its fringes, a permanent population, and established territorial sovereignty over all land areas. The Arctic also is of great strategic importance because of its central location between North America and Eurasia; the northern tip of Canada lies only about 4,000 km (2,500 mi) from the Soviet city of Murmansk on the great circle route. As a consequence of such proximity, the Arctic region is the site of many radar stations maintained by Canada, the USSR, and the US to monitor air traffic and to provide early warning of an air attack.

The continental shelf around the Arctic basin occupies more than half the ocean area, a much larger proportion than in any other ocean; the edge of the continental shelf near Franz Josef Land lies about 1,500 km (930 mi) from the Eurasian mainland. The landmasses that extend above the Arctic Circle exhibit three major types of landforms: rugged uplands and deep fjords formed by glaciation; swampy coastal plains and high ice plateaus covered by glacial deposits; and folded mountains, including the high peaks of the Canadian Rocky Mountains, Alaska's Brooks Range, and the rounded slopes of the Ural Mountains of the USSR. Principal rivers flowing into the Arctic Ocean are the Mackenzie, in Canada, and the Ob', Yenisey, Lena, and Kolyma, in the USSR. Major seas in the Arctic include the Chukchi, East Siberian, Laptev, Kara, Barents, Norwegian, Greenland, and Beaufort.

The Arctic Ocean remains frozen throughout the year (except for its fringes during summer) and is virtually icelocked from

October to June. The vast Arctic ice pack expands from an average area of 5.2 million sq km (2 million sq mi) in summer to an average of 11.7 million sq km (4.5 million sq mi) during winter. The average thickness of the ice pack is estimated at 3–3.5 m (9.8–11.5 ft). Ice "islands" up to 60 m (200 ft) thick and 30 km (19 mi) wide break away from the moving ice pack off North America and float slowly in erratic circles before disintegrating or exiting to the North Atlantic. Smaller fragments called icebergs break off glaciers in Greenland and northeastern Canada and move southward via the East Greenland and Labrador currents into Atlantic shipping lanes. An estimated 1,000 icebergs each year cross 55°N, and nearly 400 reach the Grand Banks off Newfoundland. A few icebergs have traveled as far as 4,000 km (2,500 mi) over a three-year period and have been sighted as far south as Bermuda.

The most recent Ice Age climaxed about 15,000 years ago, when continental ice sheets covered most of the Northern Hemisphere. The retreat of the glaciers was stabilized some 8,500 years ago in Europe and 7,000 years ago in North America. The warming period that followed reached its maximum in historic times during AD 800–1000, making possible the Viking colonization of Arctic lands, and from the 1880s to the 1940s, when extensive Arctic exploration occurred. However, a minor cooling trend that began in the 1940s (and was expected to last well into the 1980s) has had severe effects in the Arctic, increasing the ice-covered area substantially and reducing the annual mean air temperatures by several degrees, thereby shortening the summer season along the Arctic coast of Eurasia by nearly a month.

The Arctic experiences alternating six-month periods of winter darkness and summer daylight, including 24 hours of daylight within the Arctic Circle during the summer equinox (hence the designation "land of the midnight sun"). The region is subject to long, cold winters and short, cool summers. The snow cover is relatively light, averaging 20–50 cm (8–20 in) and lasting for about 10 months over the frozen ocean. Air temperatures above the pack ice average −30°C (−22°F) in January and near 0°C (32°F) in July. Annual mean temperatures on land vary from −12°C (10°F) at Barrow, Alaska, and −16°C (3°F) on Resolute Island, in northern Canada, to 0°C (32°F) at Murmansk, in the western USSR. Annual mean temperatures in Greenland are low because of the island's high elevation and vast interior ice sheet; they range from −40°C (−40°F) in January to −10°C (14°F) in July, temperatures significantly colder than those of the North Pole. Total annual precipitation varies from 10 to 25 cm (4–10 in) on the Arctic ice pack to 45 cm (18 in) or more in Greenland.

A climate-dependent phenomenon is the presence of perennially frozen ground, or permafrost, which has impeded human use of land in the Arctic region. Permafrost, occurring wherever ground temperatures remain below freezing for two or more years, underlies most of the Arctic landmass of Alaska and Greenland, half of that in Canada and the USSR, and parts of Scandinavia. It also has been found under coastal seabeds of the Arctic Ocean. The maximum thickness of permafrost has been measured at 500 m (1,640 ft) in Canada, 900 m (2,950 ft) in Alaska, and 1,500 m (4,920 ft) in the USSR. Alternate freezing and thawing of the outer permafrost layer shortens the growing season during the summer and causes serious engineering problems for construction and mining operations in the Arctic region.

Vegetation on the Arctic tundra, or treeless plain, is limited to mosses, lichens, sedges, and a few flowering plants which blossom during the brief spring and summer seasons. The outer edges of the Arctic ice pack support a small number of animal species by providing an overhead platform for algae and plankton, which are eaten by fish that, in turn, serve as food for seals, walruses, and birds; the food chain is continued by foxes and polar bears which feed upon young seals. Altogether, the Arctic has about 20 species of land mammals, including the moose, caribou,

reindeer, wolf, and squirrel. The arrival of migratory birds each spring increases the bird population enormously. Principal fish are cod, herring, and capelin, a true Arctic fish; all of these have great commercial value, as do shrimp and crab. Since 15 October 1975, when Iceland extended its fishing zone to 200 nautical miles, all nations bordering the Arctic have done the same, and fish catch quotas are now under national management.

The ecological cycle of Arctic life has been damaged by human encroachment, but in recent years the natural environment has been increasingly protected by the five circumpolar countries (Canada, Denmark, Norway, the USSR, and the US). In 1956, the USSR prohibited hunting of the polar bear, and in 1973 the five nations agreed to protect the bear's habitat. During construction in the 1970s of the trans-Alaska oil pipeline from Prudhoe Bay on the Arctic coast to the port of Valdez on the Gulf of Alaska, the US government required contractors to clean up the work site and to restore displaced vegetation; drillers were directed to trap and remove spilled oil. The pipeline carrying hot oil was suspended above ground level to prevent the permafrost from thawing, and crossings under the pipeline were provided at intervals for caribou and moose migrations. The Alaska Native Claims Settlement Act (1971) set aside about one-fourth of the state's area for wilderness preserves, wildlife refuges, and national parks. To prevent or control oil spills in the Arctic Ocean, Canada in 1970 authorized a 161-km (100-mi) offshore pollution control zone north of the 60° line. The USSR has established nature preserves on several islands off the Kola Peninsula, east of the Barents Sea, and on Wrangel Island. In 1973, Norway established nature reserves and national parks in its Svalbard territory in the Barents Sea, and the next year, Denmark designated the northeastern third of Greenland as a national park.

Settlement and Exploration

The Arctic region was settled some 10,000 to 12,000 years ago, after the last Ice Age, by peoples of Central Asia, probably of Mongoloid stock, who pursued animal herds northward in the wake of retreating glaciers. The ancestors of the Lapps migrated to northern Scandinavia and the Kola Peninsula, while further east diverse peoples settled along the Arctic coast. At about the same time, the forebears of the American Indians came from Asia via a land bridge across the Bering Strait or traveled along the Aleutian Islands to North America. It is believed that the Eskimos arrived in Alaska much later.

These migratory peoples adapted to the harsh Arctic environment by inventing snowshoes, the kayak, the igloo, and primitive tools. They fashioned clothes and tents of caribou or reindeer skins, perfected efficient hunting techniques, and evolved distinctive forms of social organization. Gradually, over the course of centuries, these hunter-gatherers made the transition to herding and trading; especially for the Indians and Eskimos of Canada and the US, however, intense contact with modern culture in the 20th century has meant abrupt change. In addition to Indians and Eskimos, principal indigenous Arctic population groups include the mixed Eskimo-Caucasian peoples of Greenland, the Lapps in Scandinavia, and the Samoyedic, Yakuts, Tungus-Manchurian, and Chukchi peoples of the USSR. These aboriginal peoples constituted about half of the Arctic's total population of approximately 2 million in the early 1980s.

The first explorers in Arctic waters were the Vikings (Northmen) from Scandinavia, who ventured into the North Atlantic as far as Greenland and the North American continent in the 10th and 11th centuries. It is generally accepted that the Norse chieftain Leif Ericson explored part of the northeastern North American mainland, which he called Vinland, although its actual location is disputed. During the 16th and 17th centuries, European explorers such as Martin Frobisher, William Baffin, and William Barents probed the Arctic Ocean for the fabled Northwest Passage around North America to the Orient. Arctic geographical landmarks have been named after them and for Vitus Bering, the Danish explorer who sailed in the service of Russia in 1728 through the strait that bears his name. In the late 18th century, while developing trade routes for English fur companies, Alexander Mackenzie and Samuel Hearne followed Canadian rivers to reach the Arctic coast. In 1819, William Parry sailed west through the northern Canadian islands as far as M'Clure Strait before being stopped by heavy pack ice. That year, Swedish explorer Nils Nordenskjöld became the first to complete the Northeast Passage along the Russian Arctic coast. The disappearance in 1845 of Sir John Franklin's expedition spurred further exploration and the mapping of many Canadian islands in the Arctic Ocean. Norwegian explorer Roald Amundsen successfully transited the Northwest Passage for the first time, from 1903 to 1906.

Amundsen's accomplishment shifted the emphasis of Arctic exploration to reaching the North Pole. American explorer Robert E. Peary came within 280 km (174 mi) of the goal in his 1905–06 expedition, and on 6 April 1909, he and his party, including four Eskimos, were the first men to reach the North Pole. In 1926, Adm. Richard E. Byrd, of Antarctic exploration fame, and his copilot Floyd Bennett were the first to fly over the pole, and Amundsen and Lincoln Ellsworth flew from Spitsbergen (now Svalbard) across the pole to Alaska. Much later, in 1958, the US atomic-powered submarine *Nautilus* was the first underwater vessel to navigate the North Pole, and in 1960, another US submarine, the *Skate,* became the first to surface at the pole. The Soviet icebreaker *Arktika* was the first surface vessel to reach it, in 1977.

Unresolved Arctic territorial disputes concern Norway's exclusive claim to the resources of the Svalbard continental shelf and conflicting Norwegian-Soviet claims in the Barents Sea. After the Antarctic Treaty was signed in 1959, hopes were raised for a similar agreement in regard to the Arctic, but the strategic importance of the Arctic region, its increasing economic value, and complex legal problems involving national sensitivities have thus far prevented the attainment of such an accord.

Arctic Development
The five nations with territories within the Arctic Circle have all developed the area's natural resources to some degree, but the USSR has taken the lead both in populating the region and in exploiting its rich mineral deposits and other resources. The largest Arctic city is Murmansk, with a population of about 300,000, and there are some 30 other Soviet cities and towns in the Arctic with more than 10,000 inhabitants. In contrast, the largest town on the North American mainland located north of the Arctic Circle is Inuvik, in Canada's Northwest Territories, with a population of about 3,000; Godthaab, the capital of Greenland, has less than 10,000 residents. The USSR estimated the population of what it terms its "far north" (including areas in eastern Siberia as far south as 55°N) at about 4 million in the late 1970s. Of the total, about 65% lived in mining districts or coastal settlements based on fishing and military activities, 20% were concentrated in northern river valleys, and 15% were scattered in the hinterlands. Canada's Yukon Territory and Northwest Territories have over 40% of the country's land area but less than 1% of the total population. Alaska is the largest but least populous of all the states of the US.

Beginning in the 1930s with the establishment of the northern sea route to link coastal and river settlements, the Soviet government has undertaken the exceptionally costly task of fostering industrial development of the Arctic region. Because the harsh climate, the shortage of housing and amenities, and the low level of social services have discouraged voluntary migration to the area, the Soviet government has offered special resettlement inducements to workers, such as high wages and extensive fringe benefits. As a result, Soviet migration to the far north was nearly equal to the region's natural population increase between 1940 and 1970. However, labor turnover there has been rapid, with

most new workers staying only one to three years. The most important economic activity is the mining of large nickel, copper, tin, platinum, cobalt, iron, and coal deposits. Eastern Siberia produces more than half the country's total output of nickel and much of the nation's copper, while the Kola Peninsula's apatite deposits provide at least two-thirds of the raw materials used to produce phosphate fertilizer. Eastern Siberia also produces about 90% of the USSR's annual output of diamonds and tin. In addition, valuable oil fields and about two-thirds of proved Soviet natural gas reserves are located in western Siberia. Expansion of Soviet mining operations in the Arctic region continued into the early 1980s.

The most significant economic development in the Arctic during the 1970s was the $4.5-billion trans-Alaska oil pipeline project and the exploitation of vast petroleum reserves (estimated at more than 10 billion barrels) at Alaska's Prudhoe Bay. Construction began on the 1,270-km (789-mi) pipeline to Valdez in 1974, and oil began to flow through the pipeline in 1977. Tens of thousands of American workers migrated to Alaska to take part in the project (earning the highest average wage rates in the US), and many stayed there after its completion, thereby contributing to Alaska's population increase of 32.4% during the decade. Coal reserves estimated at 5 trillion tons are located on Alaska's North Slope; coal is mined at Healy, between Anchorage and Fairbanks. Gold, copper, lead, zinc, tin, platinum, tungsten, and uranium have been mined in the past, and there are known reserves of silver, lead, nickel, cobalt, mercury, molybdenum, and asbestos. However, the remoteness of mining sites and the high production costs continued to hinder mineral development (except for oil) in the 1980s.

Valuable minerals produced in the Canadian Arctic include gold, silver, lead, zinc, copper, nickel, platinum, cadmium, and uranium. Canada also has proved oil reserves totaling 1.5 billion barrels in the Mackenzie River delta and offshore areas of the Beaufort Sea. Although Greenland also has considerable mineral resources, only lead, zinc, and coal were being mined in the early 1980s. The two largest iron mines in Scandinavia are situated in the vicinity of Kiruna, in Swedish Lapland, and in Norway, near the Soviet border. Both Norway and the USSR operate coal mines in Svalbard, and both have explored for offshore oil beneath the Barents Sea.

Lack of adequate transportation facilities long hampered Arctic development. Since World War II, however, a network of air, water, and land routes has been developed, and modern technology has made most polar areas accessible. Scheduled flights from many airfields scattered throughout the region link cities and remote towns in Alaska, Canada, and the USSR. In Greenland, where the rugged terrain makes the building of airstrips both difficult and costly, there is scheduled jet helicopter service. Air transport serves both military and civilian needs in Norway's polar region and links Svalbard with the mainland. Although water transport is seasonal because of ice-blocked channels in winter, large quantities of cargo generally move by ship. Several hundred Soviet vessels, including icebreakers, ply the 2,800-km (1,740 mi) northern sea route between Novaya Zemlya and the Bering Strait, moving an estimated 4 million tons of cargo annually during 2–4 months of navigability. The USSR and Norway use waterborne shuttles to supply Svalbard and to convey coal to their respective home ports. Canada's shipping service for Hudson Bay, the Arctic islands, and the Mackenzie River delta is provided by the coast guard and by private companies. The Alaskan ports of Prudhoe Bay and Barrow are served by ships for a two-month period in late summer. Inland waterways provide important supply links in the Soviet Arctic and northwestern Canada.

Land routes in the Arctic are relatively undeveloped in the colder regions. However, there are four railroad lines in North America that penetrate the Arctic Circle. In addition to Alaska's

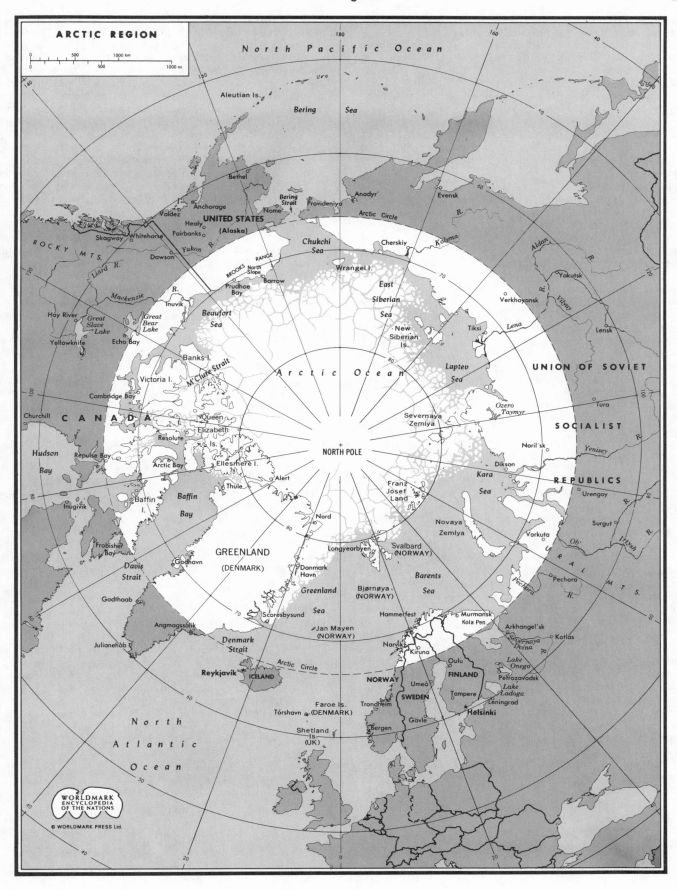

ARCTIC REGION

North Pacific Ocean

Aleutian Is.

Bering   Sea

Bethel

Anadyr'

Evensk

Anchorage

Bering Strait   Providehiya

Arctic Circle

Valdez   Nome

UNITED STATES

Healy   (Alaska)

Cherskiy

Kolyma

Aldan

Whitehorse   Fairbanks

R.

Skagway   Yukon   R.

Chukchi Sea

Yakutsk

Dawson

BROOKS   RANGE   North Slope

East Siberian Sea

Verkhoyansk

Prudhoe Bay   Barrow

Wrangel I.

Lena

Inuvik

Beaufort Sea

New Siberian Is.

Tiksi

Lensk

Mackenzie   R.

Great Bear Lake

Laptev Sea

UNION   OF   SOVIET

Hay River   Great Slave Lake

Banks I.

Ozero Taymyr

Tura

Yellowknife   Echo Bay

M'Clure Strait

Arctic   Ocean

SOCIALIST

Churchill   Cambridge Bay

Victoria I.

Severnaya Zemlya

Yenisey

C A N A D A

Queen Elizabeth Is.

Noril'sk

REPUBLICS

Hudson Bay   Repulse Bay   Resolute

Kara Sea

Dikson

Urengoy

NORTH POLE

Arctic Bay

Ellesmere I.

Franz Josef Land

Novaya Zemlya

Vorkuta

Ob

Surgut

Inugivik   Baffin I.   Baffin   Bay

Thule   Alert

Nord

URAL   MTS.

Frobisher Bay

Davis Strait   Godhavn

GREENLAND

Longyearbyen   Svalbard (NORWAY)

Pechora

Godthaab

(DENMARK)

Danmark Havn

Barents Sea

Pechora   R.

Angmagssalik

Greenland

Bjørnøya (NORWAY)

Hammerfest

Murmansk Kola Pen.

Arkhangel'sk   Kotlas

Julianehåb

Scoresbysund   Sea

Narvik

Severnaya Dvina   R.

Denmark Strait

Jan Mayen (NORWAY)

Kiruna

Lake Onega

Petrozavodsk

Arctic Circle

Oulu

Reykjavík   ICELAND

NORWAY   Umeå   FINLAND

Lake Ladoga

Leningrad

SWEDEN   Tampere

Helsinki

North

Faroe Is.   Trondheim

Gävle

Atlantic

Tórshavn (DENMARK)   Bergen

Ocean

Shetland Is. (UK)

WORLDMARK
ENCYCLOPEDIA
OF THE NATIONS
© WORLDMARK PRESS Ltd.

500   1000 km

500   1000 mi

heavily used Anchorage–Fairbanks line, there are three Canadian railroads, providing links to Churchill, on Hudson Bay; to Hay River, on the Great Slave Lake; and to Skagway, on the Alaskan border. Six Soviet railroads serve the Arctic region, including the ports of Murmansk and Arkhangel'sk. Canada's two Arctic highways connect Inuvik with Dawson and with the Great Slave Lake towns of Hay River and Yellowknife. The most heavily traveled highway is Alaska's Arctic haul road between the Yukon River and Prudhoe Bay; this road was instrumental in hauling supplies and equipment to build the trans-Alaska oil pipeline. The Soviet Arctic has few roads, but the Murmansk area in the west connects with a well-developed Scandinavian road network.

Scientific Research

Scientific research in the Arctic region is directed mainly toward economic development and military applications. Research studies have dealt primarily with the Arctic's role in global air and water circulation and with such natural phenomena as pack ice, permafrost, geomagnetism, the aurora borealis, and other upper atmospheric conditions.

International cooperation has long played a vital role in Arctic research, dating back to the 1882/83 and 1932/33 International Polar Years. The most intensive multinational scientific study of the Arctic was accomplished during the International Geophysical Year (1957/58), in which some 300 Arctic stations were set up to monitor polar phenomena. The US and USSR each launched two drifting stations on the pack ice to gather data on Arctic currents and the topography of the Arctic seabed. It was found that little marine life existed on the Arctic Ocean floor and that rocks were scattered in profusion on the ocean bottom. The land stations obtained detailed information on the aurora borealis, ionosphere, and polar magnetic field. During 1969–75, Canada and the US jointly conducted an Arctic ice experimental program involving manned and unmanned drifting stations to determine the dynamics of sea-ice movement within the polar environment.

Scientific efforts by the USSR in the Arctic have exceeded the combined activities of all the other circumpolar nations. By the late 1970s, the USSR operated at least 100 polar stations and more than a dozen specially equipped sea and air vehicles to collect data on weather, ocean currents, and sea ice, with the aim of maintaining shipping services over the northern sea route. Drifting ice stations maintained year-round make a variety of meteorological observations and conduct oceanographic and geophysical experiments. Each year, the USSR mounts air expeditions to hundreds of sites along the ice pack, emplacing nearly two dozen automatic buoys to radio data on environmental conditions to the mainland.

US Arctic research centers mainly on Alaska but extends also to northern Canada, Greenland, and the Arctic Ocean. Civilian research is coordinated by the National Science Foundation (NSF), which contracts out its research programs to universities; the principal research centers are at Fairbanks and Barrow. Small outposts to gather weather information have been established at US military facilities in Alaska and at radar stations on the 4,800-km (3,000-mi) Distant Early Warning (DEW) line extending from Alaska to Greenland. In 1983/84 the NSF allocated approximately $15 million for Arctic research studies.

The US operates an average of one drifting ice station per year in the Arctic Ocean, supplemented by automatic data buoys. Ice reconnaissance flights are conducted, as well as ocean surveys by icebreakers and submarines in the Bering and Greenland seas. In the early 1980s, the NSF was conducting a six-year project, called Processes and Resources of the Bering Sea Shelf (PROBES), to study the marine ecosystem of the Bering Sea in order to predict the environmental impact of both natural events and human activities. In the summer of 1981, the US cooperated with Denmark and Switzerland to obtain ice cores from the bottom of the Greenland ice sheet, which represents a record of the climate over the past 130,000 years. Other recent US programs include studies of the geology and geophysics of the Arctic basin and research in Alaska on so-called surging glaciers, which move forward at the unusually rapid rate of several miles a year.

Other circumpolar nations have concentrated their Arctic research on the land and continental shelf. Canada's ongoing Polar Continental Shelf Project, begun in 1959, makes intensive studies of the North American continental shelf, Arctic islands, and Arctic Ocean. From March to October of each year, Canada also conducts aerial surveys of sea ice in the Arctic Ocean, Baffin Bay, and Beaufort Sea. Norway's Polar Institute, in Oslo, supervises mapping and scientific surveys of Svalbard, Jan Mayen, and the Arctic Ocean. In Greenland, the US participates in geophysical and weather studies at Thule Air Base. Scientists from the USSR, the UK, France, and other countries also conduct geological and biological research on the Danish dependency.

BIBLIOGRAPHY

Armstrong, Terrence, *et al.* *The Circumpolar North: A Political and Economic Geography of the Arctic and Sub-Arctic.* New York: Methuen, 1978.

Auburn, F. M. *Antarctic Law and Politics.* Bloomington: Indiana University Press, 1982.

Bonner, W. N., and R. J. Berry (eds.). *Ecology in the Antarctic.* New York: Academic Press, 1981.

Bush, W. M. *Basic Documents on Antarctica.* 2 vols. Dobbs Ferry, N.Y.: Oceana, 1982.

McWhinnie, Mary A. (ed.). *Polar Research: To the Present and the Future.* Boulder, Colo.: Westview Press, 1978.

Mirsky, Jeanette. *To the Arctic: The Story of Northern Exploration from Earliest Times to the Present.* Chicago: University of Chicago Press, 1970.

Parker, Bruce C. (ed.). *Environmental Impact in Antarctica.* Charlottesville: University Press of Virginia, 1978.

Polar Regions Atlas. Washington, D.C.: Central Intelligence Agency, 1978.

Porter, Eliot. *Antarctica.* New York: Dutton, 1978.

Quigg, P. W. *A Pole Apart: The Emerging Issues of Antarctica.* New York: McGraw-Hill, 1982.

Ray, G. Carleton, and M. G. McCormick-Ray. *Wildlife of the Polar Regions.* New York: Abrams, 1981.

Sugden, David. *Arctic and Antarctic: A Modern Geographical Synthesis.* Totowa, N.J.: Barnes & Noble, 1982.

UN Economic Commission for Europe. *Human Settlements in the Arctic: An Account of the ECE Symposium on Human Settlements Planning and Development in the Arctic, Godthåb, Greenland, Aug. 18–25, 1978.* Elmsford, N.Y.: Pergamon, 1980.

World Tables

Table 1. Membership in International Organizations, 1983

UNITED NATIONS SYSTEM AND SPECIALIZED AGENCIES

AFRICA	UN	FAO	GATT	IAEA	IBRD	ICAO	ICJ	IDA	IFAD	IFC	ILO	IMF
Algeria	•	•	•	•	•	•	•	•	•		•	•
Angola	•	•				•		•			•	
Benin	•	•	•		•	•	•	•	•		•	•
Botswana	•	•	•		•	•	•	•	•		•	•
Burundi	•	•	•		•	•	•	•	•		•	•
Cameroon	•	•	•	•	•	•	•	•	•		•	•
Cape Verde	•	•			•	•	•	•	•		•	•
Central African Rep.	•	•	•		•	•	•	•	•		•	•
Chad	•	•			•	•	•	•	•		•	•
Comoros	•	•			•		•	•	•		•	•
Congo	•	•	•		•	•	•	•	•	•	•	•
Djibouti	•	•	•		•	•	•	•	•		•	•
Egypt	•	•	•	•	•	•	•	•	•	•	•	•
Equatorial Guinea	•	•			•	•	•	•	•		•	•
Ethiopia	•	•			•	•	•	•	•		•	•
Gabon	•	•	•		•	•	•	•	•		•	•
Gambia	•	•	•		•	•	•	•	•		•	•
Ghana	•	•	•		•	•	•	•	•	•	•	•
Guinea	•	•			•	•	•	•	•	•	•	•
Guinea-Bissau	•	•	•		•	•	•	•	•		•	•
Ivory Coast	•	•	•	•	•	•	•	•	•	•	•	•
Kenya	•	•	•	•	•	•	•	•	•	•	•	•
Lesotho	•	•	•		•	•	•	•	•	•	•	•
Liberia	•	•			•	•	•	•	•	•	•	•
Libya	•	•			•	•	•	•	•		•	•
Madagascar	•	•	•		•	•	•	•	•	•	•	•
Malawi	•	•	•		•	•	•	•	•	•	•	•
Mali	•	•	•	•	•	•	•	•	•	•	•	•
Mauritania	•	•	•		•	•	•	•	•	•	•	•
Mauritius	•	•	•		•	•	•	•	•	•	•	•
Morocco	•	•		•	•	•	•	•	•	•	•	•
Mozambique	•	•	•		•	•	•		•		•	
Namibia		•		•							•	
Niger	•	•	•	•	•	•	•	•	•	•	•	•
Nigeria	•	•	•	•	•	•	•	•	•	•	•	•
Rwanda	•	•	•		•	•	•	•	•	•	•	•
São Tomé and Príncipe	•	•	•		•		•	•	•		•	•
Senegal	•	•	•	•	•	•	•	•	•	•	•	•
Seychelles	•	•	•		•	•	•	•	•		•	•
Sierra Leone	•	•	•		•	•	•	•	•	•	•	•
Somalia	•	•			•	•	•	•	•	•	•	•
South Africa	•		•		•	•	•			•		•
Sudan	•	•		•	•	•	•	•	•	•	•	•
Swaziland	•	•	•		•	•	•	•	•	•	•	•
Tanzania	•	•	•		•	•	•	•	•	•	•	•
Togo	•	•	•		•	•	•	•	•	•	•	•
Tunisia	•	•	•		•	•	•	•	•	•	•	•
Uganda	•	•	•		•	•	•	•	•	•	•	•
Upper Volta	•	•	•		•	•	•	•	•	•	•	•
Zaire	•	•	•		•	•	•	•	•	•	•	•
Zambia	•	•	•		•	•	•	•	•	•	•	•
Zimbabwe	•	•	•		•	•	•	•	•	•	•	•
AMERICAS												
Antigua and Barbuda	•											
Argentina	•	•	•	•	•	•	•	•	•	•	•	•
Bahamas	•	•	•		•	•	•				•	•
Barbados	•	•	•		•	•	•			•	•	•
Belize	•				•			•		•	•	•
Bolivia	•	•			•	•	•	•	•	•	•	•
Brazil	•	•	•	•	•	•	•	•	•	•	•	•

232

SELECTED INTERNATIONAL ORGANIZATIONS

IMO	ITU	UNESCO	UPU	WHO	WIPO	WMO	CMEA	EC	G-77	LEAGUE OF ARAB STATES	NATO	OAS	OAU	OECD	OPEC	WTO
•	•	•	•	•	•	•			•	•			•		•	
•	•	•	•	•	•	•			•				•			
•	•	•	•	•		•			•				•			
	•	•	•	•		•			•				•			
•	•	•	•	•	•	•			•				•			
•	•	•	•	•	•	•			•				•			
	•	•	•	•	•	•			•				•			
	•	•	•	•		•			•				•			
•	•	•	•	•	•	•			•				•			
•	•	•	•	•	•	•			•	•I			•			
•	•	•	•	•	•	•			•				•			
•	•	•	•	•	•	•			•				•		•	
•	•	•	•	•	•	•			•				•			
•	•	•	•	•	•	•			•				•			
•	•	•	•	•		•			•				•			
•	•	•	•	•	•	•			•				•			
•	•	•	•	•	•	•			•				•			
•	•	•	•	•		•			•	•			•		•	
•	•	•	•	•		•			•				•			
•	•	•	•	•		•			•	•			•			
•	•	•	•	•	•	•			•	•			•			
•	•	•	•	•		•			•				•			
•	•	•	•	•	•	•			•				•		•	
•	•	•	•	•	•	•			•				•			
•	•	•	•	•		•			•				•			
•	•	•	•	•		•			•				•			
•	•	•	•	•	•	•			•	•			•			
•	•	•	•	•		•			•	•			•			
•	•	•	•	•	•	•			•				•			
•	•	•	•	•		•			•	•			•			
	•	•	•	•		•			•				•			
	•	•	•	•		•			•				•			
	•	•	•	•		•			•				•			
•	•	•	•	•	•	•			•				•			
•	•	•	•	•	•	•			•				•			
•	•	•	•	•	•	•			•				•			
•	•	•	•	•	•	•			•				•			
•	•	•	•	•	•	•			•				•			

Table 1. Membership in International Organizations, 1983—*cont.*

UNITED NATIONS SYSTEM AND SPECIALIZED AGENCIES

	UN	FAO	GATT	IAEA	IBRD	ICAO	ICJ	IDA	IFAD	IFC	ILO	IMF
Canada	•	•	•	•	•	•	•	•	•	•	•	•
Chile	•	•	•	•	•	•	•	•	•	•	•	•
Colombia	•	•	•	•	•	•	•	•	•	•	•	•
Costa Rica	•	•		•	•	•	•	•	•	•	•	•
Cuba	•	•	•	•		•	•		•		•	
Dominica	•	•	•		•		•	•	•	•		•
Dominican Republic	•	•	•		•	•	•	•	•	•	•	•
Ecuador	•	•		•	•	•	•	•	•	•	•	•
El Salvador	•	•	•		•	•	•	•	•	•	•	•
Grenada	•	•		•	•		•	•	•	•		•
Guatemala	•	•		•	•	•	•	•	•	•	•	•
Guyana	•	•	•		•	•	•	•	•	•	•	•
Haiti	•	•	•		•	•	•	•	•	•	•	•
Honduras	•	•		•	•	•	•	•	•	•	•	•
Jamaica	•	•	•		•	•	•	•	•	•	•	•
Mexico	•	•		•	•	•	•	•	•	•	•	•
Nicaragua	•	•	•		•	•	•	•	•	•	•	•
Panama	•	•		•	•	•	•		•	•	•	•
Paraguay	•	•		•	•	•	•	•	•	•	•	•
Peru	•	•	•	•	•	•	•	•	•	•	•	•
St. Christopher–Nevis	•						•					
St. Lucia	•	•		•	•		•	•		•	•	•
St. Vincent and the Grenadines	•		•		•		•			•		•
Suriname	•	•	•		•	•			•	•	•	•
Trinidad and Tobago	•	•	•		•	•	•		•	•	•	•
Turks and Caicos												
US	•	•	•	•	•	•	•	•	•	•	•	•
Uruguay	•	•		•	•	•	•		•	•	•	•
Venezuela	•	•		•	•	•	•		•	•	•	•

ASIA & OCEANIA												
Afghanistan	•	•		•	•	•	•	•	•	•	•	•
Australia	•	•	•	•	•	•	•	•	•	•	•	•
Bahrain	•	•	•		•	•	•				•	•
Bangladesh	•	•	•		•		•	•	•	•	•	•
Bhutan	•					•		•	•			•
Brunei												
Burma	•	•	•		•	•	•	•	•	•	•	•
China	•	•		•	•	•	•	•	•	•	•	•
Cyprus	•	•	•		•	•	•	•	•	•	•	•
Fiji	•	•	•		•	•	•	•	•	•	•	•
India	•	•	•	•	•	•	•	•	•	•	•	•
Indonesia	•	•	•	•	•	•	•	•	•	•	•	•
Iran	•	•		•	•	•	•	•	•	•	•	•
Iraq	•	•		•	•	•	•	•	•	•	•	•
Israel	•	•	•	•	•	•	•	•	•	•	•	•
Japan	•	•	•	•	•	•	•	•	•	•	•	•
Jordan	•	•		•	•	•	•	•	•	•	•	•
Kampuchea	•	•	•		•	•	•	•				
Kiribati			•									
Korea, D. P. Rep. of			•		•							
Korea, Rep. of		•	•	•	•	•		•	•	•	•	•
Kuwait	•	•	•		•	•	•	•	•	•	•	•
Laos	•	•		•	•	•	•	•	•		•	•
Lebanon	•	•		•	•	•	•			•	•	•
Malaysia	•	•	•		•	•	•	•		•	•	•
Maldives	•	•	•		•	•	•	•	•	•		•
Mongolia	•	•		•			•				•	
Nauru						•						
Nepal	•	•	•		•	•	•	•	•	•	•	•
New Zealand	•	•	•	•	•	•	•	•		•	•	•

SELECTED INTERNATIONAL ORGANIZATIONS

IMO	ITU	UNESCO	UPU	WHO	WIPO	WMO	CMEA	EC	G-77	LEAGUE OF ARAB STATES	NATO	OAS	OAU	OECD	OPEC	WTO
•	•	•	•	•	•	•			•		•			•		
•	•	•	•	•	•	•			•			•				
•	•	•	•	•	•	•			•			•				
•	•	•	•	•	•	•	•		•			•				
•	•	•	•	•		•			•			•				
•	•	•	•	•	•	•			•			•			•	
•	•	•	•	•	•	•			•			•				
•	•	•	•	•	•	•			•			•				
•	•	•	•	•	•	•			•			•				
•	•	•	•	•		•			•			•				
•	•	•	•	•		•			•			•				
•	•	•	•	•		•			•			•				
•	•	•	•	•	•	•			•			•				
•	•	•	•	•	•	•			•			•				
•	•	•	•	•		•			•			•				
•	•	•	•	•	•	•			•			•²				
•		•	•	•					•			•				
•	•	•	•	•	•	•			•			•				
•	•	•	•	•	•	•			•		•	•	•			
•	•	•	•	•	•	•		•				•				
•	•	•	•	•	•	•			•			•			•	
•		•	•	•		•			•							
•	•	•	•	•	•	•								•		
•	•	•	•	•	•	•			•	•						
•	•	•	•	•	•	•			•							
•	•	•	•	•					•							
•	•	•	•	•		•			•							
•	•	•	•	•	•	•			•							
•	•	•	•	•	•	•			•							
•	•	•	•	•	•	•			•							
•	•	•	•	•	•	•			•						•	
•	•	•	•	•	•	•			•	•					•	
•	•	•	•	•	•	•			•							
•	•	•	•	•	•	•			•	•				•		
•	•	•	•	•	•	•			•							
•	•	•	•	•		•			•							
•	•	•	•	•	•	•			•							
•	•	•	•	•	•	•			•						•	
•	•	•	•	•	•	•			•	•						
•	•	•	•	•	•	•			•							
•	•	•	•	•	•	•	•									
•	•	•	•	•	•	•			•							
•	•	•	•	•	•	•										
•	•	•	•	•	•	•								•		

Table 1. Membership in International Organizations, 1983—*cont.*

UNITED NATIONS SYSTEM AND SPECIALIZED AGENCIES

	UN	FAO	GATT	IAEA	IBRD	ICAO	ICJ	IDA	IFAD	IFC	ILO	IMF
Oman	•	•			•	•	•	•	•	•	•	•
Pakistan	•	•	•	•	•	•	•	•	•	•	•	•
Papua New Guinea	•	•	•	•	•	•	•	•		•	•	•
Philippines	•	•	•	•	•	•	•	•		•	•	•
Qatar	•	•	•	•	•	•	•			•		•
Sa'udi Arabia	•	•		•	•	•	•	•		•	•	•
Singapore	•		•	•	•	•	•	•		•	•	•
Solomon Islands	•		•		•	•	•	•		•		•
Sri Lanka	•	•	•	•	•	•	•	•		•	•	•
Syria	•	•		•	•	•	•	•		•	•	•
Taiwan												
Thailand	•	•	•	•	•	•	•	•		•	•	•
Tonga		•	•									
Turkey	•	•	•	•	•	•	•	•		•	•	•
Tuvalu												
UAE	•	•	•	•	•	•	•			•	•	•
Vanuatu	•						•					
Viet-Nam	•	•		•	•	•	•	•		•	•	•
Western Samoa	•	•			•	•	•	•		•		•
Yemen, P. D. Rep. of	•	•		•	•	•	•	•		•	•	•
Yemen Arab Rep.	•	•		•	•	•	•	•		•	•	•
EUROPE												
Albania	•	•		•			•					
Andorra												
Austria	•	•	•	•	•	•	•	•	•	•	•	•
Belgium	•	•	•	•	•	•	•	•	•	•	•	•
Bulgaria	•	•		•		•	•				•	
Czechoslovakia	•	•	•	•		•	•				•	
Denmark	•	•	•	•	•	•	•	•	•	•	•	•
Finland	•	•	•	•	•	•	•	•		•	•	•
France	•	•	•	•	•	•	•	•	•	•	•	•
German Dem. Rep.	•			•			•				•	
Germany, Fed. Rep. of	•	•	•	•	•	•	•	•	•	•	•	•
Greece	•	•	•	•	•	•	•	•		•	•	•
Hungary	•	•	•	•	•	•	•				•	•
Iceland	•	•	•	•	•	•	•	•		•	•	•
Ireland	•	•	•	•	•	•	•	•		•	•	•
Italy	•	•	•	•	•	•	•	•	•	•	•	•
Liechtenstein				•			•					
Luxembourg	•	•	•	•	•	•	•			•	•	•
Malta	•	•	•	•		•	•			•	•	•
Monaco				•		•						
Netherlands	•	•	•	•	•	•	•	•	•	•	•	•
Norway	•	•	•	•	•	•	•	•	•	•	•	•
Poland	•	•	•	•	•	•	•				•	•
Portugal	•	•	•	•	•	•	•	•		•	•	•
Romania	•	•	•	•	•	•	•			•	•	•
San Marino												
Spain	•	•	•	•	•	•	•	•		•	•	•
Sweden	•	•	•	•	•	•	•	•	•	•	•	•
Switzerland		•	•	•		•	•			•	•	
USSR	•			•		•	•				•	
UK	•	•	•	•	•	•	•	•	•	•	•	•
Vatican				•								
Yugoslavia	•	•	•	•	•	•	•	•	•	•	•	•

1. Membership suspended in 1979.
2. Joined in 1984.

SELECTED INTERNATIONAL ORGANIZATIONS

IMO	ITU	UNESCO	UPU	WHO	WIPO	WMO	CMEA	EC	G-77	LEAGUE OF ARAB STATES	NATO	OAS	OAU	OECD	OPEC	WTO
•	•	•	•	•		•			•	•						
•	•	•	•	•	•	•			•							
•	•	•	•	•		•			•							
•	•	•	•	•	•	•			•						•	
•	•	•	•	•		•			•	•					•	
•	•	•	•	•	•	•			•	•						
•	•	•	•	•	•	•			•							
•	•	•	•	•	•	•			•	•						
•	•	•	•	•	•	•			•							
•	•	•	•	•		•			•							
•	•	•	•	•		•					•			•		
•	•	•	•	•	•	•			•	•					•	
•	•	•	•	•	•	•	•		•							
			•	•					•							
•	•	•	•	•		•			•	•						
•	•	•	•	•	•	•			•	•						
•	•	•	•			•	•							•		
	•															
•	•	•	•	•	•	•		•	•		•			•		
•	•	•	•	•	•	•	•		•							•
•	•	•	•	•	•	•	•		•							•
•	•	•	•	•	•	•		•			•			•		
•	•	•	•	•	•	•		•			•			•		
•	•	•	•	•	•	•		•			•			•		•
•	•	•	•	•	•	•	•									
•	•	•	•	•	•	•		•			•			•		
•	•	•	•	•	•	•		•			•			•		•
•	•	•	•	•	•	•		•			•			•		
•	•	•	•	•	•	•		•			•			•		•
•	•	•	•	•	•	•		•			•			•		
•	•	•	•	•	•	•		•			•			•		
•	•	•	•	•	•	•		•			•			•		
•	•	•	•	•	•	•		•	•		•			•		
•	•	•	•	•	•	•		•			•			•		
•	•	•	•	•	•	•		•			•					•
•	•	•	•	•	•	•	•				•			•		•
•	•	•	•	•	•	•	•		•							•
•	•	•	•	•	•	•					•			•		
•	•	•	•	•	•	•								•		
•	•	•	•	•	•	•		•								•
•	•	•	•	•	•	•					•			•		
•	•	•	•	•	•	•			•							

Table 2: World Demographic Indicators

	POPULATION EST. 1982 ('000,000)	POPULATION GROWTH RATE 1970–81 (%)	% UNDER AGE 15 (EST.)[1]	CRUDE BIRTHRATE (EST.)[1]	CRUDE DEATH RATE (EST.)[1]	INFANT MORTALITY RATE (EST.)[1]	LIFE EXPECTANCY (YEARS, EST.)[1] FEMALE	MALE	PER CAPITA INCOME 1981 (US$)
AFRICA									
Algeria	20.1	3.3	47	46	14	118	57	55	2,140
Angola	6.8	2.5	44	48	23	154	43	40	—
Benin	3.7	2.7	46	49	19	154	48	44	320
Botswana	0.9	—	46	51	18	83	57	54	—
Burundi	4.4	2.2	44	45	23	122	46	43	230
Cameroon	8.9	2.2	43	45	20	109	46	42	880
Cape Verde	0.3	—	36	29	8	82	59	55	—
Central African Rep.	2.4	2.3	41	44	22	149	48	44	320
Chad	4.6	2.0	41	44	24	149	45	42	110
Comoros	0.4	—	43	44	14	93	48	44	—
Congo	1.6	2.9	43	45	19	129	48	44	1,110
Djibouti	0.5	—	—	49	22	—	—	—	—
Egypt	44.8	2.5	40	43	12	103	56	54	650
Equatorial Guinea	0.3	—	42	42	19	143	48	44	—
Ethiopa	30.5	2.0	43	50	25	147	41	38	140
Gabon	0.7	—	34	34	22	117	45	42	—
Gambia	0.6	—	42	49	28	198	43	39	—
Ghana	12.4	3.0	47	48	17	103	50	47	400
Guinea	5.3	2.9	44	46	21	165	45	42	300
Guinea-Bissau	0.8	—	39	40	21	149	43	39	—
Ivory Coast	8.8	5.0	45	48	18	127	48	44	1,200
Kenya	17.9	4.0	50	53	14	87	56	52	420
Lesotho	1.4	2.4	40	40	16	115	51	49	540
Liberia	2.0	3.5	41	50	20	154	49	47	520
Libya	3.2	4.1	49	47	13	100	57	54	8,450
Madagascar	9.2	2.6	44	45	18	71	48	44	330
Malawi	6.6	3.0	44	51	19	172	48	44	200
Mali	7.1	2.6	48	52	24	154	44	41	190
Mauritania	1.7	2.3	42	50	22	143	44	41	460
Mauritius	1.0	—	35	27	7	33	69	65	—
Morocco	22.3	3.1	46	45	14	107	57	54	860
Mozambique	12.7	4.2	45	45	19	115	48	44	—
Namibia	1.1	—	44	44	15	120	52	50	—
Niger	5.8	3.3	43	51	22	146	44	41	330
Nigeria	82.3	2.5	47	50	18	135	49	46	870
Rwanda	5.4	3.4	51	50	19	107	48	44	250
São Tomé and Príncipe	0.1	—	—	42	10	50	—	—	—
Senegal	5.9	2.7	44	48	22	147	45	42	430
Seychelles	0.1	—	38	28	7	27	68	62	—
Sierra Leone	3.7	2.6	41	46	19	208	48	44	320
Somalia	4.6	2.8	44	46	20	147	45	41	280
South Africa	30.0	2.8	42	36	12	96	62	59	2,770
Sudan	19.9	3.1	44	47	17	124	47	45	380
Swaziland	0.6	—	48	48	19	135	48	44	—
Tanzania	19.9	3.4	46	46	14	103	52	49	280
Togo	2.8	2.5	50	48	19	109	48	44	380
Tunisia	6.7	2.3	43	35	11	100	58	56	1,420
Uganda	13.7	2.6	45	48	16	97	54	51	220
Upper Volta	6.7	2.0	44	48	22	211	44	41	240
Zaire	30.3	3.0	45	46	19	112	48	44	210
Zambia	6.0	3.1	46	49	17	106	50	47	600
Zimbabwe	8.0	3.2	51	47	14	74	55	52	870
AMERICAS									
Antigua and Barbuda	0.1	—	—	16	6	32	—	—	—
Argentina	28.6	1.6	27	25	9	45	73	66	2,560
Bahamas	0.2	—	44	22	5	32	71	67	—
Barbados	0.3	—	31	17	8	25	72	68	—
Belize	0.2	—	49	40	12	—	—	—	—
Bolivia	5.6	2.6	42	45	18	131	53	48	600
Brazil	127.7	2.1	41	32	9	77	67	61	2,220
Canada	24.4	1.2	24	16	7	11	77	71	11,400
Chile	11.5	1.7	34	22	7	32	70	63	2,560
Colombia	25.6	1.9	40	28	8	56	64	61	1,380

	POPULATION EST. 1982 ('000,000)	POPULATION GROWTH RATE 1970–81 (%)	% UNDER AGE 15 (EST.)[1]	CRUDE BIRTHRATE (EST.)[1]	CRUDE DEATH RATE (EST.)[1]	INFANT MORTALITY RATE (EST.)[1]	LIFE EXPECTANCY (YEARS, EST.)[1] FEMALE	MALE	PER CAPITA INCOME 1981 (US$)
Costa Rica	2.3	2.8	38	29	4	24	72	68	1,430
Cuba	9.8	1.1	35	14	6	19	74	70	—
Dominica	0.1	—	—	21	5	19	60	55	—
Dominican Republic	5.7	3.0	45	37	9	68	62	58	1,260
Ecuador	8.5	3.4	45	42	10	82	62	58	1,180
El Salvador	5.0	2.9	46	35	8	53	65	61	650
Grenada	0.1	—	—	24	7	15	66	61	—
Guatemala	7.7	3.1	43	42	10	71	59	57	1,140
Guyana	0.9	—	44	28	7	44	72	67	—
Haiti	6.1	1.7	41	42	16	115	52	49	300
Honduras	4.0	3.4	48	47	12	88	59	55	600
Jamaica	2.2	1.5	40	27	6	16	72	68	1,180
Mexico	71.3	3.1	42	32	6	56	67	64	2,250
Nicaragua	2.6	3.9	48	47	12	90	57	54	860
Panama	1.9	2.3	43	27	6	34	72	68	1,910
Paraguay	3.3	2.6	45	34	7	47	65	62	1,630
Peru	18.6	2.6	44	38	11	88	58	55	1,170
St. Christopher–Nevis	—	—	—	—	—	—	—	—	—
St. Lucia	0.1	—	50	32	7	33	70	65	—
St. Vincent and Grenadines	0.1	—	—	35	7	38	—	—	—
Suriname	0.4	—	51	28	8	36	70	—	—
Trinidad and Tobago	1.1	1.4	37	25	6	26	72	66	5,670
Turks and Caicos	—	—	—	—	—	—	—	—	—
US	232	1.0	23	16	9	12	77	70	12,820
Uruguay	3.0	0.4	27	19	11	37	74	67	2,820
Venezuela	18.4	3.4	43	34	5	42	68	66	4,220
ASIA & OCEANIA									
Afghanistan	15.1	2.5	45	48	23	205	43	42	—
Australia	15.0	1.4	27	15	7	11	76	70	11,080
Bahrain	0.4	—	41	37	8	53	64	61	—
Bangladesh	93.3	2.6	42	47	19	136[2]	47	48	140
Bhutan	1.4	2.0	42	43	21	150	42	44	80
Brunei	0.2	—	34	28	4	20	66	66	—
Burma	37.1	2.2	40	39	14	101	54	51	190
China	1,000.0	1.5	32	22	7	45	70	66	300
Cyprus	0.6	—	25	22	19	18	74	70	—
Fiji	0.7	—	41	30	4	37	73	70	—
India	713.8	2.1	40	35	15	123	51	52	260
Indonesia	151.3	2.3	42	34	16	93	51	49	530
Iran	41.2	3.1	44	44	14	108	59	58	—
Iraq	14.0	3.4	49	47	13	78	57	54	—
Israel	4.1	2.6	33	24	7	14	75	73	5,160
Japan	118.6	1.1	24	14	6	7	78	74	10,080
Jordan	3.5	3.5	51	47	10	69	57	54	1,620
Kampuchea	6.1	—	42	38	19	212	49	44	—
Kiribati	—	—	—	—	—	—	—	—	—
Korea, D. P. Rep. of	18.7	2.6	40	32	8	34	65	60	—
Korea, Rep. of	41.1	1.7	38	19	5	34	65	60	1,700
Kuwait	1.5	6.3	44	42	5	39	72	67	20,900
Laos	3.7	1.9	42	44	20	129	44	41	80
Lebanon	2.7	0.6	43	30	9	41	67	63	—
Malaysia	14.7	2.5	40	30	7	31	63	60	1,840
Maldives	0.2	—	45	47	14	120	—	—	—
Mongolia	1.8	2.9	43	38	9	55	65	60	—
Nauru	—	—	—	—	—	—	—	—	—
Nepal	14.5	2.6	40	44	21	150	42	44	150
New Zealand	3.1	1.5	28	17	8	13	76	70	7,700
Oman	0.9	—	45	49	19	128	48	46	—
Pakistan	93.0	3.0	46	44	16	126	52	52	350
Papua New Guinea	3.3	2.1	44	44	16	104	52	49	840
Philippines	51.6	2.7	43	34	8	55	62	59	790
Qatar	0.3	—	37	37	10	53	56	54	—

Table 2: World Demographic Indicators—cont.

	POPULATION EST. 1982 ('000,000)	POPULATION GROWTH RATE 1970–81 (%)	% UNDER AGE 15 (EST.)[1]	CRUDE BIRTHRATE (EST.)[1]	CRUDE DEATH RATE (EST.)[1]	INFANT MORTALITY RATE (EST.)[1]	LIFE EXPECTANCY (YEARS, EST.)[1] FEMALE	MALE	PER CAPITA INCOME 1981 (US$)
Sa'udi Arabia	11.1	4.5	45	46	14	114	49	47	12,600
Singapore	2.5	1.5	28	17	5	12	72	68	5,240
Solomon Islands	0.2	—	48	44	9	78	58	56	—
Sri Lanka	15.2	1.7	39	29	7	37	65	62	300
Syria	9.7	3.7	48	46	9	62	64	61	1,570
Taiwan	18.5	—	—	23	5	—	74	70	—
Thailand	49.8	2.5	42	28	7	55	63	58	770
Tonga	—	—	—	—	—	—	—	—	—
Turkey	47.7	2.3	40	33	10	123	62	60	1,540
Tuvalu	—	—	—	—	—	—	—	—	—
UAE	1.2	16.6	28	30	7	53	61	59	24,660
Vanuatu	0.1	—	—	45	17	101	—	—	—
Viet-Nam	56.6	2.8	41	37	9	100	64	60	—
Western Samoa	0.2	—	48	37	9	40	67	63	—
Yemen, P. D. Rep. of	2.0	2.5	46	48	21	146	40	39	460
Yemen Arab Rep.	5.5	3.0	45	49	24	162	45	43	460
EUROPE									
Albania	2.8	2.5	37	29	7	47	71	68	—
Andorra	—	—	—	—	—	—	—	—	—
Austria	7.6	0.1	21	12	12	14	75	68	10,210
Belgium	9.9	0.2	21	13	12	11	76	69	11,920
Bulgaria	8.9	0.5	22	14	11	20	75	69	—
Czechoslovakia	15.4	0.7	24	16	12	17	74	67	—
Denmark	5.1	0.3	20	11	11	9	77	71	13,120
Finland	4.8	0.4	21	13	9	8	76	68	10,680
France	54.2	0.5	22	15	10	10	77	69	12,190
German Dem. Rep.	16.7	−0.2	20	15	14	12	75	69	—
Germany, Fed. Rep. of	61.7	0.0	20	10	12	13	75	69	13,450
Greece	9.8	0.9	23	16	9	19	75	71	4,420
Hungary	10.7	0.4	21	14	14	23	73	67	2,100
Iceland	0.2	—	29	20	7	5	79	73	—
Ireland	3.5	1.3	31	22	10	12	75	70	5,230
Italy	57.4	0.4	22	11	10	14	76	70	6,960
Liechtenstein	—	—	—	—	—	—	—	—	—
Luxembourg	0.4	—	20	12	12	12	75	68	—
Malta	0.4	—	24	15	9	16	72	68	—
Monaco	—	—	—	—	—	—	—	—	—
Netherlands	14.3	0.8	23	13	8	9	78	72	11,790
Norway	4.1	0.5	23	12	10	9	78	72	14,060
Poland	36.3	0.9	24	20	10	21	75	67	—
Portugal	9.9	0.8	28	16	9	26	73	67	2,520
Romania	22.6	0.9	26	19	10	32	73	68	2,540
San Marino	—	—	—	—	—	—	—	—	—
Spain	37.9	1.1	27	15	8	11	76	70	5,640
Sweden	8.3	0.3	20	12	11	7	78	72	14,870
Switzerland	6.3	0.1	20	12	9	9	78	72	17,430
USSR	270.0	0.9	24	18	10	36	74	65	—
UK	56.1	0.1	22	14	12	12	75	69	9,110
Vatican	—	—	—	—	—	—	—	—	—
Yugloslavia	22.6	0.9	25	17	9	33	72	67	2,790
WORLD AVERAGES	4,585.0	1.7[3]	35	29	11	85	64	60	—

—Nil, not available, or does not apply.

1. Figures are latest available estimates for the late 1970s or early 1980s.
2. Indications were that by 1983 the infant mortality rate in Bangladesh may have reached 400 per 1,000 live births, highest in the world.
3. Average for 1975–80.
SOURCES: World Bank; Population Reference Bureau; *UN Statistical Yearbook, 1981*. Note that for purposes of comparison, figures are taken from standardized sources and may not always accord with data cited in the separate country articles.

Table 3. World Agriculture and Nutrition, 1981　　　　241

AFRICA	LAND AREA ('000 HA)	CROP-LAND ('000 HA)	% LABOR FORCE IN AGRICULTURE	CEREALS, OUTPUT ('000 TONS)	ROOTS AND TUBERS, OUTPUT ('000 TONS)	CATTLE ('000 HEAD)	% OF CALORIE REQUIREMENT PER CAPITA*
Algeria	238,174	7,509	56	2,254	618*	1,370*	99
Angola	124,670	3,500*	58	320	2,120*	3,200*	91
Benin	11,062	1,795*	46	459*	1,801*	770*	98
Botswana	58,537	1,360*	81	66	7*	2,950*	94
Burundi	2,565	1,305*	84	277	2,207*	872*	97
Cameroon	46,944	6,930*	81	956*	2,480*	3,284*	106
Cape Verde	403	40*	57	3*	19*	12*	95
Central African Rep.	62,298	1,945*	88	105*	1,272*	1,272*	99
Chad	125,920	3,150*	84	661*	396*	3,800*	74
Comoros	217	91*	64	19*	103*	79*	81
Congo	34,150	669*	35	19*	592*	75*	103
Djibouti	2,198	1*	—	—	—	34*	—
Egypt	99,545	2,855	44	7,795*	1,281	1,912	109
Equatorial Guinea	2,805	230*	75	—	88*	4*	—
Ethiopia	110,100	13,880*	80	4,379	1,468*	26,100*	75
Gabon	25,767	452*	77	11*	231*	4*	104
Gambia	1,000	270*	78	91	7*	333*	97
Ghana	23,002	2,760*	52	714*	3,350*	950*	86
Guinea	24,586	1,570*	81	468*	783*	1,800*	84
Guinea-Bissau	2,800	285*	83	41*	40*	210*	101
Ivory Coast	31,800	3,880*	80	935*	3,230*	720*	105
Kenya	56,925	2,275*	78	2,939	1,350*	11,500	88
Lesotho	3,035	292	84	231	6*	600*	99
Liberia	9,632	371*	72	216*	361*	40*	104
Libya	175,954	2,080	17	223*	103*	185*	126
Madagascar	58,154	3,000*	84	2,126	2,517	10,150*	115
Malawi	9,408	2,320*	84	1,781	207*	850*	90
Mali	122,000	2,050*	87	1,204	116*	5,134	90
Mauritania	103,040	195*	83	80	8*	1,200*	86
Mauritius	185	107*	29	2*	13*	57*	114
Morocco	44,630	7,719*	52	2,108	396*	3,240*	105
Mozambique	78,409	3,080*	65	400*	2,962*	1,420*	81
Namibia	82,329	657*	49	48*	140*	1,700*	95
Niger	126,670	3,350*	89	1,442	254*	3,300*	91
Nigeria	91,077	30,385*	54	9,967	28,775*	12,500*	83
Rwanda	2,495	975*	90	271	1,705*	650*	98
São Tomé and Príncipe	96	36*	—	1*	15*	3*	91
Senegal	19,200	5,225*	75	928	37*	2,260	95
Seychelles	27	5*	18	—	—	2*	—
Sierra Leone	7,162	1,766*	66	435	128*	348*	93
Somalia	62,734	1,066*	80	276	37*	3,950*	88
South Africa	122,104	13,572*	29	17,502	748*	12,200*	116
Sudan	237,600	12,417*	77	3,538	306*	18,791*	93
Swaziland	1,720	204*	74	103	16*	670*	99
Tanzania	88,604	5,160*	82	1,382	5,128*	12,701	89
Togo	5,439	1,420*	68	271	1,002	240*	90
Tunisia	15,536	4,700	32	1,262	124*	950*	112
Uganda	19,971	5,680*	81	1,344	2,450*	5,000*	91
Upper Volta	27,380	2,563*	82	1,299	119*	2,800*	79
Zaire	226,760	6,314	75	825	13,588*	1,230*	104
Zambia	74,072	5,108*	67	1,118	201*	2,225	87
Zimbabwe	38,667	2,539*	59	3,422	73*	5,261*	108
TOTALS	2,966,447	181,164	66	76,329	84,990	170,930	94
AMERICAS							
Antigua and Barbuda	44	8*	—	—	—	9*	86
Argentina	273,669	35,200*	13	30,672	2,724	54,235	126
Bahamas	1,007	16*	—	1*	—	4*	96
Barbados	43	33*	17	2*	16*	19*	133
Belize	2,280	52	29	29	17*	50*	108
Bolivia	108,439	3,370*	46	480	1,237	4,100*	83
Brazil	845,651	61,950*	39	32,023	27,762	93,000*	107
Canada	922,107	44,350*	5	50,257	2,555	12,468*	127
Chile	74,880	5,530*	16	1,535	1,014	3,745	109
Colombia	103,870	5,650*	28	3,334	4,421	24,251	102

	LAND AREA ('000 HA)	CROP-LAND ('000 HA)	% LABOR FORCE IN AGRICULTURE	CEREALS, OUTPUT ('000 TONS)	ROOTS AND TUBERS, OUTPUT ('000 TONS)	CATTLE ('000 HEAD)	% OF CALORIE REQUIREMENT PER CAPITA*
Costa Rica	5,066	490*	36	340	46	2,275	114
Cuba	11,452	3,200*	24	614*	995*	5,900*	118
Dominica	75	17*	—	—	10*	4*	87
Dominican Republic	4,838	1,230*	57	525*	349	2,155*	93
Ecuador	27,684	2,620*	45	721	597	3,032	92
El Salvador	2,072	725	41	676*	31	1,211	90
Grenada	34	14	—	—	4	8	88
Guatemala	10,843	1,834	57	1,211	45	1,730	98
Guyana	19,685	380*	22	292	28*	295*	110
Haiti	2,756	890*	67	380	691*	1,200*	93
Honduras	11,189	1,757*	61	424	18*	2,336	89
Jamaica	1,083	265*	29	10*	223*	305*	119
Mexico	192,304	23,330*	40	25,574	984	31,784*	114
Nicaragua	11,875	1,516*	42	385	28*	2,301*	109
Panama	7,599	574*	35	260*	81*	1,604*	101
Paraguay	39,730	1,920*	44	750	2,124*	5,400*	122
Peru	128,000	3,400*	40	1,656	2,361	3,895	97
St. Christopher–Nevis	36	14*	—	—	3*	8*	—
St. Lucia	61	17*	—	—	11*	11	92
St. Vincent and Grenadines	34	17*	—	1*	22*	8*	98
Suriname	16,147	52*	18	244	3*	45*	118
Trinidad and Tobago	513	158*	12	31*	23*	78*	111
Turks and Caicos	43	1*	—	—	—	—	—
US	912,680	190,624	3	333,748	15,711	114,321	135
Uruguay	17,362	1,910*	16	1,243	190*	10,971*	114
Venezuela	88,205	3,755*	19	1,773*	655	10,840	99
TOTALS	3,889,035	125,741	—	489,178	65,072	394,283	—
ASIA & OCEANIA							
Afghanistan	64,750	8,050*	78	4,664	272*	3,800*	110
Australia	761,793	44,400	6	23,242	900	25,177	129
Bahrain	62	2	3	—	—	6*	—
Bangladesh	13,391	9,145*	77	21,143	1,794	35,000*	91
Bhutan	4,700	93	94	107*	19*	306*	88
Brunei	527	9*	—	10*	4*	4*	113
Burma	65,774	10,023	65	14,881	130	8,600*	106
China	930,496	99,200*	61	286,104*	145,275*	53,410*	104
Cyprus	924	432	35	123*	219	41*	136
Fiji	1,827	236*	41	24*	149*	155*	116
India	297,319	169,130*	64	149,702	16,916	182,000*	91
Indonesia	181,135	19,500*	65	36,991	16,329	6,435*	105
Iran	163,600	15,950	37	8,585	705*	8,139*	130
Iraq	43,397	5,450*	30	2,047	108*	2,624*	89
Israel	2,033	413	6	256	196	265	122
Japan	37,103	4,881	9	13,866	5,252	4,385	126
Jordan	9,718	1,380	27	96*	13*	37*	62
Kampuchea	17,652	3,046	74	1,258	164*	956	85
Kiribati	71	36*	—	—	12*	—	—
Korea, D. P. Rep. of	12,041	2,240*	47	8,685*	1,982*	960*	121
Korea, Rep. of	9,819	2,196	34	8,026	1,666	1,531	119
Kuwait	1,782	1	2	—	—	11*	—
Laos	23,080	880*	74	1,187	134*	445	95
Lebanon	1,023	348*	11	42	148*	60*	101
Malaysia	32,855	4,310*	49	2,155	507*	540*	117
Maldives	30	3*	—	—	7*	—	90
Mongolia	156,500	1,182	50	319*	55*	2,397	104
Nauru	2	—	—	—	—	—	—
Nepal	13,680	2,330*	93	3,762	347	6,973*	91
New Zealand	26,867	453*	10	915	294*	8,581*	127
Oman	21,246	41*	62	3*	—	146	—
Pakistan	77,872	20,320*	54	18,113	560	15,084	99
Papua New Guinea	45,171	366*	83	7*	1,119*	132*	85
Philippines	29,817	9,920*	49	10,896	3,612*	1,900*	108
Qatar	1,100	2	—	1*	—	10*	—

Table 3. World Agriculture and Nutrition, 1981—*cont.*   **243**

	LAND AREA ('000 HA)	CROP-LAND ('000 HA)	% LABOR FORCE IN AGRICULTURE	CEREALS, OUTPUT ('000 TONS)	ROOTS AND TUBERS, OUTPUT ('000 TONS)	CATTLE ('000 HEAD)	% OF CALORIE REQUIREMENT PER CAPITA*
Sa'udi Arabia	214,969	1,105*	61	285*	5*	410*	88
Singapore	57	8	1	—	7*	9*	134
Solomon Islands	2,754	52*	—	9*	78*	25*	81
Sri Lanka	6,474	2,147	54	2,062	723*	1,644*	96
Syria	18,405	5,684	32	3,606	272	817	108
Taiwan	—	—	—	—	—	—	—
Thailand	51,177	17,970*	73	23,084	18,255	5,062*	105
Tonga	67	53*	—	—	94*	10*	—
Turkey	77,076	28,479	56	25,322	2,900	15,894	115
Tuvalu	3	—	—	—	—	—	—
UAE	8,360	13	5	1*	1*	26*	—
Vanuatu	1,476	95*	—	1*	30*	95*	—
Viet-Nam	32,536	6,055*	71	13,145	6,550*	1,765	83
Western Samoa	285	122	61	—	—	27*	82
Yemen, P. D. Rep. of	33,297	207*	40	102	1*	120*	81
Yemen Arab Rep.	19,500	2,790	75	808*	138*	950*	91
TOTALS	3,519,778	501,027	—	685,640	228,087	397,101	—
EUROPE							
Albania	2,740	750*	61	872*	140*	476*	113
Andorra	45	1*	—	—	—	—	—
Austria	8,273	1,635	11	4,358	1,310	2,538	134
Belgium[1]	3,282	878	—	2,016*	1,426	3,116*	—
Bulgaria	11,055	4,181	34	8,495	407	1,796	144
Czechoslovakia	12,549	5,169	11	9,607	3,500	5,002*	139
Denmark	4,237	2,653	8	7,185	910	2,933	127
Finland	30,547	2,399	11	2,412	478	1,776	114
France	54,563	18,643	8	45,004	6,480	23,553	136
German Dem. Rep.	10,610	5,034	10	9,147*	10,500*	5,722	139
Germany, Fed. Rep. of	24,434	7,494	6	22,826	8,045	15,069	127
Greece	13,080	3,926	38	4,955	957	899	136
Hungary	9,234	5,333	22	12,524	1,603	1,918	134
Iceland	10,025	8	12	—	9*	60	110
Ireland	6,889	972*	19	1,821	1,100*	6,696	141
Italy	29,402	12,465	14	18,642	2,886	8,734	136
Liechtenstein	16	4	—	—	11*	9*	—
Luxembourg[1]							
Malta	32	14*	6	5*	22*	15*	129
Monaco	—	—	—	—	—	—	—
Netherlands	3,396	861	6	1,276	6,445	5,100	124
Norway	30,787	812	8	1,135*	530*	988*	118
Poland	30,454	14,901	30	19,699	42,600	11,801*	140
Portugal	9,164	3,550*	27	1,082	1,005	1,000*	126
Romania	23,034	10,497	48	19,705	4,500*	6,258*	130
San Marino	6	1*	—	—	—	—	—
Spain	49,954	20,510*	17	11,546	5,621	4,531	128
Sweden	41,162	2,979	6	5,680	1,278	1,935*	120
Switzerland	3,977	396	7	819	1,048	1,954*	130
USSR	2,227,200	231,966	17	167,306*	72,000	115,057	135
UK	24,160	6,996	2	19,306	6,108	13,109*	132
Vatican	—	—	—	—	—	—	—
Yugoslavia	25,540	7,884	39	15,238	2,500*	5,484	136
TOTALS	2,699,988	372,915	16	412,652	183,418	249,132	133
WORLD TOTALS	13,075,248	1,452,215	46	1,663,828	561,567	1,209,833	109

*Estimate or projection.

—Nil, not available, or does not apply.

1. Figures for Luxembourg are included in the Belgium totals.

SOURCES: FAO; Population Reference Bureau. Note that for purposes of comparison, figures are taken from standardized sources and do not always accord with data cited in the separate country articles. Columns may not add to totals because of rounding and omissions in sources.

| | ELECTRIC POWER | | | COAL AND LIGNITE OUTPUT | NATURAL GAS OUTPUT | CRUDE PETROLEUM | | CONSUMPTION | |
| | TOTAL | HYDRO | NUCLEAR | | | PROVED RESERVES | PRODUCTION | ('000 | CHANGE |
	('000,000 KWH)	('000,000 KWH)	('000,000 KWH)	('000,000 TONS)	(BILLION FT³)	('000 TONS)	('000 TONS)	TONS)	1970–81(%)
AFRICA									
Algeria	7,170	260	—	—	1,150,000	1,119,000	39,530*	4,380	189
Angola	1,500	1,100	—	—	—	—	7,158*	1,300	87
Benin	5	—	—	—	—	—	—	—	—
Botswana	—	—	—	—	—	—	—	—	—
Burundi	2	—	—	—	—	—	—	—	—
Cameroon	1,655	1,561	—	—	—	—	4,000*	2,566	—
Cape Verde	9	—	—	—	—	—	—	—	—
Central African Rep.	65	61	—	—	—	—	—	—	—
Chad	65	—	—	—	—	—	—	—	—
Comoros	10	—	—	—	—	—	—	—	—
Congo	165	90	—	—	—	—	3,910	410	—
Djibouti	110	—	—	—	—	—	—	—	—
Egypt	18,590	9,650	—	—	—	—	32,500	14,500	330
Equatorial Guinea	26	2	—	—	—	—	—	—	—
Ethiopia	677	480	—	—	—	—	—	601	1
Gabon	450	350	—	—	—	61,000	7,500*	1,500	64
Gambia	40	—	—	—	—	—	—	—	—
Ghana	5,053	5,000	—	—	—	—	—	950	12
Guinea	498	80	—	—	—	—	—	—	—
Guinea-Bissau	13	—	—	—	—	—	—	—	—
Ivory Coast	1,903	1,744	—	—	—	—	200	1,129	58
Kenya	1,715	1,381	—	—	—	—	—	2,332	81
Lesotho	—	—	—	—	—	—	—	—	—
Liberia	1,100	300	—	—	—	—	—	635	52
Libya	5,600	—	—	—	150,000	3,138,000	55,120	6,140	1,311
Madagascar	425	125	—	—	—	—	—	380	−33
Malawi	428	402	—	—	—	—	—	—	—
Mali	110	50	—	—	—	—	—	—	—
Mauritania	102	—	—	—	—	—	—	—	—
Mauritius	441	60	—	—	—	—	—	—	—
Morocco	5,277	1,517	—	—	—	—	15*	4,805	208
Mozambique	3,800	3,350	—	—	—	—	—	500	−33
Namibia	—	—	—	—	—	—	—	—	—
Niger	60	—	—	—	—	—	—	—	—
Nigeria	7,260	3,800	—	—	—	2,278,000	71,192	6,800	501
Rwanda	163	155	—	—	—	—	—	—	—
São Tomé and Príncipe	11	3	—	—	—	—	—	—	—
Senegal	599	—	—	—	—	—	—	750	33
Seychelles	51	—	—	—	—	—	—	—	—
Sierra Leone	235	—	—	—	—	—	—	255	−23
Somalia	75	—	—	125	—	—	—	346	—
South Africa	98,206	1,801	—	—	—	—	—	17,000	105
Sudan	1,000	500	—	—	—	—	—	1,130	36
Swaziland	—	—	—	—	—	—	—	—	—
Tanzania	715	550	—	—	—	—	—	750	3
Togo	84	19	—	—	—	—	—	500	—
Tunisia	3,020	29	—	—	—	—	5,407	1,583	36
Uganda	657	650	—	—	—	—	—	—	—
Upper Volta	115	—	—	—	—	—	—	—	—
Zaire	4,560	4,500	—	—	—	—	1,000*	370	−45
Zambia	9,100	9,000	—	1	—	—	—	747	—
Zimbabwe	4,519	4,114	—	3	—	—	—	—	—
TOTALS	187,859	52,789	—	131	1,370,000	7,524,000	227,532	72,371	156
AMERICAS									
Antigua and Barbuda	63	—	—	—	—	—	—	—	−100
Argentina	39,288	14,670	2,816	—	350,000	—	25,534	26,915	24
Bahamas	860	—	—	—	—	—	—	8,400	236
Barbados	327	—	—	—	—	—	29	193	61
Belize	55	—	—	—	—	—	—	—	—
Bolivia	1,677	1,155	—	—	70,000	—	1,029	1,009	74
Brazil	142,430	130,680	—	5	—	—	10,366	52,437	108
Canada	377,624	263,164	36,892	39	2,470,000	873,000	62,928	80,903	38
Chile	11,978	7,588	—	—	—	—	1,871	4,285	19
Colombia	23,690	16,320	—	5	140,000	—	6,925	8,044	13

Table 4. World Energy Production and Consumption, 1981—*cont.*

	ELECTRIC POWER			COAL AND LIGNITE OUTPUT	NATURAL GAS OUTPUT	CRUDE PETROLEUM			
	TOTAL ('000,000 KWH)	HYDRO ('000,000 KWH)	NUCLEAR ('000,000 KWH)	('000,000 TONS)	(BILLION FT³)	PROVED RESERVES ('000 TONS)	PRODUCTION ('000 TONS)	CONSUMPTION ('000 TONS)	CHANGE 1970–81(%)
Costa Rica	2,300	2,140	—	—	—	—	—	470	49
Cuba	10,572	60	—	—	—	—	278	6,378	48
Dominica	18	16	—	—	—	—	—	—	—
Dominican Republic	3,350	37	—	—	—	—	—	1,455	—
Ecuador	2,950	950	—	—	—	—	10,733	4,477	289
El Salvador	1,565	1,050	—	—	—	—	—	665	287
Grenada	25	—	—	—	—	—	—	—	—
Guatemala	1,995	325	—	—	—	—	206	896	19
Guyana	440	—	—	—	—	—	—	—	—
Haiti	325	225	—	—	—	—	—	—	—
Honduras	955	640	—	—	—	—	—	520	−27
Jamaica	2,325	125	—	—	—	—	—	975	−36
Mexico	73,559	24,618	—	7	1,100,000	6,003,000	115,408	55,317	154
Nicaragua	1,100	520	—	—	—	—	—	555	25
Panama	2,565	1,245	—	—	—	—	—	1,950	−47
Paraguay	975	905	—	—	—	—	—	250	34
Peru	10,100	7,800	—	—	—	—	9,552	6,890	69
St. Christopher–Nevis	32	—	—	—	—	—	—	—	—
St. Lucia	60	—	—	—	—	—	—	—	—
St. Vincent and Grenadines	29	18	—	—	—	—	—	—	—
Suriname	1,670	1,380	—	—	—	—	—	—	—
Trinidad and Tobago	2,050	—	—	—	190,000	—	9,780	10,391	−52
Turks and Caicos	11	—	—	—	—	—	—	—	—
US	2,365,062	262,434	272,674	733	19,420,000	3,602,000	421,804	614,860	14
Uruguay	3,603	2,546	—	—	—	—	—	1,746	−5
Venezuela	37,542	15,090	—	—	580,000	2,449,000	111,578	44,986	−33
TOTALS	3,140,383	755,847	312,382	790	24,510,000	13,955,000	788,021	989,140	15
ASIA & OCEANIA									
Afghanistan	1,035	715	—	—	—	—	—	—	—
Australia	103,108	18,000	—	135	400,000	322,000	19,907	28,071	18
Bahrain	1,830	—	—	—	130,000	—	2,290	12,808	3
Bangladesh	2,962	626	—	—	—	—	6	1,319	—
Bhutan	22	19	—	—	—	—	—	—	—
Brunei	405	—	—	—	300,000	—	7,933	−270	−687
Burma	1,500	915	—	—	—	—	1,685*	1,310	24
China	309,300	65,550	—	655	460,000	2,797,000	101,220	87,220	258
Cyprus	1,060	—	—	—	—	—	—	511	—
Fiji	311	—	—	—	—	—	—	—	—
India	125,900	49,155	3,170	121	—	352,000	14,925	29,528	60
Indonesia	7,750	2,820	—	—	630,000	1,296,000	78,662	25,075	112
Iran	16,900	3,000	—	—	60,000	7,844,000	65,226	29,226	11
Iraq	6,290	690	—	—	—	4,093,000	44,992	8,100	113
Israel	13,112	—	—	—	—	—	16	6,696	12
Japan	583,249	90,567	87,820	18	80,000	—	387	196,446	16
Jordan	1,237	—	—	—	—	—	—	2,172	373
Kampuchea	175	—	—	—	—	—	—	—	−100
Kiribati	6	—	—	—	—	—	—	—	—
Korea, D. P. Rep. of	36,000	23,000	—	—	—	—	—	2,000	—
Korea, Rep. of	43,667	2,709	2,897	20	—	—	—	24,750	152
Kuwait	10,336	—	—	—	270,000	9,268,000	56,502	14,614	−29
Laos	1,150	1,100	—	—	—	—	—	—	—
Lebanon	1,810	850	—	—	—	—	—	1,790	−10
Malaysia	9,541	1,334	—	—	—	—	13,650*	5,630	6
Maldives	5	—	—	—	—	—	—	—	—
Mongolia	1,750	—	—	—	—	—	—	—	−100
Nauru	26	—	—	—	—	—	—	—	—
Nepal	232	190	—	—	—	—	—	—	—
New Zealand	22,706	19,483	—	2	—	—	—	2,333	−15
Oman	965	—	—	—	—	309,000	16,300	—	—
Pakistan	16,068	9,054	150	—	420,000	—	484	4,244	−39
Papua New Guinea	1,350	430	—	—	—	—	—	—	—
Philippines	19,040	3,753	—	—	—	—	450*	9,975	97
Qatar	2,515	—	—	—	—	489,000	19,502	435	867

Table 4. World Energy Production and Consumption, 1981—cont.

| | ELECTRIC POWER | | | COAL AND LIGNITE OUTPUT | NATURAL GAS OUTPUT | CRUDE PETROLEUM | | CONSUMPTION | |
	TOTAL ('000,000 KWH)	HYDRO ('000,000 KWH)	NUCLEAR ('000,000 KWH)	('000,000 TONS)	(BILLION FT³)	PROVED RESERVES ('000 TONS)	PRODUCTION ('000 TONS)	('000 TONS)	CHANGE 1970–81(%)
ASIA & OCEANIA									
Sa'udi Arabia	11,100	—	—	—	430,000	22,923,000	491,132	30,100	3
Singapore	7,442	—	—	—	—	—	—	34,675	217
Solomon Islands	21	—	—	—	—	—	—	—	—
Sri Lanka	1,870	1,665	—	—	—	—	—	1,607	−11
Syria	3,920	2,600	—	—	—	—	8,520	6,200	214
Taiwan	—	—	—	—	—	—	—	—	—
Thailand	15,960	3,940	—	—	—	—	8	8,843	141
Tonga	12	—	—	—	—	—	—	—	—
Turkey	24,100	11,500	—	127	—	—	2,362	13,439	86
Tuvalu	—	—	—	—	—	—	—	—	—
UAE	6,050	—	—	—	230,000	—	72,872	2,400	—
Vanuatu	20	—	—	—	—	—	—	—	—
Viet-Nam	4,000	700	—	—	—	—	—	—	—
Western Samoa	39	7	—	—	—	—	—	—	—
Yemen, P. D. Rep. of	260	—	—	—	—	—	—	2,070	−70
Yemen Arab Rep.	228	—	—	—	—	—	—	—	—
TOTALS	1,480,138	318,382	102,387	969	4,040,000	54,871,000	1,019,215	613,161	46
EUROPE									
Albania	2,650	2,100	—	—	—	—	2,200*	2,200	56
Andorra	—	—	—	—	—	—	—	—	—
Austria	42,895	30,831	—	3	—	—	1,338	8,826	42
Belgium	50,755	1,084	12,859	6	—	—	—	29,257	−2
Bulgaria	36,972	3,618	9,119	—	—	—	300*	12,800	116
Czechoslovakia	74,054	5,654	4,700	124	—	—	89	18,889	88
Denmark	18,091	20	—	—	—	—	758	6,296	−38
Finland	39,070	13,420	13,970	—	—	—	—	11,114	35
France	282,480[1]	72,600[1]	113,480[1]	22	290,000	—	1,676[1]	97,304[1]	−5[1]
German Dem. Rep.	100,720	1,736	11,902	256	300,000	—	50*	20,550	97
Germany, Fed. Rep. of	368,770	21,400	51,000	221	680,000	—	4,459	85,453	−20
Greece	23,433	3,408	—	23	—	—	196	15,946	216
Hungary	24,219	168	—	—	210,000	—	2,024	9,218	54
Iceland	3,295	3,040	—	—	—	—	—	—	—
Ireland	10,909	1,242	—	—	—	—	—	603	−78
Italy	181,755[2]	45,700[2]	2,855[2]	2	490,000	—	1,466[2]	85,596[2]	−26[2]
Liechtenstein	—[3]	—[3]	—[3]	—	—	—	—	—[3]	—[3]
Luxembourg	1,195	573	—	—	—	—	—	—	—
Malta	558	—	—	—	—	—	—	—	—
Monaco	[1]	[1]	[1]	—	—	—	[1]	[1]	[1]
Netherlands	64,860	—	4,100	—	2,500,000	—	1,348	40,391	−35
Norway	92,770	92,693	—	—	920,000	750,000	23,503	7,205	22
Poland	115,006	3,014	—	196	220,000	—	315	13,825	85
Portugal	13,948	5,193	—	—	—	—	—	7,960	119
Romania	70,138	12,737	—	—	1,440,000	—	11,600*	24,700	58
San Marino	[2]	[2]	[2]	—	—	—	[2]	[2]	[2]
Spain	110,696	22,909	9,564	35	—	—	1,229	48,802	58
Sweden	103,548	60,220	37,802	—	—	—	6	14,201	21
Switzerland	51,515[3]	36,097[3]	14,462[3]	—	—	—	—	4,016[3]	−27[3]
USSR	1,326,031	186,744	68,000	704	16,420,000	8,595,000	609,000	496,000	71
UK	277,735	5,385	37,969	127	1,340,000	—	88,216	71,562	−29
Vatican	—	—	—	—	—	—	—	—	—
Yugoslavia	60,390	25,118	291	—	—	—	4,375	13,729	89
TOTALS	3,548,681	656,754	392,073	—	25,010,000	1,744,000	754,148	1,146,443	19
WORLD TOTALS	8,357,061	1,783,772	806,842	3,808	54,930,000	88,475,000	2,788,916	2,821,121	24

*Estimate or projection.
—Nil, not available, or does not apply.
1. Figures for France include Monaco.
2. Figures for Italy include San Marino.
3. Figures for Switzerland include Liechtenstein.
SOURCES: OECD; OPEC; UN *Yearbook of World Energy Statistics*; US Energy Information Administration. Note that for purposes of comparison, figures are derived from standardized sources and do not always accord with data cited in the separate country articles. Columns may not add to totals because of rounding and omissions in sources.

Table 5. World Industrial Production, 1980–81   **247**

	% LABOR FORCE IN INDUSTRY, 1980	% OF GDP IN INDUSTRY, 1981	GROWTH OF INDUSTRIAL PRODUCTION (%, 1970–81), ANNUAL AVG.	CEMENT, 1980 ('000 TONS)	CRUDE STEEL, 1980 ('000 TONS)	MOTOR VEHICLES, 1981	TELEVISION RECEIVERS, 1980 ('000)	SUGAR, 1980 ('000 TONS)	CIGARETTES, 1980 ('000,000)
AFRICA									
Algeria	25	55	7.6	4,159	345	—	75	15	15,150
Angola	16	—	—	400	—	—	—	50	2,400
Benin	16	13	—	—	—	—	—	—	—
Botswana	—	—	—	—	—	—	—	—	—
Burundi	5	16	8.5	—	—	—	—	—	—
Cameroon	7	20	9.4	227	—	—	—	58	1,340
Cape Verde	—	—	—	15	—	—	—	—	—
Central African Rep.	4	13	4.0	—	—	—	—	—	—
Chad	7	—	—	—	—	—	—	30	349
Comoros	—	—	—	—	—	—	—	—	—
Congo	26	53	13.6	34	—	—	—	20	706
Djibouti	—	—	—	—	—	—	—	—	—
Egypt	30	38	7.6*	2,994	762	—	—	620	32,500
Equatorial Guinea	—	—	—	—	—	—	—	—	—
Ethiopia	7	16	1.8	123	—	—	—	163	1,458
Gabon	—	—	—	100	—	—	1	—	315
Gambia	—	—	—	—	—	—	—	—	—
Ghana	20	12	−2.2	—	—	—	—	20	1,300
Guinea	11	33*	—	—	—	—	—	20	—
Guinea-Bissau	—	—	—	—	—	—	—	—	—
Ivory Coast	4	23	9.3	—	—	—	—	90	3,480
Kenya	10	21*	8.5	1,228	—	—	—	400	4,501
Lesotho	4	21	12.9*	—	—	—	—	—	—
Liberia	14	—	−0.7	108	—	—	—	—	140
Libya	28	71	3.1	—	—	—	—	—	3,300
Madagascar	4	14	0.3	60	—	—	—	116	1,983
Malawi	5	20*	—	92	—	—	—	156	630
Mali	12	11	2.4	26	—	—	—	19	—
Mauritania	8*	24	−4.0	—	—	—	—	—	—
Mauritius	—	—	—	—	—	—	—	504	959
Morocco	21	34	5.8	3,561	—	—	—	398	11,491
Mozambique	18	—	—	277	—	—	—	170	3,300
Namibia	—	—	—	—	—	—	—	—	—
Niger	3	32	11.4	39	—	—	—	—	—
Nigeria	19	37	6.0	1,714	—	—	208	35	11,063
Rwanda	2	22	—	—	—	—	—	—	—
São Tomé and Príncipe	—	—	—	—	—	—	—	—	—
Senegal	10	26	4.1	371	—	—	—	45	2,703
Seychelles	—	—	—	—	—	—	—	—	31
Sierra Leone	19	20	−3.6	—	—	—	—	—	1,451
Somalia	8	—	—	—	—	—	—	35	—
South Africa	29	53*	—	7,125	8,959	—	344	1,780	28,151
Sudan	10	14	3.2	181	—	—	—	195	730
Swaziland	—	—	—	—	—	—	—	328	—
Tanzania	6	15*	2.2	306	—	—	—	122	4,735
Togo	15	27	6.2	304	—	—	—	—	—
Tunisia	32	37	9.3	1,780	178	—	88	8	4,419
Uganda	6	4	−9.8	5	2	—	—	15	636
Upper Volta	13	16	2.9	—	—	—	—	30	—
Zaire	13	24	−0.8	399	—	—	—	55	2,700
Zambia	11	32	−0.4	299	—	—	—	111	1,283
Zimbabwe	15	37	—	469	898	—	—	358	3,900
AMERICAS									
Antigua and Barbuda	—	—	—	—	—	—	—	—	—
Argentina	28	38*	1.4	7,263	2,556	172,350	454	1,716	34,680
Bahamas	—	—	—	544	—	—	—	—	—
Barbados	—	—	—	—	—	—	—	135	224
Belize	—	—	—	—	—	—	—	108	63
Bolivia	24	27	3.7	260	—	—	—	262	1,300
Brazil	24	34*	9.1*	25,873	10,232	779,836	3,211	8,270	142,300
Canada	29	32	2.9	10,340	15,901	1,322,780	—	92	67,180

Table 5. World Industrial Production, 1980–81—*cont.*

	% LABOR FORCE IN INDUSTRY, 1980	% OF GDP IN INDUSTRY, 1981	GROWTH OF INDUSTRIAL PRODUCTION (%, 1970–81), ANNUAL AVG.	CEMENT, 1980 ('000 TONS)	CRUDE STEEL, 1980 ('000 TONS)	MOTOR VEHICLES, 1981	TELEVISION RECEIVERS, 1980 ('000)	SUGAR, 1980 ('000 TONS)	CIGARETTES, 1980 ('000,000)
Chile	19	35	0.7	1,583	695	—	—	65	10,510
Colombia	21	31	4.7	4,336	263	—	—	1,247	21,200
Costa Rica	23	28	7.4	440	—	—	—	220	2,452
Cuba	31	—	—	2,831	304	—	40	6,805	15,109
Dominica	—	—	—	—	—	—	—	—	—
Dominican Republic	18	27*	7.6	928	—	—	—	1,013	3,379
Ecuador	17	38	12.5	1,397	—	—	—	368	3,858
El Salvador	22	20	3.3	550	—	—	—	217	2,500
Grenada	—	—	—	—	—	—	—	—	—
Guatemala	21	—	7.3	576	—	—	—	452	2,699
Guyana	—	—	—	—	—	—	—	286	567
Haiti	7	—	7.1	243	—	—	—	65	1,094
Honduras	15	25	4.9	635	—	—	—	191	2,475
Jamaica	25	37	-3.6	144	—	—	—	236	1,283
Mexico	26	37	7.4	16,398	7,003	597,118	964	2,719	54,520
Nicaragua	20*	33	2.1	349	—	—	—	190	2,228
Panama	18	21*	4.1	499	—	—	—	200	1,083
Paraguay	20*	26	11.0	177	—	—	—	89	648
Peru	18*	41	3.4	2,994	471	—	—	537	4,034
St. Christopher–Nevis	—	—	—	—	—	—	—	36	—
St. Lucia	—	—	—	—	—	—	—	—	—
St. Vincent and Grenadines	—	—	—	—	—	—	—	—	—
Suriname	—	—	—	43	—	—	—	12	379
Trinidad and Tobago	39	52	4.0	186	—	—	—	114	1,300
Turks and Caicos	—	—	—	—	—	—	—	—	—
US	32	34	2.3	67,675	101,456	7,942,916	—	5,313	697,000
Uruguay	32	33	3.5	684	17	—	—	102	3,914
Venezuela	27	45	2.7	4,100	2,077	—	—	358	21,500
ASIA & OCEANIA									
Afghanistan	8	—	3.2*	80	—	—	—	3	—
Australia	33	—	—	5,201	7,895	391,614	332	3,415	33,146
Bahrain	—	—	—	—	—	—	—	—	—
Bangladesh	11	14	9.0	341	137	—	—	120	13,830
Bhutan	2	—	—	—	—	—	—	—	—
Brunei	—	—	—	—	—	—	—	—	—
Burma	10	13	5.6	221	—	—	—	5	2,575
China	19*	46	8.3	79,860	37,120	—	2,492	2,800	—
Cyprus	—	—	—	1,233	—	—	—	—	2,301
Fiji	—	—	—	83	—	—	—	453	549
India	13	26*	4.4	17,803	9,327	148,887	—	4,528	77,376
Indonesia	15	42	11.2	5,259	—	—	730	1,171	81,610
Iran	34	—	—	8,981	—	—	—	350	10,000
Iraq	26	—	—	5,300	350	—	—	20	7,500
Israel	36	36*	—	2,092	100	—	24	10	5,337
Japan	39	43*	5.6*	87,957	111,395	11,179,962	15,205	793	303,177
Jordan	26	30*	—	913	—	—	—	—	—
Kampuchea	—	—	—	—	—	—	—	—	4,100
Kiribati	—	—	—	—	—	—	—	—	—
Korea, D. P. Rep. of	33	—	—	8,000	3,500	—	—	—	—
Korea, Rep. of	29	39	14.4	15,631	5,790	133,084	6,819	—	70,351
Kuwait	34	71	-2.2	1,307	—	—	—	—	—
Laos	6	—	—	—	—	—	—	—	1,100
Lebanon	27	—	—	2,200	—	—	—	10	150
Malaysia	16	36	9.3	2,349	—	—	157	50	13,529
Maldives	—	—	—	—	—	—	—	—	—
Mongolia	22	—	—	178	—	—	—	—	—
Nauru	—	—	—	—	—	—	—	—	—
Nepal	2	—	—	29	—	—	—	15	164
New Zealand	35	31*	—	720	—	—	126	—	6,276
Oman	—	—	—	—	—	—	—	—	—
Pakistan	20	26	5.5	3,343	—	—	—	686	34,647
Papua New Guinea	8	—	—	—	—	—	—	—	—
Philippines	17	37	8.4	4,516	—	—	206	2,332	58,810
Qatar	—	—	—	207	—	—	—	—	—

Table 5. World Industrial Production, 1980–81—cont. 249

	% LABOR FORCE IN INDUSTRY, 1980	% OF GDP IN INDUSTRY, 1981	GROWTH OF INDUSTRIAL PRODUCTION (%, 1970–81), ANNUAL AVG.	CEMENT, 1980 ('000 TONS)	CRUDE STEEL, 1980 ('000 TONS)	MOTOR VEHICLES, 1981	TELEVISION RECEIVERS, 1980 ('000)	SUGAR, 1980 ('000 TONS)	CIGARETTES, 1980 ('000,000)
Sa'udi Arabia	14	78	10.2*	3,200	—	—	—	—	—
Singapore	33	41	9.0	1,952	—	—	1,889	—	3,147
Solomon Islands	—	—	—	—	—	—	—	—	—
Sri Lanka	14	28	4.2	633	—	—	—	26	4,900
Syria	31	31	9.8*	1,995	—	—	72	47	6,943
Taiwan	—	—	—	—	—	—	—	—	—
Thailand	9	28	9.9	5,337	454	—	249	778	30,788
Tonga	—	—	—	—	—	—	—	—	—
Turkey	13	32	6.1	14,802	1,700	—	327	1,140	51,977
Tuvalu	—	—	—	—	—	—	—	—	—
UAE	—	77*	—	—	—	—	—	—	—
Vanuatu	—	—	—	—	—	—	—	—	—
Viet-Nam	10	—	—	848	—	—	—	130	—
Western Samoa	—	—	—	—	—	—	—	—	—
Yemen, P. D. Rep. of	15	28*	—	—	—	—	—	—	—
Yemen Arab Rep.	11	16	13.9	81	—	—	—	—	—
EUROPE									
Albania	25	—	—	1,000	—	—	—	25	6,100
Andorra	—	—	—	—	—	—	—	—	—
Austria	37	39	3.2	5,455	4,624	14,920	—	441	15,260
Belgium	41	37*	3.1*	7,482	12,323	257,456	746	874	28,167
Bulgaria	39	—	—	5,429	2,565	—	91	200	85,180
Czechoslovakia	48	—	—	10,546	15,225	229,513	389	841	22,543
Denmark	35	32	1.1	1,917	196	—	77	499	9,390
Finland	35	36	3.3	1,787	2,509	—	—	125	7,035
France	39	35	2.7	29,100	23,176	3,019,370	1,928	3,913	73,125
German Dem. Rep.	50	—	—	12,440	7,308	219,400	578	662	26,008
Germany, Fed. Rep. of	46	46	—	34,551	43,838	3,897,007	4,425	2,935	160,993
Greece	28	31	4.5	13,260	1,089	—	—	198	24,889
Hungary	43	48	5.8	4,660	3,766	13,788	417	509	27,158
Iceland	—	—	—	131	—	—	—	—	—
Ireland	37	—	—	—	—	—	—	187	9,660
Italy	45	42	2.9	41,862	26,501	1,433,743	1,984	1,892	73,090
Liechtenstein	—	—	—	—	—	—	—	—	—
Luxembourg	—	—	—	325	4,624	—	—	—	—
Malta	—	—	—	—	—	—	—	—	430
Monaco	—	—	—	—	—	—	—	—	—
Netherlands	45	33	2.0*	3,745	4,959	89,933	—	951	40,705
Norway	37	41	5.0	2,093	866	—	—	—	820
Poland	39	—	—	18,428	18,648	306,700	900	1,155	93,446
Portugal	35	44	4.4	5,858	312	98	453	15	11,866
Romania	36	60*	9.2	14,607	13,175	127,000	541	600	33,000
San Marino	—	—	—	—	—	—	—	—	—
Spain	40	36	3.9*	28,752	12,553	987,474	—	968	57,800
Sweden	34	31	0.8	2,523	4,237	313,755	—	333	10,900
Switzerland	46	—	—	4,252	929	1,178	—	105	31,264
USSR	45	—	—	125,049	147,941	2,197,000	7,528	7,250	363,971
UK	42	33	0.4	14,805	11,277	1,184,205	2,357	1,347	135,908
Vatican	—	—	—	—	—	—	—	—	—
Yugoslavia	35	43	6.8	9,716	2,306	266,423	505	758	59,103
WORLD TOTALS	—	—	—	867,720	706,472	37,277,510	69,396	84,631	3,497,183

* Estimate or projection.

—Nil, not available, or does not apply.

SOURCES: World Bank; *World Motor Vehicle Data, 1982*; *UN Statistical Yearbook, 1981*. Note that for purposes of comparison, figures are taken from standardized sources and do not always accord with data cited in the separate country articles. Columns may not add to totals because of rounding and omissions in sources. For the purposes of this table, the industrial sector includes manufacturing, mining (including petroleum), construction, and utilities.

Table 6: Economic Development Assistance to 1982
(millions of US dollars)

	BILATERAL AID GRANTED BY SOURCE		MULTILATERAL AID RECEIVED BY SOURCE (1946–82)								
	OECD (1977–82)	OPEC (1977–81)	IBRD	IFC	IDA	UNDP	ADB	AsDB	IDB	EEC	TOTALS
AFRICA											
Algeria	—	493.0	934.9	—	—	55.3	13.4	—	—	55.3	1,066.5
Angola	—	—	—	—	—	15.6	—	—	—	—	24.7
Benin	—	—	—	—	84.3	24.6	74.3	—	—	70.8	260.3
Botswana	—	—	142.7	0.4	15.9	15.1	31.3	—	—	6.5	214.2
Burundi	—	—	4.8	5.6	93.0	42.9	63.5	—	—	60.3	279.4
Cameroon	—	—	492.3	14.4	233.2	42.9	33.9	—	—	223.4	1,047.4
Cape Verde	—	—	—	—	—	5.9	22.3	—	—	—	29.2
Central African Rep.	—	—	—	—	31.4	25.4	42.2	—	—	74.4	179.1
Chad	—	—	—	—	59.9	25.0	49.1	—	—	106.8	250.4
Comoros	—	—	—	—	10.2	9.7	37.2	—	—	—	57.5
Congo	—	—	76.0	3.7	57.2	24.2	33.7	—	—	79.6	276.6
Djibouti	—	—	—	—	—	4.7	—	—	—	—	5.1
Egypt	—	—	1,576.1	86.7	776.8	94.6	60.8	—	—	65.0	2,689.9
Equatorial Guinea	—	—	—	—	8.2	5.2	—	—	—	—	13.4
Ethiopia	—	—	108.6	15.5	341.6	93.6	90.9	—	—	—	699.3
Gabon	—	—	67.0	—	—	16.8	18.0	—	—	89.9	192.9
Gambia	—	—	—	—	27.5	7.0	34.2	—	—	—	70.1
Ghana	—	—	190.5	—	180.9	42.4	29.5	—	—	16.0	472.3
Guinea	—	—	73.5	—	65.9	53.3	30.4	—	—	44.4	276.6
Guinea-Bissau	—	—	—	—	9.0	14.2	28.2	—	—	—	52.5
Ivory Coast	—	—	996.1	11.4	7.5	35.2	15.7	—	—	254.7	1,328.2
Kenya	—	—	970.8	61.0	408.4	61.2	57.1	—	—	58.9	1,634.6
Lesotho	—	—	—	0.3	61.0	22.5	43.3	—	—	—	130.4
Liberia	—	—	155.7	0.6	44.0	25.3	27.4	—	—	7.4	267.9
Libya	—	751.0	—	—	—	23.7	—	—	—	—	26.0
Madagascar	—	—	32.6	12.5	257.0	45.8	47.8	—	—	192.9	599.1
Malawi	—	—	75.2	26.0	188.9	39.8	85.4	—	—	14.5	438.1
Mali	—	—	—	3.2	176.0	49.8	85.2	—	—	126.1	459.3
Mauritania	—	—	126.0	17.9	48.1	18.0	34.3	—	—	96.3	347.2
Mauritius	—	—	116.3	0.5	20.4	12.8	19.8	—	—	17.3	189.0
Morocco	—	—	1,908.5	62	52.6	60.1	26.8	—	—	56.0	2,188.0
Mozambique	—	—	—	—	—	17.9	71.7	—	—	—	99.7
Namibia	—	—	—	—	—	5.7	—	—	—	—	5.7
Niger	—	—	—	2.6	138.4	45.3	28.5	—	—	127.3	352.0
Nigeria	—	323.0	1,975.9	22.3	39.9	83.7	9.6	—	—	50.0	2,217.7
Rwanda	—	—	—	0.8	115.7	28.4	68.1	—	—	60.2	281.3
São Tomé and Príncipe	—	—	—	—	—	1.5	8.7	—	—	—	10.6
Senegal	—	—	155.7	32.8	187.5	35.6	33.7	—	—	201.6	653.1
Seychelles	—	—	—	—	—	2.6	20.2	—	—	—	23.2
Sierra Leone	—	—	18.7	2.1	34.0	34.7	36.4	—	—	—	120.2
Somalia	—	—	—	0.4	148.4	49.5	52.8	—	—	78.5	343.4
South Africa	—	—	241.8	—	—	—	—	—	—	—	242.3
Sudan	—	—	139.2	33.2	492.6	80.6	78.8	—	—	—	868.3
Swaziland	—	—	60.7	8.5	8.4	11.6	27.6	—	—	19.0	137.8
Tanzania	—	—	317.2	7.2	572.3	70.4	75.6	—	—	5.0	1,088.7
Togo	—	—	3.5	—	83.0	29.6	59.8	—	—	90.4	270.1
Tunisia	—	—	1,056.3	61.8	75.2	47.0	23.4	—	—	41.0	1,314.1
Uganda	—	—	8.4	3.2	120.5	52.7	27.2	—	—	—	228.4
Upper Volta	—	—	—	0.5	129.1	37.1	52.4	—	—	111.4	342.6
Zaire	—	—	221.6	4.9	278.5	69.3	72.6	—	—	192.4	865.6
Zambia	—	—	576.0	75.8	37.3	31.5	62.2	—	—	42.0	828.6
Zimbabwe	—	—	179.0	38.0	—	7.3	12.2	—	—	—	242.6
AMERICAS											
Antigua and Barbuda	—	—	—	—	—	—	—	—	—	—	—
Argentina	—	—	1,706.7	183.1	—	53.8	—	—	2,233.4	—	4,180.6
Bahamas	—	—	22.8	—	—	4.1	—	—	3.2	—	30.1
Barbados	—	—	35.7	—	—	5.0	—	—	56.3	7.5	104.7
Belize	—	—	—	—	—	2.5	—	—	—	—	3.4
Bolivia	—	—	289.7	9.3	109.4	40.5	—	—	676.5	—	1,134.2
Brazil	—	—	6,998.9	938.4	—	85.7	—	—	3,768.6	—	11,810.1
Canada	6,556.0	—	—	—	—	—	—	—	—	—	0.1

Table 6: Economic Development Assistance to 1982—*cont.*
(millions of US dollars)

	BILATERAL AID GRANTED BY SOURCE		MULTILATERAL AID RECEIVED BY SOURCE (1946–82)								
	OECD (1977–82)	OPEC (1977–81)	IBRD	IFC	IDA	UNDP	ADB	AsDB	IDB	EEC	TOTALS
Chile	—	—	442.1	24.5	22.9	59.3	—	—	848.5	—	1,405.0
Colombia	—	—	3,553.2	94.5	23.5	55.6	—	—	1,640.5	—	5,389.5
Costa Rica	—	—	380.9	5.2	5.5	11.7	—	—	532.3	—	938.7
Cuba	—	—	—	—	—	36.6	—	—	—	—	40.6
Dominica	—	—	—	—	—	—	—	—	—	—	—
Dominican Republic	—	—	285.4	15.7	22.1	24.8	—	—	590.7	—	944.4
Ecuador	—	—	650.2	48.1	37.5	45.5	—	—	921.3	—	1,712.1
El Salvador	—	—	214.2	1.0	28.0	21.3	—	—	456.9	—	727.4
Grenada	—	—	—	—	—	—	—	—	—	—	—
Guatemala	—	—	275.2	18.2	—	21.6	—	—	516.1	—	842.4
Guyana	—	—	79.3	2.0	28.6	18.2	—	—	111.9	—	241.9
Haiti	—	—	2.6	3.2	110.0	35.7	—	—	181.7	—	346.9
Honduras	—	—	438.5	10.4	85.1	26.1	—	—	444.6	—	1,010.4
Jamaica	—	—	463.3	16.8	—	20.4	—	—	248.3	—	750.5
Mexico	—	—	5,749.0	572.3	—	52.8	—	—	2,565.6	—	8,958.4
Nicaragua	—	—	231.0	9.5	55.6	22.3	—	—	375.5	—	699.3
Panama	—	—	382.9	8.3	—	26.1	—	—	505.8	—	927.4
Paraguay	—	—	377.5	17.0	49.8	24.3	—	—	409.9	—	885.0
Peru	—	—	1,312.5	56.0	—	50.6	—	—	977.4	—	2,411.1
St. Christopher–Nevis	—	—	—	—	—	—	—	—	—	—	—
St. Lucia	—	—	—	—	—	—	—	—	—	—	—
St. Vincent and Grenadines	—	—	—	—	—	—	—	—	—	—	—
Suriname	—	—	—	—	—	10.0	—	—	—	47.8	58.5
Trinidad and Tobago	—	—	111.5	2.4	—	17.0	—	18.8	—	10.0	160.5
Turks and Caicos	—	—	—	—	—	—	—	—	—	—	—
US	36,251	—	—	—	—	—	—	—	—	—	—
Uruguay	—	—	397.2	20.8	—	22.7	—	—	346.5	—	788.1
Venezuela	—	472.0	342.2	25.4	—	34.9	—	—	232.8	—	637.4
ASIA & OCEANIA											
Afghanistan	—	—	—	0.3	172.7	83.0	—	95.1	—	—	386.8
Australia	3,815	—	417.7	0.9	—	—	—	—	—	—	418.9
Bahrain	—	—	—	—	—	4.3	—	—	—	—	4.5
Bangladesh	—	—	54.9	4.9	1,465.4	73.2	—	890.3	—	—	2,637.9
Bhutan	—	—	—	—	—	—	—	—	—	—	2.4
Brunei	—	—	—	—	—	0.1	—	—	—	—	0.1
Burma	—	—	33.1	—	362.1	68.0	—	426.3	—	—	962.2
China	—	—	100.0	—	—	—	—	—	—	—	100.0
Cyprus	—	—	162.2	6.1	—	18.7	—	—	—	12.0	199.8
Fiji	—	—	—	—	—	—	—	—	—	—	—
India	—	—	4,095.3	231.0	8,511.6	208.3	—	—	—	—	13,367.8
Indonesia	—	—	4,635.2	135.0	941.6	104.4	—	1,807.0	—	—	7,718.7
Iran	—	381.0	1,022.7	33.3	—	60.7	—	—	—	—	1,131.3
Iraq	—	2,053.0	106.5	—	—	48.9	—	—	—	—	161.2
Israel	—	—	283.8	10.5	—	15.4	—	—	—	30.0	340.9
Japan	13,186.0	—	857.0	—	—	2.6	—	—	—	—	860.4
Jordan	—	—	185.0	95.3	86.1	39.7	—	—	—	18.0	431.5
Kampuchea	—	—	—	—	—	20.2	—	1.7	—	—	32.4
Kiribati	—	—	—	—	—	—	—	—	—	—	—
Korea, D. P. Rep. of	—	—	—	—	—	3.9	—	—	—	—	3.9
Korea, Rep. Of	—	—	3,805.0	127.4	115.6	31.8	—	1,366.0	—	—	5,461.2
Kuwait	—	4,107.0	—	—	—	3.1	—	—	—	—	3.2
Laos	—	—	—	—	32.0	32.3	—	36.8	—	—	111.3
Lebanon	—	—	116.6	9.3	—	33.9	—	—	—	35.0	202.8
Malaysia	—	—	1,371,1	8.7	—	41.8	—	700.5	—	—	2,135.3
Maldives	—	—	—	—	—	3.2	3.4	—	—	—	6.8
Mongolia	—	—	—	—	—	—	—	—	—	—	—
Nauru	—	—	—	—	—	—	—	—	—	—	—
Nepal	—	—	—	9.3	276.7	31.2	—	84.5	—	—	663.1
New Zealand	381.0	—	101.6	—	1.4	—	—	—	—	—	103.2
Oman	—	—	61.5	2.0	—	5.5	—	—	—	—	69.5
Pakistan	—	—	904.4	86.0	1,254.0	122.6	—	1,278.4	—	—	3,790.4
Papua New Guinea	—	—	99.5	7.6	82.4	14.4	—	138.2	—	7.0	350.6

Table 6: Economic Development Assistance to 1982—*cont.*
(millions of US dollars)

	BILATERAL AID GRANTED BY SOURCE		MULTILATERAL AID RECEIVED BY SOURCE (1946–82)								
	OECD (1977–82)	OPEC (1977–81)	IBRD	IFC	IDA	UNDP	ADB	AsDB	IDB	EEC	TOTALS
Philippines	—	—	3,463.5	164.4	122.2	62.6	—	1,401.3	—	—	5,248.7
Qatar	—	1,042.0	—	—	—	—	—	—	—	—	—
Sa'udi Arabia	—	25,061.0	—	—	—	26.2	—	—	—	—	28.7
Singapore	—	—	209.4	—	—	24.8	—	181.1	—	—	415.9
Solomon Islands	—	—	—	—	—	—	—	—	—	—	—
Sri Lanka	—	—	115.6	32.0	356.4	67.0	—	279.4	—	—	868.2
Syria	—	—	473.4	—	48.6	44.3	—	—	—	15.7	590.2
Taiwan	—	—	309.8	9.8	15.8	62.4	—	92.4	—	—	525.8
Thailand	—	—	2,882.0	111.2	124.8	64.7	—	1,070.1	—	—	4,298.6
Tonga	—	—	—	—	—	—	—	—	—	—	—
Turkey	—	—	3,762.2	240.5	196.2	64.8	—	—	—	625.0	4,900.4
Tuvalu	—	—	—	—	—	—	—	—	—	—	—
UAE	—	4,623.0	—	—	—	—	—	—	—	—	—
Vanuatu	—	—	—	—	—	—	—	—	—	—	—
Viet-Nam	—	—	—	—	60.0	31.4	—	44.4	—	—	196.3
Western Samoa	—	—	—	—	12.4	8.6	—	31.0	—	—	52.1
Yemen, P. D. Rep. of	—	—	—	—	84.3	26.9	—	—	—	—	120.5
Yemen Arab Rep.	—	—	—	3.2	201.3	38.9	—	—	—	—	251.4
EUROPE											
Albania	—	—	—	—	—	—	—	—	—	—	—
Andorra	—	—	—	—	—	—	—	—	—	—	—
Austria	1,245.0	—	104.9	—	—	0.3	—	—	—	—	105.5
Belgium	3,217.0	—	57.8	—	—	—	—	—	—	—	58.0
Bulgaria	—	—	—	—	—	—	—	—	—	—	—
Czechoslovakia	—	—	—	—	—	—	—	—	—	—	—
Denmark	2,406.0	—	85.0	—	—	—	—	—	—	—	85.2
Finland	583.0	—	302.2	3.1	—	0.4	—	—	—	—	305.9
France	18,046.0	—	250.0	—	—	—	—	—	—	—	250.3
German Dem. Rep.	—	—	—	—	—	—	—	—	—	—	—
Germany, Fed. Rep. of	17,368.0	—	—	—	—	—	—	—	—	—	—
Greece	—	—	489.6	66.8	—	25.4	—	—	—	341.4	924.4
Hungary	—	—	—	—	—	—	—	—	—	—	—
Iceland	—	—	47.0	—	—	1.6	—	—	—	—	48.7
Ireland	—	—	150.4	—	—	0.7	—	—	—	—	151.2
Italy	3,016.0	—	398.0	1.0	—	0.2	—	—	—	—	399.6
Liechtenstein	—	—	—	—	—	—	—	—	—	—	—
Luxembourg	—	—	—	—	—	—	—	—	—	—	—
Malta	—	—	6.0	—	—	7.5	—	—	—	3.0	16.6
Monaco	—	—	—	—	—	—	—	—	—	—	—
Netherlands	8,067.0	—	236.5	—	—	—	—	—	—	—	236.7
Norway	2,598.0	—	145.0	—	—	—	—	—	—	—	145.1
Poland	—	—	—	—	—	19.7	—	—	—	—	22.1
Portugal	—	—	771.5	11.2	—	2.0	—	—	—	380.0	1,164.9
Romania	—	—	2,183.6	—	—	19.9	—	—	—	—	2,203.5
San Marino	—	—	—	—	—	—	—	—	—	—	—
Spain	—	—	416.3	11.2	—	8.6	—	—	—	40.0	477.7
Sweden	5,418.0	—	—	—	—	—	—	—	—	—	0.1
Switzerland	1,246.0	—	—	—	—	—	—	—	—	—	—
USSR	—	—	—	—	—	—	—	—	—	—	0.1
UK	10,576.0	—	—	—	—	—	—	—	—	—	—
Vatican	—	—	—	—	—	—	—	—	—	—	—
Yugoslavia	—	—	3,184.8	327.8	—	35.8	—	—	—	50.0	3,601.5

SOURCES: World Bank; US AID. Note that for purposes of comparison, figures are derived from standardized sources and do not always accord with data cited in the separate country articles. Total column includes contributions from other UN agencies.

Table 7. World Social and Military Indicators   **253**

	ANNUAL % POP. INCREASE, 1970–81	ANNUAL % INCREASE PER CAPITA INCOME, EST. 1970–80	MILITARY SPENDING, % OF GNP, 1980	POPULATION PER PHYSICIAN, 1980	POPULATION PER NURSE, 1980	% CHILDREN IN PRIMARY SCHOOLS		% OF LITERATE ADULTS	
						MALE	FEMALE	MALE	FEMALE
AFRICA									
Algeria	3.3	3.1	2.2	2,650[2]	740[2]	94	72	60	23
Angola	2.5	—	—	15,404[2]	—	78	53	4	2
Benin	2.7	1.2	2.2	17,050	1,670	57	27	43	7
Botswana	2.8[1]	9.0	3.5	8,750[2]	—	70	84	69	63
Burundi	2.2	1.5	2.6	45,020	6,180	18	12	39	7
Cameroon	2.2	3.3	1.5	13,670[2]	1,910[2]	80	68	64	37
Cape Verde	1.7[1]	5.5	3.4	6,078[2]	—	—	—	54	34
Central African Rep.	2.3	−0.2	1.8	27,050[2]	1,760[2]	74	40	59	20
Chad	2.0	−3.6	5.0[2]	47,530[2]	3,850[2]	44	17	12	1
Comoros	3.4[1]	−2.4	—	16,500[2]	—	—	—	66	52
Congo	2.9	0.5	4.1	5,510[2]	790[2]	100	100	30	3
Djibouti	5.0*	—	—	—	—	—	—	—	—
Egypt	2.5	5.6	6.0	970	1,500	82	56	56	28
Equatorial Guinea	2.3[1]	—	—	62,000[2]	—	80	67	—	—
Ethiopia	2.0	0.6	9.7	58,490[2]	5,440[2]	23	12	8	4
Gabon	1.0[1]	3.2	0.4	2,560[2]	—	100	100	22	5
Gambia	2.8[1]	3.1	0.0	11,632[2]	—	48	23	27	3
Ghana	3.0	−2.6	0.4	7,630[2]	780[2]	47	38	51	37
Guinea	2.9	0.4	—	16,630[2]	2,490[2]	35	17	14	4
Guinea-Bissau	1.8[1]	—	6.4	6,363[2]	—	83	48	42	15
Ivory Coast	5.0	1.5	1.2	21,040	1,590	86	56	58	24
Kenya	4.0	2.4	3.8	10,500[2]	550[2]	74	68	64	35
Lesotho	2.4	8.6	0.0	18,640[2]	4,330[2]	54	80	58	82
Liberia	3.5	−0.1	1.5	9,610[2]	1,420[2]	44	28	42	9
Libya	4.1	−0.9	1.7	730	400	—	—	77	36
Madagascar	2.6	−1.6	4.1	10,170[2]	3,660[2]	74	66	41	27
Malawi	3.0	2.8	1.8	40,950[2]	3,830[2]	49	37	48	25
Mali	2.6	2.3	2.5	22,130[2]	2,380[2]	27	14	19	8
Mauritania	2.3	−1.0	15.8	14,350[2]	2,080[2]	30	16	17[3]	17[3]
Mauritius	1.6[1]	5.0	0.6	2,078[2]	—	86	85	90	79
Morocco	3.1	2.8	6.1	11,200	1,830[2]	69	42	41	18
Mozambique	4.2	—	3.5	39,110	5,600	61	38	44	11
Namibia	2.8[1]	1.7	—	—	—	—	—	45	31
Niger	3.3	−0.8	1.0	38,790[2]	4,650[2]	19[3]	19[3]	10	1
Nigeria	2.5	3.0	2.6	12,550[2]	3,010[2]	72	59	46	14
Rwanda	3.4	1.7	2.0	31,510	9,840	68	63	62	37
São Tomé and Príncipe	1.1*	−0.2	1.3	1,860[2]	—	—	—	—	—
Senegal	2.7	−0.4	2.6	13,800[2]	1,400[2]	43	28	31	14
Seychelles	1.1*	3.7	—	2,222[2]	—	—	—	56	60
Sierra Leone	2.6	−1.1	1.1	18,280[2]	2,130[2]	41	29	10	4
Somalia	2.8	1.1	6.2	14,290	2,330	26	18	10	1
South Africa	2.8	0.7	3.2	—	—	87	90	57	57
Sudan	3.1	0.9	3.0	8,800	1,410	36	26	38	14
Swaziland	2.8[1]	3.6	2.5	7,200[2]	—	76	78	64	58
Tanzania	3.4	1.1	5.0	17,560[2]	1,980[2]	58	50	78	70
Togo	2.5	0.9	2.4	18,100[2]	1,430[2]	89	58	47	18
Tunisia	2.3	5.4	1.4	3,690	890	92	70	61	34
Uganda	2.6	−4.1	1.8	26,810[2]	4,180[2]	41	33	64	32
Upper Volta	2.0	1.6	3.1	48,510	4,950	18	11	18	5
Zaire	3.0	−2.8	3.1	14,780[2]	1,920[2]	75	57	77	39
Zambia	3.1	−2.3	3.8	7,670[2]	1,730[2]	88	80	79	58
Zimbabwe	3.2	−1.5	8.4	6,580	1,190[2]	74	64	78	64
AMERICAS									
Antigua and Barbuda	1.3*	−1.7	—	2,187[2]	—	—	—	90	88
Argentina	1.6	0.7	2.4	—	—	100	100	96	94
Bahamas	2.0*	−2.9	—	530	—	—	—	90	89
Barbados	1.4[1]	3.2	0.3	1,218[2]	—	100	100	98	98
Belize	1.8*	4.8	—	1,293[2]	—	—	—	91	91
Bolivia	2.6	1.9	2.0[2]	1,850	3,070	79	70	79	58
Brazil	2.1	5.9	0.9	1,700	820	73[3]	73[3]	75	72
Canada	1.2	2.6	1.9	550[2]	90[2]	100	100	99	99
Chile	1.7	−0.5	2.4	1,920[2]	450[2]	98	100	94	91
Colombia	1.9	4.0	1.1	1,920[2]	1,220[2]	62	67	82	84

Table 7. World Social and Military Indicators—*cont.*

	ANNUAL % POP. INCREASE, 1970–81	ANNUAL % INCREASE PER CAPITA INCOME, EST. 1970–80	MILITARY SPENDING, % OF GNP, 1980	POPULATION PER PHYSICIAN, 1980	POPULATION PER NURSE, 1980	% CHILDREN IN PRIMARY SCHOOLS MALE	FEMALE	% OF LITERATE ADULTS MALE	FEMALE
Costa Rica	2.8	2.6	—	1,470²	450	91	91	92	91
Cuba	1.1	—	—	700²	360²	100	99	96	95
Dominica	−0.2*	−3.1	—	8,000²	—	—	—	94	94
Dominican Republic	3.0	3.3	1.5	4,020	2,150	69	73	75	73
Ecuador	3.4	5.3	1.8	1,620²	—	87	85	82	76
El Salvador	2.9	1.3	2.5	3,040	870²	74	73	70	63
Grenada	1.3*	−0.6	—	4,400²	—	—	—	98	98
Guatemala	3.1	2.8	0.8	8,600²	1,620²	58	50	59	43
Guyana	2.2¹	1.1	3.9	—	—	94	97	96	93
Haiti	1.7	1.8	1.4	8,200²	2,490²	42	37	33	24
Honduras	3.4	0.5	1.9	3,120²	700²	66	67	64	62
Jamaica	1.5	−2.8	0.8	2,830²	630²	91	92	90	93
Mexico	3.1	3.1	2.4	1,260	1,420	92	90	87	81
Nicaragua	3.9	−2.9	2.7	1,800	550	59	61	58	57
Panama	2.3	1.2	0.8	980²	420²	94	96	86	84
Paraguay	2.6	5.9	1.2	1,747²	—	87	84	90	83
Peru	2.6	0.2	5.7	1,390²	690²	84	81	89	72
St. Christopher–Nevis	−0.3*	1.7	—	—	—	—	—	—	—
St. Lucia	1.1*	3.0	—	2,750²	—	—	—	81	82
St. Vincent and Grenadines	3.2*	−1.0	—	—	—	—	—	96	96
Suriname	1.3¹	6.8	—	1,728²	—	79	77	68	63
Trinidad and Tobago	1.4	3.9	0.3	1,490	410	96	95	95	90
Turks and Caicos	—	—	—	2,000²	—	—	—	—	—
US	1.0	2.1	5.5	520²	150²	99	99	99	99
Uruguay	0.4	3.2	1.6	540²	190²	67	74	95	95
Venezuela	3.4	2.2	1.2	950²	370²	84	84	84	79
ASIA & OCEANIA									
Afghanistan	2.5	—	2.0²	16,730²	25,990²	27	6	26	5
Australia	1.4	1.3	2.3	560	120	100	100	99	99
Bahrain	2.8¹	5.7	1.9	991	—	84	72	68	47
Bangladesh	2.6	1.4	1.4	10,940²	24,450²	78	48	44	19
Bhutan	2.0	0.0	—	—	—	11	5	—	—
Brunei	4.0*	3.1	—	2,738	—	—	—	76	50
Burma	2.2	2.3	3.8	4,660²	4,750²	67	64	80	59
China	1.5	4.1	8.5	1,920²	1,890²	—	—	—	—
Cyprus	0.4*	—	1.6	1,125	—	64	64	95	85
Fiji	1.8¹	2.9	0.9	2,108²	—	100	200	88	77
India	2.1	1.5	2.8	3,640²	5,380²	76	50	56	28
Indonesia	2.3	4.8	2.8	11,530²	2,300²	84	76	78	58
Iran	3.1	—	14.6²	2,320²	2,520	86	58	56	30
Iraq	3.4	—	8.0²	1,790	2,140	100	97	68	32
Israel	2.6	1.3	29.1	370²	130²	100	100	93	83
Japan	1.1	3.4	0.9	780²	240²	98	98	99	99
Jordan	3.5	5.8	12.0	1889	—	94	87	76	48
Kampuchea	−1.0¹	—	—	—	—	—	—	62	10
Kiribati	1.6*	−2.5	—	—	—	—	—	—	—
Korea, D. P. Rep. of	2.6	—	8.2	440²	—	—	—	—	—
Korea, Rep. of	1.7	7.5	6.2	1,690	380	100	100	96	88
Kuwait	6.3	2.7	4.2	590	180	84	76	72	51
Laos	1.9	—	—	20,060²	3,040²	67	58	55	27
Lebanon	0.6	—	—	530²	720²	93	85	84	64
Malaysia	2.5	5.1	4.8	7,910²	940²	94	90	77	62
Maldives	3.0*	5.1	—	—	—	—	—	82	82
Mongolia	2.9	—	—	450	240	78	77	—	—
Nauru	1.3*	—	—	—	—	—	—	—	—
Nepal	2.6	-0.3	0.9	30,060	33,420	57	17	34	5
New Zealand	1.5	0.3	1.9	670	130	100	100	99	99
Oman	3.0¹	2.8	24.6	1,731	—	59	31	55	20
Pakistan	3.0	1.9	5.0	3,480	5,820	63	25	39	18
Papua New Guinea	2.1	0.1	1.3	13,590²	960²	—	—	39	24
Philippines	2.7	3.7	2.4	7,970	6,000	87³	87³	90	88
Qatar	6.5¹	−0.2	8.4	1,129²	—	—	—	33³	33³

Table 7. World Social and Military Indicators—cont. 255

	ANNUAL % POP. INCREASE, 1970–81	ANNUAL % INCREASE PER CAPITA INCOME, EST. 1970–80	MILITARY SPENDING, % OF GNP, 1980	POPULATION PER PHYSICIAN, 1980	POPULATION PER NURSE, 1980	% CHILDREN IN PRIMARY SCHOOLS		% OF LITERATE ADULTS	
						MALE	FEMALE	MALE	FEMALE
Sa'udi Arabia	4.5	9.0	14.4	1,640²	1,150²	62	36	30	2
Singapore	1.5	6.7	5.7	1,150	320	99	99	89	70
Solomon Islands	3.7*	2.9	—	6,666²	—	—	—	60³	60³
Sri Lanka	1.7	2.8	0.7	7,170	1,340	61	73	82	76
Syria	3.7	6.0	18.1	2,314	—	94	72	74	34
Taiwan	—	—	7.6²	—	—	—	—	—	—
Thailand	2.5	4.2	3.2	7,180²	2,420²	80	78	93	83
Tonga	—	0.8	—	3,333²	—	—	—	—	—
Turkey	2.3	3.0	4.5	1,630	1,130	72	73	81	51
Tuvalu	1.5*	—	—	—	—	—	—	—	—
UAE	16.6	0.2	6.4	900	340	—	—	30	19
Vanuatu	2.7*	−2.6	—	3,571²	—	—	—	—	—
Viet-Nam	2.8	—	—	4,190	2,930	—	—	—	—
Western Samoa	0.9*	—	—	2,500²	—	—	—	98	98
Yemen, P. D. Rep. of	2.5	10.7	12.8	7,390	850	84	50	48	16
Yemen Arab Rep.	3.0	6.1	8.3	11,670	4,580	38	5	16	1
EUROPE									
Albania	2.5	—	—	960²	310²	—	—	—	—
Andorra	—	—	—	—	—	—	—	—	—
Austria	0.1	3.4	1.2	400	230	85	86	99	99
Belgium	0.2	2.9	3.4	400	120	97	98	99	99
Bulgaria	0.5	—	12.4	410	190	95	94	97	93
Czechoslovakia	0.7	—	4.9	360	130	95	98	—	—
Denmark	0.3	1.7	2.5	480²	210²	99	99	99	99
Finland	0.4	2.5	1.7	530	100	86	90	99	99
France	0.5	3.0	4.0	580²	120²	100	100	99	99
German Dem. Rep.	−0.2	—	5.7	520²	—	99	100	—	—
Germany, Fed. Rep. of	0.0	2.7	3.3	450²	170²	96	96	99	99
Greece	0.9	3.7	5.4	420²	600²	96	97	96	84
Hungary	0.4	4.9	4.4	400	150	94	95	99	98
Iceland	1.1¹	3.1	0.0	518²	—	—	—	—	—
Ireland	1.3	2.6	1.8	760	120	93	94	98	98
Italy	0.4	2.5	2.4	340²	330	98	99	97	95
Liechtenstein	1.7*	—	—	1,400	—	—	—	99	99
Luxembourg	—	4.6	1.0	710	—	92	94	99	99
Malta	0.9¹	10.4	0.5	864²	—	97	98	84	80
Monaco	—	—	—	—	—	—	—	—	—
Netherlands	0.8	2.1	3.2	540²	130²	92	95	99	99
Norway	0.5	3.8	3.0	520²	90²	98	99	99	99
Poland	0.9	—	5.4	570²	240²	98	98	99	98
Portugal	0.8	1.2	3.7	540²	650²	92	93	86	76
Romania	0.9	4.3	4.4	680	270	89	84	98	95
San Marino	—	—	—	—	—	—	—	—	—
Spain	1.1	2.6	1.7	460²	330²	98	98	96	91
Sweden	0.3	1.6	3.1	490²	60²	100	100	99	99
Switzerland	0.1	0.6	2.0	410	160	82	84	99	99
USSR	0.9	—	14.6	280²	210	99	99	99	99
UK	0.1	1.8	5.1	650²	140²	97	97	99	99
Vatican	—	—	—	—	—	—	—	—	—
Yugoslavia	0.9	5.0	4.8	680	280	—	—	94	81

*Most recent annual estimate.
—Not available.
1. Estimate for 1975–80.
2. Figure is for earlier year than that specified in column heading.
3. Based on single literacy figure for both sexes.
SOURCES: World Bank; various UN and US government publications. Note that for purposes of comparison, figures are derived from standardized sources and do not always accord with data cited in the separate country articles.

Table 8: World Cultural Indicators

	SCIENTISTS AND TECHNICIANS PER 1,000,000 POP.[1]	POSTSECONDARY EDUCATION PER 100,000 POP., 1979	RADIOS PER 1,000 POP., 1980	TV SETS PER 1,000 POP., 1980	CINEMAS, SEATS PER 1,000 POP.[1]	DAILY NEWSPAPER CIRCULATION PER 1,000 POP., 1979
AFRICA						
Algeria	—	374	174	52.0	—	22
Angola	—	22	18	4.0	4.9	17
Benin	—	88	70	0.1	1.4	—
Botswana	—	134	82	—	1.2	21
Burundi	—	43	33	—	—	—
Cameroon	—	115*	89	—	3.5	—
Cape Verde	—	—	127	—	—	—
Central African Rep.	—	93	54	0.3	—	—
Chad	—	14*	22	—	2.9	—
Comoros	—	—	112	—	—	—
Congo	197	457	60	2.3	—	—
Djibouti	—	—	143	42.0	54.7	—
Egypt	—	1,345	143	33.0	5.7	—
Equatorial Guinea	—	—	275	2.8	14.0	—
Ethiopia	—	48	8	1.0	—	2
Gabon	—	307	174	16.0	—	—
Gambia	—	—	108	—	—	—
Ghana	952	86	163	5.0	1.4	31*
Guinea	—	435*	24	1.2	—	4
Guinea-Bissau	—	—	44	—	—	11
Ivory Coast	75	167*	125	38.0	5.3	7
Kenya	41	65	33	4.0	1.8	10
Lesotho	—	131*	22	—	—	1*
Liberia	—	199	171	11.0	5.1	6
Libya	—	534	45	55.0	7.7	—
Madagascar	—	268	194	5.1	—	—
Malawi	78	34	46	—	0.9	5
Mali	—	78	13	—	—	—
Mauritania	—	32*	92	—	5.9	—
Mauritius	295	128	206	81.0	48.9	79
Morocco	—	422	148	37.0	8.0	—
Mozambique	—	8	24	0.1	—	4
Namibia	—	—	—	—	—	—
Niger	20	18	47	0.1	—	—
Nigeria	50	114	73	0.9	—	—
Rwanda	—	27	40	—	0.2	—
São Tomé and Príncipe	—	—	271	—	—	—
Senegal	102	224	53	0.7	—	5
Seychelles	46	—	385	—	13.8	56
Sierra Leone	—	50*	96	6.0	—	—
Somalia	—	68	24	—	—	—
South Africa	—	—	273	68.0	—	—
Sudan	376	151	71	6.0	4.8	1
Swaziland	—	258	148	1.8	7.5	15
Tanzania	—	23	28*	0.3*	1.0	11
Togo	194	142	204	3.7	—	3
Tunisia	—	486	157	47.0	7.0	44
Uganda	—	55*	19*	5.0*	1.1	2
Upper Volta	—	20*	16	1.4	1.9	—
Zaire	—	97	26	0.3	—	—
Zambia	78	97	23	10.0	1.0	19
Zimbabwe	—	21	43	10.0	—	16
AMERICAS						
Antigua and Barbuda	—	—	227	207.0	—	—
Argentina	842	1,869	379*	190.0	22.7	—
Bahamas	—	—	464	132.0	31.8	146
Barbados	—	734*	534	198.0	29.4	85
Belize	—	—	438	—	—	41
Bolivia	—	1,041*	89	54.0	29.8	39
Brazil	507	1,072*	284	122.0	—	44*
Canada	2,478	3,539	1,109	471.0	33.0	241
Chile	442	1,166	293	110.0	13.0	87
Colombia	84	1,072	111	83.0	14.7	48

	SCIENTISTS AND TECHNICIANS PER 1,000,000 POP.[1]	POSTSECONDARY EDUCATION PER 100,000 POP., 1979	RADIOS PER 1,000 POP., 1980	TV SETS PER 1,000 POP., 1980	CINEMAS, SEATS PER 1,000 POP.[1]	DAILY NEWSPAPER CIRCULATION PER 1,000 POP., 1979
Costa Rica	146	2,558	80	72.0	—	70
Cuba	1,246	1,513	295	129.0	—	91
Dominica	—	—	438	—	—	—
Dominican Republic	—	981	41	71.0	10.5	42
Ecuador	363	3,288	317	60.0	—	49
El Salvador	—	757	322	62.0	—	—
Grenada	—	—	303*	—	47.9	—
Guatemala	148	675	40	24.0	12.0	—
Guyana	389	312	343	—	48.0	77
Haiti	—	78	20	3.2	0.6	7
Honduras	—	677*	48	13.0	—	63
Jamaica	—	470*	328	76.0	—	59
Mexico	—	1,221	285	104.0	—	—
Nicaragua	—	1,027	259	65.0	—	69
Panama	302	1,999	155	120.0	—	79
Paraguay	—	700*	62	20.0	—	—
Peru	387	1,509*	155	48.0	15.5	—
St. Christopher–Nevis	—	—	299	63.0	—	22
St. Lucia	71	—	708	15.0	—	35
St. Vincent and Grenadines	—	—	—	—	—	—
Suriname	—	—	486	103.0	—	—
Trinidad and Tobago	—	424*	263	184.0	52.4	171
Turks and Caicos	333	—	457	—	166.7	—
US	2,800	5,225	2,099	624.0	—[3]	282
Uruguay	—	1,310	562	125.0	28.1	—
Venezuela	324	1,987	385	123.0	20.7	176
ASIA & OCEANIA						
Afghanistan	—	148	71*	2.1*	1.3	—
Australia	2,520	2,219	1,026	378.0	—	336
Bahrain	—	431	343	247.0	—	—
Bangladesh	—	271	8	0.9	1.3	5
Bhutan	—	21	5	—	3.9	—
Brunei	—	—	164*	122.0*	43.6	—
Burma	74	408	20	—	4.4	10
China	—	104	57	4.2	—	—
Cyprus	—	247	498	238.0	—	—
Fiji	—	453*	475	—	69.0	87
India	88	781*	45	1.7	5.6	20
Indonesia	96	205*	41	9.0	4.5	—
Iran	—	447*	62*	56.0	9.0	—
Iraq	—	765	153	50.0	5.5	—
Israel	3,990	2,317	207	150.0	41.3	—
Japan	4,556	2,110	678	539.0	8.2	569
Jordan	156	962	168	54.0	6.5	—
Kampuchea	—	—	15*	3.7*	—	—
Kiribati	50	—	198*	—	—	—
Korea, D. P. Rep. of	—	—	—	—	—	—
Korea, Rep. of	677	1,347	393	164.0	7.8	—
Kuwait	678	980	387	400.0	13.0	—
Laos	—	32	94	—	—	—
Lebanon	59	3,159	633	237.0	—	—
Malaysia	—	291	149	64.0*	—	—
Maldives	—	—	28	7.0	—	—
Mongolia	—	729	99	3.0	—	69
Nauru	—	—	500	—	—	—
Nepal	—	276	21	—	—	—
New Zealand	2,223	2,295	889	278	33.2	345
Oman	—	—	—	—	1.0	—
Pakistan	—	185*	67	10.0	3.9	14
Papua New Guinea	—	261	65	—	—	6
Philippines	148	2,464	43	21.0	13.4	—
Qatar	—	917	545	118.0*	17.6	33

Table 8: World Cultural Indicators—*cont.*

	SCIENTISTS AND TECHNICIANS PER 1,000,000 POP.[1]	POSTSECONDARY EDUCATION PER 100,000 POP., 1979	RADIOS PER 1,000 POP., 1980	TV SETS PER 1,000 POP., 1980	CINEMAS, SEATS PER 1,000 POP.[1]	DAILY NEWSPAPER CIRCULATION PER 1,000 POP., 1979
Sa'udi Arabia	—	614	299	251.0	—	—
Singapore	312	890	192	166.0	30.3	249
Solomon Islands	—	—	90	—	3.9	—
Sri Lanka	43	143	99	2.4	12.4	—
Syria	—	1,302	218*	43.0	6.2	12
Taiwan	—	—	—	—	—	—
Thailand	—	1,027	125	17.0	6.1	—
Tonga	—	—	206	—	20.0	—
Turkey	317	611	95	75.0	15.3	—
Tuvalu	—	—	—	—	—	—
UAE	—	237	302	117.0	43.5	—
Vanuatu	40	—	165	—	13.4	—
Viet-Nam	383	267*	—	—	3.5	—
Western Samoa	1,546	—	196	16.0	36.1	—
Yemen, P. D. Rep. of	—	145*	51	18.0	11.6	—
Yemen Arab Rep.	—	74*	19	0.2	4.2	—
EUROPE						
Albania	—	577*	74	3.7	—	54
Andorra	—	—	200	118.0	72.4	—
Austria	1,373	1,707	443	296.0	—	351
Belgium	2,195	1,916	457	395.0	23.6	228
Bulgaria	5,551	1,213	242	186.0	82.1	234
Czechoslovakia	7,459	1,257	289	280.0	58.7	304
Denmark	2,983	2,086	381	368.0	22.1	367
Finland	3,360	1,752	837	374.0*	19.1	480
France	4,315	1,990	895	354.0	27.6	—
German Dem. Rep.	10,896	2,370	383	342.0	21.7	517
Germany, Fed. Rep. of	3,872	1,886	370	337.0	16.5	—
Greece	383	1,266	345	156.0	—	—
Hungary	4,602	967	252	258.0	58.5	242
Iceland	2,244	1,362*	614	275.0	42.7	557
Ireland	1,330	1,505	371*	225.0*	—	229
Italy	1,255	1,937	242	386.0	—	93*
Liechtenstein	—	—	500	269.0	—	477
Luxembourg	—	113*	512*	245.0*	—	358
Malta	—	545	376	207.0	74.3	—
Monaco	—	—	346	654.0	53.2	432
Netherlands	3,836	2,505	309	296.0	11.3	325
Norway	3,673	1,928	327	292.0	34.2	456
Poland	4,218	1,723	295*	224.0	14.7	237
Portugal	423	936	159	141.0	24.4	50*
Romania	—	873	144	167.0	11.0	181*
San Marino	—	—	381	238.0*	130.0	—
Spain	—	1,719*	256	252.0	83.4	—
Sweden	4,395	2,414*	383*	381.0	—	526
Switzerland	5,094	1,264	361	314.0	28.1	395
USSR	5,172	1,976	490	303.0*	—	—
UK	2,921	1,429	947	404.0	12.9	426*
Vatican	—[2]	—[2]	—[2]	—[2]	—[2]	—[2]
Yugoslavia	1,565	2,029	207	192.0	19.8	103

*Estimate or figure for most recent available year.
—Nil, not available, or does not apply.
1. Most recent available estimates.
2. Population too small for statistical reliability.
3. Data on number of seats NA; total of 18,772 screens reported as of April 1983.
SOURCE: UNESCO. Note that for purposes of comparison, figures are derived from standardized sources and do not always accord with data cited in the separate country articles.

Glossary of Special Terms

The following is a selected list, with brief definitions and explanations, of terms that appear frequently in these volumes. Not included below are UN organs and related agencies, which are discussed under their own headings elsewhere.

adult literacy: the capacity of adults to read and write, as defined by divergent national criteria of age and ability.

ad valorem tax: a levy based on a fixed percentage of an item's value; ad valorem taxes include sales taxes, property taxes, and the majority of import duties.

African Development Bank: IGO founded in 1963 and with its headquarters at Abidjan, Ivory Coast; coordinates its members' development finances and provides loans.

animism: the belief that natural objects and phenomena have souls or innate spiritual powers.

Asian Development Bank: IGO founded in 1966 and with its headquarters at Manila, Philippines; seeks to encourage economic growth in Asia and the Far East and provides long-term, large-scale loans, with emphasis on the developing countries.

Association of South-East Asian Nations (ASEAN): IGO founded in 1967 and with its headquarters at Jakarta, Indonesia; promotes economic cooperation among its members.

balance of payments: a systematic record of all financial transactions between one country and the rest of the world.

bank of issue: a bank empowered to issue currency.

capital account: all additions to or subtractions from a stock of investment.

capital punishment: punishment by death.

Caribbean Community and Common Market (CARICOM): IGO founded in 1973 and with its headquarters in Georgetown, Guyana; seeks the establishment of a common external tariff and common trade policy among its members, and promotes increased cooperation in agricultural and industrial development in the Caribbean region.

cash economy: see **money economy**.

central bank: a financial institution that handles the transactions of the central government, coordinates and controls the nation's commercial banks, and regulates the nation's money supply and credit conditions.

Colombo Plan: formally known as the Colombo Plan for Cooperative Economic Development in Asia and the Pacific, a multinational mutual assistance program that took effect in 1951 and has its headquarters in Colombo, Sri Lanka.

commercial bank: a bank that offers to businesses and individuals a variety of banking services, including the right of withdrawal by check.

Commonwealth of Nations: voluntary association of the UK and its present dependencies and associated states, as well as certain former dependencies and their dependent territories. The term was first used officially in 1926 and is embodied in the Statute of Westminster (1931). Within the Commonwealth, whose Secretariat (established in 1965) is located in London, England, are numerous subgroups devoted to economic and technical cooperation.

constant prices: money values calculated so as to eliminate the effect of inflation on prices and income.

Council for Mutual Economic Assistance (CMEA): also known as COMECON; IGO established to foster economic and technical cooperation within the Socialist bloc, including the USSR, most Eastern European countries, and several other nations. Founded in 1949, CMEA has its headquarters in Moscow.

Council of Europe: intergovernmental organization, founded in 1949 and with its headquarters in Strasbourg, France; promotes consultation and cooperation among European countries.

crude birthrate: the number of births in a year per 1,000 estimated midyear population.

crude death rate: the number of deaths in a year per 1,000 estimated midyear population.

current account: the flow of goods and services; payments for and receipts from imports and exports, including interest and dividends.

currency in circulation: the tangible portion of a nation's money supply, composed of bank notes, government notes, and coins.

current prices: money values that reflect prevailing prices, without excluding the effects of inflation.

customs duty: a tax imposed on the import or export of goods.

customs union: an arrangement between governments to establish a common tariff policy and remove customs barriers between them.

demand deposit: a bank deposit that can be withdrawn by the depositor without previous notice to the bank.

direct tax: a tax that cannot be shifted from the original payer to the ultimate consumer of a good or service; direct taxes include income tax and poll tax.

Economic Community of West African States (ECOWAS): IGO founded in 1975 and with its headquarters at Lagos, Nigeria; seeks to establish a common tariff policy and promote economic cooperation among its members.

endangered species: a type of plant or animal threatened with extinction in all or part of its natural range. For the Sixth Edition, listings of endangered animal species are as compiled for each country by the International Union for Conservation of Nature and Natural Resources.

European Communities (EC): collective name for a supranational organization encompassing, among other entities, the European Coal and Steel Community, established in 1952; the European Economic Community (EEC, or European Common Market), founded in 1958; and the European Energy Community (EURATOM), also established in 1958. All EC members also participate in the European Parliament, which meets in Strasbourg and Luxembourg, and the Court of Justice, which sits in Luxembourg.

European Free Trade Association (EFTA): customs union established in 1960 and with its headquarters in Geneva, Switzerland.

factor cost: a concept used in determining the value of the national product in relation to the economic resources employed.

fertility rate: the average number of children that would be born to each woman in a population if each were to live through her childbearing lifetime bearing children at the same rate as women of those ages actually did in a given year.

fly: the part of a flag opposite and parallel to the one nearest the flagpole.

foreign exchange: all monetary assets that give residents of one country a financial claim on another.

gross domestic product (GDP): the total gross expenditure, in purchasers' values, on the domestic supply of goods and services (final use).

gross national product (GNP): the total monetary value of all final goods and services a nation produces.

Group of 77 (G-77): IGO founded in 1967 to represent the interests of the developing countries and taking its name from the 77 developing nations that signed the Joint Declaration of the first UN Conference on Trade and Development (UNCTAD).

Gulf Cooperation Council (GCC): IGO founded in 1981 and with its headquarters in Riyadh, Sa'udi Arabia; aims at increasing cooperation among nations of the Persian (Arabian) Gulf region in matters of security and economic development.

hoist: the part of a flag nearest the flagpole.

indirect tax: a tax levied against goods and services; sales taxes, excise taxes, and import duties are generally regarded as indirect taxes.

infant mortality rate: the number of deaths of children less than one year old per 1,000 live births in a given year.

installed capacity: the maximum possible output of electric power at any given time.

Inter-American Development Bank (IDB): IGO established in 1959 and with its headquarters in Washington, D.C.; provides technical assistance and development financing to member nations in Latin America and the Caribbean.

intergovernmental organization (IGO): a body, such as the UN, to which only governments belong.

international reserves: cash and other international assets readily convertible into cash for the settlement of international accounts by a government.

invisibles: exports and imports of services (e.g., shipping charges, banking services, royalties, rents, interest).

Latin American Integration Association (LAIA): IGO founded in 1980 as the successor to the Latin American Free Trade Association, and with its headquarters in Montevideo, Uruguay; seeks to foster economic cooperation among Latin American nations.

League of Arab States (Arab League): IGO founded in 1945 and with its headquarters in Tunis, Tunisia (formerly in Cairo, Egypt); attempts to coordinate national and international political activities of its members, to revive and diffuse the cultural legacy of the Arabs, and to develop Arab social consciousness.

life expectancy: the expected life span of a newborn baby at any given date.

lingua franca: a language widely used as a means of communication among speakers of other languages.

Marshall Plan: formally known as the European Recovery Program, a joint project between the US and most Western European nations under which $12.5 billion in US loans and grants was expended to aid European recovery after World War II. Expenditures under the program, named for US Secretary of State George C. Marshall, were made from fiscal years 1949 through 1952.

metropolitan area: in most cases, a city and its surrounding suburbs.

money economy: a system or stage of economic development in which money replaces barter in the exchange of goods and services.

most-favored-nation clause: a provision in commercial treaties between two or more countries that guarantees that all partners to the agreement will automatically extend to each other any tariff reductions they offer to nonmember countries.

net material product: the total net value of goods and "productive" services, including turnover taxes, produced by the economy in the course of a given time period.

net natural increase: the difference between the crude birthrate and the crude death rate.

nongovernmental organization (NGO): a body, such as the International Chamber of Commerce or Amnesty International, in which organizations and individuals participate, often without government control or sponsorship.

Nordic Council: IGO founded in 1952 and with its headquarters in Stockholm, Sweden; a consultative body on matters of common interest to the Nordic (Scandinavian) countries.

North Atlantic Treaty Organization (NATO): IGO established in 1949 and with its headquarters in Brussels, Belgium; fosters cooperation in defense and other matters.

Organization of African Unity (OAU): IGO established in 1963 and with its headquarters in Addis Ababa, Ethiopia; attempts to promote African unity and development, eradicate colonialism, and coordinate members' economic, political, diplomatic, educational, cultural, health, scientific, and defense policies.

Organization of American States (OAS): IGO founded in 1948 and with its headquarters in Washington, D.C.; seeks to achieve peaceful settlement of members' disputes, promote solidarity in defense matters, and foster cooperation in the health, economic, social, and cultural fields.

Organization for Economic Cooperation and Development (OECD): IGO established in 1961 as the successor to the Organization for European Economic Cooperation, with headquarters in Paris; attempts to promote economic growth, higher living standards, and financial stability in member countries.

Organization of Petroleum Exporting Countries (OPEC): IGO founded in 1960 and with headquarters in Vienna, Austria; seeks to coordinate its members' production and pricing of crude petroleum.

Pan American Health Organization (PAHO): IGO founded in 1902 as the International Sanitary Bureau; headquarters now located in Washington, D.C. An OAS affiliate, PAHO seeks to improve health and environmental conditions in the Americas.

per capita: per person.

proved reserves: the quantity of a recoverable mineral resource (such as oil or natural gas) that is still in the ground.

public debt: the amount owed by a government.

retail trade: the sale of goods directly to the consumer.

smallholder: the owner or tenant of a small farm.

subsistence economy: the part of a national economy in which money plays little or no role, trade is by barter, and living standards are minimal.

supranational: transcending the limitations of the nation-state.

time deposit: money held in a bank account for which the bank may require advance notice of withdrawal.

turnkey project: a factory or other installation wholly built by a company of one country at a site in another country, which then assumes complete operational control over it, paying the builder in cash, credits, or a share of the proceeds.

turnover tax: a tax on transactions of goods and services at all levels of production and distribution.

value added by manufacture: the difference, measured in national currency units, between the value of finished goods and the cost of the materials needed to produce them.

value-added tax (VAT): see **ad valorem tax**.

visibles: international transactions involving movement of tangible goods.

Warsaw Treaty Organization (WTO): IGO commonly known as the Warsaw Pact; attempts to promote the collective security of its members. Founded in 1955, the alliance has its headquarters in Moscow.

wholesale trade: the sale of goods, usually in bulk quantities, for ultimate resale to consumers.

Glossary of Religious Holidays

CHRISTIAN HOLIDAYS

The chief Christian holiday is **Easter**, the annual celebration of the resurrection of Jesus Christ. Like Passover, the Jewish feast from which it derives, the date of observation is linked to the phases of the moon. Since the Christian calendar is a solar one rather than a lunar one, the date of Easter changes from year to year. Easter is celebrated on the first Sunday after the first full moon following the spring equinox; in the Gregorian calendar it can occur as early as 22 March or as late as 25 April. The Easter date determines the date of many other Roman Catholic holidays, such as Ash Wednesday, Ascension, and Pentecost.

Important Christian celebrations and feasts that invariably occur on Sunday are not listed as holidays in the country articles because Sunday itself is a holiday ("holy day") in predominantly Christian countries. In these lands it is the day of rest and worship, occurring on the day after the Jewish Sabbath, from which it derives, in commemoration of Christ's resurrection on Easter Sunday.

The names and dates of the Christian holidays listed below are almost all based on Roman Catholic observances. Some of these holidays are also observed by Protestant denominations. By contrast, all countries where Eastern Orthodox rites predominate are Communist-ruled except Greece and the Greek-held portion of Cyprus; in the Communist countries, Christian holidays are not national holidays. For religious celebrations, some Orthodox churches retain the Julian calendar, which is 13 days behind the Gregorian calendar. Orthodox holidays do not fully correspond to the list of church holidays given below.

Solemnity of Mary, Mother of God. Observed on 1 January, this celebration was, before a 1969 Vatican reform, the Feast of the Circumcision of Our Lord Jesus Christ.

Epiphany of Our Lord. Traditionally observed on 6 January but now observable on the Sunday falling between 2 January and 7 January, this feast commemorates the adoration of the Magi who journeyed to the place of Jesus' birth. In the Orthodox churches, however, it is the feast celebrating Jesus' baptism.

St. Dévôte Day. Observed on 27 January in Monaco in honor of the principality's patron saint, this day celebrates her safe landing after a perilous voyage, thanks to a dove who directed her ship to the Monaco shore.

Candlemas. A national holiday on 2 February in Liechtenstein, this observation is now called the Presentation of the Lord, commemorates the presentation of the infant Jesus in the Temple at Jerusalem. Before a 1969 Vatican reform, it commemorated the Purification of Mary 40 days after giving birth to a male child, in accordance with a Jewish practice of the time.

St. Agatha's Day. On 5 February is celebrated the feast day of the patron saint of San Marino. St. Agatha is also the patron saint of nurses, firefighters, and jewelers.

Shrove Monday and Shrove Tuesday. These two days occur just prior to the beginning of Lent (a term which derives from the Middle English *lente*, "spring"), the Christian season of penitence that ends with Easter Sunday. These are days of **Carnival**, public holidays of feasting and merriment in many lands. Shrove Tuesday is also known as **Mardi Gras**.

Ash Wednesday. The first day of Lent, observed 46 days before Easter, is so called from the practice of placing ashes on the forehead of the worshiper as a sign of penitence. In the Roman Catholic Church, these ashes are obtained from burning palm branches used in the previous year's **Palm Sunday** observation. (Palm Sunday commemorates the entry of Jesus into Jerusalem a week before Easter Sunday, and it begins **Holy Week**.) On Ash Wednesday the ashes are placed on the forehead of the communicant during Mass. The recipient is told,"Remember that you are dust, and unto dust you shall return" or "Turn away from sin and be faithful to the Gospel."

St. Patrick's Day. This holiday, observed on 17 March, is celebrated in Ireland to honor its patron saint.

St. Joseph's Day. The feast day in honor of Mary's husband is observed on 19 March as a public holiday in several countries.

Holy (Maundy) Thursday. The Thursday preceding Easter commemorates the Last Supper, the betrayal of Jesus by Judas Iscariot, and the arrest and arraignment of Jesus by the Roman authorities. In Rome, the pope customarily performs a ceremony in remembrance of Jesus' washing of his disciples' feet (John 13:5–20).

Good Friday. The day after Holy Thursday is devoted to remembrance of the crucifixion of Jesus and is given to penance and prayer.

Holy Saturday. This day commemorates the burial of Jesus and, like Good Friday, is given to solemn prayer.

Easter Monday. The day after Easter is a public holiday in many countries.

Prayer Day. This Danish public holiday is observed on the fourth Friday after Easter.

Ascension. One of the most important Christian feasts, Ascension is observed 40 days after Easter in commemoration of Jesus' ascension to heaven.

Pentecost Monday (Whitmonday). This public holiday in many countries occurs the day after Pentecost (derived from the ancient Greek *pentekostos*, "fiftieth"), or **Whitsunday**, which commemorates the descent of the Holy Spirit upon Jesus' disciples and apostles on the seventh Sunday after Easter. It derives from the Jewish feast of Shavuot. It was an important occasion for baptism in the early church, and the name "Whitsunday" originated from the white robes worn by the newly baptized.

Corpus Christi. This holiday in honor of the Eucharist is observed on the Thursday or Sunday after **Trinity Sunday**, which is the Sunday after Pentecost. In most Christian churches the Eucharist is a sacrament in which consecrated bread and wine are literally the body and blood of Jesus Christ, a belief stemming from New Testament accounts of the Last Supper.

Sacred Heart. The Friday of the week after Corpus Christi is a holiday in Colombia. The object of devotion is the divine person of Jesus, whose heart is the symbol of his love for mankind.

Day of St. Peter and St. Paul. This observance, on 29 June, commemorates the martyrdom of the two apostles traditionally believed to have been executed in Rome on the same day in AD 64, during the persecution of Christians ordered by Emperor Nero.

St. James' Day. Observed on 25 July, this day commemorates St. James the Greater, one of Jesus' 12 disciples. St. James is the patron saint of Spain.

Feast of Our Lady of Angels. This feast, on 2 August, is celebrated as a national holiday in Costa Rica in honor of the Virgin Mary. Pilgrimage is made to the basilica in Cartago, which houses a black stone statue of the Virgin.

Assumption. This holiday, observed on 15 August in many countries, celebrates the Catholic and Orthodox dogma that, following Mary's death, her body was taken into heaven and reunited with her soul.

Crowning of Our Lady of Altagracia. Another holiday in honor of Mary, this day is celebrated in the Dominican Republic on 15 August with a pilgrimage to her shrine. (**Altagracia Day**, 21 January, is also a holiday in the Dominican Republic).

Day of Santa Rosa of Lima. The feast day in honor of the first native-born saint of the New World, declared patron saint of South America by Pope Clement X in 1671, is 23 August, but in Peru she is commemorated by a national holiday on 30 August.

Day of Our Lady of Mercy (Las Mercedes). Another holiday in honor of Mary, this observance on 24 September is a holiday in the Dominican Republic.

All Saints' Day. On 1 November, a public holiday in many countries, saints and martyrs who have no special festival are commemorated.

All Souls' Day. This day, 2 November, is dedicated to prayer for the repose of the souls of the dead.

Immaculate Conception. This day, 8 December, celebrates the Catholic dogma asserting that Mary's conception, as the future mother of God, was uniquely free from original sin. In Paraguay it is observed as the Day of Our Lady of Caacupé.

Our Lady of Guadalupe. This Mexican festival, on 12 December, celebrates a miracle the Virgin Mary is believed to have performed on this day in 1531, when she appeared before an Indian peasant and commanded him to build a shrine in her honor. The shrine is now the site of a basilica in the Mexico City area.

Christmas. The annual commemoration of the nativity of Jesus is held on 25 December. A midnight Mass ushers in this joyous celebration in many Christian churches. The custom of distributing gifts to children on **Christmas Eve** derives from a Dutch custom originally observed on the evening before **St. Nicholas' Day** (6 December). The day after Christmas —often called **Boxing Day**, for the boxed gifts customarily given—is a public holiday in many countries.

St. Stephen's Day. The feast day in honor of the first martyred Christian saint is 26 December, the day after Christmas. St. Stephen is the patron saint of Hungary.

The following list shows the dates of selected movable Christian holidays between 1984 and 1990, according to the Gregorian calendar:

	ASH WEDNESDAY	EASTER	ASCENSION	PENTECOST
1984	7 March	22 April	31 May	10 June
1985	20 February	7 April	16 May	26 May
1986	12 February	30 March	8 May	18 May
1987	4 March	19 April	28 May	7 June
1988	17 February	3 April	12 May	22 May
1989	8 February	26 March	4 May	14 May
1990	28 February	15 April	24 May	3 June

JEWISH HOLIDAYS

The basic Jewish holy day is the **Sabbath**, the seventh day of each week, starting at sundown on Friday and ending at nightfall on Saturday. This is a day of rest and is devoted to worship, religious study, and the family.

Other Jewish holidays (all starting at sundown and ending at nightfall) occur on specific days of specific months of the Jewish calendar, which consists of 12 alternating months of 29 or 30 days (two months are variable), conforming to the lunar cycle of roughly 29½ days. In order to reconcile the lunar year of 353, 354, or 355 days to the solar year of 365¼ days, a 30-day month (Adar Sheni) is added 7 times within a 19-year cycle. In this way, Jewish festivals retain their seasonal origins. The following list, arranged in the order of the Jewish calendar, shows Jewish religious holidays observed in the State of Israel.

Rosh Hashanah. The Jewish New Year is celebrated on Tishri, the first month. In synagogues the sounding of the shofar (ram's horn) heralds the new year. Rosh Hashanah begins the observance of the Ten Penitential Days, which culminate in Yom Kippur. Orthodox and Conservative Jews outside Israel celebrate the next day as well.

Yom Kippur. This Day of Atonement, spent in fasting, penitence, and prayer, is the most solemn observance of Judaism. It takes place on 10 Tishri.

Sukkot. This ancient Jewish harvest festival, which begins on 15 Tishri, recalls the period in which harvesters left their homes to dwell in the fields in sukkot, or booths—small outdoor shelters of boards, leaves, and branches—in order to facilitate gathering the crops before the seasonal rains began. In religious terms, it commemorates the 40 years of wandering in the desert by the ancient Hebrews after their exodus from Egypt. The 8th day of Sukkot and the 22d day of Tishri is **Shmini Azeret/Simhat Torah**, a joyous holiday in which the annual cycle of reading the Torah (the Five Books of Moses) is completed and begun anew. Outside of Israel, Simhat Torah and the beginning of a new reading cycle are celebrated on 23 Tishri.

Hanukkah. The Festival of Lights, corresponding roughly to the winter solstice, is celebrated over an eight-day period beginning on 25 Kislev, the third month. Also known as the Feast of Dedication and Feast of the Maccabees, Hanukkah commemorates the rededication of the Temple at Jerusalem in 164 BC. According to tradition, the one ritually pure container of olive oil, sufficient to illuminate the Temple for one day, miraculously burned for eight days, until new oil could be prepared. A feature of the Hanukkah celebration is the lighting in each Jewish home of an eight-branched candelabrum, the menorah (hanukkiah). This festival, though not a public holiday in Israel, is widely observed with the lighting of giant hanukkiot in public places.

Purim. This holiday, celebrated on 14 Adar (Adar Sheni in a leap year), joyously commemorates the delivery of the Jews from potential annihilation at the hands of Haman, viceroy of Persia, as described in the Book of Esther, which is read from a scroll (Megillah). The day, though not a public holiday in Israel, is widely marked by charity, exchange of edible gifts, and feasting.

Pesach (Passover). Pesach, lasting seven days in Israel and eight outside it, begins on 15 Nisan, at roughly the spring equinox, and recalls the exodus of the Hebrews from Egypt and their delivery from bondage. The chief festival of Judaism, Pesach begins with a ceremonial family meal, or seder, at which special foods (including unleavened bread, or matzoh) are eaten and the Passover story (Haggadah) is read.

Shavuot. This festival, on 6 Sivan, celebrates the presentation of the Ten Commandments to Moses on Mt. Sinai and the offering of the first harvest fruits at the temple in Jerusalem. The precursor of the Christian Pentecost, Shavuot takes place on the 50th day after the first day of Pesach.

The Jewish calendar begins with the traditional date of Creation, equivalent to 3761 BC on the Christian calendar. The following table gives the Jewish year the equivalent starting dates in the Gregorian calendar for selected holidays from 1984/85 through 1990/91:

	ROSH HASHANAH	YOM KIPPUR	HANUKKAH	PESACH
5745	27 Sept. 1984	6 Oct	19 Dec.	6 April 1985
5746	16 Sept. 1985	25 Sept.	8 Dec.	24 April 1986
5747	4 Oct. 1986	23 Oct.	27 Dec.	14 April 1987
5748	24 Sept. 1987	3 Oct.	16 Dec.	2 April 1988
5749	12 Sept. 1988	21 Sept.	4 Dec.	20 April 1989
5750	30 Sept. 1989	9 Oct.	23 Dec.	10 April 1990
5751	20 Sept. 1990	29 Sept.	12 Dec.	30 March 1991

MUSLIM HOLIDAYS

Like the Jewish calendar, the Islamic calendar consists of 12 months alternating between 29 and 30 days. A normal year is 354 days: a leap day is added to the last month (Dhu'l-Hijja) 11 times during a 30-year cycle in order to keep the calendar in conformity with the phases of the moon. Like the Jewish day, the Islamic day runs from sundown to sundown. Unlike the Jewish calendar, however, the Islamic calendar makes no attempt to align itself with the solar year by the periodic addition of an extra month; therefore, over the course of time, Islamic festivals may occur at any season. Like the Christian and Jewish calendars, the Islamic calendar has a seven-day week. Friday is the principal day of worship; although work is not forbidden on that day, it is suspended during the midday prayer session. The following list gives Muslim holy days that are observed as public holidays in one or more of the predominantly Muslim countries. Except where noted, a transliteration style reflecting pronunciation practice in the Arab countries is given. Not given here are certain special Muslim holidays in Iran, the only Muslim country in which the Shi'i form of Islam predominates.

Muslim New Year. Although in some countries 1 Muharram, which is the first month of the Islamic year, is observed as a holiday, the new year is in other places observed on the 14th of Sha'ban, the eighth month of the year. This practice apparently stems from pagan Arab times. Shab-i-Bharat, a national holiday in Bangladesh on this day, is held by many to be the occasion when God ordains all actions in the coming year.

'Ashura. This fast day was instituted by Muhammad as the equivalent of the Jewish Yom Kippur but later became voluntary as Ramadan replaced it as a penitential event. It also commemorates Noah's leaving the ark on Mt. Ararat after the waters of the Great Flood had subsided. In Iran, the martyrdom of Husayn, grandson of Muhammad, is commemorated with passion plays on this day.

Milad an-Nabi. The traditional birthday of Muhammad is celebrated on 12 Rabi al-Awwal, the third month of the Islamic year.

Laylat al-Miraj. This holiday, celebrated on 27 Rajab, the seventh month, commemorates Muhammad's miraculous night journey to heaven, during which he received instructions from Allah on the requirements for daily prayer.

Ramadan. The first day of Ramadan (the ninth month) is a public holiday in many countries, although the religious festival does not officially begin until the new moon is sighted from the Naval Observatory in Cairo, Egypt. The entire month commemorates the period in which the Prophet received divine revelation and is observed by a strict fast from sunrise to sundown. This observance is one of Islam's five main duties for believers.

Laylat al-Qadr (Night of Power). This commemoration of the first revelation of the Koran (Qur'an) to Muhammad usually falls on 27 Ramadan.

'Id al-Fitr. The Little Festival, or Breaking-Fast Festival, that begins just after Ramadan, on 1 Shawwal, the 10th month, is the occasion for three or four days of feasting. In Malaysia and Singapore, this festival is called Hari Raya Puasa; in Turkey, Şeker Bayramı.

'Id al-'Adha'. The Great Festival, or Sacrificial Feast, celebrates the end of the special pilgrimage season, or Hajj, to Mecca and Medina, an obligation for Muslims once in their lifetime if physically and economically feasible. The slaughter of animals pays tribute to Abraham's obedience to God in offering his son to the Lord for sacrifice; a portion of the meat is supposed to be donated to the poor. The feast begins on 10 Dhu'l-Hijja and continues to 13 Dhu'l-Hijja (14 Dhu'l-Hijja in a leap year). In Malaysia and Singapore, this festival is celebrated as Hari Raya Haji; in Indonesia, Lebaran Haji; in Turkey, Kurban Bayramı.

The Islamic calendar begins with the entry of Muhammad into Medina, equivalent to AD 622 on the Christian calendar. Shown below are the Islamic years 1405–11 and their equivalent starting dates:

1405—27 September 1984
1406—16 September 1985
1407—6 September 1986
1408—26 August 1987
1409—14 August 1988
1410—4 August 1989
1411—24 July 1990

HINDU HOLIDAYS

Hindu holidays are based on various lunar calendars, with an extra month inserted at intervals that vary from year to year, in order to keep festivals from shifting in relation to the seasons. The bright half of the month is that in which the new moon advances to the full moon; the dark half lasts from full moon to new moon. It is said that no nation has more festivals than India. Most are of only local or regional importance, but the following are national holidays in India and other countries with large Hindu populations.

Raksha Bandhan. During this festival, which usually falls in August, bracelets of colored thread and tinsel are tied by women to the wrists of their menfolk, thus binding the men to guard and protect them during the year. It is celebrated on the full moon of Sravana.

Ganesh Chaturthi. The festival, honoring Ganesh (Ganesa), god of prosperity, is held on the fourth day of the bright fortnight of the month of Bhadrapada, corresponding to August or September.

Durga Puja. This holiday honors the Divine Mother, wife of Shiva and the principle of creation, in her victory over the demon Mashishasura. It is held during the first 10 days of the bright fortnight of Asvina (Navaratri), a period corresponding to September or October. The last day is Dussehra, an autumn festival that celebrates the victory of the god Rama over Ravana, king of demons.

Dewali (Deepavali; Divali). Dewali is the Hindu Festival of Lights, when Lakshmi, goddess of good fortune, is said to visit the homes of humans. The four- or five-day festival comes at the end of Asvina and the beginning of Karttika, a time corresponding to October or November.

Shivarati (Mahashivarati). Dedicated to the god Shiva, this holiday is observed on the 13th day of the dark half of Magha, corresponding to January or February.

Thaipusam. A holiday in Malaysia, Thaipusam honors Subrimaya, son of Shiva and an important deity in southern India. The three-day festival is held in the month of Magha according to when Pusam, a section of the lunar zodiac, is on the ascendant.

Holi. A festival lasting 3 to 10 days, Holi closes the old year with processions and merriment. It terminates on the full moon of Phalguna, the last month, corresponding to February or March.

BUDDHIST HOLIDAYS

Buddhist religious practice stems from the Hindu belief that every new-moon or full-moon day should be set apart for observance. In Buddhism, the half-moon days also have special status. In Sri Lanka, each Poya day—the day of the rise of the full moon of each month of the Buddhist calendar—is a public holiday. The following observances are common in Southeast Asia.

Songran. The Buddhist New Year is a three-day springtime water festival, in which images of the Buddha are bathed.

Vesak. This last full-moon day of Visakha highlights a three-day celebration of the birth, enlightenment, and death of the Buddha. It falls in April or May.

Waso (Varsa; Vassa). This holiday begins the Buddhist equivalent of Lent, a period between July and October (the rainy season in Southeast Asia), during which Buddhist monks may not leave their cloisters. The season starts with the full moon of the month of Asalha and ends with a festival during the full moon of the month of Thadingyut.

Abbreviations and Acronyms

AD—Anno Domini
ADB—African Development Bank
AsDB—Asian Development Bank
AFL-CIO—American Federation of Labor–Congress of Industrial Organizations
AID—Agency for International Development [of the US]
AM—before noon
AM—Amplitude modulation
ANZUS—Security Treaty of Australia, New Zealand, and the United States of America
Arch.—Archipelago
ASEAN—Association of Southeast Asian Nations
ASSR—Autonomous Soviet Socialist Republic
avg.—average
b.—born
BC—Before Christ
BCEAO—Central Bank of the West African States (Banque Centrale des États de l'Afrique de l'Ouest)
BEAC—Bank of the Central African States (Banque des États de l'Afrique Centrale)
BENELUX—Benelux Economic Union (Belgium-Netherlands-Luxembourg Economic Union)
Bibliog.—bibliography
BIS—Bank for International Settlements
BLEU—Belgium-Luxembourg Economic Union
Br.—British
Brig.—brigadier
c.—circa (about)
C—Celsius
CACM—Central American Common Market
Capt.—Captain
CARE—Cooperative for American Remittances to Everywhere, Inc.
CARICOM—Caribbean Community and Common Market
CCC—Customs Cooperation Council
CDB—Caribbean Development Bank
CEAO—West African Economic Community (Communauté Économique de l'Afriqué de l'Ouest; replaced UDEAO)
CEMA—see CMEA
CENTO—Central Treaty Organization
CERN—European Organization for Nuclear Research
CFA—Communauté Financière Africaine
CFP—Communauté Française du Pacifique
CGT—Confédération Générale du Travail
CIA—Central Intelligence Agency [of the US]
c.i.f.—cost, insurance, and freight
cm—centimeter(s)
CMEA—Council for Mutual Economic Assistance
Co.—company
Col.—colonel
COMECON—see CMEA
comp.—compiled, compiler
Cons.—Conservative
Corp.—corporation
cu—cubic
cwt—hundredweight
d—daily
d.—died
DDT—dichlorodiphenyltrichloroethane
Dem.—Democratic
DPT—diphtheria, pertussis, and tetanus
Dr.—doctor
DPRK—Democratic People's Republic of Korea (North Korea)
DRV—Democratic Republic of Viet-Nam (North Viet-Nam)
dwt—deadweight tons
e—evening
E—east

EAC—East African Community
EAEC—see EURATOM
EC—European Communities
ECA—Economic Commission for Africa [of the UN]
ECAFE—see ESCAP
ECE—Economic Commission for Europe [of the UN]
ECLA—Economic Commission for Latin America [of the UN]
ECOSOC—Economic and Social Council [of the UN]
ECOWAS—Economic Community of West African States
ECSC—European Coal and Steel Community
ECWA—Economic Commission for Western Asia [of the UN]
ed.—editor, edited, edition
EEC—European Economic Community (Common Market)
EFTA—European Free Trade Association
e.g.—exempli gratia (for example)
ESCAP—Economic and Social Commission for Asia and the Pacific [of the UN]
ESRO—European Space Research Organization
est.—estimate(d)
et al.—et alii (and others)
etc.—et cetera (and so on)
EURATOM—European Atomic Energy Community
f.—founded
F—Fahrenheit
FAO—Food and Agriculture Organization [of the UN]
ff.—following
fl.—flourished
FM—frequency modulation
f.o.b.—free on board
Fr.—France, French
FRG—Federal Republic of Germany (West Germany)
ft—foot, feet
ft³—cubic foot, feet
Ft.—Fort
G-77—Group of 77
GATT—General Agreement on Tariffs and Trade
GCC—Gulf Cooperation Council
GDP—gross domestic product
GDR—German Democratic Republic (East Germany)
Gen.—General
GHz—gigahertz
gm—gram(s)
GMT—Greenwich Mean Time
GNP—gross national product
GRT—gross registered tons (tonnage)
GSP—gross social product
HMSO—Her Majesty's Stationery Office [of the UK]
ha—hectare(s)
I.—Island
IADB—see IDB
IAEA—International Atomic Energy Agency
IATA—International Air Transport Association
IBRD—International Bank for Reconstruction and Development (World Bank)
ICAO—International Civil Aviation Organization
ICC—International Control Commission
ICFTU—International Confederation of Free Trade Unions
ICJ—International Court of Justice (World Court)
IDA—International Development Association
IDB = IADB—Inter-American Development Bank
i.e.—id est (that is)
IFAD—International Fund for Agricultural Development
IFC—International Finance Corporation
IGO—intergovernmental organization
IGY—International Geophysical Year
ILC—International Law Commission

ILO—International Labor Organization
IMCO—*see* IMO
IMF—International Monetary Fund
IMO—International Maritime Organization (formerly IMCO)
in—inch(es)
Inc.—incorporated
Indep.—Independent
INTELSAT—International Telecommunications Satellite Consortium
INTERPOL—International Criminal Police Organization
IRU—International Relief Union
Is.—islands
ITU—International Telecommunication Union
IUCN—International Union for the Conservation of Nature and Natural Resources
IWC—International Whaling Commission; International Wheat Council
kg—kilogram(s)
kHz—kilohertz
km—kilometer(s)
km/hr—kilometer(s) per hour
kw—kilowatt(s)
kwh—kilowatt-hour(s)
L.—Lake
LAFTA—Latin American Free Trade Association
LAIA—Latin American Integration Association
lb—pound(s)
Lieut.—lieutenant
Ltd.—limited
m—meter(s); morning
m^3—cubic meter(s)
mg—milligram(s)
MHz—megahertz
mi—mile(s)
mm—millimeter(s)
mph—mile(s) per hour
MPR—Mongolian People's Republic
Mt.—Mount
Mtn.—mountain(s)
Mw—megawatt(s)
N—north
NA—not available
NATO—North Atlantic Treaty Organization
n.d.—no date
n.e.s.—not elsewhere specified
Neth.—Netherlands
NGO—nongovernmental organization
n.i.e.—not included elsewhere
NMP—net material product
NZ—New Zealand
OAPEC—Organization of Arab Petroleum Exporting Countries (subgroup of OPEC)
OAS—Organization of American States
OAU—Organization of African Unity
OCAM—African and Malagasy Common Organization
OECD—Organization for Economic Cooperation and Development
OIHP—International Office of Public Health (Office International d'Hygiène Publique)
O.M.—Order of Merit
ONUC—*see* UNOC
OPEC—Organization of Petroleum Exporting Countries
oz—ounce(s)
p.—page
PAHO—Pan American Health Organization
PC of A—Permanent Court of Arbitration
PDRY—People's Democratic Republic of Yemen (South Yemen)
PL—Public Law
PLO—Palestine Liberation Organization
PM—after noon
pop.—population
Port.—Portugal, Portuguese
pp.—pages
PRC—People's Republic of China
r.—reigned
R.—river
Ra.—Range

Rep.—Republic
rev.—revised
ROC—Republic of China (Taiwan)
ROK—Republic of Korea (South Korea)
RVN—Republic of Viet-Nam (South Viet-Nam)
s—South
S.A.—Société Anonyme
SDRs—Special Drawing Rights
SEATO—Southeast Asia Treaty Organization
SELA—Latin American Economic System (Sistema Económica Latinoamericano)
Sgt.—sergeant
SHAPE—Supreme Headquarters Allied Powers Europe
SPC—South Pacific Commission
sq—square
SRV—Socialist Republic of Viet-Nam
SSR—Soviet Socialist Republic
St.—Saint
TB—tuberculosis
TV—television
UAE—United Arab Emirates
UAR—United Arab Republic
UCC—Universal Copyright Convention
UDEAC—Central African Customs and Economic Union (Union Douanière et Économique de l'Afrique Centrale)
UDEAO—*see* CEAO
UEAC—Central African Economic Union (Union des États de l'Afrique Centrale)
UHF—ultra high frequency
UK—United Kingdom of Great Britain and Northern Ireland
UMOA—West African Monetary Union (Union Monétaire Ouest Africaine)
UN—United Nations
UNCHS—Center for Human Settlements (Habitat)
UNCOK—UN Commission in Korea
UNCTAD—UN Conference on Trade and Development
UNCURK—UN Commission on the Unification and Rehabilitation of Korea
UNDOF—UN Disengagement Observer Force
UNDP—UN Development Program
UNEF—UN Emergency Force
UNEP—UN Environment Program
UNESCO—UN Educational, Scientific and Cultural Organization
UNFICYP—UN Force in Cyprus
UNFPA—UN Fund for Population Activities
UNHCR—UN High Commissioner for Refugees
UNICEF—UN Children's Fund
UNIDO—UN Industrial Development Organization
UNIFIL—UN Interim Force in Lebanon
UNITAR—UN Institute for Training and Research
UNMOGIP—UN Military Observer Group for India and Pakistan
UNOC—UN Operation in the Congo
UNRRA—UN Relief and Rehabilitation Administration
UNRWA—UN Relief and Works Agency for Palestine Refugees
UNSO—UN Sahelian Office
UNTSO—UN Truce Supervisory Organization
UNU—UN University
UNV—UN Volunteers
UPU—Universal Postal Union
US—United States of America
USIA—US Information Agency
USSR—Union of Soviet Socialist Republics
VHF—very high frequency
vol., vols., Vol., Vols.—volume(s)
w—west
WEU—Western European Union
WFC—World Food Council
WFP—World Food Program
WFTU—World Federation of Trade Unions
WHO—World Health Organization
WIPO—World Intellectual Property Organization
WMO—World Meteorological Organization
WTO—Warsaw Treaty Organization; World Tourism Organization
YAR—Yemen Arab Republic (North Yemen)

Conversion Tables*

LENGTH

1 centimeter	0.3937 inch
1 centimeter	0.03280833 foot
1 meter (100 centimeters)	3.280833 feet
1 meter	1.093611 US yards
1 kilometer (1,000 meters)	0.62137 statute mile
1 kilometer	0.539957 nautical mile
1 inch	2.540005 centimeters
1 foot (12 inches)	30.4801 centimeters
1 US yard (3 feet)	0.914402 meter
1 statute mile (5,280 feet; 1,760 yards)	1.609347 kilometers
1 British mile	1.609344 kilometers
1 nautical mile (1.1508 statute miles or 6,076.10333 feet)	1.852 kilometers
1 British nautical mile (6,080 feet)	1.85319 kilometers

AREA

1 sq centimeter	0.154999 sq inch
1 sq meter (10,000 sq centimeters)	10.76387 sq feet
1 sq meter	1.1959585 sq yards
1 hectare (10,000 sq meters)	2.47104 acres
1 sq kilometer (100 hectares)	0.386101 sq mile
1 sq inch	6.451626 sq centimeters
1 sq foot (144 sq inches)	0.092903 sq meter
1 sq yard (9 sq feet)	0.836131 sq meter
1 acre (4,840 sq yards)	0.404687 hectare
1 sq mile (640 acres)	2.589998 sq kilometers

VOLUME

1 cubic centimeter	0.061023 cubic inch
1 cubic meter (1,000,000 cubic centimeters)	35.31445 cubic feet
1 cubic meter	1.307943 cubic yards
1 cubic inch	16.387162 cubic centimeters
1 cubic foot (1,728 cubic inches)	0.028317 cubic meter
1 cubic yard (27 cubic feet)	0.764559 cubic meter

LIQUID MEASURE

1 liter	0.8799 imperial quart
1 liter	1.05671 US quarts
1 hectoliter	21.9975 imperial gallons
1 hectoliter	26.4178 US gallons
1 imperial quart	1.136491 liters
1 US quart	0.946333 liter
1 imperial gallon	0.04546 hectoliter
1 US gallon	0.037853 hectoliter

WEIGHT

1 kilogram (1,000 grams)	35.27396 avoirdupois ounces
1 kilogram	32.15074 troy ounces
1 kilogram	2.204622 avoirdupois pounds
1 quintal (100 kg)	220.4622 avoirdupois pounds
1 quintal	1.9684125 hundredweights
1 metric ton (1,000 kg)	1.102311 short tons
1 metric ton	0.984206 long ton
1 avoirdupois ounce	0.0283495 kilogram
1 troy ounce	0.0311035 kilogram
1 avoirdupois pound	0.453592 kilogram
1 avoirdupois pound	0.00453592 quintal
1 hundred weight (cwt., 112 lb)	0.50802 quintal
1 short ton (2,000 lb)	0.907185 metric ton
1 long ton (2,240 lb)	1.016047 metric tons

ELECTRIC ENERGY

1 horsepower (hp)	0.7457 kilowatt
1 kilowatt (kw)	1.34102 horsepower

TEMPERATURE

Celsius (C)	Fahrenheit−32 × 5/9
Fahrenheit (F)	9/5 Celsius + 32

BUSHELS

	LB	METRIC TON	BUSHELS PER METRIC TON
Barley (US)	48	0.021772	45.931
(UK)	50	0.02268	44.092
Corn (UK, US)	56	0.025401	39.368
Linseed (UK)	52	0.023587	42.396
(Australia, US)	56	0.025401	39.368
Oats (US)	32	0.014515	68.894
(Canada)	34	0.015422	64.842
Potatoes (UK, US)	60	0.027216	36.743
Rice (Australia)	42	0.019051	52.491
(US)	45	0.020412	48.991
Rye (UK, US)	56	0.025401	39.368
(Australia)	60	0.027216	36.743
Soybeans (US)	60	0.027216	36.743
Wheat (UK, US)	60	0.027216	36.743

BAGS OF COFFEE

	LB	KG	BAGS PER METRIC TON
Brazil, Colombia, Mexico, Venezuela	132.28	60	16.667
El Salvador	152.12	69	14.493
Haiti	185.63	84.2	11.876

BALES OF COTTON

	LB	METRIC TON	BALES PER METRIC TON
India	392	0.177808	5.624
Brazil	397	0.18	5.555
US (net)	480	0.217724	4.593
US (gross)	500	0.226796	4.409

PETROLEUM

One barrel = 42 US gallons = 34.97 imperial gallons = 158.99 liters = 0.15899 cubic meter (or 1 cubic meter = 6.2898 barrels).

EXPLANATION OF SYMBOLS

Data not available ...
Nil (or negligible) —
Figures on tables not included in totals and subtotals are usually given in parentheses ( ).
A fiscal or split year is indicated by a stroke (e.g., 1974/75).

* Includes units of measure cited in the text, as well as certain other units employed in parts of the English-speaking world and in specified countries.

Index to Countries and Territories

This alphabetical list includes countries and dependencies (colonies, protectorates, and other territories) described in the encyclopedia. Countries and territories described in their own articles are followed by the continental volume (printed in *italics*) in which each appears, along with the volume number and first page of the article. For example, Argentina, which begins on page 5 of *Americas* (Volume 3), is listed this way: Argentina—*Americas* 3:5. Dependencies are listed here with the title of the volume in which they are treated, followed by the name of the article in which they are dealt with. In a few cases, an alternative name for the same place is given in parentheses at the end of the entry. The name of the volume *Asia and Oceania* is abbreviated in this list to *Asia*.

Index to the United Nations and Related Agencies

WORLDMARK ENCYCLOPEDIA OF THE NATIONS
© WORLDMARK PRESS Ltd.

ARCTIC OCEAN

Ellesmere

Greenland
(DENMARK)

Banks
Victoria

Baffin

Alaska
(US)

HUDSON
BAY

Newfoundland

CANADA

St. Pierre & Miquelon
(FRANCE)

Montreal
ICAO

UNITED STATES

★ London
IMO
★ Paris
UNESCO
Bern
UPU

★■ Geneva

New York
UN Headquarters
UNDP
UNFPA
UNICEF
UNITAR

Washington ★
Bermuda
(UK)
IMF
IFC
World Bank

UNHCR
UNCTAD
GATT
ILO
WHO
ITU
WMO
WIPO
ECE

PORTUGAL

Azores
(PORT)

Gibraltar

SPAIN

Rom

WFC
WFP
FAO
IFA

MEXICO

GULF OF
MEXICO

BAHAMAS

Turks and
Caicos
(UK)

ATLANTIC

OCEAN

Madeira Is.
(PORT)

Canary Is.
(SPAIN)

Western Sahara

MOROCCO

ALGERIA

Hawaiian Is.
(US)

CUBA

Cayman Is.
(UK)

DOMINICAN

HAITI

Puerto Rico (US)
Br. Virgin Is. (UK)
US Virgin Is. (US)
Anguilla (UK)
ST. CHRISTOPHER AND NEVIS
ANTIGUA AND BARBUDA
Guadeloupe (FRANCE)
DOMINICA

MAURITANIA

MALI

NIG

BELIZE

JAMAICA

CARIBBEAN

GUATEMALA
EL SALVADOR
HONDURAS

St. Martin
(FR and NETH)
Montserrat (UK)

CAPE
VERDE

SENEGAL
GAMBIA
GUINEA-BISSAU

UPPER
VOLTA

NIGER

NICARAGUA

SEA

Martinique
(FRANCE)

ST. LUCIA
BARBADOS

SIERRA LEONE

GUINEA

IVORY
COAST

GHANA

NIGER

COSTA RICA

PANAMA

GRENADA
ST. VINCENT AND THE GRENADINES

TRINIDAD
AND TOBAGO

LIBERIA

CAMER

VENEZUELA

GUYANA

SURINAME

EQUATORIAL GUINEA

SÃO TOME & PRÍNCIPE

GA

COLOMBIA

Guiana

Annobón

Cabin

Clipperton I.

Northern
Line Is.

Christmas I.

Galápagos Is.
(ECUADOR)

ECUADOR

PACIFIC OCEAN

PERU

BRAZIL

Ascension (UK)

ATLANTIC OCEAN

Southern
Line Is.

Îles Marquises

French

BOLIVIA

St. Helena
(UK)

Tahiti
Society Is.

Tuamotu Is.

Polynesia

Cook Is.
(NEW ZEALAND)

Gambier Is.

Trinidade (BRAZIL)

Tubuai Is.

Pitcairn Is. (UK)

Easter I.

PARAGUAY

Tristan da Cunha (UK)

Gough (UK)

Santiago
ECLA

CHILE

Juan Fernández Is.
(CHILE)

ARGENTINA

URUGUAY

Bou
(NORW

Falkland Is.
(Islas Malvinas)
(UK)

South Georgia
(UK)

South Sandwich Is.
(UK)

● UNITED NATIONS ORGANS,
SPECIALIZED AGENCIES AND
OTHER AUTONOMOUS
ORGANIZATIONS WITHIN
THE SYSTEM

■ UNITED NATIONS DEVELOPMENT
PROGRAM FIELD OFFICES

★ UNITED NATIONS INFORMATION
CENTERS / SERVICES

▲ PEACEKEEPING OPERATIONS /
OBSERVER MISSIONS

WEDDELL SEA

Antarctica

PRINCIPAL ORGANS OF THE UNITED NATIONS

New York:	General Assembly	Trusteeship Council
	Security Council	Secretariat
	Economic and Social Council	
The Hague:	International Court of Justice	

OTHER UNITED NATIONS ORGANS

Geneva:	UNHCR	– Office of the United Nations High Commissioner for Refugees
	UNCTAD	– United Nations Conference on Trade and Development
Nairobi:	UNCHS	– United Nations Center for Human Settlements (Habitat)
	UNEP	– United Nations Environment Program
New York:	UNDP	– United Nations Development Program
	UNFPA	– United Nations Fund for Population Activities
	UNICEF	– United Nations Children's Fund

	UNITAR	– United Nations Institute for Training and Research
Rome:	WFC	– World Food Council
	WFP	– Joint UN / FAO World Food Program
Tokyo:	UNU	– United Nations University
Vienna:	UNIDO	– United Nations Industrial Development Organization
	UNRWA	– United Nations Relief and Works Agency for Palestine Refugees in the Near East

REGIONAL COMMISSIONS

Addis Ababa:	ECA	– Economic Commission for Africa
Baghdad:	ECWA	– Economic Commission for Western Asia
Bangkok:	ESCAP	– Economic and Social Commission for Asia and the Pacific